THE PAPERS OF
Clarence Mitchell Jr.

THE PAPERS OF
Clarence Mitchell Jr.

Volume II, 1944–1946

Denton L. Watson, *editor*

Elizabeth M. Nuxoll, *associate editor*

OHIO UNIVERSITY PRESS

ATHENS

Ohio University Press, Athens, Ohio 45701

Ohio University Press books are printed on acid-free paper ⊗ ™
The paper used in this publication meets the minimum requirements of the
American National Standard for Information Sciences—Permanence of Paper
for Printed Library Materials, ANSI Z39.48-1992.

13 12 11 10 09 08 07 06 05   5 4 3 2 1

Publication of *The Papers of Clarence Mitchell Jr.* has been made possible by a grant
from the National Historical Publications and Records Commission of the
National Archives and Records Administration and by the sponsorship of
the State University of New York College at Old Westbury.

This project was supported by the Harry Frank Guggenheim Foundation.

Dust jacket: Photo of Clarence Mitchell Jr. by Surlock Studio,
courtesy of Elmer Henderson Papers.

Frontispiece: Drawing of Clarence Mitchell Jr. Copyright *Los Angeles Times,* 1969.
Reprinted by permission.

Library of Congress Cataloging-in-Publication Data
Mitchell, Clarence M. (Clarence Maurice), 1911–1984.
  [Papers. Selections]
  The papers of Clarence Mitchell, Jr. / Denton L. Watson, editor,
Elizabeth M. Nuxoll, associate editor.
    p. cm.
  Includes bibliographical references and index.
  ISBN 0-8214-1603-0 (cloth : v. 1 : alk. paper) — ISBN 0-8214-1604-9 (cloth : v. 2 : alk. paper)
  1. Mitchell, Clarence M. (Clarence Maurice), 1911–1984—Archives. 2. African Americans—Archives. 3.
Civil rights workers—United States—Archives. 4. African Americans—Civil rights—History—20th
century—Sources. 5. African Americans—Legal status, laws, etc.—History—20th century—Sources. 6.
Civil rights movements—United States—History—20th century—Sources. 7. United States—Race rela-
tions—History—20th century—Sources.   I. Watson, Denton L. II. Nuxoll, Elizabeth Miles, 1943–   .
III. Title.
  E185.97.M63A25 2005
  323'.092—dc22

                                                                    2005022302

To Rose, Victor, and Dawn

The Papers of Clarence Mitchell Jr.

Volume I, 1942–1943
Volume II, 1944–1946
Volume III, 1946–1954
Volume IV, 1954–1960
Volume V, 1961–1978

ADVISORY BOARD

CONTENTS

Volume I

Volume II

DOCUMENTS

1944

*Reports and Headquarters Memoranda of Clarence M. Mitchell Jr.
as Associate Director of Field Operations,
Fair Employment Practice Committee (FEPC)*

1945

Reports and Memoranda of Clarence Mitchell Jr. as Director of Field Operations, FEPC

1946

APPENDIXES

THE PAPERS OF
Clarence Mitchell Jr.

Memorandum on Conference
with General Accounting Office

January 5, 1944

TO: Mr. Malcolm Ross
Chairman

FROM: Clarence M. Mitchell
Associate Director of Field Operations

SUBJECT: Conference with General Accounting Office

On the above date, pursuant to your letter of December 27 to Mr. Lindsay Warren, Comptroller General, we met with Mr. Frank Yates, Assistant Comptroller General of the United States, and Mr. E. Ray Ballinger, Director of Personnel, at the General Accounting Office, to discuss the policy of GAO on employment of loyal American citizens of Japanese origin. We also discussed the non-discrimination clause in Government contracts.[1]

With regard to the first item, Mr. Yates stated that the General Accounting Office would consider the employment of American citizens of Japanese ancestry who are qualified for various jobs if investigations have shown them to be loyal. He also said that he would try to work out some instructions for his field offices on the subject.

On the question of the non-discrimination clause in contracts, Mr. Yates stated that his office would try to get either photostatic copies of such contracts, except secret and confidential, as we request, or state definitely whether a given contract contained the non-discrimination clause. Information on whether the secret and confidential contracts contain the clause will be furnished on request, he stated. He also said that, in most instances, his office would prefer to give the statement rather than a photostatic copy because of the difficulty in getting documents photostated.

Mr. Yates suggested that Mr. A. Banks Thomas, Acting Attorney Conferee, should be called or visited by the representative of our office who wishes information on contracts. Mr. Thomas will need the number of the contract, the name of the contractor, the name of the contracting department of the Government, and the approximate date of the contract. This will facilitate finding such contracts, Mr. Yates said. The number of the contract can be secured from the contracting agency.

Mr. Yates promised to notify Mr. Thomas that FEPC would be calling or writing for such material from time to time.[2]

cc: Elmer W. Henderson

MS: copy, HqR67, Central Files. Reports, U.S. Government 1, General, A–M.

1. For Mitchell's earlier efforts to ease employment discrimination against Japanese Americans, see 11/17/43; 2/4, 2/5/44; headnotes on Relationships with Federal Agencies and on Japanese Americans.

2. See Mitchell's oral report on this meeting to the Committee in Transcript of Proceedings, 1/15/44, 46–48, HqR65, Central Files.

Weekly Report

1–7–44

Mr. Will Maslow
Clarence M. Mitchell
Report of Assignments for Week Ending January 8, 1944

EMANUEL H. BLOCH

The following matters were assigned to Mr. Bloch for handling:

1. Memorandum from Mr. A. Bruce Hunt on Atlanta Gas Light Company.
2. University of Georgia, School of Aviation, 7-GC-170.

Mr. Bloch is handling docketing and other duties of Mr. Eugene Davidson. Hence, no FDR's have been submitted to him for review and action. Such as would normally go to him are handled by me.

STANLEY METZGER

The following FDR's have been assigned to Mr. Metzger for review and handling:

Region VI—8
Region XI—1
Region XII—9

Mr. Metzger is also preparing a memorandum on the stenographic record of the Corpus Christi cases handled by Dr. Castaneda.

I have been unable to make any other assignments to Mr. Metzger because he has not had any stenographic service and has been working on matters assigned by you.

CLARENCE M. MITCHELL

This week, I had a conference with Mr. Jonathan Daniels, at the State Department, concerning the Western Electric case.[1] I accompanied the Chairman [Ross] to the General Accounting Office to discuss GAO policies with reference to the hiring of Japanese and also obtained from that office the commitment that information on whether contracts contained non-discrimination clauses will be given to us upon request. A memorandum on this has been prepared.[2]

I also discussed with Mr. Edward Lawson his handling of the Standard Oil case in New York, 2-BR-61, and General Electric. Mr. Lawson informed me that he would make a visit to General Electric headquarters at Schenectady in the near future.

I have reviewed and taken action on problems listed in weekly reports.

The following FDR's have been reviewed and acted upon by me:

> Region I—1
> Region II—14
> Region III—5
> Region V—1
> Region X—3

I am in the process of preparing a summary on DFO cases which will be in your hands Monday, January 10.[3]

MS: copy, HqR3, Office Files of George M. Johnson. M.

1. For an example of Mitchell's earlier activity on this case, see 8/5/43.
2. See Mitchell's memoranda of 11/17/43, and notes, 2/4, 2/5/44; headnote on Japanese Americans.
3. Memorandum not found.

Memorandum on Telephone Conversations with Mr. J. B. Knotts, of Bethlehem Steel Company, and Alexander Allen, Baltimore Urban League

Jan. 8, 1944

Mr. Will Maslow

Clarence M. Mitchell

Telephone Conversations with Mr. J. B. Knotts, of Bethlehem Steel Company, and Mr. Alexander Allen, Baltimore Urban League.

Following information which I had received from the Baltimore Urban League that colored riveters were being laid off at Bethlehem Steel Company, I called Mr. J. B. Knotts, management's representative in charge of industrial relations, at the company. Mr. Knotts stated that it was not correct that colored riveters were to be discharged. He said that he was trying to talk some of them out of leaving. He explained that the company is ahead of its schedule, and riveters have to be taken off riveting and put on other jobs. The men, he stated, insist upon being given releases. Mr. Knotts stated that the company did not want them to go as it would be needing them later as riveters. He also said that this did not mean that all Negro riveting gangs would be dismissed.

I suggested that Mr. Knotts talk with the men on the problem as it had been presented to me originally. He agreed to arrange a meeting to talk with the men involved. I told Mr. Knotts that the men complained the alleged dismissals were not handled on a seniority basis.

After talking to Mr. Knotts, I called Mr. Alexander Allen, of the Baltimore Urban League. I informed Mr. Allen of my conversation with Mr. Knotts and suggested that he also meet with the men involved.

I handled the matter because I was unable to talk with anyone in Region IV at the time. A copy of this is being sent to Mr. Hook for whatever follow-up may be necessary.

Rogers

cc: Mr. Frank Hook\

MS: copy, HqR38, Central Files. (entry 25) Memoranda, Maslow, Will, 1944.

Memorandum on Jurisdiction over Employees in Motion Picture Theaters

DATE: Jan. 8, 1944

TO: MR. GEORGE M. JOHNSON
               Deputy Chairman

FROM: CLARENCE M. MITCHELL
               Associate Director of Field Operations

SUBJECT: JURISDICTION OVER EMPLOYEES IN MOTION PICTURE THEATERS

Attached is the file on a case involving a motion picture theater in Indianapolis, Indiana. Mr. George Williams, Business Agent for Local Number 194-A, I. A. T. S. E., charges that he was dismissed by his employer, Mr. Dudley Williston, after presenting certain grievances.

As I read this complaint, it appears that the real basis for Mr. Williams' action is his discharge in connection with union activity. However, I shall appreciate a ruling from you on whether motion picture theaters are within our jurisdiction.
Attachment

MS: LH, DI, HqR84, Correspondence Relating to Cases. (L–S) Motion Picture Theater, Indianapolis, Ind.

This case was another example of the fine line the Committee constantly drew in considering jurisdictional issues. Here Johnson, in a 1/12/44 response to Mitchell, ruled that the Committee had no jurisdiction over motion picture *theaters*. However, at its meeting on 3/18/44, Johnson recorded that the Committee "decided that its jurisdiction extended to the Motion Picture Industry because that industry was listed as 'essential' by the War Manpower commission. The Committee held that it would regard an industry as a 'war industry' if it is classified as essential by WMC, unless there are facts present which warrant a different conclusion." Johnson memorandum, 4/5/44, HqR5, Office Files of George M. Johnson. Shishkin. For a broader treatment of these questions, see the headnote on Jurisdictional Issues.

Memorandum on Illinois Ordnance Plant Strike, Herrin, Illinois

Jan. 10, 1944

Mr. George M. Johnson
    Deputy Chairman
Clarence M. Mitchell
    Associate Director of Field Operations
Illinois Ordnance Plant Strike, Herrin, Illinois

In keeping with our conversation, I have drawn up this memorandum on the above-mentioned strike.

Mr. Charles T. Estes, of the Conciliation Service, U.S. Department of Labor, called on Friday, January 7, and informed you that a strike was in progress at the plant. He stated that the disturbance began when one Negro Inspector was employed on the production line. At that time, forty-five whites left the job and were discharged. Later, only four of these whites returned when those discharged were offered reemployment, Mr. Estes stated, and some 2,000 went on strike.

The company is a Government-owned, contractor-operated establishment. The Sherwin Williams Company is the contractor. Apparently, it has a contractual relationship with District 50 of the United Mine Workers.

A call was made to Mr. Charles Fell, a member of the International Executive Board of District 50 of the United Mine Workers. Mr. Fell stated he would check on the situation.

We informed Mr. Henderson and Mr. Ross in Chicago of our actions here. They stated that Miss Joy Schultz, of Mr. Henderson's office, was to be assigned to investigate the situation in Herrin. Mr. Henderson also stated that he had talked with War Department representatives concerning the strike.

Later, Mr. Fell called you to say that he had talked with his representatives in the locality, who stated that there was no race problem involved in the strike. Mr. Fell's representative stated that the company had <u>two</u> Negro Inspectors on the production line and that these individuals went beyond their line of duty to give orders to white persons in another section. The individuals receiving the orders were women, expressed resentment, walked off the job, and were discharged. Later, they were given an opportunity to return to work. Four of them did so. Mr. Fell was optimistic about possibilities for settling the whole matter.

Mr. Estes was advised of the Union representative's version of the controversy and reiterated his version that the employment of the Negro as Inspector was the cause of the work stoppage. He stated that he had suggested to company officials that segregation might be the solution. He stated further that he may have "muddied the waters" by this suggestion, but pointed out that race relations were very bad in the area. Mr. Estes was advised that the Committee had never recommended segregation as the solution to discriminatory employment problems.

A teletype message from Mr. Henderson, dated January 8, stated that the strikers had returned to the plant and that a full report would follow.

cc: Davidson
      Metzger

MS: copy, HqR77, Office Files of Eugene Davidson. Strikes.
   On the Illinois Ordnance Plant strike, see the headnote on Strikes and Work Stoppages.

St. Louis & San Francisco Railroad Company, Fort Scott, Kansas

1/12/44

Mr. George M. Johnson
Clarence M. Mitchell
St. Louis & San Francisco Railroad Company, Fort Scott, Kansas
9-BR-132

We have received a memorandum from Mr. Roy A. Hoglund, Regional Director in Kansas City, stating the following:

> "We have just received a complaint, transmitted through Bruce Hunt, Atlanta, from a complainant who alleges dismissal on the basis of racial prejudice from the St. Louis & San Francisco Railroad Company at Fort Scott, Kansas, December 1939."
>
> "Inasmuch as this dismissal occurred two years before the issuance of the Executive Order creating the President's Committee on Fair Employment Practice, would we have jurisdiction in the case? We have docketed the case, but are withholding any action until we are further advised."

I shall appreciate a ruling from you on what disposition should be made of Mr. Hoglund's inquiry.[1]

MS: copy, HqR38, Central Files. (entry 25) Memoranda, Johnson, George M., 1/44–.

1. See the headnote on Jurisdictional Issues.

Memorandum on Employment of All-Negro Deck Crew by Texas Oil Company

DATE: 1–12–44

TO: Mr. George M. Johnson

FROM: Clarence M. Mitchell

SUBJECT: Employment of All-Negro Deck Crew by Texas Oil Company
           2-BR-423

Mr. Edward Lawson, Director of Region II, states that the Texas Oil Company has asked the War Shipping Administration for all-Negro deck crews to man some of its tankers.[1]

I understand that, when Mr. Ross was in New York, he discussed this situation with Mr. Craig S. Vincent, Atlantic Coast representative of the War Shipping Administration. It is also my understanding that Mr. Vincent does not believe the idea a good one.

I shall appreciate it if you will give us a ruling on whether we should inform Mr. Lawson that this plan is discriminatory.

MS: HqR39, Central Files. (entry 25) Memoranda, Region II.

1. On 2/9/44, Mitchell responded to Lawson that, in sum, the Committee believed the plan was discriminatory. The FEPC had no authority to attack segregation, only discrimination in employment. Nevertheless, as a result of its bitter experience in the Alabama Dry Dock case in 6/43 (see

Trimble/Mitchell report and notes in appendix 1), where it accepted segregated ways in order to end the violence there, it adopted the policy that "in cases of segregation, the staff should eliminate discrimination, and then refer case to the Committee for final disposition." HqR4, Office Files of George M. Johnson. Policy. See 1/12, 1/29/44; headnotes on Jurisdictional Issues, on Relationships with Federal Agencies (section on the War Shipping Administration), and on the Oil Industry.

Weekly Report

Jan. 14, 1944

Mr. Will Maslow
Clarence M. Mitchell
Report for Week Ending January 15, 1944

OUTSTANDING EVENTS AND PROBLEMS.

This week, Captain Atkins, of the Navy Department, reported to Mr. George Johnson, Deputy Chairman, on a controversy at Dravo Shipbuilding Company, Neville Island, Pennsylvania. Thirty-five Negro workers were discharged in connection with a wage dispute. At present, no FEPC action seems necessary, but we are keeping in touch with the situation. Mr. Elmer Henderson, Director of Region VI, reported that the strike involving Negro workers in the Illinois Ordnance Plant at Herrin, Illinois, has been settled.[1]

IMPORTANT CONTACTS WITH REGIONAL OFFICES, OTHER DIVISIONS, AND OTHER GOVERNMENT AGENCIES.

Because of a request from Region II, a ruling is being sought from the Deputy Chairman on whether proposed employment of all-Negro deck crews on ships of the Texas Oil Company is discriminatory. Region II has also asked whether certain Army hiring regulations on Japanese are discriminatory. Additional information has been requested. The Regional Director of Region II proposes that he be given jurisdiction over all War Shipping Administration cases on the East Coast. Additional information is being requested.[2]

A question involving the operating agreement with WMC arose in Region V. This matter is fully explained in a memorandum being prepared.[3]

Region VI is being advised that the Deputy Chairman has ruled we have no jurisdiction over motion picture theater employment complaints.[4]

A question of jurisdiction over a case involving the St. Louis and San Francisco
Railway in Region IX has been submitted to the Deputy Chairman for a ruling.[5]

Region X raised a question on the handling of railway complaints, and the hearings division indicates that a special new instruction is being prepared on this. Requests for additional office space and personnel matters in Region X have also been
acted upon and explained in attached memorandum.[6]

ASSIGNMENTS TO CENTRAL STAFF.

Mr. Bloch:

1. Region III—Memorandum re Philadelphia Quartermaster Depot.
2. Region VII—Memorandum on Brookley Air Field, 7-GR-141.
3. Region VII—Memorandum re Amanda Lee Crosby.
4. Region VII—Memorandum re Iron Workers Local, 7-UR-59.
5. Region VII—Memorandum re Railroad Retirement Board, 7-GR-168.

I do not expect early action on these since Mr. Bloch is working on Smith Committee matter for the Director of Field Operations.

Mr. Metzger:

The following assignments were completed by Mr. Metzger:

1. Memorandum on Disposition of Corpus Christi, Texas cases.
2. Memorandum reviewing and recommending further action on Charles
   Schwab v. Hydraulic Machinery, Inc., 5-BC-1213.
3. F.D.R.'s previously assigned.

New assignments given to Mr. Metzger include:

1. Memorandum from Region XII on Mexican Consul.
2. Memorandum from Region IX re St. Louis Aircraft Company.
3. War Department—6-GC-138.
4. Taking necessary action on Weekly Reports from Regions IX, XI, AND XII.
   Also, the following FDR's:
   Region VI—15
   Region VIII—1
   Region XII—2

Mr. Mitchell:

Assignments completed are attached or included in this report.

I have reviewed and taken action on questions raised in Weekly Reports other than those being handled by Mr. Metzger.

The following FDR's have been reviewed and acted upon:

> Region V—3
> Region X—23

NEW R.D'S, FIELD LETTERS, OR FIELD INSTRUCTIONS

I have prepared and sent out the following R.D's:

> Date and Summary of Complaint—No. 47
> Satisfactory Adjustment—No. 48
> Language in FDR's—No. 49

cc: Bloch
        Davidson
        Metzger

MS: copy, HqR6, *Office Files of Emanuel H. Bloch. Weekly Reports.*

1. See the headnote on Strikes and Work Stoppages.

2. On this development, see Mitchell to Johnson, memorandum concerning report from Edward Lawson, director of Region II; 1/12/44; Mitchell to Johnson, memorandum, 1/22/44; headnote on the Oil Industry.

3. Memorandum not found, but see Ross's detailed memorandum to McNutt on this problem, 2/9/45, in HqR67, U.S. Government, War Manpower Commission; headnote on Relationships with Federal Agencies.

4. See Mitchell to Johnson, memorandum, 1/8/44, note 1.

5. See 1/12/44 memorandum on this subject.

6. Memorandum not found.

Memorandum on Wilhelm Klasing vs. General Chemical Company

Jan. 14, 1944

Mr. George M. Johnson
    Deputy Chairman

Clarence M. Mitchell
Associate Director of Field Operations
Wilhelm Klasing Versus General Chemical Company, 6-BA-20

Since Mr. Crockett has made some recommendations on this case, I thought you might wish to let him read Mr. Lawson's latest memorandum.

If Mr. Crockett does not wish to make any other suggestion on the basis of this new information, please return the case to me, and I shall take the necessary follow-up action.

Attachment

MS: copy, HqR83, Correspondence Relating to Cases. (A–K) General Chemical Company.

The Klasing case was an alienage case involving a German who had been living in the U.S. for several years. He charged that the company discharged him because he was not a citizen and was thus in violation of E.O. 8802. Upon the FEPC's intervention, the company offered him back his job, but he declined to return because he would not have received back pay. The FEPC therefore closed the case as "withdrawn by complainant." See Mitchell to Henderson, 3/9/44, and Crockett's memorandum of 11/24/43, both filed with this text.

Memorandum on H.C.R. 105, Texas

DATE: Jan. 18, 1944

TO: Mr. Will Maslow

FROM: Clarence M. Mitchell

SUBJECT: H. C. R. 105, Texas

After a careful review of the correspondence from the Good Neighbor Commission concerning H. C. R. 105 in Texas, I have arrived at the conclusion that this is a very unfortunate piece of legislation.[1] In my opinion, it is less than a gesture in the direction of settling the problem of discrimination against Latin Americans in Texas.

Also, because it places such an emphasis upon the Caucasian race throughout its context, I do not believe it would be advisable for us to mention it in any of our official correspondence.

MS: HqR66, Central Files. U.S. Government, Aliens in Defense, Specific Groups, Mexican Workers.

1. The Texas legislature adopted HCR 105 in 1943. The bill said that the state's public policy opposed discrimination against Mexicans. In a telegram on 4/12/44 to Hoglund, Mitchell said he had learned from A. M. Motley and Vernon McGee of the WMC that the WMC's previous discriminatory instruction in Denver regarding the recruiting of Mexicans for Pasco, Washington, had been rescinded. For the FEPC's broader attempt to protect Latin Americans against discrimination by the Denver USES, see 4/12/44. HqR66, Central Files. U.S. Government, Aliens in Defense, Specific Groups, Mexican Workers.

Memorandum on Discrimination in Shipyards

Jan. 21, 1944

Mr. Will Maslow
Clarence M. Mitchell
Discrimination in Shipyards

In a memorandum to Mr. Haas, dated August 3, 1943, Mr. Ross stated the following:

"I think we ought to press the point made to Admiral Vickery—that tripartite Committees might well be established to consider discrimination problems in all shipyards.

"I will speak to Dan Ring when he returns and let you know."

I do not know whether any follow-up action was taken on this, but it sounds like a good idea. I hope that we can explore it further.

MS: copy, HqR38, Central Files. (entry 25), Memoranda, Maslow, Will, 1944.
    See the headnotes on the Shipbuilding Industry and on Relationships with Federal Agencies.

Memorandum on Discriminatory Practices
in Standard Oil Building

DATE: Jan. 21, 1944

TO: Mr. Theodore A. Jones
    Administrative Officer
FROM: Clarence M. Mitchell
    Associate Director of Field Operations
SUBJECT: Discriminatory Practices in Standard Oil Building

Attached is a memorandum from Mr. Frank E. Hook, Director of Region IV. You will note that it makes certain statements concerning facilities in the building.[1]

I am referring his memorandum to you for appropriate consideration.
Attachment

MS: LH, DI, HqR83, Correspondence Relating to Cases. (A–K) Discriminatory Practices in Standard Oil Building.

For responses to this case, see Mitchell, weekly report, 1/22/44; George Johnson to Maslow, 1/22/44, filed with this text.

1. Hook reported:

The Government agencies including the FEPC has leased space on the second, third, fourth, fifth and sixth floors of the above mentioned building.

A lunch room counter is operated in the west end of the building on the second floor. The proprietress of the lunch counter is carrying on discriminatory practices against colored people and especially employees of the Government agencies located in the building.

I have been informed by the PBA that the contract leased for the Government space in the building does not contain a nondiscriminatory clause, even though it has been ruled to be mandatory. There have been recent renewals and amendments to the contract lease.

The question of our jurisdiction has arisen. I do not have copies of the lease. They can be obtained, however, from the PBA. The situation is becoming rather intense and is a matter that should be determined without delay.

In addition to the discriminatory practices of the tenants occupying the lunch room space, the Standard Oil Company is practicing further discriminatory practices by locking the toilet facilities on the second floor and giving keys out to only white occupants of the second floor. These toilet facilities were opened and available until the FEPC moved into the building and until colored girls commenced using these toilet facilities.

I have taken the matter up with the PBA and they advised me that it is a legal question. I, therefore, respectfully request that some members of the Legal Staff be assigned to make a research of the provision of the lease and determine the question of jurisdiction. (Hook to Maslow, memorandum, 1/7/44, HqR83, Correspondence Relating to Cases. (A–K) Discriminatory Practices in Standard Oil Building.

Weekly Report

Jan. 22, 1944

Mr. Will Maslow

Clarence M. Mitchell

Report for Week Ending January 22, 1944

OUTSTANDING EVENTS AND PROBLEMS

In company with the Deputy Chairman and Mr. Ernest G. Trimble of the Hearings Division, I appeared before the Sub-committee on Production in Shipyards [Shipbuilding Plants] of the House Committee on Merchant Marine and Fisheries. The Sub-Committee was interested in obtaining information on how discrimination in West Coast shipyards may affect production.[1]

A strike occurred at the Youngstown Sheet and Tube Company's Indiana Harbor Works in Region VI this week. Mr. Elmer Henderson, Regional Director, has been active on the case because racial issues were involved in the walkout. Mr. Henderson reports that the parties involved have reached an agreement, and he will send in a final report on it when this agreement is consummated.[2]

Region X has raised a number of questions in connection with discrimination by oil companies in Texas. These cases now appear to be at the point where further field action on them will bring us no results. I am reviewing them for the purpose of recommending action by the Committee.[3]

For some weeks, we have been negotiating with the War Manpower Commission on a problem raised by Region IV. The problem is that the WMC Regional Director refuses to give FEPC access to USES 270 Reports. The WMC office also does not submit 510 or Form 42 Reports, as provided for in the FEPC-WMC agreement. After a conversation with Mr. Glenn Brockway's office this week, I have reached the conclusion that further negotiations with anyone below the level of Mr. McNutt or Mr. Appley will be a waste of time. Accordingly, I have prepared for the Chairman's signature a draft of a letter to be sent to Mr. McNutt on this matter.[4]

IMPORTANT CONTACTS WITH REGIONAL OFFICES, OTHER DIVISIONS, AND OTHER GOVERNMENT AGENCIES

All regional offices have been requested to send in copies of their operating agreements with the War Manpower Commission. These will be assigned to Mr. Bloch for analysis and recommendations.

Regional Directors and Dr. Carlos E. Castaneda, Special Assistant to the Chairman on Latin American Affairs, have been notified that a meeting of directors will be held in Washington February 10, 11, and 12. Notice of this meeting is being sent to other divisions with the request that any matters to be included on the agenda should be submitted by February 1.

On January 7, Region IV submitted a memorandum concerning discrimination in the lunch room located in the Standard Oil Building.[5] Since this matter involved the Administrative Office, I referred it to Mr. Jones. Subsequently, I talked with a member of the Legal Division. I then referred the matter to the Deputy Chairman because of legal questions raised. Region IV has also requested that the copy of the Lunt Report be sent to them for their review. However, I have not seen a copy of this report myself. As soon as it is obtained, I shall transmit it to the regional office.[6]

A request from Region VII concerning the Atlanta Journal has been referred to Mr. McKnight, Director of Region V. Also sent to Region V was a recommendation in connection with the case of Charles Schwab, 5-BC-1215. Memoranda setting forth central office recommendations in connection with WMC placement programs and strikes based on racial problems were sent to Region V this week.[7]

In further reference to questions concerning paid pre-employment training for the Alabama Dry Dock and Shipbuilding Company, a statement of Maritime Commission policy was sent to Region VII.[8] Also, at the request of the Director of Region VII, a statement of Committee policy on the post-employment records of the General Motors Company was sent out.[9]

Recommendations that Corpus Christi Latin American cases be closed were transmitted to Region X this week. Also, the War Department has been requested to give further information in connection with the Engineers Exchange, 10-GN-158.

The full report on the current status of the Western Cartridge case has been requested from Region VI.[10]

Further action on a complaint involving the Marine, Firemen, Oilers, Watertenders, and Wipers Union has been requested by Region XII. A letter has been sent to Admiral Land, of the Maritime Commission, on this matter. Also, Region XII's request for information on alienage and compliance matters has been answered.

ASSIGNMENTS TO CENTRAL STAFF.

Mr. Bloch:

1. Complaints against Railroad Retirement Board in Region II.
2. Mercedes Reid vs. Civil Service Commission, 2-GR-195.
3. FDR's assigned:
   Region I—3
   Region II—23
   Region III—21

As you requested, I asked Mr. Bloch about the status of his memorandum on important regional cases. I have not received this as yet because he is working on other matters assigned by you.[11]

Mr. Metzger:

1. Chevrolet Division of General Motors, 9-BR-135.
2. Ruling from Deputy Chairman on General Chemical Company.
3. USES, Richmond, California, 12-GR-6.
4. (For Mitchell) U. S. Army Air Force Depot, 5-GR-211–15.
5. Follow-up action on strike at Youngstown Sheet and Tube Company, Indiana Harbor Works.
6. FDR's assigned:
   Region V—24 (For Mitchell)
   Region VI—9
   Region XII—7

Mr. Mitchell:

The following important assignments are not yet completed:

1. Status of DFO cases.
2. Agendum for meeting of regional directors.
3. Memorandum on important oil cases in Region X.[12]

Assignments completed are attached or included in this report.

I have reviewed and taken action on questions raised in Weekly Reports other than those being handled by Mr. Metzger.

NEW R. D.'S OR FIELD INSTRUCTIONS

I have prepared and sent out the following R.D.'s:

1. Administrative Order No. 18, OPA—No. 52
2. Monthly Reports from Companies—No. 54 (For R&A)
3. Editorial Comment on the FEPC—No. 55
4. Case Action Forms—No. 56
5. Pushing Employment of Negroes—No. 58

Field Instruction No. 31 on Tension Areas has been submitted to the Administrative Office for duplicating.[13]

cc: Block
     Davidson
     Metzger

MS: copy, FEPC RG 228, *Office Files of Clarence Mitchell, DNA.*

1. The heart of the testimony presented by George M. Johnson and Mitchell reported the extensive racial discrimination in the Boilermakers Union, which covered 65 percent of shipyard workers. Referring to the extensive research done by Herbert Northrup, a professor at Cornell University, into discrimination by labor unions, Johnson said that at the shipyards African American workers were barred from regular membership. Instead, they were required to join a separate and unequal auxiliary in order to work there. If they refused, they had to leave their jobs. See "Production in Shipbuilding Plants," 1/19/44, H. Res. 52, *Hearings,* (78) H1037-1-C, 1171–84; Mitchell's testimony, 1181; 6/26/44, note 1; headnote on the Shipbuilding Industry and the Boilermakers Union.

2. See the headnote on Strikes and Work Stoppages.

3. A problem was that the Texas Oil Company required all-black deck crews. See Mitchell's texts at 1/12, 1/14, 1/25/44; headnote on the Oil Industry.

4. For a report on this conference, see Mitchell, memorandum, 4/12/44. See also the section on the WMC and USES in the headnote on Relationships with Federal Agencies.

5. On segregation at the Standard Oil building, see Mitchell to Jones, memorandum, 1/21, with attached memorandum of 1/7/44 from Frank Hook.

6. See the headnote on Street and Local Railways.

7. See the headnote on Strikes and Work Stoppages.

8. See "Defense Training for Negroes in Birmingham, Alabama," and "The Participation of Negroes in the National Defense Training Program in Alabama," both reports in HqR66, Central Files. U.S. Government, Mexicans (Miscellaneous); Weaver, *Negro Labor,* 51–53.

9. See the headnote on Race, Creed, Color or National Origin on Employment Application Forms.

10. On the significance of the Western Cartridge case, involving a company in East Alton, a community where "No Negroes were allowed to work in the plant or live," see the headnote on Major Cases in St. Louis and sources cited there.

11. See memorandum, 1/27/44.

12. See memorandum, 1/25/44.

13. For Field Instruction 31, subsequently renumbered 32, on Racial Tension areas, see HqR78, Field Instructions. (entry 46), nos. 20–39. The RDs listed—in Memoranda Sent to Regional Directors (entry 45), FEPC RG 228, DNA—were not microfilmed.

Memorandum on Important Unadjusted Cases in Region X

Jan. 25, 1944

Mr. Will Maslow

Clarence M. Mitchell

Important Unadjusted Cases in Region X

I. Latin-Americans:

Dr. Carlos E. Castaneda, who was Acting Regional Director at the time, held conferences with the Shell, Humble, and Sinclair Oil Companies at Houston, Texas, in December of 1943. At that time, Dr. Castaneda made the following statement concerning the Shell Company:

"Mr. P. E. Foster, Manager of Refineries for the Shell Company at Houston, and Mr. G. H. Causler, representative of the Oil Workers, both stated that no changes would be made in a discriminatory upgrading program now in effect at the company."

This program according to Dr. Castaneda, "dead ends all Latin-Americans at the level of janitor and gard[e]ner."[1]

The position of the Union is as follows:

"The Union at this time does not propose to change without first having a hearing or order, as we consider ourselves and the company both in violation of the Executive Order."

"The position of management of the company is that the consequences of any change in this respect are so far reaching and would have such detrimental results that we do not see any reason for change."

Previously, on December 23, Mr. P. E. Keegan of the Industrial Relations Department at Shell informed our examiner, Mr. Clay Cochran, that the company pays Latin-Americans and Negroes a lower wage than whites. Dr. Castaneda has described the Sinclair Oil Company and the Humble Oil Company as cooperative. We have the following cases against these companies:[2]

Texas Oil Company, Port Arthur, Texas

1. 10-BR-85 (hire)
2. 10-BR-86 (hire)

Sinclair Refining Company, Houston, Texas

1. 10-BR-135 (wage & upgrading)
2. 10-BR-32 (wages)
3. 10-BR-91 (?)
4. 10-BR-207 (wages)

Shell Oil Company, Houston, Texas

1. 10-BR-65 (upgrading)
2. 10-BR-64 (upgrading)
3. 10-BR-66 (upgrading)
4. 10-BR-67 (discharge)

Humble Oil Company, Baytown, Texas

1. 10-BR-84 (wages)
2. 10-BR-83 (wages)
3. 10-BR-82 (classification)
4. 10-BR-81 (upgrading)

II. Negro Complaints:

After almost twenty months of negotiations, the Consolidated Vultee Aircraft Corporation, 10-BR-28, still refuses to upgrade Negroes on a basis comparable to white employees. We also have two complaints against this company in New Orleans, Louisiana.[3]

The Delta Shipyard at New Orleans still refuses to upgrade Negro employees. Information obtained from USES 270 Reports show Negroes confined to unskilled jobs and an unwillingness on the part of the company to upgrade them. The Committee issued directives to this company on June 20, 1942.

The Todd Johnson Dry Docks at Algiers, Louisiana, and Galveston, Texas, are also listed as refusing to upgrade Negro employees.

MS: copy, HqR66, Central Files. U.S. Government, Aliens in Defense, Specific Groups, Mexican Workers.

1. On Latin Americans, see the headnotes on the FEPC and Unions, on the Oil Industry, and on Mexican Americans.

2. The following handwritten notations appear in the right margin of the memorandum:

> Texas Oil: "To be closed for insuf. Evidence. CEC 4/1/44."
>
> Sinclair Refining: "Satisfactorily adjusted. FDR's coming. CEC 2/1/44."
>
> Humble Oil: "Satisfactorily adjusted—CEC 2/1/44."

3. For texts immediately related to complaints by blacks, see 5/5, 8/14/44. For background, see the headnotes on the Aircraft Industry and on the Shipbuilding Industry.

Memorandum on Unions at the Federal Cartridge Company in Minneapolis, Minnesota

Jan. 26, 1944

Mr. George M. Johnson
> Deputy Chairman

Clarence M. Mitchell
> Associate Director of Field Operations

Unions at the Federal Cartridge Company in Minneapolis

The Twin City Ordnance Plant, which is operated by the Federal Cartridge Company, has bargaining agreements with the Federal Labor Union Number 23230 and District Lodge Number 77 of the International Association of Machinists. These agreements were made in May of 1943, according to the War Department.

Other unions at the company, but holding no bargaining agreements, are the International Association of Fire Fighters, AFL; International Union of Operating Engineers, Local 3436, AFL; UERMWA, CIO, Local 1152; General Drivers Union, Local 120; and Fireman and Oilers Union, Local 48 of St. Paul, and Local 490 of Minneapolis.

MS: copy, HqR3, Office Files of George M. Johnson. M.
See 2/12/44; headnote on the FEPC and Unions.

Memorandum on Cases Referred to Director of Field Operations

DATE: Jan. 27, 1944

TO: Mr. Will Maslow

FROM: Clarence M. Mitchell

SUBJECT: Cases Referred to Director of Field Operations

The following cases, referred to the Director of Field Operations for handling, are still unadjusted and are in the hands of the individuals listed, (excluding railroad and boilermaker cases).

MR. BLOCH

1. Mt. Ranier Motor Base, 12-GR-15. Complaint of a Negro who says he was refused employment because of his race. Report requested from War Department. Assigned 10/23/43.

2. War Department, Fort Knight, Oakland, California, 12-GR-7. Negro complainant states she was refused employment. Assigned.

3. American Bemberg Corporation, 7-BA-122. A German-born complainant states he was discharged because of alienage. Assigned 11/13/43.

4. Collins & Aikman, 3-BR-73, USES complaint charges company did not accept Negroes. Fleming making investigations since complaint was forwarded to DFO from Region II. Assigned 12/14/43.

5. Office of Censorship, 2-GN-285. Bulgarian complainant states she was refused employment because of her national origin. Loyalty report requested. Assigned 11/6/43.

6. Office of Education, 2-GR-434. Regional office of FEPC states discriminatory form is being used by schools in accepting applicants for vocational training for war work. Letter sent to the U.S. Office of Education on December 17, 1943. No response as yet. Assigned 12–10–43.[1]

7. Navy Department, Pearl Harbor Navy Yard, 7-GR-168. Negro complainant states she was refused employment in Hawaii after qualifying in Civil Service examination. Assigned 1–18–44.

8. Civil Service Commission, 2-GR-195. Negro complainant charges she was refused referral to employment. Referred to DFO 1/12/44. Assigned 1/19/44.

MR. DAVIDSON

1. Clinton Engineer Works, 7-BN-116. Latvian complainant charges she was dismissed because of her national origin. Assigned 10/21/43.

2. Quartermaster Market Center, 3-GC-244. Complainant charges he was dismissed from employment because he is a Jew. Assigned 8/6/43.

3. Athenia Steel Company, 3-BC-225. Discriminatory application form. Assigned 11/19/43.

MR. JOHNSON

1. Kansas City Stock Yards Company, Question of jurisdiction sent in by Region IX. After the President of the company verbally agreed to cooperate in adjusting discriminatory practice, he turned the matter over to his lawyers, who now question our jurisdiction. Referred to Mr. Johnson 12/31/43.

2. Oakland Port of Embarkation. Negro complainant alleges he was refused employment solely because of his race. War Department reported on November 19, 1943, on this matter. Congressman Tolan's office interested in behalf of complainant. Assigned 5/28/43. War Department report of November 19 to Mr. Johnson.

MR. METZGER

1. Hydraulic Machinery, Incorporated, 5-BC-1213. Jehovah's Witness charges he was discharged because of creed. Assigned 12–29–43. Returned to region 1–17–44 for further action.

2. General Chemical Company, 6-BA-20. Complainant charges he was dismissed because of alienage. Assigned

3. Anaconda Mining Company, Butte, Montana, 11-BR-20. Negro complainant states he was refused employment.

4. U. S. Army Air Forces (War Department), Cleveland, Ohio, 5-GR-211–215. Negro complainants charge refusal to hire. Referred to DFO 1/6/44. Assigned 1/18/44.

5. Chevrolet Division, General Motors, 9-BR-135. Refusal of company to keep post-employment records of non-white employment. Referred to DFO 1–10–44.

MR. MITCHELL (for Mr. Maslow)

1. Delco-Remy, 6-BC-296. Complaint of Jehovah's Witnesses charging they were dismissed because of creed. Referred to Region V by DFO. Assigned 12/15/43.

2. General Motors-Delco-Remy Corporation, 6-BC-275-82. Complainants charge they were dismissed because they are Seventh Day Adventists. Matter referred to Region V by DFO. Assigned 12/15/43.

MR. MITCHELL

1. Sinclair Contractors, 11-BR-21. USES 510 on this company states it refused to accept Negro applicants. Company reply states its representative was recruiting for another contractor. We have asked for name of company for whom recruiting was being done. Also, have requested that Sinclair Company inform its representative that he should refrain from recruiting in a discriminatory manner. Assigned 11/9/43.

2. United States Maritime Enrolling Office, 10-GR-11. Complainant charges he was denied a referral to employment. Inquiry sent to War Shipping Administration 12/30/43. No reply as yet. Assigned 9/14/43.

3. Comptroller General, 6-GR-248. War Relocation Authority stated GAO in Chicago refused to accept American citizens of Japanese origin referred for employment. Conference with Assistant Comptroller General, Chairman, and myself on January 5, 1944.[2] Assigned 11/17/43.

4. Treasury Department, 3-GC-179. Complainant charges she failed to obtain employment at a War Loan Office in Philadelphia because she is a Jew. We originally thought we would have a conference with Treasury on this and other cases, but no other cases were referred to us by regional offices. Matter then taken up by letter December 29, 1943. Reply from Treasury dated January 18 denies discrimination. Letter states complainant was too young, but another Jewish applicant was hired.

5. U.S. Army Engineers, Northwest Division, 12-GR-112. Matter referred to War Department for action. Negro complainant states he was refused right to register for job in Alaska. Assigned 11/23/43.

6. Metcalfe-Hamilton Construction Company, 12-BR- Negro complainant says he is being discriminated against in Canada. Further information requested on December 29, 1943.

7. Columbus & Greenville Railway Company, 7-BR- . Railway union charges company refuses to grant pay increase because a number of employees affected are Negroes. Assigned 12/7/44.

8. William Otsuki, citizen of Japanese origin, charges he was denied admission to Maritime Commission training service in Denver, Colorado. Letter to WSA 12/30/43. Assigned 12/20/43.

MR. MITCHELL (For Mr. Bloch)

1. 2-GN-262. Complaint by Japanese-American Committee for Democracy that Japanese-Americans had been denied War Shipping Administration training.

War Shipping Administration announced its policy was one of no discrimination. This forwarded to complainant organization 1/4/44. Comments asked. Assigned 1/4/44.

MS: LH, DI, HqR3, Office Files of George M. Johnson. M.
   1. Handwritten notation in right margin: "Reply received Jan. 22."
   2. For Mitchell's report on this meeting, see 1/5/44.

Memorandum on Mrs. Joy Davis's
Comments on Cases

Date: Jan. 27, 1944

TO: Mrs. Marjorie Lawson
        Mr. John A. Davis

FROM: Clarence M. Mitchell

SUBJECT: Mrs. Joy Davis' Comments on FDR 10-BR-53, 10-GR-150,
           10-GR-151, and 10-GR-146

1. North American Aviation, Inc., 10-BR-53. There is nothing in this report to prove that discrimination had actually taken place. The USES statement and the hiring policies of the company must be weighed against the complainant's original statement that he was told he was too young. In addition, the USES asked that the complainant be referred to its office a second time. The FEPC regional office made an effort to contact the complainant but was unsuccessful in doing so. In the absence of any further information from the complainant, the regional office acted properly in dismissing the case on merits. The complaint was filed October 6, 1943.

2. USES, 10-GR-150–151.* This complaint was filed December 27, 1942. The Bureau of Placement should have acted on this promptly. However, unless we could determine whether the complainants are still available and able to give full statements, further investigation of these particular cases would be a waste of time. Use of discretion in handling such cases is a valuable asset to our regional directors. The regional office is under no illusions about USES policy in Texas.[1]

* 10-GR-151 was filed 2/5/43

3. Fort Worth Quartermaster Depot, 10-GR-146. This complaint was referred to the Committee by the Civil Service Commission. From the information given, there did not seem to be sufficient evidence of discrimination. An effort was made by our office to contact the complainant. It was unsuccessful and, hence, the case was closed. The complaint was filed 5-18-43.

MS: LH, DI, HqR38, Central Files. (entry 25) Memoranda, Lawson, Marjorie.
  1. See the section on the WMC and USES in the headnote on Relationships with Federal Agencies.

Weekly Report

Jan. 29, 1944

Mr. Will Maslow
Clarence M. Mitchell
Report for Week Ending January 29, 1944

OUTSTANDING EVENTS AND PROBLEMS

A listing of the DFO cases was completed this week. It showed a total of thirty cases being handled by the central office upon referral from regional offices. This was as of January 27.

Regions IX and X show an accumulation of problem cases which appear unadjustable unless a hearing is held. Mr. Stanley Metzger of the central staff will be in St. Louis on Monday, January 31, to review and take further action on outstanding cases in that area. A memorandum prepared by me shows that in Region X cases involving the Shell, Humble, Sinclair, and Texas Oil Companies seem to have reached the point where further action from the Committee is imperative. These cases involve Latin-Americans, primarily, but there are some Negro complainants, also. Cases involving the Consolidated Vultee Aircraft Corporation, the Delta Shipyard, and the Todd Johnson Dry Docks concern Negro complainants exclusively. In these cases, unwillingness on the part of the companies to adjust grievances of long standing seem to indicate the necessity of Committee action.[1]

On January 12, 1944, the Deputy Chairman was informed of a plan formulated by the Texas Oil Company to use all-Negro deck crews. It is my understanding that this matter has been discussed with Mr. Edward Lawson, Director of Region II. The Deputy Chairman indicates that, on the basis of information submitted, "it is apparent that the plan is discriminatory."[2]

IMPORTANT CONTACTS WITH REGIONAL OFFICES, OTHER DIVISIONS, AND OTHER GOVERNMENT AGENCIES

The Deputy Chairman has been requested to make a ruling on whether a complaint involving the R. R. Donnelly and Sons Company (8-BR-1) is within the jurisdiction of the Committee. The company is one of the large printing concerns of the country.[3]

The Deputy Chairman has also been requested to consider the possibility of working out an agreed statement of facts on the Los Angeles Street Railway case (12-BR-11503).

A complaint from Mr. Neal McGillicuddy, of the United Electrical Workers, CIO, has been sent to Region II for further action. Mr. McGillicuddy charges that Negro employees of the Remington Arms Company are being laid off in a discriminatory manner.

Region II indicated in its Weekly Report of January 22 that WMC would be asked to discontinue 510 Reports under certain circumstances. We have requested that Mr. Lawson, the Director, continue receiving 510's under all circumstances.

We have forwarded to Region IV a digest of telephone conversations between myself and officials of the Bethlehem Steel Company and Baltimore Urban League concerning alleged dismissals of Negro workers.[4]

No reply has been received in connection with the letter to Governor Paul V. McNutt, Chairman of the War Manpower Commission, regarding the Region IV WMC Director's refusal to supply ES 270 information and 510 Reports.[5]

Regions X's request of January 12 for information concerning the handling of cases involving Sabbatarians has been answered.[6]

In Region IV questions have arisen concerning additional office space and additional personnel. It appears that these matters have been settled. If any further action is needed on them, it will be taken up at the time of the regional directors' meeting.

Regional Director Brin states that 510 Reports are now coming in from Louisiana. I believe that this may be attributed to field trips by Mr. L. Virgil Williams and other action on the part of our office in Dallas. This is an encouraging sign.

ASSIGNMENTS TO CENTRAL STAFF

Mr. Bloch:

No new assignments have been made to Mr. Bloch, aside from the review of FDR's and Weekly Reports from Regions I, II, III, and VII. Previous assignments are held up because of a lack of stenographic service. It is hoped that this will be remedied during the coming week.

FDR's assigned:

> Region II—4
> Region III—25

Mr. Davidson:

Action of the Assistant Director of Field Operations is, of course, reported on his own initiative. However, he has agreed to share with me the additional work load created by the field trip of Mr. Stanley D. Metzger. In keeping with this, the U.S. Department of Health, IX-GR-20, DFO, has been transmitted to Mr. Davidson for handling.

Miss Kahn:

1. The following FDR's have been handled by Miss Kahn under my supervision:

   Region V—25

2. Also, under my supervision, Miss Kahn has reviewed and made recommendations on undocketed complaints against U. S. Insular Bases.

New assignments given to Miss Kahn:

At the request of the Hearings Division, Miss Kahn is reviewing Weekly Reports from Region XII under my supervision.

Mr. Metzger:

Assignments completed by Mr. Metzger include:

1. Summary of St. Louis cases for Committee.
2. Review of and recommendations on correspondence concerning non-discrimination clause in the lease between the Board of State Harbor Commission, San Francisco, California, and the Food Distribution Administration.
3. Recommendations on Los Angeles Street Railway Company, 12-BR-1150.
4. Recommendations on St. Louis Aircraft Company (9-BR-52) and Strickland Aircraft Company (9-BR-51).
5. Recommendations to the field on General Chemical Company (6-BR-20).

New assignments to Mr. Metzger are:

1. Review of Weekly Reports from Regions VI, IX, XI, and XII.
2. FDR's assigned:
   Region VI—2
   Region XII—6

Mr. Mitchell:

The following assignments were completed by me:

1. DFO case on Ronald I. Shiosaki.[7]
2. General Accounting Office (6-GR-248)
3. Treasury Department (3-GC-179) returned to the region for appraisal of report by Treasury Department.
4. Memorandum on important cases in Region X.[8]
5. Status of DFO cases.[9]

Important assignments not yet completed:

1. Agendum for regional directors' meeting.

New assignments:

1. Guy F. Atkinson Company (12-BR-23 DFO).
2. Reviewing and taking action on matters raised in Weekly Reports from Regions IV, V, and X.
3. FDR's reviewed and acted upon:
   Region VI—6

MS: copy, HqR6, _Office Files of Emanuel H. Bloch. Weekly Reports._

1. See Mitchell, report, "Unadjusted Cases in Region X," 1/25/44.

2. See 1/12/44 memorandum, and notes.

3. See the headnote on Jurisdictional Issues.

4. Digest not found, but for earlier discussions regarding this firm, see report of 8/6/43 and digests of 7/31 and 8/43, in appendix 1.

5. See the section on the WMC and USES in the headnote on Relationships with Federal Agencies.

6. See the headnote on Creedal Discrimination.

7. Shiosaki was discharged from his job as a cost accountant with Shotwell Manufacturing Company following intervention by the War Department. This case, involving a loyalty investigation of a Japanese American excluded from employment by the War Department, was conducted under the terms of the FEPC agreement with the provost marshal's office discussed by Mitchell in his 5/6/43 memorandum and of a follow-up agreement with Colonel Alton C. Miller, director, Personnel Security Division, Office of the Provost Marshal General, 9/3/43, in HqR67, Central Files. Reports, U.S. Government, War Department, M–Z. See also 2/4/44; and, for similar cases involving Italian and German Americans, Mitchell's 2/17/44 report. For background, see the headnotes on National Origin, Alienage, and Loyalty and on Japanese Americans.

8. See memorandum, 1/25/44.

9. See weekly report, 1/27/44.

Memorandum on Field Instructions
of General Accounting Office Regarding
American Citizens of Japanese Ancestry

CONFIDENTIAL

February 4, 1944

MEMORANDUM

TO: Mr. Malcolm Ross
              Chairman

FROM: Clarence M. Mitchell
              Associate Director of Field Operations

SUBJECT: Field Instruction of General Accounting Office
              in re. American Citizens of Japanese Ancestry

On the above date, I called Mr. E. Ray Ballinger, Director of Personnel for the General Accounting Office, concerning a field instruction which Mr. Frank Yates, Assistant Comptroller General, had promised us would be gotten out to the GAO regional offices on the hiring of citizens of Japanese ancestry. Mr. Ballinger stated that the instruction has been sent out and that Mr. Lindsay Warren, Comptroller General, was reluctant to send a copy to another Government agency. Mr. Ballinger agreed to read the instruction over the telephone, and this is the gist of it:

It is a memorandum, Number 19, dated January 22, 1944, entitled "American Citizens of Japanese Ancestry." The memorandum states that the matter of employment of citizens of Japanese ancestry has been discussed from time to time. It also states that the General Accounting Office will not deny employment to such persons solely because of national origin. Citizens of Japanese ancestry are to be appointed on the basis of merit when there is no question of their loyalty. Further, the memorandum provides that, if a citizen of Japanese ancestry is declared by the War Relocation Authority to be loyal but the appointing officer has some doubts, the case is to be referred to Mr. Ballinger for further investigation and consideration.

Under the circumstances, I presume it is unnecessary to insist upon receiving a copy of the actual instruction itself.

MS: copy, HqR1, Office Memoranda. M.

In his 1/7/44 report, Mitchell noted the meeting he and Ross had with GAO officials. See also 2/5/44; headnote on Japanese Americans.

Weekly Report

Feb. 5, 1944

Mr. Will Maslow

Clarence M. Mitchell

Weekly Report for Week Ending February 5, 1944

OUTSTANDING EVENTS AND PROBLEMS

In the report of January 29, it was mentioned that Region X has pending and un-adjustable cases involving the Sinclair, Humble, Shell, and Texas Oil Companies.[1] A report received from Dr. Carlos E. Castaneda, Special Assistant to the Chairman, states that the Humble and Sinclair cases are settled. This means that the companies are correcting wage discriminations and other complaints, principally involving Latin-Americans. The Shell Company case is still unadjusted, and the case has been referred to the Director of Field Operations. The Special Assistant to the Chairman feels that the cases involving the Texas Oil Company are too old for current handling. Dr. Castaneda indicates further that the Houston and Brown Shipbuilding Companies in Houston, Texas, apparently have ceased discriminating against Latin-Americans but still discriminate against Negroes.

Region VI has submitted a report on its settlement of the Youngstown Sheet and Tube Company strike, which occurred when a Negro was employed as an Engine Hostler Helper in a department in the plant which had not previously employed colored persons.

We are still awaiting a statement from Governor Paul V. McNutt, Chairman of the War Manpower Commission, in reply to a letter from the Chairman [Ross] concerning the refusal of the WMC's Region IV Director [Henry Triede] to give ES 270 information and 510 Reports to FEPC's Region IV.[2]

IMPORTANT CONTACTS WITH REGIONAL OFFICES, OTHER DIVISIONS, AND OTHER GOVERNMENT AGENCIES

This week, Mr. E. Ray Ballinger, Director of Personnel for the General Accounting Office, informed the Associate Director of Field Operations [Mitchell] that the GAO has sent out a field instruction to its regional offices on citizens of Japanese ancestry. This is in conformity with our agreement at a previous conference with the General Accounting Office.[3]

The Director of Field Operations [Maslow] has requested the Deputy Chairman [Johnson] to rule on whether, "When an employer discriminates against a Jehovah's Witness because of the latter's refusal to buy War Bonds, is this discrimination based upon creed, which is forbidden by Executive Order 9346."[4]

Regions II and III are considering a possible division of territory which will place the northern counties of New Jersey under the jurisdiction of New York. A proposed division has been worked out by the Associate Director of Field Operations.

We have not yet had a reply from Region III on the status of the Pennsylvania Bell Telephone Case. A reminder has been sent to the Regional Director [Fleming].

Region IV has been informed that the Capital Transit case should be transmitted to the Director of Field Operations for further handling.[5] We have also requested Region IV to submit the latest report and recommendations on the Chesapeake and Potomac Telephone case in Baltimore, Maryland.

Questions raised by Region VI in connection with the Pullman Company of Chicago, 6-BR-166 and 266, have been answered.

Region X's question in connection with the General Alkali cases of Corpus Christi, Texas, has been answered. The cases are to be dismissed on merit.

For his information, we have transmitted to the Director of Region XII [Kingman] a report on the status of the Los Angeles Street Railway Company case.[6]

ASSIGNMENTS TO CENTRAL STAFF

Mr. Bloch:

Mr. Bloch has completed the following assignments:

1. Interview with Washington representative of Railroad Retirement Board.
2. Listing of Major Cases in Regional Offices.
3. Elimination of discriminatory information on application forms of Railway Mail Service.
4. Memorandum on Federal policy against discrimination by reason of race, color, creed, and national origin.[7]

New assignments:

1. Metcalfe-Hamilton Construction Company, 2-BR-544—DFO.
2. Reviewing Weekly Reports—Regions I, II, III, and VII.
3. FDR's assigned:
   Region II—10

Mr. Davidson:

1. The Assistant Director of Field Operations has agreed to handle questions raised by Region VI on national origin.
2. FDR's assigned:
   Region VI—5

Miss Kahn:

Miss Kahn is absent from the central office, but, before leaving, completed her assignment of reviewing Weekly Reports from Region XII for the Legal Division.

Mr. Metzger:

Mr. Metzger is absent on a field assignment in St. Louis and has sent in a report on the U.S. Cartridge Company, 9-BR-13, 62, 69, 87, and 97, located there.[2]

Mr. Mitchell:

Assignments completed:

1. Vivian B. Moreton vs. Navy Department, 7-GR-168.
2. Reviewing and acting upon Weekly Reports from Regions IV, V, VI, VIII, IX, XI, and XII.

New assignments:

1. Shell Oil Company, 10-BN-64, DFO.
2. Kasuo Yamashita vs. State Department, 2-GR-519, DFO.
3. Digest of agreements between FEPC and other Government agencies for the Deputy Chairman.

MS: copy, FEPC RG 228, Office Files of Clarence Mitchell, DNA.

1. For Mitchell's earlier report on these cases, see 1/25/44. See also the extensive background materials in HqR66, Central Files. U.S. Government, Aliens in Defense, Specific Groups, Mexican Workers; headnote on Mexican Americans.

2. See the section on the WMC and USES in the headnote on Relationships with Federal Agencies.

3. For earlier references, see 11/17/43, 1/5, 1/7, 2/4/44; headnote on Japanese Americans.

4. At its 3/4/44 meeting, the Committee declined "jurisdiction of cases based on religious grounds unless it" was shown that there was a violation based on "some established precept of the creed." See Minutes of 3/4/44, HqR1, Summary Minutes of Meetings; headnote on Creedal Discrimination.

5. See the headnote on Street and Local Railways.

6. This report was prepared by the legal department at Mitchell's request (see 1/29/44 report). The report has not been found, but George Crockett's instruction to Mitchell of 3/8/44 on how to proceed with the investigation is in HqR2, Office Files of Malcolm Ross. Difficult Cases. Also filed with this text is a "Compliance after Formal Complaint" text that provides a chronological development of the case.

7. For the National Policy against Racial or Religious Discrimination, see 2/8/44 in appendix 1.

8. See the headnote on Major Cases in St. Louis.

Memorandum on Monthly Summary Reports

February 9, 1944

MEMORANDUM

TO: Mr. Bloch
        Miss Kahn
        Mr. Metzger

FROM: Clarence M. Mitchell
        Associate Director of Field Operations

SUBJECT: Monthly Summary Reports, as Discussed in Our Staff Meeting
        of Monday, January 24, 1944

Please prepare a monthly summary report on FDR's which you have handled. Indicate by region major problems raised and the types of settlement reached. This should be a narrative statement in which you may also add your general views concerning the effectiveness of our operations, as evidenced by the FDR's.

Some illustrations of the things which should be treated in your summary statement are:

1. Delays in the handling of cases.
2. Whether the complainant has been handled properly.
3. Errors in following Field Instructions.
4. Collateral investigations.
5. Whether standards of settlement are too low or too high.

cc: Davidson
        Maslow

MS: copy, HqR6, Office Files of Emanuel H. Bloch. (A–Z), Clarence Mitchell (Assignments Completed).

Memorandum on Experiences
with the War Manpower Commission,
as Reported by FEPC Regional Directors

February 10, 1944

MEMORANDUM

TO: Mr. Will Maslow

FROM: Clarence M. Mitchell

SUBJECT: Experiences with WMC, as Reported by FEPC Regional Directors

The following is a brief digest of the working relationships between the War Manpower Commission and the Regional Directors of FEPC as reported in our conference on Thursday, February 10, 1944. Regional Directors were requested to report on the following items.[1]

1. Do you have access to ES 270 Reports?
2. Do you receive ES 510 Reports?
3. Has the WMC appointed a Liaison Officer?
4. Has WMC sent out a special Regional Instruction on the national Operating Agreement between FEPC and WMC?
5. Is there general cooperation from WMC?

For the sake of clarity, I include the information that ES 270 Reports are statistical and narrative reports on projected labor requirements of specific plants, as well as information on current numbers of persons employed. The ES 510 is a form which the USES uses to indicate that it has received a discriminatory order from an employer. It is a docketable complaint under FEPC field instructions.

Mr. Edward Lawson, Acting Regional Director of Region I (the New England states) and Director of Region II (New York State), reported complete cooperation from the War Manpower Commission on all counts. He has full access to ES 270 Reports, receives ES 510 Reports regularly, and there are two WMC Liaison Officers. In addition, Mrs. Anna Rosenberg, Regional Director in II for WMC, has sent out a model operating instruction, and Mr. Joseph Smith, WMC Region I Director, has sent out a slightly less effective one.

Mr. G. James Fleming, Director of Region III (Pennsylvania, New Jersey, and Delaware), reported that he has access to the ES 270 Reports. So far, he has received ES 510 Reports from Philadelphia only, as WMC officials in Delaware and New Jersey are reluctant to submit ES 510's. A good relationship exists between Mr. Fleming and the Regional WMC Director. A special operating instruction has been sent out and a liaison representative has been appointed.

Mr. Frank E. Hook, Director of Region IV (The District of Columbia, Maryland, Virginia, West Virginia, and North Carolina) is denied access to ES 270 Reports by Mr. Henry Triede, Regional Director of WMC. The WMC has not sent any ES 510 Reports to FEPC. The national WMC instruction on the operating agreement has not been sent to the local WMC offices in Region IV, nor has any special instruction been sent out on the National FEPC-WMC Agreement. There is a Liaison Officer between FEPC and WMC who cooperates so far as he can within the limitations prescribed by Mr. Triede. Mr. Hook reported that some WMC offices cooperate at the local level.

Mr. William T. McKnight, Director of Region V (Michigan, Ohio, and Kentucky) reported that he has access to ES 270 Reports and that, in the last four months, he has received 160 ES 510's from the WMC. The WMC has appointed liaison representatives in his region and special operating instructions have been sent out by the Regional Director of WMC.

Mr. Elmer W. Henderson, Director of Region VI (Illinois, Indiana, and Wisconsin) reported good cooperation from WMC. He stated that a special instruction has been sent out to state directors by Mr. William H. Spencer, Director of WMC. Liaison duties are handled by the Director of Manpower Utilization in Region VI. In Wisconsin, the Deputy State Director of WMC serves as Liaison Officer. Mr. Henderson stated that he does not receive many 510 Reports in his region. In his capacity of Acting Director of Region VIII, Mr. Henderson reported he has very few cases in this region (comprising the states of Minnesota, Iowa, the Dakotas, and Nebraska) but his relationships with WMC are good there.

Mr. A. Bruce Hunt, Director of Region VII (South Carolina, Georgia, Florida, Alabama, Mississippi, and Tennessee) reported that the majority of local USES offices in the region appear to be unaware of the FEPC. He stated that he has access to ES 270 information, but has not received any ES 510's as yet. However, he believes they will be forthcoming later. The national operating instruction of WMC has been sent out with other special directions. A Liaison Officer has been appointed. Mr. Hunt said that he has a good working relationship with the Deputy Regional Director of WMC.

Mr. Roy A. Hoglund, Director of Region IX (Missouri, Oklahoma, Arkansas, and Kansas), reported that he gets ES 270 information at the Regional level. In St. Louis, he stated, he can obtain the information he requests on them although he is not permitted to see the actual report. A Liaison Officer has been appointed, but no ES 510 Reports come in. Mr. Hoglund made no report on Region XI (Montana, Idaho, Utah, Wyoming, and Colorado) where he is Acting Regional Director.

Mr. Leonard M. Brin, Director of Region X (Louisiana, Texas, and New Mexico), reported that WMC has sent out a weak operating instruction. WMC has appointed a Liaison Officer, but he (Mr. Brin) has received only three ES 510's. The WMC has sent in one Form 42, reporting discriminatory training practices.

Mr. Harry L Kingman, Director of Region XII (California, Arizona, Nevada, Washington, and Oregon) reports an increasingly good working relationship with the WMC.

Several Liaison Officers have been appointed and special operating instructions sent out. The San Francisco area is getting a good number of 510's, and conferences to be held in other parts of the region are likely to result in an increasing flow of 510's. Access to ES 270's is satisfactory. WMC sanctions will occasionally be forthcoming on FEPC request.

MS: copy, LH, HqR3, Office Files of George M. Johnson. M.

1. On the first FEPC regional directors meeting, held 2/10–2/12/44, see report, 2/17/44. For background to this text, see the section on the WMC and USES in the headnote on Relationships with Federal Agencies.

Memorandum on Information on Charles L. Horn

2–12–44

ROUGH DRAFT

MEMORANDUM

TO: Mr. Malcolm Ross

FROM: Clarence M. Mitchell

SUBJECT: Information on Mr. Charles L. Horn

I first knew of Mr. Horn while living in St. Paul, Minnesota.[1] At that time, a mutual friend suggested that I should urge Mr. Horn to employ some Negroes at his plant in Anoka, Minnesota, which is the Federal Cartridge Company. In 1938, or thereabout, I raised this question with Mr. Horn. He indicated that his plant did not discriminate against Negroes, and none were at that time because there were not many Negroes living in the City of Anoka. From my knowledge of Anoka, I knew this to be a fact.

When Mr. Horn began operating the Twin Cities Ordnance Plant, Mr. Cecil E. Newman, Editor of the Minneapolis Spokesman and St. Paul Recorder (two Negro newspapers) told me that Mr. Horn expected to hire a number of Negroes. Mr. Newman and Mr. Horn have been friends for a number of years and very shortly Mr. Horn kept his commitment. At first, some difficulties arose in the employment of colored persons, and the whole program was threatened. In order to prevent any retarding of the program, Mr. Horn urged Mr. Newman to come on the staff as a personnel representative. Mr. Newman did this and is still so engaged. There are approximately 1,200 Negroes who have been or are employed at the company. There have been some recent curtailments in cartridge production which have resulted in some lay-offs. Mr. Horn has not only committed himself to the full employment of Negroes without discrimination in his own plant, but he has been most vigorous in attempting to persuade other employers to follow his example. I should judge that he is a man in his fifties, who would do an excellent job if appointed to the Committee. He is very popular, personally, in the Twin City area among Negroes.

MS: draft, HqR3, Office Files of George M. Johnson, M.

1. Mitchell also testified regarding Horn at the FEPC meeting of 2/11/44, where the Committee approved Horn's nomination as the FEPC's candidate for a successor to Samuel Zemurray as a business representative on the FEPC. Roosevelt did subsequently appoint him to the post. See Transcript of Proceedings, 2/11/44, 2–10, HqR65, Central Files.

Memorandum on Visit to Baltimore on Western Electric Case

Feb. 16, 1944

Mr. Malcolm Ross

Clarence M. Mitchell and Ernest G. Trimble

Visit to Baltimore on Western Electric Case

We went to Baltimore on the above date to meet with Brigadier General A. A. Farmer, who is in charge of the Western Electric Company for the War Department. Also at the meeting was Lieutenant Colonel W. E. Thurman. General Farmer stated that the company is currently operating at top efficiency level; most of the employees are back at work; and there has been no change in the arrangement of facilities at the plant. He said, however, he was assured from investigations conducted by the F. B. I. and Army Intelligence that, when the Army moves out, some of the workers will leave the plant unless there is a plan provided for some separation of Negroes and whites in the use of lavatory facilities. General Farmer was asked whether the investigations had shown what the reaction of Negroes would be if a segregated lavatory scheme was introduced. General Farmer stated that some of the investigators felt that a large number of Negroes would not object to the separate facilities. Mr. Mitchell told General Farmer that he did not share the views of the investigators concerning the reaction of the Negroes on the basis of information which he had received from first-hand sources.

General Farmer stated that a new man, Mr. Jack Gainey, is in charge of personnel. Apparently, he has replaced Mr. C. C. Chew. Also, Mr. V. L. Dorsey, of the PBEA, has been replaced by Mr. H. G. Hennighausen. Colonel Thurman appeared to regard Mr.

Hennighausen as more stable than Mr. Dorsey. Mr. Mitchell feels that there is very little to choose from when considering the relative merits of Mr. Dorsey and Mr. Hennighausen.

Colonel Thurman presented what he said was the company's plan for a solution of the problem. First, the company intends to maintain the restaurant facilities as before. There will be new facilities installed with smaller tables, but Negroes and whites alike will use these facilities, under the plan. Another part of the plan calls for the establishment of locker units with wash rooms and toilets attached. General Farmer stated that the company had been given assistance in obtaining the additional steel required for lockers and that the Western Electric Company would spend approximately $500,000 in getting improved locker and lavatory facilities throughout the plant. Under this unit system, Negroes would be assigned to a locker unit on one side of the building and the whites to units on the opposite side. There would be no signs designating Negro or white facilities, but Colonel Thurman said the company hoped that persons using certain locker units would use the lavatory facilities attached to such units. Mr. Mitchell asked whether those planning this new scheme had taken into consideration the possibility of difficulties which individuals would face if they were working in one part of the plant and their locker unit with its lavatory facility was in another part. Colonel Thurman said that under the plan the facilities would be conveniently located as far as it was possible to do so, and it would be unlikely that persons would be disadvantaged by the arrangement.

It was agreed that Mr. Trimble would remain in Baltimore and go through the plant to try to ascertain the attitude of the colored employees on the question of separate or joint facilities.

In the afternoon, Mr. Trimble went with General Farmer to the latter's office in the Cable Building and started the afternoon's work by talking with Mr. John Shea, the Works Manager. Mr. Shea gave the same report about the reasons for the proposed plan for separate facilities that General Farmer and Colonel Thurman had given us in the forenoon. He said that the plan was that of the management. This was worked out, Mr. Shea said, after management had become convinced that trouble would develop when the military was removed from the plant if joint facilities were continued. He explained that, in his opinion, the community is opposed to joint facilities for colored and white and that he was reminded of this everytime he went to the Rotary Club or a meeting of the Chamber of Commerce. He had recently been to a social gathering, he said, including members of the Johns Hopkins University faculty and that at this gathering the faculty members made the same charge that he received from the business elements of the community, namely, that Western Electric was upsetting the pattern of the community on the race question. He also read from an article in the Baltimore Sun for December 31, 1943, which was to the same effect.

Mr. Shea was asked about the type of physical examination that the company gave prospective employees and whether or not a Wassermann test was given to determine the presence of venereal diseases. He at first said that such tests were given but called the medical office to check on his memory. He got the report that local tests were not given except a visual physical examination, but that the company's doctors did take samples of blood, which were sent to the Public Health Department of Baltimore for analysis. The test that the City Department of Health employed, he was told, was the Klein test which is supposed to be more accurate than the Wassermann. It was also reported to him, however, that while the City Health Department is making the test a new employee is put on the job and is released if the test reveals the presence of such a disease.

Mr. Trimble then went through the Cable Building and the Wire Building and talked to a number of the colored employees, both male and female, to find out how they felt on the question of separate or joint facilities for the two races. (General Farmer had told us that a number of colored employees were in favor of separate facilities). He talked to approximately 27 colored employees chosen at random. Nearly all the male employees expressed themselves as being opposed to the establishment of separate facilities. Quite a few of the female employees indicated that they would not object to separate facilities. At the same time, some of the employees who expressed this opinion obviously felt rather bitter about the treatment which they received from the white employees. He got the feeling that even though they said that they would accept separate facilities, nevertheless, some of them would be somewhat resentful if separate facilities were established. Quite a few among the employees interviewed did feel that a strike would probably occur if the military were withdrawn and joint facilities were continued. A smaller number did not think that a strike would develop.

Mr. Trimble's purpose in interviewing them was solely to determine their attitude on the question of facilities, and he scrupulously refrained from saying anything that might influence their decision one way or another. He did not even indicate to them that any plan for separate facilities was contemplated. The results of his interviews can be summarized as follows: Most of the colored people would resent the establishment of separate facilities; some of them also felt that a strike might develop if and when the military was removed if joint facilities were continued. If separate facilities were established, he believed the effect on the colored employees would be one of resentment and lowering of morale but that that would be the extent of their objection. As to whether the white employees would strike if joint facilities were retained, he believes it is impossible to determine except by trial.

MS: copy, FR45, Region IV. Closed Cases 108–215, Western Electric Co., Point Breeze Plant, Baltimore, Md.

For Mitchell's involvement in this case and for background on the racial tensions over toilet facilities and the army takeover of the plant, see Mitchell's memoranda of 8/26, 11/11, 12/14/43, 3/14, 4/5/44; Transcript of Proceedings, 4/1/44, 96, HqR65, Central Files; headnote on Strikes and Work Stoppages.

Weekly Report

Feb. 17, 1944

Mr. Will Maslow

Clarence M. Mitchell

Weekly Report for Week Ending February 12, 1944

OUTSTANDING EVENTS AND PROBLEMS

The Regional Directors of the President's Committee on Fair Employment Practice met in Washington on February 10, 11, and 12. One of the important results of this meeting was a statement on the working relationships existing between the Committee's representatives and WMC regional offices in the field. In most regions, the agreement between WMC and the Committee seems to be operating in good order. Region IV was one of those in which a poor working relationship exists. As yet, we have had no reply from Governor Paul V. McNutt, Chairman of the War Manpower Commission, concerning problems in Region IV.[1]

Recommendations and summary statements concerning parties charged in the St. Louis area were received from Mr. Stanley D. Metzger this week.

Cases involving discrimination against American citizens of Japanese ancestry who sought employment on Merchant vessels have been referred to Mr. Ralph A. Bard, Assistant Secretary of the Navy, by the Chairman.

IMPORTANT CONTACTS WITH REGIONAL OFFICES, OTHER DIVISIONS, AND OTHER GOVERNMENT AGENCIES

A stenographic summary of the meetings of Regional Directors has been prepared and is now being edited before distribution.[2]

War Department reports on loyalty investigations in the cases of Vincent A. Cutietta, 5-GA-185, R. Soellner, and William Gohr have been given to Mr. Davidson for transmittal to the region.[3]

The report on the Railroad Retirement Board, prepared by Mr. Bloch, has been transmitted to Region VII. Also, an R. D. memorandum, Number 75, prepared by Mr. Bloch on the Railroad Retirement Board has been sent to all regional offices.

ASSIGNMENTS TO CENTRAL STAFF

Mr. Bloch:

1. Retail Credit Company, 3-BR-524 (DFO).
2. Preparation of digest of WMC regional operating instructions.
3. The following FDR's:
   Region I—1
   Region II—8
   Region III—13

Mr. Davidson:

1. The following FDR's :
   Region VI—17
   Region VIII—1
   Region XII—1

Miss Kahn:

Miss Kahn is out of the office.

Mr. Metzger:

Mr. Metzger is still in the field investigating the St. Louis area cases. We have received current reports from him.

Mr. Mitchell:

Assignments completed include:

1. Digest of reports of operating relationships between FEPC and WMC in regional offices.
2. Digest of agreements between FEPC and other Government agencies for the Deputy Chairman.[4]

New assignments include:

1. Preparation of record on regional directors' meeting.

MS: copy, FEPC RG 228, Office Files of Clarence Mitchell. DNA.

1. See Mitchell, report, 2/10/44.

2. For a report on the regional directors' meeting, see 2/28/44, note 4.

3. Maslow noted that Gohr and Soellner were two of three people who had filed complaints alleging that their discharges by their respective employers following action by the War Department were discriminatory. Maslow noted that the FEPC's involvement in the matter was in line with an agreement between the Committee and Colonel Alton C. Miller, Personnel Security Division of the Provost Marshal General's office. Maslow to Major Sidney Suffrin, Labor Branch of the Industrial Personnel Division of the Army Service Force, War Department, 11/8/43. Gohr and Soellner had appeared before the Industrial Employment Review Board on 5/18, 5/21/43, respectively, but received no notice of the board's findings. Both men were aeronautical engineers and naturalized citizens living in St. Louis County, Missouri. Texts are in HqR67, Central Files. Reports: U.S. Government, War Dept., M–Z.

4. This digest has not been found, but for a later version covering agreements through 12/44, see HqR68, Office Files of John A. Davis. Agreements with Federal Agencies. For background, see the headnote on Relationships with Federal Agencies.

Weekly Report

Feb. 19, 1944

Will Maslow

Clarence M. Mitchell

Weekly Report for Week Ending February 19, 1944

OUTSTANDING EVENTS AND PROBLEMS

L. V. Williams, Examiner on the staff of Region X, called on February 17 and stated that he had received a wire from the New Orleans Urban League concerning the Delta Shipbuilding Company.[1] The wire stated that one Negro employee of the yard had been chased off the job, and 1,000 Negroes had left in protest. Mr. Williams was leaving immediately for New Orleans to investigate the situation.[2]

In company with Mr. Ernest G. Trimble, of the Legal Division, I went to Baltimore on Wednesday, February 16, to talk with General A. A. Farmer, who is operating the Western Electric Company for the War Department. We discussed various aspects of the case, and I have prepared a special report on it.[3]

IMPORTANT CONTACTS WITH REGIONAL OFFICES, OTHER DIVISIONS, AND OTHER GOVERNMENT AGENCIES

It is noted that Region VI now has the services of Mr. Arnold Aronson, Executive Director of the Bureau of Jewish Employment Problems, on a consultant basis.

I discussed with Regional Director McKnight and Regional Director Hunt the latter's problem with the discriminatory advertising of the <u>Atlanta Journal</u>. Mr. Hunt felt that action on this matter would have to come from Mr. Ross if it will be successful. Meanwhile, Mr. McKnight has an appointment pending with one of the owners of the paper and will report to us on what he is able to accomplish.

I also discussed with Mr. Hunt the case of Mrs. Vivian Noretan, 7-GR-168 (DFO). This complainant was seeking employment at the Pearl Harbor Navy Yard and charged she had been discriminated against because of her race. The Navy Department reports that she has been offered employment. Mr. Hunt stated he had attempted to contact her but as yet has not been able to do so.[4]

ASSIGNMENTS TO CENTRAL STAFF

Mr. Bloch:

Completed assignments include:

1. U. S. Office of Education, 2-GR-434 (DFO).
2. Monthly summary of FDR's.

New assignments include:

1. Basic Magnesium, 12-BR-58 (DFO), and 12-BR-129–132 (DFO).
2. Weekly Reports for Regions II, III, and VII.

Mr. Davidson:

New assignments include:

1. Selective Service, Oakland, California, 12-GR-1 (DFO).

Miss Kahn:

Miss Kahn is out of the office.

Mr. Metzger:

Mr. Metzger is still in the field investigating the St. Louis area cases.

Mr. Mitchell:

Completed assignments include:

1. Reviewing the following FDR's:
   Region V—2
   Region VI—10
   Region VIII—1
   Region XII—8

2. Reviewing and taking action on Weekly Reports from Regions IV, V, VI, and XII.

I have not received reports from Regions VIII and IX as yet.

MS: copy, FEPC RG 228, Office Files of Clarence Mitchell, DNA.

1. In a memo to Ross, John A. Davis describes Delta's use of state troopers as guards as a "dangerous situation" that had resulted in "three cases of peremptory violence" against blacks. Because Delta had taken no action against the guards, two thousand blacks walked off the job and refused to return. A day and a half later the general manager and the personnel manager persuaded them to do so. Davis says he worked out a program with the Delta managers for controlling the problem that involved holding "weekly meetings on the race question with supervisors, superintendents and guards." They also agreed to fire any guards who were persecuting blacks. Davis to Ross, memorandum, 2/29/44, HqR1, Records of the Office of the Chairman, D. For the problems involving the guards, see 5/5/44.

2. The running story on this struggle can be seen at 2/28, 3/6, 5/1, 5/5, 8/14, 11/22/44, 1/8, 1/9, 1/12/45. See also the headnote on the Shipbuilding Industry; Northrup, *Organized Labor and the Negro*, 210–31, 233, 242, 255.

3. See Mitchell's memorandum of 2/16. For background, see the headnote on Strikes and Work Stoppages.

4. For the FDR on this case, see 3/17/44, in HqR60, Central Files. Reports, FDRS, Region VII.

Memorandum on Committees Determining Essentiality of Industries

Feb. 21, 1944

Will Maslow

Clarence M. Mitchell

Committees Determining Essentiality of Industries

At the national level, the War Manpower Commission's committee to determine whether an activity or industry is essential is composed of representatives from the War Manpower Commission, the War Department, the Navy Department, the War Production Board, the Department of Agriculture, and Selective Service.[1]

Mr. Ewing of the War Manpower Commission, who heads a sub-committee of this group, informed me that similar committees are not required at the local level. However, there is one in Kansas City and another in Chicago. These function on a regional level and act on cases referred by local area directors of the WMC.

MS: copy, HqR67, Central Files. Reports, U.S. Government, War Manpower Commission.
  1. Determination of what industry was essential to the war effort was related to questions of jurisdiction, which are discussed in the headnote on Jurisdictional Issues.

Memorandum on Jurisdiction over Hospitals

2–22–44

Mr. George Johnson, Deputy Chairman

Clarence M. Mitchell, Associate Director of Field Operations

Jurisdiction over Hospitals

The following question has been raised by Mr. Kingman in his weekly report of the thirty first.

"In case we receive USES #510 complaints against state or municipal hospitals, do we take jurisdiction? Hospitals are rated essential by the WMC and we have complaints of flagrant employment discrimination against several. Should our procedure in handling a complaint against a state-operated hospital like the University of California Hospital be different from that in the case of a private hospital?"[1]

Is this sufficient information to make a determination? If you need more facts we will get them from Mr. Kingman.

MS: copy, HqR63, Central Files. Reports, Rulings, General.
  1. See 5/5, 5/8, 5/17, 5/20, 5/24, 10/16/44; related texts in the file; headnote on Jurisdictional Issues.

Memorandum on Complaints against the Panama Canal

DATE: Feb. 24. 1944

TO: Mr. Will Maslow

FROM: Clarence M. Mitchell

SUBJECT: Complaints against the Panama Canal

Beginning in 1941 and up until January of 1943, the Committee has received and sent correspondence concerning complaints involving the Panama Canal area. In the main, these complainants charge that Negroes in the United States who seek employment in the Canal area are refused solely because of their race. Apparently, this discrimination stems from wage discrimination and segregation in the Canal Zone and the Republic of Panama.

This material is very useful for background purposes, but it does not appear that any further action can be taken on it at the present time because of the time which has elapsed since the complaints were made. I am, therefore, suggesting that we consider this a closed file but make use of its contents if complaints are received in the future.[1]
Attachment

MS: LH, DI, HqR84, Correspondence Relating to Cases. (L–S) Panama City Situation.

1. This file is apparently misplaced in the FEPC Papers, and no related materials are filed with this text. The Panama file was closed, as Mitchell advised. See report of 2/28/44.

Memorandum on Successful Cases Recommended for the *New York Times* Article

DATE: Feb. 26, 1944

TO: Mrs. Marjorie M. Lawson

FROM: Clarence M. Mitchell

SUBJECT: Successful Cases Recommended for the NEW YORK TIMES Article:

I am sending you this list of successful cases with the caution that the names of companies are listed simply to authenticate the case.[1] I presume you do not intend to use them in the publication.

1. <u>Kelley Field, San Antonio, Texas, 10-GN-35 and 10-GN-37.</u>

A Government establishment in the Southwest was charged with failure to up-grade three Latin-American employees solely because of their national origin. The Committee took the matter up with the agency involved, and it was discovered that the complainants were entitled to upgrading. Two were raised from laborer classifications to general mechanic helpers, and a third was given an administrative promotion to which he was entitled. The complaints were given to the Committee on September 21, 1943, and the complainants indicated they were satisfied with the adjustment on November 11.

2. <u>United States Employment Service, 10-GN-10.</u>*

A naturalized American of Italian origin charged he was refused referral to a job because of his national origin.* The complainant was a skilled machinist and was unable to obtain employment in his field because of this action by the employment agency. The complainant reported on December 14, 1943, that he was employed by a shipyard after referral from the employment agency and was satisfied with his job, as the result of FEPC action.

3. <u>North American Aviation Company, 10-BA-70.</u>

An aircraft firm in the Southwest was having difficulty in the employment of Mexicans who were not citizens because the processing of alien questionnaires was slow. The FEPC representative in the area reviewed the past history of similar cases and asked that the process of determining the loyalty of such persons be accelerated. As a result of this request, the particular complainant was able to get a job nine days after the FEPC inquiry, and a promise was made by the investigating agency that greater speed would be used in the future. Other cases show that the promise has been kept. Since October, 1943, when the Committee first took up the situation with the company management, more than 50 Mexicans who are not citizens of the United States have been hired. (See FEPC news release December 7, 1943).[2]

4. <u>Matson Navigation Company, 12-BA-117.</u>

A Marine machinist, who was an alien from Belgium, complained to the Committee on November 12, 1943, that he had not been hired by the personnel officer of a navigation company because of his non-citizenship. An investigation by the FEPC showed that the company wanted the complainant to fill out application papers for clearance, but, apparently, because of a misunderstanding, he had thought he was being refused employment altogether. The complainant took the action required by the company, and on November 29, he

* The date the complaint was filed is not given because there has been considerable delay due to the fact that the Committee did not have a regional office in the area.

stated, "I am very happy to inform you that I have obtained from the authorities the permit required. I am now engaged by the company."

5. Naval Air Station, 12-GC-52.

A Government employer dismissed a complainant because of her desire to have Saturdays off to meet the requirements of her religion. She was a Seventh Day Adventist. She filed a complaint with the FEPC on July 21, 1943. On the same date, the FEPC requested that the complainant be kept on the job until completion of an investigation of a countercharge by the employer that the complainant was absent without permission. The FEPC discussed the case with the Government agency on October 21, and it was agreed that the complainant would be reinstated. On November 2, the complainant was re-appointed to her position with the same title and pay she had received previously and with Saturdays off. The complainant wrote to FEPC on November 5 to express thanks for having secured re-employment. The party charged also wrote stating that preliminary reports have indicated that the complainant and her supervisors are well satisfied with her work.

6. Hegemen Harris Company, 2-BC-233.

An eastern contracting company handling many large construction jobs in cities throughout the United States and the Republic of Panama submitted an order for typists to the United States Employment Service on November 11, 1942, stating that "Christian" were preferred. The local United States Employment Service office obtained a promise of relaxation , but a follow-up report revealed that it received no further orders from the company. The case was turned over to the FEPC on March 6, 1943. When the FEPC investigated the matter, the firm denied the allegations of the USES. The FEPC took the matter up with the president of the company, who assured the FEPC that all hiring would be done without regard to race, creed, color, or national origin. A subsequent checkup by the FEPC revealed that the company had called upon the USES for two clerical workers. Jewish girls were referred in each instance and accepted without question by the company.[3]

7. Richmond Shipyard, Pre-Fabrication Plant, 12-BR-153.

An individual employed in a West Coast shipyard complained to the FEPC on December 7, 1943, that he had been discharged because he was a active leader of Negroes who had filed a complaint with the Committee on November 2, 1943, alleging discriminatory practices in the advancement and upgrading of Negroes. The Committee was still in the process of working on the complaint of the employees filed on November 2. One of the complainants mentioned in the November 2 charges had notified the Committee on December 2 that he was dismissed because of his activities in connection with the attempts to upgrade the Negro employees. FEPC investigation showed that the complainant dismissed on December 7 was apparently discharged without the knowledge of the general manager of the plant. In a conference on December 9, the company agreed to reinstate the complainant dismissed on December 2 and give him back pay. It refused to reinstate the complainant dismissed on December 7. The FEPC accepted the decision of the company with regard to the complainant dismissed on December 2 but refused to accept the negative decision with regard to the individual dismissed on December 7. A conference was held with the party charged on December 13. Representatives of the complainant's union were also present at the negotiations. FEPC agreed to withhold any of its action pending the outcome of negotiations between the union and management under the terms of the union's collective bargaining agreement. On January 12, the complainant was reinstated by the company with back pay. In addition to the reinstatement of both complainants, the general manager and vice president of the company issued written instructions to all management and supervisory personnel regarding equal employment opportunities for workers regardless of race, creed, color, or national origin.

8. <u>Atlantic Basin Iron Works, 2-BR-232.</u>

The United States Employment Service notified the FEPC on March 18, 1943, that a shipbuilding firm on the East Coast was refusing to accept Negroes referred for employment. This particular firm had long been known as one which would not employ Negroes. Although the Employment Service reported the case in March of 1943, it asked that FEPC take no action until the War Manpower Commission had had an opportunity to correct the discrimination. After the WMC was unable to correct the discrimination, the FEPC took the matter up with company officials and obtained an agreement that Negroes would be hired. The United States Employment Service and a local office of the National Urban League referred Negro workers to the company after the FEPC conference. A checkup by FEPC on September 3 indicated that of fourteen qualified Negro workers referred to the company, five were hired. The question was again taken up with the company management, and a subsequent checkup on November 1 showed that of thirty-eight non-whites referred by the United States Employment Service, twenty-four had been employed. Of eighteen persons referred by the office of the Urban League, ten were hired. The FEPC closed the case as satisfactorily adjusted on November 24, 1943.

9. <u>Chicago Surface Lines, 6-BR-113, and Chicago Motor Coach Company, 6-BR-114.</u>

The FEPC received complaints against a surface transportation line and a motor coach company in a large midwestern city. The complaints charged that Negroes were not permitted to operate street cars or buses. The charges were filed with the FEPC by a community organization in behalf of colored persons who had sought employment. On October 5, 1943, the surface line company agreed to accept applications from Negroes for positions of platform men. Negroes were subsequently employed without difficulty. The motor coach company advised the FEPC on October 30 that "In reply to your letter of October 23, advising that you are in receipt of a complaint of discrimination on the part of (this) company against Negroes seeking employment as bus operators, and in line with our telephone conversation of October 25 that we were at that very moment interviewing applicants for appointment as bus drivers, I wish to advise that the following named men have entered our school of instruction on October 29." The letter then listed the names of five individuals who had entered the training.[4]

10. IHCB and CLU of A, 12-UR-74 and 12-UR-75.

Two complainants charged that they went to a western city from a distant point in response to telegrams asking for union members to work on a construction job. The complainants alleged that, although they were union members in good standing and had been instructed to make the trip by their local, when they arrived they were told that no jobs were available in their particular skill and they should accept jobs in a lower category. The complainants refused to do this and placed their complaints with the FEPC on September 17, 1943. When the FEPC investigators talked with union officials, the complainants advised that, as a result of this conversation, the union agreed to pay each of them $150 for time lost and inconvenience caused if they signed a receipt absolving the union of any blame. Other Negroes who were involved accepted the $150, but the complainants who had given their case to FEPC did not accept it on the ground that it was inadequate. The union, in addition, had agreed that it would secure employment for all of the Negroes involved in the controversy. Three of the Negroes accepted this employment, but the two complainants obtained work elsewhere. FEPC investigations showed that a total of six persons had complaints similar to the individuals who gave the original charge. One of these left the city in disgust, thereby reducing the number to five.

MS: LH, FEPC RG 228 (entry 8-PI-147), Office Files of Malcolm Ross. Difficult Cases, box 67, DNA.

1. No *New York Times* article based on this material has been found. On the FEPC policy of not using the names of companies in public relations materials, see the two memoranda of 7/24/43.

2. See the headnote on National Origin, Alienage, and Loyalty.

3. See the headnote on Creedal Discrimination.

4. See the headnote on Street and Local Railways.

Weekly Report

Feb. 28, 1944

Mr. Will Maslow
Clarence M. Mitchell
Weekly Report for Week Ending February 26, 1944

OUTSTANDING EVENTS AND PROBLEMS

Difficulty arose in Region VII this week when one of the examiners attached to the Atlanta office attempted to visit the Bell Aircraft Company, Marietta, Georgia, and also when he requested the War Department representative in the plant to participate in a conference with the contractor-operator, as provided in Field Instruction No. 19. Not only was he denied access to the plant, but the War Department representative also refused to participate in the conference. This matter was taken up with the Civilian Aide to the Secretary of War, who was unable to obtain clearance for the Atlanta examiner to visit the plant. A request for this clearance has been sent to Wright Field in Dayton, Ohio, in keeping with a suggestion made by the Civilian Aide which, he said, was based on an Army Air Forces regulation.[1]

Region VII also noted this week four cases satisfactorily closed, although we have not as yet received FDR's on these cases. One of them involved a private company, and three involved the United States Employment Service.

The Director and the Associate Director of Field Operations had a conference with Mr. J.H. Bond, Deputy Executive Director of the War Manpower Commission, concerning WMC-FEPC relationships in the field. Mr. Bond stated that the problem in Region IV involving Mr. Henry Triede, Regional Director for WMC, had been settled. This means that FEPC's Region IV now has access to ES 270 Reports and also should receive ES 510 Reports. Mr. Frank Hook, Director of Region IV for FEPC, informed me that he has received two 510 Reports from WMC this week. Mr. Bond has sent out a special memorandum to all WMC regional directors on the "Disclosure of Information to the Committee on Fair Employment Practice." With certain minor exceptions, this new memorandum should clarify relationships in the field and give FEPC representatives access to WMC reports.

Mr. Leonard M. Brin, Director of Region X, reported that the walkout at the Delta Shipbuilding Company at New Orleans, mentioned in my report of last week, appears to be settled. However a new problem is brewing at the Republic Oil and Refining Company of Texas City, Texas, which is seeking to hire Negroes as laborers for the first time at a rate of sixty-five cents an hour when its union contract provides for a rate of eighty-three cents an hour for laborers. White employees have informed the company that they will walk out if this action is taken.[2]

IMPORTANT CONTACTS WITH REGIONAL OFFICES, OTHER DIVISIONS, AND OTHER GOVERNMENT AGENCIES

Complaints against the Pennsylvania Bell Telephone Company in Pittsburgh have been investigated, and it appears that no hearing will be necessary at this time.

Region IV has been notified that further regional action should be taken in the case of the Millhiser Bag Company, 4-BR-216 (DFO).

The file on the Anaconda Copper Mining Company, 11-BR-20 (DFO), has been returned to Region IX with recommendations for further action. Also, a War Department report on the case of Laura Le Catoe et al., 9-GR-93, has been sent to Region IX.

At the request of Region X, a communication has been addressed to the North American Aviation Company, concerning Seventh Day Adventists (10-BC-174 and 10-BC-175) who were dismissed in Dallas for religious reasons. A copy of this letter is being sent to Region XII for its information in the event that the North American Company headquarters in California should call about it.[3]

The Guy F. Atkinson Company, 12-BR-23 (DFO), has been referred to the War Department for investigation.

ASSIGNMENTS TO CENTRAL STAFF

Mr. Bloch:

Completed Assignments:

1. The following FDR's have been reviewed and acted upon by Mr. Bloch:
   Region II—25
   Region III—19

2. Review of satisfactorily adjusted FDR's for January, 1944.

New Assignments:

1. Screen Actors' Guild, 12-UA-1126 (DFO).
2. Government Printing Office, 4-GR-206–209 (DFO).
3. The following FDR's:
   Region II—27
   Region III—19
4. Review of Weekly Reports for Regions I, II, III, and VII.

Miss Kahn:

New Assignments:

1. Review of successfully completed Jewish cases.
2. Review of material on regional director's meeting and preparation of digest thereof.[4]
3. The following FDR's (under Mr. Mitchell's supervision):
   Region V—20
   Region VI—1

Mr. Metzger:

Mr. Metzger is out of the office on St. Louis cases but was able to recommend the closing of the General Chemical Company case, 6-BA-20 (DFO). His check-up in this case shows the importance of contacting the complainant in satisfactory adjustment cases, and an R. D. Memorandum is being prepared on this.

Mr. Mitchell:

Assignments Completed:

1. Preparation of a digest of satisfactorily adjusted cases for the Chairman and Deputy Chairman. Ten (10) cases were digested for the Chairman, who expects to use some of them in an article for the New York Times. Eighteen (18) cases were selected for the Deputy Chairman, who decided to use seven (7) of them in a special pamphlet. Three of these were digested by me and the remainder by Mr. Davidson and the Deputy Chairman.[5]
2. FDR's reviewed and acted upon:
   Region VI—9
   Region X—19
   Region XII—29
3. Reviewing and acting upon Weekly Reports from Regions IV, V, VI, VIII, IX, X, XI, and XII.
4. The review and closing of the file on the Panama Canal Zone.
5. Recommended closing of Oakland Port of Embarkation case approved.

MS: copy, FEPC RG 228, Office Files of Clarence Mitchell, DNA.

1. For background on Field Instruction 19, 10/4/43 (on relationships with the War Department), see the section on the War Department in the headnote on Relations with Federal Agencies. For the text, see appendix 1. It is likely that the attached Field Instructions, 19A and 19B, were attempts to remedy the problems Mitchell noted.

2. For the progressive development of this case, see 2/19, 3/6, 5/1, 5/5, 8/14/44, 1/8, 1/9, 1/12/45.

3. See the headnote on Creedal Discrimination.

4. "Digest of Regional directors' meeting," HqR6, Office Files of Emanuel H. Bloch. Conference of Regional Directors (2/10, 11, 12/44).

5. No article based on these materials was found.

Memorandum on the Policies of the *Atlanta Journal*, Atlanta, Georgia

Feb. 28, 1944

Mr. Will Maslow

Clarence M. Mitchell

Policies of the <u>Atlanta Journal,</u> Atlanta, Georgia

I have discussed the attached report from Mr. McKnight with Mr. A. Bruce Hunt. Mr. Hunt, at the time of our discussion, said that this matter would have to be handled by Mr. Ross personally if the outcome is to be successful. However, Mr. McKnight states that his conference with one of the owners of the paper will be between February 29 and March 4, 1944, unless an earlier date is requested.

I believe that it is advisable for Mr. McKnight to go ahead with his plans, and, if he is unsuccessful, the matter can then be taken up by Mr. Ross.

Attachment

MS: copy, HqR83, Correspondence Relating to Cases. Region VII, Atlanta Journal.

This case involved the use of racial designations in employment ads by the *Atlanta Journal* and the *Atlanta Constitution,* a policy the FEPC opposed because it was discriminatory. The newspapers either had separate help-wanted columns labeled "whites" or "colored," or they used racial numeric codes for employment ads—"31" in the *Constitution* and "41" in the *Journal*—to indicate "Help wanted, male, white." The case was brought to Mitchell's attention by McKnight, the regional director based in Dayton, Ohio, who sent Mitchell a copy of a letter to Glenn L. Cox, one of the owners of the *Constitution,* who also was living in Dayton.

Hunt, the director of Region VII, which covered Atlanta, had sent McKnight a copy of his report, which was sparked by numerically coded ads in the *Journal* and *Constitution* from the J. A. Jones Construction Company for workers for its war project in Knoxville. Hunt said he had examined the USES files on the company and had found no indication there that it was discriminating on the project. To the contrary, Hunt reported, the USES had been referring both races to the Jones Company for employment. The USES informed Hunt that the two newspapers were responsible for placing the ads in the "white column," a practice that violated EO 8802.

Subsequently, McKnight told Mitchell that Cox's office in Dayton had told him that neither Cox nor anyone else at the Dayton Evening News Publishing company, in which Cox apparently also had proprietary interests, had "any authority to discuss or change the policies of the Atlanta *Journal* and advised that all matters concerning the publication of said newspaper be handled locally."

In a memorandum of 3/28/44 to Hunt, Mitchell said:

Needless to say, I am disappointed with the outcome and regret that it is as you feared it would be.

In some of your recent reports, there has been an indication that you are in the process of settling this problem. If you are, I presume no further action by the central office will be necessary. On the other hand, if you wish Mr. Ross to take some action, please indicate what you believe should be done.

The exchange of memoranda is in HqR83 with the text. See also HqR4, Office Files of George M. Johnson. Policy.

Request for Further Action, Shell Oil Refinery, Houston, Texas

Mar. 1, 1944

Mr. Will Maslow

Clarence M. Mitchell

RFA, Shell Oil Refinery, Houston, Texas, 10-BN-64 (DFO)

The following is a report on the Shell Oil Company at Houston, Texas. My opinion and the positions taken by the Union Local and the management indicate that a hearing is necessary if we are to obtain compliance with Executive Order 9346. I am, therefore, requesting that this be transmitted to the Deputy Chairman for handling in the Legal Division.[1]

DESCRIPTION OF THE PARTY CHARGED:

The Shell Oil Company operates a refinery at Houston, Texas. The file shows that as of May 13, 1943, there were employed 1,850 persons. Of these, 236 were women and 114 were non-whites. All of the non-whites were in unskilled jobs. In a conference with management on December 28, 1943, Dr. Carlos E. Castaneda, then Acting Regional Director of Region X, was informed that the company had about thirty or forty Mexican workers employed. The company has a contract with Local 367 of the Oil Workers' International, CIO.

SUMMARY OF THE COMPLAINT:

On May 14, 1943, there was a conference between officials of the Shell Oil Company, representatives of Local 367 of the Oil Workers' International, and Mr. Adolfo Dominguez.[2] Mr. Dominguez summarized the conference by indicating that there was apparent discrimination against Negroes and Mexicans in that they were not up-graded in spite of contractual provisions for advancing employees in the labor department to other departments. The contract between the company and the union provides that "promotions, demotions, and transfers shall be made in accordance with the seniority chart agreed upon and in effect at the time of (the) agreement. Any changes there-to shall be agreed upon between the management and the workmen's committee." The seniority chart referred to is included in the file and shows a line of progression by which white yardmen or laborers may go into all varieties of jobs in the refinery. The line of progression for Negro and Mexican laborers goes to janitors and gardeners and no further.

On October 13, 1943, Mr. Dominguez wrote a letter to Dr. Castaneda stating that seven employees had been suspended for insubordination. These employees were Juan R. Alba, Alberto Gonzalez, Genaro Obregon, Luis Pena, Sabas Serna, Gumercindo Carrisales, and Enrique Flores. The Mexican Consul said that the men refused to do a job in the pipe-fitting department because the company wanted to pay them eighty-seven cents an hour when the minimum rate in the department was ninety-seven cents an hour. At the same time, the company was supposed to be advertising in the local papers (October 12 and 13, 1943) for general helpers at ninety-seven cents an hour.[3]

BACKGROUND OF COMPLAINT:

Cases against the Shell Oil Company are an outgrowth of investigations in the Southwest involving oil companies and other types of industries. The company follows a general pattern of discrimination in the area. However, recently Region X, which has the responsibility for the Houston area, reported satisfactory adjustments in cases involving the Sinclair and Humble Oil Companies.

PRIOR CASES AGAINST PARTY CHARGED:

None.

EFFORTS TO OBTAIN COMPLIANCE:

Through various letters and visits, FEPC has been attempting to obtain adjustment of the company's discriminatory practices since May of 1943. The most recent and culminating contact with the party charged was had by Dr. Castaneda in his meeting on December 28, 1943, and Mr. Leonard Brin, who received a letter dated January 27, 1944, from the Oil Workers International Union, setting forth its position, and, also, a letter from the company dated January 28, enclosing a copy of the company's seniority chart and agreement with Local 367 of the OWI. The position of the company was stated by Dr. Castaneda to be as follows: "The position of management and the company is that the consequences of any change in this respect are so far-reaching and would have such detrimental results that we do not see any reason for change." The position of the Union was that "The Union at this time does not propose to change without first having a hearing or order as we consider ourselves and the company both in violation of the Executive Order."

NAMES AND TITLES OF OFFICIALS CONFERRED WITH:

1. Mr. P. E. Foster, Manager, Houston Refinery, Shell Oil Company.
2. Mr. P. E. Keegan, Manager of Industrial Relations, Shell Oil Company.
3. Mr. J. J. Hickman, Secretary-Treasurer, Local 367, Oil Workers International Union.
4. Mr. G. H. Cansler, President, Local 367, Oil Workers International Union.

POSITIONS AND CONTENTIONS OF PARTY CHARGED:

Both the company and the union contend that the discriminatory practice at the Shell Oil Refinery is typical of the area. The company insists that any change in its treatment of Negroes and Mexicans should be made along with other companies in the Gulf area. The union agrees with the company in this conclusion and expresses the fear that it will be detrimental to the union's interest if compliance is obtained by a membership vote. The union also makes the charge that the Shell management refused to modify or eliminate discriminatory features of its chart "unless the Union would take full responsibility for whatever results might follow." The union also states, "We feel that if the Committee on Fair Employment Practice issues a directive and the Union offers compliance, the Company will feel obligated to fall in line." The union states further that, at the time of its first conference in 1943, only two or three Mexicans and no Negroes belonged to Local 367. Since that time, according to the union, the majority of Mexicans in the Shell Plant have joined the Local, but there are still no Negro members.

ADJUSTMENTS ALREADY MADE:

None.

PENDING ISSUES:

The adjustment of specific complaints and elimination of discriminatory upgrading plan.

RECOMMENDATIONS:

In view of all the foregoing facts, I recommend that a hearing be held on this case.

MS: copy, HqR85, Correspondence Relating to Cases. (Sh–Z) Shell Oil Company.
1. See the headnote on the Oil Industry.
2. Domínguez was the Mexican consul in Houston.
3. For background on such wage discrimination, see the headnote on Mexican Americans.

Weekly Report

March 6, 1944

Mr. Will Maslow

Clarence M. Mitchell

Weekly Report for Week Ending March 4, 1944

OUTSTANDING EVENTS AND PROBLEMS

Two regional successes in handling difficult problems which may have resulted in some extreme racial tension are noted in the reports of the current week. Regional Director Brin of Dallas indicated that the problem at the Republic Oil Refining Company, Texas City, Texas, mentioned in last week's report, has been settled.[1] The company indicates that it is hiring Negroes at the rate of eighty-three cents an hour rather than sixty-five cents, as it had originally planned to do. It will be recalled that white workers had threatened a walkout if the Negroes were hired at the sixty-five cents rate. Mr. Brin indicates the situation is now in hand. Also in Region X, the Delta Shipbuilding Company presented a problem mentioned in last week's report. Mr. Brin indicates that this is currently in hand, but he does not state that all of the problems involved have been finally settled. I am preparing a letter to Admiral Vickery concerning the Delta Shipbuilding Company, which we can send as soon as we have a full report on the whole case from Mr. L. Virgil Williams, the examiner who visited the yard.[2]

In Region III, the Director, Mr. Fleming, reported last week that Mr. Manly, an examiner on his staff, was active in the settlement of a walkout which had resulted in a shutdown of the Carnegie Steel Plant, Clairton, Pennsylvania. Mr. Fleming's report of March 4 states that Mr. Manly prevented a spread of the shutdown which would have affected adversely production in the area for approximately thirty days.[3]

At this point, it seems advisable to call attention to similar problems which are acute in various sections of the country. In Region XII, the Los Angeles Street Railway case, 12-BR-1150, DFO, and the problems of discrimination by the Hanford Engineering Company at Pasco, Washington, represent possible sources of racial tension.[4] Also in Region XII, the unresolved problems at Las Vegas in connection with the Basic Magnesium Company are of importance.

In Region X, the North American Aviation Company's policy at Dallas has resulted in considerable ill feeling between the racial groups employed at the plant. This matter has been directed to the attention of the company by Mr. Brin, the Regional Director, and I have discussed it with the CIO Committee to Abolish Discrimination.

In Region IX, the U. S. Cartridge Company, and the Western Cartridge Company at East Alton in Region VI are also in this group.[5]

At the Kingsbury Ordnance Plant, La Porte, Indiana, difficulties based upon segregated employment policies are a problem for the Director of Region VI.

The employment policies of Bell Aircraft Company in Atlanta and problems connected with the strike at the Western Electric Company in Region IV are still before us. In all of these cases, the regional offices are at work to correct the problems which have arisen, but it is well to keep them in mind as potential trouble spots.

Mr. Hunt, Director of Region VII, has called to our attention certain violations of our agreement with the War Manpower Commission on the part of local WMC offices in his region. However, he has not indicated that he desires any Washington action at this time.

IMPORTANT CONTACTS WITH REGIONAL OFFICES, OTHER DIVISIONS, AND OTHER GOVERNMENT AGENCIES

Region IX has been informed that it does have jurisdiction over the Kansas City Stockyards case, as ruled by the Legal Division.[6]

We have been advised by Mr. Brin, the Director, that there are no unadjustable cases in Region X, except 10-BC-174 and 10-BC-176, referred to the DFO on February 1, 1944.

Other questions arising on Weekly Reports of Regional Directors have been answered and are attached.

ASSIGNMENTS TO CENTRAL STAFF

Mr. Bloch:

Completed Assignments:

1. The following FDR's have been acted upon by Mr. Bloch:
   Region I—2

Region II—7
Region III—28

Mr. Bloch's comments on some of these Final Disposition Reports are attached.

1. Memorandum on Screen Actors Guild, 12-UA-1126.
2. Prohibition against racial, religious, or color discrimination in federal Civil Service.

New Assignments:

1. Civil Service Commission, 2-GR-411, DFO.
2. Revision of memorandum on major cases submitted February 1, 1944.
3. Bridgeport Hospital, 1-BR-47, DFO.
4. U.S. Naval Medical Supply Depot, 2-GR-194, DFO.
5. Army Air Forces, 12-GR—, DFO (No number assigned as yet).
6. The following FDR's:
   Region I—2
   Region II—4
   Region III—28
7. Checking on year old cases in Regions III and VII.

Miss Kahn:

Completed Assignments:

Miss Kahn has reviewed, under my supervision, the following FDR's:
Region V—22
Region VI—13

2. She has also reviewed and submitted comments on the Curtis Company, 9-BR-72, DFO.

New Assignments:

1. Checking on year old cases in Regions VI, VIII, IX, and XII.
2. St. Louis Ordnance Department, 9-GR-138, DFO.
3. Marinship Company, 12-BR-240, DFO.
4. Review of files on 12-UR-203, 12-UR-16, 12-UR-32, 12-GR-55.
5. The following FDR'S:
   Region VI—7
   Region XII—16

Mr. Mitchell:

Assignments Completed:

1. Preparation of Shell Oil file for submission to Hearings Division.

2. Arranging clearance for Regional Director Hunt to Bell Aircraft Company, Atlanta, Georgia.[7]
3. Discussions with CIO on union problems at North American Aviation Company in Dallas, Texas.

Other assignments completed are attached.

MS: copy, FEPC RG228, Office Files of Clarence Mitchell. DNA.

1. For background and cross-references, see 2/28/44 report; headnote on the Oil Industry.

2. For activities involving Delta Shipbuilding, see 2/19, 2/28, 3/27, 5/1, 5/5, 8/14, 11/22/44, 1/8, 1/9, 1/12/45.

3. On Manly's role in the settlement of the Clairton strike and other race related walkouts, see John Davis's memorandum of 5/25/44 on FEPC Action on Race Strikes and notes in appendix 1.

4. For coverage of problems of racial tensions and related walkouts, see the headnote on Strikes and Work Stoppages. On the situation at Hanford Engineering, a part of the Manhattan Project, see the introduction and documents cited there.

5. See the headnote on Major Cases in St. Louis.

6. See the headnote on Jurisdictional Issues.

7. See the headnote on the Aircraft Industry.

Memorandum on Cases on Which a Hearing Is Requested by the Regional Office

March 11, 1944

Mr. George M. Johnson

Clarence M. Mitchell

Cases on Which a Hearing is Requested by the Regional Office

The New York office has sent in the attached files on the following cases:

1. Shelter Island Oyster Company, 2-BC-284
2. Metro Envelope Company, 2-BR-47
3. Colt's Patent Firearms Company, 1-BC-25
4. Colt's Patent Firearms Company, 1-BC-45

You will note in my memorandum of today to Mr. Maslow I suggested that these cases should be turned over to the Legal Division. He has agreed, and the files are transmitted herewith for whatever action they merit.[1]
Attachments* Files (4)

MS: copy, HqR38, Central Files. (entry 25) Memoranda, Johnson, George M., 1/44–.

1. No hearing was held on these cases.

Weekly Report

March 14, 1944

Mr. Will Maslow

Clarence M. Mitchell

Weekly Report for Week Ending March 11, 1944

OUTSTANDING EVENTS AND PROBLEMS

During the past week, the Chairman and the Associate Director of Field Operations held conferences in connection with the Western Electric Company in Baltimore, Maryland. One of these conferences was with Mr. Jack Gainey, Personnel Manager of the Point Breeze Works of the Western Electric Company. Another was with Mr. Charles Fahey, Solicitor General of the United States. It appears that the Army will withdraw from operations during the week ending March 18.[1]

A conference was held with Mr. Ivan Willis, Director of Industrial Relations for the Curtis Wright and Wright Aeronautical Companies in the offices of the Chairman on Thursday, March 9. Mr. Willis expressed the desire of the company to cooperate in the settlement of problems at the St. Louis plant of the Curtis Wright Company.[2]

A very optimistic note was struck by Region XII in its report that the Richmond Shipyard, on March 6, indicated that President McGowen, of the Boiler Makers Union, made a commitment to Mr. Joseph Keenan, of the War Production Board, that Negro workers would not be discharged for non-payment of auxiliary dues pending settlement of the Boiler Makers case.[3]

IMPORTANT CONTACTS WITH REGIONAL OFFICES, OTHER DIVISIONS, AND OTHER GOVERNMENT AGENCIES

During the past week, the following cases were referred to the Hearing Division:

1. Shelter Island Oyster Company, 2-BC-284 DFO.
2. Metro Envelope Company, 2-BR-47 DFO.
3. Colt's Patent Firearms Company, 1-BC-25 DFO.
4. Colt's Patent Firearms Company, 1-BC-45 DFO.
5. Marinship Corporation, 12-BR-240 DFO.

A report was sent to Region II on U. S. Naval Medical Supply Depot, 2-GR-194 DFO.

ASSIGNMENTS TO CENTRAL STAFF

Mr. Bloch:

Completed assignments:

1. U. S. Naval Medical Supply Depot, 2-GR-194 DFO.
2. Recommendations on Bridgeport Hospital, 1-BR-47 DFO.
3. The following FDR's :
   Region II—11
   Region III—6

New assignments:

1. Miller Printing Machine Company, 3-BR-72 DFO.
2. Port of Embarkation, 7-BR-205.

Miss Kahn:

New assignments:

1. Review of case file on Marine Firemen, Oilers, Watertenders & Wipers Association, 12-UR-118 DFO.
2. The following FDR's:
   Region VI—3
   Region IX—8
   Region X—6
   Region XII—11

Mr. Metzger:

Completed assignments:

1. Draft of letter to War Department on McQuay-Norris case, 9-BR-79 through 84.
2. Recommendation for hearing on Marinship Corporation, 12-BR-240 DFO.
3. Memorandum to Region XII on Shipfitters' Local A-33.
4. Memorandum to Region XII on Puget Sound Navy Yard, 12-GR-55 DFO.
5. The following FDR's:
   Region VI—9
   Region XII—16

Mr. Metzger was not given any new assignments because he left for a field trip.

Mr. Mitchell:

Completed assignments:

1. Pearl Harbor Navy Yard, 7-GR-168, returned to region for closing. (DFO case).
2. Curtis Company, 9-BR-72 DFO, returned to region for further action.
3. Memorandum on DFO cases.
4. Memorandum on DFO cases from Region XII.[4]
5. Reviewing and acting upon questions contained in Weekly Reports from Regions II, IV, VI, VII, IX, and XII.

White copies of action by Messrs. Bloch and Metzger are attached, in addition to my own.
Attachments

MS: copy, HqR6, Office Files of Emanuel H. Bloch. Weekly Reports.

1. For substantive background on this case, see 8/26, 11/11, 12/14/43, 2/16/44; headnote on Strikes and Work Stoppages.

2. See the headnote on the Aircraft Industry and sources cited there.

3. See the headnote on the Shipbuilding Industry and the Boilermakers Union.

4. Neither of Mitchell's memoranda has been found.

Weekly Report

March 18, 1944

Mr. Will Maslow
Clarence M. Mitchell
Weekly Report for Week Ending March 18, 1944

OUTSTANDING EVENTS AND PROBLEMS

This week, a strike occurred at the Monsanto Chemical Company in the vicinity of East St. Louis, Illinois. It appears that Negro workers walked out of the plant following a dispute concerning transportation facilities. The issues are not entirely clear at this point since we have not had a written report from Region VI, in which the problem occurred. One serious note was struck when the War Department indicated that a Department of Labor Conciliator is alleged to have stated that the white workers agreed to bring production up to normal without the Negroes. The information concerning the Conciliator's alleged statement was referred to Mr. Henderson, Director of Region VI, for whatever action it merits.[1]

A second problem arose at the Anniston Warehouse Corporation in Anniston, Alabama, when a War Department representative actively discouraged FEPC-Management cooperation. This matter was directed to the War Department on March 16.[2]

Region VII reported that, in Anniston, the USES seems wholly unaware of the fact that it was acting improperly when it followed discriminatory racial specifications in filling jobs. The Region reports that three (3) 510 Reports were received from the USES in Atlanta on March 10. All were prepared at the request of the Committee's representatives. This indicates that much is to be desired from the War Manpower Commission in Region VII so far as our operating agreement is concerned.

IMPORTANT CONTACTS WITH REGIONAL OFFICES, OTHER DIVISIONS, AND OTHER GOVERNMENT AGENCIES

The Exchange and Service Club, 2-GR-141 DFO, was returned to the Region for closing.

Region III was officially advised that the Committee did not intend to hold a hearing on the Pennsylvania Bell Telephone Company case. This information had been given to the region before, but the memorandum was to confirm a previous verbal statement.

Region V was informed that cases against the Hydraulic Machinery Company, 5-BC-1215, and the Hoover Ball Bearing Company, 5-BC-1222, both of which involve Jehovah's Witnesses, are not within our jurisdiction because of action taken by the Committee at its meeting of March 4.[3]

Region VI was advised that a question raised by the Director concerning the Central Soya Company, 6-BC-38 DFO, was not within the jurisdiction of the Committee. This case, also, involved a Jehovah's Witness who was seeking an appeal of his draft classification.

Questions raised by Region VI in its Weekly Report of February 26 were answered and the answers are attached.

Queries from Regions IX and XI, submitted by Mr. Hoglund, were answered. These involved the St. Louis and San Francisco Railroad, 9-BR-132, the Anaconda Copper Mining Company, 11-BR-20, and the Denver office of the War Manpower Commission. Copies of these statements to Mr. Hoglund are attached.

Suggestions and information on matters in his Weekly Report of March 11 were submitted to Mr. Brin, Director of Region X.

Information was sent to Region XII, at its request, on the following matters:

1. Los Angeles Street Railway case 12-BR-1160.
2. Mt. City Copper Company, 12-BR-25.
3. Information on memoranda sent to the Region.
4. Oakland Port of Embarkation file.
5. In response to a request by the Examiner-in-Charge [Robert E. Brown] of the Los Angeles office, information was sent concerning the Boiler Makers case.

The Director of Region XII [Kingman] mentioned that a special investigation is being made by the Army at Pasco, Washington. I requested that an extra copy of this report be sent to us when it is completed.

DFO CASES

We began the week ending March 18 with thirty (30) pending DFO cases being handled by our examiners and eight (8) additional cases being handled by the Legal Division. Of the cases being handled by our examiners, two (2) were returned to the regions for further action (Retail Credit Company, 3-BR-524, and Sinclair Contractors, 11-BR-21). Of the cases being handled by the Legal Division, one (1) was dismissed for no jurisdiction (Central Soya Company, 6-BC-38), and Exchange and Service Club, 2-GR-141, was returned to the region with closing recommended. This leaves a balance of twenty-eight (28) DFO cases being handled by our examiners and six (6) being handled by the Legal Division.

ASSIGNMENTS TO CENTRAL STAFF

Mr. Bloch:

Completed Assignments:

1. Memorandum on major cases.
2. Memorandum on Civil Air Regulations Affecting Aliens.
3. Railway Mail Service, 2-GR-558 DFO.
4. Miller Printing Machine Company, 3-GR-72 DFO.
5. Memorandum re. Requirements for Citizenship in Shipping.
6. The following FDR's:
   Region I—2
   Region II—18

New Assignments:

Mr. Bloch has two new field assignments, one in Dallas, Texas, and one in Las Vegas, Nevada. He is leaving the office today.

Miss Kahn:

Completed Assignments:

1. Memorandum on Jewish cases.
2. Memorandum on outstanding cases.
3. Summary of file on Marine Firemen, Oilers, Watertenders and Wipers Association, 12-UR-118 DFO.
4. The following FDR's (under my supervision):
   Region V—46
   Region VI—14
   Region IX—1
   Region X—6
   Region XII—25
5. Report on Regional Directors' Conference (being typed).

New Assignments:

1. Review of file on case of Laura Hooper et al.

Mr. Metzger:

Mr. Metzger is out of the office on a field trip.

Mr. Mitchell:

Completed Assignments:

1. Recommended closing of Exchange and Service Club, 2-GR-141 DFO.
2. Reviewing and acting upon Weekly Reports from regional offices.
3. The following FDR's:
   Region VII—36
   Region X—6

MS: copy, HqR6, Office Files of Emanuel H. Bloch. Weekly Reports.

1. For ongoing activity on this development, see 4/3/44 and related subsequent texts. See also the headnote on Strikes and Work Stoppages.

2. Regional director A. Bruce Hunt had complained that the War Department representative, Maj. H. F. Ogden, an Army officer at the Anniston Warehouse Corporation, which operated the Anniston Ordnance Depot, had raised numerous objections to a general settlement Hunt and John Hope II believed they had reached with company management. At issue were complaints of discriminatory work orders and discriminatory layoffs and reinstatements aggravated by segregated work arrangements. Ogden's actions included insistence on checking Alabama laws regarding segregation, challenging the credentials of Hunt and Hope, and preventing them from taking a copy of statistics prepared at their request, all of which led to a breakdown of negotiations. See Hunt to Maslow, 3/11; Mitchell to Truman K. Gibson Jr., 3/16/44; related texts, in HqR83, Correspondence Relating to Cases. (A–K) Anniston

Warehouse Corp., Anniston Ordnance Depot, Region VII. For related documents see 4/13, 4/17, 5/1, 5/8, 5/17/44, 1/25/45. For background, see the section on the War Department in the headnote on Relationships with Federal Agencies.

3. See 3/30/44, note 2; headnote on Creedal Discrimination.

Eleanor F. Rogers, Memorandum to Clarence Mitchell on His Telephone Call to Mr. James Grady, WSA

DATE: March 21, 1944

TO: Mr. Clarence M. Mitchell

FROM: Eleanor F. Rogers

SUBJECT: Your Telephone Call to Mr. James Grady, WSA

On the above date, you made a telephone call to Mr. James Grady, who has administrative responsibility for the United Seamen's Service. The call was made because of a memorandum from Mr. Leonard M. Brin, Director of Region X, to the effect that Negro merchant seamen were denied access to rest camps operated by the United Seamen's Service, in the State of Louisiana. The United Seamen's Service is a private corporation sponsored by the War Shipping Administration, according to Mr. Grady. The Chairman of the Board of Directors is, he stated, Admiral Emory S. Land. The Board meets once a year in New York. The Executive Committee, of which Mr. Arthur Paige is the head, meets every two weeks. Mr. Grady stated that the idea behind these rest camps is to provide a place where the men can relax and be able to go back to sea within two or three weeks.[1]

You asked Mr. Grady if he was familiar with the Ordinance which the Mayor of Pass Christian, Mississippi, mentioned and which specifies the separation of the races in that City. Mr. Grady stated that he did not have a copy of the ordinance with him but he had one in the files. This was brought to him, and he promised to send us a copy of it.

Mr. Grady stated that any situation which would aggravate the condition would not be good. He went on to say that, in order to operate economically, there are only five (5) rest centers. A sixth one, he said, is to be opened in Los Angeles this week. The men are sent to rest centers where there are vacancies and where it is determined that they will be best advantaged. Mr. Grady stated that transportation to the rest centers is provided free so that half of the buildings will be fully used. A Negro seaman who is denied admission to Pass Christian may go to some other center (transportation free), according to Mr. Grady. Each center has, he said, the same general setup, and an effort is being made to avoid having them institutionalized.

In answer to your query as to whether the institution is under Federal direction in any way, Mr. Grady stated that the United Seaman's Service accepts the administrative responsibility. This agency, he stated, participates in many ways in which Government could not.

You then asked Mr. Grady who pays the cost of construction. He stated that the United Seaman's Service does not buy or build the centers. They are leased from year to year. Private contributors who are ship owners, ship builders, seamen, and other public-spirited citizens pay about 5/7 of the cost. The War Shipping Administration pays about 2/7 of the cost, he stated.

MS: copy, HqR85, Correspondence Relating to Cases. United Seamen's Service, Region X.

1. This case involved segregation, over which the Committee had no jurisdiction, as opposed to discrimination, over which it did under Executive Order 8802. See note 1 of 1/29/44, where the FEPC's policy on segregation v. discrimination is explained, and the introduction for a full discussion of the Committee's efforts to deal with the dichotomy.

Memorandum on Cutbacks in Ammunition Production

March 22, 1944

Mr. Malcolm Ross
    Chairman
Clarence M. Mitchell
    Associate Director of Field Operations
Cutbacks in Ammunition Production

Recent layoffs in small arms and ammunition plants have affected Negroes adversely in the St. Louis, Missouri area.[1] We have received other complaints alleging that individuals were dismissed in a discriminatory manner in spite of seniority provisions in contracts. The following is the picture on the basis of reports from regional offices to date:

1. The U. S. Cartridge Company in St. Louis, Missouri, laid off 728 Negroes in December, 1943. It is charged that only 161 should have been laid off if proper seniority had been observed.

2. The McQuay-Norris Company, which has a record of discriminating against Negroes over a two-year period, had a layoff of 1,500 workers schedule for February 17, 1944. It is not ascertained how many of these were non-white.

3. The Denver Ordnance Plant, operated by the Remington Arms Company, has an arrangement whereby terminated employees, irrespective of race, are given the privilege to bump employees in lower job classifications. The Regional Director reports: "While plan basically is non-discriminatory, Negroes having been more recently upgraded may suffer heavier losses than whites in higher classifications."

4. Remington Arms Company, Bridgeport, Connecticut, has dismissed all of 250 non-white workers who were employed at the plant. There have been numerous charges alleging discrimination in the layoffs, but Regional Director Lawson states that, in general, Negro workers were among the first laid off because they had the least seniority.

5. The Twin City Ordnance Plant, Minneapolis, Minnesota, expected to lay off 100 Negroes out of 623 employed as of January 1. Layoffs in the plant are strictly on the basis of seniority and, in this instance, because Negroes have accumulated considerable seniority, it appears that they will not be discharged in large numbers.

6. At Evansville, Indiana, Negro employees of the Chrysler-operated ordnance plant were the last to be laid off due to the operation of departmental seniority and the fact that they were concentrated in the Packing Department.

MS: HqR48, Central Files. Reports.

1. These cutbacks reflected the general difficulties of reconversion. For African Americans, who were new to industrial employment, facing the prospect of the end of war production was especially painful and traumatic. Weaver, *Negro Labor,* 264–305.

Weekly Report

March 27, 1944

Mr. Will Maslow
Clarence M. Mitchell
Weekly Report for Week Ending March 25, 1944

OUTSTANDING EVENTS AND PROBLEMS

The Weekly Report of Region IX, for the Week Ending March 18, shows that a problem which formerly existed in St. Louis concerning the use of ES 270 Reports has been corrected. Previously, the Regional Director was able to secure information from these

Reports in the WMC regional office at Kansas City but was unable to secure it at the local level in St. Louis. Mr. Hoglund reports that instructions have been issued by the WMC Regional Director requiring that the St. Louis WMC office make ES 270 information available to FEPC representatives at such times as it is needed. Our Regional Director has also discussed with the WMC Regional Director certain complaints against the USES office in St. Louis. The WMC promised an investigation.

In Region XII, the Regional Director has obtained from the Sacramento Transit Company a commitment for full compliance with Executive Order 9346. However, he advises that there should be no publicity on this until he meets with the employees of the company on April 6.

IMPORTANT CONTACTS WITH REGIONAL OFFICES, OTHER DIVISIONS, AND OTHER GOVERNMENT AGENCIES

This week, we requested the War Department to designate a representative to cooperate with Regional Director Fleming in the settlement of a case against the Miller Printing Machine Company, Pittsburgh, Pennsylvania, (3-BR-72, DFO). Although this is a privately-owned and privately-operated plant, the War Department's assistance was requested because it appeared that the company's position was such that little could be accomplished without joint action of FEPC and the War Department.

Because of a reminder from Region VI, we communicated with the War Relocation Authority in connection with Civil Service policies affecting the employment of citizens of Japanese ancestry.[1]

At the request of Region X, we are beginning action at this level on the Delta Shipbuilding Corporation case (10-GR-128–187, DFO). A letter was prepared for the Chairman's signature to Admiral Vickery. This letter requests that the Maritime Commission designate a representative to discuss this whole case with a representative of FEPC in Washington. Because the company has its property policed by guards who are under the supervision of the State of Louisiana, there have been several racial clashes, and the situation is tense.[2]

The Special Assistant to the Chairman on Latin-American Affairs [Castañeda] has been advised that the Committee, in its meeting of March 18, voted to hold a hearing on the Shell Oil Company case, (10-BN-64 DFO). The Deputy Chairman informed me that a full statement of the Committee's action will be forthcoming when the minutes of the meeting are transcribed. Dr. Castaneda was also advised that a news release on the satisfactory adjustment of cases involving the Humble and Sinclair Oil Companies has been approved.[3]

Region II was asked to make a re-check on the following companies: (1) Carl Norden, Inc., (2) The Continental Can Company, and (3) Fairchild Aviation Company. All of these companies were sent directives in May of 1942 to correct certain discriminatory practices. The re-check was suggested by the Division of Review and Analysis.

A note of congratulations was sent to Region III for its handling of the Carnegie-Illinois Steel Company strike at Clairton, Pennsylvania. The report, submitted by Mr. Manly, who was in charge of the handling, is an excellent document.[4]

Region V requested that Mr. Ernest G. Trimble, of the Legal Division, return to Cincinnati for further negotiations with companies between March 27 and 30. Later, the Region requested that Mr. Trimble postpone his visit for a few days. The Deputy Chairman has approved Mr. Trimble's visit.

Region V has been advised, also, that the Army has replied on the Air Forces cases, 5-GR-211–215, DFO. The comment of the Region was requested.

At the request of the War Department, we asked Mr. Henderson, Director of Region VI, to indicate whether he is still desirous of compliance reports from the Elwood Ordnance Plant in Indiana.

At the request of Region VI, we have communicated with Captain S. H. Ingersoll, Commanding Officer of the U. S. Naval Air Station, Anacostia, D.C., concerning a contract given to a Chicago firm in which the non-discrimination clause was marked out.

A letter has also been sent to Mr. J. H. Bond, Deputy Executive Director of the War Manpower Commission asking that he indicate whether the War Manpower Commission is asking General Motors Corporation to give non-white statistics on ES 270 Reports.[5]

At the request of the Division of Review and Analysis, we have asked Mr. A. Bruce Hunt, Director of Region VII, to recheck employment policies of the Vultee Aircraft Corporation at Nashville, Tennessee. This company was sent a directive by the committee on November 17, 1942.[6]

The following questions raised by the Director of Region XII were answered: (1) Request for transcript of discussion at the Boiler Makers convention, and (2) Request for information in connection with the Los Angeles Street Railway case. It is noted that the Region has settled the Mezetta case, 12-BR-187. This case was a difficult problem, and Mr. Pestano, a new examiner on the staff of Region XII, deserved commendation for his handling of it. This commendation was addressed to the Region.

DFO CASES

We began the week ending March 25 with twenty-eight (28) DFO cases being handled by our examiners. An additional six (6) cases were being handled by the Legal Division. During the week, we received five (5) additional cases. Four (4) of these are being handled by our examiners and one (1) by the Legal Division. This makes a total of thirty-two (32) cases being handled by examiners and seven (7) by the Legal Division. Our case load for all regions for the week ending March 18 was 2219. The previous week, it was 2,195. This represents an increase of twenty-four (24) cases.

ASSIGNMENTS TO CENTRAL STAFF

Mr. Bloch:

Mr. Bloch is absent from the office on a field trip.

Mr. Davidson:

Mr. Davidson has agreed to handle the following FDR's:

> Region III—8
> Region X—5

Miss Kahn:

Completed Assignments:

1. Review of file on Brooklyn Navy Yard.
2. Review of case of Laura Hooper vs. the War Department.
3. Preparation of material for Appropriations Committee.
4. Arrangement of material for use in Appropriations Committee hearing.[7]

New Assignments:

1. The following FDR's were assigned for review under my supervision:
   Region II—15
2. R. J. Dorn Company, 10-BR-169, DFO.
3. New York Navy Yard, 2-GR-390, DFO.

Mr. Metzger:

Mr. Metzger is still in the field in connection with preparations for the St. Louis hearing.

Mr. Mitchell:

Completed Assignments:

1. Memorandum on cutbacks in ammunition production.
2. Agreements with other government agencies for Budget Hearing.
3. Review of Weekly Reports from all regions.

4. The following FDR's were reviewed and acted upon:
Region I—4
Region II—10
Region III—13
Region IV—2
Region V—3
Region VI—10
Region VII—2
Region VIII—1
Region XII—6

New Assignments:

1. Delta Shipbuilding Corporation, 10-BR-127, DFO.

MS: copy, FEPC RG 228, Office Files of Clarence Mitchell, DNA.

1. See the headnote on Japanese Americans.

2. On continuing activities against Delta, see Mitchell to Ross, memorandum, 5/5/44; headnote on the Shipbuilding Industry. E. S. Land, chairman of the Maritime Commission, responded to Ross on 3/6/44 that L. R. Sanford of the commission had discussed the matter involving Delta with Johnson, Mitchell, and Trimble. He said that, based on information he had received, steps were being taken to adjust the complaint. Noting this meeting in a memorandum to Hunt on 5/11/44, Mitchell said that in addition to discussions on Delta, the group had discussed problems at the Alabama Dry Dock Company and the J. A. Jones Construction Company yard in Brunswick, Georgia. See HqR66, Central Files. U.S. Government, Maritime Commission.

3. At a meeting on 3/18/44, the Committee voted that an examiner should hold a commissioner-type hearing. HqR1, Summary Minutes of Meetings.

4. For the excellent report, see Manly to Fleming, 3/7/44, HqR77. See also HqR83, Correspondence Relating to Cases. (A–K) Carnegie-Illinois Steel Corp.

5. In reply to the letter Mitchell addressed to J. H. Bond on 3/20/44, Vernon McGee, deputy executive director of WMC, reported on 3/28/44 that, although the WMC agreed with Mitchell's recommendation that General Motors should maintain postemployment records on nonwhite employees, it had no authority to require employers to do so. HqR83, Correspondence Relating to Cases. (A–K) General Motors, Region V. For further consideration of the issue, see Mitchell at 1/22/44, note 7, 4/12/44; later texts on GM; headnote on Race, Creed, Color, or National Origin on Employment Application Forms.

6. The directive followed a hearing in Birmingham on 6/18/42. The complaint charged that Vultee hired only whites, with the exception of African American janitors; that its manager of industrial relations had on 2/5/41 written a letter stating that it was inadvisable to include African Americans in Vultee's workforce; that the company's policy in this respect was unchanged; that experienced African American mechanics had been refused employment by the company and that it had also recently refused training to another African American with shop experience, though whites were then being trained. Furthermore, Vultee had a preferential hiring agreement with Local 735 of the IAM, which barred African Americans from membership. See HqR3, Summary Hearings, Birmingham, Ala., 6/18/42, Vultee Aircraft; headnote on the Aircraft Industry.

7. For Theodore Jones's report on the FEPC testimony before the House Subcommittee on Appropriations in 3/44 where he said, "In all we had between eight and nine hours of grilling," see Transcript of Proceedings, 4/1/44, 73–81, HqR65, Central Files. Queries at this hearing regarding FEPC authority over aliens from enemy countries led to a suspension of FEPC action on alienage cases (see the headnotes on Jurisdictional Issues and on National Origin, Alienage, and Loyalty). For the subsequent debates in the House on FEPC appropriations, see Maslow, memorandum, 5/27/44, in appendix 1.

Memorandum on Appointment
of a Hearing Commissioner

DATE: March 27, 1944

TO: Mr. George M. Johnson

FROM: Clarence M. Mitchell

SUBJECT: Appointment of a Hearing Commissioner

It has occurred to me that frequently in our relationships with the public the presence of an outstanding Catholic handling some of our deliberations would be advisable and helpful. I am suggesting, therefore, that Father Paul H. Furfey, of Catholic University, would be desirable as a Hearing Commissioner in some cases which are not important enough to be presented to the full Committee.[1]

I have not approached Father Furfey on his willingness to serve, but, knowing of his convictions in connection with the problems of race, I feel that he would be inclined to accept. Of course, he probably would not wish to serve on a full-time basis.

If you think it advisable, I shall determine whether he is receptive to such an assignment.

MS: LH, DI, HqR3, Office Files of George M. Johnson. M.

1. This was another example of Mitchell's admiration for the commitment of Roman Catholics to social justice. Regarding his relationship with Father Francis J. Gilligan when he was executive director of the St. Paul Urban League, see Watson, *Lion in the Lobby*, 121.

Memorandum on Staff Conferences

March 30, 1944

TO: Mr. Malcolm Ross, Chairman
          Mr. Will Maslow, Director of Field Operations

FROM: Clarence M. Mitchell
          Associate Director of Field Operations

SUBJECT: Staff Conferences

After careful thought, I am submitting this memorandum to request that we have staff conferences. I realize that we have many other matters before us, and I have tried to postpone it until after such things as the budget hearings and various Committee investigations. However, the recent request of the Smith Committee for my Form 57 has been the factor which has made it difficult to hold off any longer.[1]

There seems to be a tendency to hold small meetings from time to time with various staff members. I have been in on a few of these myself. However, more frequently they are gatherings one stumbles into. I have a feeling that some of the policies which affect the entire staff are decided in these meetings and also feel that I, personally, could accept some of the decisions with more enthusiasm if I felt that all points of view had been properly aired. Some examples of what I refer to are as follows:

1. THE METHOD BY WHICH THE PERSONS ATTENDING THE RECENT BUDGET HEARING WERE SELECTED.

In an informal way, I had a rough idea of what was going on, but I am still in the dark about what our planning and presentation included in an over-all sense.

2. THE COMMITTEE'S DECISION IN THE JEHOVAH'S WITNESSES CASES.

My interest in the work of the Committee is over and above simply the problem of one minority in this country. I feel that some important religious principles were involved in these cases, even though I do not personally agree with the tenets of the Witnesses. I do not feel that I had an adequate opportunity to express my views before the Committee acted.[2]

3. VARIOUS ADMINISTRATIVE AND HEADQUARTERS MEMORANDA.

From time to time, there are various memoranda circulated which require staff members to conform to certain rules and regulations. These are not particularly onerous, but they do seem somewhat arbitrary.

Other reasons could be listed but I do not wish to burden you with many when the few illustrate what I believe to be an important point. The personal pronoun has been used in this because I have not talked this over extensively with other staff members and cannot presume to speak for them.

I have conviction about the worth of what we are doing, and, because I do, I am honored when called to give an accounting, whether that accounting be required by a member of the Executive branch of Government or the Smith Committee of Congress. However, I must confess my esprit de corps suffers when I must unearth rather than observe our policy making.

cc: Johnson
        Jones

MS: copy, MP.

1. On the Special Committee to Investigate Executive Agencies, headed by Howard Smith of Virginia, see the headnote on Jurisdictional Issues. Mitchell's reference was to the Civil Service Commission's form 57, which was standard and a part of all Security Division forms. Item 41(a) asked, "Were any of the following members of your family born outside Continental U.S.A.? Wife, Husband, Father, Mother." It continued, "If so, indicate which by marking the appropriate space and show under Item 45 for each (1) full name, including maiden name of the wife or mother; (2) birthplace; (3) native citizenship; and (4) if U.S. naturalized, date of naturalization." Item 41(b) asked, "Have you any relatives, by blood or by marriage (excluding persons in the U.S. armed forces) now living in a foreign country?" Transcript of Proceedings, 3/4/44, 25–26, HqR65, Central Files. U.S. Government, Aliens in Defense, General (A–N).

2. At its 3/4/44 meeting, the Committee discussed the appropriate policy it should adopt regarding the refusal of Jehovah's Witnesses to buy war bonds and their subsequent discharge from their jobs. The Committee agreed to decline jurisdiction of such cases based on religious grounds unless it was shown that the action taken violated "some established precept of the creed."

In cases where a Jehovah's Witness had requested deferment and the employer refused to request the local draft board to grant such deferment or refused to appeal from an unsatisfactory decision, "the Committee agreed that the refusal to appeal a denial of the deferment is not ground for a complaint on the theory that a person had been discriminated against because of creed," even though the complainant was a Jehovah's Witness. Minutes of 3/4/44, HqR1, Summary Minutes of Meetings. See also weekly report, 3/18/44; memorandum, 3/30/44; headnote on Creedal Discrimination.

Weekly Report

April 3, 1944

Mr. Will Maslow
Clarence M. Mitchell
Weekly Report for Week Ending April 1, 1944

OUTSTANDING EVENTS AND PROBLEMS

Region III reports three strike situations in the State of Pennsylvania. One of these is at the Sun Ship Company, Chester, Pennsylvania, where, on March 22, and 23, work stoppages occurred because Negro employees were dissatisfied with upgrading and hiring policies of the company.[1] On March 23, the Regional Director received a report that a strike loomed at the Allen Wood Steel Company, Conshohocken, Pennsylvania. Workers were protesting against the upgrading of a colored man. A third strike appeared possible at the McIntosh Hemphill Foundry Company, Midland, Pennsylvania. This threat of a strike was based on the alleged discriminatory dismissal of a Negro worker. Region III is keeping in contact with these problems.

Region VI reports that a conference in East St. Louis on March 31 was designed to find solutions for problems presented by Negro workers who went on strike at the

Monsanto Chemical Company March 11 and remained off the job until March 21. Unfortunately, the conference was virtually broken up by the actions of a representative [George Streator] of the War Production Board, according to the Regional Director [Henderson]. A full report on this matter has been requested, and it should be taken up with the War Production Board as soon as we receive this report.[2]

A strike at the General Cable Company, St. Louis, Missouri, was not as serious as it at first appeared, according to Mr. Hoglund, the Regional Director. Mr. Hoglund stated that a short work stoppage occurred and lasted for about half an hour on March 17 when it was rumored that Negro women would be hired by the company. FEPC negotiations with the company are continuing. Additional labor difficulties appear possible at the General Box Company in Kansas City, Missouri, where Negro employees have asked for a strike vote following dismissals which they believe to be unfair and because of union activity. This matter is not within our jurisdiction, but the Regional Director is keeping aware of what goes on. The Region (IX) announced a satisfactory adjustment of cases against the Missouri-Pacific Railroad. A news release has been authorized on this settlement.[3]

IMPORTANT CONTACTS WITH REGIONAL OFFICES, OTHER DIVISIONS, AND OTHER GOVERNMENT AGENCIES

Information obtained by the Associate Director of Field Operations from former Ambassador Joseph Grew and Admiral Russell R. Waesche indicates that we may shortly expect settlement of cases 2-GR-519 and 11-GR-18 DFO, both of which involve American citizens of Japanese ancestry seeking employment on merchant vessels.[4]

Complaints from Region II alleging discrimination in the Navy Yard in Brooklyn have been sent to Assistant Secretary of the Navy Ralph A. Bard.[5]

Region II has been advised that the Committee has no jurisdiction over the Clinton County Board of Supervisors in New York.

The Division of Review and Analysis request for information on the National Smelting Company in Cleveland has been sent to Region V.

A report on information concerning the Atlanta Journal has been sent to Region VII.

The full text of the Committee's decision and the file in the Screen Actors Guild case, 12-UA-1128, has been sent to Region XII.[6]

DFO CASES

We began the week ending April 1 with thirty-nine (39) DFO cases. Of these, thirty-two (32) were being handled by examiners and seven (7) by the Legal Division. During the week, we received ten (10) new cases and closed three (3) of those being handled by examiners. This makes a total of forty-seven (47) DFO cases. Of these, thirty-six are being handled by examiners and eleven by the Legal Division. Our case load for all regions for the week ending March 25 was 2,213. The previous week it was 2,219. This represents a decrease of six (6) cases.

ASSIGNMENTS TO CENTRAL STAFF

Mr. Bloch:

Mr. Bloch is still absent from the office on a field trip.

Miss Kahn:

Completed Assignments:

1. R. J. Dorn Company, 10-BR-169 DFO.
2. The following FDR's :
   Region II—15
   Region V—17
   Region VI—1

New Assignments:

1. Request of Region X for Post Office statement on discrimination.

Mr. Metzger:

1. Completed Assignments:
   Region II—15
   Region III—9
   Region V—2
   Region VI—4
   Region IX—3
   Region X—1
   Region XII—10

New Assignments:

1. United Seamen's Services
2. Collector of Customs, 3-GC-590 DFO.
3. D. C. Fire Department, 4-GC-89-DFO.
4. Norfolk Naval Hospital, 4-GR-164 DFO.
5. The following FDR's:
   Region II—6
   Region III—19
   Region V—2

Region VI—4
Region IX—5
Region X—1
Region XI—1
Region XII—13

Mr. Mitchell:

New Assignments:

1. Army Communications Service, 3-GR-547 DFO.
2. Aberdeen Proving Ground, 4-GR-283DFO.
3. Cardinal Engineering Company, 2-BR-568 DFO.
4. The following FDR's:
   Region II—3
   Region XIX—2
   Region XI—2
   Region XII—8
5. Reviewing and taking action on Weekly Reports from all regions

MS: copy, FEPC RG 228, Office Files of Clarence Mitchell, DNA.

1. For earlier accounts of shootings at Sun Shipbuilding on 6/16/43, see Dorothea de Schwernitz to Philip L. Gorman, memorandum, 6/28/43, RG 179, WPB, WPB323.42, Shipyards-Labor—Strikes and Disputes, DNA. See also the headnote on Strikes and Work Stoppages.

2. For the beginning of this problem at Monsanto, see 3/18/44. For reports on this incident, see Harry H. C. Gibson to Elmer Henderson, memorandum, 4/10/44, and Stanley Metzger's 4/15/44 memorandum based on it, regarding the activities of George Streator in the Monsanto Chemical Company case of 3/13/44, both in HqR84, Correspondence Relating to Cases. (L–S) Monsanto Chemical Co., Region VI. Gibson's reports state that Streator "effectively prevented anything constructive from being done" at a meeting called to settle outstanding grievances of African American employees against the company that had led to a work stoppage. At the meeting, a leader of the Chemical Workers International Council blamed the stoppage on "subversive elements, that is, work by communists under the guise of the CIO," and Streator had supported that position. Gibson further reported that Streator disputed the sincerity of many of the African Americans, depicted them as divided and lacking leadership, and blamed the strike on an organizational fight between the CIO and the AFL, "with the CIO representatives stirring up the Negro employees." Gibson claimed that the union officials then used Streator's remarks to designate "subversive elements" as the complete cause of the work stoppage, which Gibson asserted was in fact primarily due to the desire of black workers to receive "equal opportunities for upgrading along with the white employees."

3. See the headnote on Strikes and Work Stoppages.

4. On 4/1/44 Admiral Waesche informed Ross that the Coast Guard had been authorized as of 4/1/44 to act as a clearing house for determining the eligibility of Japanese-American citizens for employment in the maritime industry in all waters except the Pacific and Indian Oceans. Waesche also reported the procedures to be followed to obtain clearance. See Field Instruction No. 20-A, HqR78, Field Instructions, Aug. 1943–May 1945, 20–39, and the headnotes on Japanese Americans and on Relationships with Federal Agencies.

5. For a report on problems at Brooklyn Navy Yard, which involved issues of racial identification badges, intimidation of minority workers, and time off on religious days, see Alice Kahn's memorandum to Mitchell, 3/28/44, in which she recommends that the naval officials in Washington take up the discrimination cases. HqR38, Central Files. (entry 25) Memoranda, Mitchell, Clarence.

The reason for Kahn's recommendation evidently was that she knew the nine navy yards were operated directly by cabinet officials who would direct compliance. Kryder, *Divided Arsenal*, 124–26, 127; Weaver, *Negro Labor*, 21, 35, 100. See also the numerous texts included in HqR84, Correspondence Relating to Cases. (L–S) Navy Identification Badges (esp. Ross to Bard, 4/29/44, undated draft, and Bard to Ross, 5/17/44); headnote on Race, Creed, Color, or National Origin on Employment Application Forms.

6. On 3/18/44 the Committee had declined to take jurisdiction over the complaint against the Screen Actors Guild involving SAG's refusal to admit aliens to its Class B membership, although it did admit them to its Class A membership. Class A membership in the local comprised regular actors, while Class B membership was limited to extras. However, it asserted its jurisdiction over the motion picture industry as a whole. The full text of the ruling follows:

(a) That the Committee will regard an industry a "war industry" if it is classified as essential by WMC, unless there are facts present which warrant a different conclusion.

(b) That the Committee has jurisdiction over all types of employment in a war industry but declines to take jurisdiction in this particular case because the casual and intermittent nature of the work of extras makes its relationship to the war effort too remote.

(c) The Committee recognizes a distinction between workers who are employed only casually and intermittently (one day out of five in this case) and employees regularly but not constantly employed such as longshoremen, as well as employees regularly employed in unskilled occupations such as janitors.

See Minutes of 3/18/44, HqR1, Summary Minutes of Meetings; Transcript of Proceedings, 3/18/44, 30–38, HqR65, Central Files; and, on the importance of this ruling, the headnote on Jurisdictional Issues.

Eleanor F. Rogers, Digest of Telephone Call from Mr. Blackwell, Non-Partisan Committee, Baltimore, Maryland

April 5, 1944

Mr. Clarence M. Mitchell

Eleanor F. Rogers

Digest of Telephone Call from Mr. Blackwell,
Non-Partisan Committee, Baltimore, Maryland

On the above date, Mr. Blackwell called with regard to the situation at Western Electric.[1] He stated that Mr. Alexander Allen, Industrial Secretary of the Baltimore Urban League had asked him to call you.

Mr. Blackwell stated that he was one of the participants in the conference with Mr. C. C. Chew, Manager of Industrial Relations for Western Electric. Mr. Blackwell said that those present were not satisfied with the plan for segregated locker room facilities and this was made clear to Mr. Chew. Mr. Blackwell stated that he asked Mr. Chew whether the latter thought "harmonious relations" could be built up by segregated facilities, and Mr. Chew admitted that in his opinion it could not be done. Mr. Blackwell stated that new lockers are being set up and given alphabetical designations. Toilet facilities are attached to the locker rooms and persons will be assigned to lockers and expected to use the facilities attached to them. Negroes would be entirely separated from whites. He said this plan would go into effect as soon as the new facilities are completed—within ten or fifteen days. This is in the Wire Building, Mr. Blackwell said, adding that he did not know about the other buildings. He said they were informed by Mr. Chew that the new cafeteria facilities would not be segregated.

Among those present at the meeting, Mr. Blackwell said, were Messrs. Chew, Stoll (for the company), and the following workers: Elwood Robertson, Seaborn, Wright, Gershin, Herbert Watts, and Barnes, the last named having arrived about ten minutes after the meeting began. Messrs. Robertson and Wright did most of the talking, according to Mr. Blackwell.

In explaining how the conference was arranged, Mr. Blackwell stated that Mr. Watts called Mr. Chew Monday night asking for permission to talk with him. Mr. Chew asked how many persons would be present. When Mr. Watts informed [him] his six, he was quoted as saying that six would constitute a committee and, although he would talk with individuals, he would not talk with a committee. Mr. Chew asked that he be called again Tuesday morning, but Mr. Blackwell explained that it was considered best to go to his office without calling, which the group did, and they were admitted to Mr. Chew's office after he had apparently summoned Mr. Stoll. Mr. Blackwell said that Mr. Chew was informed that the group had petitions signed by colored persons who were opposed to the segregated setup, but Mr. Chew refused to accept the petitions. About 500 persons had signed at the time of the meeting, Mr. Blackwell stated, but they now have over 1,000 signatures.

In summary, Mr. Blackwell stated that the group definitely did not say they would accept the segregated facilities. Mr. Chew, according to Mr. Blackwell, was asked to talk to the colored workers but stated that he did not know that he had the power to do so, but that he would find out and let the group know whether he could talk at a meeting of just employees.

MS: copy, FR45, Region IV. Closed Cases, Western Electric Co., Point Breeze Plant, Baltimore, Md.

1. See the other digest of a telephone call of this date to Alexander Allen and sources cited there. Charles Blackwell and Eugene Barnes were leaders and the other workers mentioned were members of the Non-Partisan Committee, a group opposed to the creation of segregated facilities at the Point Breeze plant.

Eleanor F. Rogers, Digest of Clarence Mitchell's Telephone Call to Mr. Alexander Allen, Baltimore Urban League, Baltimore, Maryland

April 5, 1944

Mr. Clarence M. Mitchell

Eleanor F. Rogers

Digest of Your Telephone Call to Mr. Alexander Allen,

Baltimore Urban League, Baltimore, Maryland

On the above date, you called Mr. Alexander Allen with regard to a wire which Mr. Ross had received from Miss Rogers, Secretary of the Non-Partisan Committee. You informed him that you had talked with Mr. Ganey in New York, who said that Mr. Barnes had a conference with Mr. Chew, of Western Electric, at the plant yesterday.

Mr. Allen stated that a committee of workers went in to see Mr. Chew and Mr. Barnes was among them, but the group was not representing the Non-Partisan Committee. You told Mr. Allen that Mr. Ganey said it was his understanding that the whole situation with regard to segregated locker room facilities at the plant had been explained to the satisfaction of the Non-Partisan Committee. Mr. Allen said this was not true; that Mr. Chew refused to meet with the Non-Partisan Committee, stating that he would meet with individuals but no group. Mr. Allen further stated that Mr. Chew tried to "rope" in the people present by telling them that they would be segregated but it is not segregation.

Mr. Allen stated that the telegram sent to FEPC was also sent to Major Summers in the War Department, Under Secretary of War Robert J. Patterson, Dr. Frank Graham, NWLB, The United Electrical Workers, CIO, Baltimore, and the United Federation of Labor in Baltimore.[1]

Mr. Allen stated that Mr. Pete Bosch of the CIO made the statement read by you over the telephone (re. War Department policy).

At your suggestion, Mr. Allen agreed to get in touch with Mr. Barnes and have him tell you what went on in the conference with Mr. Chew. You suggested that he get other people attending the conference to sign a joint statement indicating what their views were on the conference and whether they agreed with the statements of Mr. Chew.

MS: copy, FEPC FR45, Region IV. Closed Cases 108–215, Western Electric Co., Point Breeze Plant, Baltimore, Md.

1. This telegram and other related texts are included in the file. On the opposition of the Non-Partisan Committee, headed by Eugene Barnes and Maybelle Rogers, to the segregated facilities demanded by the Point Breeze Employees Association, see Mitchell's memoranda of 8/26, 11/11, 12/14/43, 2/16, 3/14/44; the digest of the other telephone conversation of this date with Blackwell of the Non-Partisan Committee; headnote on Strikes and Work Stoppages.

Memorandum on Forthcoming Meeting of Division Heads

DATE: April 12, 1944

TO: Mr. George M. Johnson
        Deputy Chairman

FROM: Clarence M. Mitchell
        Associate Director of Field Operations

SUBJECT: Your Forthcoming Meeting of Division Heads

It is an unending source of amazement to me how a small agency such as ours must have a limited meeting of division heads <u>from which persons whose duties place them in key positions are excluded. Previously I have discussed this with you and now</u> wish to make a formal request for admission to these meetings.

I have read the memorandum concerning the proposal that FEPC have two divisions, one of which will be devoted to public relations. Any regional director who is doing his job (and in my opinion each is a good man), does not need the type of public relations program proposed. <u>We need the respect of complainants and parties charged. We will earn this respect as we deliver and as they observe us in action. I have never regarded the excellent work which Miss Schultz has been doing as anything more than what we should expect of every good examiner.</u>

I am sending copies of this memorandum to all who were eligible to attend the meeting when I last talked with you about it.

CC: Messrs. Maslow, Jones, Bourne and Davis

MS: LH, DI, FEPC RG 228, Office Files of Clarence Mitchell, DNA.

Memorandum on Conference with WMC Officials

April 12, 1944

Mr. Will Maslow
    Director of Field Operations
Clarence M. Mitchell
    Associate Director of Field Operations
Conference with WMC Officials

On the above date, we met with Mr. Vernon McGee, Deputy Executive Director, WMC, and Mr. A. W. Motley, Director, Bureau of Placement, WMC, to discuss the following items:

1. Alleged discriminatory recruitment practices of the Hanford Engineering Company in Pasco, Washington.
2. Failure of General Motors Corporation to supply non-white information on ES 270's.[1]
3. Failure of WMC Regions IV, VII, and X to file ES 510 Reports against employers who violate the requirements of Executive Order 9346.
4. Tendencies of USES offices in Region VII to pretend that discriminatory specifications have been eliminated, but, at the same time, to fill orders in a discriminatory manner.

Mr. McGee and Mr. Motley assured us that the previous instructions which permitted discrimination against Latin-Americans in the Denver USES on the part of the Hanford Engineering Company have been rescinded. They stated that Latin-Americans have been recruited for work at Pasco, Washington, and promised to give us figures showing the number. Mr. Motley stated that in Texas very few Latin-Americans had been recruited. A great many of the available workers had gone into agricultural jobs in accordance with seasonal demands before the discriminatory practices of the company were corrected.

Mr. Motley promised that during a forthcoming visit to Detroit he will talk with Mr. Cushman, State Director of WMC, concerning General Motors' policy of refusing to supply information on non-white employees for the 270 Reports. Mr. Motley expressed the hope that Mr. Cushman might be able to do something to correct this problem.

When we discussed the failure of Regions IV, VII, and X to submit 510 Reports, Mr. McGee stated he felt that Region IV intends to send in such reports. For this reason, he suggested it would not be advisable to discuss the matter with Mr. Henry E. Treide, Regional Director of WMC, at this time.

A promise was made by Mr. McGee that he would talk over the 510 question and discriminatory practices of local USES offices with Mr. Dillard Lassiter [Lasseter], Regional Director, WMC, in Atlanta, and Mr. J. M. Bond, Regional Director in Dallas. Both of these men are to be in Washington on Thursday, April 13, for a Regional Directors' Conference. Mr. McGee declined to issue a new instruction at this time and stated that he, also, felt a discussion of the problem at the general sessions of the WMC Regional Directors would not accomplish as much as a more or less private conference with Messrs. Lassiter and Bond.

MS: copy, HqR1, Office Memoranda. M.

1. See Vernon McGee, WMC deputy executive director, to Mitchell, 3/28/44, HqR83, Correspondence Relating to Cases. (A–K); Mitchell to Hoglund, telegram 4/12/44, HqR1, Office Memoranda. M; Mitchell to Maslow, report, 3/27/44; headnote on Race, Creed, Color, or National Origin on Employment Application Forms.

Weekly Report

April 13, 1944

Mr. Will Maslow
Clarence M. Mitchell
Weekly Report for Week Ending April 8, 1944

OUTSTANDING EVENTS AND PROBLEMS

In the report for the week ending April 1, 1944, it was indicated that a strike was threatening at the General Box Company in Kansas City, Missouri. This matter was not within our jurisdiction but, since between sixty and eighty per cent of the employees were Negroes, our regional office was requested to render any assistance necessary in the settlement of the case by the War Labor Board. The Regional Director, Mr. Hoglund, advised us this week that the walkout did not occur and the parties involved have submitted the dispute to arbitration.[1]

A somewhat similar problem in St. Louis, Missouri, but within our jurisdiction, appears to be progressing satisfactorily. It has been previously mentioned that white workers had expressed opposition to the employment of Negroes at the General Cable Company in St. Louis and staged a brief slow down of production. The Regional Director's report on the situation states, "The Management of the Company is emphatic in stating its desire to integrate Negro women workers . . . and . . . with unified effort on the part of the Company, the Union, and the Signal Corps, we are hopeful that a satisfactory adjustment can be reached."[2]

Region III reports that the Transport [Transit] Workers Union has taken steps to have a conference with the Director of Industrial Relations [A. A. Mitten] of the Philadelphia Transit [Transportation] Company concerning compliance with FEPC's directive on the employment of Negroes as platform workers.[3]

The region also reports threats of disruption of production in the Pittsburgh area at the Dravo Corporation and the Clairton branch of the Carnegie-Illinois Steel Corporation. Those problems do not involve Negro workers only, but the regional office is standing by to render whatever assistance it can.[4]

The Detroit office of Region V reports that eighty-seven colored workers who were laid off by the L. A. Young Spring and File Company during the week of March 4 have been recalled to work. Apparently, the situation has improved.

IMPORTANT CONTACTS WITH REGIONAL OFFICES, OTHER DIVISIONS, AND OTHER GOVERNMENT AGENCIES

The Division of Review and Analysis has been requested to furnish monthly summaries on strikes or potential strikes which involve matters necessitating action by FEPC.

The Legal Division has been asked to answer questions involving Committee rules or regulations raised by attorneys for the R. J. Dorn Company, case 10-BR-169. The Legal Division has also been asked to indicate whether the United Seamen's Service, U. S. S. Hotel Carol, New Orleans, and Camp Kittiwake, Pass Christian, Mississippi, are within the jurisdiction of FEPC. In both of these cases, Negro seamen have been discriminated against solely because of race. The War Shipping Administration has been keeping a file on cases where Negroes have been rejected from Camp Kittiwake, and this file will be made available to the Committee upon request.[5]

The War Department has been requested to take action on our previous communication of March 16 concerning the Anniston Ordnance Depot. In this case, a War Department representative interfered with operations of the Director of Region VII at the Anniston Ordnance Depot, Anniston, Alabama.[6]

Region II has been advised that a field visit will be made by Mr. Stanley D. Metzger in connection with problems at the Cardinal Engineering Company, 2-BR-566.

The Bureau of Printing and Engraving, 4-GC-117 DFO, has been returned to Region IV for further processing.

Questions raised by Region IV in connection with the Capital Transit case, Army and Navy establishments, and the Point Breeze Employees Association of Baltimore have been handled in a special memorandum to the region.

Region V has been requested to take follow-up action on General Motors cases, 6-BC-275 though 282 and 6-BC-296 DFO.

Questions raised by Regional Director McKnight on comments concerning FDR's were handled in a memorandum dated April 7, a copy of which is attached.

Mr. McKnight was also advised on dates for payroll changes in connection with Mr. Daniel Donovan's transfer to New York.

Region IX was advised that the Director of Field Operations [Maslow] plans to take action in connection with complaints against the UCCWA in that region.

The Region (IX) was also advised that all requests for WLB action on cases would have to be cleared with the central office before going to WLB.

Special questions raised by Regional Director Brin concerning the W. F. Baldwin Company, 10-BR-186, are being handled with the assistance of Region IX.

We have requested the Director of Region XII [Kingman] to make a follow-up check on a communication we sent to the North American Aviation Company concerning cases 10-BC-174 and 175 DFO.

An R. D. memorandum was prepared on Region XII's handling of discriminatory advertising.

DFO CASES

We began the week ending April 8 with 47 DFO cases. Of these, 36 were being handled by examiners and 11 by the Legal Division. During the week, we received five (5) new cases and closed two (2)—one of those being handled by examiners and one of those being handled by the Legal Division. This makes a total of 50 DFO cases. Of these, 39 are being handled by examiners and 11 by the Legal Division. Our case load for all regions for the week ending April 1 was 2,169. The previous week it was 2,143. No statement is made concerning the increase or decrease because it was necessary to readjust our figures in the central office on the basis of new data received from the field.

ASSIGNMENTS TO CENTRAL STAFF

Mr. Bloch:

Mr. Bloch is still in the field.

Miss Kahn:

Completed Assignments:

1. Compilation of Mexican Book.
2. Summary of Pasco Company Case.
3. Review of DFO Cases.
4. Naval Observatory, 4-GR-259.
5. Post Office, 10-GR-210.
6. General Motors Case.

New Assignments:

1. The following FDR's:
   Region II—2
   Region IV—1
   Region VI—3

Mr. Metzger:

Completed Assignments:

1. Memorandum on Revision of Field Instruction No. 7, re. Jurisdiction.[7]
2. Mt. Ranier Motor Base, 12-GR-15 DFO.
3. Norfolk Naval Hospital, 4-GR-164 DFO.
4. Conference with Commissioner W. F. Johnson, Bureau of Customs, re. Sabbatarians.

New Assignments:

1. American South African Lines, 12-BR-1005 DFO.
2. AFL Operators Union, 12-UR-1006 DFO.

273

3. Tankers Association, 12-UR-1047 DFO.
4. The following FDR's:
   Regions II—15

Mr. Mitchell:

Completed Assignments:

1. Bureau of Engraving and Printing, 4-GC-117 DFO.
2. Reviewing and acting upon problems raised in all Weekly Reports from regional offices.

Copies of other assignments completed are attached.

MS: copy, FEPC RG 228, Office Files of Clarence Mitchell, DNA.

1. For background on the NWLB, see 11/11/43; for its interactions with the FEPC, see the headnote on Relationships with Federal Agencies.

2. See the headnote on Major Cases in St. Louis.

3. See the headnote on Street and Local Railways.

4. See the headnote on Strikes and Work Stoppages.

5. On these cases, see also 3/21, 3/27, 4/3, 10/12, 11/21/44.

6. See 3/18, 4/17/44.

7. For Field Instruction 7, dated 9/11/43, see HqR78, Field Instructions, 8/43–5/45 (entry 46), Field Instructions 1–19. For the background, see the headnote on Jurisdictional Issues.

Weekly Report

April 17, 1944

Mr. Will Maslow
Clarence M. Mitchell
Weekly Report for Week Ending April 15, 1944

OUTSTANDING EVENTS AND PROBLEMS

Region VII reports that the Moore Dry Dock Company, mentioned in its Weekly Report of January 24 as upgrading 113 Negro employees to higher paying repair work because of Committee action, now has increased this number to 240.

Region IX indicates that a Captain Morgan of the U. S. Army Signal Corps, Labor Division, is working on the problem presented by the General Cable Company, St.

Louis, Missouri, case 9-BR-165. In this case, employees have made statements opposing the introduction of Negro women. Captain Morgan, according to the Regional Director, is conducting a personal investigation among leaders of white employees who have been most vocal in opposition to the employment of colored women.[1]

In an otherwise gloomy picture, Region VII notes that the regional office of WMC stopped service on a discriminatory order which had been marked for clearance for the Reynolds Metal Company of Macon, Georgia. The establishment is a Naval ordnance plant, and the order had gone to four cities outside of the Macon area before it was stopped at the request of FEPC.

The Director and the Associate Director of Field Operations conferred with Mr. Vernon McGee, Deputy Executive Director, WMC, and Mr. A. W. Motley, Acting Director, Bureau of Placement, WMC, on April 12, concerning problems involving the relationship between FEPC and WMC. A special memorandum on the visit was prepared and is attached.[2]

IMPORTANT CONTACTS WITH REGIONAL OFFICES, OTHER DIVISIONS, AND OTHER GOVERNMENT AGENCIES

The Treasury Department was requested this week to issue instructions designed to permit Sabbatarians to have favorable consideration when they seek time off to observe their Sabbath.[3]

The War Department was reminded of our problem at the Anniston Ordnance Depot at Anniston, Alabama. It will be recalled that, in this case, a War Department official prevented proper functioning of our Regional Director.[4]

The War Production Board indicates that housing facilities to be provided for Negro employees of the Sun Shipbuilding Company in Chester, Pennsylvania, have been curtailed. It was felt by WPB that the curtailment was improper since there had been an acute need for such housing previously. At the WPB's request, I asked Mr. Fleming, our Regional Director, to give us the picture of Negro employment at this time. A memorandum on this is attached.

Mr. Fleming has been advised of recent favorable comments received from Region IX concerning the Post Office.

Cases involving the Pennsylvania Central Airlines, 4-BC-187 and 4-BR-176, and the Norfolk Naval Hospital, 4-GR-164, have been returned to the region for further action.

Region VII's request for information on Civil Service agreements has been answered.[5]

Region IX was advised by teletype of WMC relaxation of previous discriminatory instructions which were being followed by the Denver WMC in the recruitment of workers for Pasco, Washington.

Questions concerning the Treasury Department and Post Office, 10-GR-210 and 10-GR-250, have been answered.

We have asked Region X to supply us with further information on the laundry industry which is considered locally essential by WMC.[6]

The file on the Mt. Ranier Motor Base, 12-GR-15, has been returned to the region for further action.

War Department information concerning the Sacramento Air Service Command, 12-GR-278, has been referred to Regions II and XII. Because the complainant is now residing in Region II, Mr. Lawson has been requested to obtain his comments.

A very excellent report on the Los Angeles office has been filed by Mr. Stanley D. Metzger. This report is an analysis of the work of the office for the period beginning January 1 and ending March 31. Mr. Metzger is requested to do a similar analysis on Region IV and the Detroit office of Region V.

DFO CASES

We began the week ending April 15 with 50 DFO cases. Of these, 39 were being handled by examiners and 11 by the Legal Division. During the week, we received five (5) new cases and closed nine (9)—seven of those being handled by examiners and two of those being handled by the Legal Division. This makes a total of 46 DFO cases. Of those, 33 are being handled by examiners and 13 by the Legal Division. Our case load for all regions, excluding IV and XI, for the week ending April 8 was 1,901. The previous week, it was 2,124. No significance can be attached to these figures because current readjustments make it impossible to determine increase or decrease.

ASSIGNMENTS TO CENTRAL STAFF

Mr. Bloch:

Mr. Bloch returned to the office Thursday, April 13, and is still working on Basic Magnesium.

Miss Kahn:

Miss Kahn was assigned to Region IV Monday, April 10.

Mr. Metzger:

Completed Assignments:

1. Instructions to Chicago and letters to Mr. Joseph Keenan, Office of Labor Production, WPB, and Assistant Secretary of the Navy Bard on Missouri Valley Bridge and Iron Company, Evansville, Indiana.
2. Memorandum on activities of Mr. George Streator re. Monsanto Chemical Company.[7]
3. Draft of proposed rules and regulations for FEPC.
4. Memorandum on legal effect of FEPC directive.

5. Memorandum analyzing work of Los Angeles office, period January 1 through March 31.
6. Answered questions contained in Region IX's Weekly Report for week ending April 8.
7. Letter to Mr. Daniel W. Bell, Under Secretary of the Treasury, re. Treasury policy on Sabbatarians.
8. St. Louis Ordnance Depot, 9-GR-138 DFO.
9. Sacramento Air Service Command, 12-GR-278 DFO.

Mr. Mitchell:

Completed Assignments:

1. Reviewing and taking action on matters raised in Weekly Reports from Regions.

Copies of other assignments complete are attached.

MS: copy, FEPC RG 228, Office Files of Clarence Mitchell, DNA.

1. For follow-up activity, see 5/17/44; for background and cross-references, see the headnote on Major Cases in St. Louis.

2. See 4/12/44 ("Conference").

3. See the headnote on Creedal Discrimination.

4. See 3/18, 4/13/44; the section on the War Department in the headnote on Relationships with Federal Agencies.

5. See FEPC FR80, Region VII, Administrative Files (A–Z), Civil Service Commission; the section on the U.S. Civil Service Commission in the headnote on Relationships with Federal Agencies.

6. See the headnote on Jurisdictional Issues.

7. On this report, dated 4/15/44, see notes to Mitchell's report of 4/3/44.

Memorandum on Important Cases Being Handled at Regional Level

April 21, 1944

MEMORANDUM

TO: Mr. Malcolm Ross, Chairman
Mr. George M. Johnson, Deputy Chairman

FROM: Clarence M. Mitchell
Associate Director of Field Operations

SUBJECT: Important Cases Being Handled at Regional Level

277

Attached is a list of the most important cases which are being handled by our regional offices as of April 18, 1944. It is my intention to keep this report current by weekly changes. Since it is a new report, I am trying to keep it flexible for some time until we can determine the best way of handling it. For the first few weeks, supplements will be prepared showing new cases or new action on those listed. Such supplements will show the date of the original report to which they should be attached. At the end of the month, a new complete list will be prepared. Ultimately, we hope to have this report form stabilized as that it can be mimeographed and sent to the regional offices.[1]

Meanwhile, any suggestions for improving either the form or the content will be appreciated.

Attachment

MS: copy, HqR39, Central Files. (entry 25) Memoranda, Ross, Malcolm, 1944.

1. For the information included in the attached list and subsequent weekly supplements through 5/22/44, see "Important Cases Being Handled at Regional Level," 4/22–5/22/44, in appendix 1.

Weekly Report

April 24, 1944

Mr. Will Maslow

Clarence M. Mitchell

Weekly Report for Week Ending April 22, 1944

OUTSTANDING EVENTS AND PROBLEMS

Adjustment of complaints against the Texas and Pacific Railway has been announced by Region X. These complaints involve the upgrading of Negro employees in boiler maker and machinist trades.[1]

Region VII reports that a school for the training of Negroes in war occupations will be established in Jacksonville, Florida. The school will accommodate 600 students.

A new street railway case is now being handled by Region VI. It is the Gary Street Railway Company at Gary, Indiana. Complaints charge refusal to employ Negroes on platform operations.[2]

Two strikes—one at Akron, Ohio, and the other at Toledo—require attention in Region V. Latest reports from Akron indicate that the strike, which involved 200

Negro employees at the Goodyear Aircraft Corporation, approaches settlement. There is no late information on the Toledo strike, which occurred on Saturday, April 22, at the Chevrolet Transmission Plant. White workers left the job when Negro women were upgraded.[3]

A complaint of long standing involving American citizens of Japanese ancestry received positive action this week from the United States Coast Guard. American citizens of Japanese ancestry contend they are unable to obtain employment on merchant vessels solely because of their ancestry. A report from Admiral Waesche, of the Coast Guard, this week gives hope of settling these cases in Region II and XI.[4]

IMPORTANT CONTACTS WITH REGIONAL OFFICES, OTHER DIVISIONS, AND OTHER GOVERNMENT AGENCIES

Cases 4-UR-285 and 4-BR-248, concerning the Wright Automatic Tobacco Packing Machinery Company in North Carolina, have been returned to Region IV for further handling at the suggestion of the Legal Division.

Detailed inquiries concerning Final Disposition Reports on cases originating from USES 510 Reports have been answered in a memorandum addressed to Mr. McKnight, Director of Region V. A report analyzing the work of the Detroit office has also been sent to Region V.

At the request of the War Department, we have obtained information from Mr. Henderson, Director of Region VI, that statistical data from the Elwood Ordnance Plant may now be discontinued. The War Department is being informed.

Information concerning inclusion of non-discrimination clauses in Naval contracts has been forwarded to Region VI for further checking.

Complaints received from citizens of Tampa, Florida, who visited the office during the week, have been forwarded to Mr. Hunt in Atlanta. Theses citizens charge discrimination by the Tampa Shipbuilding Company.

Region XII has been requested to close case 12-UR-118, involving the Marine Firemen, Oilers, Watertenders and Wipers Association.

DFO CASES

We began the week ending April 15 with 46 DFO cases. Of these, 34 were being handled by examiners and 12 by the Legal Division. During the week, we received five (5) new cases and closed five (5)—three of those being handled by examiners and two of those being handled by the Legal Division. This makes a total of 46 DFO cases. Of these, 34 are being handled by examiners and 12 by the Legal Division. Our case load for all regions for the week ending April 15 was 2,083. The previous week it was 2,092. This represents a decrease of nine (9) cases.

ASSIGNMENTS TO CENTRAL STAFF

Mr. Bloch:

Completed Assignments:

1. The following FDR's:
   Region I—4
   Region II—6
   Region III—8
   Region VII—30

New Assignments:

1. Office of Postal Censorship, 2-GA-675 DFO.
2. Army Communications Service, 3-GR-547 DFO.
3. Cardinal Engineering Company, 2-BR-566 DFO.
4. Undocketed complaint of Walter Fisher (Region II)—jurisdiction question re. alienage by reason of alien status.
5. The following FDR's:
   Region I—4
   Region II—7
   Region III—10

Mr. Metzger:

Completed Assignments:

1. Answering questions raised in Weekly Report of Region IX.
2. Letters to Maritime Commission for Chairman's signature re. Wagner Electric Company, 9-BR-157.
3. Analysis of Detroit Sub-Regional Office.
4. Letter to Post Office Department on Seattle Post Office.
5. Review of files on Southern Pacific Railroad Company, 12-BR-154, 267, 234.
6. The following FDR's:
   Region I—2
   Region II—14
   Region VI—10
   Region IX—3
   Region XII—4

New Assignments:

1. The following FDR's:
   Region I—3
   Region II—16
   Region VI—18

Region IX—3
Region XII—5
2. U. S. Treasury Department, Fiscal Service, 12-GR-262, DFO.

Mr. Mitchell:

Completed Assignments:

1. Reviewing and taking action on matters contained in Weekly Reports from Regional Offices.
2. The following FDR's:
   Region III—1
   Region IV—7
   Region VI—8
   Region VIII—1
   Region IX—2
   Region X—8
   Region XII—18
3. Copies of other assignments completed are attached.

New Assignments:

1. Electronics Mechanics, Inc. (Undocketed, Region II), re. American citizens of Japanese ancestry.
2. The following FDR's:
   Region IV—6
   Region X—26

MS: copy, FEPC RG 228, Office Files of Clarence Mitchell, DNA.

1. See the headnote on the FEPC and Unions.

2. See the headnote on Street and Local Railways.

3. See the headnote on Strikes and Work Stoppages.

4. See the headnote on Japanese Americans; the section on the War Department in the headnote on Relationships with Other Agencies.

Memorandum on Railroad Settlements
by Regional Offices

April 28, 1944

Mr. Will Maslow
  Director of Field Operations

Clarence M. Mitchell
    Associate Director of Field Operations
Railroad Settlements by Regional Offices

Pursuant to your request, I have prepared this memorandum on railroad settlements from Regions IX and X. Certain elements of discrimination are not completely eliminated. For example, in one of the Texas and Pacific cases, a Negro was fired after he was in a fight with a white man. The somewhat meager evidence before us indicates that the white man started the trouble. As you know, we have received new complaints against the Missouri-Pacific in connection with Mexicans and Negroes seeking transfers to stewards' jobs. The cases adjusted follow:

1. Texas and Pacific Railroad, International Association of Machinists, Boiler Makers Union, Brotherhood of Railway Carmen, Blacksmiths, Electrical Workers, and Sheetmetal Workers, Fort Worth, Texas. Our Dallas office reports that the Negro complainants charged: (a) Negro machinist helpers and boiler maker helpers were not upgraded in accordance with their seniority. (b) Negroes were not permitted to obtain training for certain higher skills covered by the unions mentioned.

    The unions and management agreed that Negroes would be given the opportunity to learn all parts of the craft and to operate all machines which formerly had not been available to them. The company agreed to post notices when there are openings in higher grades of work. This means that Negroes will have an opportunity to do all the work classified as "A" in the six crafts, covered by the unions previously mentioned.

2. Missouri-Pacific Railroad Roundhouse and Shops, Kansas City, Missouri. In this case, Negro complainants charged the company with discriminatory policies which prevented Negroes from being upgraded from the classification of laborer. The complainants also alleged discriminatory employment policies resulting from inadequate facilities.

    As a result of FEPC negotiations, the following upgrading has been effectuated among Negroes:

DECEMBER, 1943

(a) Machinist	5
(b) Class B Machinist	1
(c) Machinist Helper	1
(d) Boilermaker	1
(e) Class B Boilermaker	2
(f) Boilermaker helper	1
(g) Boilermaker	5

JANUARY 1, 1944

(a) Class B to Class A Boilermaker   1

(b) Class B to Class A Machinist   1

(c) Machinist helper to machinist   1

(d) Engine washer to Machinist helper   1

(e) Laborer to Machinist helper   2

(One boilermaker declined promotion)

2. <u>Denver and Rio Grande Western Railroad Company, Denver, Colorado</u>. In this case, the company inserted a discriminatory advertisement in the <u>Denver Post</u> and the <u>Rocky Mountain News</u> on February 20, asking for white cooks and cook's helpers. Applicants were not required to have had experience.

On March 17, the regional office in Kansas City wrote to the company concerning this type of advertisement. Mr. Wilson McCarthy, one of the Trustees of the railroad, made the following reply on March 21:

"I have had this complaint investigated and find that the publication was made, as stated.

"On behalf of the Trustees and Management of the Denver and Rio Grande Western Railroad, I desire to assure you that we are in accord with the spirit of the Executive Order referred to, and that we desire in every way to avoid any employment practices that may be discriminatory as to the color of our employes. Our Personnel and Commissary Departments have been directed to refrain from the use of any advertisement containing discriminatory specifications as to race, color, creed or national origin; and it is our purpose to see that these instructions are strictly adhered to.

"Thanking you for calling the matter to our attention, I am confident you will have no further complaints of this nature in the future."

MS: copy, HqR38, Central Files. (entry 25) Memoranda, Maslow, Will, 1944.
This is a follow-up to the hearings that the Committee held 9/15–18/43 on discrimination involving upgrading, job assignments and seniority rights of African Americans in the operating divisions and shops in the railroad industry. In December it issued directives against both the railroads and the unions that said the Southeastern Carriers Conference Agreement, under which the discrimination was practiced, must be set aside. For highly selected background documents, see "Progress Report–Railroad Hearings," Bartley C. Crum to Haas, memorandum, 9/4/43, HqR1, Office Files of Malcolm Ross. B; the Committee's most recent discussions of the hearings in Transcript of Proceedings, 10/18/43, 125, HqR64, Central Files; FEPC advance news release, 12/1/43, HqR4, Office Files of George M. Johnson. Railroad Findings; the railroads' letter responding to the FEPC's directives of 11/18/43, HqR1, Office Files of Malcolm Ross. Committee Meetings; FEPC news release, 12/13/43, FEPC RG 228, IE-2-48-25-3, Trimble, box 469, also in HqR86, Press Releases. Railroads; NAACP, *Annual Report*, 1943, 19–21; *Steele v. Louisville*, 323 U.S. 192 (1944); *Tunstall v. Brotherhood of Locomotive Firemen and Enginemen*, 323 U.S. 210 (1944); *Wallace Corporation v. National Labor Relations Board*, 323 U.S. 248 (1944); Johnson's assessment to the staff of the *Steele, Tunstall*, and *Wallace* cases (n.d.), HqR5, Office Files of George M. Johnson. Undesignated (blank) folder. See also an expanded discussion of the impact of the hearings on the railroads and the Supreme Court's decisions on Mitchell's work in the introduction.

Weekly Report

May 1, 1944

Mr. Will Maslow
Clarence M. Mitchell
Weekly Report for Week Ending April 29, 1944

OUTSTANDING EVENTS AND PROBLEMS

At the request of the Jones and Laughlin Steel Company, Examiner Manly, of Region III, went to Pittsburgh to investigate problems connected with a strike at the company's Hazelwood By-Products Plant. Negro employees left the job and charged that they were denied opportunities to be upgraded to jobs as pushers. Upon learning that Mr. Manly was en route to Pittsburgh, the Negro workers returned to the job. No report has as yet been received from the region as to the outcome of negotiations on the charge of discrimination based on race.

Region V reports that the strike at the Chevrolet Transmission Plant in Toledo, Ohio, mentioned in last week's report, has been settled. Details on the settlement have not yet been received. Region V also has a strike in Detroit at the Palmer-Bee Company because a citizen of Japanese ancestry was hired. The company indicated that not many workers were involved in the walkout and, apparently, additional loyal citizens of Japanese ancestry will be hired by the company.[1]

There is a report from Region IX (dated April 22) stating that discrimination against Mexicans in the recruitment of workers by the Olympic Commissary (Hanford Engineering Company) at Pasco, Washington, has been discontinued in Denver, Colorado. This verifies information previously obtained in a conference with the War Manpower Commission.[2]

IMPORTANT CONTACTS WITH REGIONAL OFFICES, OTHER DIVISIONS, AND OTHER GOVERNMENT AGENCIES

A follow-up letter was sent to the Maritime Commission on April 27, concerning the Delta Shipbuilding Company of New Orleans, Louisiana. Serious problems involving Negro workers at the company await action by the Maritime Commission.[3]

A conference concerning complaints against the Brooklyn Navy Yard was held in the central office Saturday, April 29, with representatives of the Navy Department. The Director of Field Operations, Mr. Bloch of the central staff, and Mr. Lawson of Region II joined the Chairman in this conference.[4]

The Director of Field Operations and Mr. Metzger of the central staff met with Post Office officials on April 27 to discuss complaints against post offices in Los Angeles, California, and Seattle, Washington.[5]

A new case, 10-BR-238, against the North American Aviation Company of Dallas, Texas, has been submitted to the Legal Division.

The War Department's request to discontinue the preparation of employment statistics by the Elwood Ordnance Plant, Elwood, Indiana, has been granted.

At the request of Region VII, further action was taken by the central office concerning the Bell Aircraft Company, Marietta, Georgia. This consisted of advising Region II to contact Bell officials in Buffalo, New York, which contact was made by Mr. Lawson, Director of Region II. Mr. Vaughn Bell, Vice President of the company, informed Mr. Lawson that the company would cooperate in the handling of problems at the Marietta plant.

Region VII was informed via teletype that the War Department now has a report on the Anniston Ordnance Plant at Anniston, Alabama. In this case, the War Department official who previously interfered with the Regional Director's efforts to obtain information now states that this information will be available. A full report is being sent by the War Department.[6]

Region X has been advised that we have requested follow-up action by Region XII on cases 10-BC-174 and 175, involving the North American Aviation Company at Dallas, Texas. Region XII is expected to contact the company's headquarters at Inglewood, California.

The Guy F. Atkinson Company file, 12-BR-23 DFO, and the Fort Knight file, 12-GR-7 DFO, have been returned to Region XII as possible satisfactory adjustments.

DFO CASES

We began the week ending April 29 with 46 DFO cases. Of these, 34 were being handled by examiners and 12 by the Legal Division. During the week, we received two (2) new DFO cases, and we closed four (4). Of the closed cases, three (3) were handled by examiners and one (1) by the Legal Division. This makes a total of 44 DFO cases, with 31 being handled by examiners and 13 by the Legal Division. Our case load for all regions (excluding Region V's Cleveland Office) for the week ending April 22 was 1,851. The previous week, excluding the Cleveland office in Region V, it was 1,871. No increase or decrease is given at this time because of the readjustment of figures sent in by regional offices.

ASSIGNMENTS TO CENTRAL STAFF

Mr. Bloch:

Completed Assignments:

1. Ruling on Jurisdiction of Undocketed Complaint of Walter Fisher (Region II).
2. Office of Postal Censorship, 2-GA-675 DFO.

3. The following FDR's:
   Region I—2
   Region II—23
   Region III—24
   Region VII—0

New Assignments:

1. The following FDR's:
   Region I—2
   Region II—10
   Region III—16

Mr. Metzger:

Completed Assignments:

1. Conference with Post Office officials; returned to Region XII the Los Angeles and Seattle cases.
2. Answered questions in Weekly Report of Region IX.
3. Memoranda to field re:
   a. Des Moines Report, Region VI.
   b. Hannon Machine Works, 12-BR-220.
   c. American Trading and Production Corporation, 2-BR-479.
   d. Boston Navy Yard, 1-GR-55.
   e. Muncie Sub-Office, Cincinnati Ordnance District, 6-GR-146.
   f. Koontz—Wagner Electric Company, 6-BR-56.
   g. St. Louis Post Office, 9-GR-48.
4. Letter to War Shipping Administration re. Wagner Electric Company, 9-BR-157.
5. Referred to Region X for investigation cases 12-UR-1006, 12-BR-1005 and 12-UR-1047, involving AFL Operators Union, American South African Lines and Tankers Association respectively.
6. Analysis of Region IV's FDR's and Weekly Reports for period January 1 to March 31, 1944.
7. The following FDR's:
   Region VI—4
   Region XII—5

New Assignments:

1. The following FDR's:
   Region VI—14
   Region VIII—2
   Region XII—2

Mr. Mitchell:

Completed Assignments:

1. Fort Knight, War Department, 12-GR-7 DFO.
2. Guy F. Atkinson Company, 12-BR-23 DFO.
3. Memorandum on Railroad settlements by Regional Offices.[7]
4. Review of all regional Weekly Reports, with special action on IV, V, and X.
5. The following FDR's:
   Region IV—5
   Region V—9
   Region X—8

New Assignments:

1. The following FDR's:
   Region IV—5
   Region V—9
   Region X—8

Copies of other completed assignments for Mr. Bloch and Mr. Mitchell are attached.

Attachments

MS: copy, FEPC RG 228, Office Files of Clarence Mitchell, DNA.

1. See the headnotes on Strikes and Work Stoppages and on Japanese Americans.

2. See the headnote on Mexican Americans.

3. In his field trip report of 2/22/44, on a recent incident at the Delta yard in New Orleans, Virgil Williams recommended that the Washington FEPC office request the Maritime Commission to "to make a complete and thorough investigation of the whole problem" because "it seems a bit timid" and inclined to side with the state troopers, who deplored the termination of its two members who were accused of beating two black Delta workers in racial clashes. Williams said the crux of the problem seemed to be the state troopers whom Delta had hired as guards and assigned to the yard to protect workers and equipment. In his cover memorandum of 3/16/44, Williams said an assistant to Maj. W. K. Graham, industrial relations director, U.S. Maritime Commission in New Orleans, had said that, based on his conversation with Mitchell, the assistant believed that Mitchell's picture of recent racial incidents at the Delta yard in New Orleans was "highly colored," or biased. On the other hand, Regional Director Brin had concluded that it was the assistant's attitude that "was one of bias against the Negroes" and had so told Williams. HqR83, Correspondence Relating to Cases. (A–K) Delta Shipbuilding. For subsequent developments in the case, see Mitchell to George Johnson, memorandum, 5/5/44. For immediately related cases, see 2/19, note 1, 3/6, 5/5, 5/8, 8/14, 11/22/44, 1/8, 1/9, 1/12/45.

4. See 4/3/44, note 3.

5. On 4/29/44 Maslow asked the Los Angeles FEPC office to further investigate the local post office discrimination case and to obtain "a detailed comparison of efficiency ratings, seniority, and types of work done" there. He also requested an analysis of the case. HqR84, Correspondence Relating to Cases. U.S. Post Office, Los Angeles, Cal. For an update, see Mitchell to Johnson, 9/23/44, "Visit of Los Angeles Complainant in Post Office Case."

6. See related materials filed at HqR83 with above text; see also 3/18, 4/13, 4/17/44.

7. See 4/28/44.

Memorandum on Philadelphia Post Office

May 3, 1944

Mr. George M. Johnson

Clarence M. Mitchell

Philadelphia Post Office, Case Number 3-GR-413

Mr. Joseph F. Gallagher, Postmaster of Philadelphia, questions the jurisdiction of the President's Committee on Fair Employment Practice over complaints involving the Post Office Department. You will note from the attached copy of his letter of April 28 and Mr. G. James Fleming's memorandum of May 1 that the fullest possible answer is needed to his letter.[1]

Mr. Fleming has asked that the Legal Division of FEPC draw up an appropriate reply to the Postmaster's letter. It will be appreciated if this action will be taken at the first opportunity.[2]

Attachments

MS: copy, HqR38, Central Files. (entry 25) Memoranda, Johnson, George M., 1/44–.

1. Garland's letter to Fleming and Fleming's reply of 5/13/44 to him and related texts are in HqR84, Correspondence Relating to Cases. (L–Se) Philadelphia Post Office, 3-GR-671. On immediately related activities, see Mitchell's 5/8/44 weekly report to Maslow. For background, see the section on the Post Office Department in the headnotes on Relationships with Federal Agencies.

2. George W. Crockett, in a memorandum of 5/5/44 to Johnson, provided the following response:

In his letter of April 28, 1944, denying the Committee's jurisdiction, the Postmaster at Philadelphia, Mr. Gallagher, refers to those paragraphs of Executive order 9346 which are numbered 1 and 2. From this he concludes that, since the Post Office Department "is not a contracting agency and is not concerned with vocational and training programs for war production," the Executive Order is inapplicable.

It is quite obvious that Mr. Gallagher, without any apparent justification, is limiting his analysis of the Executive Order to that portion of the Order which follows the "Now, Therefore" clause. Even so, his conclusion does not take into consideration the language of the paragraph numbered 4 of the Order. This paragraph reads:

"The Committee shall formulate policies to achieve the purposes of this Order and shall make recommendations to the various Federal Departments and agencies . . . which it deems necessary and proper to make effective the provisions of this Order" (emphasis supplied).

The above underlined language of Executive Order 9346 is taken, almost verbatim, from Executive Order 8802, the predecessor of Executive Order 9346. It has been interpreted by the highest authority, the President himself, to be a grant of power to the Committee to investigate charges of alleged discrimination on the part of officials of the several departments of the Federal Government. In his letter of March 28, 1942, addressed to the Chairman of the Committee, the President, after quoting the above language, concluded:

"The policy of the United States Government on the subject of racial discrimination was clearly enunciated in Executive Order 8802, and the application of that policy in the Federal Government was made perfectly clear in my letter of September 3, 1941. I suggest, therefore, that you ascertain, by direct reports from them (the several Federal agencies), the degree of progress which has been achieved by the respective departments and agencies. I am confident you will receive the full cooperation of the heads of departments and agencies in supplying the information you desire."

There is attached hereto a copy of the President's communication of September 3, 1941, "TO HEADS OF ALL DEPARTMENTS AND INDEPENDENT ESTABLISHMENTS." [Copy in appendix 1.]

Upon receipt of the President's communication, and on September 20, 1941, the Postmaster General wrote to the President as follows:

"In reply to your letter dated September 3, 1941, relating to lack of uniformity and possibly some lack of sympathetic attitude towards the problems of minority groups, I wish to assure you that the subject-matter will have my attention."

Thereafter, and on October 22, 1941, the Postmaster General also wrote to the Chairman of the Committee that:

"As recommended by you, the Department will furnish you with copies of complaints that are received with reference to alleged discriminations and advise you of the action taken in such cases."

It is evident, we think, from the above communications, that the President and the Post Office Department recognized the applicability of Executive Order 8802 to the United States Post Office Department. Since Executive Order 9346 does not differ in this particular from its predecessor, Executive Order 8802, the logical inference is that Executive Order 9346 likewise embraces the Post Office Department.

Indeed, on June 2, 1943, barely five days after Executive Order 9346 was issued and published, the Postmaster General, in a message to all postal personnel, called attention to the subject of alleged discrimination by Postmasters and other supervisors against various employees because of "Party affiliations, race, creed, and color . . ." (See "Postal Bulletin" for June 2, 1943.) Subsequent to the issuance of the above mentioned message by the Postmaster General, and on December 10, 1943, the Committee conducted a formal hearing and thereafter advised the Post Office Department and the Civil Service Commission of the discriminatory practices found to exist in the Post Office at Newport News, Virginia, and the conclusions reached with respect to the elimination of these practices. In this hearing the local Postmaster and the Post Office Department were represented by Mr. Vincent Miles, Solicitor for the United States Post Office Department. Neither on this occasion nor in subsequent negotiations following the above hearing has there been any indication that the Post Office Department does not recognize the jurisdiction of this Committee over cases of alleged discrimination in the Postal service in violation of Executive order 9346. On the contrary, the Post Office Department has taken affirmative steps to bring its employment practices at the Newport News Post Office into conformity with the requirements of the Executive Order.

Finally, we think attention should be called to the attached opinion given the Committee on September 25, 1942, by the General Counsel, War Manpower Commission. You will observe that, after reviewing the power of the President both under United States Civil Service Laws and Constitutional Provisions, the conclusion is stated that the jurisdiction of the President's Committee under Executive Order 8802, extends to all of the Executive Departments and independent establishments in the Federal Government. A fortiori, the Committee's jurisdiction under Executive Order 9346 must be accorded the same breadth.

We have responded to Mr. Gallagher's communication in this detailed manner because we are reluctant to assume that he intentionally disagrees with the views and policy of the Post Office Department regarding cooperation with this Committee. It is suggested that the documents referred to in this memorandum be called to his attention. Should he, nevertheless, feel constrained to adhere to the opinion expressed in his letter of April 28, the matter might well be referred formally to the Postmaster General with the Committee's recommendation that Mr. Gallagher be instructed to furnish to our Regional Director the requested information. (HqR3, Office Files of George M. Johnson. Maslow.)

Memorandum on Strike at Hazelwood By-Products Plant, Jones and Laughlin Steel Company, Pittsburgh, Pennsylvania

DATE: May 4, 1944

TO: Mr. Will Maslow

FROM: Clarence M. Mitchell

SUBJECT: Strike at Hazelwood By-Products Plant, Jones and Laughlin
           Steel Company, Pittsburgh, Pennsylvania

On Tuesday, April 25, Mr. Harvey, Chief of Industrial Relations at the above-mentioned plant,[1] called to state that a strike of Negro workers was in progress. He requested assistance from FEPC in settling the problem. He originally stated that the Negro employees were seeking to displace white employees in the job of pusher at the plant. These white employees had been on the job since 1939, Mr. Harvey stated. He indicated that the Steel Workers Union, representing the employees, had presented a grievance on this matter a year ago, but the chief problem is that there is a small turnover and, although the company would like to place Negroes on the job as push-ers, it has been unable to do so because there has been no turnover. According to his version, the Negro employees were seeking to create the vacancies by having white employees dismissed.

We called Mr. Fleming in Philadelphia on this matter and learned that the first walkout occurred on the midnight shift Sunday night, April 23, at which time fifty-three (53) Negro employees left the job. Following this, the Negroes returned to work on the morning shift Monday but the midnight shift failed to report on Monday night. By Tuesday morning, the eight o'clock shift, also made up of Negroes, had not reported for work and there was every indication that the four o'clock shift would not report for duty.

According to Mr. Fleming and Mr. Manly, of the Philadelphia office, the workers were disgruntled because on two occasions white pushers had been ill and, therefore, unable to report for duty, but white workers from outside the shop, although em-ployed by the company, had been brought in to fill these jobs temporarily. Mr. Flem-ing and Mr. Manly agreed that it would be important for FEPC to look into the matter and also mentioned that, if the strike continued, there would be a serious shutdown in other departments which depended on the work of the By-Products Plant.

It was agreed that Mr. Manly would go to Pittsburgh. When the workers were in-formed by Mr. Fleming that Mr. Manly was en route, they agreed to return to the job at 1:30 P. M., according to Mr. Milton Jacobs, Assistant Chief of Industrial Relations for the Plant, who talked with me via long distance about the strike.

Negotiations were to proceed upon the arrival of Mr. Manly, who went to Pittsburgh by plane and was to arrive there at 5:00 P. M.

MS: LH, DI, HqR63, Central Files. Tension Reports, Region III.

1. Mitchell mentioned this development in his 5/1/44 weekly report. See Mitchell's 9/4 and 9/29/43 memoranda on activities involving this company; regional director's excerpts from his weekly reports on the Jones and Laughlin Steel Corporation in HqR77, Office Files of Eugene Davidson. Strikes.

Mitchell prepared an excerpt from his Strike Data Report of 5/44, which has not been found, as follows:

> On April 23, 1944, the midnight shift of Negro workers at this plant refused to work when a foreman brought in a white worker from another department to fill a temporary vacancy in one of the better jobs. The matter was adjusted, but on the following night a similar occurrence took place, and this time a real strike ensued. A Federal Conciliator was called in, but failed to persuade the men to return to work. Thereupon, on April 25, the Jones and Laughlin management contacted the regional office of the FEPC. An FEPC Examiner arrived in Pittsburgh late that afternoon. He found that because of the strike at the By-Products Plant, the rolling mill and the blast furnance had already been forced to close, and that the rest of the huge Jones and Laughlin Plant was even then in the process of closing. The Examiner immediately met with the strikers and had them form a negotiating committee. Then, before allowing negotiations to be opened, he required the strikers to return to work in order that production of vitally needed steel might suffer no further delay.
> When this was done negotiations involving the company, the union and the strikers were opened. The chief cause of the trouble was found to be the lack of a job progression plan in the By-Products Plant. By April 28 the Examiner, together with the company and the union, had worked out a plan satisfactory to all and which will eliminate job progression as a source of trouble.

See HqR76, Office Files of Eugene Davidson. Strikes.

Memorandum on Conference with Mr. L. R. Sanford, Director of Construction, Gulf Region, U.S. Maritime Commission, Regarding Delta Shipbuilding Company, New Orleans, Louisiana

DATE: May 5, 1944

TO: Mr. George M. Johnson

FROM: Clarence M. Mitchell

SUBJECT: Conference with Mr. L. R. Sanford, Director of Construction, Gulf Region, U. S. Maritime Commission, re. Delta Shipbuilding Company, New Orleans, Louisiana

On the above date, with Mr. Ernest G. Trimble of the Legal Division and Mr. Stanley D. Metzger of Field Operations, we met in a conference with Mr. L. R. Sanford,

Director of Construction, Gulf Region, U. S. Maritime Commission, concerning the Delta Shipbuilding Company, New Orleans, Louisiana. This conference was arranged following a call to you on May 4 from Lieutenant William A. Weber, Assistant to Commissioner Vickery, U. S. Maritime Commission. Lieutenant Weber stated that Mr. Sanford was in the city and would like to discuss the problems at the Delta Shipbuilding Company, outlined in Mr. Ross' letter of March 25 to the Maritime Commission.[1]

Briefly, Mr. Ross' letter pointed out that certain acts of violence had occurred in the Yard which resulted in a walkout of Negro workers. These acts had the active participation of the guard force, in some instances. In other instances, there was indifference on the part of these policing officials when Negroes were being beaten by whites. Mr. Ross also pointed out that the Committee directives, issued to the company on October 8, 1942, had not been compiled with. We discussed these matters in our meeting of today in your office.

The results of our discussion, as I understand them, are:

1. Mr. Sanford stated that the guards at the Yard are deputized by the State of Louisiana and paid out of company funds. He also said that the company has authority to dismiss such guards for improper actions under the present arrangement. However, for other reasons, according to Mr. Sanford, the present relationship with the State of Louisiana in regard to the hiring of the guards is to be discontinued in the near future. He believes that this will correct the problem of unwarranted acts of violence against Negroes by members of the guard force.

2. Mr. Sanford agreed that the Delta Shipbuilding Company was not using Negroes in skilled capacities, as required by the Committee directives. He volunteered the explanation that the use of Negroes in such jobs might provoke racial outbreaks which would interfere with production. The Committee representatives pointed out that full utilization of the Negro labor supply in accordance with abilities of individuals is consonant with all out production and is an important factor in the promotion of morale.

3. We discussed the specific case of Mr. David Robinson, who, on January 12, 1944, was referred to the Boiler Makers Union in New Orleans by the USES. Mr. Robinson was sent to the Delta Shipbuilding Company by Mr. Pat Dailey of the Boiler Makers Union. Mr. Dudenhefer of the Delta Shipbuilding Company turned down the applicant on the ground that there were no openings in the occupation of welder trainee. Thereupon, the USES in New Orleans filed a 510 Report, dated February 11, 1944. Mr. Sanford promised to investigate this case when he returns to New Orleans.

4. It was suggested that Mr. Leonard Brin of the Dallas office of FEPC would be glad to work with the Maritime Commission in securing full compliance with the Executive Order. The FEPC representatives stressed the importance of having contractors know that the contracting agencies regard Executive Orders 8802 and 9346 as policies which must be followed. Mr. Sanford agreed to work with Mr. Brin and stated that he would send a wire to our Dallas office indicat-

ing when a conference may be held in New Orleans. Because of new duties which he has assumed in the Great Lakes area, Mr. Sanford was not certain of when he would be able to hold the conference but expected that it would be within two weeks.

5. We discussed the question of whether the use of Negroes in skilled jobs at the Delta Shipbuilding Company should be on a segregated basis. We also pointed out that segregation was impractical in that such problems as the filling of vacancies in segregated setups, the introduction of undesirable competition between Negroes and white workers, and observance of seniority in times when it is necessary to lay off workers because of cutbacks were all factors which make segregated work schemes unworkable in the long haul. We pointed out that in the Sun Shipbuilding Company, Chester, Pennsylvania, the J. A. Jones Construction Company at Brunswick, Georgia, and the Alabama Dry Dock and Shipbuilding Company in Mobile, Alabama, patterns of segregation break down in order to maintain a flexible working force.

It was suggested that any effort to settle the problems at the Delta Shipbuilding Company should be approached with these things in mind and that every effort should be made to avoid a segregated setup.

MS: LH, DI, HqR3, *Office Files of George Johnson. Will Maslow.*

For earlier developments in this case, see memoranda, 5/1/44, 8/14, 11/22/44, 1/8, 1/9, 1/12/45 and other related texts; headnote on the Shipbuilding Industry.

1. In a letter to Ross on 5/6/44, E. S. Land, chairman of the Maritime Commission, said that as a result of the 5/5/44 FEPC meeting with Sanford, he was informed that steps were "being taken with the hope that the matters referred to" might be adjusted. Land, however, said it was George Johnson who was at the meeting, not Metzger, as Mitchell reported. Mitchell attached a copy of Land's letter to a memorandum of 5/11/44 to Bruce Hunt, regional director in Atlanta, in which he reported that he, Johnson, and two other staff members again discussed the Delta Company at the 5/11/44 meeting. Mitchell said the FEPC delegation also discussed Alabama Dry Dock and the J. A. Jones Construction Company. Regarding the Jones Company, he said Sanford mentioned that it was necessary to change its three-shift operation to two nine-hour shifts. The company, however, was reluctant to do so "because a large number of its Negro employees" were concentrated on the night shift. Mitchell to Hunt, memorandum, 5/11/44, HqR66, Central Files. U.S. Government, Maritime Commission—1.

Ross's letter, as well as a follow-up, can be found in HqR83, Correspondence Relating to Cases. (A–K) Shipbuilding.

Memorandum on Jurisdiction in Hospital Cases

DATE: May 5, 1944

TO: Mr. George M. Johnson

FROM: Clarence M. Mitchell

SUBJECT: Jurisdiction in Hospital Cases

Attached is a copy of a memorandum to Mr. Henderson, concerning jurisdiction over hospitals, which is self-explanatory.[1]

In view of the fact that this question may arise in other regions, it will be appreciated if we may have copies of the opinions in these cases for distribution to the regional offices.

Attachment

MS: LH, HqR63, Central Files. Reports, Rulings, General.
    1. See related texts, 2/22, 5/8, 5/17, 5/20/44; headnote on Jurisdictional Issues.

Weekly Report

May 8, 1944

Mr. Will Maslow
Clarence M. Mitchell
Weekly Report for Week Ending May 6, 1944

OUTSTANDING EVENTS AND PROBLEMS

Region XII reports that, through the cooperative efforts of the State Manpower Director, the Richmond (California) office of the USES is now submitting 510 Reports on companies and unions that have openly violated Executive Order 9346, but which, prior to this time, have not been reported. The Region rightfully considers this an important step forward in its relationships with WMC. A clearance for 5,900 workers for the Richmond Shipyards for crafts from which Negroes are barred has been revoked by the War Manpower Commission following FEPC conferences on the subject.

Region X reports action on cases involving the Lone Star Defense Corporation and the Red River Ordnance Depot at Texarkana, Texas, lo-BR-190 and 10-GR-189 respectively. The investigation is still in process, but it is pleasing to note activity in an area which has been a source of complaint in the past but on which little satisfactory action had been taken.

Prospects of adjusting a case involving St. Louis University, 9-GR-25 DFO, seemed brighter this week when Regional Director Hoglund announced that he has communicated with the President of the University concerning acceptance of Negroes in ESMWT courses.[1]

The segregated plant arrangement of the Curtis-Wright Corporation in St. Louis appears to be limiting the use of Negro employees. The regional office reports that, while general plant expansion is to run from 12,000 to 17,000, the plan for increasing Negro employees indicates the hiring of 400 to 1,000 persons. We have advised the Region that help from the central office is available if needed.

Region V reports cooperation from the U.S. Department of Labor Conciliation Service in supplying information on strike situations which occurred in Youngstown, Toledo, Dayton, and Cincinnati. All of these strikes involve the upgrading of Negro women, according to the regional office. A strike occurred at the Chrysler Tank Arsenal in Detroit, the regional office reports. The controversy centered around management's right to transfer Negro women to the foundry as sweepers. The Committee has not yet entered the case in an official fashion.[2]

IMPORTANT CONTACTS WITH REGIONAL OFFICES, OTHER DIVISIONS, AND OTHER GOVERNMENT AGENCIES

A visit to the Treasury Department this week by Mr. Metzger of the central staff appears to have had satisfactory results. Treasury informed its office in Portland that it would have to give consideration to a Negro complainant who had been refused employment solely because of race. The handling of this matter by Mr. Metzger deserves commendation.

We have requested the War Department to take follow-up action on the case of Mr. Sylvester E. White, 12-GR-112 DFO.

The Legal Division has been requested to draw up a reply to Mr. Joseph F. Gallagher, Postmaster of Philadelphia, who questions the jurisdiction of FEPC over complaints filed against the Post Office.[3]

The Legal Division has been asked to give attention to further problems in connection with the Committee's jurisdiction over hospital cases.[4]

A note of commendation has been sent to Region IV for the improved quality of its Weekly Reports, as shown by the report dated April 22.

A case involving the Naval Observatory, 4-GR-259, has been returned to Region IV for further action. Also, material in the central office on Western Electric Company, Baltimore, has been sent to the Region.

Additional information from the War Production Board on the Missouri Valley Bridge and Iron Works, Evansville, Indiana, has been sent to Region VI.

Region VI has also been advised that its case against the United States Civil Service Commission, 6-GR-232, should be dismissed on merits.

A matter involving the Will and Baumer Candle Company, 6-BC-67, appears to require a jurisdictional ruling. The Region has been asked to furnish information for this purpose.

The full report on the War Department's investigation of problems at the Anniston Ordnance Depot has been sent to the regional office in Atlanta for comment. The Region was asked to obtain such statistical data as the War Department report said is now available.[5]

A case involving the Columbus and Greenville Railway Company has been closed this week. Although the union which filed the complaint in the beginning indicates it now has satisfactory relations with the party charged, elements of doubt arose and the Region was advised to close the case as "withdrawn by complainant."

Region X has been advised that the North American Aviation Company will conduct an investigation of cases 10-BC-174 and 175 through one of its California representatives. This representative was in Dallas on May 6.

Mr. Brin, Director of Region X, was also advised of a conference in the central office with Mr. L. R. Sanford, Director of Construction for the Gulf Region, U.S. Maritime Commission, concerning the Delta Shipbuilding Company. The file is being returned to the region for action.[6]

DFO CASES

We began the week ending May 6 with 44 DFO cases. Of these, 31 were being handled by examiners and 13 by the Legal Division. The Legal Division has two new cases and has closed none. Of the cases handled by examiners, four were closed and two new cases were received. Thirty (30) cases being handled by examiners and 15 by the Legal Division make a total of 45 DFO cases. Our case load for all regions (excluding Region II because of an adjustment of figures) for the week ending April 29 was 1,825. The previous week, it was 1,770, excluding Region II. No statement of increase or decrease is given at this time because of the readjustment of figures sent in by regional offices.

ASSIGNMENTS TO CENTRAL STAFF

Mr. Bloch:

Completed Assignments:

1. Memorandum on Request for Interpretation of Ruling Regarding Seventh Day Adventists, Case No. 1-GC-60.[7]
2. The following FDR's:
   Region I—1
   Region II—19
   Region III—10

New Assignments:

1. Beth Israel Hospital, New York, (War Department Application Form).
2. The following FDR's:
   Region II—19
   Region III—15

Mr. Metzger:

Completed Assignments:

1. Fiscal Division, Treasury Department, 12-GR-262 DFO.
2. Mt. City Copper Company, 12-BR-25 DFO.
3. Answered questions contained in Weekly Report of Region X.
4. Memorandum to Region X on Dallas Post Office.
5. The following FDR's:
   Region X—14
   Region XII—7

New Assignments:

1. Mt. City Copper Company, 12-BR-25 DFO.
2. The following FDR's:
   Region X—6
   Region XII—8

Mr. Mitchell:

Completed Assignments:

1. Columbus and Greenville Railway Company.
2. Delta Shipbuilding Corporation, 10-BR-128 and 187 DFO, Conference on.
3. Reviewing and taking action on Weekly Reports from Regions.

New Assignments:

1. Kentucky Chemical Industries, Inc., 5-BR-260 DFO.
2. The following FDR's:
   Region IV—1
   Region VI—14

MS: copy, FEPC RG 228, *Office Files of Clarence Mitchell*, DNA.

1. Other texts dealing with Engineering Science Management War Training courses are at 12/17/42 and 5/24/44.

2. See the headnote on Strikes and Work Stoppages.

3. See notes to 5/3/44 text for the Legal Department's response on the Philadelphia Post Office case. For background, see also the section on the Post Office Department in the headnote on Relationships with Federal Agencies.

4. See the headnote on Jurisdictional Issues.

5. Truman K. Gibson's report on the War Department investigation of Regional Director Hunt's complaints about its role in the case questioned Hunt's version of events and asserted that the charges had not been substantiated. See Gibson to Mitchell, 4/29, which was forwarded to Hunt on 5/2/44. For Region VII's response, see John Hope II to Mitchell, 5/16/44, HqR83, Correspondence Relating to Cases. (A–K) Anniston Warehouse Corp., Anniston Ordnance Depot, Region VII. For related texts, see 3/18, 4/13, 4/17, 5/1, 5/17/44.

6. See memoranda of 5/5, 8/14/44.

7. For a broader treatment of the problems faced by the Seventh-day Adventists, see the headnote on Creedal Discrimination. This particular case involved a charge against the Springfield Armory that it refused to promote workers who were Seventh-day Adventists purportedly because they were excessively absent from work, as Saturday is their day of worship. The armory maintained that the War Department's memorandum no. 55 on Policy on Religious Holidays covered only certain holy days, such as Jewish holy days and Good Friday, and did not include Sabbatarians.

Maslow, however, in a ruling that Lawson had requested, noted that the War Department's policy explicitly permitted "absence from work to those whose conscience leads them to spend certain holy days in religious devotion." He continued:

> This language is clear and unambiguous. Its scope and effect are comprehensive. Permission to absent oneself from work applies to "those whose conscience leads them to spend certain holy days in religious devotion." Nothing in the purport, language or intent of the policy enunciated in the Memorandum would warrant its application only to certain sects or only to certain holy days. Any elusive attempt to so narrow the effect of the War Department's policy leads to ambiguity and confusion and flies in the face of well-recognized canons of grammatical and statutory construction.

Consequently, Maslow said, the FEPC rejected the armory's contention. The full text of the memorandum, "Request for Interpretation of Ruling Regarding Seventh Day Adventists," case 1-GC-60, 5/1/44, is in HqR76, Central Files. Reports, U.S. Government. It is probably based on the memorandum that Bloch prepared.

Memorandum on Western Cartridge Company, East Alton, Illinois

DATE: May 11, 1944

TO: Mr. George M. Johnson

FROM: Clarence M. Mitchell

SUBJECT: Western Cartridge Company, East Alton, Illinois

Following our conversation concerning the above-mentioned company on May 10, I checked with the War Manpower Commission and the National Labor Relations Board concerning the past relationships each agency had with the company. The following items are of importance:

1. "A confidential report prepared by Mr. W. J. Murphy, Area Supervisor, (USES) in re Western Cartridge Company, Alton, Illinois, June 17, 1941, states that, 'Western Cartridge anticipates hiring no colored people, for the reason, as stated by Mr. Haddleton and Mr. Weiland, (company representatives), that to date it has not been the policy or practice of the firms in East Alton to hire colored people. There is no written law that colored workers cannot be hired; it is just an attitude of the community. I asked Mr. Haddleton what about the five per cent

colored population in Alton; would it be possible to take on some of these people in his company? His reply was that they preferred not to do so. His thinking is that as jobs are given to the white people, it is quite possible that the colored workers in Alton could move into the vacancies created (in non-war employment).'"

2. The NLRB's intermediate report on hearings involving the Western Cartridge Company, Local 22574, Chemical Workers, AF of L, and Local 333, Moulders and Foundry Workers, AF of L, is dated February 25, 1942. The following statements are based on the contents of this report:

   a. From 1915 to 1921, the company had individual contracts with its employees. These contracts were discontinued in 1921 but were revived in 1933. No labor organization existed in the plant until spring of 1937 when the company began negotiating with certain workers. On June 25, 1937, an independent union was established. The Trial Examiner for NLRB, Horace A. Ruckel, considered this independent union to be company dominated.

   b. On August 2, 1941, the company signed a contract with the Chemical Workers of the AF of L.

The record of this company reveals that its policy of refusing to hire Negroes was enunciated to the Government prior to the time it had a contract with a union other than the independent union. It is difficult to see how the company can avoid the responsibility of discriminatory practices against Negroes seeking employment.

MS: LH, DI, HqR1, Documents File. M.

For background and cross-references on the Western Cartridge case, see the headnote on Major Cases in St. Louis.

Weekly Report

May 17, 1944

Mr. Will Maslow

Clarence M. Mitchell

Weekly Report for Week Ending May 13, 1944

OUTSTANDING EVENTS AND PROBLEMS

An illustration of good cooperation between the Civil Service Commission and FEPC was presented from reports sent in by Region III during the past week. These reports were on the employment of a Negro complainant by the Navy Department. The job opening was in a naval office at the New York Shipbuilding Company in Camden, New Jersey. Originally, the applicant was denied employment solely because of her race. Through intervention of the Civil Service Commission and FEPC, the complainant was hired and reports that she is now adjusted to her surroundings.

A work stoppage at the Chrysler Tank Arsenal in Detroit, which was mentioned in last week's report, has been settled. Negro employees staged a stoppage when two colored women were transferred to jobs as sweepers. The women were returned to their former employment. FEPC took no part in this settlement but observed happenings and remained available for any help needed in the adjustment of the problem.

Regional Director McKnight of Cleveland suggests that the central office contact Mr. F. W. Luikart, formerly Associate Regional Director of the U.S. Civil Service Commission in Cleveland. Mr. Luikart is assuming duties as Chief of the Investigations Division of the Civil Service Commission in Washington. While in Region V, he cooperated frequently with Regional Director McKnight of FEPC. It is suggested that Mr. Bloch make this contact with Mr. Luikart.

As a result of central office discussions, it has been agreed that the following agencies will be handled by the designated central staff representative:

Mr. Bloch: Navy Department, War Production Board, War Labor Board,
            U.S. Civil Service Commission.

Mr. Metzger: Post Office Department, Treasury Department, National Labor
            Relations Board.

Mr. Mitchell: War Department, Maritime Commission, General Accounting
            Office, War Manpower Commission.[1]

Under this arrangement, persons on the central staff will continue to handle problems arising from specific groups of regions, but they will be regarded as specialists in the affairs of the agencies assigned to them.[2]

Regional Director Hoglund of Kansas City reported a new development in the General Cable Company case, 9-BR-165 (St. Louis). In this case, a work stoppage occurred on March 17 when white workers heard that the company intended to employ Negro women. The stoppage lasted for one-half hour, according to Mr. Hoglund. During the period between March 17 and May 6, Mr. Hoglund, Captain Morgan of the Signal Corps Labor Division, U.S. Army, company representatives, and union officials have been working to make possible the integration of Negro women without difficulty. The case has now been referred to the Director of Field Operations for further action because Captain Morgan has informed our regional office that the "Washington Headquarters advised him there was no obligation on the part of the Army or the Signal Corps to compel the enforcement of the Executive Order, that under no circumstances would they sanction any action which might impair production schedules at the Cable Company, and therefore Captain Morgan and his office were to observe a 'hands off' policy." This situation is the reverse of the problem we had at Anniston, Alabama, where the local War Department representative attempted to interfere with the adjustment of cases, according to the Regional Director. This matter requires immediate action at the Washington level. Such action will be taken.[3]

Mr. Brin, Director of Region X, reports that he is now establishing a basis for follow-up action in connection with our Delta Shipbuilding case.

IMPORTANT CONTACTS WITH REGIONAL OFFICES, OTHER DIVISIONS, AND OTHER GOVERNMENT AGENCIES

The Legal Division's opinion on the baking and dairy industries has been forwarded to Region III for appropriate action. Region III also asked for advice from the Legal Division in connection with Post Office cases. In addition to the Legal Division's opinion, a rough draft of a letter to the Postmaster was drawn up in the central office in order that we might be certain of complete agreement on policies expressed therein. This letter was sent to Mr. Fleming for whatever use he wished to make of it.[4]

A note of appreciation was sent to Region V for its good working relationship with the U.S. Conciliation Service on strike problems. The Region was also advised to take further action on the case involving the Engineers Depot, Cambridge, Ohio, 5-GR-282. In this case, the Regional Director felt that complainants had been intimidated. Region V was asked to continue the processing of a case against the Kentucky Chemical Industries, 5-GR-260 (Cincinnati). The party charged in this case expressed the view that it believed the case had been closed following a visit by an examiner from Mr. McKnight's staff. Thereupon, Mr. McKnight forwarded the case to the central office for action. He was advised that further action should be taken from the regional office. A copy of the memorandum dealing with this is attached.

Region VI has been advised that discriminatory advertising favoring minority groups should be handled as any other type of discriminatory advertisement.

Further word on jurisdiction over hospitals has been sent to Regions XII and II. In both of these regions, the Directors have problems of discrimination involving hospitals. It has been suggested that cases falling within the description contained in the Legal Division's memorandum as possibly under the Committee's jurisdiction should be sent to the central office for a ruling.[5]

DFO CASES

We began the week ending May 13 with 45 DFO cases. Of these, 30 were being handled by examiners and 15 by the Legal Division. The Legal Division has no new cases but closed two (2). Of the cases handled by examiners, two were closed and five new cases were received. This makes a total of 48 DFO cases in which 35 are being handled by examiners and 13 by the Legal Division.

ASSIGNMENTS TO CENTRAL STAFF

Mr. Bloch:

Completed Assignments:

1. Memorandum on and letter to complainant in Sacramento Air Service Command case, 12-GR-278 DFO.
2. Letter to attorney for Cardinal Engineering Company, case 2-BR-566 DFO.
3. Follow-up memorandum to Region III on Collins and Aikman Corporation, 3-BR-78 DFO.
4. Letter to attorney for Metro Envelope Company, 2-BR-47 DFO.
5. The following FDR's:
   Region II—22
   Region III—7

New Assignments:

1. The following FDR's:
   Region I—7
   Region II—14
   Region III—2
   Region VII—7

Mr. Metzger:

Completed Assignments:

1. New Orleans Port of Embarkation (Undocketed).
2. Memorandum to Region VI on American South African Lines, etc., 12-BR-1005, 12-UR-1006, and 12-UR-1047 DFO.
3. Letter to Treasury Department re Collector of Customs, 3-GC-590 DFO.
4. Field trip to Norfolk, Virginia, on complaints against Naval Air Station.
5. The following FDR's:
   Region X—9
   Region XII—6

New Assignments:

1. Southern Pacific Lines, 10-BR-281 DFO.
2. McDonald Aircraft Company, 9-BR-169 DFO.
3. Wagner Electric Corporation, 9-BR-157 DFO.
4. General Cable Company, 9-BR-165 DFO.
5. New Orleans Port of Embarkation, (Undocketed).
6. The following FDR's:
   Region X—8
   Region XII—1

Mr. Mitchell:

Completed Assignments:

1. Kentucky Chemical Industries, Inc., 5-BR-280 DFO.
2. Engineers Depot, Cambridge, Ohio, 5-GR-282.
3. Reviewing and taking action on Weekly Reports from Regions IV, V, VI, and VIII.
4. The following FDR's:
   Region V—28
   Region VI—4

New Assignments:

1. The following FDR's:
   Region V—28
   Region VI—4
2. Foss and Luke Taylor, 6-BC-391 DFO.

Father Roche:

Father Roche is currently preparing strike data and codifying the Field Instructions, Field Letters, and R. D.'s.

MS: copy, FEPC RG 228, Office Files of Clarence Mitchell, DNA.

1. This division, making Mitchell the liaison with the War Department, placed him in direct contact with Truman K. Gibson, for whom he had little or no respect. For example, on 7/14/44, Mitchell wrote Gibson requesting that Capt. Robert D. Morgan, a representative of the Signal Corps in Kansas City, Missouri, be allowed to cooperate with the FEPC regional representative in obtaining compliance by the General Cable Company in that city with EO 9346, concerning the hiring of African American women. Gibson dismissed Mitchell's request by responding that Morgan's detailed report on the case showed that he had cooperated fully with the FEPC. Consequently, said Gibson, there did not appear to be anything further Morgan or the War Department could do in the matter until the FEPC had "exhausted all of its resources in attempting an adjustment." Gibson letter to Mitchell, 9/6/44, FEPC FR91, Region IX, St. Louis. Closed Cases, D–Z, General Cable. For further complaints about Gibson, see also Mitchell to Ross, memorandum, 12/14/44. On Gibson's treatment of the FEPC's complaint regarding the R.C. Mahon Company of Detroit, see Maceo Hubbard to Francis Haas, memorandum, 7/10/43, HqR38, Central Files. Memoranda, Haas, Francis J.

2. On this division of labor among field operations staff, see also Mitchell's 5/12/44 memorandum to Bloch and Metzger, which added that whenever special problems arose and it was necessary to contact any of those agencies, the assigned person would join the director of field operations or other staff members in the visit. Under the most recent staff assignments, Mitchell agreed to handle reports from regions IV, V, VI, and VII. He turned over region XII to Metzger in exchange for Region VI. The shift was made owing to the overflow of work from Mitchell's regions. Regional assignments varied depending on staff availability and workload. Mitchell to Bloch and Metzger, memorandum, 4/29/44. Both memoranda are in HqR38, Central Files. Bloch, Emanuel.

3. See 3/18, 5/8/44; headnotes on Strikes and Work Stoppages and on Major Cases in St. Louis.

4. In an initial opinion on this question on 5/4/44, Crockett noted in a footnote that the term *industry* as the Committee had used it in directives could include companies engaged in transportation or communication or "a particular concern in a given industry." For a broader discussion, see HqR3, Office Files of George M. Johnson; headnote on Jurisdictional Issues.

Crockett's later and fuller opinion of 5/8/44, which Mitchell forwarded to Fleming on 5/12/44, noted that since Fleming did not request an opinion on a specific case, it was suggested that, pending adoption of rules and regulations, "cases arising in the Philadelphia office and involving the Committee's jurisdiction over the food industry, should be handled on a case by case basis." Doubtful ones were to be referred to the central office. Crockett noted that the manufacturing or processing of foodstuffs was essential to the war effort. That conclusion was supported by the creation of the War Food Administration under EO 9322 on 4/19/43. But it did not necessarily follow that every manufacturer and processor was engaged in "war industry" under the terms of EO 9346. Mitchell's memorandum to Fleming and Crockett's 5/8/44 opinion are in HqR83, Correspondence Relating to Cases. (A–K).

On jurisdictional questions involving the Post Office Department, see 5/3, 5/8/44.

5. See 2/22/44 and related texts cited in notes therein; headnote on Jurisdictional Issues.

Memorandum on Hospital Cases, Region I

Date: May 20, 1944

TO: Mr. George M. Johnson

FROM: Clarence M. Mitchell

SUBJECT: Hospital Cases, Region I—1-BR-69, 1-BR-72, 1-BR-74 and 1-BC-75, DFO

In each of the above-mentioned cases, the regional office has requested a ruling on whether these institutions are within the jurisdiction of the Committee. I requested the regional office to include any information which would indicate that cases of this type fall within the category mentioned in Mr. Crockett's memorandum on jurisdiction over private hospitals dated March 13, 1944. The Region reports in each case that there is some doubt about whether the institution caters primarily to war workers.[1]

On the basis of this doubt mentioned by the Region and using Mr. Crockett's memorandum as a measuring rod, I would feel that these cases are not within our jurisdiction.[2] However, since the Legal Division is currently at work on jurisdictional problems, it will be appreciated if a determination will be made in each of these cases so that we may advise the Region of whether we will accept jurisdiction over them.[3] Attachment (File)

MS: LH, DI, FEPC FR2, Region I. Closed Cases G–Z, Peter Bent Brigham Hospital, 1-BR-69.

1. Crockett's memorandum of 3/13/44, regarding a Bridgeport hospital case, argued that, although the WMC classified hospitals as "essential" activities, they were not in most cases closely connected to war production and that the FEPC should not assume jurisdiction over either state or private hospitals unless they were primarily engaged in the care of war workers. This formulation was ultimately adopted by the FEPC, both for hospitals and for industries in general. See FR1, Region I. Closed Cases A–F, Beth Israel Hospital and Bridgeport Hospital Case; texts of 2/22, 5/5, 5/8, 5/17, 5/24, 10/16/44; headnote on Jurisdictional Issues.

2. These cases, which involved Peter Bent Brigham, Beth Israel, and Massachusetts General Hospitals, concerned complaints regarding questions of race or religion on employment applications. See

the files for these hospital cases in FR1, Region I. Closed Cases A–F; and FR2, Region I. Closed Cases G–Z; and the final disposition reports on them in HqR56, Central Files. Reports, FDRs, Region I.

3. Johnson affirmed that in each of these cases the FEPC was without jurisdiction. Johnson to Mitchell, memorandum, 10/6/44, FR2, Region I. Closed Cases G–Z, Peter Bent Brigham Hospital, 1-BR-69.

Weekly Report

May 24, 1944

Mr. Will Maslow

Clarence M. Mitchell

Weekly Report for Week Ending May 20, 1944

OUTSTANDING EVENTS AND PROBLEMS

A notable illustration of compliance on the part of a large company on the West Coast was furnished this week in case 12-BR-1021, involving the Shell Oil Company. Although the case belonged to the Los Angeles office, the Regional Director [Kingman] had a conference with a representative of the company's top office, which resulted in compliance affecting twenty-nine installations in various California cities. The Region indicates that a follow up check will be made on this compliance in August. A note of commendation has been sent to the Region for this excellent work.[1]

Region X has an acute problem in New Iberia, Louisiana. A complainant was forced to leave the city when local authorities learned that he complained to FEPC concerning discriminatory training in New Iberia. The Director of the Region indicates that this case is being referred to the central office for further action. The Chairman also called the Department of Justice concerning this matter and learned that an affidavit had already been filed with that agency.

Region IX reports that it has received its first 510 Report. This Report was sent in by the Kansas City USES office against the Aluminum Company of America. The Regional Director is hopeful about additional 510's being sent in. He also mentions that he has received 510's from Region XI.[2]

The National Lead Company, case 9-BR-159, is mentioned by the Director of Region IX in his Weekly Report. A representative of this company in Washington has indicated that he desires a conference with the central office on the case.

Two widely different reports came in from the regions this week on Pasco, Washington. Region VI reports that the company is recruiting in a non-discriminatory manner. On the other hand, Mr. Hunt of Region VII advises that in Jacksonville,

Florida, white persons only are recruited for the company. It is not clear whether this is because of the War Manpower Commission or the employer. In any event, the Regional Director is taking appropriate follow-up action.

IMPORTANT CONTACTS WITH REGIONAL OFFICES, OTHER DIVISIONS, AND OTHER GOVERNMENT AGENCIES

Region I has sent in four hospital cases for a determination of whether they are within the jurisdiction of the Committee. These have been referred to the Legal Division for a ruling.[3]

Region III has been advised that the War Department is attempting to arrange a conference concerning the Miller Printing Machine Company, 3-BR-72 DFO. The case has been returned to the region for handling.

The case of Foss and Luke Taylor, 6-BC-391, has been returned to Region VI for further handling. This involves a Jehovah's Witness who was dismissed from his employment. The Region was also advised that the Civil Services Commission is still processing case 6-GR-4 concerning the Army Air Force Technical Training Command.[4]

Region IX has been advised that complainants with cases against St. Louis University, ESMWT courses, should again apply for admission in view of the school's change of policy.

DFO CASES

We began the week ending May 20 with 46 DFO cases of which 33 were being handled by examiners and 13 by the Legal Division. The Legal Division has six new cases—two of them having been referred to it by Field Operations examiners. During the week, it closed one case. Of the cases handled by examiner[s], four were closed and five new cases received. This makes a total of 52 DFO cases, of which 34 are being handled by examiners and 18 by the Legal Division.

ASSIGNMENTS TO CENTRAL STAFF

Mr. Bloch:

Completed Assignments:

1. Weekly Reports for Regions I, II, III, and VII reviewed and acted upon.
2. The following FDR's:
   Region I—1
   Region II—27
   Region III—6

New Assignments:

1. Railroad Retirement Board, 2-GR-571 DFO.
2. Retail Credit Company, 3-BR-524 DFO.
3. The following FDR'S:
   Region I—1
   Region II—27

Mr. Davidson:

Mr. Davidson has agreed to handle the following FDR's:

Region IV—15

Mr. Metzger:

Completed Assignments:

1. Bechtel, Price, and Callahan, 12-BR-67 DFO, referred to Legal Division.
2. Southern Pacific Lines, 10-BR-281, DFO, referred to Legal Division.
3. Reviewing and acting upon Weekly Reports from Regions IX and XII.
4. The following FDR's:
   Region XII—22

New Assignments:

1. Lockheed—Plant Protection, 12-BR-1009 DFO.
2. Bechtel, Price, and Callahan, 12-BR-67 DFO.
3. The following FDR's:
   Region X—6
   Region XII—13

Mr. Mitchell:

Completed Assignments:

1. Miller Printing Machine Company, 3-BR-72 DFO.
2. Foss and Luke Taylor, 6-BC-391 DFO.
3. Reviewing and taking action upon Weekly Reports from Regions IV, V, and VI.

New Assignments:

1. Will and Baumer Candle Company, 6-BC-67 DFO.

2. The following FDR's:
   Region IV—4
   Region VI—1

Father Roche:

Completed Assignments:

1. Index for Field Instructions, R.D.'s. etc.[5]
2. Handling of special cases in Region IV.
3. Reviewing and taking action upon FDR's from Regions IV, V, and VI.

MS: copy, FEPC RG 228, Office Files of Clarence Mitchell, DNA.

1. For the FEPC's continued difficulties regarding Shell Oil's operations in Texas, see the headnote on the Oil Industry.

2. See the section on the WMC and USES in the headnote on Relationships with Federal Agencies.

3. See 5/20/44, and notes.

4. See the headnote on Creedal Discrimination.

5. For an updated version of this index, see Subject Index to Field Instructions (FI), Field Letters (FL), and Regional Directors' Memoranda (RD), 8/6/43–3/15/45, HqR78, Field Instructions, 8/43–5/45 (entry 46).

Memorandum on National Lead Company, St. Louis, Missouri

May 29, 1944

MEMORANDUM

TO: Mr. George M. Johnson
           Deputy Chairman

FROM: Clarence M. Mitchell
           Associate Director of Field Operations

SUBJECT: National Lead Company, St. Louis, Missouri, 9-BR-159

In view of our forthcoming meeting with Mr. D. W. Robertson, Vice President of the National Lead Company, on Thursday, June 1, 1944, I thought it advisable to summarize the highlights of a conference with Mr. D. K. Pickens, who described himself as [a] "government relations" representative for the National Lead Company. Mr. Metzger and Father Roche joined me in a conference in your office on Thursday, May 25.

Mr. Pickens stated that the plant employs approximately 500 persons and that 31% of these are Negroes. Previously, he had informed me over the telephone that 41% of the employees were Negroes, but he stated that a subsequent check had shown this figure was in error and that 31% is the correct figure. Briefly, the problem Mr. Pickens presented was that the company has certain departments where the employees are all white. He described these departments as the Mechanical Department, the Titanium Department, the Acid Plant, and the Power Plant. Negroes are used in the Laboring, Shipping, Packing, and Stock Piling Departments.

The Committee's regional office in Kansas City, Missouri, has been negotiating with the company to permit upgrading of Negroes. Mr. Pickens stated that it would be impossible to upgrade Negro employees at this time because certain key employees will leave the company if Negroes are introduced in the departments under dispute. He stated that approximately 100 white employees form the nucleus of those who would object. These people, he said, are former members of an AF of L union and are hostile to the present union which is Local 212 of the United Gas, Coke, and Chemical Workers, CIO. Mr. Pickens said that the company has had a series of labor problems since 1938, some of which resulted in open street battles between employees of the plant. He mentioned that the company had taken motion pictures of some of these fights and that the local police had not done much to stop them.

Mr. Pickens alleged that the white employees who would object to Negroes in certain departments would not make their views public because they would fear reprisals from the CIO union in the plant. On the other hand, he stated that he was convinced that the objectors would walk out if Negroes were introduced. He insisted that FEPC should accept the company's word on this state of things. When he was asked to indicate what he desired from us, he stated the he thought there should be a waiting period of approximately ninety days, at the expiration of which the company would be able to inform FEPC of whether any progress could be made on the utilization of Negroes in new departments. He stated that the plant officials are planning to introduce Negroes into the "Black Ash" Department, which is under one of the four departments previously mentioned as white only. This action, he stated, would involve ten persons, and the company is considering the possibility of moving all the whites out and replacing them with Negroes.

Mr. Metzger suggested that the company could take a positive step in the right direction by permitting Negroes to bid on job openings which would become available in the departments now wholly white. He also suggested that this could be worked out in conference between FEPC, the company officials, and union representatives in St. Louis. Mr. Pickens was not entirely hostile to this proposal but insisted that it should not take place for at least ninety days. Thereupon, I informed him that our operations under the Executive Order required that we take action on problems of discrimination. I stated that my conversations with him and information from the Region left me with the conclusion that the company and the union were on record as opposed to discrimination. I informed him that the objections of the white workers were so vague at this point that we could not put our hands on them. Mr. Metzger and Father Roche agreed with this position on the basis of information revealed in our conversation with Mr. Pickens. The company representative then proposed that Mr. Robertson, the Vice President, come in for a conference with us.

MS: LH, DI, MP.
    See the discussion of this case in the headnote on Major Cases in St. Louis. For related texts, see 7/27, 8/2, 8/8/44, 2/10, 5/7/45.

Eleanor F. Rogers, Digest of Clarence Mitchell's Telephone Conversation with Mr. William T. McKnight, Cincinnati, Ohio

June 6, 1944

Mr. Clarence M. Mitchell

Eleanor F. Rogers

Digest of Your Telephone Conversation with Mr. William T. McKnight, Cincinnati, Ohio

On the above date, you called Mr. McKnight, who was in Cincinnati at the Wright Aeronautical Plant, with regard to a strike of 5,000 white employees of the plant over the transfer of Negroes to the main plant.

You informed Mr. McKnight that Mr. Ross had just talked with Mr. R. J. Thomas, President of the U.A.W., via long distance telephone. Mr. George Addes was already in Cincinnati, Mr. McKnight said. Mr. McKnight said that he was very much impressed with the attitude and cooperation of Colonel F. W. LaVista, Resident Representative of the Army Air Forces, who, he stated, is from Brooklyn. He stated further that union men are favorable in their opinion of Colonel LaVista.

About two-thirds of the four o'clock shift reported, Mr. McKnight stated, adding that he was meeting each shift as it came on duty. On every shift, the workers reported but did not start to work, and management, according to Mr. McKnight, says it will probably be thirty-six hours before it can get production started because the foundry is down. You asked Mr. McKnight if the Negro employees were on the job, and he stated that they were there but there is no work for them. The union, Mr. McKnight stated, charges that although it is against its wishes, some supervisors and stewards are telling the workers to go home.

Colonel Strong, Mr. McKnight informed you, flew in with Mr. Addes from Detroit. He said that the company had sent for moving pictures to keep the people inside to appeal to their patriotism. There are, he said, 35,000 people employed at the plant.

Mr. McKnight said that he had announced that he is there as an observer to be used at the request of management or the Army. There is, he stated, full cooperation between management, the union, the Army, and the Conciliation Service. He had been present at all conferences, Mr. McKnight stated.

Mr. McKnight said that the Times Star and Post carried strong editorials concerning the strikers.

The spark was set off, Mr. McKnight stated, by the moving of seven Negroes. Until two days ago, the Negroes had worked exclusively in the north plant. The proposed integration of Negroes into the main plaint has been discussed for four months, he said. The plan was approved by management, union leaders, and the Army representative. Mr. McKnight also said that the company feels it must have its working force fully integrated by October, 1944, in order to have a completely flexible working force. At this point, Mr. McKnight stated that he feels that union politics figure into the situation. He stated that there is an attempt to remove Mr. B. Beckam, Chairman of the union's bargaining committee, or to undermine his prestige. Mr. Beckam, he said, had been very cooperative.

Negroes were working on production operations, Mr. McKnight stated. He added that Colonel LaVista said the men had been carefully selected, their work had shown that they were capable, and they are of good character. Also, they were assigned to seven idle machines.

Mr. McKnight concluded by saying that things seemed to be "shaping up." He said that he would send in clippings that have been published thus far and would call you tomorrow morning between nine and ten o'clock.

* * * * * * * * * * * * * * *

On Wednesday, June 7, Mr. McKnight called as he had previously promised and stated that a large number of the plant employees returned to work but only to punch their time cards. He stated that he had joined Army, union, company, and Government representatives in conferences which lasted until 3:00 a. m., June 7. He stated that the strikers listen to all the arguments and then go home.

At present, the matter has been certified to the War Labor Board and Mr. McKnight thought that it would be useless for him to remain in Cincinnati any longer. He summarized the situation by saying that the company is made up of three plants—the north plant, the central plant, and the south plant. Negroes have been working on production jobs in the north plant for some time. Also, a number of whites are employed there. The company foundry is in that plant. About a month ago, Mr. McKnight said, the company made its first effort to change the pattern of sending all Negro production workers to the north plant. (It should be noted that Negro maintenance workers are employed in all the plants.) At that time, two Negroes were sent to work in the central plant. About 175 whites protested and the Negroes were sent back to the north plant. Mr. McKnight stated that Colonel Strong feels the company made a mistake in backing down at that time. He feels that the white workers then decided that whenever Negroes were placed in the shop they would walk out and thereby force the company to remove the colored persons. However, management is now determined to keep the Negroes on the job in the central plant, and there is some indication that, if the company retreats from this position, the Negro employees will walk out.

MS: copy, HqR63, Central Files. Reports, Tension Area Reports, Region V.
   See 6/9/44; headnotes on Strikes and Work Stoppages and on the Aircraft Industry.

Eleanor F. Rogers, Memorandum on Clarence Mitchell's Telephone Call to William T. McKnight, Cleveland, Ohio, Regarding Strike at Wright Aeronautical Corporation

June 9, 1944

Mr. Clarence M. Mitchell

Eleanor F. Rogers

Your Telephone Call to Mr. William T. McKnight, Cleveland,
Ohio, re Strike at Wright Aeronautical Corporation

On the above date, you called Mr. McKnight to inform him that the OWI had just gotten a ticker flash that ninety per cent of the strikers at Wright Aeronautical Corporation in Lockland, Ohio, were back at work and to inquire if he would verify this percentage. Mr. McKnight stated that he could not, at the time, state just what per cent of the workers were back on the job. However, he stated that last night sixty per cent of yesterday's crew had stayed on and practically all of last night's shift. He said that he would verify the percentage and wire you back.

Mr. McKnight stated that no one (management, union officials, the War Department representatives, or Government representatives) has wavered from the original position taken, and the Negroes will remain on the machines. The War Labor Board had, he said, ordered the strikers back to work. Mr. McKnight stated that he had talked with Colonel LaVista. Management and the union had, he informed you, gotten together in a joint order stating that the workers report by midnight Friday or be fired and that the program of integrating Negroes into the center plant would be continued. He stated that a complete report will be in tomorrow morning. Mr. McKnight stated that, in order to achieve its objective of having Negroes integrated, the Army was willing to forego some new installations it was planning for the plant and let management reduce its force.

Mr. McKnight stated that he has an appointment to talk with the Chief of Military Intelligence and Colonel LaVista Monday. It was felt by him that the satisfactory settlement of this situation would add greatly to the prestige of the Committee in the Cincinnati area.

MS: copy, HqR63, Central Files. Reports, Tension Area Reports, Region V.
    See 6/6/44; headnotes on Strikes and Work Stoppages and on the Aircraft Industry.

Memorandum on Brotherhood of Railway Clerks and Missouri-Kansas-Texas Railroad

DATE: June 10, 1944

TO: Mr. George M. Johnson

FROM: Clarence M. Mitchell

SUBJECT: Brotherhood of Railway Clerks—M.K.T., 10-UR-168 and
        Missouri-Kansas-Texas Railroad, 10-BR-318

The files on the above-numbered cases are herewith referred to the Legal Division for whatever action is deemed appropriate.

Attachments—(Files)

MS: LH, DI, MP.
    Although Mitchell's reports and memoranda do not reflect his full involvement in railroad cases, they did consume a representative amount of his time. Ultimately, as in this case, he referred them to the legal division.
    See, for example, the cases involving the Gulf-Colorado and Santa Fe Railway and the Southern Pacific Railroad. A common characteristic in these cases was that they involved the Brotherhood of Railway Trainmen. In the Gulf-Colorado case, for example, which Mitchell referred to Maceo Hubbard, acting director of the legal division, on 5/16/45, Hubbard in a 5/29 memorandum to Maslow noted that the company and the union nearly a year earlier had entered into an agreement that ultimately would take away the jobs of African American porter-brakemen throughout the system and give them to "regular brakemen as permanent vacancies" arose. This practice was set by a decision of the National Railroad Adjustment Board on 4/20/42. The agreement by Gulf-Colorado was entered into because of the NRAB award "and represented a compromise between the order of the Board and the company's former policy representing porter-brakemen, for although under the agreement brakemen's duties were not taken from all Negro porter-brakemen, they were taken from some of them. Furthermore, it was a method by which the award of the Board would be put into effect gradually." Both the Hubbard 5/29/45 memorandum to Maslow and a 3/23/45 memorandum from Johnson to Mitchell are in HqR5, Office Files of George M. Johnson. Maceo Hubbard. See also the discussion of railroad cases in the headnote on the FEPC and Unions.

313

Memorandum on West Coast Shipbuilding Companies

June 26, 1944

Mr. George M. Johnson

Clarence M. Mitchell

West Coast Shipbuilding Companies

Attached are the files on cases 12-UR-32 and 12-UR-203. In each of these instances, the complainants allege that there has been union discrimination.

It does not appear that these cases can be adjusted until the main complaints involving the Boiler Makers' Union are settled. Therefore, I am referring them to you with the request that they be included in the over-all settlement.[1]

Attachments (Files-2)

MS: copy, HqR38, Central Files. (entry 25) Memoranda, Johnson, George M. 1/44–.

1. The Boilermakers Union cases could be divided into three categories: (a) those originating prior to and considered at the hearing in 11/43; (b) those originating prior to but not considered at the hearing; and (c) those arising since the hearing. These complaints, like those mentioned in Mitchell's memorandum of 7/21/44, were apparently among the new posthearings cases. See the section on the Boilermakers in the headnote on the FEPC and Unions.

In a memorandum to Johnson, Frank Reeves noted that at least 64 percent of workers (slight variation from Johnson at 1/22/44, note 1) in the shipbuilding industry were engaged in skills that came under the jurisdiction of the International Boilermakers Union. As of November 1943, he said, 348,466 persons were engaged in the industry, 29,069 of whom were nonwhite. The records of the San Francisco office listed twenty-one cases involving individual and organizational complaints pending against seven shipbuilding companies and eight locals of the Boilermakers Union in northern California, Oregon, and Washington. Reeves said the problem in the San Francisco Bay area was especially complicated by court actions that had been taken independently by groups of shipyard workers seeking to enjoin the companies and union from worsening discrimination policies and practices that the Committee in its hearing had found to be in violation of EO 9346. He said the effect of the related uncertainties, as the regional office reported, was that:

> The Boilermaker situation, ever since the public hearings held on the coast [11/15–20/43], has become more serious and aggravated. When the Negroes saw that the FEPC could not take direct action against the union, they employed the injunction method. However, injunctions have only resulted in firmer resistance by the local Boilermakers Unions so that even though Negroes cannot be discharged after an injunction has been placed against the union and the company, no prospective or new employees can be hired. The injunction clearly does not cover this situation. What has happened is that, the Boilermaker Council representing all the Boilermakers Locals in the Bay area has gotten together and decided not to accept into the auxiliary or refer new Negro hires. While we have no specific data as to how many Negroes have been turned down through this "conspiracy," we have reasons to believe that the numbers are very high. We have been informed of a number of instances where Negroes with their families have moved into the area expecting to be employed in the shipyards and have had to return because they could receive no employment. Some very positive and definitive action is necessary before the situation grows out of hand.

See related materials in HqR5, Office Files of George M. Johnson. Frank Reeves.

The regional office reported, furthermore, that there was evidence that the union, pending the court's ruling on the application for an injunction against its plan, would "pick-off" blacks who were leading the opposition to the auxiliaries. The regional office expressed its appreciation for the Committee's efforts to obtain compliance with the directive it issued on 12/9/43 as a result of the hearings in Portland and Los Angeles. "However, the Regional office has been and is being subjected to constant pressure."

Memorandum on Strike at Pratt Whitney Plant, Kansas City, Missouri

DATE: June 30, 1944

TO: Mr. Will Maslow

FROM: Clarence M. Mitchell

SUBJECT: Strike at Pratt Whitney Plant, Kansas City, Missouri

In keeping with our telephone conversation with Mr. Roy A. Hoglund, Regional Director at Kansas City, I am suggesting that, at this time, we refrain from any action which would place the Committee in this particular situation.[1] It is my feeling that the company has acted in a highly improper and arbitrary fashion, if the facts as set forth in Mr. Hoglund's telegram are correct.

MS: LH, DI, HqR63, Central Files. Reports, Tension Area Reports, Region IX.
   1. See the headnote on Strikes and Work Stoppages for sources and selected cross-references.

Memorandum on WMC Priority Referral System

June 30, 1944

Mr. Will Maslow

Clarence M. Mitchell

WMC Priority Referral System

The following is a supporting argument for Section A of your memorandum dated June 28, concerning the WMC priority referral system.[1]

It is my understanding that the priority referral system is being instituted by the War Manpower Commission because of acute male labor shortages. If such shortages exist, there must be full use of all manpower. We are now past the stage where individual prejudices and customs of local communities can set the pattern for employment.

Our experience, especially in the South, has shown that many shortages could be corrected in part if the employer would make an intelligent use of all his workers and would also hire without discrimination in local communities. As long as employers can obtain even a fraction of the new workers they say they need, discrimination will continue. When the Government takes the position that no priority will be given if workers are excluded in violation of Executive Order 9346, employers will find a way to make proper use of the minority group labor supply.

I do not believe that the granting of a partial priority will have the desired effect on speeding up the elimination of discriminatory practices. There are many areas in which employers will make requests for an excess of workers knowing that there is a possibility of the requests being pared down because of discriminatory practices. It is also important that the employment ceilings be lowered in plants which discriminate because this inevitably will mean that the total number of employees will dwindle because of separations due to the draft and the loss of workers who obtain releases for justifiable reasons. These workers cannot be replaced without priority referral. Again, it will mean that there will be a speeding up of the proper use of available manpower.

These suggestions may appear somewhat drastic, but, after three years of promises and reliance upon educational processes, we are discovering that some individuals will not be fair in their handling of the problem. Hence, it now appears that all available machinery should be brought to bear upon the recalcitrants.

MS: *copy, HqR67, U.S. Government: War Manpower Commission.*

1. In his memorandum of 6/28/44 to Ross, Maslow explained that on 7/2/44 the WMC would be instituting a nationwide priority referral system that the FEPC could eventually use to impose sanctions. The gist of the system was:

> 1. Employers throughout the country may hire MALE workers only through USES "or in accordance with arrangements approved by the USES."
> 2. Employment ceilings for all 184 labor shortage areas in the country will be imposed (Group I and Group II areas).
> 3. Referrals to establishments in these 184 areas will be made in accordance with priorities established by manpower priority committees. In other areas, the WMC area director will refer workers to jobs "in the order of the relative importance of those jobs to the war effort."

Of the five recommendations Maslow made to Ross, Section A, the one on which Mitchell was commenting, stated the following:

> In Group I or Group II areas, a discriminatory refusal to hire or upgrade qualified members of a minority group in violation of WMC Field Instruction No. 21, dated September 3, 1943 and Executive Order 9346 shall result in a suspension of the manpower priority and in the lowering of the employment ceiling. This suspension should remain in effect until the discrimination ceases. In Group III and Group IV areas, USES should suspend any manpower priority and in addition discontinue all referrals to a discriminatory employer until the discrimination ceases. Upon the recommendation of FEPC, WMC shall temporarily suspend such priority pending a final determination by FEPC after hearing. After such final determination, WMC shall either revoke or reinstate the priority, according to the recommendation of FEPC.

On the priority referral system and the enforcement of the nondiscrimination policy, see also Mitchell's memoranda of 7/14/44, 3/28/45. For the background, see the section on the WMC and USES in the headnote on Relationships with Federal Agencies.

Memorandum to Will Maslow on Matters Requiring Action during His Absence

July 3, 1944

MEMORANDUM

TO: Mr. Will Maslow

FROM: Clarence M. Mitchell

SUBJECT: Matters Requiring Action During Your Absence

It is my understanding following our conversation on the above date that the following matters are of importance and require some action during your absence from the office:[1]

1. The Committee has authorized a hearing in the case of the Seafarers' Union, and you wish the files transferred to the Legal Division for further study.[2]

2. The Committee authorized Mr. Ross to work out a plan with the War Manpower Commission in connection with the priority referral program of WMC. Also, you mentioned that certain special action should be taken in connection with the handling of classified advertising under the priority referral plan. A WMC Form 63 is also to be studied in this connection because of certain information it is supposed to contain on prevention of discriminatory referrals. You have suggested that it would be well to obtain approval for Mr. Lawson's agreement with the War Manpower Commission on priority referrals.

3. A proposed letter to Mr. Harry B. Mitchell, of the Civil Service Commission, is to be gotten out as soon as possible.

4. Dr. Castaneda's reports on the mining industry in the Southwest should be analyzed and a determination should be made of whether it is important to have him come into the central office following this analysis. Also in connection with the Southwest investigations, you suggest that, if union grievance machinery is working effectively, it will not be necessary for us to go into a given case.[3]

5. You requested that I make a determination of whether the Machinist Local on the West Coast has received a wire from Mr. Harvey Brown concerning a problem called to our attention by Mr. Kingman. Also, in this connection, it is my understanding that a special memorandum is being prepared for a subcommittee of FEPC, which will have a conference with Mr. Brown.

6. The Philadelphia Transit Company contract has been ratified and follow-up action will be necessary to see that Negroes are employed as previously agreed upon.

7. A determination should be made of whether a hearing is to be held in connection with the Shell Oil case.

cc: Davidson
       Johnson
       Jones

MS: copy, MP.

1. While Maslow was gone for a two-week vacation, Mitchell served as acting director of field operations. See Maslow's memorandum to field directors, 7/3/44, FR42, Region IV, Administrative Files, A–Z.

2. In 5/42 the War Shipping Administration, in conjunction with the Seafarer's International Union, AFL, and other maritime unions, adopted a "Statement of Policy" that froze existing collective bargaining agreements for the duration of the war. Based on that policy, the SIU continued specifying "white" and "Negro" in its requests for seamen. Background SIU résumé from the Committee decision based on a 9/6/45 hearing, HqR2, Office Files of Malcolm Ross. Difficult Cases 2.

3. See Castañeda's 7/4/44 report to Maslow, as well as his 7/6/44 "Checklist on Memoranda Sent During Field Trip On Area Wide Mining Industry Investigation in Texas, New Mexico and Arizona," and other related materials, all in HqR38, Central Files. Memoranda, Castañeda.

Memorandum on Personnel Matters within Field Operations

July 3, 1944

MEMORANDUM

TO: Mr. Will Maslow

FROM: Clarence M. Mitchell

SUBJECT: Personnel Matters within Field Operations

It is my understanding, as a result of our conference on the above date, that you have the following views in connection with specific personnel matters:

1. Regional Director McKnight should be reclassified, as of July 7, to $4600.

2. Examiner Grinnage, currently employed on a WAE basis in Philadelphia, should remain in that status until September 30.

3. Mrs. Seymore, of the San Francisco office, should remain in her present status until the expiration of two months.

4. You propose the reclassification of Examiner Ellinger, of Region X, from $3200 to $3800 and that he serve as Acting Regional Director.

5. You propose the hiring of Mr. Meske, of the NLRB, for work in the Dallas office.

6. Mr. Brin is available for a short-term assignment at a $3800 rate in Region VII. It is my understanding Mr. Hunt feels he would be of some use in special investigations at Brunswick, Georgia.

7. Examiner Risk, of the New York office, is to be transferred from the New York offices to Philadelphia as of July 5. It is my understanding that Mr. Fleming will handle his reclassification from $3200 to $3800.

8. There is a possibility of the resignation of Mr. Stanley Metzger, of the Field Operations Staff. It is my suggestion that, as soon as we have learned of Mr. Metzger's final decision, the vacancy should be posted so that eligible persons in the field may have an opportunity to apply for it.

9. It is my understanding that Mr. Emanuel Bloch, of the central office, is applying for a vacancy in the Legal Division.

cc: Davidson
       Johnson
       Jones

MS: copy, MP.

Memorandum on Jurisdiction over Radio Stations

·   July 7, 1944

Mr. George M. Johnson
Clarence M. Mitchell
Jurisdiction over Radio Stations

Region IV, of FEPC, has sent in a request for information on whether we have jurisdiction over discriminatory radio advertising.[1] The Regional Director reports that, on June 26 through the medium of Alice Lane's advertising program, Station WNDC made the following announcement between the hours of 10:30 and 11:00 A.M., "Station WNDC wants a strong, healthy boy for summer work, white."

It will be appreciated if you will let me know whether such cases should be processed by our regional offices.

MS: copy, HqR63, Central Files. Reports, Rulings, General.

1. This request, no doubt, was prompted by the Committee's ruling—at its 5/27/44 meeting in a case involving the *Dallas Morning News*—that "newspapers of general circulation are not 'war industries.'" Nevertheless, the Committee voted to submit the question to the attorney general with a request that he assist in coordinating such issues in keeping with EO 9346. HqR1, Summary Minutes of Meetings.

Drawing a very fine line between the First Amendment activities of radio broadcasting systems and their actions related to war employment practices, which were covered by EO 9346, the Committee established the following policy: "The news dissemination and entertainment services of radio systems are not within the scope of FEPC's jurisdiction. On the other hand, radio communication services are subject to FEPC jurisdiction."

The attorney general evidently upheld the Committee's position, because in the same 10/27/44 memorandum, Johnson listed it as one of several jurisdictional issues handled by the legal department. In the same memorandum, he also provided the Committee's ruling on discriminatory advertisements:

> The committee deems that for an employer within its jurisdiction to publish advertisements for employment which specify that only workers of a particular race or color or creed or national origin are desired, or in any way specifies a particular race, color or creed or national origin, is discriminatory with respect to hire and employment, and as such violates Executive Order 9346. Such publication is no less a violation because the employer involved employs members of the particular race that the discriminatory advertisement seeks to bar. (HqR5, Office Files of George M. Johnson. [H–Telephone Company], Maceo Hubbard.)

See also the headnote on Jurisdictional Issues.

Eleanor F. Rogers, Memorandum of Clarence Mitchell's Telephone Call from Mr. Roy A. Hoglund and Mr. Ernest G. Trimble, St. Louis, Missouri

July 7, 1944

Mr. Clarence M. Mitchell

Eleanor F. Rogers

Telephone Call from Mr. Roy A. Hoglund and
Mr. Ernest G. Trimble, St. Louis, Missouri

On the above date, Mr. Hoglund called from St. Louis, Missouri, with regard to USES cooperation during the forthcoming hearings and other matters. Mr. Trimble was also on the line in St. Louis and Mr. Reeves in Washington.[1]

Mr. Trimble stated that we should get permission from the USES for one man to bring records and testify on all the companies involved. Mr. Hoglund stated that the

Area Representatives of WMC did not know how much information they were authorized to disclose.

You suggested that Mr. Hoglund get Mr. McDonald, WMC Regional Director, to authorize the release of the information. You informed Mr. Hoglund that Mr. Wertz of WMC in Washington has assured us that Mr. Lewis Clymer will testify. You suggested that Mr. Clymer should designate someone who would be friendly and who would have the information needed. You agreed to contact Mr. Wertz again if Mr. McDonald refuses to permit someone to testify on the employment data needed.

You told Mr. Hoglund that a Mr. Carl Pretscheold, formerly with the St. Louis Dispatch and now with PM, called Mr. Ross to find out if we knew anything about the situation at Pratt Whitney Company, Kansas City, Missouri. The IAM is supposed to have an agreement with the company that Negroes are not to be used in certain jobs. The IAM does not have a closed shop agreement with the company, according to Mr. Hoglund, but it will not admit Negroes to membership. Mr. Hoglund stated that although he does not know what percentage of Negroes are employed in skilled jobs by the company, there are quite a few so employed. He stated that there is a rumor that the contract has a discriminatory clause in it, but he has no verification of the rumor and, at present, the union is still negotiating for a contract.

Mr. Hoglund stated that the matter requires careful investigation, and they are tied up at present. However, he stated that they would be in Kansas City Monday, July 10, and he wanted to know if this would be time enough. Mr. Hoglund said he will get something out to you on Monday regarding this matter.

You informed Mr. Hoglund that you have received word that the Welders and Carpenters are discriminating against Negroes. Mr. Hoglund said he does not know that they are.

Mr. Hoglund said that Negroes want to file complaints against the union (IAM). He said that he did not believe that such cases should be docketed at present. You informed him that we would not have to docket these complaints, but they could be sent to Washington and used in connection with a conference to be held with Mr. Harvey Brown of the Machinists Union. Mr. Hoglund said that latest developments are that Negroes are reported to be filing complaints with NLRB alleging that the IAM should not be the bargaining agent because it does not represent them. The IAM, he said, has bargaining rights but no contract. You asked Mr. Hoglund if the IAM has bargaining rights with the entire plant or just a unit. Mr. Hoglund replied that the Service Union represents the maintenance employees and the IAM represents production employees.

You talked with Mr. Louis Silverberg, of the NLRB, concerning the bargaining relationship at the Pratt Whitney Plant. He stated that the IAM won an election on April 26, 1944. Apparently, it represents other AF of L unions as well as its own interests. The Carpenters have a separate bargaining agreement. Mr. Silverberg said he did not know of a complaint from Negro workers alleging that the IAM did not properly represent them.

ROGERS

MS: copy, HqR37, Central Files. (entry 25) Hearings, St. Louis.

1. At its meeting on 6/13/44, the Committee voted to hold hearings on the St. Louis cases on 7/14 and 7/15/44. At its 5/27/44 meeting, the Committee had recommended the following cases for hearing: U.S. Cartridge Company, McQuay-Norris Company, Carter Carburetor Company, Amertorp Corporation, Bussman Manufacturing Company, and Wagner Electric Company. At its 9/30/44 meeting, the Committee assigned cases to its members accordingly: Amertorp, Sara Southall; Bussman and McDonald Aircraft, Boris Shishkin; Carter Carburetor, Charles Hamilton Houston; McQuay-Norris and U.S. Cartridge, Charles Horn and Houston; Wagner Electric, John Brophy; St. Louis Shipbuilding, Milton Webster. In 1945 the Committee devoted extensive attention to the St. Louis cases because of their expected significance for postwar employment. HqR1, Summary Minutes of Meetings; headnote on Major Cases in St. Louis.

Memorandum on Conference with Representatives of Industrial Union of Marine and Shipbuilding Workers Regarding Merrill-Stevens Dry Dock Company, Jacksonville, Florida

July 10, 1944

Mr. Malcolm Ross

Clarence M. Mitchell

Conference with Representatives of Industrial Union of Marine and Shipbuilding Workers re Merrill-Stevens Dry Dock Company, Jacksonville, Florida

On the above date, the following persons met with us to discuss problems at the Merrill-Stevens Dry Dock Company: Mr. Michael Ross, of the International office of the union; Mr. W. R. Thorpe; Mr. Archie L. Brockins; Mr. Wallace S. Raspberry; Mr. Edward H. Orleman; and Mr. Sol Syde; all of Jacksonville. These gentlemen complained about working conditions at the shipyard and mentioned that Mr. Raspberry had been fired by management when it was learned that he was on the Committee coming to Washington to discuss the situation.

The Yard employs 2,100 persons, and 1,700 of these are members of the CIO, according to Mr. Syde. There are approximately 550 Negro employees. The CIO has bargaining rights with the company. Apparently, this is the result of a second election on the same issue. It appears that, a year ago, the union won an election, but this was later challenged by the company. Three weeks ago a new election was held, and again the CIO won. The individuals present stated that there are only 40 or 50 Negroes above the laboring classifications. Although colored persons do advanced kinds of skilled work and instruct whites, they are not paid wages in keeping with the duties performed, it was alleged. Mr. Raspberry's case was cited as an illustration of this type of discrimination. It was stated that he was receiving $1.08 an hour as a boiler maker helper while whites doing similar work receive $1.40 an hour. According to those present, Mr. Raspberry had charge of a group of Negroes as a leaderman. In this capacity, he signed a slip for an individual seeking time off, it was stated. The company took advantage of this incident and charged that he exceeded his authority when he signed the slip. On Saturday, July 8, he was dismissed on this charge. Those present contended that the real cause was his membership on the committee which visited us.

Three Negroes were recently upgraded to positions of trainees at 75¢ an hour following an investigation by Mr. A. Bruce Hunt of our Atlanta office, it was stated. The names of these Negroes are: Dallas, Jones, and Smith. As trainees, these men received 93¢ an hour, but they were demoted to 75¢ an hour and placed in a gang with Negro sealers who get 80¢ an hour, according to the complaint. This was the company's way of disciplining them for filing a complaint, it was stated.

The company has work from the Army Transport Service at present. This is conversion of ships into hospital vessels. The union representatives said they had filed complaints on the problems of discrimination with Mr. A. Bruce Hunt but felt that there should be some over-all attack on the company's policy of underpaying its Negro workers. Mr. Raspberry said he would submit a written complaint to us.

Following our meeting with the men, I checked with the Maritime Commission to determine whether it holds contracts in the Yard. I was informed that it is possible that some of these contracts may have come over to the Maritime Commission from the War Shipping Administration, but this is not a certainty.

As soon as we have determined the status of the case from Mr. Bruce Hunt, I shall be in a position to propose further action if he believes it is needed.[1]

cc: Mr. Hunt

MS: copy, HqR84, Correspondence Relating to Cases. (L–S) Merrill Stevens Dry Dock Co., Region VII.

1. For later reports on this case, see 1/23/45 memorandum on the case load of Region VII and texts filed with this document.

Memorandum on Conference with
Judge Charles M. Hay, Executive Director,
War Manpower Commission

DATE: July 14, 1944

TO: Mr. Malcolm Ross

FROM: Clarence M. Mitchell

SUBJECT: Conference with Judge Charles M. Hay, Executive Director, War Manpower Commission

On the above date, we met with Judge Hay and Miss Bernice Lotwin, Assistant General Counsel for the War Manpower Commission. We discussed the FEPC recommendations made in connection with the War Manpower's priority referral system, these recommendations having previously been approved by the Committee at its meeting of July 1.[1]

Miss Lotwin discussed the recommendations beginning in reverse order. Our recommendation "D" is taken care of by current regulations of the War Manpower Commission, Miss Lotwin stated. She said that workers who quit because an employer conforms to the policies of Executive Order 9346 are not at present given releases. This means that such strikers may not immediately take other essential jobs. She expressed the view that our objectives could be accomplished if the Committee wrote a letter to the War Manpower Commission asking whether current regulations prevent workers who strike when minority groups are utilized from getting releases. We pointed out that a regular instruction from WMC would be stronger than a letter to the Committee.

With regard to "C", it was proposed by the War Manpower officials that FEPC representatives have the right to offer information to the Area Directors of the War Manpower Commission when a firm seeks a priority rating. The Commission would instruct its employees to give full consideration to the views of FEPC. Neither Judge Hay nor Miss Lotwin favored the inclusion of a Committee representative at the actual meetings. Judge Hay made the suggestion that the War Manpower officials would be allowed to have FEPC representatives present if, in the opinion of WMC, it would be necessary. Again we expressed disapproval of such an approach.

It was agreed that Section B would be given study by the War Manpower Commission, but neither Judge Hay nor Miss Lotwin indicated a definitely favorable reaction to it.

Miss Lotwin made the proposal, when discussing "A," that, in her opinion, it would be better to give releases to employees when employers refuse to cooperate in the observance of Executive Order 9346. She expressed the view that this would be more effective than refraining from giving the employer a priority. We disagreed with her view.

Judge Hay agreed to check carefully on the problem in the Los Angeles Street Railway case. You requested that a War Manpower revocation of the company's priority would be very helpful. You also suggested that you would like to have another conference when Bruce Hunt of Region VII could be present to discuss these problems. You left with the War Manpower officials a copy of Mr. Hunt's statement on the problem.

It was agreed that War Manpower would carefully review our recommendations and get in touch with us on them.

MS: LH, DI, HqR84, Correspondence Relating to Cases. St. Louis Cases.

1. On the WMC's priority referral system and the FEPC's recommendations regarding it, see Mitchell's memorandum of 6/30/44 and texts cited there.

Memorandum on Area-Wide Mining Industry Investigation in the Southwest

DATE: July 17, 1944

TO: Mr. George M. Johnson

FROM: Clarence M. Mitchell

SUBJECT: Area-Wide Mining Industry Investigation in the Southwest

Attached is a file of reports from Dr. Carlos E. Castaneda on his investigations in the Southwest. At my request, Mr. Stanley D. Metzger, of the Division of Field Operations, prepared a memorandum summarizing this file. It is also attached. After you have read Mr. Metzger's summary and possibly refer to any documents in the file which you deem important, I should like to discuss this case with you in order that we may either submit it to the Division or take any other Field Operations' action which is deemed appropriate.

You will note that Mr. Metzger feels that the individual cases are not very dramatic and, possibly, they could be adjusted without the basic problem's being corrected. He recommends the testimony of an expert on the conditions in the area. At the time of his recommendation, Mr. Metzger had in mind Mr. Orville Larsen, International Representative of the Mine, Mill and Smelter Workers, Miami, Arizona. Mr. Metzger felt that Mr. Larsen could testify on industry-wide conditions in Arizona, and a similar union official could testify on conditions in New Mexico.

Attachments

  File

  Metzger memo dated 7–12–44

[Attachment]

July 12, 1944

Clarence M. Mitchell, Associate Director of Field Operations

Stanley D. Metzger, Senior Fair Practice Examiner

Area Wide Mining Industry Investigation of Dr. Castaneda

Pursuant to your request, I have reviewed the files and reports forwarded to the central office by Dr. Castaneda.[1]

Following is an analysis by companies of his reports:

I. Phelps-Dodge Copper Corporation, Morenci, Arizona.

Eleven complaints were docketed at this operation of the Phelps Dodge Corporation. Seven of them appeared to have been disposed of satisfactorily to Castaneda. Of the remaining four, a) Sandoval, involves a refusal to classify and pay him as a welder foreman; b) <u>Gaylor</u>, involves a rent reduction from his pay because he is an Indian; c and d) <u>Garcia</u> and <u>Roybal</u>, involve the refusal to employ Mexican women.

Kuzell, Labor Relations Director for Phelps-Dodge interests in Arizona, admitted, in a conference with Castaneda, that Mexicans were barred from the Power House Division, Electrical Department, Machine Shop, welding and as machine operators. Kuzell further admitted that the company's refusal to employ Mexican women was discriminatory, but stated that he was afraid of repercussions by Anglo women if Mexican women were employed.

Generally, the company's position is that the regular grievance procedures outlined in their contracts with the unions should be used to take care of individual cases of alleged discrimination in upgrading.

II. Phelps-Dodge Copper Corporation, Bisbee, Arizona (Copper Queen Mine)

No individual complaints were docketed on this operation. Castaneda's report is a general discussion of conditions in the community and mine. He states that he has been informed that until 1943, there were no Mexicans in the underground operations, or in skilled or semi-skilled surface jobs. At present, Mexicans are employed in these classifications to some extent.

III. Phelps-Dodge Copper Corporation, Douglas, Arizona. (Copper Queen Branch, Smelting Division)

No individual complaints were docketed on this operation. Castaneda observes that, generally, no Mexicans are employed in the Mechanical Department, Powerhouse, or Electrical Department.

IV. Kennecott Copper Corporation, Hurley, New Mexico

Sixteen complaints were docketed on this operation. Of these, ten appear to have been satisfactorily disposed of by Castaneda and the company. Six are still outstanding, and, in Castaneda's opinion, will be valid complaints. These are: a) <u>Galaz</u>, involving the refusal to upgrade to Helper in the Electrical Department; b) <u>Valenzuela</u>, involving a refusal to upgrade a Car Dropper to Brakeman in March, 1942. An existing contract between the company and the Brotherhood of Railway Trainmen states that Car Droppers cannot use their seniority on positions of Brakemen, Switchmen, Switchman tender, or Lookout man; c) <u>Arredondo</u>, involving the refusal to upgrade from common laborer to second-class helper in the Machine Shop. Common labor is in a pool, and while a common laborer may apply for machine shop upgrading, his experience on the track gang does not qualify him for such upgrading. Track labor forms a pool, and a common laborer must be transferred to a given department in order to secure promotion; d, e, and f) <u>Heredia</u>, <u>Ruiz</u>, and <u>Sepulveda</u>, involve the refusal to upgrade Car Droppers to Brakemen under the same circumstances as the Valenzuela case.

Castaneda states that, generally, no Mexicans are employed as Plummer Journeymen, Blacksmiths, or Brakemen.

V. Phelps-Dodge Copper Corporation, Ajo, Arizona.

No individual complaints were docketed on this operation. Castaneda observes that the Mexican employees are afraid of reprisals if they file complaints. He notes that no Mexicans are employed as foremen, as apprentices in the Mechanical Department, and that Mexicans are no higher than powdermen in the mining operations.

VI. Phelps-Dodge Copper Corporation, Clarksdale, Arizona.

No individual complaints were docketed on this operation. Castaneda observes that the general conditions here are the same as elsewhere in mining towns.

VII. Phelps-Dodge Copper Corporation, Jerome, Arizona

No individual complaints were docketed on this operation. Castaneda observes that conditions here are better than at other mining centers in the state, with Mexicans far more integrated in the community and less discrimination.

VIII. Kennecott Copper Corporation, Hayden Division, Arizona.

Four complaints were docketed on this operation. These appear to have been disposed of by Castaneda and the company, or were not very strong. This is a small operation, employing only one hundred and sixty-five persons, of whom approximately fifty percent are Mexicans.

IX. Kennecott Copper Corporation, Ray Division, Arizona.

Fourteen complaints were docketed on this operation. Castaneda states that seven of these were not satisfactorily answered by the Company. I believe that only two of these were not satisfactorily answered. At any rate, I believe that the remaining does not constitute prima facie cases on the present state of evidence. These two are: a) *Porras,* involving the refusal to transfer to the job of Timberman. The company states that Porras requested a transfer from Chute Blaster ($7.16) to Trackman ($6.86). It states that his services are needed more as a Trackman than as a Timberman. In view of the cut in pay, it is questionable whether Porras's request for transfer was voluntary; b) *Alvarez,* involves a demotion from Brakeman to Mucker. The company states that it is not acquainted with the facts in the case. Castaneda indicates that further information should be sought from the complainant.

X. American Smelting and Refining Company. Hayden, Arizona

Six complaints were docketed on this operation. These are questionable cases on the present state of the evidence. Castaneda advises that we postpone a determination on these cases until he informs the complainants of the company's statement on each case.

XI. Miami Copper Company, Miami, Arizona

Six complaints were docketed on this operation. All were considered to be satisfactorily answered by the company, according to Castaneda. He was impressed with the company's sincerity in ridding itself of discrimination and gives the company a clean bill of health.

XII. Inspiration-Consolidated Copper Company, Inspiration, Arizona.

Fifteen complaints were docketed on this operation. Castaneda states that fourteen out of the fifteen appear to be valid, that in each case, it is the company's word against the complainant's, with no resolutions of the facts possible at this time, but with the company's position weak in all cases. I agree with Castaneda's opinion. Castaneda states that the company does not admit any discrimination, and refuses to do anything. Subsequent to his conference with the company, Castaneda wrote the company stating that the conference revealed to him that no Mexicans were employed as Repairman Helpers, Oilers, Craneman, Roller Operators, or Lead Burner Helpers. He asked how many Mexicans were employed in such classifications and whether the company will employ them if they are qualified. The file does not reveal any reply by the company to Castaneda's letter.

On July 4, 1944, Dr. Castaneda rendered his Summary Report on his investigation. This report contains five recommendations. These are, briefly: 1) that FEPC request charts showing lines of promotion from each of the companies, together with a statement that no employees will be denied promotion in accord with the charts because of his race, creed, color, or national origin; 2) that FEPC request copies of union contracts from each of the local unions, and request that a non-discrimination clause should be included therein, if not already there; 3) that FEPC send to the companies and the unions a "simple statement" explaining the jurisdiction of FEPC, and "how and when" cases involving discrimination are to be referred to FEPC; 4) that FEPC, after analyzing the companies statements in each of the cases discussed by them with Castaneda, request the company to make a satisfactory adjustment "in those cases in which their explanation is unsatisfactory"; 5) that "if they refuse to change their policy in regard to upgrading," FEPC hold a hearing in Phoenix or Denver "as soon as possible."

I believe that 1, 2, and 3 of Dr. Castaneda's recommendations are probably beneficial, although not the most important of his recommendations. As to No. 4, I do not believe that it is possible, on the present state of the evidence, to determine with any degree of accuracy whether the companies' explanations are satisfactory or unsatisfactory in many of the individual upgrading cases. Owing to lack of time, Dr. Castaneda was forced to conduct a very limited investigation; customarily, he secured the written complaint from a complainant outlining the facts as the complainant saw them, and then conferred with the companies, getting their story as they saw the facts. On this state of the record, it is very difficult, and unwise, to make a formal request on these cases at this time. This is especially so because the entire pattern of discrimination in the industry is intimately tied up with these individual cases.

Further, I am very doubtful whether this case by case system will be effective either in eliminating discrimination informally or in the presentation of a hearing. Rather, I believe that any hearing should be keyed to expert testimony on general conditions, general classifications from which Mexicans are excluded, with individual cases thrown in as illustrative material, and for some immediate relief to be procured shortly following the hearing. I do not believe that a hearing should be keyed to individual grievances and their redress. In the first place, we have relatively few individual cases after the sifting that was done by Dr. Castaneda and the company. Each individual case can be made into a law suit of its own at a hearing, and such a hearing can easily be bogged down in a morass of detail. Further, the individual complaints we have are both too few and not colorful enough to pitch the problem in the key which is necessary. In addition, with the exception of a very few cases where the companies are bound by contracts with unions (as in the BRT cases), the companies would undoubtedly adjust the few individual cases which are outstanding in advance of the hearing in order to forestall it. The adjustment of these cases either now or at such a time would certainly do nothing to eliminate the widespread discrimination in the industry. It would, however, serve to tie up the FEPC, if it proceeds on the individual case method of handling such a hearing. I recommend, therefore, that Dr. Castaneda be called in to Washington to discuss this matter at length with Mr. Ross and Mr. Maslow with the above ideas in the forefront at such a discussion.[2]

Recommendation No. 5 has received my comments in the above discussion on recommendation No. 4.

MS: LH, DI, HqR19, Records Relating to Hearings. Southwest (Mexicans).

1. For other selected textual sources, see HqR2, Office Files of Malcolm Ross. Materials from July 6 and 7 Meetings; HqR4, Office Files of George M. Johnson, Deputy Chairman, 11/41–10/45, Evelyn N. Cooper; HqR19, Records Relating to Hearings. Mining. See also Mitchell to Johnson, memorandum, 7/17/44, and other related texts; headnote on the Mining Industry.

2. On the strategic significance of Metzger's recommendation, see Daniel, *Chicano Workers,* 170–72. While the CIO represented workers at most of the mining companies, the Brotherhood of Railroad Trainmen, along with the AFL and the CIO, had separate contracts at the Kennecott Copper Company in New Mexico. Almaráz, *Knight without Armor,* 235.

Memorandum on Complaints against the Seafarers International Union

DATE: July 19, 1944

TO: Mr. George M. Johnson

FROM: Clarence M. Mitchell

SUBJECT: Complaints Against the Seafarers International Union

It is with considerable pleasure that I transmit to you a memorandum dated July 17, which was prepared by Mr. Emanuel Bloch of the Field Operations' staff. Mr. Bloch has done an excellent job in digesting and presenting the material in a rather complicated file. I have read his memorandum very carefully and feel that it will contribute greatly to the understanding of this problem.[1]

Since the Committee expects to have a hearing on this matter, the entire file and Mr. Bloch's memorandum are submitted to you for appropriate disposition.[2] I shall appreciate it if we can talk this matter over before you leave for the hearing in St. Louis. Knowing that you are rather tied up with a number of other matters, I shall be happy to go over this after office hours or on a Sunday if that will be more convenient for you. Attachment (File)

MS: LH, DI, HqR6, Office Files of George M. Johnson. Unarranged Material, Seafarers International Union.

1. Bloch's memorandum of 7/17/44 has not been found, but in a subsequent memorandum of 8/25/44, filed with this text, Bloch told Johnson that after "re-reading and re-analyzing" the SIU file, he reaffirmed his decision that a hearing should be scheduled and held as soon as practicable. He said difficulty could reasonably be expected in the presentation of the evidence to substantiate the complaints because the aggrieved persons worked on ships and the "vast majority of them" would be outside the limits of the country at any specified date. Nevertheless, that difficulty should not deter the Committee from proceeding to a hearing. A strong prima facie case could be presented without their presence, he said.

2. The FEPC, in its decision of 9/6/45 resulting from the hearing, found that the evidence sustained the allegations that the SIU was in violation of EO 9346, and it formulated the usual cease-and-desist directive. In an undated follow-up report, evidently prepared by Bloch, the Committee said the "SIU never complied with the requirements of the decision. Negotiations to bring it into compliance were fruitless and the SIU" was "still in default." See HqR2, Office Files of Malcolm Ross. Difficult cases; the section on the Seafarers International Union in the headnote on the FEPC and Unions.

Memorandum on Complaints against the International Association of Machinists

DATE: July 19, 1944

TO: Mr. George M. Johnson

FROM: Clarence M. Mitchell

SUBJECT: Complaints Against the International Association of Machinists

I have reviewed the files of the central office on cases 12-UR-174, 12-UR-263, and 12-UR-265, and the central file of correspondence on the Union. The review was made for the purpose of determining whether material in the central office covers the suggestions raised in your memorandum of July 8.[1] In addition, I am sending a memorandum to all Regional Directors with the request that any material bearing on the items mentioned in your memorandum be sent to the central office. The following is an analysis of the data I have gotten from the files already in the hands of the Director of Field Operations. I am listing it in accordance with the headings given in your memorandum of July 8.

1. **Areas in Which Negroes are Admitted to Membership Without Discrimination or Limitation.**

   The material before us does not show any specific case in which Negroes are currently admitted to membership without discrimination. There are several references to instances in which Negroes are admitted to membership in Machinists locals without discrimination, but these are not verified. The nearest approach to a condition of full participation by Negroes in the business of a local is furnished by Lodge 79 of Seattle, Washington, which holds a contract with the Seattle-Tacoma Shipbuilding Corporation. Mr. Kingman, in a Request for Further Action Report dated May 13, 1944, states that some twenty (20) Negroes are still active in the union and entitled to all the rights and privileges. These colored members were initiated following the 1940 convention of the International Association of Machinists. At the time, the local lodge was under the impression that it had the right to initiate such Negro members. Since that time, active interference by the International Union has prevented the admission of other Negro members.

2. **Areas in Which Negroes are Permitted to Work Upon Payment of a Permit Fee.**

   Again, as in one, Local 79 of the Machinists Union is the best illustration on this point. Negroes are permitted to work by paying a fee of $1.25, according to statements in the record. This is paid on a monthly basis. Mr. Kingman states, in his Request for Further Action Report of May 13, 1944, that Lodge 79 allows Negroes to be upgraded without discrimination and, apparently, handles grievances for them. There is no statement on whether the amount of the permit fee is the equivalent of the total monthly dues paid by regular members. I shall have to ask Mr. Kingman to supply this information.

   In general, the same description can be given for case 12-UR-265, which involves the IAM Aeronautical Mechanics Lodge 751 of Seattle, Washington. According to Mr. Kingman's Request for Further Action Report dated May 27, 1944, this is a relatively new local and it does clear Negroes for work although it has never admitted any to full membership.

3. **Areas in Which Negroes are Barred From Employment Altogether in Skills Under the Jurisdiction of IAM.**

A memorandum from Mr. Pestana, of the San Francisco office, dated July 8, 1944, and addressed to Mr. Kingman sets forth the relative positions of the IAM in Seattle and the same organization's lodge in Richmond, California. There is before us case 12-UR-174 against the Machinists Union's Local 824 of Richmond. Mr. Pestana points out that this union refuses to clear Negroes for work at all. Also, we have a teletype from Region XII, dated July 12, 1944, which states that the local in the area has received a statement from Mr. Harvey Brown, President of the International Association of Machinists, with regard to its discriminatory policy. In spite of this statement, the union intends to continue its discrimination, according to the regional office of FEPC.

4. The Position of Officials of IAM with Respect to the Problem Before Us.

Apparently, the best position taken by any local is that of Lodge 79. It appears that the sole reason why Negroes are not now initiated into full membership is because of intervention by the International Union. As far back as September 14, 1942, we have a letter from Mr. I. A. Sandvigen, Business Representative of the Lodge, indicating that Negroes are acceptable for full membership.

Both Lodge 79 and Lodge 751 indicate that Negroes will be cleared for jobs, but Lodge 751 feels that any effort to change the ritual so that Negroes may be admitted to membership may result in a split of the IAM.

The attitude of the local in Richmond, California, which is Lodge 824, is clearly defiant and non-cooperative. Apparently, the local considers its position buttressed by the actions of the International in that the file on case 12-UR-174 contains a letter from Mr. Albert B. Nelson, Business Representative of the Local. Mr. Nelson states that the January, 1944, issue of the Monthly Journal of the Machinists contains a statement of the policy of the international organization. Among other things, this statement indicates that the Machinists will not comply with the directives issued by the Committee in the railroad cases.[2]

5. Nature of Complaints Which the Committee Has Received.

The complaints before the Committee at present include USES 510 Reports filed against Local 824 in Richmond, California. Also, we have specific complaints from individuals protesting against the policies of Lodge 79 in Seattle. These persons indicate that they are paying $1.25 monthly for work permits but are denied admission to the union. We have one case against Lodge 751. It is the complaint of Miss Pauline Houston, 103–20 Avenue South, Seattle. She alleges that she has made an effort to become a member of the union but has been unable to gain admission.

MS: LH, HqR83, Correspondence Relating to Cases. (A–K) International Association of Machinists.
1. Johnson's memorandum of 7/8/44 and related materials, including the 9/14/42 letter from Sandvigen, are in this file in HqR83. See also Mitchell to Johnson, memorandum, 9/6/44, "FEPC Com-

plaints Involving the Machinists"; memorandum, 1/8/45, "Types of Complaints against the International Association of Machinists"; other texts dealing with this union elsewhere in this volume; headnotes on the FEPC and Unions and on the Shipbuilding Industry.

2. See 9/6/44.

Memorandum on Associated Shipyards, Seattle, Washington

July 21, 1944

Mr. George M. Johnson

Clarence M. Mitchell

Associated Shipyards, Seattle, Washington, 12-BR-251 DFO

The attached Request for Further Action is referred to the Legal Division for handling in connection with the overall Boiler Maker cases.[1] It does not appear that anything can be accomplished by Field Operations on this problem until it adjusted at the national level.

Attachment (File)

cc: Mr. Kingman

MS: copy, HqR38, Central Files. (entry 25) Memoranda, Johnson, George M. 1/44–.

1. The problems involved here were similar to those that had been documented at the Kaiser Company; the Oregon Shipbuilding Corporation in the Vancouver, Washington–Portland, Oregon area; the California Shipbuilding Corporation; Western Pipe and Steel Company; the Consolidated Steel Corporation (Shipbuilding Division) in the Los Angeles area; and locals of the Boilermakers Union. For background on Boilermakers and shipbuilding industry cases, see 6/26/44; headnotes on the FEPC and Unions and on the Shipbuilding Industry.

Memorandum on Conrady Construction Company

DATE: July 22, 1944

TO: George M. Johnson, Deputy Chairman

FROM: Clarence M. Mitchell, Associate Director of Field Operations

SUBJECT: Conrady Construction Company, 2-BR-886

In accordance with point one of the Summary of Essential Actions taken by the Committee at its meeting held on April 20, 1944, I am submitting to you for your legal opinion the question of our jurisdiction over the subject company.[1]

The Conrady Construction Company is a corporation "owned by an individual" doing carpentry sub-contracting. There are six in its personnel. The firm is listed as "essential" by the War Manpower Commission. Investigation discloses that this is a private corporation holding no U. S. Government contracts or "any other contacts."

MS: LH, DI, HqR83, Correspondence Relating to Cases. (A–K) Conrady Construction Company.

1. Johnson informed Mitchell on 7/28/44 that, based on Bloch's analysis, Conrady had no government contracts and was not engaged in war production or in activities essential to the maintenance of war production industries and therefore the Committee did not assume jurisdiction over it. Johnson's response and Mitchell's memorandum to Lawson, 8/2/44, informing him of the ruling, are filed with this text. For the context, see the headnote on Jurisdictional Issues.

Memorandum on Evansville Shipyard

July 25, 1944

Mr. George M. Johnson

Clarence M. Mitchell

Evansville Shipyard, 6-BR-478 DFO

Attached is the file on the Evansville Shipyard. This case involves a local of the Boiler Makers International. It is, therefore, referred to the Legal Division for appropriate handling.[1] You will note that Mr. Henderson, the Regional Director, suggests that we contact the Navy Department and the Boiler Makers International.

If you deem it appropriate, I shall be glad to work with whomever handles this matter in the Legal Division.

Attachment (File)

cc: Mr. Henderson

MS: copy, HqR38, Central Files. (entry 25) Memoranda, Johnson, George M., 1/44–.

1. For similar referrals on Boilermakers Union cases, see 6/24, 7/21/44. For background, see the headnote on the FEPC and Unions.

Eleanor F. Rogers Memorandum
on Call from Mr. Roy A. Hoglund, St. Louis, Missouri, Regarding Strike at National Lead Company, St. Louis

July 27, 1944

Mr. Clarence M. Mitchell

Eleanor F. Rogers

Call From Mr. Roy A. Hoglund, St. Louis, Missouri, re
Strike at National Lead Company, St. Louis

On the above date, Mr. Hoglund called from St. Louis, Missouri, to inform you that Negro employees of the National Lead Company went out on strike on the seven o'clock shift because of the failure of the company to upgrade or hire Negroes in certain classifications. Mr. Hoglund stated that, so far as he could ascertain, all of the Negroes were out. He had talked with Mr. Pfauts, Manager of the plant. There is a picket line at the end of the car line where workers get off to go to the plant, Mr. Hoglund said.[1]

You informed Mr. Hoglund that you had called Mr. Martin Wagner, of the United Gas, Coke and Chemical Workers, who informed you that he had gotten in touch with his people in the area. Mr. Wagner said he was told that everything was going along smoothly. You asked Mr. Hoglund if he had seen Mr. Joe Applebaum, International Representative of the Union, or Mr. Thomas Mosley, International Board Member, both of whom are in the area, according to Mr. Wagner. Mr. Hoglund had not talked with Mr. Mosley, but he had talked with Mr. Applebaum. Mr. Wagner also stated, you told Mr. Hoglund, that FEPC had not been in touch with the union, according to representatives of CIO. Mr. Hoglund stated that this was incorrect because he had met with union officials last Friday, July 21. Mr. Pfauts, he stated, called him yesterday to inform him of the strike. Mr. Hoglund stated that he then got in touch with the Negro leaders in an effort to persuade them not to go on strike, which efforts were continued until late last night. The Negroes agreed that if a meeting were held last night and some commitment made, they would hold off a strike. Mr. Hoglund stated that he called Mr. Pfauts and the president of the local. Management agreed to attend the meeting and did so but the union's officials said they could not meet last night.

Mr. Hoglund stated that the Negroes have no confidence in the union at the plant. He stated further that there was a meeting yesterday afternoon between management and union. He knew this, Mr. Hoglund stated, because the president of the company had called him and stated that the Negroes were not represented. Mr. Hoglund said that Negroes told him that they were not informed of the meeting nor were they invited to participate. It is Mr. Hoglund's impression that management and union officials are in collusion in the matter and will "pass the buck" if they can.[2]

You asked Mr. Hoglund if the question of whether or not Negroes would go on strike arose at last Friday's meeting. Mr. Hoglund stated that Mr. Theodore Brown (FEPC Examiner) met with a delegation of Negroes some time ago (about three weeks) when Negroes were threatening to walk out. Mr. Brown persuaded them not to walk out at that time.

Although FEPC cannot process the complaints at this point, Mr. Hoglund was advised that attempts to persuade the strikers to return to the job should continue and that all of the Government agencies which will be concerned with settling the strike should be apprised of all the facts. Such agencies would be WMC, WPB, WLB, and Conciliation.[3] Mr. Hoglund stated that, although the WPB representative is not in St. Louis, he called said representative last night and informed him that the Negroes were going out on strike.

Mr. Hoglund estimated that between two and three hundred Negroes were out on strike. You advised him to point out to management and the union that they need to give some assurance to the striking employees so that they can have some confidence in them.

You informed Mr. Hoglund that you would call Mr. Wagner and inform him of this conversation and developments.

MS: copy, HqR63, Central Files. Reports, Tension Area Reports, Region IX.
  1. See 5/29, 8/2, 8/8/44; headnotes on Major Cases in St. Louis and on Strikes and Work Stoppages.
  2. See the headnote on the FEPC and Unions.
  3. See the headnote on Relationships with Federal Agencies.

Memorandum on Services of Mr. Bloch for Field Operations

July 28, 1944

MEMORANDUM

TO: George M. Johnson
        Deputy Chairman

FROM: Clarence M. Mitchell
        Acting Director of Field Operations

RE: Services of Mr. Bloch for Field Operations

Because of my absence from the office for a short vacation and owing to the resignation of Mr. Metzger, I will appreciate it if you will permit Mr. Bloch to continue working on a part time basis for the Division of Field Operations until August 28 when I return to the office.

As I understand it you have already given him two assignments in the Legal Division and we would expect Mr. Bloch to arrange his Field Operations work so that it would not conflict with the assignments given by you.

MS: LH, DI, MP.

Memorandum on Strike at American Steel Castings Company, Granite City, Illinois

DATE: July 31, 1944

TO: Mr. Will Maslow

FROM: Clarence M. Mitchell

SUBJECT: Strike at American Steel Castings Company, Granite City, Illinois

On July 20, we received a report that 300 Negro chippers were out on strike in this plant.[1] The nature of this walkout is confused to some extent but it appears that a wage dispute was involved. The War Labor Board ordered the individuals back to work, and they returned to the job.

Attached is a telegram received from Regional Director Roy A. Hoglund on the strike. Subsequently, the workers have again walked out, but this time because of alleged abuse by a foreman. The later walkout has tied up operations of the entire plant.

[attachment]

JULY 24, 1944

TELETYPE

MR. CLARENCE M. MITCHELL
HAVE JUST CONFERRED WITH REGIONAL OFFICE WAR LABOR BOARD CONCERNING STRIKE OF CHIPPERS AT AMERICAN STEEL CASTING COMPANY,

GRANITE CITY, ILLINOIS. STRIKE WAS UNAUTHORIZED AND RESULTED FROM ALLEGED DELAY IN ISSUANCE OF WAR LABOR BOARD DIRECTIVE IN LABOR DISPUTE. ONLY CHIPPERS, ALL NEGROES, WALKED OUT. ENTIRE PLANT FORCED TO CLOSE. DIFFICULTY IN GETTING WORKERS BACK, ACCORDING TO WAR LABOR BOARD, WAS CONFUSED BY INJECTION OF RACIAL ISSUES. WAR LABOR BOARD ISSUED ORDER TO REOPEN PLANT JULY 19 AND SUSPENDED RECALCITRANT STRIKERS. PLANT REOPENED JULY 20. TODAY REPORTED SEVENTY-FIVE CHIPPERS WENT TO WORK ON FIRST SHIFT AND ALL EXPECTED TO RETURN FOR LATER SHIFTS, EXCEPTING TWELVE CHIPPERS SUSPENDED.

ROY A. HOGLUND, KANSAS CITY.

Rec'd by
E. Rogers
5:00 P.M.

MS: LH, DI, HqR63, *Central Files. Reports, Tension Area Reports, Region VI.*
    1. See the headnotes on Strikes and Work Stoppages and on the Steel Industry.

Memorandum on Strike at National Lead Company, St. Louis, Missouri

August 2, 1944

Mr. Will Maslow
Clarence M. Mitchell
Strike at National Lead Company, St. Louis, Missouri

On July 27, the Negro employees of the National Lead Company went on strike because of alleged failure to upgrade them in various departments. The union at the plant is the United Gas, Coke and Chemical Workers (CIO).

I have discussed the problems at the plant with Mr. Martin Wagner, of the union. Also, Mr. Hoglund and Mr. Brown of our Kansas City office have been making strenuous efforts to get these employees to return to the job, although they are not processing the complaints because of the Committee's ruling in this regard.

There was considerable talk of tension in the area, but Mr. Hoglund and Mr. David Grant of St. Louis both felt that, while there is tension in St. Louis, it was not accentuated by the strike at the National Lead Company.

MS: *copy, HqR63, Central Files. Reports, Tension Area Reports, Region XIV.*

See 5/29, 7/27, and 8/8/44 texts and the headnotes on Major Cases in St. Louis and on Strikes and Work Stoppages.

Memorandum on Case of Miss Olga Tate vs. War Department, Gravelly Point

August 2, 1944

Mr. George M. Johnson

Clarence M. Mitchell

Case of Miss Olga Tate vs. War Department, Gravelly Point, 4-GR-289

Attached is a Request for Further Action from Region IV concerning the above case. You will note that the Region suggests that there be a conference between various persons involved and a representative of FEPC.[1]

Because of the somewhat complicated nature of this case, and also because the War Department has conducted one investigation, it is suggested that it be considered for a possible hearing. It is, therefore, referred to the Legal Division for that purpose. I do not believe that much could be accomplished by a conference.

Attachment (File)

cc: Mr. Evans

MS: copy, FR42, Region IV. Active Cases, War Department 4-GR-289, Office of Fiscal Director, Olga Tate, DFO.

1. See Joseph H. B. Evans to Maslow, 7/6/44, and related documents, filed with this text. Miss Tate's complaint, dated 4/12/44, alleged discrimination caused her discharge after a white fellow worker accused her and another black woman, Mrs. Maurice Fenwick, with threatening her with physical violence during a bus incident. Evans's request for further action cited a general pattern of War Department denial of the existence of discrimination and inadequate opportunities for presenting witnesses for her case during the War Department's investigation. See also the section on the War Department in the headnote on Relationships with Federal Agencies.

Report on Investigation of Philadelphia Transit Company Strike

August 4, 1944

Mr. Will Maslow, Director of Field Operations

Clarence M. Mitchell, Associate Director, Field Operations
Investigation of Philadelphia Transit Company Strike

At your suggestion, upon learning of the strike of transit workers in the City of Philadelphia, I left Washington on Tuesday, August 1st to lend all possible assistance to the Regional Office in handling any part of the problem which involved FEPC.[1] I wish to state that on arriving I found the Regional Office busily engaged in attempts to resolve the problem. Mr. G. James Fleming, the Regional Director and his staff, were in possession of all important information available and kept their office open well into the night, in order to be of greatest service. The following is a brief account of some of the important matters which came to my attention while there.

The strike of the Employees of the Philadelphia Transit Company began on the morning of Tuesday, August 1, 1944. Newspaper accounts indicate that only a few street cars and buses were affected in the beginning, but that flying squads of strikers "persuaded" other employees to leave their jobs. This information seems substantiated by statements made to FEPC by employees and also by announcements made by officials of the Transport Workers Union. There was a dismal failure of the city to prevent workers on strike from interfering with those who wanted to work.

The company had placed eight Negroes in training as of Sunday, July 30. Three of these trainees visited the F.E.P.C. office and gave the following account of what happened.

On Sunday, they took their first instructions at the company's station at 810 Dauphin Street. Monday, they worked at 3rd and Wyoming Streets, where they were taught the use of equipment. Tuesday, they were supposed to take cars on the street. This last was prevented because of the strike, but the men have been reporting for work each day. They contend that the majority of workers at the training section have been highly cooperative and even during the strike there have been no instances of unpleasant exchanges between themselves and the persons on strike. The three men who visited the F.E.P.C. office were Lewis Sylvester Thompson, 1410 N. 25th Street, formerly a welder; Rufus Garrison Lancaster, 4002 Ogden Street, formerly a porter; and William J. Barber, 3708 Mt. Vernon Street, formerly a track worker. Each morning since the strike began, they have been reporting to the barn at 59th and Callowhill Streets. There are no whites in the training class with them, according to their statement. It was their expectation that they would be ready to operate street cars for passengers within twenty-one days after their first instruction. However, before taking passengers it would be necessary to take a final test.

The company, F.E.P.C. and the Regional Office of the War Manpower Commission met on the first day of the strike. Those present at the conference, which was held in the Regional Office of the War Manpower Commission, were: Dr. A. A. Mitten, representing the company; G. James Fleming, Regional Director of F.E.P.C.; Joseph Sharfsin, special counsel for F.E.P.C.; Frank McNamee, regional director of WMC; and William A. Smith, WMC minorities representative in Region III. At that meeting the following notice was proposed by the company:

NOTICE

Stoppage of PTC service has crippled every war industry in the Philadelphia area. Service must be restored immediately to prevent critical interference with vital war production.

The first duty of this company is to provide service to the war effort and the public.

Therefore, provisions of the notice dated July 7, 1944, regarding changes in employment practices to comply with the directive of the War Manpower Commission are suspended.

This notice was the company's proposal to return to its former system of denying Negroes jobs on platform operations. It was rejected by F.E.P.C. and the War Manpower Commission.

Throughout the day, various efforts were made by the Army, Navy, War Labor Board, War Production Board, F.E.P.C. and interested citizens to get the strikers to return to work. Representatives of these agencies visited various barns to urge workers to return to the job. The efforts were unsuccessful. However, great difficulty was encountered in getting radio time for speakers. Mr. James P. Casey, regional representative of the Office of Labor Production of the War Production Board, was scheduled to urge the workers to return to their jobs, but his radio time was cancelled, at the request of the Mayor of Philadelphia, according to information received by the Regional Director of F.E.P.C.

The strikers made full use of the company property for various meetings. Since it was evident that it would be difficult to get them to return to work and such meetings merely served as a setting for inflammatory speech making, I suggested that the company should prevent the strikers from using its barns. I conveyed this information to Mr. Buck White, counsel for the company, who insisted that the strikers were not in the barns, but were just outside. I also mentioned this to Mr. Orville Bullitt, regional director of the War Production Board and urged that he use his influence to get the company to bar its property to the strikers. Later, the company announced that it would prevent the strikers from using the barns.

F.E.P.C. proposed that there be a meeting of the Government agencies concerned with the problem. It was suggested that this meeting could be held in the Mayor's office to enlist his cooperation in reaching a solution. An informal discussion of the matter took place in the Regional Office of the War Labor Board. The Board representatives, Mr. Sylvester Garret and Eli Rock, indicated that they did not wish to attend a meeting with the Mayor. It was suggested by Mr. Mitchell of F.E.P.C. that the cars be operated by such loyal union men as could be found. Mr. Mitchell also suggested that the full force of the Philadelphia police system back up such action. Others present feared, however, that protection from the police would not be adequate—thereby causing more trouble. It was then agreed that Messrs. Mitchell, Sharfsin and McNamee would meet with the Mayor to present the problems to him. At 11:00 p.m. a meeting was held with the Mayor in the City Hall. The following announcement was made by the Mayor:

"At a meeting held in my office I was informed by Frank McNamee, regional director of the War Manpower Commission, and Joseph Sharfsin and Clarence Mitchell, representing the FEPC, that the C.I.O. and the following Federal agencies—the War Labor Board, FEPC, and the War Manpower Commission—have concluded that nothing effective can be done locally to end the transit stoppage.

"They further informed me," the Mayor said, "that Mr. Garrett will certify the case for further action to the chairman of the National War Labor Board."

He also stated that such announcement seemed perfectly proper because he did not see what he could do in the situation.

Mr. Bullitt, called F.E.P.C. on Wednesday morning and suggested that a committee of strikers wished to meet with him. Mr. Bullitt expressed the opinion that the men might go back to work, if they thought that they could save face. Under this "face-saving" plan the strikers were to be given an opportunity to appeal the F.E.P.C. directive requiring the company to follow the requirements of Executive Order 9346. Also, the Negroes would be "off for a few days until things cooled down." Mr. Bullitt was informed by Mr. Mitchell that the issue had been heard on an appeal from an F.E.P.C. action based on an agreed statement of facts. Also Mr. Mitchell, Mr. Fleming and Mr. Sharfsin rejected the idea of keeping the Negro trainees off of the cars. Mr. Bullitt met with the strikers, but subsequent events showed that he was unable to get them to return to work.

On Tuesday night there were a great many rumors about racial clashes. Unquestionably the strike was an explosive issue in the Negro community. A feeling of deep resentment was expressed on every hand and it was not difficult to hear numerous arguments on this score. However, there was a tendency of out-of-town newspapers to exaggerate the possibility of racial outbreaks. In addition, many rumors were in circulation, i.e., as Mr. Sharfsin and I left the office to visit the Mayor, a man came up to us and stated that he hoped we were not going in the direction of Tenth and Christian Streets. "There is a serious riot in that neighborhood," he said. This was found to be untrue. An elevator operator in one of the buildings told us that a transit worker had been killed. This also was untrue, but it had been related to us as an indisputable fact. The few clashes which did occur happened in neighborhoods which for the most part give trouble each night. It is true that some persons were arrested for actions growing out of their feelings about the strike but the majority of those responsible were not involved in any unusual disorders. Nevertheless some newspapers tried to make it appear that every group of Negroes arrested were persons trying to start a race riot. I mentioned this to Mr. Jack Smith of the Associated Press and pointed out that the reiteration of such stories would really promote a riot.

Fortunately a heavy rain began on Wednesday morning, keeping many people off the streets. On Wednesday night volunteers from the union attempted to run some of the street cars. This operation lasted for a brief period but was shut down because of insufficient men. The regional director also states that there was insufficient police protection from the City as well as some opposition from cashiers who would not let passengers board the trains.

I left the City Wednesday night to return to Washington.

MS: copy, FEPC RG 228 (entry PI 147), Office Files of Malcolm Ross, Philadelphia Rapid Transit, box 71, DNA.

1. See N. Jeanne Clifton's 8/7/44 recording of Mitchell's telephone conversation on the Philadelphia strike; headnotes on Street and Local Railways and on Strikes and Work Stoppages; "Philadelphia— Postwar Preview?" editorial, *Crisis*, 7/44, 280; Spaulding, "Philadelphia's Hate Strike," *Crisis*, 7/44, 281–83, 301; *NYT*, 7/9/44, 38, 7, plus extensive coverage and commentary throughout 8/44; *Newsweek*, 8/14/44, 36–37; *Time*, 8/14/44, 22–23.

In his analysis, Davis concluded that "nobody acted fast enough or took the strike seriously enough at the outset." Based on newspaper reports, he found it inconceivable that the Transport Workers Union could not have known that the strike was developing. So, had the TWU been more vigorous in preventing the strike, "they could well have copied Mike Quill's tactics during the Interborough [subway] strike in New York on the race issue." In sum, he felt the real issue was the "determination of a gang of rabble-rousers and desperate job-holders of the old company union to regain paying positions and to control the CIO union." Davis to Mitchell, memorandum, 8/5/44, HqR38, Central Files. (entry 25) Memoranda, Mitchell, Clarence. For other reports on the level of violence, see Hill, *Black Labor*, 297–99, 301–2; Winkler, "Philadelphia Transit Strike," 86–87.

Report on Conference with Jonathan Daniels Regarding Philadelphia Transit and Los Angeles Street Railway

August 4, 1944

Personal Files

Clarence M. Mitchell

Conference with Jonathan Daniels re: Philadelphia Transit
and Los Angeles Street Railway

On the above date I met with Mr. Daniels to discuss the status of the Philadelphia Transit case and Los Angeles Street Railway.[1] Mr. Daniels reiterated his pledges given over the telephone to me the day before. These pledges were that the government would not back down in its enforcement of the Executive Order 9346, which led to the upgrading of Negroes in Philadelphia on the transit system.

He showed me a telegram from Mayor Fletcher Bowron of Los Angeles. This wire, which was several pages, urged that the forth-coming hearing be cancelled. The Mayor expressed the view that it would cause possible racial conflict and felt that the police force in Los Angeles would be inadequate to control the situation. Mr. Daniels asked my opinion on what should be done. I informed him that the Los Angeles hearings had been postponed twice at the request of the Mayor. I also stated that in this instance the attention of the Nation had been focused on the Philadelphia situation, if the Government retreated in the Los Angeles Street Railway, it would appear that we had become frightened because of irresponsible opposition. This, I informed him, would greatly weaken our position with employers all over the country and would have a dangerously adverse affect on Negroes throughout the country.

Mr. Daniels suggested that it might be possible to hold a closed hearing in view of the hostile newspapers in the community. I pointed out that closed hearings are reserved for government agencies and that since newspapers are hostile, it would be very advisable to have a public hearing so that from at least one source our story would not be garbled. He then asked whether it would be possible to hold in abeyance the issuance of directives, for a few weeks. I pointed out that directives are never issued immediately after the hearing, and that if the normal course of events takes place, such directives would not be issued immediately after the public hearings. He seemed somewhat reassured at this point and indicated that he would appreciate it if Mr. Ross would communicate with Mayor Bowron for the purpose of letting the latter know what our procedures are.

I agreed to call Mr. Daniels later in the day after he talked with Mr. Ross. I did call him on Saturday, August 5, he stated that he had talked to Mr. Ross and the latter saw Mayor Bowron yesterday. Mr. Daniels said it was his understanding that Mr. Ross was to have a second meeting with Mayor Bowron and representatives of the company, following this meeting Mr. Ross was to call Mr. Daniels.

Again Mr. Daniels assured me that there would be no interference with the Los Angeles hearing, but it was hoped that they would be handled in a careful fashion. He also reiterated his assurance that the government would stand firm in its actions against the strikers in the Philadelphia transit case.

MS: copy, MP.

1. See immediately related texts; Mitchell to Maslow, 8/4/44; Jeanne Clifton's transcript of Mitchell's 8/7/44 conversation on the PTC case; headnote on Street and Local Railways.

N. Jeanne Clifton Memorandum to Clarence Mitchell on His Conversations on Philadelphia Transportation Company Case

August 7, 1944

Mr. Clarence M. Mitchell

N. Jeanne Clifton

Philadelphia Transportation Company case.*

On Saturday afternoon, August 5, 1944, Regional Director Fleming called you to report the latest occurrences in connection with the above subject. Mr. St. Clair Bourne, who was in Philadelphia was on the other phone.

*Transcript of Mitchell's telephone conversation.

Mr. Fleming reported that shortly before his call, Mr. Joseph Sharfsin had reported that WCAU had informed him that time was being allotted the strikers in the case at 7:00 p.m. that evening to give their side of the story to the public, that WCAU wanted someone to give the other side of the story and Mr. Sharfsin had agreed to do this. Mr. Fleming stated he said this would be all right, but FEPC would have to give an opening statement to the effect that Mr. Sharfsin was speaking as a private citizen and not as a representative of FEPC. You (Mr. Mitchell) told Mr. Fleming and Mr. Bourne, who had explained the same story, that you were against the idea of a radio broadcast and thought the whole thing should be called off. Mr. Fleming said FEPC could not control this, since the radio station felt they had a perfect right to broadcast both sides of the story, just as the newspapers have a right to print both sides.

At about this time Mr. Sharfsin was called to the phone and he stressed his own personal feeling for the city of Philadelphia and thought this was the time that the right point of view should be given to the public. He thought it would be a great mistake to have the strikers to give their point of view without the other point of view being explained to people, he said are in ignorance on the whole subject. You disagreed with him, and reminded him that WCAU had waited some time to feel that the public should have both sides of the story, that during the first of the week when FEPC wanted time on the radio, it had not been cleared until OWI gave assistance. You also pointed out that later this broadcast was not given, and not until Wednesday (the second day of the strike) did WCAU have a discussion by the interested parties. Mr. Sharfsin said that he was not concerned with petty issues in this matter, and that he would go on the air even if he had to pay for the time himself. You informed him that you would do all that you could to stop the broadcast.

While Mr. Davidson in Washington, Mr. Bourne and Mr. Fleming continued talking on the phone, you called Mr. Victor Rotnem of Justice Department and explained the whole story to him. He thought it was not a good idea at all and suggested that his men in Philadelphia be told the story so they could work on the matter. He also suggested that you call Commissioner Clifford J. Durr of FCC.

You then called General E. S. Greenbaum of War Department and he said this would be a most unfortunate move since the Army was moving in and this would disrupt their program. General Greenbaum at first said if the strikers are going on the air "we had better go on" (War Department), he then said, "No, that would be a debate." He indicated he would contact Philadelphia immediately to urge that the broadcast be called off.

You talked with Mr. James McGranery of the Justice Department who explained that General Hayes was going on the radio to inform the strikers that they must return to work or be fired. Later Mr. McGranery called again and you informed him that our representatives in Philadelphia said they were unable to get in touch with Mr. Schweinhaut and Mr. James Gledson. Mr. McGranery agreed to call them himself and you also told him that it was your understanding that Mr. McMenamin and the other strike leaders were going to WCAU at 7:00 o'clock. Mr. McGranery said that he would call the station and stop the broadcast.

Mr. Jonathan Daniels called and said he thought that it should be made clear that Mr. Fleming was the representative of FEPC in the area, and no one else was authorized to speak for FEPC. He was afraid that Sharfsin could not be disconnected from FEPC at this late date since he had represented it the first of the week. He suggested you continue to press War Department with the importance of the whole thing. You explained that you were urging Mr. Sharfsin to stay off the air and that our Philadelphia office was making it clear that he would not be an FEPC spokesman if he did talk.

You called Mr. Ted Poston of OWI, who agreed that this would be an unfortunate move and agreed to call his Philadelphia man to see that the program had OWI clearance.

Mr. Blackie Meyers of TWU called from Philadelphia to say that the Transport Workers Union and the Army were to go on the air to talk about the case, that McMenamin had heard of this and wanted time, that WCAU said he could go on if they could get someone to take the opposite side and Sharfsin said he would take the other side. Mr. Meyers urged that FEPC do all in its power to prevent Mr. Sharfsin from going on the air. You explained that the matter was being given attention here in Washington.

Mr. Fleming then called and stated that since talking with you he had called the War Department in Philadelphia to ask whether it believed Mr. Sharfsin's broadcast would be helpful. The War Department said that it would not be helpful and Mr. Sharfsin agreed to withdraw. Mr. Fleming also said that the broadcast of the strikers was "off." Later, Mr. Poston said the representative of OWI in Philadelphia, a Mr. Tall, had assured him that the broadcast was off. Mr. Fleming called a few hours later however and said that he understood one representative of the strikers did get on the air but simply made an appeal for the workers to return to their jobs. You informed Mr. Poston of this and he indicated that he would check on the matter further.

You informed me on Monday, August 7, that Mr. Fleming called you on Sunday to indicate that operations were resumed and that Mr. McMenamin had been arrested along with Messrs. Thompson, Carney and Dixen. Mr. Fleming also informed you that Mr. McMenamin was arrested on his way to the radio station with a statement urging that the workers should return to their job, but that the upgrading of Negroes should be postponed for the duration and one year thereafter. When the men were arrested, Mr. Fleming said only Thompson could furnish bail. Subsequently the others were released on bond after it had been posted. Each bond was $2500.

MS: copy, HqR3, Office Files of George M. Johnson. M.

For background, see immediately related texts; Mitchell to Maslow, 8/4; Mitchell to Personal Files, 8/4/44; headnote on Street and Local Railways.

Memorandum on Sub-regional office, Seattle, Washington

August 7, 1944

MEMORANDUM

TO: Will Maslow
Director of Field Operations

FROM: Clarence M. Mitchell
Associate Director of Field Operations

RE: Sub-regional office, Seattle, Washington

At my request the Division of Review and Analysis prepared the attached statement on the Region XII case load in the states of Washington and Oregon. You will note that nearly a third of the case load falls in these two states. I obtained this information in order that we might fully explore the possibility of opening an office in the Northwest.[1]

MS: copy, HqR38, Central Files. Memoranda, Maslow, Will, 1944.

1. Bernard Ross, a resident of the area, was recruited as examiner in anticipation of the opening of a Northwest office. No such office was opened, but Ross stayed in Region XII as an examiner. See subsequent activities involving Ross and Region XII at 8/10/45 and in the biographical directory.

Memorandum on Arnold Agency

DATE: August 7, 1944

TO: Mr. George M. Johnson

FROM: Clarence M. Mitchell

SUBJECT: Arnold Agency, 12-BR-1106

The Regional office has referred this case to Washington in an effort to determine whether private employment agencies come under our jurisdiction. It will be appreciated if you will indicate whether this matter is one for consideration by the Committee.

Attachment—file

MS: LH, HqR83, Correspondence Relating to Cases. (A–K) Arnold Agency.
    For related texts see Johnson to Reeves, 8/25; Reeves to Johnson, 8/15/44; Johnson to Mitchell, 9/2/44; and Mitchell to Robert E. Brown, 9/9/44, all in same location as above text. See also Johnson's opinions on "Jurisdictional Problems Handled by the Legal Division," 10/27/44, HqR5, Office Files of George M. Johnson. (H–Telephone Company), Maceo Hubbard, and 12/4/44, "Matters Requiring Immediate Consideration by the Legal Division," HqR38, Central Files. Memoranda—3, Legal Division. The significance of Mitchell's concerns in the above text was earlier established by the memorandum of agreement between the Committee and the provost marshal general that barred the release of any information on a person's race, color, creed, or national origin in connection with their being considered for employment. See Lawrence Cramer's memorandum of 4/27/43 to all staff on the subject as well as the Memorandum of Understanding between the President's Committee on Fair Employment Practice, the WMC, and the provost marshal general, War Department, 3/10/43, both in HqR67, Central Files. Reports, U.S. Government. War Department, A–L.

Memorandum on Strikes in the St. Louis Area

DATE: **August 8, 1944**

TO: **Mr. Will Maslow, Director, Field Operations**

FROM: **Clarence M. Mitchell, Associate Director, Field Operations**

SUBJECT: **Strikes in the St. Louis area**

On Saturday August 5, I talked with Mr. Roy Hoglund of our regional office concerning strikes at the National Lead Company, St. Louis and Liggett & Meyers Tobacco Company and the General Steel Castings Company in Granite City, Illinois. Mr. Hoglund indicated that National Lead workers have gone back on the job, but will meet with the union on Monday, August 7. The other two plants were out at the time I talked with Mr. Hoglund.

Later in the day I talked with Mr. Kenneth Sauser, Philadelphia representative of General Steel Castings. He said he understood that the Negro workers who were out there had returned to the job. He said however, they had been in once before and had walked out so he was not certain they would remain. Our regional office in Chicago has been at work on this case, but reports that the issues involved are not racial, in that the foreman is accused of abusing workers both Negro and white. It just happens that the bulk of the striking workers are Negroes.

I have no information on the issues in the Meyers Tobacco case, but 400 Negroes are out.

MS: LH, DI, HqR63, Central Files. Reports, Tension Areas Reports, Region IX.
See the headnote on Strikes and Work Stoppages; John A. Davis, report on race strikes, 5/25/44, in appendix 1.

Memorandum on Montgomery Ward and Company

DATE: August 8, 1944

TO: Mr. George M. Johnson

FROM: Clarence M. Mitchell

SUBJECT: Montgomery Ward and Company

From the attached memorandum you will note that the Sixth Region has received a complaint against the Montgomery Ward Company in Chicago. They request an opinion on whether a company of its character would fall within the jurisdiction of the Committee. It is transmitted to you for an opinion.

Attachments—2

MS: LH, DI, HqR84, Correspondence Relating to Cases. Montgomery Ward & Company (Region IV).
See Henderson to Maslow, 5/29, 8/4/44; Henderson to Maslow, telegram, 7/19/44. For Maslow's response, which indicated a lack of jurisdiction unless the cases were directly related to the few contracts the company had with the government, see Reeves to Johnson, 10/25/44; Johnson to Maslow, 1/26/44; Mitchell to Henderson, 11/4/44, which are all in the file. See also the headnote on Jurisdictional Issues.

Memorandum on Los Angeles Railway Directive

August 10, 1944

Mr. Malcolm Ross   Mr. George M. Johnson

c/o FEPC Reg. Office   c/o FEPC Reg. Office

San Francisco, California   Los Angeles, California

AP Dispatch in today's Washington Star Date Line Los Angeles August 10 as follows: Quote The Fair Employment Practice Committee issued a directive last night ordering the Los Angeles Railway Corp. to cease alleged discrimination against Negroes in its hiring of streetcar conductors, motormen and bus drivers.

Paragraph. "It is understood," said a committee statement, "that a reasonable time will be necessary to eliminate the discriminatory practices found to exist. . . . But the Committee will take affirmative steps to obtain compliance."

Paragraph. The railway corporation agreed to take immediate steps to bring its policies and practices into conformity with the national policy of nondiscrimination.

Paragraph. The company issued no denial of the charges at the hearing ended yesterday. Both company and AFL union representatives told the committee that enforcement of Negro hiring would cause disruption of transportation. Unquote.[1]

In conferring with War Department and White House August 5 I indicated that committee directives customarily are not issued immediately after hearings. Anticipate inquiries. Please send clarification.[2]

Clarence M. Mitchell
Asso. Dir. Field Operations

MS: copy, HqR39, Central Files. (entry 25) Memoranda, Ross, Malcolm, 1944.

1. For a copy of the press release that Maceo Hubbard, hearing examiner for the case, telegraphed to Mitchell, see HqR84, Correspondence Relating to Cases. (L–S) Los Angeles Railway. Maslow sent all regional directors a copy of the findings and directives in the LARY case that were issued in Los Angeles on 8/10/44, following the company's response on 8/9/44 that it would not file any exception and would proceed to implement the order. He explained, "When the parties formally stated for the record that they had no exceptions to the findings and directives, they were made final." He added, "The speed with which the Committee acted is of course unprecedented and due in part to the fact that the parties in effect consented to the issuance of the directive." Maslow, Field Letter 29, 9/7/44. See also the headnotes on Strikes and Work Stoppages and on Street and Local Railways; findings, directives, and other related texts in HqR21, Records Relating to Hearings., Los Angeles Railway Corporation.

2. On Mitchell's conference with White House representative Jonathan Daniels on this subject, see his memorandum of 8/4/44. Mitchell praised the Committee's quick action during the FEPC meeting of 9/9/44. See Transcript of Proceedings, 9/9/44, 65, HqR65, Central Files.

Memorandum on Goodyear Aircraft Corporation

DATE: August 11, 1944

TO: Mr. George M. Johnson

FROM: Clarence M. Mitchell

SUBJECT: Goodyear Aircraft Corporation, 5-BR-350

The Regional Director [McKnight] believes that no further accomplishments can be made at his level. He requests that a hearing be held. The case is therefore referred to the Legal Division for appropriate action.[1]

Attachment—file

MS: LH, DI, HqR83, Correspondence Relating to Cases. (A–K) Goodyear Aircraft Corporation.

1. After referral, first to Ernest Trimble, then to Maceo Hubbard, this case, a complaint from the UAW regarding refusal to upgrade a black machinist, was presented to the Committee at its meetings of 9/7 and 9/9/44. At that time the Committee recommended that before resorting to a hearing, further efforts be made to resolve the case through negotiations with the company and with the UAW-CIO. A hearing on Goodyear Aircraft Corporation was held in Akron, Ohio, on 5/14/45. See the related correspondence filed with this text in HqR83; Transcript of Proceedings, 9/9/44, 19–21, HqR65, Central Files; hearings transcript and related texts in HqR22.

Memorandum on Retail Credit Company

August 14, 1944

MEMORANDUM

TO: George M. Johnson
       Deputy Chairman

FROM: Clarence M. Mitchell
       Associate Director of Field Operations

RE: Retail Credit Company
       2-BC-782
       3-BR-524
       3-BC-710

These cases involve the Retail Credit Company, a firm which does investigatory work for various business establishments.

In case 2-BC-782 it is charged that the company has a list of discriminatory questions on its employment application blanks. Among these are racial descent of parents and religious affiliation.

In case 3-BR-524 the company is charged with questioning the complainant regarding racial descent on an application for employment with the Radio Corporation of America.

The third case, 3-BC-710 is based on a letter from the American Jewish Congress which charges that the company advertised for investigators in a newspaper and requested that the nationality of the applicant be stated. In addition, it is alleged that the company's application for employment form contains the question "What is your religious affiliation"?

There is some question of whether the Retail Credit Company is within the jurisdiction of the Committee. Accordingly I am referring these cases to the legal division for a determination. You will note that on May 19 we had prepared memoranda which we intended to send to Atlanta for a check on the problems involved with the company's headquarters. However, we are holding these up pending a determination of jurisdiction.

MS: LH, DI, FR38, Region III. Closed Cases, Retail Credit Co. (second file).

Complaints against the Retail Credit Company date back to December 4, 1942, when John Beecher, FEPC regional representative, informed Cramer of a complaint he had received from Carl Weinberg, a Jewish applicant for a job at Grumman Aircraft Corporation. Weinberg said he and a Gentile man, both equally qualified as specialists in automobile electrical repair, had applied for similar positions. "The Gentile worker was hired on the spot," Beecher told Cramer, while the interviewer, employed by the Retail Credit Company, told Weinberg he had to do background checks on him. Weinberg said the investigator's first question to his wife was, "Is your husband Hebrew?" Beecher visited the company's office in Hempstead, Long Island, and discovered that it had a set national policy for dealing with "War Industries" applicants. He said its questionnaire noted "racial descent" (twice) and "racial predominance of neighborhood" and asked, "Is he an active church goer?" Beecher said he subsequently learned that not only Grumman, but also Brewster Aircraft and Fairchild Aviation used Retail Credit Company for their investigations. HqR66, Central Files. U.S. Government Agencies, Application Forms. Other documentation of the extent to which Retail Credit Company was a problem can be found in FR38, Region III. Closed Cases, Retail Credit Co. (second file). However, the Legal Division ruled and the Committee affirmed that the FEPC had no jurisdiction over private employment agencies and Retail Credit companies. See Johnson to Legal Division, memoranda, 10/27/44, HqR5, Records of the Legal Division, Office Files of George M. Johnson. Maceo Hubbard; 12/4/44, HqR38, Central Files. Memoranda—3. Legal Division. For additional background, see the headnotes on Jurisdictional Issues and on Race, Creed, Color, or National Origin on Employment Application Forms.

Memorandum on Delta Shipbuilding Company

Date: 8-14-44

To: George M. Johnson
               Deputy Chairman

From: Clarence M. Mitchell
               Associate Director of Field Operations

Subject: Delta Shipbuilding Company, 10-BR-128

Attached is a memorandum to the central office from Mr. Ellinger of Region X.[1] Since this case involves a Committee directive, I suggested that he prepare all available information to be submitted to the Committee at its next meeting. This matter is submitted to you for your information. I will appreciate the return of Mr. Ellinger's memorandum.

MS: LH, DI, HqR83, Correspondence Relating to Cases. (A–K) Delta Shipbuilding.

On the Delta Shipbuilding case, see 1/29, 2/28, 3/6, 3/27, 5/1, 5/5, 5/18, 11/1, 11/22/44, 1/8, 1/9, 1/12, 1/15/45; headnote on the Shipbuilding Industry.

1. In his memorandum of 8/2/44, Ellinger said it was not his intention to close the case until he had evidence of compliance regarding the upgrading and training of welders. He asked Mitchell whether, if that was accomplished, he should close the case. The following is a copy of Ellinger's 7/6/44 memorandum to the files:

Conference with L.R. Sanford, Major Walter K. Graham, James Davis, and R. B. Ackerman, July 6, 1944, at the office of the Maritime Commission.

Mr. Sanford opened the meeting by explaining that since the FEPC hearings in Birmingham in 1942, the Maritime Commission and Delta had been attempting to work out upgrading and hiring of Negro workers. Since Mr. Sanford's discussion with Clarence Mitchell and others of the national office, he has conferred with officials of the Delta company and has developed plans for the use of Negro painters and welders. Davis, Personnel Manager of the company, described these plans in detail. They had already upgraded 75 Negro painters to first-class craftsmen and were preparing to use from 300 to 400 Negro welders. This was a goal set up to be achieved as training is completed. An immediate group of 40 to 60 experienced welders who were available will be employed. A paid training program at the Catholic University has been instituted and recruitment from near-by cities is under way.

When asked if I approved these suggestions as compliance with the directives of the Committee, I stated that the Committee's directives spoke for themselves and that a report of this action by the company should be sent to the Committee in accordance with the directives. However, I pointed out that I felt it was definitely a step in the right direction and that the matter had been skillfully handled by the officers of the company.

The question of segregation was discussed at length. It is intended that the welders will be used on a segregated shift at the beginning. However, it was definitely understood that there was to be no inflexibility on this position and that it will be the goal, if practicable, to integrate Negro welders in the places of greatest usefulness. Major Graham explained the experience at Mobile and made many practical, useful, and positive suggestions.

The company has made arrangements to hire and pay its guards, starting the first of August, removing them completely from the jurisdiction of the state. The specific case of David Robinson was discussed briefly but was informally settled on the basis that Robinson has already been offered a welding trainee job under the new plan.

The atmosphere of this conference was very cooperative and direct. It was obviously the intention of the company to fulfill its obligations now. They emphasized that conditions had changed materially from the previous experiences that they had had, first, because of the increased shortage of workers and second, because of the greatly decreased racial tension in New Orleans.

The company agreed to report about 8/1 to the regional office on its experience in handling the upgrading of Negro welders. See HqR83, Correspondence Relating to Cases. (A–K) Delta Shipbuilding. (Filed along with the text is the Summary of the Hearings and Findings and Directives.)

Johnson's memorandum of 3/6/45 to Maslow showed that, in addition to the issues pertaining to the complaint in this case, there were important policy issues involved that further revealed how the FEPC functioned:

The questions raised [by Ellinger] as to whether under the circumstances of these cases the field staff should insist upon compliance with outstanding directives issued by the old Committee ultimately may have to be resolved by the [new] Committee itself, but it is believed that the Division of Field Operations and the Legal Division both should indicate what in their opinion the conclusions should be. The following questions seem to be relevant:

(1) What is the length of time that the unsatisfactory directives have been outstanding.
(2) What purpose originally was sought to be achieved by the particular directives. (Certain directives issued by the old Committee were designed to elicit statistical information, which is now available through other sources such as ES-270 reports.)
(3) What is the current employment picture at the plant in question as well as the present practices and policies of the party charged.
(4) What is the most appropriate procedure for disposing of the outstanding directives. (Should it be decided that any useful purpose would be served by insisting that the

outstanding directives be complied with, it may be appropriate to recommend to the Committee that the directives be dismissed upon a recommendation from the Regional Director where it appears that such Regional Director has conferred with representatives of the party charged and reached an agreement which will in effect amount to compliance with the formal directives.)

Johnson suggested that Maslow discuss the matter with members of his staff and that he would do the same with his. Then both would consider providing a recommendation to the Committee. HqR5, Office Files of George M. Johnson. A Bruce Hunt. For background, see the headnote on Shipbuilding Industry.

Memorandum on Mr. Lawson's Request on DFO Cases

August 18, 1944

MEMORANDUM

TO: Will Maslow
         Director of Field Operations

FROM: Clarence M. Mitchell
         Associate Director of Field Operations

RE: Mr. Lawson's request on DFO cases

I am in hearty agreement with Mr. Lawson that some action should be taken to expedite the handling of DFO cases. This action, however, is very simple and is linked with my oft-repeated suggestions on the distribution of work in the central office.

Under the arrangement previously set up we could give expeditious handling to such cases that might be referred to the Director of Field Operations. However, because of frequent instances in which examiners assigned to the handling of DFO cases have been taken off their duties my personal work load has increased and cases assigned to the examiners have not received necessary attention.

I recognize that part of this is due to the pressure of work in connection with the Smith Committee hearing and other matters with which Mr. Lawson is familiar. However, I believe that we must make a decision to keep our central staff examiners on the work assigned to them if we are to avoid being bogged down.

This question at the moment is somewhat academic since both Mr. Metzger and Mr. Bloch, who normally would be handling DFO cases with me, are no longer in

Field Operations, the former being with the OPA and the latter having assumed his new duties in the Legal Division. My suggestions are applied to the future.[1]

MS: LH, DI, HqR38, Central Files. (entry 25) Memoranda, Maslow, Will, 1944.
  1. On the division of labor among DFO staff, see 5/17/4.

Memorandum on WMC Clearance for Bell Aircraft in Atlanta, Georgia

August 19, 1944

MEMORANDUM

TO: Will Maslow
         Director of Field Operations

FROM: Clarence M. Mitchell
         Associate Director of Field Operations

RE: WMC clearance for Bell Aircraft in Atlanta

In keeping with your request I called Miss Bernice Lotwin, Assistant General Counsel, WMC, concerning the information we received from Mr. Bruce Hunt regarding clearance given to Bell Aircraft in Region VII.[1]

Miss Lotwin said that she sent a wire to Mr. Dillard Lasseter on this matter but had not received a reply. She suggested that we check with her again on Tuesday since Mr. Lasseter was away from the region at a conference of regional directors.

Since I will not be in the office on Tuesday I presume you will make a follow-up check with her.

cc: Hunt

MS: copy, HqR38, Central Files. (entry 25) Memoranda, Maslow, Will, 1944.
  1. The FEPC opposed the WMC's giving clearance for a company to recruit additional workers from other parts of the country if it was discriminating against locally available minority workers. See the section on the WMC and USES in the headnote on Relationships with Federal Agencies and the headnote on the Aircraft Industry.

Memorandum on FEPC Complaints Involving the International Association of Machinists

September 6, 1944

MEMORANDUM

TO: Mr. George M. Johnson
     Deputy Chairman

FROM: Clarence M. Mitchell
     Associate Director of Field Operations

SUBJECT: FEPC COMPLAINTS INVOLVING THE INTERNATIONAL ASSOCIATION
     OF MACHINISTS

In keeping with the suggestion made in your memorandum of July 8, 1944, I have reviewed the files of the central office on cases involving lodges of the International Association of Machinists. In addition, I have obtained material from Regional Directors indicating the nature of cases before them. The following is a presentation of the data, in accordance with the headings given in your memorandum of July 8:[1]

I. AREAS IN WHICH NEGROES ARE ADMITTED TO MEMBERSHIP WITHOUT DISCRIMINATION OR LIMITATION.

Mr. Edward Lawson, Director of Regions I and II (New York and Boston), has sent in the following report:

"Both in New York State and in New England, Negroes are accepted to membership in the International Association of Machinists without restriction or discrimination. In New York State there are approximately 100 to 150 members of the Machinists Union, and in upstate New York there are about 100 more. In New England there are several hundred, mostly concentrated in the Boston Navy Yard and the Watertown Arsenal. Most of the Negro members of this union in Regions I and II are not full-fledged machinists but are helpers or production workers. However, there is nothing to prevent them from advancing to higher categories of work.

"According to Mr. John Sullivan of the New York Regional Office of the IAM, Negroes are admitted to membership in the IAM here under the regular procedures of the union. He says that there is nothing in the constitution or in the ritual of the union which would exclude a Negro from membership.

"As you may know, the New York State law makes it a penal offense to bar a person from union membership because of his race, creed, color or national origin. The New England states do not have such laws, so far as I know; however, the question of admittance of Negroes to IAM membership has never come up in the New England area, although a large number of the plants there have IAM contracts."

Lodge 79 of Seattle, Washington, which holds a contract with the Seattle-Tacoma Shipbuilding Corporation, has some twenty (20) Negroes who are still active in the union and are entitled to the rights and privileges of full membership, according to Mr. Harry Kingman, Director of Region XII (San Francisco). These colored members were initiated following the 1940 convention of the Internation[al] Association of Machinists. At that time, the local lodge was under the impression that it had the right to initiate such Negro members. Since that time, active interference by the International union has prevented the admission of other Negroes.

The position of the International is set forth in a Request for Further Action Report, dated May 13, 1944, from Mr. Kingman. This report quotes Mr. Eric Peterson, General Vice-President of the International, as follows:

> "Our Organization as well as other International and National Labor Unions takes the position that the Fair Employment Practice Committee is without authority to compel Labor Unions to accept for members persons not eligible according to the Organizations' laws. As long as Lodge No. 79 does not interfere with the employment of Negroes there can be no justification for complaint on the part of the individuals who have been denied membership because of the policy and laws of our organization."

II. AREAS IN WHICH NEGROES ARE PERMITTED TO WORK ONLY UPON PAYMENT OF A PERMIT FEE.

Lodge 79, which has been previously mentioned, is an appropriate illustration of this procedure. Under the present arrangement, Negroes are permitted to work by paying a fee of $1.25. This is paid on a monthly basis. Mr. Kingman states in his Request for Further Action Report of May 13, 1944, that Lodge 79 allows Negroes to be upgraded without discrimination and, apparently, handles grievances for them. A supplementary memorandum from Mr. Kingman, dated July 27, 1944, states that Mr. Harold Johnson, Assistant Business Agent of Lodge 79, gave him the following information on fees charged Negroes and whites: "Helpers (both Negro permit men and bonafide members of the union), $1.25 per month dues. Negro permit men, however, do not pay an initiation fee. Journeymen (both Negro permit men and bonafide Members of the union), pay $2.00 per month. Negro Journeymen also do not pay an initiation fee."

In case 12-UR-285, which involves the IAM Aeronautical Mechanics Lodge 751 of Seattle, Washington, Negroes are cleared for work although they are not permitted to full membership. Mr. Kingman gives the following statement on this Lodge:

> "Mr. Sullivan, one of the Business Agents for Local 751, stated that his union has two basic categories of dues for its members. These categories are Production Workers, (who are the equivalent of helpers), and Journeymen. The helpers, whether they are Negro permit men or bonafide members, pay $1.50 per month. Journeymen, whether they are bonafide members of the union or permit men, pay $1.75 per month. Negro permit men are not required to pay initiation fees."

According to Mr. Kingman, the representatives of Lodge 79 and Lodge 751 state that the dues paid by Negro permit men and the bonafide members of the union are "ear marked" for such purposes as per capita payment to the International Association of Machinists, Insurance fund, the Central Labor Council, Washington Machinists Council, and the State Federation of Labor. Negro members are not allowed to participate in nor do they directly receive benefits from any of these. Mr. Johnson of Lodge 79 stated that he would discuss this matter with Mr. Sanvigen, Business Agent, because he "felt that the matter ought to be straightened out," and that Negroes should not be forced to pay dues "for purposes which are of no benefit to them."

III. AREAS IN WHICH NEGROES ARE BARRED FROM EMPLOYMENT ALTOGETHER IN SKILLS UNDER THE JURISDICTION OF THE IAM.

We have before us case 12-UR-174 against the Machinists' Lodge 824 of Richmond, California. Mr. Frank Pestana, an examiner on the staff of Region XII, points out that this Lodge refuses to clear Negroes for work at all. Also, we have a teletype from Region XII, dated July 12, 1944, which states that the Lodge has received a communication from Mr. Harvey Brown, President of the IAM, regarding its discriminatory policy. In spite of Mr. Brown's communication, the Lodge intends to continue its discriminatory practice, according to the regional office of FEPC. The action of this Lodge prevents Negroes from obtaining employment in machinist trades at the following companies: Richmond Shipyards, Rheon Manufacturing Company, American Radiator and Standard Sanitary Company, and the Pacific Enamel Works.

The Philadelphia office (Region III) reports the following complaint, 3-UR-685, which involves Lodge 243 of the Machinists at the A. B. Farquhar Company, York, Pennsylvania. The complaint alleges that Negro employees of the company are refused membership by the union and, further, that said employees are denied upgrading by the company because of "pressure by the union." Where Negro employees have applied for membership and attempted to pay joining fees, these fees were returned by Lodge 243, according to the regional office. These cases are still being investigated by the regional office.

The Washington office (Region IV) calls attention to case 4-UR-285, which is a complaint involving the Wright Automatic Tobacco Packing Machinery Company at Durham, North Carolina. The case dates back to March, 1942, when the company, in an answer to a letter from Mr. Sidney Hillman of the War Production Board, stated that it had a non-discriminatory policy with regard to hiring. On April 21, 1942, the company stated that it has a contract with Lodge 721 of the IAM, and that, under the interpretation of the contract, Negro workers cannot be employed on production work. The text of the union's communication, dated April 20, 1942, is as follows:

> "In reply to your question of this date, Lodge 721 of the International Association of Machinists admits to its membership only competent, white candidates. It would, therefore, be impossible for your company to employ in the mechanical depart-

ments persons of other race than white under the terms of the contract you hold with Lodge 721.

"We trust that the above statement will define our position on this question."

The letter is signed by Mr. E. W. Donahue, President of Lodge 721, and Mr. J. A. Cardne, Recording Secretary. On November 28, 1943, Mr. Frank Hook, who at that time was Regional Director, and Mr. Joseph H. B. Evans, the present Regional Director, conferred with Mr. Harvey Brown, President of the IAM, on this case. Files in Mr. Brown's office showed that the local union was asked to withdraw the letter it had written to the company. However, Mr. Brown was unable to produce a reply to the letter sent to the local lodge by the International.

The Dallas office (Region X) reports that Negroes are specifically barred from membership in all railroad lodges of the IAM. A separate Federal charter is provided for Negro employees at the Consolidated Aircraft Company in Fort Worth, Texas. The IAM represents employees at this plant. The Region is currently processing case 10-UR-333, which involves the lodge representing workers of the Texas and Pacific Railroad. The Regional Director states that the issue involves the attempt of the local chairman of the IAM to prevent Negro machinists from performing certain operations on the railroad. The International Representative of the IAM, a Mr. Mulholland, agreed that this action of the lodge was wrong and stated that the local leaders would not interfere with full utilization of Negro workers. It was also agreed in a conference called by FEPC that Negro workers would be allowed to use the union's bargaining machinery through a separate Negro committee. In the current case, the Texas and Pacific colored employees charge that the agreement reached with Mr. Mulholland is not being adhered to.

IV. THE POSITION OF OFFICIALS OF THE IAM WITH RESPECT TO THE PROBLEM BEFORE US.

The best positions are those of the New England and New York lodges, as set forth by our regional office and mentioned under I. It appears that the sole reason why Negroes are not admitted to Lodge 79 is due to the intervention of the International union. As far back as September 14, 1942, we have a letter from Mr. I. A. Sandvigen, Business Representative of the Lodge, indicating that Negroes are acceptable for full membership.

Lodge 761 feels that any effort to change the ritual so that Negroes may be admitted to membership may result in a split of the IAM.

The attitude of the Lodge in Richmond, California (824) is clearly defiant and non-cooperative. Apparently, the Lodge considers its position buttressed by the action of the International in that the file on case 12-UR-174 contains a letter from Mr. Albert B. Nelson, Business Representative of the Lodge, in which Mr. Nelson states that the January, 1944, issue of the Machinists' Monthly Journal contains a statement of the policy of the International Organization. Among other things, this statement indicates that the Machinists will not comply with the directives issued by the Committee in the railroad cases.

V. NATURE OF COMPLAINTS WHICH THE COMMITTEE HAS RECEIVED.

There are twenty-six (26) active cases against the IAM. These cases include charges against lodges of the IAM in the railway industry, as well as complaints involving ship-building and aircraft companies. Some are complaints by individuals, others by groups of persons, and some are reports of discrimination received from USES offices. Railway complaints charging failure to upgrade because of IAM are:

3-UR-636	6-UR-519
3-UR-637	10-UR-333
4-UR-11	11-UR-32
4-UR-12	11-UR-33
4-UR-14	11-UR-42
6-UR-254	11-UR-45

Other complaints charging failure to hire, upgrade, or admit to membership are:

3-UR-685	12-UR-263
3-UR-686	12-UR-265
4-UR-285	12-UR-361
12-UR-1127	12-BR-275
12-UR-1032	12-UR-174
12-BR-343	12-BR-317
12-BR-321	

Complaints charging IAM with attempting to organize a Negro auxiliary:

9-BR-152

Since the preparation of this memorandum, it has become apparent that we must negotiate with the Machinists' Lodge 698 in Detroit, Michigan, if we are to obtain correction of discriminatory practices in the hiring of mechanics for the trucking industry. At present, we do not have a docketed case against this Lodge, but the Detroit office states that officials of the War Manpower Commission have been informed by the union that it will not permit the employment of Negroes as mechanics for the maintenance of trucking equipment. Our office in Detroit has a number of cases in which Negro applicants for mechanical jobs have been turned down. However, Mr. Edward Swan, the Examiner-in-Charge, states that none of these cases shows that the applicants have been told that they cannot be hired because of the policies of the machinists' union. The Examiner-in-Charge and Mr. William T. McKnight, Director of Region V (Cleveland), plan a conference with officials of Lodge 698 to obtain a statement on the Lodge's position.[2]

MS: copy, HqR1, Documents File. M.

1. Johnson instructed Mitchell to prepare this background for Boris Shishkin and Charles Hamilton Houston, whom the Committee had appointed to meet with the international president of the IAM. See 1/15/45 for subsequent activities.

2. Mitchell summarized these findings before the FEPC meeting of 9/7/44. See Transcript of Proceedings, 9/7/44, 56–65, HqR65, Central Files; 9/18/44 report. For the context, see the section on the International Association of Machinists in the headnote on the FEPC and Unions.

Memorandum on Complaints against the Post Office Department

DATE: Sept. 7, 1944

TO: Mr. George M. Johnson
               Deputy Chairman

FROM: Clarence M. Mitchell
               Associate Director of Field Operations

SUBJECT: COMPLAINTS AGAINST THE POST OFFICE DEPARTMENT

The regional offices of FEPC have referred to Washington a total of seventy-one (71) complaints against five major post offices. Efforts to adjust these through negotiations at the local level have been unsuccessful. The Post Offices involved are located in Houston and Dallas, Texas; Los Angeles, California; Seattle, Washington; and Philadelphia, Pennsylvania.

On April 27, 1944, Mr. Will Maslow, Director of Field Operations, and Mr. Stanley Metzger, Fair Practice Examiner assigned by me to handle post offices cases, conferred with Mr. K. P. Aldrich, First Assistant Postmaster General; Mr. Vincent M. Miles, Solicitor; and three other Post Office officials. The purpose of the conference was to discuss the Seattle and Los Angeles cases. The postal officials stated that the problem in Seattle had been adjusted. This case was one in which the Postmaster was charged with keeping a separate file of Negro and white applicants. However, with the exception of Mr. Miles, who was described by Mr. Metzger as the only official present who seemed "aware" of the Committee's role, the officials of the Post Office were not cooperative. In a memorandum on the conference, dated April 29, 1944, Mr. Metzger stated:

> "There was marked hostility on the part of Post Office officials toward any 'interference' by FEPC on their postal policies. It was suggested by one of the officials present that a great many of the complaints filed with FEPC were simply the work of communists."

A summary of the complaints follows:

1. <u>Dallas, Texas.</u>

   There are ten (10) complaints in this case charging that Negroes are not hired as clerks, that Negro laborers are refused promotions, and that Negroes are not hired as guards. The regional office of FEPC reports that there are thirty-five (35) Negroes employed as mail handlers and, also, an unspecified number of Negro custodial workers.

2. <u>Houston, Texas.</u>

   FEPC has eleven (11) complaints against this post office charging refusal to hire or upgrade Negroes above the job of carrier and denial of transfer privileges accorded to white workers. The regional office of FEPC reports that there are 200 Negroes employed as carriers.

3. Philadelphia, Pennsylvania.

The most important case before us concerns the Philadelphia Post Office. There are forty-six (46) complaints alleging that Negroes are excluded from certain departments, that they are not properly upgraded, and that they are not given supervisory jobs. The Postmaster has broken off negotiations with FEPC on the ground the Post Office is not within the Committee's jurisdiction. Of the 5,000 persons employed in the Philadelphia Post Office, 20% are non-white.

4. Los Angeles, California.

The complaints in Los Angeles charge that Negroes are not properly upgraded. The Committee has received wires, dated September 1, 3, and 5, urging that a hearing be held on the cases. We do not have the file in the Washington office as yet, so we are unable to give the number of Negroes employed.

5. Seattle, Washington.

Although the Post Office states that the practice of keeping separate lists of Negro and white applicants has been discontinued in Seattle, FEPC is unable to obtain any statistics on the number of Negroes employed and the jobs they hold.

In view of the reception accorded Messrs. Maslow and Metzger, it does not appear that much can be accomplished unless there is a conference with the Postmaster General. It is recommended that a sub-committee of FEPC visit the Postmaster General with appropriate staff members to obtain the following:

1. Consideration and correction of the individual complaints, as well as the policies which cause the problem.

2. Instructions to local Postmasters that they must cooperate with FEPC in the settlement of valid complaints.

3. Establishment of a working procedure in Washington for the handling of complaints which are not resolved at the local level.

MS: LH, DI, HqR3, Office Files of George M. Johnson. M.

Mitchell presented a summary of this report during the FEPC meeting of this date and recommended a meeting with the postmaster general. At that meeting the Committee authorized Ross, Mitchell, and such other persons as the chairman designated to meet with the postmaster and seek a conference with the attorney general in order to get a supportive ruling from him on FEPC jurisdiction over post offices. See Transcript of Proceedings, 9/7/44, 45–51, HqR65, Central Files. For the outcome, see the section on the Post Office Department in the headnote on Relationships with Other Agencies.

Memorandum on General Baking Company and Ward Baking Company Cases

Sept. 16, 1944

Mr. Will Maslow

Clarence M. Mitchell

General Baking Company, 3-BR-538; Ward Baking Company, 3-BR-539 and 3-BR-403

Attached are the files on the General Baking Company and the Ward Baking Company, together with a memorandum for your signature to Mr. Johnson.[1]

In the interest of saving time, I believe that it would be desirable for you to make transmittals to the Legal Division directly yourself, since they are to be prepared for your signature. I make this suggestion because it is not practical to revise such memoranda of transmittal as some times you indicate should be done.

Attachments (Files)

MS: copy, HqR38, Central Files. (entry 25) Memoranda, Maslow, Will, 1944.

    1. Attachments not found. For the background, see the headnote on Jurisdictional Issues.

Weekly Report

Sept. 18, 1944

Mr. Will Maslow

Clarence M. Mitchell

Weekly Report for Week Ending Saturday, September 16, 1944

Because of the volume of work in the central office during the period in which the Committee was up for an appropriation in Congress and because of subsequent staff changes, I have been unable to prepare a weekly report since May, 1944. However, the activities during that period are documented by various reports and memoranda, which are available for inspection. A recent redistribution of work in the central office offers something of an opportunity to resume operations on a basis approximating normalcy. Hence, the weekly reports are resumed.[1]

OUTSTANDING EVENTS AND PROBLEMS

The following important cases are being handled by me personally and involve problems of long standing:

1. U.S. Post Office cases in Houston, Dallas, Los Angeles, Seattle, and Philadelphia. A draft of a letter has been prepared for the Chairman's signature asking for a conference with the Postmaster General,[2] as the Committee agreed in its meeting on September 7.*

2. We are handling complaints against the International Association of Machinists from Regions III, IV, IX, X, and XII. In its meeting on September 9, the Committee received a summary of these cases, prepared by me, and a subcommittee is to meet with Mr. Harvey Brown, President of the IAM, on them.[3]

3. In keeping with our agreement with the War Department on cases involving Government-owned and privately-operated plants, I have submitted complaints against the Consolidated Vultee Corporation, Fort Worth, Texas, to the War Department for action. The Region has recommended that a hearing be held in this case.[4]

5. The failure of the General Motors Corporation to submit statistics on non-white employment is unresolved. It does not appear that anything short of Committee action will dispose of this problem.[5]

In addition to the cases mentioned above, I am now handling seventeen (17) other DFO cases.

The following Final Disposition Reports have been reviewed by me:

> Region IX—29
> Region XI—3
> Region XII—9

We have returned to the regional offices the following DFO cases:

1. Retail Credit Company, 2-BR-782.
2. Retail Credit Company, 3-BR-710 and 3-BR-524.
3. Knickerbocker Canvas Company. (II)
4. Columbia Broadcasting Company, 12-BR-1329.
5. Graham Construction Company, 4-BR-297.
6. Southern Pacific Lines, 10-BR-281.

cc: Davidson
     Johnson
     Jones

MS: copy, FEPC RG 228, Office Files of Clarence Mitchell, DNA.

1. For the appropriations committee hearing in March and the FEPC's preparation for it, see report, 3/27/44; for the subsequent debates over FEPC appropriations in 5/44, see Maslow, summary,

*Drafted letter being held up pending ruling from Attorney General.

5/27/44, in appendix 1. On the staff diversions and changes affecting Mitchell's work, see, for example, texts of 3/14, 3/18, 4/3, 7/3, 7/28/44.

In a memorandum of 1/31/45, Eugene Davidson noted that on 9/12/44 Mitchell transferred all active DFO cases in Regions I, II, III, IV, V, IX, and XI to him, with the exception of a few cases on which Mitchell had started action and wished to complete. As of 1/3/45 all new DFO cases from regions IX and XI were again handled by Mitchell. See HqR76, Office Files of Clarence Mitchell. Will Maslow.

2. For the conference with the postmaster general, see report, 11/27/44. For the background, see the section on the Post Office Department in the headnote on Relationships with Federal Agencies.

3. See Mitchell, memorandum, 9/6/44.

4. No hearing was held. See the headnote on the Aircraft Industry.

5. On race-related employment statistics, see the headnote on Race, Creed, Color, or National Origin on Employment Application Forms.

Memorandum on General Motors' Policy on Supplying Employment Statistics

DATE: Sept. 18, 1944

TO: Mr. George M. Johnson

FROM: Clarence M. Mitchell

SUBJECT: General Motors' Policy on Supplying Employment Statistics

You will note from the attached memoranda and correspondence from Region IX that the problem of obtaining information on non-whites employed by the General Motors Company is still unresolved. We have made several efforts to get this information, with the help of the War Manpower Commission. These efforts have been unsuccessful.

I shall appreciate it if you will indicate whether this matter should be prepared for presentation to the Committee in order that we may make an appropriate disposition of this and other cases.

It is possible that you may have a suggestion for disposing of it immediately. If so, I should also like to discuss that.

Attachments

MS: LH, DI, HqR1, Committee Meetings.

The following texts were filed with this text: Hoglund's Request for Further Action on the Chevrolet-Division of General Motors, 1/10/44; his letter to Chevrolet, 12/30/43; the reply, 1/4/44; Hoglund's response, 1/5/44; the firm's reiteration of its previous stance, 1/8/44. Johnson referred the file to Maceo Hubbard on 9/19/44. For the contents of these letters and the overall background, see the headnote on Race, Creed, Color, or National Origin on Employment Application Forms.

Memorandum on Visit of Los Angeles Complainant in Post Office Cases

DATE: Sept. 23, 1944

TO: Mr. George M. Johnson

FROM: Clarence M. Mitchell

SUBJECT: Visit of Los Angeles Complainant in Post Office Cases

On Wednesday, September 13, 1944, Miss Sylvia Smith of Los Angeles, California, came into the office to discuss complaints which have been filed against the Post Office by various employees in Los Angeles. Miss Smith stated that she was in Washington for the purpose of getting assistance in the adjustment of the cases from all possible sources. She discussed, briefly, the problem in Los Angeles, and I told her of the Committee's plans for a visit with the Postmaster General on the cases.

Among other things, Miss Smith mentioned that Station K, which is in the Negro section of Los Angeles, has a colored superintendent and assistant superintendent. However, this is an exception to the general rule in that Negroes are not promoted in keeping with their ability in other sections of the city, she stated. The Terminal Annex, which employs about sixty per cent Negroes, does not have any Negro supervisors and, even during the Christmas holidays, Negroes are not appointed as Christmas foremen, she said. She mentioned the names of a Mr. Bowdon and a Mr. Skanks, who have been eligible for promotions for some time on the basis of seniority. However, while these men are victims of the policy which prevents promotion of Negroes, according to Miss Smith, they are not currently interested in being promoted, because the former has a business which prevents him from accepting a promotion and the latter is about to retire.

There is a tendency to concentrate Negroes in the handstamp section, according to Miss Smith, and the flat alley, where newspapers and magazines are handled.

In one of the letters received from the Los Angeles complainants, it is mentioned that a Mr. Oliver has recently been appointed in a supervisory position. Miss Smith stated that this appointment is a probationary post and was made since the complainants have been trying to get their problems adjusted. Mr. Oliver supervises very few men, according to Miss Smith, whereas white employees are assigned large numbers of individuals to supervise, especially in the Terminal Annex. According to Miss Smith, Mr. Oliver received a small raise amounting to about $100 in connection with the probationary appointment, whereas the normal raise for supervisory positions would be around $300.

During the discussion, Mr. Arnold, of the Postal Alliance, who was with Miss Smith, mentioned that Negro clerks have been appointed in Dallas, Texas. However, upon checking with our regional office, I have learned that the Negroes were appointed as mail handlers and not as clerks.

MS: LH, DI, FEPC RG 228, Office Files of Clarence Mitchell, DNA.
See 5/1/44, note 5; the section on the Post Office Department in the headnote on Relationships with Federal Agencies.

Memorandum on Additional Personnel in Regional Offices

Sept. 23, 1944

Mr. Will Maslow

Clarence M. Mitchell

Additional Personnel in Regional Offices

If the pendency figures currently before us reflect a true picture of the regional offices, it appears that Cleveland, Philadelphia, Detroit, and Atlanta have the greatest need for some additional help in the handling of the back log of cases.

Accordingly, I am suggesting that, when we receive additional help, the first field visits should be made to those offices for the purpose of clearing up cases pending for more than six months.

My only reason for being hesitant to accept the pendency figures as an absolute reflection of the case load is based on a conversation I had with Mr. Davidson. He feels that, in some instances, cases pending are fewer than the figures show. Mr. Lawson, of Region II, who was present at the time, had a similar feeling concerning his own region.

cc: Mr. Davidson
       Mr. Johnson

MS: copy, FEPC RG 228, Office Files of Clarence Mitchell, DNA.

Weekly Report

Sept. 25, 1944

Mr. Will Maslow

Clarence M. Mitchell

Weekly Report for Week Ending Saturday, September 23, 1944

OUTSTANDING EVENTS AND PROBLEMS

The War Manpower Commission conference this week with Messrs. McGee and Werts represents one of the outstanding problems of Regions VII and X. I have submitted my observations on this conference in a separate memorandum, which, I hope, will be followed up by appropriate Committee action.[1]

Following failure of the Justice Department to take action in the complaint involving the St. John's River Shipbuilding Company, Jacksonville, Florida, this case has been submitted to Admiral Russell R. Waesche, of the Coast Guard, since a member of that body was involved.

The Chairman has signed a communication prepared by me requesting a conference with the Postmaster General [Frank C. Walker]. We are now awaiting the Postmaster General's reply.

During visits to the West Coast in 1942 and 1943, I accumulated certain data on the City of Portland, Oregon, which, I believe, we should consider in any conferences we have on the problems of that city.[2]

A request for information on payment of back wages for Government employees improperly dismissed and subsequently reinstated was submitted to the Civil Service Commission as a result of a suggestion from Region XII. The Commission has sent us a reply stating that back wages will not be paid to employees improperly dismissed, and this information has been sent to the regional office.

I wish to remind you of my memorandum on the use of field personnel, in view of pendency data submitted by the Division of Review and Analysis.[3]

ASSIGNMENTS

The following DFO cases have been returned to regional offices:

1. Goodyear Aircraft Company, 5-BR-350.
2. Union Pacific Railway Lines, 9-BR-336.
3. Metcalfe-Hamilton Construction Company, (2-BR-544)
   (2-BR-483)
   (12-BR-202)
4. General Electronics, Inc., 2-GR-709 et al.

The following new DFO cases are being handled by me:

1. Brotherhood of Railroad Trainmen, 6-UR-338.
2. Illinois Central Railroad & Brotherhood of Maintenance of Way Employees, AFL, 6-BR-601 & 6-UR-586.
3. U. S. Army Air Forces Depot, 5-GR-362.

The following Final Disposition Reports have been reviewed by me:

Region XII—10

DFO cases presently being handled by me total 19.

cc: Davidson
     Davis
     Johnson
     Jones

MS: copy, FEPC RG 228, Office Files of Clarence Mitchell, DNA.

1. Memorandum not found.

2. On Mitchell's visits to Portland in August 1942 and in October 1943, see his memoranda of 10/10/42, note 1, and 10/18 through 10/23/43.

3. See memorandum of 8/23/44.

Memorandum on Phelps-Dodge Relationship with WMC

Sept. 27, 1944

Mr. Will Maslow

Clarence M. Mitchell

Phelps-Dodge Relationships with WMC

I note in the attached correspondence that Mr. Bond, in a letter dated August 30, described the WMC relationship with the Phelps-Dodge Company as "exceptionally harmonious up to the time of this incident."[1]

It occurs to me that this is another indication of WMC's failure to appreciate its responsibility in the South. I do not see how they could be having an "exceptionally harmonious" relationship with the company, which appears to be consistently violating the Executive Order if the War Manpower Commission considers Executive Order 9346 as operative.

Attachment (File)

MS: copy, HqR67, Central Files. Reports, U.S. Government, War Manpower Commission.

1. On Phelps-Dodge's antiunionism and egregious discriminatory policies and practices, see Almaráz, Knight without Armor, 243–45, 247; and Daniel, Chicano Workers, 81–83, 88–105.

Memorandum on Matters to Be Discussed with Regional Director McKnight

Sept. 28, 1944

Mr. Will Maslow
Clarence M. Mitchell
Matters to be Discussed with Regional Director Mc Knight

During my stay in Columbus, I shall discuss the following matters with Regional Director McKnight[1] at your request:

1. The status of his plans for naming consultants in his region.
2. Whether he believes a sub-office should be established in Cincinnati.
3. The status of the problems involving the Detroit trucking industry.[2]
4. Travel problems due to shortage of funds.
5. The possibility of obtaining from WMC a statement on discriminatory hiring patterns similar to that recently announced by Region II of WMC.
6. Prospects of State legislation providing for a Michigan FEPC.
7. Personnel matters—including Examiners, Abbott, Weitz, Clore, and Swan.
8. Status of case load.
9. Cutback problems in the region.
10. Present relationship with WMC.

MS: copy, HqR38, Central Files. Memoranda, Maslow, Will, 1944

1. For an overview of FEPC actions in Region V, in which McKnight was regional director and Edward Swan examiner in charge of the Detroit suboffice, see Kersten, *Race, Jobs, and the War,* 75–111.

2. On the problems of the Detroit trucking industry, see the section on the Teamsters in the headnote on the FEPC and Unions and the sources cited there.

Memorandum on Industries with Postwar Significance

October 7, 1944

TO: Mr. Malcolm Ross
FROM: Clarence M. Mitchell
SUBJECT: Industries with Post-War Significance

Following our conversation on Thursday, October 5, Mr. Davidson and I made a check on the docketed cases in the regions for which we have immediate responsibility. The following is an analysis based on the industrial categories which the Division of Review and Analysis indicates will have post-war employment possibilities.[1] This list, of course, should be checked with each region, and we shall do so immediately.

We have omitted firms engaged in aircraft production, unless the companies were making some other product before the war. Also, we have omitted shipbuilding in all of the regions. Firms engaged in the manufacture of small arms and ammunition have also been left out. It is possible that the regions may suggest that we include certain of these firms when they receive this material. The regions which I have reviewed and my knowledge of the cases concerned show that the most important concentration of work should be in transportation and public utilities, oil and non-ferrous metals, mining and smelting.

REGION VI

BASIC METALS AND RUBBER

The region has 19 active cases in this category. These include such industries as the American Bridge Works at Gary, Indiana; and the Tubular Alloy Steel Company, Gary, Indiana; and the Carnegie-Illinois Steel Company.

COMMUNICATIONS EQUIPMENT

The region has four cases in this category involving such firms as the Western Electric Company and the Hammond Instrument Company.

FOOD AND TOBACCO

There are eight cases in Region VI charging firms in this category with discriminatory practices. Among the firms are the Wilson Company and the Quaker Oats Company.

METALLIC NON-MUNITIONS

As I understand the description of this category, as given by the Division of Review and Analysis, it includes industries which may be currently engaged in war production but which, following the war, will return to the production of such things as automobiles, ice boxes, agricultural equipment, etc. In this group, Region VI has 15 cases. These include the General Motors Corporation's Buick Division at Melrose Park, Illinois, the Dodge Chicago Plant, and the Caterpillar Tractor Company.

PAPER AND PRINTING

There is one case in Region VI involving the Cuneo Press.

TEXTILE, APPAREL AND LEATHER

The region has two cases against firms engaged in the manufacture of garments and one against the Freeman Shoe Company.

TRANSPORTATION AND PUBLIC UTILITIES

There is a heavy concentration of important cases in this category. Forty of these cases involve railroads, such as the New York Central, Pennsylvania, Chicago and Northwestern, and the B & O Chicago Terminal. The region also has one complaint against the Sangamo Electric Plant at Springfield, Illinois; five against the Bell Telephone Company; five involving the trucking industry; and one against the Gary, Indiana Street railway. This makes a total of fifty-two cases in this group.

OTHER MANUFACTURING

There are three cases in this group against the Johnson and Johnson Company, the A. B. Dick Company, and a chemical manufacturing company.

The total case load for the region as of _____ is _____. These cases are _____ per cent of the total.[2]

REGION VII

BASIC METALS AND RUBBER

The region has eleven cases against the Firestone Tire and Rubber Company, currently engaged in aircraft production. It also has two iron and steel cases.

PAPER AND PRINTING

The region has two cases against the Brunswick Pulp and Paper Corporation of Brunswick, Georgia.

TRANSPORTATION AND PUBLIC UTILITIES

The bulk of the regions cases in this group (128) are against railway companies. There are also six cases against trucking firms.

OTHER MANUFACTURING

There are nineteen cases against the Swift Manufacturing Company; seventeen against the Buckeye Cotton Oil Company; and two cases against the Tri-State Compress Company. These cases principally involve failure to upgrade and wage discrimination.

REGION VIII

FOOD AND TOBACCO

There are three cases against firms engaged in food processing.

METALLIC NON-MUNITIONS

Two of the regions most difficult cases are against the Northern Pump Company of Minneapolis. Although this firm is engaged in war production at present, it has important peace-time implications.

TRANSPORTATION AND PUBLIC UTILITIES

There are three railroad cases in this region.

OTHER MANUFACTURING

There is one case against a chemical company in Region VIII.

REGION X

BASIC METALS AND RUBBER

The region has one case against the Firestone Company at New Orleans and two iron and steel cases.

NON-FERROUS METALS, MINING, AND SMELTING

There are forty-five cases against mining and smelting companies in the region.

TRANSPORTATION AND PUBLIC UTILITIES

There is a telephone case in this region against the Southern Bell Company and one against the Western Union Company.[3] There are also eight railroad cases.

OTHER MANUFACTURING

There are seven cases against oil refineries and one case against the Murray Gin Company.

REGION XII

Los Angeles

BASIC METALS AND RUBBER

There are two cases in this category—one involving a rubber company and the other iron and steel.

METALLIC NON-MUNITIONS

The Los Angeles office has three cases in this group.

NON-FERROUS METALS, MINING, AND SMELTING

In this group, there are fifty-five cases, principally in Arizona.

TEXTILE, APPAREL, AND LEATHER

The office has two complaints against garment industries.

TRANSPORTATION AND PUBLIC UTILITIES

There are two pending cases against the Southern California Telephone Company, five steam railway cases, two electric transportation cases (Pacific Electric Company), two cases against trucking firms, and one case against the Grey Hound Bus Lines.

OTHER MANUFACTURING

There are two cases against oil refineries, two cases against chemical firms, one against a paint manufacturing firm, and one against a firm making medical supplies.

San Francisco

BASIC METALS AND RUBBER

The region has one case in this group.

FOOD AND TOBACCO

In this category, there is one case involving a food concern.

METALLIC NON-MUNITIONS

The region has six cases against firms manufacturing machinery and heating equipment.

PAPER AND PRINTING

There is one case listed in this category.

TEXTILES, APPAREL, AND LEATHER

There is one case in this group against a garment firm.

TRANSPORTATION AND PUBLIC UTILITIES

There are four steam railway cases, one case against a bus company, and one case against a trucking company. There are four cases against the Pacific Telephone and Telegraph Company.

OTHER MANUFACTURING

It is important to note that, in this region, there are two pending cases involving the steamfitters union.

In analyzing these cases, we have been aware that adjustments in some of the industries mentioned, particularly the railroads, may not be accomplished in any comparatively short time. It should be pointed out, however, that, apart from the basic problem involved in the railway cases now before the Stacy Committee,[4] it has been possible to adjust some railroad complaints received. It is also believed that, by concentration, we may expect to adjust cases against public utilities, such as the telephone company.

MS: draft, FEPC RG 228 (entry 40, PI-147), Office Files of Clarence M. Mitchell, Clarence M. Mitchell, DNA.

1. See also Davidson to Ross, 10/9/44, "Industries with Post-war Significance," report for Regions I–V, IX, and XI supplementing Mitchell's report. Davidson's memorandum is provided as an attachment to Mitchell's 10/10/44 memorandum to George Johnson. Davidson explained that he had omitted the railroad cases. HqR76, Office Files of Will Maslow. Malcolm Ross.

At its 10/11/44 meeting the FEPC agreed that the staff, in processing cases, should give priority to the most important cases. HqR1, Summary Minutes of Meetings. It was agreed that as a general rule, the priority should be as follows: first, industries which have the greatest postwar significance and in which minority group members are not now employed in large numbers; second, industries with post-war significance in which minority groups have found considerable employment opportunities; third, war production industries with little post-war significance. It was emphasized that this priority arrangement should be used only as a guide, and that suggestions should be solicited from the region.

2. Spaces left blank in manuscript.

3. The Southern Bell complaints involved women who, responding to ads in the Louisville Courier-Journal, applied for training or jobs as operators and were told by the company's personnel that it was not employing or training African Americans. See Reeves to Johnson, memorandum, 8/12/44; McKnight, memorandum, 5/20/44, both in HqR5, Office Files of George M. Johnson. Frank Reeves. See also 11/27, note 2; 12/2/44, note 2. For context, see the headnote on the Telephone Industry.

4. On the Stacy Committee and the railway cases, see the headnote on the FEPC and Unions.

Weekly Report

Oct. 9, 1944

Mr. Will Maslow

Clarence M. Mitchell

Weekly Report for Weeks Ending September 30 and October 7, 1944

OUTSTANDING EVENTS AND PROBLEMS

At the request of the Chairman, I have been at work on a statement concerning the industrial areas in which work by the Committee's field staff is likely to have post-war significance. This problem is to be the subject of further staff conferences.[1]

We have returned to Region II the file on the General Electronics Company, 2-BR-709 et. al. Since we returned the file, the War Department has given us a list of the complainants who were reinstated following a military investigation.

In this connection, it should be mentioned that the War Department is causing increasing impatience in the regional offices by delaying its reports to us. Recently, I have been allowed to see some of the reports of investigations made by War Department representatives. These reports are not encouraging, and I feel that we are now at the place where we must ask the Department to change our working agreement so that FEPC investigations of Government-owned, Government-operated plants may be made in full at the regional level.[2]

The Railroad Retirement Board advises that it is giving attention to our request for action on complaints in Regions II and IV.

A letter from the Coast Guard indicates that an investigation will be made of the complaint against the St. John's River Shipbuilding Company in Jacksonville, Florida. The Coast Guard contends, however, that one of the main persons accused was not on the Government pay roll as of the date on which the incident occurred.

ASSIGNMENTS

The following DFO cases have been returned to regional offices:

1. Second Army Air Forces, 5-GR-91.
2. Selective Service Board 73, 12-GR-1.
3. Baltimore and Ohio Roundhouse, 6-BR-613.
4. Army Air Forces, 5-GR-[illegible]62.

The following Final Disposition Reports have been reviewed by me:

Region VI—51
Region VIII—1
Region VII—31
Region X—20
Region III—36

DFO cases presently being handled by me total 16.

cc: Davidson
      Davis
      Johnson
      Jones

MS: copy, HqR3, Office Files of George M. Johnson. (A–M), Mitchell.

1 See 10/7/44.

2. See the section on the War Department in the headnote on Relationships with Federal Agencies; 10/4/43, "War Department," with attachments, in appendix 1.

Memorandum on FEPC Cases with Postwar Significance

October 10, 1944

MEMORANDUM

TO: Mr. George M. Johnson
            Deputy Chairman

FROM: Clarence M. Mitchell
            Associate Director of Field Operations

SUBJECT: FEPC Cases with Post-War Significance

As you will recall, we had a discussion on Thursday, October 5, with Messrs. Ross and Davidson concerning the possibility of getting a picture of FEPC cases which would have post-war significance if settled.[1]

Mr. Davidson and I have made a check on the docketed cases and selected those which fall in the industrial categories which the Division of Review and Analysis indicates will have post-war employment possibilities. These cases (including complaints against steam railroads) are 43.2% of our total case load, or 911 cases. We omitted firms engaged in aircraft production, unless the companies were making some other product before the war. Also, we omitted shipbuilding, although the Division of Review and Analysis indicates that certain phases of the shipbuilding program will have important expansion following the defeat of Germany. Firms engaged in the manufacture of small arms and ammunition have also been left out entirely.

We included the following industries: iron and steel; metal non-munitions; rubber; transportation; communication; food processing; mining and smelting; oil; textiles, apparel and leather; lumber and furniture; chemical and allied products; and other manufacturing.

We have also prepared a detailed breakdown on each region, which we shall send out for correction or additions by the Regional Directors.

[Attachment]

October 9, 1944

Mr. Malcolm Ross
Chairman

Eugene Davidson
    Asst. Director of Field Operations
Industries with Post-War Significance

Supplementing Mr. Mitchell's memorandum to you on the above subject, I submit as an attachment hereto a listing of cases which seem to have post-war significance in the regions for which I have direct responsibility viz. Regions I through V, and IX and XI. I have omitted the listing of railroad cases and have made no attempt to determine the sizes of the companies involved nor any other factors which might make the cases more or less significant.

The following statistical summary may be of value:[2]

REGION I

Total Active Cases	16
Total Active Cases with Post-War	
Significance	7
Percentage	43.8

REGION II

Total Active Cases	263
Total Active Cases with Post-War	
Significance	69
Percentage	26.2

REGION III

Total Active Cases	275
Total Active Cases with Post-War	
Significance	86
Percentage	31.3

REGION IV

Total Active Cases	121
Total Active Cases with Post-War	
Significance	42
Percentage	34.7

The percentage of cases with post-war significance by region is as follows:

REGION	TOTAL CASE LOAD	POST-WAR CASES	PER CENT OF TOTAL
I	16	7	43.8
II	263	69	26.2
III	275	86	31.3
IV	121	42	34.7
V (Cleveland)	128	66	51.6
V (Detroit)	105	54	51.4
VI	229	105	45.9
VII	346	187	54.0
VIII	15	9	60.0
IX	185	98	53.0
X	115	66	57.4
XI	34	20	58.8
XII (Los Angeles)	137	80	58.4
XII (San Francisco)	139	22	15.8
	2,108	911	48.2

In analyzing these cases, we have been aware that adjustments in some of the industries mentioned, particularly the railroads, may not be accomplished in any comparatively short time. It should be pointed out, however, that, apart from the basic problem involved in the railway cases now before the Stacy Committee, it has been possible to adjust some railroad complaints received. It is also believed that, by concentration, we may expect to adjust cases against public utilities, such as the telephone company.

MS: copy, FEPC RG 228 (entry 40, PI-147), Office Files of Clarence M. Mitchell, box 458, Malcolm Ross.

1. For earlier analysis, see Mitchell to Ross, memorandum, 10/7/44; for reference to that analysis, see Mitchell report, 10/9/44.

2. Handwritten corrections entered to the right of the original figures have been silently incorporated, as directed.

Memorandum on Contact with Smith Committee Regarding NLRB Visit

Oct. 11, 1944

Mr. Will Maslow

Clarence M. Mitchell

Contact with Smith Committee re. NLRB Visit

On the above date, Mr. Evans, of Region IV, informed me that Miss Alice Kahn of his office had an appointment at the NLRB with Dr. Watson, in the Statistical Division. Miss Kahn was investigating a complaint filed by a Miss Tucker.

According to Mr. Evans, Miss Kahn called him to say that a representative of the Smith Committee wished to sit in on the conference. She wanted to know what should be done about it. Mr. Evans instructed her to proceed with the conference, then talked with me about the situation. I called Mr. Haynes, of the Smith Committee, and asked him whether he had a representative at the NLRB on the case. Mr. Haynes said that he knew nothing about it and the only other person who would be carrying on an investigation would be Mr. Ford of the Committee. It developed that Mr. Ford was not aware of anything connected with the matter either.

We then called Miss Kahn to give her this information and it developed that the person present was a Mr. Edwin Brown, a private lawyer, representing the complainant. According to Miss Kahn, both the lawyer and the complainant stated that he, Mr. Brown, was representing the complainant at the request of Congressman Howard Smith. Dr. Watson's Secretary had mistakenly assumed that Mr. Brown was from the Smith Committee,[1] according to Miss Kahn.

cc: Ross
       Johnson

MS: copy, HqR3, Office Files of George M. Johnson. (A–M), Clarence Mitchell.
    1. On the Smith Committee, see the headnote on Jurisdictional Issues and the sources cited there.

Memorandum on DFO Cases

Oct. 12, 1944

Mr. Will Maslow
Clarence M. Mitchell
DFO Cases

The following DFO cases are being handled by me:

1. Camp Pendleton, Post Engineers, 4-GR-249. Received from region 8-2-44. Letter to War Department 8-8-44. Follow-up letter 9-22-44. Acknowledgment from War Department 9-26-44. Memorandum to region re status 9-27-44.
2. Consolidated Vultee Aircraft Corporation, 10-BR-235, 279, 336, 278. Received from region 6-29-44. Referred to Legal Division 7-11-44. Returned

by Legal Division 9-14-44. Letter to War Department 9-18-44. Acknowledgment from War Department 9-25-44. Memorandum to region re status 9-25-44.

3. Mt. Ranier Motor Base, 12-GR-15. Referred from region 6-2-44. Referred to Legal Division 7-13-44. Returned to Field Operations 7-19-44. Letter to War Department 7-25-44. Follow-up letter to War Department 9-27-44. Visit to War Department 10-11-44.

4. R.A. Nicol Company, 12-BR-395. Pursuant to Field Instruction No. 33, referred to Region II 8-7-44.[1]

5. Railroad Retirement Board, 2-GR-571. Referred from region 5-18-44. Assigned to Bloch 5-20-44. Letter to Railroad Retirement Board 8-11-44. Wire to Railroad Retirement Board 9-27-44. Wire from Railroad Retirement Board 10-4-44. Regions notified 10-5-44.

6. Richmond Army Service Depot, 4-GR-328, 329, 330, 363, and 163. Received from region 7-3-44. Referred to War Department 7-12-44. Follow-up letters to War Department 8-8-44 and 9-28-44. Visit to War Department 10-11-44. Region received copies of each follow-up letter.

7. Sacramento Air Service Command, 12-GR-278. Received from region 2-28-44. Assigned to Bloch 3-3-44. Letter to War Department 3-9-44. Report sent to region 4-13-44. Referred to Legal Division 8-7-44. Returned by Legal Division 9-19-44 following Committee discussion. Letter to War Department for additional information 9-25-44. Memo to region 9-25.

8. St. John's River Shipbuilding Company, undocketed. Referred from Region VII 6-22-44. Report from Department of Justice 8-30-44. Letter to Coast Guard 9-23-44. Reply from Coast Guard 9-29-44. Copies of correspondence sent to region in each instance.

9. Line Material Company, 5-BR-167 through 171 and 5-BR-180 through 182. Referred from region 6-29-44. Referred to Legal Division 7-11-44. Returned to Field Operations 9-28-44. Holding pending conference with Legal Division.

10. American Bemberg Corporation, 7-BA-122. Held by central office. Case dates back to 1942. Action suspended because this is an alienage case.[2]

11. USES, New Iberia, Louisiana, 10-GR-93. Referred from Region 5-10-44. Assigned to Metzger 5-25-44. Solution of this case will depend in some measure on what action the Department of Justice takes. At this point, there is no indication of anything other than a possible Grand Jury investigation in November.

The following DFO cases have been referred to the Legal Division:

1. American Red Cross, 2-BN-777. Referred from region 4-14-44. Referred to Legal Division 8-15-44.

2. Associated Shipyards, 12-BR-251. Referred from region 7-17-44. Referred to Legal Division 7-21-44.

3. Bechtel, Price & Callahan, 12-BR-67. Referred from region 5-9-44. Referred to Legal Division 5-17-44.

4. Brotherhood of Railroad Trainmen, 6-UR-338. Referred from region 9-7-44. Referred to Legal Division 9-26-44.

5. California Shipbuilding Company, 12-BR-1115. Referred from region 11-26-43. Referred to Legal Division 12-23-43.
6. Chevrolet Division, General Motors, 9-BR-135. Referred from region 1-10-44. Referred to Legal Division 1-25-44 and 9-18-44.
7. George L. Detterbeck Company, 6-BR-264. Referred from region 7-11-44. Referred to Legal Division 7-25-44.
8. D.C. Fire Department, 4-GR-89. Referred from region 3-29-44. Referred to Legal Division 4-17-44.
9. R.J. Dorn Company, 10-BR-169. Referred from region 3-18-44. Referred to Legal Division 4-3-44 and 6-30-44.
10. Evansville Shipyard, 6-BR-478. Referred from region 7-19-44. Referred to Legal Division 7-25-44.
11. Office of Fiscal Director, War Department, 4-GR-239. Referred from region 7-6-44. Referred to Legal Division 8-2-44.
12. Quality Family Laundry, undocketed, Region II. Referred from region 5-30-44. Referred to Legal Division 6-30-44.
13. Shelter Island Oyster Company, 2-BC-284. Referred from region 3-7-44. Referred to Legal Division 3-11-44.

In addition, the Legal Division has four (4) cases involving the Boiler Makers Union. This does not include hearing cases.[3]

Since the last memorandum on DFO cases was prepared, I have closed seventeen (17) cases.

MS: copy, HqR38, Central Files. (entry 25) Memoranda, Maslow, Will, 1944.

1. Field Instruction 33, 2/28/44, directed that complaints regarding maritime operators and unions on the East Coast be referred to the FEPC's New York office. See HqR78, Field Instructions, 8/43–6/45; 11/21/44 text.

2. See the headnotes on Jurisdictional Issues and on National Origin, Alienage, and Loyalty.

3. See the section on the Boilermakers in the headnote on the FEPC and Unions.

Weekly Report

October 16, 1944

Mr. Will Maslow
Clarence M. Mitchell
Weekly Report for Week Ending Saturday, October 14, 1944

OUTSTANDING EVENTS AND PROBLEMS

Attached is a memorandum on an incident reportedly involving the Smith Committee and the National Labor Relations Board. In this situation, an FEPC representative was given the mistaken impression that a lawyer hired by a complainant was representing the Smith Committee. This emphasizes the importance of obtaining identifications of persons who contact FEPC on matters connected with official investigations.[1]

This week, I prepared a memorandum on the status of DFO cases being handled by me. Since my previous memorandum on such cases, which was dated August 28, 1944, I have closed seventeen (17) cases.[2]

The Maritime Commission has cooperated in obtaining a satisfactory adjustment of the Cardinal Engineering Company case, 2-BR-566. Relations with the Commission have been cordial and in general satisfactory.

ASSIGNMENTS

The following DFO cases have been returned to regional offices during this week:

1. Hospital cases, Region I, 1-BR-69, 1-BR-72, 1-BR-74, and 1-BC-75.
2. Maritime Nursery Schools, 12-BR-335.
3. Child Care Center, 12-BR-387, 12-BR-397.
4. Boiler Makers Union, Local 104 (Filipino).

The following Final Disposition Reports have been reviewed by me:

Region VI—14   Region XII—8

cc: Messrs. Davidson, Davis, Johnson, Jones

MS: copy, FEPC RG 228, Office Files of Clarence Mitchell, DNA.
1. See 10/11/44.
2. See 10/12/44.

Memorandum on Line Material Company

DATE: Oct. 19, 1944

TO: Mr. George M. Johnson
FROM: Clarence M. Mitchell
SUBJECT: Line Material Company, 5-BR-167 through 171 and 5-BR-180 through 182

I have read Mr. Reeves memorandum on these cases and find myself in disagreement with it.[1]

The file shows that on November 4, 1943, Mr. William Clark, Chairman of the Grievance Committee of Local 767, UER & MWA, complained to us about the company's hiring policy. Mr. William Harris, of Local 767, also took the trouble to send us an affidavit notarized by Helen F. Baker. I do not observe in the file any statement from the company which charges that the Union is responsible for the alleged attitude of white employees. In my opinion, it would be unwise to involve the Union further by requesting it to face the company with its statement of policy. Apparently, this has already been done by the Union itself without success.

In cases of this kind, the responsibility seems clearly upon the employer, and I am respectfully returning this with the hope that the Committee will give consideration to it as a possible hearing case.

Attachment (File)

MS: LH, DI HqR84, Correspondence Relating to Cases. (L–S) Line Material Co., Zanesville, Ohio.

1. Frank D. Reeves's memorandum to Johnson of 9/26/44, forwarded to Mitchell on 9/28/44, is filed with this text, along with other related materials. It recommended returning the case to the regional office of the Division of Field Operations for discussion with international officials of the United Electrical Radio and Machine Workers of America before scheduling a hearing. All the cases derived from complaints by African American women whose applications for factory employment were rejected by the company. The firm argued that it employed the largest number of nonwhite workers in the area but that resistance to working with black women was far stronger than that against black men and that a walkout of their white workers would result if they attempted to hire black women. Absence of adequate toilet facilities to permit separate restrooms for each race was cited as a contributing factor.

At its meeting of 11/11/44, the FEPC authorized a "Hearing Examiner type hearing" on the case, which was held in 1/45. Maceo Hubbard, the hearing examiner, directed Line Material Company to "recruit and hire new employees, including Negro women, without discrimination." The firm complied by integrating black women into its production line within a month. See the hearing on Line Material Company, in HqR21, Records Relating to Hearings; Kersten, *Race, Jobs, and the War,* 87–88.

Memorandum on Conference with War Manpower Commission, Region X

DATE: Nov. 1, 1944

TO: Mr. Will Maslow

FROM: Clarence M. Mitchell

SUBJECT: Conference with War Manpower Commission, Region X

On Thursday, October 26, 1944, Mr. Ellinger, Dr. Castaneda, and I met with Mr. J. M. Bond, Regional Director of the WMC in Dallas. We discussed the submission of ES 510 Reports to FEPC.

After considerable discussion, Mr. Bond stated that these reports would be submitted to us and that the War Manpower Commission would not expect us to withhold information from the employer concerning where we had received such reports. He also stated that he will instruct his Area Directors to cooperate with FEPC by making visits to plants in certain cases rather than submitting 510 Reports.

Mr. Bond expressed the view that a joint visit from FEPC and the WMC Area Director would be more effective than FEPC's going in alone on a 510 Report. It remains to be seen which of these two approaches will be more effective in Region X.

MS: LH, DI, HqR38, Central Files. (entry 25) Memoranda, Maslow, Will, 1944.

For the background, see the section on the War Manpower Commission in the headnote on Relationships with Federal Agencies.

Memorandum on Regional Views on R.D. No. 124

Nov. 1, 1944

Mr. Will Maslow

Clarence M. Mitchell

Regional Views on R.D. No. 124

While on my trip to St. Louis, Dallas, and Kansas City, I talked with the Directors of Regions VI, IX, and X concerning our R. D. on the order of processing cases. Each of the Regional Directors seemed to feel that it is the practical approach, and we discussed the most important problems of the regions in the light of this R. D.[1]

Region IX expressed the view that one of its most important industries is the shoe industry. It also has electrical companies in the area which will have important postwar significance. So far, the major cutbacks have affected the U. S. Cartridge Company in St. Louis, the North American Aviation Company in Kansas City, and the Remington Arms Company in Kansas City. In each of these cutbacks, some Negroes were affected, but, in Remington Arms and North American, the Regional Director felt there was no disproportionately large number of Negroes laid off.

Region X gave a full statement on its important cases, and these will be discussed in a separate memorandum.[2] However, the oil, sulphur, and magnesium industries were mentioned as areas in which significant post-war gains can be made.

MS: copy, HqR38, Central Files. (entry 25) Memoranda, Maslow, Will, 1944.

1. For RD 125, see Memoranda Sent to Regional Directors (RDs), 9/43–5/45, FEPC RG 228 (entry 45), DNA. On the FEPC's prioritization of cases in accordance with their significance in the postwar economy, see 10/7, 10/9, 10/10/44.

2. Memorandum not found.

Memorandum on Appointment of Regional Director for Dallas Office

Nov. 1, 1944

Mr. Malcolm Ross

Clarence M. Mitchell

Appointment of Regional Director for Dallas Office

Following my visit to the Dallas office, I have reached the conclusion that it is of great importance that we take some prompt action in filling the vacancy of Regional Director for that area.

In my opinion, both Dr. Castaneda and Mr. Ellinger are of value to the Committee; each has a number of contacts in the region and each has done valuable work for us.[1] After reviewing the work of these two men since the Dallas office opened and since each came on the payroll, I feel that I should recommend Dr. Castaneda for the position of Regional Director. I propose that we designate Mr. Ellinger as Examiner-in-Charge of the Dallas office with the responsibility for handling Texas and Louisiana and maintaining liaison with the War Manpower Commission and labor groups.

Mr. Ellinger is a friendly person who gets along well with many people. However, he has a tendency to accept offers of cooperation and pledges of support at face value. This has been shown in his handling of cases involving the Texas-Pacific Railroad, the Delta Shipbuilding Company,[2] the Daneiger Oil Company, and the War Manpower Commission. I feel that Dr. Castaneda would serve as an important check on many of these matters for us.

In my opinion, we must be prepared for adverse criticism regardless of who serves as Regional Director. Region X will be a source of trouble for us for many months to come. It is my opinion that further delay in clarifying our office setup in the area will result in misunderstandings which may further handicap our program.

I shall appreciate an opportunity to discuss this fully with you, Mr. Johnson, Mr. Maslow, and Mr. Davidson at your first opportunity.

MS: copy, HqR39, Central Files. (entry 25) Memoranda, Ross, Malcolm, 1944.

1. At this time Castañeda served as special assistant to the secretary of FEPC for Latin American affairs, while Ellinger was acting regional director since the resignation of Leonard Brin in 7/44. Castañeda became regional director of Region X in 1945, while Ellinger became director of newly created Region XIII, headquartered in New Orleans.

2. On Ellinger's appraisal of Delta Shipbuilding, see notes to 5/5/44.

Weekly Report

Nov. 13, 1944

Mr. Will Maslow

Clarence M. Mitchell

Weekly Report for Weeks Ending 10/21, 10/28/44, 11/4, and 11/11/44

During this period, I have been absent from the office for approximately ten days making field visits to the Kansas City and Dallas regional offices, as well as the sub-regional office in St. Louis, Missouri. Reports on matters handled during these visits have been submitted previously or are among the attached white copies.[1]

We have before us the unresolved problems affecting the Post Offices and the Machinists' Union. In the former, we have taken no action, because we have been unable to obtain an appointment with the Postmaster General.[2] We have had no further word from Mr. Shishkin, of the Committee, concerning further handling of complaints against the Machinist's International.[3]

ASSIGNMENTS:

As agreed in our discussion with Mr. Davidson on Monday, November 13, assignments to the new central staff examiner, Mr. Hayes Beall, will be channeled through me in order to insure an even distribution of the work load.

The following DFO cases have been returned to regional offices during this period:

1. Camp Pendleton, Post Engineers, 4-GR-249.
2. USES, New Iberia, Louisiana, 10-GR-93.
3. Bechtel, Price, Callahan, 12-BR-67.
4. Montgomery Ward and Company.
5. Bolling Field, 4-GR-156.

The following new DFO cases have been received:

1. Illinois Central Railroad, 6-BR-359.
2. Delco Remy Division, General Motors, 6-BC-6, 6-BC-275, 276, 277, 278, 280, 281, and 282. This is the second referral of all of these cases except 6-BC-6.

The following Final Disposition Reports have been reviewed by me:

Region VI—25
Region VIII—6

Region X—11
Region XII—53

cc: Messrs. Davidson, Davis, Johnson, Jones

MS: *copy, FEPC RG 228, Office Files of Clarence Mitchell, DNA.*

1. Most of these memoranda have not been found, but see Mitchell's 11/1/44 reports on Dallas.

2. Mitchell obtained this meeting with Post Master General Frank C. Walker on 11/25/44 as he reported in his memorandum of that date to Ross. Information on the meeting is also contained in his report to Maslow of 11/27/44. For further developments, see 12/2, 12/9, 12/11, 12/12/44; headnote on Jurisdictional Issues and the section on the Post Office Department in the headnote on Relationships with Federal Agencies.

3. See the section on the International Association of Machinists in the headnote on the FEPC and Unions.

Memorandum on Suggested Field Trip for Mr. Beall

Nov. 17, 1944

Mr. Will Maslow
Clarence M. Mitchell
Suggested Field Trip for Mr. Beall

Mr. Ellinger's memorandum, dated November 10, gives a bird's-eye view of major cases with post-war importance.[1]

I recommend that Mr. Beall go to Dallas on January 9 and remain until January 30 for the purpose of giving assistance in the handling of these cases. I suggest this period because it will not be broken by any holidays and all of the time can be used.

If you agree with this, I should like to notify Mr. Ellinger so that he will begin formulating plans for the best use of Mr. Beall's help.

MS: *copy, HqR38, Central Files. (entry 25) Memoranda, Maslow, Will, 1944.*

1. On efforts to collect regional views and information on the FEPC policy to prioritize cases of postwar importance, see 10/7, 11/1/44.

Memorandum on Seventh-Day Adventists against Delco-Remy Division, General Motors

Nov. 18, 1944

Mr. Will Maslow

Clarence M. Mitchell

Complaints of Seventh Day Adventists against Delco Remy Division, General Motors, 6-BC-6, 275, 276, 277, 278, 280, 281, and 282

I have reviewed this file and Mr. Henderson's Request for Further Action report.

It does not appear that the company has taken action in line with the Committee's policy, as set forth in the summary of September 14, 1943. In my opinion, a hearing should be held, and I so recommend.

Attachment—File

MS: copy, HqR83, Correspondence Relating to Cases. (A–K) General Motors, Delco-Remy Corp.

1. See appendix 1 for texts directly related: Bloch to Johnson, 11/30/44, and Johnson to Maslow, 12/6/44. In the file, see Maslow to Johnson, 11/20/44; Johnson to Bloch, 11/22/44; Henderson to Mitchell, 12/14/44; Mitchell to Henderson, 12/20/44. See also the headnote on Creedal Discrimination.

Weekly Report

Nov. 20, 1944

Mr. Will Maslow

Clarence M. Mitchell

Weekly Report for Week Ending Saturday, November 18, 1944

Following conversations with you, I have requested regional offices to submit to us the status of any telephone cases they are handling. In most instances, these cases have reached a stalemate, and it appears that the only solution is a hearing.[1]

I have also requested Mr. Davidson to bring in specific recommendations on cases in Cincinnati, since it is my belief that we will have difficulty operating in that area unless we have hearings on important unresolved cases.[2]

At the request of Region VII, I have asked the Navy Department to assist in correcting the discriminatory practices at the Reynolds Corporation in Macon, Georgia.

Our experiences in recent weeks with the War Department show that our present relationship is of no real value. In an effort to facilitate the handling of cases, I have made trips to the War Department for the purpose of reviewing files. After reviewing such files, I have attempted to rely on informal agreements, in addition to written requests, for the accomplishing of results. It now appears that nothing has been gained by such visits, and shortly I shall present a recommendation on this problem.[3]

Currently, we are planning to have Mr. Beall, the new examiner, work for a week in Philadelphia and, during the month of January, go to Dallas for the purpose of assisting Region X in its case handling.

ASSIGNMENTS

The following DFO cases have been returned to regional offices:

1. D. C. Fire Department, 4-GR-89.
2. Army Engineers, Northwest Division, 12-GR-112.
3. Railroad Retirement Board, 4-GR-368, 2-GR-571, and 2-GR-671, transmitted to Region VI for action with Railroad Retirement Board.

The following case has been referred to the Legal Division:

1. Department of Agriculture, 7-GR-78.

The following new cases have been received by me during the past week:

1. Delco Remy Division, General Motors, 6-BC-6, 275, 276, 277, 278, 280, 281, and 282.
2. Wilson and Company, 6-BC-592.
3. Murray Gin Company, 10-BR-327.

The following FDR's have been reviewed and acted upon by me:

Region VI—8　　　　　　Region XII—13

cc: Messrs. Davidson, Davis, Johnson, Jones,

MS: copy, FEPC RG 228, *Office Files of Clarence Mitchell*, DNA.

1. For the background, see the headnote on the Telephone Industry. For examples of current reports on telephone cases, see the third progress report, 11/7/44, of G. James Fleming regarding Bell Telephone Company, Pittsburgh, and Harry H.C. Gibson's memorandum to Elmer Henderson regarding Illinois Bell Telephone Company, 12/18/44, both in HqR76, Office Files of Will Maslow, Director, 9/43–5/45, Relations with Other Agencies; Kingman to Mitchell, 11/28/44, Status of Telephone Cases, FEPC RG 228 (entry 39, PI-147), Office Files of Will Maslow, box 456, DNA.

2. For background on discrimination in Cincinnati, see Kersten, *Race, Jobs, and the War*, 88–91; Kersten, "Publicly Exposing Discrimination."

The Cincinnati hearings were held 3/15–17/45, with Emanuel Bloch as trial examiner. The companies investigated were Crosley Radio Corporation, Baldwin Piano Company, Cambridge Tile Company, F. H. Lawrence, Kirk and Baum Manufacturing, Schaible Corporation, Streitmann Biscuit Company, and Victor Electric Company. Of these, only Cambridge Tile, Kirk and Blum, and Schaible, all of which settled prior to the hearings, changed their discriminatory employment practices during the war.

On the Cincinnati cases, see the hearings records in HqR21 and 22; two reports by Emanuel Bloch, both entitled "Cincinnati Cases," in HqR2, Office Files of Malcolm Ross. Difficult Cases, Cincinnati; and HqR6, Office Files of Emanuel H. Bloch, Hearing Examiner, 6/44–1/46 (A–Z; also Unarranged Materials), Cincinnati Cases.

3. It appears likely that Field Instruction 19B of 11/24/44 (in appendix 1, following no. 19), which Maslow sent to all regional directors, is Mitchell's recommendation. For the context, see the section on the War Department in the headnote on Relationships with Federal Agencies.

Memorandum on the Status of DFO Cases

Nov. 21, 1944

Mr. Will Maslow

Clarence M. Mitchell

Status of DFO Cases

The following is the status of thirty (30) DFO Cases against eighteen (18) parties charged, which are being handled by me:

1. Philadelphia Post Office, 3-GR-671. This case was received on May 23, 1944. The latest action was a letter to the Postmaster General on September 22, 1944. We are awaiting an appointment with the Postmaster General.[1]
2. Railroad Retirement Board, 2-GR-571, 671 and 4-GR-368. These three cases were received on May 18, 1944, and October 17, 1944. The latest action was taken when the files were sent to Region VI on November 13, 1944, for a conference with the Chairman of the Railroad Retirement Board.
3. Richmond Army Service Forces Depot, 4-GR-163, 4-GR-328, 4-GR-329, and 4-GR-363. These cases were received from the region on August 2, 1944. We have had two reports from the War Department concerning them. We are now awaiting some additional information from the region.
4. Illinois Central Railroad, 6-BR-359. This case was received on October 27, 1944. After a conference with the Deputy Chairman, we are preparing a letter to be sent to the company. Mr. Beall is preparing the letter, which was assigned to him on November 21, 1944.
5. Wilson and Company, 6-BC-592. This case was received on November 3, 1944. We addressed a letter to the company on November 14, 1944.
6. American Bemberg Corporation, 7-BA-122. This case was received on November 13, 1943. It was referred to the War Department for a loyalty investigation

on November 18, 1943. It is my understanding that the War Department misplaced the file. It was reported found on November 18, 1944. However, we have no information by letter as yet. Since this is an alienage case, the processing of it is held up.[2]

7. St. John's River Shipbuilding Company, 7-BR-409. This case was received on June 22, 1944, and assigned to me on August 19, 1944. We have negotiated with the Department of Justice, the Coast Guard, and the Maritime Commission concerning it. On October 25, 1944, the Maritime Commission indicated it would send a report to us following its investigation.

8. Dallas Post Office, 10-GR-250. This case was received on May 22, 1944. See comments on 3-GR-671.

9. Consolidated Vultee, 10-BR-235, 10-BR-279, 10-BR-336, and 10-BR-278. This case was received on June 29, 1944. It has been considered by the Legal Division, but we are making one more effort to obtain adjustment through the War Department. The War Department acknowledged our letter of September 18, 1944, on September 25, 1944, but as yet we have no word of favorable action.[3]

10. Houston Post Office, 10-GR-319, 320, and 321. These cases were received on June 17, 1944. See comments on 3-GR-671.

11. Murray Gin Company, 10-BR-327. This case was received on October 21, 1944. It involves a contact with CIO officials who are, at present, out of the city.

12. Sinclair Refining Company, 10-BR-322. This case was received on August 15, 1944, and referred to Region II for further handling on August 22, pursuant to Field Instruction 33.[4]

13. Mt. Ranier Motor Base, 12-GR-15. This case was received on June 2, 1944, and has been studied by the Legal Division. We have also taken it up with the War Department. Currently, we are awaiting further information from Region XII.

14. International Association of Machinists, 12-UR-174, 12-UR-263, and 12-UR-265. These cases were received on July 4, 1944. A Sub-Committee is supposed to visit Mr. Harvey Brown, of the I.A.M., on them. However, we have not had action on them as yet.[5]

15. Sacramento Air Service Command, 12-GR-278. This case was received on February 28, 1944. The latest of a long series of actions was a conference with the General Greenbaum on October 31, 1944.

16. R. A. Nicol Company, 12-BR-395. This case was received on July 8, 1944, and referred to Region II on August 7, 1944, pursuant to Field Instruction 33.[6]

17. Seattle Post Office, 12-GR-259. This case was received on July 10, 1944. See comments on 3-GR-671.

18. Los Angeles Post Office, 12-GR-1168. This case was received on September 12, 1944. See comments on 3-GR-671.

The following is a list of seventeen (17) cases in the hands of the Legal Division:

1. Quality Family Laundry, undocketed. This question of jurisdiction was received May 30, 1944, and referred to the Legal Division on June 30, 1944.

2. Shelter Island Oyster Company, 2-BC-284. This case was received on March 7, 1944, and referred to the Legal Division on March 11, 1944.

3. Office of Fiscal Director, War Department, 4-GR-289. This case was received on July 6, 1944 and referred to the Legal Division on August 2, 1944.

4. George L. Detterbeck Company, 6-BR-264. This case was received July 11, 1944, and referred to the Legal Division July 25, 1944.

5. Western Cartridge Company, 6-BR-273. This case was received June 9, 1944, and referred to the Legal Division June 14, 1944.

6. Delco Remy Division, General Motors, 6-BC-6, 275, 276, 277, 278, 280, 281, and 282. These cases were returned to the region on July 7, 1944, for further contact with the complainants and the party charged. They were returned to the DFO on November 8, 1944, and referred to the Legal Division on November 20, 1944.

7. Brotherhood of Railroad Trainmen, 6-UR-338. This case was received on September 9, 1944, and referred to the Legal Division on September 26, 1944.

8. Evansville Shipyard, 6-BR-478. This case was received July 21, 1944, and referred to the Legal Division on July 25, 1944.

9. Department of Agriculture, 7-GR-78. This case was received November 14, 1944, and referred to the Legal Division November 16, 1944.

10. Chevrolet Division, General Motors, 9-BR-135. This case was received January 10, 1944, and referred to the Legal Division January 25 and September 18, 1944.

11. R. J. Dorn Company, 10-BR-169. This case was received, originally, March 18, 1944, and referred to the Legal Division April 3, 1944. The Committee reaffirmed the position taken by Examiner Williams April 20. A letter was then written to the company's attorney May 15, 1944, and a reply received May 30, 1944, stating immediate compliance impossible. The case was returned to the Legal Division June 30, 1944.

12. Boilermakers Local 9, 12-UR-16. This case was received February 15, 1944, and referred to the Legal Division March 8, 1944, to be held pending over-all settlement of Boiler Maker cases.

13. Boilermakers Local 513, 12-UR-32. This case was received February 15, 1944. See 12-UR-16 (above).

14. Shipfitters Union, Local A-33, 12-UR-203. This case was received February 15, 1944. See comments on 12-UR-16.

15. Associated Shipyards, 12-BR-251. This case was received July 17, 1944, and referred to the Legal Division July 21, 1944. See comments on 12-UR-16.

16. California Shipbuilding Company, 12-BR-1115. This case was received November 26, 1943, and referred to the Legal Division December 23, 1943. See comments on 12-UR-16.

17. Boilermakers Union, Local 92, 12-UR-1116. This case was received November 26, 1943, and referred to the Legal Division December 23, 1943. See comments on 12-UR-16.

MS: copy, HqR38, Central Files. (entry 25) Memoranda, Maslow, Will, 1944.

1. See the section on the Post Office Department in the headnote on Relationships with Federal Agencies.

2. On the suspension of FEPC action on alienage cases, see the headnotes on Jurisdictional Issues and on National Origin, Alienage, and Loyalty.

3. See the headnote on the Aircraft Industry.

4. The instruction, dated 2/28/44, on "Complaints Involving Maritime Operators and Unions," directed that such complaints be handled by the New York office. See 10/12/44; HqR78, Field Instructions, 8/43–6/45.

5. On these Machinists Union cases and the Boilermakers Union cases listed below, see the headnote on the FEPC and Unions

6. See note 4 above.

Memorandum on Strike of
Negro Teamsters in New Orleans, Louisiana

DATE: Nov. 22, 1944

TO: Files

FROM: Clarence M. Mitchell

SUBJECT: Strike of Negro Teamsters in New Orleans

On Friday, November 17, I talked with Mr. W. Don Ellinger, via long distance telephone, concerning the strike of Negro teamsters in New Orleans.

Mr. Ellinger stated that the men left their jobs on November 1 and were still out at the time of our conversation. According to his statement, the Teamsters Union is making an effort to replace all of the Negroes who went on strike, but, so far, has been able to replace only 200 at the Delta Shipbuilding Company and there remain 450 places to be filled at this plant. He estimated that approximately 200 Negroes from other companies are also out in sympathy with the men from Delta.[1]

MS: LH, DI, HqR83, Correspondence Relating to Cases. (A–L) Delta Shipbuilding Company.

1. On Delta Shipbuilding cases, see 2/19, 2/28, 3/6, 5/1, 5/5, 8/14/44, 1/8, 1/9, 1/12/45; headnote on the Shipbuilding Industry.

Memorandum on Sacramento Air Service Command

Nov. 22, 1944

Mr. Will Maslow

Clarence M. Mitchell

Sacramento Air Service Command, 12-GR-278

Following our conference with General Greenbaum and Mr. Truman Gibson on this case, I feel that nothing can be accomplished by further negotiations with the War Department on it.[1]

I therefore recommend that, unless the Committee is willing to hold a hearing, as Mr. Hubbard recommended, the case should be closed as "other." If you do not feel that we should again request a hearing, I will return the file and notify the region to close the case.[2]

Attachment—File

MS: copy, HqR84, Correspondence Relating to Cases. Sacramento Air Depot.

1. This is another indication of the depth of Mitchell's frustrations with Gibson, the black civilian aide, whom he regarded as a roadblock to fighting discrimination in the War Department. See the section on the War Department in the headnote on Relationships with Federal Agencies.

2. See related documents: Bloch to Mitchell, 7/27/44; Hubbard to Johnson, 8/19/44; Mitchell to Harry N. Conyers, 8/7/44, all filed with this text.

Memorandum on Proposed Hearing on Machinists Local 824

DATE: Nov. 22, 1944

TO: Mr. George M. Johnson

FROM: Clarence M. Mitchell

SUBJECT: Proposed Hearing on Machinists Local 824, Case 12-UR-174

You will note from the attached memorandum from Mr. Kingman that a hearing has been recommended in this case.

This is one of several problems involving Machinists, which the Committee has considered and on which a sub-Committee was supposed to work.[1]

I pass Mr. Kingman's recommendation on to you with the hope that we may be able to get the sub-Committee to take some action or that the Committee will go forward with a hearing.

Attachment

MS: LH, DI, HqR8, Office Files of Frank D. Reeves. (Q–Z), Misc.

1. The FEPC subcommittee assigned to confer with the Machinists Union consisted of Boris Shishkin and Charles Hamilton Houston. See 9/6/44; Transcript of Proceedings, 9/9/44, 56, 63–64, HqR65, Central Files. For background, see the section on the International Association of Machinists in the headnote on the FEPC and Unions.

Memorandum on Conference with Postmaster General and Postal Officials

November 25, 1944

ROUGH DRAFT

TO: Mr. Malcolm Ross

FROM: Clarence M. Mitchell

SUBJECT: Conference with Postmaster General and Postal Officials

On the above date, we met with Postmaster General Frank C. Walker in his office on the subject of complaints we have received from our regional offices against post offices in Los Angeles, Dallas, Houston, Philadelphia, and Seattle.

The most important question for discussion with Mr. Walker was whether the Committee has jurisdiction over the Post Office Department. We cited a specific problem we had in the City of Philadelphia, where the Postmaster denied that the Committee had any jurisdiction over complaints against his office. Mr. Walker called in Mr. Joseph F. Gartland, Director of Budget and Administrative Planning. Mr. Gartland stated that the Postmaster in Philadelphia had been informed that the Committee does have jurisdiction over complaints of discrimination involving the Post Office. Mr. Walker also stated that he wanted to assure FEPC of the Post Office Department's desire to cooperate with us.

We then went to a meeting of the various assistants to the Postmaster General and other persons responsible for personnel action which lasted 2 hours. In this meeting, we obtained a commitment from Mr. Gartland that the First Assistant Postmaster [Kildroy P. Aldrich] would send to us a statement on the steps taken by the Post Office Department to make clear the Committee's jurisdiction over it.

At Mr. Gartland's request, you presented a brief history of the Committee, its methods of handling complaints, and its relationships with other Government agencies. Mr. Gartland had previously stated that the Post Office officials knew about the Executive Order, but he thought a review of it would be helpful. In my opinion, this review was very much needed and I believe that we now deal with them on a better basis than previously.

We then turned to the question of our operating relationships. Mr. Gartland began by saying that the Post Office had a system of operating which had been in effect for 150 years and, therefore, was a very good system which would not be changed unless a better system could be offered. He stated that no investigations of complaints are made at the request of outside Government agencies unless the request is first presented to the Post Office Department at the Washington level. We cited our agreements with the War and Navy Departments and indicated that the nature of our operations require the handling of complaints on a local level with the officials involved. You stated that we would be glad to notify the Post Office Department in Washington when we receive complaints against local establishments but we did wish to exercise the right to follow up on such complaints with the local postal officials through our regional representatives. Mr. Gartland expressed his opposition to such a plan and stated that he wished the investigation of all complaints against the Post Office would be authorized from Washington upon request of FEPC. We discussed this matter at great length, but did not reach an agreement. You finally suggested that you would put your views in writing and send them to Mr. Gartland. I shall prepare a proposed working relationship.

We discussed the highlights of cases against the Philadelphia, Dallas, Houston, Los Angeles, and Seattle Post Offices. You stated that we would submit the current cases to Mr. Gartland because they have been pending for some time, but that this is not to be interpreted as a waiver of the right [of] FEPC to deal with the individual Postmasters.

In Dallas, Negroes, among other things, seek assurance that, if they accept War Service Appointments as carriers or clerks, they will have reemployment rights in their old jobs, which, in this case, are mail handlers. The First Assistant Postmaster General said that this is the policy of the Post Office Department and such persons will have assurance of reemployment in their old jobs at the close of hostilities. From his phrasing, it appears that this is a national policy of the Post Office Department by which the Postmaster in Dallas must be bound.

We discussed the Houston, Texas, problem of Negroes on the eligible clerks register as a result of regular Civil Service examinations, who have been passed over by the Postmaster in making appointments. We cited a Civil Service letter indicating that twenty-six (26) War Service Appointments had been made outside of the register when, according to the Negro complainants, certain colored persons were still available as eligibles on the register but were not appointed solely because of race. This is one of the matters I am to take up with Mr. Gartland for more extensive investigation.

Briefly, we discussed the highlights of complaints regarding upgrading, which have been filed by persons in Philadelphia.

We did not touch upon the Los Angeles cases, except in passing. Mr. Gartland agreed that each individual case in all of these Post Offices would be investigated by the First Assistant Postmaster General. He also agreed to meet with me from time to time on such matters.

I raised a question concerning supplying FEPC with statistical data. Mr. Gartland said that the Post Office Department is attempting to establish machinery for collecting this material but he did not give a definite date on which such machinery will go into operation.

We explained the importance of having some official statement from the Post Office Department concerning its employment of non-whites. It was my understanding that

Mr. Gartland would make an effort to give us an estimate pending the time that his more detailed study goes into effect.

MS: draft, HqR84, Correspondence Relating to Cases. (L–S) Post Office Department (General).
This text includes corrections and interlineations incorporated as Mitchell directed. The Committee authorized Ross and Mitchell to conduct this conference during its meeting of 9/7/44 (see Mitchell's memorandum of that date, and notes). For progressive developments, see also 11/13, 11/27, 12/2, 12/9, 12/11, 12/12/44; headnote on Jurisdictional Issues and the section on the Post Office Department in the headnote on Relationships with Federal Agencies.

Weekly Report

Nov. 27, 1944

Mr. Will Maslow
Clarence M. Mitchell
Weekly Report for Week Ending Saturday, November 25, 1944

OUTSTANDING EVENTS AND PROBLEMS

In company with the Chairman, I visited the Postmaster General on Saturday, November 25. We discussed pending cases against Post Offices in Philadelphia, Los Angeles, Dallas, Houston, and Seattle. One important result of this conference was acknowledgment by the Post Office Department of the Committee's jurisdiction. This jurisdiction had been challenged by the Postmaster in Philadelphia. We also resolved a question of whether Post Office laborers who accept War Service appointments as carriers or clerks are entitled to reinstatement to their old jobs at the close of the emergency period. The Post Office officials agreed that, as a matter of national policy, such persons will be entitled to reinstatement. These cases are by no means resolved at this point, and it appears that we will have to undertake further and lengthy negotiations with postal officials. I am preparing a proposed working relationship, which Mr. Ross agreed to send to Mr. Joseph F. Gartland, Director of Budget and Administrative Planning.[1]

As mentioned in my report of November 20, I have requested regional offices to inform us of the status of telephone cases which they have pending. So far, we have received reports from Region III, concerning the New Jersey Bell Telephone Company; Region VI, on the Illinois Bell Telephone Company; Region VII, involving a Jehovah's Witness; and Region X, on the Southwestern Bell and Southern Bell Telephone Companies. A detailed report on these cases is being prepared.[2]

The War Department has replied to our letter of November 22, concerning the status of cases involving the Consolidated Vultee Corporation at Fort Worth, Texas. The Department states that, "A report was requested under date of September 21, 1944, but to date no reply has been received. I am today requesting that telegraphic inquiry be made as to the status of this matter." This letter from the War Department was dated November 23 and signed by the Civilian Aide to the Secretary of War.

We have forwarded to Region XII a brief statement on a problem affecting war workers in Renton, Washington. This problem is currently before the National Housing Agency in that three Negro women were ejected there, discriminatorily by whites. These persons were employees of Boeing Aircraft Corporation, according to our information, but, as yet, we have no further details.

By agreement between Mr. Davidson and myself, Mr. Hayes Beall is currently in the Philadelphia office, where he will assist the Regional Director in the processing of cases. This will serve as a training period for Mr. Beall and, at the same time, should give some assistance to Mr. Fleming. At my request, Mr. Beall will also contact officials of the General Cable Company in New York, New York, concerning an unresolved case against that company, which was referred to us by the St. Louis office.

We have answered, by memorandum, a request concerning separate facilities in war plants. This request came from Region IX.

ASSIGNMENTS

The following DFO cases have been returned to regional offices:

1. Gulf-Colorado and Santa Fe Railroad, 10-BR-368.
2. Richmond Army Service Forces, 4-GR-363 and 4-GR-330.

The following FDR's have been reviewed and acted upon by me:

Region VI—8
Region VIII—1
Region XII—6

cc: Messrs. Davidson, Davis, Johnson, Jones

MS: copy, FEPC RG 228, Office Files of Clarence Mitchell, DNA.

1. In his 3/20/45 report, Mitchell noted that the Post Office Department confirmed an understanding that he and Ross, at their 11/25/44 meeting, had reached with it—that employees who accepted war service appointments were entitled to their old jobs at the cessation of hostilities if they could not be retained in the positions to which they had been promoted.

For the Committee's initial response to the challenge by Philadelphia postmaster Joseph Gallagher, see 5/3/44.

2. Mitchell's detailed report is at 12/2/44. It is supported by earlier reports from regional directors and other staff. One not mentioned there is that from Lawson to Maslow on the New York Telephone Company, 10/17/44. Lawson said that, based on the company's ES-270 report, which provided information on its employment policy, it had thirty thousand workers as of 5/44, of whom 156 were African

Americans. Nonwhites were employed in clerical, service, messenger, and customer representative jobs. The ES-270 also showed that the telephone company had trouble recruiting operators because of low wages; that, periodically, it had recruited women interested in being trained as operators at high schools and churches; and that its "Policy of not using Negroes as operators may cause difficulty in meeting labor needs." The ES-270 further stated that the "Company will hire Negroes in all occupations but operator," because of their "speech and diction limitations." Lawson's report included excerpts that demonstrated these discriminatory hiring practices. HqR3, Office Files of George M. Johnson. Will Maslow.

See progressive developments on the broad-based problems at 11/13, 11/20, 11/25, 12/2, 12/9, 12/11, 12/12/44. The regional reports substantiated Evelyn Cooper's assessment of 3/7/45, in appendix 1.

Memorandum on Committee Cases against Telephone Companies

December 2, 1944

Mr. Will Maslow
Director of Field Operations
Clarence M. Mitchell
Associate Director of Field Operations
Committee Cases Against Telephone Companies

As stated in my Weekly Report of November 27, I have received statements from several of our Regional offices concerning complaints against telephone companies.[1] As you know, Mr. Davidson, when he was in Region V, discussed the Ohio Bell,[2] Michigan Bell, and Southern Bell cases with Mr. McKnight. I presume Mr. Davidson will make his own report of these cases. You also know that in Region II, the telephone company has employed its first Negro operator and intends to employ others.

The following is a digest of the material before us from the other regions:

REGION III

Case 3-BR-646 against the Bell Telephone Company of New Jersey has been referred to the Central Office for further action. In this case, three complainants have filed affidavits alleging that they sought positions as operators in Atlantic City in response to newspaper advertisements the week of October 4 to 9, 1943. Their applications were accepted, they allege, but they were not called for consideration or training.

Subsequently, the company, during the week of April 10, 1944, advertised for operators, stating that no experience was required.

On October 4, Mr. Andrew P. Monroe, Vice-President of the company, conferred with Mr. Fleming, in the latter's office, concerning these complaints. Mr. Monroe stated that the company's program of gradual integration of non-whites where and when the company felt it to be wise was the final answer to FEPC. The company refused to use the colored applicants as operators.[3]

Mr. Fleming states that he has submitted a progress report on Case 3-BR-347 involving the Bell Telephone Company of Pittsburgh.[4]

REGION IV

The complaints in this Region are against the Chesapeake & Potomac Telephone Company of Baltimore, Maryland. Negro applicants charge that they were not hired for positions as operators. The company has refused to change its policy.[5]

REGION VI

We do not have a specific report from Mr. Henderson, as yet, on the problem of employing Negro operators in the Illinois Bell System. In a Final Disposition Report dated November 9, 1944, on Case 6-BR-319, Mr. Henderson states the following:

"The total employment of 19,836 includes 91 non-whites. According to a recent ES 270 report, non-white women are used as clerks, tellers, service representatives, dining service attendants, and janitresses. Non-white men are used as coin-box collectors, building service men, installers, and one non-white man is a supervisor."

The particular case, which was the subject of the Final Disposition Report, involved a man who charged the company with failure to upgrade from a job of window washer. This case was dismissed on its merits.[6]

REGION VII

In a report dated November 20, the Region states that it has a telephone case involving a Jehovah's Witness, who was employed by the American Telephone and Telegraph Company for 23 years. This individual charges that he was dismissed last Spring because of his creedal connection.

The Region asks whether it should continue the investigation of the case. I have informed them that the inquiry should continue.

REGION IX

There are three complaints against the Southwestern Bell Telephone Company. Two are against the St. Louis Office and one against the office in Topeka, Kansas.

No contact has been made with the St. Louis Office but the Region states that it has had a conference with the Bell officials in Topeka and also with the officials in the Kansas City office, which has jurisdiction over the Topeka office.

All of these cases, 9-BR-1100, 9-BR-1154, and 9-BR-400, are complaints involving race, but the Region does not indicate whether the complainants sought jobs as operators.

REGION X

Dr. Ca[s]taneda reports that two cases were docketed against the Southwestern Bell Telephone Company involved alienage, 10-BA-123 and 10-BA-124. The first was in November 1943 and was filed by Mrs. Minerva M. Aranda. She was offered a job but refused it because it interfered with her household responsibilities. The case was dismissed on merits.

The other case involved Tomas Salas, who alleged that he was refused employment. However, when an effort was made to have the complainant re-apply after company stated that it would give him an opportunity to work, it was learned that he had volunteered for the Navy and could not be reached.

REGION X (NEW ORLEANS)

Mr. Ellinger reports that there is a case against the Bell Telephone Company of New Orleans which arose from the complaint of Miss June Richardson, who charges that in August of 1943, she applied at the Southern Bell Company in answer to an advertisement. She states that she talked with a Mr. Eber who referred her to another man. The second man told her that the only jobs open to Negroes were those as maids, elevator girls, and cleaning buildings at night. According to her statement, she alleged that she was refused solely because of her race.

Mr. Ellinger met with Mr. R. V. Davis of the Atlanta Office of the Southern Bell Company and Mr. H. G. Bartee of the New Orleans Office on September 13 by appointment.

He states that the company admits that it has no plans of hiring Negro operators in spite of non-discriminatory instructions issued in 1942 in their memorandum dated November 22. Mr. Ellinger stated that he expected to have another conference with the telephone officials.

REGION XII

This Region has four cases against telephone companies in San Diego, Los Angeles, and Monrovia, California. Case numbers 12-BR-1042, 12-BR-1191, 12-BR-1416, and 12-BR-1419. In all of them, Negro complainants allege that they have been refused employment as operators. A copy of the report is attached to this memorandum.[7]

So far, it does not appear that any progress can be made in settling these cases on the Regional level, although they have not been referred to the Central Office as yet.

In one of the cases, the USES is supposed to have a commitment indicating that the complainant will be considered for a position as a telephone operator trainee, if she is qualified.

Attachment

MS: copy, HqR85, Correspondence Relating to Cases. Telephone Company Cases.

1. See the coordinate text of 11/27/44 and Evelyn Cooper's memorandum on Telephone Company Cases, 3/7/45, in appendix 1; headnote on the Telephone Industry.

2. The Ohio Bell case resulted from the company's assertion to a black applicant who had responded to an ad for receptionists that it did not intend to hire black women in the immediate future. The Ohio Federation of Telephone Operators, an independent union, furthermore said that while it permitted the employment of African Americans in various service and clerical capacities, it would not allow their employment as telephone operators. Even so, the company said, it did not practice discrimination because it had increased the number of black employees from 76 in 4/42 to 155 on 1/14/44. Reeves to Johnson, memorandum, 8/7/44, HqR5, Office Files of George M. Johnson. Frank D. Reeves. Reeves said that unlike Ohio Bell, Southern Bell did "not present a clearly defined discriminatory policy and practice." Furthermore, the age of the complaints, which dated back to 1/11 and 1/13/43, presented a problem. He therefore recommended on technical grounds that the cases be returned to the Division of Field Operations for further consideration. HqR5, Office Files of George M. Johnson. Frank D. Reeves. See also 10/7/44, note 2.

3. See subsequent developments at 12/11/44, 1/2, 2/14, 3/8, 3/13, 5/21/45.

4. For earlier developments, see 12/21/43. In his third progress report of 11/7/44, Fleming said the company had not increased the number of its black workers since its progress report of 2/9/44 because of a "particularly high" turnover among this segment of its employees, which did not result from bad treatment. HqR76, Office Files of Will Maslow. Relations with Other Agencies.

5. See 7/5/43 for earlier activity. In an update of 9/14/43 to Lewis W. Clymer, WMC regional fair practice examiner, Mitchell said the company limited its hiring of blacks to coin collectors, clerical workers, and linemen. It refused to hire them as operators. Its stated reason, which was commonly expressed throughout the telephone industry, was that "the proximity of the operators would make for racial disturbances." HqR38, Central Files. Memoranda, Clymer, Lewis.

6. Harry Gibson in a 12/18/44 report listed eleven cases pending against Illinois Bell. Following a meeting with J. N. Stanbery, general personnel manager, Gibson reported that the company's position was that it was willing to comply with EO 9346, but it "wished to take conservative and cautious methods in the integration of Negroes into the various departments." This, of course, said Gibson, was "too gradual and conservative," even though Illinois Bell at the time employed African American women in responsible positions other than as operators at one of its branch offices. Despite the company's nervousness, a black woman subsequently hired and who was being trained as a teller for Illinois Bell's business office, told Gibson she was impressed with friendly treatment she was receiving from her coworkers and supervisory officials. Gibson concluded, "The fact that her presence has apparently not been resented by white fellow workers will aid in overcoming management's timidity about having Negroes and whites work together in white-collar positions." See Gibson to Elmer Henderson,

12/18/44, HqR76, Office Files of Will Maslow. Relations with Other Agencies. This report is also cited at 5/21/45.

7. Kingman reported, 11/28/44, that the FEPC had five recorded cases against the Pacific Telephone and Telegraph Company. Based on a conference on 9/28/44 with the company, Kingman said, there was apparent agreement accordingly: "The Pacific Telephone and Telegraph Company has approximately 17,000 employees of whom only 35 are nonwhites; there are no Negro women employed as telephone operators; the Company is experiencing a manpower shortage and has been granted a top hiring priority by the War Manpower Commission; the Company is obligated to comply with Executive Order 9346."

There was, however, Kingman said, disagreement over the scope of the nondiscrimination order. "Representatives of the Company insisted that in choosing among occupationally qualified applicants for employment the Company reserves the right to consider the factors of race and creed in arriving at a decision as to whether the applicant is the 'best fitted' or the 'most suitable' candidate for the job." The FEPC, of course, challenged that assertion as a violation of EO 9346. HqR76, Office Files of Will Maslow. Relations with Other Agencies.

Weekly Report

Dec. 4, 1944

Mr. Will Maslow

Clarence M. Mitchell

Weekly Report for Week Ending Saturday, December 2, 1944

OUTSTANDING EVENTS AND PROBLEMS

A summary of the telephone cases was completed this week and set forth the problems in Regions III, IV, VI, VII, IX, X, and XII. This memorandum was sent to you.[1]

We have received a letter from the United States Office of Education indicating that a training program for Negroes may be started in Macon, Georgia. The Office of Education indicates surprise at the War Manpower Commission's report of discriminatory practices. I have talked with Admiral Crisp's office concerning this matter, also, since the Navy is expected to take action which will insure the hiring of trainees by the Reynolds Corporation after instruction is underway. The Admiral has been on the west coast and our problem is being handled by a Lieutenant Considine, who states that he was formerly with the National Labor Relations Board. Lt. Considine promised a report as quickly as possible.

We have also had word, via telephone, from Mr. Truman Gibson, Civilian Aide to the Secretary of War, concerning the Consolidated Vultee case. Mr. Gibson informed me that he hopes to get the War Department's report to us by December 6.

This week, there was a report from the War Department on a threatened strike at the San Diego Electric Railway Company. The hiring of a Negro platform trainee was supposed to be the cause of the strike. A wire was sent to Region XII on the matter and it developed that our office was in contact with the company. Although we have not yet had a full report on the matter, at this point, it does not appear that the trainee was placed at FEPC's request.

On December 4, I received information that the Associated Press had requested its New York representative to file a report on, "the telephone strike because of the hiring of Negroes." A check with the New York office showed that this report was incorrect. The New York office talked with Mr. O. A. Taylor, Vice-President in charge of Industrial Relations, who stated that four colored girls reported for duty and two were disqualified after physical examinations. The remaining two were sent to work at the Pennsylvania Exchange, Mr. Taylor said. It appears that the threatened strike of Memphis operators over wage questions was the basis of the rumor.

ASSIGNMENTS

The following DFO cases have been returned to regional offices:

1. Basic Magnesium, Inc., 12-BR-58, 12-BR-129–132, incl.
2. Brotherhood of Maintenance of Way Employees, AFL, 6-UR-586. Illinois Central Railroad, 6-BR-601

The following case has been referred to the Legal Division:

1. Wilson & Company, 6-BC-592

The following FDR's have been reviewed and acted upon by me:

Region VI—5
Region VII—5
Region VIII—1
Region XII—14

cc: Messrs. Davidson, Davis, Johnson, Jones

MS: copy, FEPC RG 228, Office Files of Clarence Mitchell, DNA.
  1. See 12/2/44.

Memorandum on Telephone Conversation with Mr. Dillard Lassiter, War Manpower Commission

December 6, 1944

MEMORANDUM

TO: Mr. Malcolm Ross
          Chairman

FROM: Clarence M. Mitchell
          Associate Director of Field Operations

SUBJECT: Telephone Conversation with Mr. Dillard Lassiter,
          War Manpower Commission

On the above date, I talked with Mr. Dillard Lassiter,[1] Regional Director of the War Manpower Commission in Atlanta. He was in Washington for a Regional Director's meeting.

We discussed the war training for the Reynolds Corporation in Macon, Georgia. Mr. Lassiter stated that it was his understanding that a class would begin shortly for Negro applicants. He also said that he expected FEPC to pursue the matter of getting the Reynolds Corporation to hire these persons after the training is completed. I told him we are already in touch with the Navy Department on this matter and hope for an adjustment.

Mr. Lassiter also expressed his appreciation for Dr. Dodge and asked me to let you know that he is happy to work with our new Regional Director. Mr. Lassiter said that he expects to have a conference of his state directors in Tampa, Florida and will urge them to extend full cooperation to Dr. Dodge.[2]

MS: LH, HqR1, Office Memoranda, 10/42–1/45. M.

1. The spelling elsewhere is Lasseter.

2. David Witherspoon Dodge replaced A. Bruce Hunt as regional director in Atlanta in October 1944. In his autobiography, Dodge reported "good cooperation from the Atlanta office of the WMC's southern regional director [Dillard Lasseter] but it was a different story with many of the state directors who made it evident they did not intend to help implement FEPC policies. Some made promises which they never intended to fulfill. Others stalled along, paying little or no attention to my correspondence with them, asking for more time to prevent the needed decisive action. To some of them the Regional Director sent sharp letters" demanding prompt action on complaints. Even so, no action was taken.

Dodge explained that, as "cogs" of the local political machines, the WMC regional directors "doubtless considered it part of their job to keep FEPC harmless whenever possible." Nevertheless,

Dodge said, "FEPC did a much better job in the South than reasonably could have been expected of it." Dodge and Cooke, *Southern Rebel*, 150–51. See 1/23, 2/6/45.

Memorandum on Telephone Conversation Regarding General Cable Company

December 6, 1944

MEMORANDUM

TO: Files

FROM: Clarence M. Mitchell

SUBJECT: Telephone Conversation re General Cable Company

On Tuesday, December 5, Mr. Theodore Brown of the St. Louis office, called concerning the General Cable Company. He stated that on Saturday night, December 2, there was a fight at the plant between Negroes and whites. He stated that a colored girl is supposed to have passed a coat to a white man and dropped it on the floor. The man slapped her, according to Mr. Brown's information, and later began beating her. A number of Negroes came to her assistance, Mr. Brown stated, and in the fight that ensued, the white man was stabbed. He is not expected to live.

The company's version of this is that the white man had been discharged and had made an indecent remark to the colored girl. She is supposed to have hit him with a coat hangar and later, other colored persons joined in the fray.

This incident was cited by the company as a reason for not placing Negro women on production.[1]

MS: copy, HqR1, Office Memoranda. M.

1. For an earlier view of the company's position on race relations there, see Dwight Palmer's letter to Edwin B. Meissner, chairman, St. Louis Race Relations Commission: "The policy of our corporation, during my term of office as President, has been to employ people of all nationalities, races and creeds, without discrimination, and to upgrade on skill and merit alone. Negroes are in our employ at all of our ten plants, and it so happens that at one of our locations better than half of the total number of employees are of the Negro race. At no time had I heard that there was any question as to whether we did or did not employ Negroes. The item of presumed but erroneous issue was whether or not we would upgrade the Negroes along with all other racial groups." Palmer's policy provides a window to his position on race relations, which proved important to resolving racial difficulties at his firm. Palmer letter, 4/14/45, to Meissner, HqR76, Office Files of Will Maslow. General Cable Company. See also the headnote on Major Cases in St. Louis.

Memorandum on Strike at Pullman Standard Car Shipbuilding Division, Chicago, Illinois

December 8, 1944

MEMORANDUM

TO: Mr. Malcolm Ross
        Chairman

FROM: Clarence M. Mitchell
        Associate Director of Field Operations

SUBJECT: Strike at Pullman Standard Car Shipbuilding Division, Chicago, Illinois

In our telephone conversation with Mr. Elmer Henderson on Thursday, December 7, he stated that a strike occurred at the Pullman Standard Car Shipbuilding Division on Tuesday, December 5, when a Negro employee was upgraded to a supervisory position in the Pipe Fitting Department.[1]

The union representing workers at the plant is Local 2928 of the United Steel Workers, C.I.O. It is opposed to the strike and has urged all of the individuals off the job to return.

Mr. Henderson stated that the Negro employee was placed on the job when a vacancy occurred, and supervises the work of approximately four whites and three Negroes. There is one white individual who was supposed to have been a candidate for the job, and is therefore, disgruntled. His name is John Anhorn.

There are approximately three hundred workers in the Pipe Fitting Department and the Division employs a total of four thousand persons. Approximately eleven hundred are on strike, Mr. Henderson said. The company has Navy contracts.

MS: *copy, HqR62, Central Files. Reports, Tension Area Reports, Region VI.*
    1. See subsequent resolution of the problem at 12/11/44; headnote on Strikes and Work Stoppages.

Memorandum on Complaints against the Los Angeles Post Office

December 9, 1944

MEMORANDUM

TO: Mr. Malcolm Ross
            Chairman

FROM: Clarence M. Mitchell
            Associate Director of Field Operations

SUBJECT: Complaints Against the Los Angeles Post Office

The following is a resume of charges filed against the Los Angeles Post Office by members of the Special Committee on Discrimination in the Los Angeles Branch of the National Alliance of Postal Employees:

The Committee states that its first conference with the Postmaster, Mrs. Mary D. Briggs, was held on June 29, 1943. At that time, various problems were presented to the Postmaster, according to the material before us, and the Committee members cited a statement issued by the Postmaster General on June 2, 1943, as part of the reason why they hoped some of the matters complained of would be adjusted. This statement of the Postmaster General discusses problems of discrimination and appeared in the Postal Bulletin.

In the conference with the Los Angeles Postmaster, the committee members state that they pointed out that no Negro had ever been advanced beyond the rank of special clerk in the Terminal Annex. Numerous other matters such as work requests and types of assignment were also discussed.

On July 6, 1943, the Committee met with Mr. C. L. Reck, Superintendent of Mails, and submitted a list of approximately thirty Negro clerks "who had never been promoted to foremanship in spite of long years of successful service."

The Committee from the Postal Alliance held a second meeting with Mr. Reck on September 14, 1943. Apparently this conference did not have satisfactory results, and on November 15, 1943, complaints were filed with the Los Angeles Office of F.E.P.C. The specific charges are as follows:

1. Negroes are concentrated in the undesirable jobs. It is stated that the Rating Table was the subject of a survey by the Alliance Committee and it was found that an average of seven Negro girls, two Negro men, and one white man worked there each night. At no time was a white female employee observed working at the Rating Table.

   A similar survey of the Flat Alley, which is said to be an undesirable assignment requiring the clerks who work there to stand at all times, revealed an average of ten Negro girls and five Negro men working there each night. At no time during the survey was a white employee observed working in the Flat Alley.

   The Hand Stamp Section on the night shift is manned entirely by Negroes it is charged.

   There is a complaint from Mr. Saul J. Hill, alleging that approximately twenty Postal clerks, all white, were appointed as temporary foremen during the 1943 Christmas rush. Mr. Hill is said to have received an offer to serve as a Christmas foreman in the Hand Stamp Section at night. In refusing to accept this offer, Mr. Hill is quoted as telling the Assistant Superintendent of Mails that his reason for refusing was due to the fact that the Hand Stamp section was regarded as a segregated unit. Mr. Hill told the Assistant Superintendent of Mails, he would be willing to accept temporary foremanship on the Hand Stamp Section if a Negro clerk would be given the supervision over the Facing Tables and Cancelling Machines. The Assistant Superintendent of Mails is said to have promised to talk the matter with higher authorities and notify Mr. Hill later. Nothing was ever mentioned to Mr. Hill again on this matter.

2. Negroes are not permitted to work in numerous departments. A case growing out of this alleged pattern has resulted in the resignation of a Negro employee, although there is some indication that policy of the particular department in which he worked has been corrected. The Alliance Committee describes this case as follows:

On the night of November 10, 1943, together with other Negro employees and eight or ten white employees, Benjamin Woods was assigned by Supervisor Osborne to work Metered Mail on mezzanine at the Terminal Annex. Supervisor Grant reassigned the Negroes to dumping sacks. Woods is quoted as saying that after this "obvious display of discrimination by Supervisor Grant" he would rather go home than dump any more sacks. He then returned to Mr. Osborne for another assignment. On November 12, 1943, Mr. Woods received a communication from Mr. Reck charging him with insubordination. He replied to the charges and requested a hearing. On November 20, 1943, the hearing was conducted and Mr. Grant is said to have admitted that he removed Woods from the Metered Mail Section and replaced him with a white employee named Gerald Wallace. At the conclusion of this hearing, Mr. Reck denied that discrimination existed but instructed Mr. Grant to reassign Mr. Woods to Metered Mail. Mr. Woods was assigned to Metered Mail on November 22, 1943, but was removed by a Mr. Lark. Mr. Lark is said to have told Woods that the reason for removing him was that the men on Metered Mail were older in the service. Mr. Woods offered to prove that a substitute white clerk, younger than he, was on Metered Mail. At that time, Mr. Lark is said to have replied that he was too busy. As a result of these instances and the way in which he was handled, Mr. Woods resigned his postal employment on November 22, 1943, it is stated.

The F.E.P.C. received a letter dated February 23, from the Postmaster, Mrs. Briggs, in which the following statement is made:

"At this conference (between F.E.C.P. and Postal Officials) all of the items in your brief were carefully gone into and it was determined that none of the complaints had any proof in fact other than the complaint that only white clerks were being used in the handling of Metered Mail. This unwitting oversight on the part of the supervisors on the work floor has been corrected."

In view of the fact that the Postmaster admits that white employees only were admitted to work on Metered Mail, it appears that there is some need for a new inquiry on the case of Mr. Woods.

3. Negroes are not permitted to work as foremen or junior foremen in the Terminal Annex. It is charged that a Mr. James A. Randall, white, was appointed foreman, but eleven Negro clerks had seniority over him as the time of his appointment. A junior foremanship was given to Mr. Gaston Bertonneau who entered the service on October 21, 1929. It is stated that eighty-one Negro clerks had seniority over him but were not given the proper consideration for the appointment. Persons mentioned as passed over in this appointment are: Mr. Norman Shivers, who entered the service on January 9, 1943 [1923], Mr. William H. Gordon who entered the service May 11, 1943 [1923], and Mr. Custis Garrott who entered the service on November 27, 1922. Mr. Garrott has passed his scheme examination 100% four times in succession and has maintained an average of 99 to 100% in the city scheme. His efficiency ratings for the past "few years" have averaged approximately 96. The Alliance Committee states that during the conference with the Superintendent of Mails, Mr. Reck and the Assistant Postmaster, Mr. Strechley, "We were informed that this matter would be adjusted and that we would be given satisfaction."

The Alliance Committee states that subsequently the Superintendent of Mails told them that four senior Negro clerks had been approached and offered consideration for foremanships, but each had declined. It appears that these persons were advanced in age and the position would have required that they take "a graveyard tour as Junior foremen."

Mr. Reck is said to have told the Committee from the Alliance that the names of three new men had been submitted to the Washington office and that all were white. The Committee from the Alliance states that one of those white men was Mr. Claude F. Houseman, who entered the service on November 23, 1923 and that between Mr. Houseman, and Mr. Buell A. Thomas, the youngest (in seniority) of the four Negro clerks who were approached by the Superintendent of Mails, there were at least fifty-two Negro clerks who had seniority over him (Mr. Houseman). The second foremanship went to Mr. Lee Denbo who entered the service on March 1, 1928 and had less seniority than at least sixty-five Negro clerks. The third position as foreman was given to Mr. Roy W. Robbins. Sixty Negro clerks had seniority over Mr. Robbins, it is charged. The complaint states that the Superintendent of Mails did not contact any of the colored persons who had seniority over the white individuals who were appointed, except the first four Negroes who declined to accept the positions.

4. There are apparent attempts to maintain a quota of Negro employees. It is stated that Negro women are told that a number of applicants are ahead of them. However, white women are given immediate employment. The following is the Postal Alliance's version of an example of this type of action:

Mrs. J. C. Moore applied for work, had three years of college training and passed a Civil Service Examination. She was told that a number of girls had applied ahead of her and was shown a number of applications. However, a white friend of Mrs. Moore's named Mrs. Della, went to the Post Office the following day and was put to work at once. Later, two white women and a Negro woman went to the Post Office together. The white woman were offered jobs but the Negro woman was told that no help was needed. This matter was set forth in a letter to the committee dated September 2 [22], 1944.

cc: Mr. Joseph F. Gartland
Region XII

MS: copy, HqR84, Correspondence Relating to Cases. (L–S) U.S. Post Office, Los Angeles, California.
   Included in this file is the complete report of all charges and complaints filed by Sidney Moore, chairman of the Special Committee to Investigate Promotional Discrimination, the National Alliance of Postal Employees. This and other related materials are filed with the published text. As he notes at 12/11/44, Mitchell submitted this digest to Gartland, chief of operations board of the Post Office Department. See other developments at 11/13, 11/25, 11/27, 12/2, 12/11, and 12/12/44; and the headnote on Relationships with Federal Agencies.

Weekly Report

December 11, 1944

Mr. Will Maslow
Director of Field Operations
Clarence M. Mitchell
Associate Director of Field Operations
Weekly Report for the Week Ending December 9, 1944

OUTSTANDING EVENTS AND PROBLEMS

Digests of complaints against the Post Offices in Los Angeles and Philadelphia have been submitted to Mr. Joseph F. Gartland, Chief of the Operations Board of the Post Office Department. There are two other digests on Dallas and Houston which will be submitted this week.[1]

On December 5, I had a conference with Mr. George Weaver of the National C.I.O. concerning the Murray Gin Company of Dallas, Texas. Mr. Weaver agreed to discuss this case with the Steel Workers Union and inform me of any progress made. Because of the nature of the contract between a local of the Steel Workers Union, Negroes are not permitted to go above the classification of Laborer.

At the request of Region VII, I talked with Mr. Dillard Lassiter,[2] Regional Director of the War Manpower Commission, when he was in Washington. Mr. Lassiter told me that he expects the Macon Vocational School to begin operation in the near future. There now remains the problem of getting Navy cooperation to see to it that the persons who finish training are employed.[3]

At the suggestion of Mr. Fleming, Regional Director of III, and Mr. Davidson, I am seeking a conference with the New Jersey Bell Telephone Company. Mr. Fleming thought that since the New York settlement, a conference with the company would be helpful.[4]

ASSIGNMENTS

The following DFO cases have been returned to regional offices:

1. R.A. Nicel Company, 12-BR-395
2. Illinois Central Railroad, 6-BR-359

The following DFO cases were returned from the Legal Division:

1. Delco Remy Division—General Motors, 6-BC-6, 275–278, 280–282.

The following case was referred to Region XII at the request of Region VIII:

1. E. W. Elliott Company, 8-BR-53.

The following new cases have been received by me during the past week:

1. New Jersey Bell Telephone Company, 3-BR-646 (Received from Mr. Davidson)
2. District Engineer, Miami, Florida

The following FDR's have been reviewed and acted upon by me:

Region VI—4	Region VII—1
Region X—2	Region XII—21

cc: Messrs. Davidson, Davis, Johnson, Jones

MS: *copy, FEPC RG 228, Office Files of Clarence Mitchell, DNA.*

1. For progressive development, see 11/13, 11/25, 11/27, 12/2, 12/9, 12/12/44. For the background, see the section on the Post Office Department in the headnote on Relationships with Federal Agencies.

2. The general spelling is Lasseter.

3. See 12/6/44 memorandum.

4. See the headnote on the Telephone Industry.

Memorandum on Strike at Pullman Standard Car Shipbuilding Division, Chicago, Illinois

December 11, 1944

MEMORANDUM

TO: Mr. Malcolm Ross
   Chairman

FROM: Clarence M. Mitchell
   Associate Director of Field Operations

SUBJECT: Strike at Pullman Standard Car Shipbuilding Division, Chicago

On Saturday, December 9, Mr. Henderson called concerning the strike out at the Pullman Standard Car Shipbuilding Division in Chicago.

He stated that the stoppage was breaking up rapidly and of the eleven hundred workers out, all, except approximately four hundred, had returned to the job. Part of the four hundred wanted to work, but could not do so because certain key-men were still out.

Mr. Henderson said the company fully expects to have the whole situation under control by the beginning of the week. The Negro employee who was upgraded is still on the job.

MS: LH, DI, HqR1, Office Memoranda, 10/42–1/45—M.
 See previous report at 12/8/44; headnote on Strikes and Work Stoppages.

Memorandum on Minutes of the Meeting with the Post Office Operations Board

December 12, 1944

MEMORANDUM

TO: Mr. Malcolm Ross
   Chairman

FROM: Clarence M. Mitchell
        Associate Director of Field Operations
SUBJECT: Minutes of the Meeting with Post Office Operations Board

There are two matters which are not taken care of in the minutes sent to us by the Chairman of the Operations Board.[1]

The first, is information given by one of the officials present, on the right of the laborers to be restored to their former jobs if they accept war service appointments as carriers or clerks. You will recall, that one of the officials present, stated that such assurance is given to individuals by the over-all Post Office policy. Since this is an important element in our Dallas case, I believe we should remind Mr. Gartland that this was left out in the report.

The second thing, is the estimate of Negroes employed by the Post Office Department. On page 1739 of the minutes submitted to us, Mr. Gartland is quoted as estimating the number of Negro employees as 10,000 of a total of 370,000 persons. However, in the closing paragraph of the minutes, where we discussed the question of statistics, no mention is made that Mr. Gartland agreed to submit an official estimate to us. Of course, we could regard the figure of 10,000 as an official estimate since it is contained in the minutes. I have given this to the Division of Review and Analysis for its report.

MS: copy, HqR84, Correspondence Relating to Cases. Post Office (Minutes of Meeting of Operations Board).

1. For the minutes of this meeting, at which Ross, Mitchell, and Gartland spoke, see "Excerpts from the Proceedings of the Operations Board of the Post Office Department Meeting of November 25, 1944," filed with the above text. For related activities see 11/13, 11/25, 11/27, 12/2, 12/9, 12/11/44.

Memorandum on Current DFO War Department Cases

December 14, 1944

MEMORANDUM

To: Mr. Malcolm Ross
           Chairman
From: Clarence M. Mitchell
           Associate Director of Field Operations
Subject: Current DFO War Department Cases

Pursuant to our discussion in your office, I am submitting the following current cases which we are handling with the War Department:

1. Richmond Army Service Forces Depot

The principle complaint in this case centers around the discriminatory policy of the Depot which confines Negroes to certain jobs. We have a specific complaint from a colored woman who apparently was mistaken for white and hired as a checker. She contends that when it was discovered that she was a Negro, she was removed from her job and rehired as a janitress.

This case has been in the office of the Civilian Aide [Truman K. Gibson] since July 14, 1944. We have received an unsatisfactory report on it on October 16, after sending two follow-up letters in July.

In two other cases against this same establishment, the complaints have been withdrawn because of the delay. In a third case, the complainant is seeking a release from the establishment because the War Department held a hearing on his case which he considered of no value. We have asked that we be notified of this hearing but our only source of information on it so far, has been the complainant.[1]

2. Mt. Ranier Motor Base

This case has been before us since 1943. At one point, we dismissed it on merits because of information received from the War Department. It was reopened when the individual who was a party to the discrimination against the complainant filed an affidavit with our San Francisco office. This affidavit sets forth the manner in which the complainant was discriminated against. We referred it to the War Department on July 25, 1944.

Although the War Department itself admits that the complainant was denied the job because of his race, it is contended that the individual who denied him employment was not authorized to take such action. In addition, the War Department seeks to place the entire blame on Mr. Gordan Hanson, the individual who filed the affidavit with us.

3. District Engineer - Miami, Florida

On December 4, we communicated with the War Department concerning the District Engineer, Miami, Florida. In this case, a Negro was hired in St. Paul for work on a project outside of the country under the direction of the Miami, Florida District Engineer.

We have photostatic copies of the contract which he signed and photostats of letters indicating that preparations were being made for a pay allotment to the complainant's wife. Since this case has been referred to the War Department only recently, it is not possible to say what will be the result. However, I cannot expect that much will come of it in view of our past relations.

4. Consolidated Vultee Aircraft, Ft. Worth, Texas

We have a number of complaints against the Consolidated Vultee Aircraft, Ft. Worth, Texas. Because this is a Government owned privately operated establishment, the War Department was requested to assist in the adjustment of complaints.

On September 18, I sent a letter to the Civilian Aide concerning the problem and asked that some attempt be made to correct it. On December 11, I met with the War Department representatives and learned that although there had been many endorsements by War Department officials, our request for action had not produced any results.

The Civilian Aide interposed a new suggestion asking that the Committee contact the company's top officials in San Diego. Although we will take this action, I believe that it will not produce results, unless the War Department takes steps to make the contractor comply with the non-discrimination clause in his contract.

MS: LH, HqR39, Central Office Files (Entry 25), Memoranda, Ross, Malcolm, 1944.

1. This is one of the two instances in this report alone in which Mitchell's expresses his unhappiness with Gibson's performance. For other confirmation of his lack of respect for Gibson, see 2/5/45 and FDR 2/23/45.

Memorandum on Threatened Strike at McQuay Norris Core Plant, St. Louis, Missouri

December 14, 1944

MEMORANDUM

TO: Mr. George M. Johnson
Deputy Chairman

FROM: Clarence M. Mitchell
Associate Director of Field Operations

SUBJECT: Threatened Strike at McQuay Norris Core
Plant, St. Louis, Missouri

On December 13, Mr. Theodore Brown of our St. Louis office called me at home to say that approximately two hundred Negro workers in the McQuay Norris Core

Plant in St. Louis are threatening to go on strike. The cause of the threatened strike is failure of the company to upgrade them; and also, the plant's failure to include Negro workers on the new jobs which are available because of increased need for cores.

Mr. Brown said that the company had advertised extensively for workers and has urged its employees to bring their relatives and friends in for jobs. The Negro employees still remain in the Material Department. This plant makes ninety per cent of the cores used by the company. Mr. Brown said any tie-up would, therefore, be very serious. He stated that he was having a meeting with the employees later on in the evening. I urged him to work with the union at the plant in avoiding a work stoppage and told him that we would do everything possible to remedy the problem. It is expected that the Negro employees will be holding a meeting on Sunday, December 17.

MS: LH, DI, HqR20, Records Relating to Hearings. McQuay-Norris Manufacturing Co.
  See 12/18/44; headnotes on Strikes and Work Stoppages and on Major Cases in St. Louis.

Weekly Report

December 18, 1944

Mr. Will Maslow
    Director of Field Operations
Clarence M. Mitchell
    Associate Director of Field Operations
Weekly Report for the Week Ending Saturday, December 16, 1944

OUTSTANDING EVENTS AND PROBLEMS

This week, I communicated with the central office of the Consolidated Vultee Company at San Diego, California, concerning employment at Fort Worth. This action was taken at the suggestion of the War Department. I have been informed that the War Department is continuing its inquiry on this case.[1]

The threatened strike at the McQuay Norris Company in St. Louis appears to have been averted by coordinated action by the St. Louis and Washington offices. This matter was directed to the attention of the National C.I.O. officials with the hope of getting full cooperation from the local (UAW) union.

The Chief of the Operations Board of the Post Office [Joseph F. Gartland] has acknowledged receipt of the complaints against the Post Offices in Durham, North Carolina; Los Angeles; Houston and Philadelphia. A report on the various complaints is promised.

At the request of Region VII, a contact was made with the War Manpower Commission and the U. S. Office of Education on the establishment of vocational training courses in Macon, Georgia. We have notified the region that the WMC assured us that these courses will get underway within three weeks. The region has been asked to verify this information.

Mr. Hayes Beall is currently working on a digest of transit cases now being handled by the regional offices.

ASSIGNMENTS

The following DFO cases have been returned to regional offices:

   1. General Motors—Delco Remy, 6-BC-6, 275, 276, 277, 278, 280, 281, and 282.

The following case was referred to the Legal Division this week:

   1. Mt. Ranier Ordnance Depot, 12-GR-15

The following case was assigned to me this week:

   1. Post Office Department, Durham, North Carolina,

The following FDR's have been reviewed and acted upon by me:

Region VI—3	Region XII—12
Region VIII—1	

cc: Messrs. Davis, Davidson, Johnson, Jones

MS: copy, FEPC RG 228, Office Files of Clarence Mitchell, DNA.
   1. See memorandum of 12/14/44.

Memorandum of Telephone Conversation with Mr. Theodore Brown Regarding McQuay Norris

DATE: 12/18/44

TO: Files

FROM: Clarence M. Mitchell

SUBJECT: Telephone Conversation with Theodore Brown Re McQuay Norris

On December 16, Mr. Theodore Brown informed the Chairman and myself via long distance telephone that the threatened walkout of Negro employees at the McQuay Norris Company seems to be averted. He stated that the newspapers carried front page articles on the issuance of FEPC directives against the company and this appears to have convinced the workers that something was being done about their problem.[1]

Mr. Brown also mentioned that he has a conference scheduled with the St. Louis Public Service on the question of using Negroes as platform operators. Mr. Brown said that at present, the union appears to be cooperative but it does not have a real following among the rank and file workers of the company.[2]

MS: LH, DI, HqR63 Central Files. Reports, Tension Area Reports, Region IX.
    1. See 12/18/44; headnotes on Strikes and Work Stoppages and on Major Cases in St. Louis.
    2. See the headnote on Street and Local Railways.

Memorandum on Meeting with the Maritime Commission on Gulf Region Shipbuilding Companies

December 19, 1944

MEMORANDUM

TO: Mr. Will Maslow
        Director of Field Operations

FROM: Clarence M. Mitchell
        Associate Director of Field Operations

SUBJECT: Meeting With the Maritime Commission on Gulf Region
        Shipbuilding Companies

On Monday, December 18, I met with Mr. Daniel Ring, Director of Shipyard Labor Relations, Maritime Commission; Mr. Russell Cooley, Special Assistant to the Director, Division of Shipyard Labor Relations; and Major Walter Graham, Regional Labor Representative of the Maritime Commission in the Gulf area. Mr. Hayes Beall of the central staff of Field Operations was with me. We discussed the following yards: Delta Shipbuilding Company, New Orleans; Todd-Johnson Dry Docks, New Orleans; and the St. Johns River Shipbuilding Company, Jacksonville, Florida. We outlined briefly the problems in each case and left with Mr. Ring a summary of our relations with these companies.

The problem at the Delta Shipbuilding Company concerns employment of Negroes as welders. Major Graham presented a list of occupations in which Negroes are currently employed by the Company. This appears very favorable in some respects and the Maritime Commission is sending us a copy of it. However, the Major stated that the Company is unprepared to give a specific promise that Negroes will be used as welders because it has not fully sold the supervisory force on this matter. I took the position that since 1942, the company has had ample opportunity to sell its supervisors and there should be no further delay. Major Graham volunteered the information that 115 Negro welders are being released by the Higgins Company because of cutbacks. These people are available for employment at Delta where welders are needed. Mr. Ring asked Major Graham to report on whether Delta makes use of these individuals by the first of next week (December 26). Mr. Ring stated that if the company did not find it possible to convince its supervisory force, he would take the matter up with the full Commission. Major Graham then said, that in his opinion, the company wanted to do the right thing and might "even now be hiring the Negroes". I felt that Mr. Ring's position was clear and positive. The Maritime Commission is to report to me on this matter next week. I have notified Mr. Ellinger of Mr. Ring's position and a copy of this memorandum is being sent to him.

We discussed also the recent commitment received on September 14, 1944, when Mr. W. Don Ellinger of the Regional office conferred with officials of the Todd-Johnson Dry Dock Company and representatives of the International Union of Marine and Shipbuilding Workers. It was agreed that the Maritime Commission would be cooperative in seeing to it that this contractor lives up to the agreement. However, it will be necessary to obtain similar cooperation from the Army and Navy if we run into difficulties, since those agencies also have contracts in the Yard.

We presented the problem of the St. Johns River Shipbuilding Company in Jacksonville, Florida, and pointed out that there, the Metal Trades Council has informed our Regional office that there will be violence if Negroes are employed on welding and burning jobs. Mr. Ring stated that the Maritime Commission would determine the extent to which the company is responsible for this problem, but added that the Committee will have to handle the union question itself. I have requested Mr. Beall to prepare a separate memorandum for presentation to the Legal Division with the recommendation that a hearing be held in this case.

cc: Messrs. Ross
          Johnson
          Beall
          Dodge
          Ellinger

MS: copy, HqR1, Office Memoranda. M.

See the section on the Maritime Commission in the headnote on Relationships with Federal Agencies and the headnote on the Shipbuilding Industry.

Memorandum on Conference with
Dr. L. S. Hawkins, U.S. Office of Education

December 20, 1944

MEMORANDUM

TO: Mr. Will Maslow
     Director of Field Operations

FROM: Clarence M. Mitchell
       Associate Director of Field Operations

SUBJECT: Conference With Dr. L. S. Hawkins,
          U.S. Office of Education

On Thursday, December 21, I am to meet with Dr. Hawkins for the purpose of discussing the program for vocational training for war production workers.[1] Specifically, I will take up the training program in Macon, Georgia and Fort Worth, Texas. I shall also ask that the U.S. Office of Education instruct its regional representatives to inform our regional directors whenever new training programs are sent in for approval by states in which there are separate schools. In this manner, we can make a prompt determination of whether the proposal includes training for Negroes as well as for whites. Catching the problem at this point should enable us to insure more satisfactory handling of such matters.

Also, it is my understanding that extensive courses bearing upon the coal mining industry have been set up in the State of West Virginia. I shall make a determination of whether such courses are also available to Negroes in that area.

On January 1, 1945, a change in the procedure for authorizations to obligate funds for pre-employment courses will go into effect. This change was mentioned in a telephone conversation by Mr. Van Wyck, Chief of Training for the War Manpower Commission. I shall discuss this with Mr. Hawkins also.

MS: LH, DI, HqR67, Central Files. Reports, U.S. Government-1, General, N–W.

1. For initiation of the FEPC's struggle against discrimination in training programs, see Mitchell's 12/29/44 memorandum for his report of this meeting and note at 11/28/42.

Weekly Report

December 27, 1944

Mr. Will Maslow
> Director of Field Operations

Clarence M. Mitchell
> Associate Director of Field Operations

Weekly Report for the Week Ending Saturday, December 23, 1944

OUTSTANDING EVENTS AND PROBLEMS

As a result of our conferences with the Maritime Commission concerning the Delta Shipbuilding Company, Negro welders are to be hired January first or second in the New Orleans yard. These persons are to be employed on an integrated basis, according to the Maritime Commission. Mr. Ellinger has been informed of this development and requested to keep in touch with the Maritime Commission officials on it.[1]

The Navy Department, in a letter dated December 22, states that the Commanding Officer at the Reynolds Corporation plant in Macon, Georgia, has been told to call to the company's attention, the necessity for complying with Executive Order 9346 in its hiring and training policies. This matter has been forwarded to Dr. Witherspoon Dodge.

The last of the DFO Post Office cases has been sent to the Office of the Postmaster General for investigation. The proposed agreement with the Post Office is now in final form and ready for transmittal by the Chairman.[2]

On Thursday, December 21, I conferred with Dr. L. S. Hawkins, Chief of Vocational Training for War Production Workers, concerning a new working relationship with the U.S. Office of Education. The results of this conference are set forth in a separate memorandum. It appears that the Office of Education will furnish us with much of the information we desire.[3]

ASSIGNMENTS

The following DFO cases were returned from the Legal Division:

1. Baltimore & Ohio Roundhouse, 6-BR-613
2. Southern Pacific Lines, 10-BR-281.

The following new cases have been received by me during the past week:

1. University of North Carolina College Laundry, 4-BR-449; 461; 462.
2. Maryland Bolt and Nut Company, 4-BR-370.
3. New York Central Railroad Company, 5-BR-114.

The following WFA has been received on a case previously referred:

1. St. Johns River Shipbuilding Company, 7-BR-409.

The following FDR's have been reviewed and acted upon by me:

Region III—7   Region XII—5
Region VI—4

cc: Messrs. Davidson
Davis
Johnson
Jones

MS: copy, FEPC 228, *Office Files of Clarence Mitchell, DNA.*
 1. See memoranda of 5/5, 12/19/44; headnote on the Shipbuilding Industry and the section on the Maritime Commission in the headnote on Relationships with Federal Agencies.
 2. See the section on the Post Office Department in the headnote on Relationships with Federal Agencies.
 3. See memoranda of 12/20, 12/29/44.

Memorandum on Conference with U.S. Office of Education, December 21, 1944

December 29, 1944

MEMORANDUM

TO: Mr. Will Maslow
     Director of Field Operations

FROM: Clarence M. Mitchell
     Associate Director of Field Operations

SUBJECT: Conference With U.S. Office of Education
             December 21, 1944

Because of difficulties growing out of our relations with the Macon Vocational School, I had a conference with Dr. L. S. Hawkins, Chief of Vocational Training for War Production Workers, U.S. Office of Education.[1] Mr. Edgar P. Westmoreland, Special Representative Defense Vocational Education, was also present at the conference. Dr. Hawkins was very optimistic about the training program in Macon, Georgia and fully expected that it would be underway within three weeks, as stated by the War Manpower Commission.

In addition, I requested that the Office of Education supply us with information on courses approved for war production training. In this manner, our regional directors will be able to obtain from the War Manpower Commission, statements on whether such courses in the separate school states are being set up for non-whites. After the War Manpower Commission reports that such courses have not been established for non-whites, our regional directors should then request a Form 42 from the WMC and docket a case. In my opinion, this information will enable us to get at the training problem before the courses for whites are actually set up and therefore, will be more practical.

Dr. Hawkins stated that beginning February 1, all of the pre-employment training courses will be reviewed by the U.S. Office of Education and lists of such courses now in progress will be sent to us at that time.

The Office of Education has extensive courses in West Virginia for the training of individuals interested in the coal mining industry. It was agreed that FEPC would receive a listing of the location of these courses. When I receive it, I will send it to Region IV for further checking with the War Manpower Commission to determine whether similar courses will be established for qualified non-whites.

It was agreed also that the Office of Education check on training courses given for the benefit of the Consolidated Vultee Aircraft Company in Fort Worth, Texas and furnish us with a listing of this type of training. When we receive this information we will send it to Mr. Ellinger.

MS: LH, DI, HqR67, Central Files. Reports, U.S. Government, General, N–W.

1. Mitchell informed Maslow that he would be meeting with Dr. Hawkins to discuss the vocational training program for war workers. Mitchell to Maslow, memorandum, 12/20/44. The U.S. Office of Education was one of four agencies responsible for training workers for essential war industries. For extensive discussion of related racial problems, see Weaver, *Negro Labor;* Doxey Wilkerson, "The Training and Employment of Negroes in National Defense Industries"; Branson, "Training of Negroes for War Industries in World War II." See also the headnote on Relationships with Federal Agencies.

Memorandum on International Brotherhood of Teamsters, Chauffeurs, Warehousemen of America, Local 533

December 30, 1944

Mr. Will Maslow
      Director of Field Operations

Clarence M. Mitchell
      Associate Director of Field Operations

International Brotherhood of Teamsters, Chauffeurs
      Warehousemen of America, Local 533—12-UR-327

I am attaching a proposed letter to Mr. Tobin on the question of his union's attitude toward American citizens of Japanese ancestry. However, before this letter is sent, we should have a determination of whether the company which employed Mr. Baba is within the Committee's jurisdiction.[1]

I am today writing to Mr. Kingman for information to indicate why his office believes that this company is within the Committee's jurisdiction.
Attachment

MS: copy, HqR63, Central Files. Reports, Rulings, General.
  1. See the headnote on Japanese Americans.

Weekly Report

January 2, 1945

Mr. Will Maslow
      Director of Field Operations

Clarence M. Mitchell
      Associate Director of Field Operations

Weekly Report for the Week Ending Saturday, December 30, 1944

OUTSTANDING EVENTS AND PROBLEMS

In keeping with the previously made plans, I shall go to the Atlanta office on the evening of January 15 and remain until January 19. It will be appreciated if any matters which should be taken up with the Regional Director will be given to me by Saturday, January 13.

The New Jersey Bell Telephone Company has sent in a lengthy but uncooperative reply to our efforts to settle Region III's cases involving the company.[1] It appears that this matter can be resolved only by hearing.

We have received from Region XII a complaint involving the Teamsters Union in Nevada. In view of the problem we have with this union in Detroit, it appears that we should get some positive action on our unresolved cases.

ASSIGNMENTS

The following new case was received by me during the past week:
International Brotherhood of Teamsters, Chauffeurs, Warehousemen of America, Local 533, 12-UR-377

The following cases have been returned to the Regional offices:

1. Baltimore and Ohio, Chicago Terminal Railroad Company 6-BR-613
2. Southern Pacific Railroad, 10-BR-281
3. Sinclair Refining Company, 10-BR-332

Through an error the following DFO cases were reported as being handled by me in my weekly report of December 23. Actually these cases came into my office but were transmitted to Mr. Davidson who handled them:
University of North Carolina Laundry, 4-BR-449; 461; 462.
Maryland Nut and Bolt Company, 4-BR-370.
New York Central Railroad Co., 5-BR-114
The following FDR's have been reviewed and acted upon by me:

Region VI- 16	Region VII- 17
Region XII- 9	

cc: Messrs.   Davidson
             Davis
             Johnson
             Jones

MS: *copy, FEPC RG 228, Office Files of Clarence Mitchell, DNA.*
   1. For excerpts of New Jersey Bell's response to Mitchell, see 3/8/45.

Memorandum on Excerpts from Reports on Discriminatory Practices of Shipyards in the Southeast

January 2, 1945

MEMORANDUM

TO: Mr. Malcolm Ross
            Chairman

FROM: Clarence M. Mitchell
            Associate Director of Field Operations

SUBJECT: Excerpts from Reports on Discriminatory Practices
            of Shipyards in the Southeast

In keeping with our conversation on the above date, I am submitting this material which I hope will be useful:

1. During the month of September, 1944, 25 Negroes employed as riveters and reamers at the Wainwright Shipyard in Panama City, Fla., were chased off the job by 100 whites. The J. A. Jones Construction Company which owns the yard, charges that it wishes to make full use of Negroes but is prevented from doing so by the Boilermakers Union.

2. On December 7, 1944, Regional Director Dodge was told by Mr. J. Rae Simpson, business agent for the Jacksonville Metal Trades Council that:

   "Negroes would not be accepted as welders and burners in the St. John River Shipbuilding Company and violence would follow attempts to place them in these jobs."

3. In justifying a move to house whites in a project intended for Negroes at Tampa, Florida, the F.P.H.A. in a report dated December 18, 1944, states that:

   "The Don Thompson Vocational School of Tampa has trained 231 Negroes in a year and a half but none of these obtained employment in Tampa Shipyards and had to go elsewhere to work. The F.P.H.A. has already housed 50 white families in the 500 unit project originally built for Negro immigrant war workers. It is expected that a total of 220 units will be used by whites."

MS: copy, HqR3, Office Files of George M. Johnson. Clarence Mitchell.
See the headnote on the Shipbuilding Industry and the Boilermakers Union.

Memorandum on Consolidated Vultee Aircraft Corporation of Fort Worth, Texas

January 4, 1945

Mr. Will Maslow
Director of Field Operations
Clarence M. Mitchell
Associate Director of Field Operations
Consolidated Vultee Aircraft Corporation of Fort Worth, Texas

As stated in my memorandum of December 12,[1] at the War Department's suggestion, I communicated with Mr. Harry Woodhead, president of the Consolidated Vultee Aircraft Corporation in San Diego, California.

I have received a reply from Mr. F. A. Lauerman, Director of Industrial Relations, who states that Mr. Woodhead asked him to handle this matter. The company professes a desire to "continue to cooperate with the President's Committee on Fair Employment Practice." However, all of the problems raised are evaded by the local manager, Mr. R. G. Mayer, as indicated by his letter of November 18 and Mr. Lauerman in his letter of December 22.

The following are the unresolved issues before us:

1. That Negroes are not admitted to the training and upgrading program of the company.
2. Negro employees are confined to unskilled jobs and denied opportunities to be upgraded.
3. The company does not employ Negro women.

The International Association of Machinists has the bargaining rights in the company. One Negro employee, who was a member of a federal labor union for Negroes in the plant, was dismissed but was later reinstated as the result of action brought by the IAM. The union contended that the employee, H. C. Carroll, had been dismissed because of his union activities.

Since this is a Government owned privately operated plant, I have made an effort to settle the case with the aid of the War Department. I do not expect that the War Department is very active on this matter, but I am sending a copy of Mr. Lauerman's letter to the Civilian Aide. Under the circumstances, I believe that the best interest of the war effort will be served if there is an immediate hearing on this case. I trust that you will make this recommendation to the Legal Division.[2]
Attachments

MS: copy, HqR83, Correspondence Relating to Cases. (A–K) Consolidated Vultee Aircraft Co.

This text evidently supersedes one of 1/3/45 to Maslow that included the first two paragraphs of this text and the last two sentences of the last paragraph. A copy of that version is also in HqR83, Correspondence Relating to Cases. (A–K) Consolidated Vultee Aircraft Co. For other related texts, see 2/12, 4/12, 4/23/45.

1. No memorandum of that date has been found, but see Mitchell's memorandum of 12/14/44 on War Department cases.

2. See Mitchell to Gibson, 1/3/45, and related texts filed with this document; the section on the War Department in the headnote on Relationships with Federal Agencies.

Memorandum on General Cable Company

DATE: January 6, 1945

TO: Mr. George Johnson
           Deputy Chairman

FROM: Clarence M. Mitchell
           Associate Director of Field Operations

SUBJECT   General Cable Company, 9-BR-1155

Attached are additional complaints we have received from individuals in St. Louis against the General Cable Company which is now in the hands of the Legal Division.[1] The complainants are as follows:

Mrs. Lessie Oliver
Mrs. Alberta Smith
Mrs. Mattie L. Williams
Mrs. Annie Mae Connaly
Mrs. Mary Little
Mrs. Dorothy Shepard
Miss Candace Little

Attachments

MS: LH, DI, FEPC RG 228, Office Files of Clarence Mitchell, DNA.
1. On this important case, see the headnote on Major Cases in St. Louis.

Memorandum on Types of Complaints against the International Association of Machinists

DATE: January 8, 1945

TO: Mr. George M. Johnson
           Deputy Chairman

FROM: Clarence M. Mitchell
          Associate Director of Field Operations
SUBJECT: Types of Complaints Against the International Association of Machinists

There are three types of complaints before FEPC at this time against the International Association of Machinists.[1] Specific cases are discussed in the attached summary. The categories are as follows:

1. Those cases in which, because of a closed shop contract, Negroes are barred from employment because the International Association of Machinists will not permit them to work. This is the situation in Richmond, California; Durham, North Carolina and Detroit, Michigan.

2. Complaints in which it is alleged that the local lodge of the International Association of Machinists prevents the upgrading of Negroes as is illustrated in the Fort Worth, Texas and York, Pennsylvania cases.

3. Cases in which it is charged that Negroes are denied membership in the union although they are employed by a company holding a contract with the IAM. This is the situation in Seattle and in Kansas City. In the Seattle cases, Negro employees pay the same monthly fees as whites but do not pay an initiation fee. In one of the Seattle lodges, Negro employees were formerly admitted but it is alleged that they are now kept out because of the action by the International union.

Attachment

SUMMARY OF COMPLAINTS AGAINST
INTERNATIONAL ASSOCIATION OF MACHINISTS

The following is a listing of FEPC cases pending in which complainants charge that they have been discriminated against solely because of their race:

1. On January 25, 1944 a USES 510 report was filed with the Regional office of the Committee on Fair Employment Practice in San Francisco. This report charged that the policies of Lodge 824 in Richmond, California prevented employment of Negroes in the Richmond Shipyard. It is also alleged that the policies of this lodge restricted the employment of Negroes in the following companies: Rheem Manufacturing Company, American Standard and Radiator Sanitary Company, and the Pacific Enamel Works. This case has been presented to Mr. Harvey Brown, president of the Machinists. On July 12, 1944, Mr. Brown sent a telegram to the lodge urging cooperation. The region advises that there has been no change in the policies of the union and has referred the case to Washington.

2. Lodge 79, which has a contract with the Seattle-Tacoma Ship, was named in a complaint filed July 7, 1944 by Chester Barry Smith and Willy L. Hopkins. The complainants, who are Negroes, charge that they have been denied membership in Hope Lodge 79. Representatives of our office in Region XII have met with the union and were advised that some Negroes are already members of the union, but further initiations were halted by the International office. Our office was informed that the International headquarters of the union stated to the local lodge that the word "white" in the ritual would include whites, Chinese, Filipinos, Hawaiians, and Indians but would specifically exclude Negroes. Negro employees state that they pay a permit fee which is the same amount as the monthly dues of the white employees who are admitted to full membership in the union. The union admits that it is correct that the Negro members pay the same monthly amount in exchange for permission to work but says Negroes do not pay any initiation fee. This case was also referred to Washington as unadjustable at the local level.

3. On January 20, 1944, the San Francisco office of FEPC received complaints from Miss Pauline Houston and Mr. Vernon Johnson of Seattle against the Aeronautical Mechanics Lodge No. 751, IAM. The complainants, who are employees of the Boeing Aircraft Company with which the union has a bargaining relationship, charge that they were refused membership solely because of their race. These complainants state that they pay a permit fee which is the same amount as the monthly dues of the white employees who are admitted to full membership in the union. The union admits that it is correct that the Negro members pay the same monthly amount in exchange for permission to work, but says Negroes do not pay any initiation fee. On April 28, FEPC representatives met with Grand Lodge Representative, James A. Duncan; C. L. Bentley, Vice President of District 751 and A. J. Cline. The problem was discussed and the union officials took the position that admission of Negroes to membership by a change in the ritual would result in a split in the IAM. This case was referred to Washington as unadjustable.

4. The Kansas City office of FEPC received five complaints against Lodge 314 of the IAM on October 30, 1944. The following individuals signed the complaints: James E. Alsbrok, Helen Latimore, Alfretta Wilson, Frankie Mae Foster, and Juanita Mullen. These individuals charged that they made application to Lodge 314 for membership because it has a bargaining relationship with the Pratt and Whitney Company. They alleged that they were refused this membership solely because of their race. The region has referred this matter to the Central office. All complainants work at the plant.

5. The regional office of FEPC in Dallas, Texas received a complaint on November 1, 1944 on the IAM at the Texas Pacific shops in Fort Worth. The complainants charged that the local chairman of the IAM attempted to prevent Negro machinists from performing certain operations on the railroad. A con-

ference was held with Mr. Mulholland, an International representative of the IAM, who agreed that the action of the lodge was wrong and stated that the local leaders would not interfere with full utilization of Negro workers. This case was closed but negotiations were resumed when the Negro complainants charged that the agreement reached with Mr. Mulholland was being violated. This matter is still in the hands of the regional office.

6. On October 29, 1943, the regional office of FEPC in Washington docketed a case against Lodge 721 of the IAM in Durham, North Carolina. This lodge has a closed shop contract with the Wright Automatic Tobacco Packing Machinery Company at Durham. In the course of negotiations with the company, resulting from its failure to employ Negro workers, the union wrote the following letter to the company on April 20, 1942:[2]

"In reply to your question of this date, Lodge 721 of the International Association of Machinists admits to membership only competent white candidates. It would therefore be impossible for your company to employ in the mechanics department, persons of other race than white under the terms of the contract you hold with Lodge 721."

On November 22, 1943 Mr. Frank Hook, who was at that time Regional Director for FEPC and Mr. Joseph H. B. Evans, the present Regional Director, conferred with Mr. Harvey Brown on this case. Mr. Brown stated that the local union was asked to withdraw the letter it had written to the company but he was unable to show a reply to the letter sent to Local Lodge 721 by the International. This case has been referred to the Central office as unadjustable.

7. The FEPC Philadelphia office received a complaint on April 5, 1944 from Charles Washington, Frank Anderson, Charles W. Sexton, Eddie Kearse, Charles Berry, John Stoney, Earl Ritter, R. K. Arguines, Toiling Ritter, Bernard Jones, Joseph G. Bayer, Joseph Washington, David Sexton, and Corlean Jameison against Lodge 243 of the IAM which has a bargaining relationship with the A. B. Farquhar Company of York, Pennsylvania. The complaint allege[s] that Negro employees of the company are denied membership by the union and further, that certain employees are denied upgrading by the company because of pressure by the union. The complainants allege that they applied for membership and intended to pay joining fees but these fees were returned by Lodge 243. This case is still being processed by the regional office in Philadelphia.

8. The Detroit office of FEPC has informed us of a problem involving Lodge 698 of the IAM in Detroit. It is alleged that Negro mechanics are not employed for the maintenance of trucking equipment because of the policies of the union. This matter is still in the hands of the regional office.

9. There are twelve unresolved complaints against the Machinists Union in the railroad industry. These complaints are a part of the general problem considered by the Committee in the railroad hearings on September 15–18, 1943.

MS: LH, DI, HqR3, Office Files of George M. Johnson. M.

1. See the section on the International Association of Machinists in the headnote on the FEPC and Unions; Mitchell to Johnson, memorandum, 9/6/44; Mitchell, report, 1/5/45.

2. This case was referred to FEPC by the WMC before the establishment of a regional office. Hence, it was not docketed until 1943.

Memorandum on Employment of Negro Welders at Delta Shipbuilding Company

DATE: January 8, 1945

TO: Mr. Will Maslow
Director of Field Operations

FROM: Clarence M. Mitchell
Associate Director of Field Operations

SUBJECT: Employment of Negro Welders at Delta Shipbuilding Company

Major Walter Graham of the Maritime Commission was in the city today and called me concerning the Delta Shipbuilding case. He stated that it was the company's intention to put the Negro welders on the job Saturday, but a number of important labor leaders were out of the city and the company was afraid to risk a work stoppage.[1]

Shortly before he called me, Major Graham said, he talked with Mr. R. B. Ackerman of the Delta Shipbuilding Company via long-distance and learned that the company will put the Negro workers on at 1 o'clock p.m. today. Mr. Ackerman stated that he had discussed the whole situation with shop for[e]men and supervisors and felt greatly encouraged by their attitude.

Major Graham stated that fifteen Negroes will be employed at first, but believes the total number will reach two hundred in a short period. These persons will be employed on a non-segregated basis according to Major Graham. He said that he expects no trouble.[2]

I suggested to him that it will be well for Dr. Dodge, our director in Region VII to know him personally, since there are a number of problems in Florida which will fall under Major Graham's jurisdiction. Major Graham said he had heard of Dr. Dodge, but had not met him and looks forward to seeing him.

MS: LH, DI, HqR83, Correspondence Relating to Cases. (A–K).

1. Ellinger informed Mitchell that a representative of Delta had told him that fifteen African American welders would report for work that day and that no trouble was anticipated. The company, he said, had suggested that the sending out of a news release on the development be delayed for a week.

Ellinger to Mitchell, telegram, 1/8/45. Mitchell told Daniel S. Ring, director of Shipyard Labor Relations at the Maritime Commission, that the news that the Delta Shipbuilding Company in New Orleans was hiring African American welders was very welcome and that he believed that step would have "an important effect on our operations in the Gulf area." Mitchell to Ring, 1/12/45. Both documents are also in HqR83, Correspondence Relating to Cases. (A–K). For related texts, see 8/14, 11/22/44, 1/9, 1/12/45. For additional background, see the section on the Maritime Commission in the headnote on Relationships with Federal Agencies and headnote on the Shipbuilding Industry.

2. In a memorandum of 2/1/45 to Johnson, Maslow said that Delta had effected substantial improvements although as far as he knew the company had never issued any reports of compliance as the FEPC's directive issued earlier required. Responding on 2/3/45, Johnson said that while Delta's final disposition report indicated that it now employed blacks in skilled positions and as a result it could be said that it was complying with the Committee's directives, it was not clear that it and the related unions had reached a satisfactory agreement on the question. For a full assessment of the issues involved, see both documents in HqR3, Office Files of George M. Johnson. Will Maslow.

Weekly Report

January 9, 1945

Mr. Will Maslow
   Director of Field Operations
Clarence M. Mitchell
   Associate Director of Field Operations
Weekly Report for the Week Ending Saturday, January 6, 1945

OUTSTANDING EVENTS AND PROBLEMS

We have been somewhat on the anxious seat about the Delta Shipbuilding Company in New Orleans. Fifteen Negro welders were to begin duty on Saturday. The Maritime Commission called to say that the welders would begin on Monday, January 8.[1]

Region VII was sent information on Tampa, Florida, which I obtained from the National Housing Agency following receipt of a telegram from the Tampa March on Washington. Although Negroes are not being used properly in the area, apparently they are available. Mr. Brin is investigating the situation.

An evasive letter was received from the Consolidated Vultee Aircraft Company in San Diego concerning problems at the plant it operates in Fort Worth. I am glad that this matter is headed for a hearing, since both the War Department and the company have been very dilatory in handling complaints presented by us.[2]

As requested by Mr. Ellinger, I have arranged a conference for Mr. Beall with the Brown Shipbuilding Company in Houston. This conference is scheduled for January 12.

The Navy Department indicates that it is suggesting to the Bureau of Ships that certain pay roll data be supplied to FEPC by the Brown Shipbuilding Company in New Orleans. This action was requested of the Central office by Mr. Ellinger.

What appeared to be an airtight case against the War Department seems to be explained away again. However, this time it appears that the War Department has good grounds for rejecting the complainant in that he is supposed to have had a criminal record. The complaint was filed from St. Paul, Minnesota against the Miami District of Engineers.[3]

ASSIGNMENTS

The following new cases were received by me during the past week:

1. Arabian-American Oil Company, 12-BC-454.[4]
2. Bechtel, McCone & Parsons, 12-BR-468.

The following cases have been referred to the Legal Division:

1. Consolidated Vultee Aircraft Corporation, 10-BR-235, 278, 279, and 336.
2. St. Johns River Shipbuilding Company, 7-BR-409.

The following case has been reported closed by the region on December 14, 1944:

1. Seattle Post Office Department, 12-GR-259.

The following FDR's have been reviewed and acted upon by me:

Region VI-	13	Region X-	1
Region VII-	6	Region XII-	29
Region IX-	7		

cc: Messrs. Johnson
Davidson
Davis
Jones

MS: copy, FEPC RG 228, Office Files of Clarence Mitchell, DNA.

1. For immediately related texts, see 5/1, 5/5, 8/14, 11/22/44, 1/8, 1/12/45.

2. For immediately related texts, see 1/3, 1/4, 1/9, 2/12, 4/12, 4/23/45.

3. On this complaint, see Mitchell's memorandum, "Current DFO War Department Cases," 12/14/44, in which he lashes out at Truman Gibson. Regarding the complainant's criminal record, see Gibson to Mitchell, 2/2/45, and the FDR of 2/23/45. HqR83, Correspondence Relating to Cases. (A–K) District Engineer, Miami, Florida.

4. Both the Aramco and the Bechtel, McCone, and Parsons cases involved refusal to hire African Americans and Jews for assignments to the firms' contracts in Saudi Arabia. Regional Director Leonard Brin told Maslow that Aramco felt that hiring blacks "would upset the entire Arabian economy," that it would require building fifteen thousand houses for all Arabs who would demand equal-

ity with American Negroes, that their presence would impede the entire oil company development, and that all jobs are "potential foremen." Brin's telegram and related materials are in HqR83, Correspondence Relating to Cases. (A–K) American Arabian Oil (General).

At Mitchell's request, John Davis conducted the investigation and reported:

I talked to Dr. [Ralph] Bunche, of the State Department, and with Dr. Walter L. Wright, head of the Historical Section of the U.S. Army. Dr. Bunche did not consider himself an authority, but his final opinion was almost the same as that of Dr. Wright.

Dr. Wright is the former president of Roberts College in Istanbul and a former professor of Asiatic History at Princeton University. In addition, before going to the War Dept., he was the head of OSS's Near East Division. He has lived in the Near East for approximately 15 years and speaks Turkish, and Arabian, as well as French, Spanish and German.

He informed me that with proper management neither Negroes nor Jews should raise any problems in Saudi Arabia. Ibn Saud has taken a forthright position on Zionism and is one of the national leaders against the Zionist movement. In addition to that, the Jewish question in Arabia is now a subject of extreme tension because of the present political implications. But an American Jew would never be recognized by Arabians as being a Jew; he would be considered just another American. Most Jews with whom the Arabians are familiar are Yemenites and are extremely dark.

With regard to Negroes, most Negroes with whom the Arabs are familiar are slaves, having been brought to Saudi Arabia as the result of the Abysynnian slave forays against U'ganda. These slaves, however, are not slaves in the American sense, since they operate as body servants and as major domos for their masters. Many of them operate as statesmen and have achieved positions of national importance. It is quite customary for them to give orders to Arabs. Furthermore, the Arabians have absolutely no race consciousness and inter-marriage is quite a common thing. (Davis to Mitchell, memorandum, 1/13/45, HqR38, Central Files. [entry 25] Memoranda, Mitchell, Clarence).

Evelyn Cooper confirmed Davis's report. Cooper to Johnson, memorandum, 2/22/45. Mitchell, on 2/23/45, then told Cooper that he had been informed that Aramco had no contracts with the government. In effect, that meant the FEPC had no jurisdiction over it. These and related materials are in HqR83, Correspondence Relating to Cases. (A–K) American Arabian Oil (General).

Memorandum on Telephone Conversation with Mr. Ring Regarding Delta Shipbuilding Company

DATE: January 12, 1945

TO: Files

FROM: Clarence M. Mitchell

SUBJECT: Telephone Conversation with Mr. Ring Re Delta Shipbuilding Company

On January 11, Mr. Daniel Ring, Director of Shipyard Labor Relations, Maritime Commission, called me to say that on January 8, fifteen Negro welders were employed at the Delta Shipbuilding Company and by January 12, a total of forty-five would be employed. He stated that it is expected that two hundred will be used by the company.

MS: LH, DI, HqR83, Correspondence Relating to Cases. (A–K) Delta Shipbuilding Company.
For immediately related texts, see 5/1, 5/5, 5/8, 5/17, 8/14, 11/1, 11/22/44, 1/8, 1/9, 1/15/45.

Weekly Report

January 15, 1945

Mr. Will Maslow
   Director of Field Operations
Clarence M. Mitchell
   Associate Director of Field Operations
Weekly Report for the Week Ending Saturday, January 13, 1945

OUTSTANDING EVENTS

For the sake of continuity I mention that the Delta Shipbuilding case which was included in the report of last week has been settled successfully and Negro welders are now employed.[1]

Region XII has sent in a critical statement concerning working relationships with the Navy Department. We have asked for more specific information and when we receive it we will be able to take it up with the Navy Department.

D.F.O. cases against the Railroad Retirement Board have been returned to Regions II and IV. It will be interesting to note what progress is made under our new understanding.

After meeting with Messrs. Houston and Shiskin I have prepared a new summary of Machinists cases which, as I understand it, will be left with Mr. Harvey Brown for study.[2]

ASSIGNMENTS

The following cases have been received by me during the week:

1. U. S. Naval Drydocks, 12-GC-1701.
2. Goodyear Aircraft Corporation, 5-BR-350.

The following cases have been returned to the regions:

1. Railroad Retirement Board, 4-GR-368, 2-GR-571, 2-GR-671.
2. U. S. Naval Drydocks, 12-GC-1701.
3. District Engineers, 7-GR-526 (VIII).

The following FDR's have been received and acted upon by me:

Region VI-	10	Region IX-	4
Region VII-	8	Region X-	15
Region XII-	21		

cc: Mr. Johnson
       Mr. Davidson
       Mr. Jones
       Mr. Davis

MS: copy, MP.

1. See Regional Director Don Ellinger's final disposition report on this case, 1/19/45; the section on the Maritime Commission in the headnote on Relationships with Federal Agencies and the headnote on the Shipbuilding Industry.

2. Some weeks earlier, the Committee had appointed two of its members, Boris Shishkin and Charles Hamilton Houston, to meet with IAM president Brown on a number of complaints alleging that locals of the union were violating EO 9346. In an effort to expedite the processing of those complaints, George Johnson provided an example of the problem from Region VII that the Committee faced:

On Thursday, December 7, Dr. Dodge left Atlanta for a trip to Jacksonville, Pensacola, and Panama City, Florida, where he is investigating several cases. In Jacksonville he conferred with officials of the St. Johns River Shipbuilding Company with regard to Cases Nos. 7-BR-90, 409, 470, 508, and 516. He was told by these officials that due to the fact that the Company has a closed shop contract with the Metal Trades Council of the A.F. of L., all employees are furnished directly through the Union; and that skilled Negro mechanics are not acceptable as members of the various unions present. For this reason, it was stated, the Company cannot hire such Negroes. The Company avowed that it has a policy of nondiscrimination and that the unions alone are responsible for the alleged discrimination cited in the above cases.

According to Dr. Dodge, Mr. J. Rae Simpson, Business Agent of the Metal Trades Union, stated that his union did not accept Negro members and that for this reason Negro welders, burners, etc. could not be assigned to jobs along with white employees; that if such action were attempted, there would be violence resulting in the Negroes being thrown into the river. He added: "However, these Negroes can get jobs at the Brunswick and Charleston yards where they have unions, so that we cannot be accused of discrimination."

Dr. Dodge feels that nothing more can be done on the regional level to settle these cases. (Johnson to Shishkin and Houston, memorandum, 12/19/44)

Johnson provided Shishkin and Houston with a copy of Mitchell's memorandum of 9/6/44, which he prepared at the request of the Committee for use by them in their conference with Brown. HqR4, Records of the Legal Division, Office Files of George M. Johnson. Committee Matters. For Mitchell's more recent memorandum on the union, see 1/8/45; for context, see the section on the International Association of Machinists in the headnote on the FEPC and Unions.

Weekly Report

January 23, 1945

Mr. Will Maslow
    Director of Field Operations

Clarence M. Mitchell
    Associate Director of Field Operations
Weekly Report for the Week Ending Saturday, January 20, 1945

OUTSTANDING EVENTS AND PROBLEMS

During the past week I have had the pleasure of visiting the Atlanta office and feel very optimistic about the way its work is going. I am preparing a detailed report on my opinions of the office and matters which constitute problems.[1] However, briefly, I wish to say that the following matters struck me as most important:

The WMC is cooperating to some extent with our office. Conditions are not still ideal but infinitely better than they are in Regions IV and X at this time. Mr. Lasseter, the Regional Director of the War Manpower Commission, has sent out a very pointed statement to local USES offices which is helpful in getting them to follow the requirements of our operating agreement.[2] It is encouraging also to note the number of 510's which are coming in. These are not always properly made out but there is an effort to do what is required and this is progress.

While in Atlanta I conferred with a representative of the Bell Aircraft Corporation. I am convinced that if specific requests we made are not accomplished within the coming week, this case should be sent to the DFO and we should recommend that it be the subject of a hearing. Because the plant is Government owned and privately operated, it will be necessary to submit the case to the War Department before a hearing. This case illustrates the serious problems which confront Region VII. During the course of their negotiations they have made considerable progress and some of the more important aspects of the situation have been remedied. However, the remedy has not been sufficient so they are unable to close the case at this point.[3]

The region also requested that I arrange a conference with the Maritime Commission on the Southeastern Shipbuilding Company. I have done this and hope that some satisfactory handling will result.

ASSIGNMENTS

The following new cases have been received by me during the past week:

1. Southern Bell Telephone & Telegraph Company, 10-BR-344.
2. U. S. Customs Service, 10-GR-384.
3. Boilermakers Union, Local 104, 12-UR-499.

The following FDR's have been reviewed and acted upon by me:

Region XII-   4   Region VI-   5

cc: Mr. Johnson
       Mr. Jones

Mr. Davidson
Mr. Davis

MS: *copy, FEPC RG 228 (entry 40 PI-147), Office Files of Clarence Mitchell, Will Maslow, DNA.*
1. See Mitchell to Maslow, memorandum, 1/23/45, "Case Load of Region VII."
2. On Lasseter's instructions to state directors and their responses, see Mitchell, memorandum, 12/6/44, and notes.
3. See the headnote on the Aircraft Industry and the section on the War Department in the headnote on Relationships with Federal Agencies.

Memorandum on Case Load of Region VII

January 23, 1945

Mr. Will Maslow
        Director of Field Operations
Clarence M. Mitchell
        Associate Director of Field Operations
Case Load of Region VII

When I visited the Atlanta Office I intended to review all of the current cases there.[1] However, because of the numerous matters before us I could only review the most important cases. Complaints against the Bell Aircraft Corporation in Marietta, Georgia, involve failure to hire skilled Negro workers and failure to employ Negroes as trainees. The company operates a training course for Negroes which was established as a result of FEPC efforts, but four courses are offered for whites while only one is offered for Negroes. The Negro course is not full at this time because the company employs colored individuals on a segregated basis and the section for them is supposedly filled.[2] The Reynolds Metal Corporation at Macon, Georgia, is charged with failure to employ Negro trainees on a paid basis. The Regional office is currently working for the establishment of a training program and reports that 116 Negroes are available for instruction. I had one meeting with officials of Bell Aircraft on pending cases and I was already familiar with the details of complaints against the Reynolds Metal Corporation. These two companies, and certain shipbuilding companies mentioned in this memorandum, are the most important docketed cases in Region VII.[3]

Our discussions show that there will be many new training cases in the near future because the regional office had not engaged in a consistent effort to correct previous discrimination. This is no criticism because the office has had its hands full on many other matters.

The following represents cases on which the Regional Director and I are in agreement. These are not all of the region's cases, but they are important.[4]

POSSIBLE HEARING CASES*

1. Tampa Shipbuilding Company, 7-BR-315, 317, 318, and 319; also 7-GR-321 and 7-UR-314, against the USES and Boilermakers Union respectively.

   Mr. Brin is to visit the company and the union concerning the specific complaints which allege that Negroes are not employed in trades under the jurisdiction of the Boilermakers Union. An RFA is to be prepared on these cases as soon as Mr. Brin reports that his visit to the parties charged have produced no favorable results. It is expected that these cases with the possible exception of that against the USES will be ready for a hearing by the Committee.[5]

2. J.A. Jones Construction Company (Wainwright Yard) Panama City, Florida, 7-BR-506. In this company, Negroes were employed as riveters but were later chased out of the yard by white workers. The company states that it is willing to employ Negroes in skilled capacities but is prevented by doing so by the Boilermakers Union. Dr. Dodge is to docket a case against the union and prepare an RFA if no progress is made. This case is also at the point where a hearing seems necessary.

3. The Mingledorf Shipbuilding Company, 7-BR-493, Savannah, Georgia. This yard, which has a Navy contract, refuses to hire Negroes at maximum skills. There is also a case docketed against the Boilermakers Union (7-UR-484) charging that it interferes with the employment of Negro workers. Immediately after I left Atlanta, the Navy Department sent a representative [Captain George M. Keller] in to discuss this case with Mr. George McKay. Dr. Dodge is optimistic about the union's attitude but unless the assistance of the Navy Department results in progress, the case will be referred to Washington for a possible hearing.[6]

4. Savannah U.S. Employment Service, 7-GR-421. The region believes that this office of the USES conspired with the Southeastern Company in Savannah (7-BR-58) to prevent the hiring of Negroes in skilled capacities. The regional office requested that I arrange a meeting with the Maritime Commission on this case in Savannah. I have done this and unless there are favorable results from this meeting, the case will be referred to the Central office with the recommendation that a hearing be held against the company and the USES.

CASES TO BE SENT TO D.F.O.

1. Tennessee Eastman Corporation, Knoxville, Tennessee, 7-BR-432 through 476. The basic issue in these cases is the refusal of the party charged to employ Negro women at their maximum skills. Trainees are also refused employment although whites are being used extensively. In one instance, a Negro woman

*A separate report is made on Bell Aircraft, Marietta, Georgia[.]

was employed as a secretary but was removed from her job as a result of pressure from white employees. This is a secret military project and the regional office has encountered considerable difficulty in getting any information on the hiring policies and the current employment figures. Mr. Hope has been in touch with a Lt. Flaherty who is a Naval officer but represents the Army in labor matters. The party charged argues that integration of Negro employees is in process but details were not given because of the alleged secrecy of the project. I suggested that approximately ten additional days be given for the furnishing of necessary information and if it is not received, the cases should be sent to the DFO.[7]

2. There is a case against the Post Office, 7-GR-101. After discussing this matter, I suggested that it be referred to the DFO for action in Washington.

3. Fulton Sylphon Company, 7-BR-84. This is a 1943 case charging discriminatory dismissal. After a review of the file, it appears that the matter should be sent to Washington for further study. In my opinion, it will be necessary to dismiss this case as other, but before doing so, I wanted to carefully review the file.[8]

4. Buckeye Cotton Oil Company, Memphis, Tennessee, 7-BR-10. I have suggested that after one more contact with the party charged in this case, the matter be referred to the DFO for further action.

5. Swift Manufacturing Company, 7-BR-65, 75, 155, and 157. This file, because of its age and numerous denials by the party charged, is a considerable problem in Region VII. I have recommended that it be sent to the DFO for further study and recommendation.

OTHER IMPORTANT CASES BEING HANDLED BY THE REGION

1. Bechtel, McCone & Parsons Aviation Corporation, Birmingham, Alabama, 7-BR-489. In this case a training program for Negroes seeking employment at Bechtel, McCone & Parsons was discontinued. Mr. McKay reports that the WMC is willing to cooperate with him in getting it reopened.

2. Fisher Aircraft, Memphis, Tennessee, 7-BR-287–289, and 472. In this case the regional office has done an excellent job of cooperating with a local of the UAW which has a contract with the plant. Recent wage adjustment by the War Labor Board should facilitate the settlement of these cases and if so, the region will have some excellent satisfactory adjustments to its credit. Mr. Hope is going to Memphis on these and other matters in the near future.[9]

3. Aluminum Company of America at Alcoa, Tennessee, 7-BR-474, 475. These complaints involve wage discrimination and other problems of upgrading. No contact has been made with the party charged as yet because of the difficulty of reaching the plant.

4. Ferguson and J.A. Jones Construction Company, 7-BR-177 and 7-BR-483. These construction companies are in Tennessee. It appears that the region obtained a satisfactory adjustment of complaints charging refusal to hire Negroes as carpenters. The adjustment must be verified by a letter which the Regional Director hopes to receive. He has information from a Mr. Reed, who initiated the complaint, that fifty colored carpenters have been placed on the job. Mr. Reed did not indicate clearly which job is now open to colored carpenters and for that reason, an FDR has not been written. I suggested that in construction cases, the region should make use of the telegrams and long distance phone contacts since the work is of short duration and unless there is speedy action it will be over before a contact is made.

5. A. T. & T., 7-BC-522. This is a complaint of a Jehovah's Witness against the American Telegraph and Telephone Company in Atlanta. It appears that the individual has a good case and he is seeking reinstatement to his job at the telephone company. Mr. Hope and Dr. Dodge have been working on this problem and it may be that some adjustment can be expected in the near future.[10]

6. Merrill-Stevens Drydock Company, Jacksonville, Florida, 7-BR-230, 228, 229, 231, and 471. This is a CIO yard and the complaints have been filed with the Committee by the Union. However, there is one 510 report submitted by the USES charging that the company refused to employ a Negro as a welder. A discussion on these cases showed that many of the allegations are more instances of discrimination because of union membership if they have merit at all. For example, one of the complainants charges that two crews of workers (both Negroes) receive different wages for doing the same work. The union alleges that the higher paid crew is made up of "company pets" while the latter is made up of union men. We have taken these cases up with the company and explanations of each have been submitted. Dr. Dodge will be in Jacksonville next week and I suggested that he have a meeting with the complainants and the union to discuss these matters further. In my opinion, a discussion should result in a dismissal on merits in most of these cases.

7. Seaboard Airline, 7-BR-434, 171. This is a complaint against a railroad which is being processed at the regional level because it was not a matter referred to the President by the Committee. The same would apply to cases 7-BR-165, against the Nashville, Chattanooga & St. Louis Railroad; 7-BR-214 against Missouri Pacific; and 7-BR-196 against the ABC Railroad.[11]

8. The International Union of Operating Engineers, 7-UR-76. This is a case in which the union is charged with failure to permit Negroes to work on a construction project. The construction project is closed and the complaints are no longer available. The union denies that it discriminated against them. Under the circumstances, I have suggested that the case be closed as other because it is not clear that the union has a non-discrimination policy although it states that it does.

9. Williams Construction Company, 7-BR-184, 195. These are old cases which involve a construction project now closed. It will be necessary to dismiss them as <u>other</u> and I have so recommended.

10. Kennedy Central Hospital, Memphis, Tennessee, 7-CR-485–7. In this case Negro employees charge that they were dismissed when they sought increases in wages and the regional office believes that there is an over-all pattern of wage discrimination which results in the freezing of all Negro workers at a wage considerably below that of white employees. Mr. Hope is to get additional information from the Civil Service Commission on the job classification at my suggestion. He will also make a return visit to the party charged when he is next in Memphis. These cases appear somewhat difficult and may require considerable time before they are closed.

IMPORTANT U.S.E.S. CASES

1. United States Employment Service, 7-CR-436, Meridian, Miss. In this case the local office of the USES was charged with failure to submit 510 reports and also it was alleged that the office did not make proper referral of Negro workers. After discussing this with Dr. Dodge, I believe that it should be dismissed as a satisfactory adjustment and have so recommend to him. <u>The local office now submits 510's and the manager has persuaded a textile employer to use Negro women</u>. This action came after a forthright letter from Mr. Lasseter, Regional Director of WMC. He stated that if the USES did not comply with the provisions of the agreement between WMC and FEPC, he could offer no safeguard against a possible hearing by FEPC.

2. Birmingham U.S. Employment Service, Alabama, 7-CR-285. This case involves failure of the USES to live up to the terms of the operating agreement. Mr. McKay is to take a tour of the main USES office with the State Director at which time he will visit the Birmingham office on this complaint.

3. Birmingham U.S. Employment Service, Alabama, 7-CR-317. In this case a complainant alleges that she was refused referral to a job for which she was qualified. After discussing the file with Dr. Dodge, I have reached the conclusion that it should be dismissed on merits. The USES wrote a letter indicating that even though the complainant had made an improper charge, it would be very glad to refer her to a job for which she is qualified if she will register. She has not done so at this time.

4. Chattanooga U.S. Employment Service, Tennessee, 7-CR-400. In this case the complainant alleged that she could not get war work through the USES. I have recommended that it be dismissed for insufficient evidence after reviewing the file.

5. Chattanooga U.S. Employment Service, Tennessee, 7-CR-403. In this case the State Director of the Employment Service has refused to comply with a request of Mr. Lasseter that [the] FEPC-WMC operating agreement be made effective in the local USES. It appears that this matter will be a showdown between the regional office of WMC and the State Office. So far, it appears that Mr. Lasseter has done his part in this matter.

6. Knoxville U.S. Employment Service, Tennessee, 7-CR-227. In this case, the USES was advertising in a discriminatory manner. Mr. McKay had a telephone conversation with the manager of the office and was told that the policy has been changed. It appears that this is a satisfactory adjustment and I have recommended a check of newspapers by the regional office to determine whether the practice has actually been changed. If so, the case will be closed as satisfactorily adjusted.

7. 7-GA-202. This is a case against the Atlanta USES which appears to have the necessary elements for a satisfactory adjustment. However, because it is a matter of alienage, I have suggested that it be referred to the DFO for consideration and disposition.

8. 7-GR-285. This is a complaint against the Birmingham U.S. Employment Office charging discriminatory advertising. A review of the file shows that it is ready for closing as satisfactory adjustment.

9. 7-GR-201 is against the Atlanta Office of the USES charging failure to refer Negroes to the Atlantic Steel Company. A review of the file and discussion with the Regional Director shows that this case is ready for satisfactory adjustment and I have recommended that it be closed on those grounds.

10. Atlanta U.S. Employment Service, 7-CR-218. In this case the USES is charged with failure to follow the WMC-FEPC operating agreement. Discussion with the Regional Director and a review of the files shows that corrective steps have been taken and the case can be closed as satisfactorily adjusted.[12]

11. Pensacola U.S. Employment Service, Florida, 7-GR-426. On the basis of information revealed by a visit from Dr. Dodge and other material in the file, this case now can be closed as satisfactorily adjusted. It alleged that the USES was not following the FEPC-WMC agreement.

12. Jacksonville, Florida, U.S. Employment Service, 7-GR-441. In this case, the USES failed to submit a 510 report on the St. Johns Shipbuilding Company. A review of the file shows that it can now be closed as satisfactorily adjusted.

13. Jacksonville, Florida, U.S. Employment Service, 7-GR-320. This was a case of discriminatory advertising on the part of the USES. The file and reports from Dr. Dodge shows that the WMC has taken corrective steps in this matter and the case can be closed as satisfactorily adjusted.

14. Nashville, U.S. Employment Service, 7-GR-404. In this case the WMC is charged with failing to live up to the terms of our operating agreement. Mr. Hope is to make a visit to the party charged when he is next in Nashville.

15. Miami, Florida, U.S. Employment Service, 7-GR-322. This office is now submitting 510's to FEPC. However, there are certain aspects of the case which will require further study and I have suggested that it be referred to me in Washington for further action.

16. Brunswick U.S. Employment Service, 7-GR-420. Charges against this office of the USES have resulted in an investigation by FEPC and now appears ready for satisfactory adjustment.

MS: copy, FEPC RG 228, Box 458, Office Files of Clarence Mitchell, Will Maslow, DNA.

1. Mitchell's review of cases in Region VII was part of his continuing effort to achieve the greatest efficiency in the processing of complaints. Directly related to this effort was a report of 9/22/44 to Maslow from Eugene Davidson in which the assistant director of field operations provided information on the progress that was being made on DFO cases based on the agreement that he and Mitchell had made. FEPC RG 228, Office Files of Clarence Mitchell, box 458, DNA. Among others, see 5/17, 8/18, 10/12/44 for earlier reassignments and updates on DFO cases involving Mitchell.

2. See Weaver, *Negro Labor*, 111–13, 125, 127; headnote on the Aircraft Industry.

3. See weekly report of 1/23/45.

4. No separate memorandum on Bell Aviation was found, but see weekly report of 1/23/45. Files on Bell Aviation and most of the other cases referred to in this memorandum were in FR81, Region VII. Active Cases (A–Z).

5. For background on the union issues relating to shipyards, see the headnotes on the FEPC and Unions and on the Shipbuilding Industry. On the Tampa Shipbuilding case, on which, like the other cases discussed below, ultimately no hearing was ever held, see texts at 3/16/43, 4/24/44, 1/2, 2/5/45. Leonard Brin's reports on his field investigations as a temporary field examiner in Florida in late 1944 are filed in HqR80, Region VII, Field Reports, and with the files of the various Florida shipbuilding cases in FR81.

6. On Mingledorff Shipbuilding, see texts of 2/14, 2/20, 2/26, 3/13, 5/21/45; related texts in FR81, Region VII. Active Cases (A–Z), Mingledorff Shipyard.

7. Tennessee Eastman Corporation held a contract with the top-secret Manhattan Project, which was developing the atomic bomb. It had requested 2,300 trainees and 300 clerical workers from USES but refused to consider blacks for these positions. Following negotiations with Witherspoon Dodge and John Hope II, the company claimed it did employ blacks at higher positions than that of common laborer and stated, "It is our policy to employ Negroes in all capacities which are consonant with the practices and customs of the general area. A careful review of our use of Negroes convinces us that we have given full effect to such a policy." Region VII referred the case to the Division of Field Operations because it was not able to obtain access to the plant or to obtain information on black employment there on which to evaluate the discrimination complaints it received. Mitchell attached so much importance to the postwar significance of the case that it was one of those he requested Dodge to keep open when the regional office closed at the end of 1945. On this case, see texts at 2/6, 6/5/45; Mitchell to Col. Ralph Gow, 5/7/45, and other related texts in Tennessee Eastman Corporation files in FR81, Region VII. Active Cases (A–Z). On another Manhattan Project contractor in Tennessee investigated by the FEPC, Clinton Engineering, see 5/21/45. For context, see discussion on the Atomic Industry in the introduction.

8. This and other emphases are in original.

9. On the significance of NWLB rulings against discriminatory wage structures, see the headnotes on Relationships with Federal Agencies and on the Mining Industry.

10. See the headnote on Creedal Discrimination.

11. On the railroad cases referred to the president and by him to the Stacy Committee, see "Implementing the Order" section of the introduction. The FEPC continued to handle other railroad complaints in the usual manner.

12. See the section on the WMC and USES in the headnote on Relationships with Federal Agencies.

Memorandum on Matters Discussed with the Director of Region VII

January 25, 1945

Mr. Will Maslow
> Director of Field Operations

Clarence M. Mitchell
> Associate Director of Field Operations

Matters Discussed with the Director of Region VII

The following is a digest of my discussions with Dr. Witherspoon Dodge, Director of Region VII, while I was in Atlanta:

1. **Docketing and consolidation of cases.**

    I discussed the necessity for proper docketing and consolidation of all cases in the region. Mrs. Sally Chubb, who handles the docketing, explained the system used and I am satisfied that the case load now reflects a true picture of complaints docketed in accordance with our rules.

2. **Conference on cases.**

    As you will note in my memorandum dated January 23, I reviewed the principle cases before the region at this time. These were broken down into categories of those ready for referral to the Director of Field Operations, those representing possible hearing cases and those on which recommendations for further action by the region were made.

3. **Relationships with contracting agencies.[1]**

    We discussed the relationships with the WMC at considerable length and also held a meeting with the Regional Director, Mr. Lasseter. As you know, the regional office of WMC still offers some problems which must be solved, but on the whole, there is distinct progress, and a spirit of cooperation which should be helpful to our office. It no longer appears necessary to have a hearing against the USES office at this time. I have requested the regional office to send us a list of the USES offices in which they have observed segregated patterns.

Relations between our office and the Army have been fair. There has been some interference with our work as was evidenced in Anniston, Alabama, but on the whole, the War Department has not presented many obstacles in our path. On the other hand, active cooperation in such cases as Bell Aircraft Company is lacking. We have several cases which require War Department assistance and these should prove whether it will be necessary to discuss our relationships further with the office of the Under Secretary of War.

Relations with the Navy Department and the Maritime Commission are still in the primary stages and it is not possible to comment on them. The regional office of FEPC will have to deal with two Maritime Commission regions since the Philadelphia office of the Maritime Commission handles Atlantic Coast complaints with the exception of those in Florida. The Florida, Alabama, and Mississippi problems are handled by the Maritime Commission office in New Orleans. We have specific cases which require assistance from the Navy Department and the Maritime Commission and the successful processing of these will indicate cooperation.

The regional office was unanimous in its dissatisfaction with the Civil Service Commission. It is felt that the agreement which exists between the 5th Region of the Civil Service Commission and our office in Atlanta is entirely unsatisfactory. The examiners felt that any cases submitted to the Civil Service Commission would be explained away. I am preparing a letter requesting the regional office to negotiate a new agreement with the Civil Service Commission.[2]

4. **Liaison with Negro community.**

Because the Negro population is the largest minority in the region, it was important to determine whether the office appears to have acceptance at least in its home city of Atlanta. My observations show that our office is highly respected by the Negro community and there is a growing confidence in its ability to handle cases submitted. One problem which presents itself, however, is that a great deal of fine work on cases may result in settlement of some of the more pressing problems but frequently the settlement does not contain enough to warrant a satisfactory adjustment under our rules. It should be noted that with the help of the War Manpower Commission and through negotiations in Washington, certain aspects of complaints against Bell Aircraft Company were settled but over-all problems remain and it has not been possible to close these cases as satisfactory adjustments.

I was not certain of our liaison with Negro citizens in Florida and I suggested that Mr. Hope should go there for the purpose of strengthening these relationships. Mr. Brin mentioned that he had considerable difficulty in finding certain Negro complainants and that on several occasions, individuals were very reluctant to give him any information about the Negro community. Once, he sought a complainant by asking for him in a group of men who were standing on a street corner. Mr. Brin said everyone denied knowing where the individual was, but it developed later that the man Mr. Brin sought was among those to whom he was talking.

5. Personnel matters.

I asked Dr. Dodge whether he was satisfied with the services of Mr. Brin. He stated that Mr. Brin is of value to his office.[3]

We discussed the stenographer problem in full. My conclusion is that there must be no change in the present arrangement. I have requested job descriptions from each of the employees and such descriptions are attached.

We have a very valuable employee in Mrs. Chubb. She has come to us from the War Manpower Commission and is very familiar with its procedures. Actually, a number of her duties are those of a Junior Examiner. Needless to say, this is a valuable asset to an office which has the serious problem facing Region VII and so much territory to cover. Her value will increase as we docket new training cases since she worked in the office of the WMC Chief of Training, Region VII.

Mrs. Thelma Horton Ingram serves as secretary to the examiners and Miss Karyl Keen Klinger is primarily secretary to Dr. Dodge. Both of these young women are very capable and it would be a serious loss to the office if either is taken away.

The morale of the office is very high and I feel that we can make real progress in the region provided we do not disturb the situation by any curtailment of its personnel.

6. Change in regional boundaries.

I discussed with Dr. Dodge the possibility of releasing a portion of his territory to the new proposed Region XIII.[4] He suggested that the State of Mississippi could be released but it would be inadvisable to release Mobile, Alabama since it is very convenient to cover it from Pensacola, Florida, as he now does. The release of Mississippi will not greatly harm the region's case load, but by giving constant attention to areas like Pascagoula, Region XIII might be able to service better the few complaints we now have from that state.

MS: copy, HqR38, Central Files. (entry 25) Memoranda, Maslow, Will.

1. See the headnote on Relationships with Federal Agencies.

2. Letter not found, but see texts related to this negotiation in FR80, Region VII. Administrative Files (A–Z), Civil Service Commission.

3. On Brin's temporary assignment to investigate cases in Florida, see FR80, Region VII. Administrative Files (A–Z), Leonard Brin.

4. Region XIII was created in 2/45, with Don Ellinger as acting director based in New Orleans. Mississippi was transferred to the new region, then transferred back to Region VII when Region XIII closed down in August. For correspondence related to Mississippi cases, see FR80, Region VII. Administrative Files (A–Z), Regional Offices.

Memorandum on Region VII's Suggested Revision of Complaint Form

Date: January 25, 1945

To: Mr. Will Maslow
    Director of Field Operations
From: Clarence M. Mitchell
    Associate Director of Field Operations
Subject: Region VII's Suggested Revision of Complaint Form

During my visit the Regional Director and staff in Atlanta discussed the complaint form in detail.[1] All persons of the Regional office felt that the complaint form as presently set up is too complicated for the educational level of individuals who file charges in the region. Since all persons present were convinced that these changes should be made, it is my belief that even if it is necessary to give Region VII permission to have its own form, we should do so. The following revisions were suggested by the region:

The quoted statement, "Pursuant to Executive Order 8802, etc." should be placed at the end of the form instead of at the beginning. The address of the Regional office should be substituted for this.

Where it is stated "Private employer" under 2, it is suggested that the words "Private Company" be used and the words "Labor Union" instead of "Labor Organizations."

For "Type of business" it is suggested that the wording be "Kind of business" and in the parenthetical examples be listed as follows:

(Such as textile mill, shipyard, airplane factory, employment service, street car company, or other.)

Under "4," it is suggested that beneath the words, "Name of person discriminated against" in block letters should be the words, "Print name." It is also suggested that "Sex" be eliminated since there are boxes for male and female.

Under "6," it is stated that the following should be given also: "Reason for discrimination—because you are:" and then the appropriate categories should be listed. Instead of "Lack of citizenship" there would be substituted "Non citizen."

Under "7," it is suggested that the words be: "What kind of discrimination do you charge"?

"8" would read, "Give full details of your complaint."

In the second sentence of the parenthetical suggestion, it is recommended that the following be substituted:

("Give name and title of person or persons who talked to you and state your job qualifications.")

In the last sentence reading, "Are there any members of your minority group employed," it is proposed that the substitute sentence read, "Are members of your minority group employed. If so, on what jobs."

Region felt that No. 10 should be where the individual signs his name and gives his address, etc. The present No.10 should be 11 and both should be spread across the page instead of side by side.

It was also felt, primarily by Mr. Brin, but in a measure by the others, that "Comments of the interviewer" which is now 12, should be left off altogether and used on a separate page if necessary.

After talking with the Regional office about these suggested revisions, I am convinced that it would be desirable to change the form as the members of the staff recommend. It is their contention that the educational level of the complainants is so low that the language of the present form is very confusing. I cannot say that the changes made by the region seem any clearer to me, but since the regional staff was unanimous in the proposed changes, I believe it would be desirable to go along with them.

MS: LH, DI, HqR38, Central Files. (entry 25) Memoranda, Maslow, Will.

1. See 1/23/45 report and memorandum.

Weekly Report

January 30, 1945

Mr. Will Maslow
    Director of Field Operations
Clarence M. Mitchell
    Associate Director of Field Operations
Weekly Report for the Week Ending Saturday, January 27, 1945

OUTSTANDING EVENTS AND PROBLEMS

I have discussed with the Legal Division certain steps which are necessary for preparation of cases in Region VII which are ready for hearing. The informal suggestions of the Legal Division were incorporated in a memorandum dated January 26 and sent to the Region.[1]

We have received a report from the War Department finally on cases against the Richmond Army Service Forces Depot, Richmond, Virginia. It appears that one of the cases may be satisfactorily adjusted and some progress has been made in the overall hiring policies of the Depot. However, the report is characteristically evasive and generally reflects an attitude of covering up rather than cooperation.[2]

ASSIGNMENTS

The following cases were returned to the Region during the past week:

1. Richmond Army Service Forces Depot, 4-GR-163, 328, and 329.

The following case was referred to the Legal Division:

2. International Brotherhood of Teamsters, Chauffeurs, Warehousemen of America, Local 533, 12-UR-327.

The following FDR's have been received and acted upon by me during the past week:

Region VI-   5   Region X-   3

cc: Mr. Davidson
     Mr. Davis
     Mr. Johnson
     Mr. Jones

MS: copy, FEPC RG 228, Office Files of Clarence Mitchell, DNA.

1. See Mitchell to Dodge, memorandum on Proposed Hearing on Shipbuilding Cases, 1/26/45, FR80, Region VII. Miscellaneous.

2. See the section on the War Department in the headnote on Relationship with Federal Agencies.

Memorandum on Negro Trainees Finishing Vocational War Training in Tampa, Florida

DATE: February 5, 1945

TO: Mr. George Johnson
         Deputy Chairman

FROM: Clarence M. Mitchell
         Associate Director of Field Operations

SUBJECT: Negro Trainees Finishing Vocational War Training in Tampa, Florida

I hope that it may be helpful to know that approximately six hundred Negroes have finished training in Tampa, Florida which would qualify them for the war employment especially at the Tampa Shipbuilding Company. I have discussed this with Mr. Bloch and Mrs. Cooper and it will be a part of the Tampa Shipbuilding file.

Attachment[1]

MS: LH, DI, HqR3, Office Files of George M. Johnson.
    1. L. S. Hawkins, Director, Vocational Training for War Production Workers, U.S. Department of Education, to Mitchell, 2/1/45, in response to Mitchell's letter of 1/25/45 requesting enrollment figures for war production workers courses at the Don Thompson Vocational School in Tampa.

Memorandum on Problems of FEPC-WMC Relationships in Regions IV and X

February 6, 1945

Mr. Will Maslow
    Director of Field Operations
Clarence M. Mitchell
    Associate Director of Field Operations
Problems of FEPC—WMC Relationships in Regions IV and X

I am preparing this material as memorandum to you, but it is understood that following our discussion this afternoon the contents will be revised and left with Mr. McNutt in the meeting on Wednesday.

Since the FEPC-WMC Operating Agreement was signed in September 1943, we have experienced some operating problems with WMC and USES offices in Regions IV, VII, IX, and X.[1] It is pleasing to note that in Region IX our present operating relations are improving and local offices of the United States Employment Office are beginning to submit reports on discriminatory employment practices.

In Region VII, the Regional Director of the WMC [Dillard Lasseter][2] recently issued the following statement to some of the local offices of the United States Employment Service which were willfully refusing to comply with the Agreement:

"It is imperative that Forms USES 510 be submitted in proper form immediately. Otherwise the local office . . . is going to be cited by the FEPC for a hearing, in which event it will be impossible for this office to intercede or be of service in the matter.

"Therefore you are instructed to have these forms prepared and submitted at the earliest possible date."

Thus, we can say that progress is being made in Regions IX and VII and such progress gives considerable encouragement to employers and labor unions who wish to cooperate in the furtherance of requirements of Executive Order 9346.

In Region IV and Region X our relationships have not improved and there is a danger that they will become progressively worse unless some corrective action is taken by Central Office of the WMC. In Region IV the following problems are before us at this time:

1. Instances of discrimination in employment by war contractors are not reported to FEPC as required by section D-1 of the Operating Agreement.
2. The Regional Office of FEPC states that in general there is no cooperation extended by Regional Director, Mr. Treide.
3. The Regional Office of FEPC states that Negroes are not employed for the job of interviewing veterans.

In Region X the following matters are before us:

1. The War Manpower Commission refuses to submit USES Forms 510 reporting discrimination by war contractors.
2. FEPC obtained a commitment of no discrimination from the Sefton Fibre Can Company of New Orleans. When this company attempted to place a non-discriminatory order with the USES it was prevented from doing so by Employment Service officials.
3. The USES office in New Orleans refuses to employ Negroes as interviewers.
4. Local Offices of the United States Employment Service fail to offer jobs to Negroes, if, in the opinion of the local USES office, a firm will not employ colored persons or, if, in the opinion of the local interviewer, Negroes should not have the jobs for which orders exist in the office.
5. The practice of having a segregated employment office for Negro applicants results in failure to refer Negroes to jobs for which they are qualified.

MS: copy, HqR3, Office Files of George M. Johnson. Will Maslow.

1. Evans, director of Region IV, reported to Maslow that despite instructions contained in WMC Field Instruction 31 of 9/3/43, the FEPC had not been able to secure the type of cooperation that would make the arrangement effective. The reason, he said, was reservations by Regional Director Triede that had interfered with a "vigorous insistence that his regional officers follow" the agreement. The build-up of the FEPC's case load, he said, was hampered because "practically no cases" had been referred to Region IV, where discrimination was known to exist by USES offices and the WMC office. Evans to Maslow, memorandum, 2/6/45. See also draft of confidential report on Region X, which, among other things, blamed the "unwillingness or inability of persons of responsibility . . . to distinguish between tradition and duty." HqR3, Office Files of George M. Johnson. Will Maslow. On the operating agreement, see the section on the WMC and USES in the headnote on Relationships with Federal Agencies.

2. See 12/6/44, 1/23/45.

Weekly Report

February 6, 1945

Mr. Will Maslow
    Director of Field Operations
Clarence M. Mitchell
    Associate Director of Field Operations
Weekly Report for the Week Ending Saturday, February 3, 1945

OUTSTANDING EVENTS AND PROBLEMS

This week the War Department informed us that Brigadier General Harris of Army Air Forces was in Fort Worth, Texas on problems affecting the Consolidated Vultee Aircraft Corporation. General Harris was supposed to get in touch with Mr. Ellinger of our office. I wired Mr. Ellinger on this and I am now awaiting a report on the results of any conferences held.[1]

We have also requested the War Department to give consideration in the settlement of problems which we have met in processing cases against the National Carbon Company in St. Louis and the Tennessee Eastman Company in Knoxville, Tennessee. In the National Carbon case the party charged is currently recruiting workers and we have asked the War Department to remind the contractor that compliance with the Executive Order is necessary at this time because we hope to avoid a situation in which all workers are hired before the company abandons a non-discriminatory policy.[2]

We have not received a reply from the Post Office Department concerning cases submitted for investigation. A follow-up letter has been sent to Mr. Gartland, Chief of the Operations Board.

ASSIGNMENTS

The following case has been referred to the Legal Division:

1. Boilermakers Union, Local 104, 12-UR-499.

The following case has been received by me during the past week:

1. Midland Radio and Television Schools, 9-BR-454.

The following case was closed by the region but it is being noted here since it had been closed while held by the Central Office:

2. California Shipbuilding Company, 12-BR-1115—Closed December 4, 1944.

The following case was docketed by the region and is being processed as part of the St. John's River Shipbuilding Company complaint 7-BR-409: (For information only)

    1. Boilermakers Union, 7-UR-554.

The following FDR's have been received and acted upon by me:

Region VI-	6	Region IX-	4
Region XII-	6		

cc: Mr. Davidson
      Mr. Davis
      Mr. Johnson
      Mr. Jones

MS: copy, FEPC RG 228, Office Files of Clarence Mitchell, DNA.

    1. See 2/12, 2/14, 2/20, 4/23/45.

    2. The newly created National Carbon Company, whose headquarters was in Cleveland, was a subsidiary of Union Carbide and Carbon Corporation. Mitchell noted in his 3/20/45 report that National Carbon was "a vital plant." See also texts at 2/19, 2/20, 2/26, 3/20, 3/29, 4/12, 5/18, 5/21/45; headnote on Major Cases in St. Louis.

Memorandum on Joint FEPC-WMC Action in Denial of Priority Referral

DATE: February 8, 1945

TO: Mr. George M. Johnson
              Deputy Chairman

FROM: Clarence M. Mitchell
              Associate Director of Field Operations

SUBJECT: Joint FEPC-WMC Action in Denial of Priority Referral

The War Manpower Commission sometimes asks FEPC to submit a written statement on whether a given party charged is discriminating. The WMC makes such requests prior to invoking sanctions against an employer whose hiring policies appear to be out of line with the requirements of Executive Order 9346. In my opinion it would be advisable to give Regional Directors the right to summarize FEPC experiences with the party charged and, if the facts warrant, conclude the written summary with the following statement: "In my opinion and on the basis of the facts before me at this time, this party charged is discriminating against minority groups."

As an indication of the type of situations which sometimes face our Regional Directors, I quote the following passage from a WMC memorandum concerning the Norris Stamping and Manufacturing Company in San Francisco. The statement follows:

"At this conference (with Rutledge of FEPC) the situation involving the Norris Stamping and Manufacturing Company's refusal to use Negroes was thoroughly discussed. Our WMC people took the position that they are ready at all times to carry out WMC's obligations under its memorandum of understanding with FEPC, provided the FEPC and the procurement agencies involved would undertake to carry out their share of the burden without leaving WMC 'out on a limb' while awaiting action by the other agencies. Particular reference was made to the Los Angeles Railway case in which the Southern California WMC State Office was subjected to a great deal of criticism and abuse for having refused a priority to LARY and maintaining that stand for some period of time while awaiting action by FEPC . . . WMC Personnel made it clear to Mr. Rutledge that as soon as we had assurance that the other agencies were ready to step in and carry a discrimination case to its logical conclusion WMC would promptly set and impose sanctions at its command in aid of the concerted effort."

MS: LH, DI, HqR1, Documents File. Committee Minutes, February 12, 1945.

For the context, see the section on the WMC and USES in the headnote on Relationships with Federal Agencies.

Memorandum on Conference with Governor Paul V. McNutt, Chairman of the War Manpower Commission

February 9, 1945

Mr. Will Maslow
    Director of Field Operations

Clarence M. Mitchell
    Associate Director of Field Operations

Conference with Governor Paul V. McNutt, Chairman of War Manpower
    Commission

I thought it would be advisable to have a brief record on our conference with Governor McNutt and Mr. Robert Goodwin, Executive Director, hence, I have prepared this memorandum.[1] Those representing FEPC were: Mr. Ross, Mr. Jones, Mr. Davis, you, and I.

Mr. Ross opened the meeting by explaining that you would present some of our regional problems with the War Manpower Commission and Mr. Davis would discuss some educational planning desired by FEPC. You outlined the failure of Regions IV and X to live up to the terms of the FEPC-WMC Operating Agreement. In doing so, you mentioned failure to submit ES 510 Reports, failure to submit and process orders in segregated offices, and failure to utilize Negroes in professional capacities especially in the job of interviewer.[2]

I mentioned that at the beginning of our operating relationships we had considerable difficulty with Regions IV, VII, IX, and X. I pointed out that in other Regions we have enjoyed a good working relationship for some time, according to information submitted by our Regional Directors. However, I indicated that current relationships between our regional personnel and WMC personnel in Region[s] VII and IX have improved and we are getting more cooperation. Thus, we have before us principally, the problem of getting a better type of cooperation from Regions IV and X.

Mr. Davis pointed out the FEPC finds that it is necessary to be in on the planning of certain aspects of the WMC Manpower Priority Program if we are to make adequate program plans on a broad scale. He mentioned specifically the need for having admission to the meetings of the War Manpower Commission in Washington and also to priority committees of the WMC where such committees are making plans for the servicing of important industries.

I stated that while we realize that membership in the WMC is determined by the President, we also understood that certain individuals are present in the meetings because they are working in fields closely related to manpower problems. Governor McNutt expressed the view that perhaps it would be better for the committee to be represented at the operating level since the Commission itself is concerned with broader policies. I suggested that we would prefer to be represented in both places. Mr. Ross stated that, in his opinion, it would be helpful to know something about the over-all planning of WMC by having access to the meetings of the Commission. Governor McNutt agreed that FEPC would have admission to those meetings and also that it was understood we would tie in at the operating level through Mr. Goodwin and on the planning level with Mr. Collis Stocking.

During the meeting some discussion arose concerning FEPC's failure to give prompt processing to ES 510 Reports in Region V. Mr. Goodwin pointed out that, in his experience, FEPC did not have sufficient staff to handle the heavy volume of 510 Reports submitted. Mr. Jones replied that staff is allocated by the Bureau of Budget on the basis of work load and that as WMC holds up 510 Reports it prevents FEPC from getting additional staff to do the necessary jobs. He (Mr. Jones) also informed Governor McNutt that in the planning of FEPC's budget, it would be necessary to have a close working relationship with the War Manpower Commission and to know something about the Commission's plans along budgetary lines. He stated that already he had had a conference with the WMC Budget Officer. Governor McNutt appeared to receive this suggestion favorably and discussed it with Mr. Ross and Mr. Jones for a short time after the meeting.

While no specific commitment was made on whether the War Manpower Commission would require Mr. Treide, Regional Director of IV and Mr. Bond, Regional Director of X, to cooperate more fully with FEPC, I feel that we can expect some favorable results and should take follow up action with Mr. Goodwin within the next two weeks.

Near the close of the conference, Mr. Davis mentioned that FEPC's inquir[i]es showed that approximately 400,000 additional Negro workers could be found in the labor market if there is proper utilization of minority groups. This seemed to impress Governor McNutt considerably. Mr. Ross left with Governor McNutt the prepared memorandum on WMC problems.

I believe there was one significant accomplishment in obtaining an agreement that FEPC shall have admission to meetings of the Commission. It is my understanding that the problem of whether FEPC's representatives shall attend meetings of the priority Committees will be taken up with Mr. Goodwin later on. He did not say that he was opposed to our attending such meetings, but did not seem fully convinced that it would be the best place for our representatives to achieve the results sought.

cc: Mr. Davidson
      Mr. Johnson

MS: copy, Office Files of George M. Johnson. M.

1. This was one of the series of meetings that FEPC staffers held with their WMC counterparts early in the year on relations between the two agencies. In addition to Mitchell's 2/6, 2/14, and 2/28/45 texts, see McKnight's Region V summation for Davidson, 2/10/45, of their conference with Goodwin. Regarding the failure of WMC to refer many 510 reports to FEPC for investigation, McKnight concluded that that WMC regarded "FEPC as an appeals and enforcement agency," so WMC "did not refer cases to FEPC so long as its own representatives thought there was a chance of bringing about a satisfactory adjustment." McKnight reported, furthermore, "that most employers were antagonistic toward FEPC and did not wish their representatives to come into their plants." He added that Goodwin felt that USES, in dealing with the FEPC, "had to be mindful of its place in the post war period when it would have to rely on these same employers for its continued existence." At that time, EO 9346 would no longer be in effect. See HqR76, Office Files of Will Maslow. Relations with other Agencies.

In preparing for this meeting Ross proposed to McNutt on 2/9/45 that an FEPC representative be permitted to attend the WMC's weekly meetings as an observer and be allowed to participate in discussions of proposed manpower policies when they affect the use of minority workers. Such participation would enable the FEPC to give advice on proposed control programs as they affected the utilization of minority workers. Where minority workers were not being used, such participation would also enable the FEPC to give advice on industrial and community situations. Ross noted that the FEPC had been systemically gathering data on community attitudes and had "developed a store of information on techniques which can be used in the hiring of Negro workers." He added that some of the Committee's regional employees were experts in this area. See HqR67, Central Files. U.S. Government: War Manpower Commission. See also the section on the WMC and USES in the headnote on Relationships with Federal Agencies.

2. In line with these concerns, see reports by Kingman, 4/26/45, and by Evans, 4/3/45, in HqR76, Office Files of Clarence Mitchell. WMC-FEPC Relations.

Memorandum on Information on Consolidated Vultee Aircraft, Fort Worth, Texas

February 12, 1945

Mr. Emanuel Bloch

Clarence M. Mitchell

Information on Consolidated Vultee Aircraft, Ft. Worth, Texas

On Friday, February 9, I talked with Mr. Ellinger via long distance concerning the Consolidated Vultee Aircraft Company. He stated that he had a conference with General Harris of the Army Air Forces as I requested.

It appears that Army Air Forces made certain suggestions for settling the case and Ellinger is to send us a full report on these suggestions. He told me that he informed the company and the Army representatives that because the case had been sent to Washington, he could not make a final commitment whether the arrangements made would be satisfactory. I shall let you know as soon as I receive this report.

MS: copy, HqR83, Correspondence Relating to Cases. (A–K) Consolidated Vultee Aircraft Co.
See 2/6, 2/14, 2/20/45; headnote on the Aircraft Industry.

Weekly Report

February 14, 1945

Mr. Will Maslow

    Director of Field Operations

Clarence M. Mitchell

    Associate Director of Field Operations

Weekly Report for the Week Ending Saturday, February 10, 1945

OUTSTANDING EVENTS AND PROBLEMS

During the past week we have been in touch with the Navy Department concerning the Mingledorff Shipbuilding Company at Savannah, Georgia. We are requesting that the contracting agency give assistance in having the non-discrimination clause of the contract enforced. Captain Keller of the Navy Department appears cooperative on this score.

It is interesting to note that Region VII reports that another Navy contractor, the Reynolds Metal Corporation may begin hiring Negroes for its paid training program during the coming week. Captain Keller and others in the Navy Department were influential in informing the Reynolds Corporation that the Navy Department would require that the non-discrimination clause be followed.

Region VII is faced with a serious problem at the Southeastern Shipbuilding Company at Savannah. I have arranged a meeting between Mr. McKay and Mr. Burns of the Maritime Commission, but it appears that the contractor will be reducing force and the problem of upgrading Negroes will be more difficult because of this reduction.

It is surprising and I hope constructive that the War Department, following my previous request, has at last taken action in the Consolidated Vultee case at Ft. Worth, Texas. Conferences were held between Mr. Ellinger of our office and Army officials. Mr. Ellinger has submitted a plan for the beginning of upgrading Negroes. After looking at this plan, I am not impressed with it, but since Mr. Ellinger feels that it will represent progress, I believe we should talk with the Legal Division about it now that the case is being considered for a possible hearing.[1]

The New Jersey Bell and Chesapeake & Potomac Telephone cases were referred to the Legal Division for action this week.[2]

As you know, I was present at a conference with Governor McNutt, Chairman of the War Manpower Commission, during this week and the happenings of the conference were outlined in a separate report.[3]

In order that there may be no break in the continuity I am mentioning that we are still pressing the Post Office Department for replies to our request for action in cases on Los Angeles, Dallas, Houston, Philadelphia, Fredericksburg, and Durham. We have had communications this week from Mr. Gartland, Chief of the Operations Board and Mr. Aldrich, First Assistant Postmaster General.

ASSIGNMENTS

The following cases were received by me during the past week:

1. Southern Pacific Railroad, 10-BR-281
2. Brotherhood of Railroad Trainmen, 10-UR-435

The following cases were referred to the Legal Division by me during the past week:

1. New Jersey Bell Telephone Company, 3-BR-646
2. Chesapeake & Potomac Telephone Company, 4-BR-3, 4-BR-410.

The following FDR's were reviewed and acted upon by me:

Region VI-	7	Region IX-	14
Region VII-	3	Region X-	13
		Region XII-	18

cc: Mr. Davis
   Mr. Davidson
   Mr. Johnson
   Mr. Jones

MS: copy, FEPC RG 228, Office Files of Will Maslow, DNA.

1. See Outline of Plan Relative to Increasing Employment of Negro Men and Women, Consolidated Vultee Aircraft Corporation, Fort Worth, Texas, n.d., HqR83, Correspondence Relating to Cases. (A–K) Consolidated Vultee Aircraft Co.; headnote on the Aircraft Industry.

2. See Mitchell's memorandum of 3/8/45 and Evelyn Cooper's of 3/7/45 in appendix 1.
   In a memorandum of 5/15/45 to Joseph Evans, regional director, Mitchell noted that Evelyn Cooper had met with Leo Craig, vice president of the American Telephone and Telegraphy Company, concerning complaints of discrimination the FEPC had received. "Recently," he said, indicating that this was a fruit of the meeting, New Jersey Bell agreed to employ black operators. As of 5/15/45, the pledge had not been honored, but "it is our hope that some will be on the job within thirty days." HqR5, Records of the Legal Division (entry 14), Office Files of George M. Johnson. Telephone Company. See 5/21/45 for his ultimate success on the New Jersey Bell case. For Evans's reply, see 3/13/45, note 4.

3. See Mitchell's report of 2/9/45 and notes.

Memorandum on Conference with War Department on St. Louis

February 19, 1945

Mr. Malcolm Ross
   Chairman
Clarence M. Mitchell
   Associate Director of Field Operations
Conference With War Department on St. Louis

On Thursday, February 15, there was a conference between the Committee on Fair Employment Practice and Brigadier General E. S. Greenbaum, Executive Officer in the Office of the Under Secretary of War. Those present from the War Department in addition to General Greenbaum were: Colonel Reed, Major Keck, Major Goulard, and Major Hubbell of Army Ordnance; Colonel Gow, Director of the Industrial Personnel Division, Truman Gibson, Civilian Aide to the Secretary of War; and Lemuel Foster, Race Relations Analyst in the Industrial Personnel Division. Those from FEPC in addition to yourself were: Will Maslow, Theodore Jones, Emanuel Bloch, and myself.

The following represents the understandings reached in the conference:

1. General Greenbaum stated that the U. S. Cartridge Company needs 5600 workers. The War Department stated that roughly 30% of all hires would be Negroes and that both Negroes and whites would work together on an integrated basis in new but not old departments. This would amount to approximately 1,600 new Negro workers. Since it is possible that the limitation of 1,600 would result in some discrimination against Negro applicants, the War Department intimated that referrals to U. S. Cartridge might be limited to some extent by the USES. <u>FEPC made no agreement to countenance the limiting of the referral of Negro applicants</u>. We pointed out that not only would this violate the Executive Order but would also disrupt our working relationships with the War Manpower Commission. We made the counter proposal that the army give assistance in clearing up discriminatory practices in other St. Louis plants which would thereby result in a more even distribution of Negroes throughout the city. General Greenbaum agreed to our proposal and we are to furnish him with the names of the companies needing the War Department's attention.

2. The situation at the McQuay Norris plant was discussed and the War Department stated that the company proposed an educational campaign which it hoped would finally result in better utilization of Negro workers. These plans were contained in a confidential letter sent to the War Department. The number of persons needed at the McQuay Norris Company is considerably less than the number needed at the U. S. Cartridge Company. However, the War Department agreed to cooperate in adjusting this problem also. Cooperation was also promised on the Bussman, Carter Carburator, and Wagner Electric Companies.

3. It was agreed that FEPC would submit statements on the discriminatory policies of the following companies:

   a. Emerson Electric
   b. National Carbon Company[1]
   c. General Cable Company
   d. Curtis Wright Company.

   Although no directives have been issued against these companies, the War Department agreed to consider the problems they present since it would insure a better working out of the U. S. Cartridge company's new hiring plan. We agreed to send information on these companies to General Greenbaum immediately.

4. We discussed the Western Cartridge case briefly. The War Department stated that the company needs 2,100 additional workers but wants all of them to be

white. We reached no agreement on any joint FEPC-War Department attack on the Western Cartridge problem. However, it was mentioned that a hearing involving this company will be resumed shortly.[2]

MS: copy, HqR67, Central Files. Reports, U.S. Government, War Department, M–Z.

1. Regional Director Hoglund provided in his FDR of 5/3/45 a detailed account of his negotiations with the War Department to resolve discrimination complaints at the National Carbon Company. As Mitchell noted herein, the National Carbon Company was also discussed at this meeting. HqR60, Central Files. FDRs, Region IX.

2. For related activities involving the St. Louis war production plants, see also 2/6, 2/19 (Complaints), 2/20, 2/26, 3/20, 3/29, 4/12, 5/18, 5/21/45. For background, see the headnotes on Major Cases in St. Louis and on Relationships with Federal Agencies.

Memorandum on Complaints against Major St. Louis War Department Contractors

February 19, 1945

Mr. Malcolm Ross
    Chairman
Clarence M. Mitchell
    Associate Director of Field Operations
Complaints Against Major St. Louis War Department Contractors

The following is a brief summary of complaints against major St. Louis contractors which are being processed in the St. Louis office of FEPC.[1] These complaints were not included in our St. Louis hearings.[2]

1. General Cable Company, 9-BR-1155, 1252, 1253, 1286, and 1311. This company, as of today, employs a total of 4235 persons, of these 1548 are female workers. There are 368 non-whites employed by this company. Although the plant employs a great many women, it does not hire Negro women for production work and we have been unable to make progress in our dealings with the company's management in St. Louis or its headquarters in New York. The bulk of the non-white employees are men, some of whom are engaged in production. A few colored women are used in non-production work. The plant has a contract with the Army Signal Corps.

2. The Curtis Wright Company, 9-BR-1086, 1153. This company employs a total of 11,540 persons of whom 4,503 are females. Non-whites total 593. Although the company employs Negro men and women for production jobs it limits them

to approximately fifteen departments out of more than one hundred. The company operates two plants, one of which does not employ any Negro production workers. It has a contract with Army Air Forces.

3, Emerson Electric Company, 9-BR-1285, 1238. This company employs a total of 7202 persons of whom 3003 are females and 456 are non-whites. Complaints before FEPC allege that company refuses to hire Negro women and does not upgrade Negro men. During the course of our negotiations with this company we have made some progress in that Negro males have been upgraded to one type of production work, gear cutting. Recently, following negotiations with Mr. W. L. Symington, president of the company, and our St. Louis office, an agreement was reached which provided for the employment of Negro women on production work. However, any review of St. Louis' failure to make full use of the available Negro supply should include this company because it represents one of the largest employers in the area. It should be stated, however, that our local office feels that there is a greater chance for settling complaints against this company than there is for settling the charges against the others included in this memorandum. The company has a contract with the War Department.

4. The National Carbon Company, 9-BR-1454. This contractor is currently recruiting workers for employment in St. Louis. At present there are 392 persons employed, 270 of whom are females. There are 19 non-whites employed. The company refuses to hire Negroes in any capacities other than material handlers and maids. The plant has recently begun operations and expects to reach a peak employment of twelve hundred persons. When peak employment is reached nine hundred women will be on the pay roll. It is especially important that something be done to bring this contractor into compliance with Executive Order 9346 because, at this point, it should be relatively easy to recruit Negro workers while whites are being hired. It has a contract with the Signal Corps of the Army.

5. The National Lead Company, 9-BR-1159, 1394. This company employs a total of 714 persons of whom 170 are non-whites. There are 50 female employees at the plant. The company refuses to give proper upgrading to its Negro employees and excludes them from the Mechanical, Titanium, Acid, and Power Departments. This has caused considerable unrest among the Negro workers. The company admits that it fills vacancies in the departments mentioned by recruiting whites from outside, while refusing to upgrade Negro employees. This plant does not have a direct contract with the Army or Navy, but one of its major sub-contracts is with the Atlas Powder Company, an Army contractor.

MS: copy, HqR67, Central Files. Reports, U.S. Government, War Department, A–L.

1. Maslow told Greenbaum he was sending him a copy of Mitchell's memorandum, in keeping with their 2/15/45 conversation. Maslow explained that a settlement of these complaints would ease "to a considerable extent" the labor shortage in St. Louis. He said that, with the exception of the Na-

tional Lead Company, all the St. Louis companies had contracts with the War Department. "Although the National Lead Company does not have a direct contract with the War Department, we have been informed by the plant management that a great part of its production is for companies holding contracts with the War Department." He added that he was sending additional copies of the Committee's directive issued to Amertorp Corporation, Bussman Manufacturing Company, Carter Carburetor Corporation, McQuay-Norris Manufacturing Company, St. Louis Shipbuilding and Steel Company, U.S. Cartridge Company, and Wagner Electric Corporation. Those companies were the subjects of hearings on 8/1–2/44. Although the Amertorp Corporation and the St. Louis Shipbuilding Company did not hold War Department contracts, he said, the Committee was sending him copies of the directives issued to them for his information. Maslow to Greenbaum, 2/19/45. For additional information on these cases and on the St. Louis Hearings, see HqR2, Office Files of Malcolm Ross. Difficult Cases; HqR38, Central Files. Memoranda, Johnson, George, M—3, 1944. For an analysis of the St. Louis Cases, see Metzger to Maslow, memorandum, 5/24/44, HqR5, Office Files of George M. Johnson. Shishkin. See also "Summary of the Evidence with Opinion and Order on Hearings Held in St. Louis, Missouri–August 2, 1944," in HqR3, Office Files of Malcolm Ross. Committee Meeting, 9/3/44. See also 2/6, 2/19 (Conference), 2/20, 2/26, 3/20, 3/29, 4/12, 5/18, 5/21/45; headnote on Major Cases in St. Louis.

2. Emphasis in original. The Committee authorized the hearings at its 5/27/44 meeting. See Reeves to Johnson, memorandum on "St. Louis Hearings," 6/5/44, HqR38, Central Files. Memoranda, Johnson, George, M-3, 1944; follow-up report on the companies that were the subjects of the 8/1–2/44 hearings, HqR2, Office Files of Malcolm Ross. Difficult Cases.

Weekly Report

February 20, 1945

Mr. Will Maslow
   Director of Field Operations
Clarence M. Mitchell
   Associate Director of Field Operations
Weekly Report for the Week Ending Saturday, February 17, 1945

IMPORTANT EVENTS AND PROBLEMS

The most significant event of this week was our meeting with Brigadier General E. S. Greenbaum on problems in St. Louis. As you know, we have submitted to the War Department, following this conference, information on the status of cases in St. Louis. It is hoped that the War Department's cooperation will result in a settlement of these complaints.[1]

In a somewhat back-handed fashion the Post Office Department has reported on its investigation of a complaint in Fredericksburg, Virginia. I am informing the region that this case may be closed as a satisfactory adjustment because the complainant was asked to state whether he was still interested in employment at the Post

Office and the First Assistant Postmaster General [Kildroy P. Aldrich] states that the local postmaster will follow the requirements of Executive Order 9346.

I have communicated with the Navy Department concerning the Mingledorff Shipbuilding Company in Savannah and hope that this will enable us to settle the case satisfactorily.

Although the Consolidated Vultee Aircraft Corporation in Ft. Worth has submitted a plan for employment of Negroes on a segregated basis, discussions with the Legal Division have led to a final conclusion that this plan is not satisfactory and should not cause a postponement of the proposed hearing involving this company.[2]

It appears that the impending lay-offs in the shipbuilding industry are becoming more serious and will vitally affect our operations. For example, the St. Johns River Shipbuilding Company at Jacksonville; the Southeastern Shipbuilding Company at Savannah; the Todd Houston Company at Houston; and the Alabama Drydock Company all have drastic lay-offs pending. We will need to give prompt and vigorous attention to such complaints as are now before us if we hope to have any settlement of them. In addition we are facing a larger problem of what to do with the workers who will be displaced.[3]

For some mysterious reason I was invited to speak at the Miner Teachers College this week and, while I cannot say that those who heard me enjoyed the speech, I did received a free lunch.

ASSIGNMENTS

The following cases have been received by me:

1. Key System, 12-BR-170, 462, 464 (2/2/45).
2. Amalgamated Association of Street Electric Railway and Motor Coach Employees of America, 12-UR-534 (2/2/45).
3. Chesapeake and Potomac Telephone Company, 4-BR-417 (Received through Mr. Davidson).

The following case was returned to the region to be closed for lack of jurisdiction:

1. Zip Baggage & Express Company, 9-BR-435.

The following cases were referred to the Legal Division:

1. Southern Pacific Railroad, 10-BR-281.
2. Brotherhood of Railroad Trainmen, 10-UR-435.

The following FDR's have been reviewed and acted upon by me:

Region VI-	1	Region VII-	5
Region XII-	4		

cc: Mr. Davidson
     Mr. Davis
     Mr. Johnson
     Mr. Jones

MS: copy, FEPC RG 228, Office Files of Clarence Mitchell, DNA.
   1. See also 2/19, 2/20, 2/26, 3/29, 4/12, 5/18, 5/21/45; headnote on Major Cases in St. Louis.
   2. See 2/6, 2/12, 2/14/45; headnote on the Aircraft Industry.
   3. See the headnote on the Shipbuilding Industry.

Weekly Report

February 26, 1945

Mr. Will Maslow
   Director of Field Operations
Clarence M. Mitchell
   Associate Director of Field Operations
Weekly Report for the Week Ending Saturday, February 24, 1945

IMPORTANT EVENTS AND PROBLEMS

This week the WMC, in response to my request for information, informed me that training for the Reynolds Metal Corporation in Macon, Georgia began last week. This is the case on which we have been asking joint Navy Department, U. S. Office of Education, and War Manpower action. I sent a teletype to the region to verify this information.

A new report was submitted this week by the Post Office Department on Durham, North Carolina. The Post Office Department reported that the two complainants were hired and that the postmaster will observe the requirements of Executive Order 9346. It denied that the Post Office in Durham had submitted a discriminatory order to the USES. From the explanation it appears that the Employment Service is to blame. I have asked the region to check on whether the USES included the discriminatory provision in the report. Meanwhile, we have received a new case involving the San Antonio Post Office which has been sent to the Chief of the Operations Board, Mr. Gartland.

The Navy Department has sent a letter stating that it is giving consideration through the Bureau of Ships to our proposals concerning the Mingledorff Shipbuilding Company in Savannah.

I have also discussed with the Maritime Commission our complaints against the Todd Houston Company. I expect some helpful action out of Mr. Ring's office on this case, although it is difficult to tell how significant this will be since a cutback is scheduled for this company.

Cases involving a number of St. Louis contractors have been sent to General Greenbaum for War Department assistance as was agreed in our conference of February 15.[1]

The St. Louis office sent in three new cases against the General Cable Company which were referred to the Legal Division on Saturday, February 24, for inclusion in the cases set for a hearing. In this connection I discussed briefly with Mr. Johnson, the Deputy Chairman, the necessity for setting a dead line after which new complaints cannot be considered for inclusion in any given hearing. In my opinion this is a very needed action since I presume it must cause some difficulty when a statement of charges goes to an employer and thereafter new complaints are submitted.

ASSIGNMENTS

The following cases were received from the regions:

1. San Antonio Post Office, 10-GR-363.
2. U.S. Naval Drydock, 12-GC-1101 (Assigned to Examiner Beall).

The following cases were returned to the regions:

Chesapeake and Potomac Telephone Company, 4-BR-417.
Fredericksburg Post Office, 4-GR-85.
Durham Post Office, 4-GR-446.
Key Company, 6-BR-83.

The following cases were referred to the Legal Division:

1. Goodyear Corporation, 5-BR-350[.]
2. Key System, 12-BR-170, 462, 464. (February 2, 1945)
3. Amalgamated Association of Street Electric Railway & Motor Coach Employees of America, 12-UR-534 (February 2, 1945):

The following case was returned from the Legal Division:

1. Key Company, 6-BR-83.

The following FDR's were reviewed and acted upon by me:

Region VI-	16	Region VII-	2
Region XII-	4		

cc: Mr. Davidson
       Mr. Davis

Mr. Johnson
Mr. Jones

MS: copy, FEPC RG 228, Office Files of Clarence Mitchell, DNA.
1. See related texts at 2/19 (Conference with War Department in St. Louis), 2/19 (Complaints against Major St. Louis War Department Contractors), 2/20, 5/18, 5/21/45.

Memorandum on Conference with Robert Goodwin, Executive Director of the War Manpower Commission

Date: February 28, 1945

To: Mr. Will Maslow
        Director of Field Operations

From: Clarence M. Mitchell
        Associate Director of Field Operations

Subject: Conference with Robert Goodwin, Executive Director
         of the War Manpower Commission

On Tuesday, February 27, John A. Davis, Director of Division of Review and Analysis; Joseph H. B. Evans, Director of Region IV; and I met with Mr. Robert Goodwin, Executive Director of the War Manpower Commission to discuss problems in Regions IV and X, as well as follow up on certain matters taken up with Governor McNutt in our conference on February 9.

After reading the letter addressed to Mr. Ellinger in Region X concerning ES 510 reports, Mr. Goodwin stated that it was clearly out of line. This letter, as you know, provided that WMC would submit 510's to FEPC but on the condition that we would not show them to the employer or use them in a public hearing. Mr. Goodwin promised to correct this.

Mr. Evans discussed fully his problems in Region IV and mentioned specifically the fact that no 510 reports are received and that certain special ES 270 data is denied him although at one time he was receiving some of it. The latest difficulty with the Regional Director of WMC in Region IV, as described by Mr. Evans, was the former's failure to give FEPC the right to look at a 270 report on the Chesapeake and Potomac Telephone Company in Baltimore. Mr. Triede, the WMC Regional Director, previously refused FEPC access to ES 270 data on the Capital Transit Company. Mr. Evans also discussed the segregated setup at the USES and Mr. Goodwin promised to check on all of these matters. He will give us a report on what he is able to accomplish. He stated that he had hoped to talk with Mr. Triede before our conference, but he was unable to reach him (Mr. Triede) because the Regional Director of WMC was ill. I suggested that it possibly would be helpful if Mr. Goodwin could have a meeting between Mr. Evans and Mr. Triede and in such a session reach mutually satisfactory understandings. Mr. Goodwin felt this was a good idea as did Mr. Evans.

Mr. Davis discussed FEPC's desire to be represented at meetings of WMC priority committees in the role of a consultant agency. Mr. Goodwin expressed some concern about whether FEPC's presence might lead the WMC representatives to feel that FEPC and not WMC had the obligation to push for full utilization of labor without discrimination when firms sought priority ratings. Mr. Davis made it clear the FEPC is not seeking to relieve War Manpower of any of its responsibilities along this line but would serve to strengthen and expand this responsibility, especially in areas where it is not now recognized.

Mr. Davis describes Mr. Goodwin's position as follows:

> "Mr. Goodwin's position was that he preferred our men to work through the War Manpower representative on the Manpower Priorities committee. By this he did not mean the Chairman of the Committee in his capacity as Chairman, but rather the Manpower representative himself. He was concerned about our men turning up with information on situations which the WMC had not cleared up. He also pointed to regions such as his own where there is a large minority staff working on utilization, which would perhaps resent our taking over the entire responsibility of utilization of minorities.
>
> "I explained to Mr. Goodwin that his own region was quite the exception. I also indicated that we were only interested in the consultation role and that we did not expect to interject ourselves, except when we indicated that we had a problem and would like to be consulted. To this extent, we were willing to do away with the language in A of the memorandum which indicated that we could participate at Manpower Priority Committee meetings whenever we deemed it desirable without first notifying WMC and the Committee of our interest. I also pointed out that the Committee was intent upon exercising its recommendation powers under the Executive Order and to the extent that it did, it was bound to get into the question of utilization. The point was discussed only to make it clear that WMC and FEPC have a joint responsibility. Mr. Goodwin summed up by indicating that he was not opposed to our serving in a consultative capacity, but that he wished to protect his own staff, both with regard to the utilization function and with regard to whatever temporary compromises were necessary in order to get the overall manpower job done. He indicated that he would draw up his proposals in reply to Section A, B, and C of number 2 of the memorandum."[1]

There was some discussion on FEPC's tying in with the planning program of WMC through Mr. Collis Stocking, Chief of Reports and Analysis Service. Mr. Goodwin said that he would speak to Mr. Stocking about Mr. Davis' suggestion and it was agreed that in a day or two, Mr. Davis would call Mr. Stocking and work out a relationship. Mr. Goodwin mentioned, however, that he was thinking of certain changes in the planning program which would have to be taken into consideration.

On the whole I felt that our conference was productive and certainly Mr. Goodwin gave us a full opportunity to discuss our problems. I have the impression that unless he is "ham-strung" by certain other forces within the War Manpower Commission, he will attempt to do a constructive job and we should make an effort to maintain a cordial relationship with him.[2]

MS: copy, FEPC RG228 (entry 39), Office Files of Will Maslow, DNA.

1. In his own memorandum to Ross on this subject, Davis precedes the report Mitchell includes verbatim herein with the explanation that his part in "the discussion was concerned with working out methods to effectuate the programs which we developed with regard to WMC." HqR5, Office Files of George M. Johnson. Misc.

2. For follow-up action, see Joseph H. B. Evans to Maslow memorandum, 4/11/45. Evans said that Victor Daly told him that, regarding the availability of ES270 reports, the WMC's position was that the Region IV WMC was only required to furnish the Region IV FEPC with figures showing the total number of employees and the number of nonwhite employees in any plant. Regarding the submission of 510 reports, Daly said the WMC's position remained the same. There was no change in the way they were being handled. That meant, Evans concluded, "that no 510s will be referred to FEPC." See HqR76, Office Files of Will Maslow. Relations with Other Agencies. For context, see the section on the WMC and USES in the headnote on Relationships with Federal Agencies.

Weekly Report

March 5, 1945

Mr. Will Maslow
 Director of Field Operations
Clarence M. Mitchell
 Associate Director of Field Operations
Weekly Report for the Week Ending Saturday, March 3, 1945

IMPORTANT EVENTS AND PROBLEMS

For a second time in two weeks I am listing the Macon Vocational Training Program under important events in this weekly report.[1] I do this because an entirely new series of events presented themselves this week showing the type of opposition we face in moving forward in Region VII. After the War Manpower Commission, the Navy, and our office had ironed out the question of getting Negroes employed at the company, the local school board finally gave in and agreed to assist in the establishing of a course. This week I discovered in checking with the War Production Board, at the request of the region, that certain data needed for the granting of a priority had been sloppily and improperly presented by the local representatives either in the training field (non-Federal employees) or the War Production Board in Atlanta. This presentation resulted in the cancellation of a priority request for lathes and drill presses and the granting of a lower priority for sewing machines. I am glad to report that we were able to straighten out these kinks with the assistance of a very able and energetic person in the War Manpower Commission, Mrs. Marie Smoot, Administrative Analyst. The Textile Division of the War Production Board in Washington was also cooperative. It now appears that the training will get underway and Region VII will deserve considerable credit for its persistent work on this case.

I treat this at some length because the work done by the regional office on cases of this kind shows up on a statistical report as one case. However, the one case in this instance was many times more difficult and time consuming than several dozen other cases in a more favorable area. For the sake of continuity as soon as I am informed that the Negro individuals are actually in the classes, I will include that information in a future weekly report.[2]

At the risk of seeming sentimental on this point, I wish to include the thought that it is cases of this kind which translate telephone calls, memoranda, and conferences into the tangible result of individuals on jobs who previously had no chance of getting them because of race.

At my request the U. S. Office of Education this week submitted a report on the number of training courses offered for the Consolidated Vultee Corporation in Fort Worth, Texas. I have submitted these to the Legal Division as a supplement to the file. Also, I wired the Legal Division's position on the proposed plan for using Negroes to Mr. Ellinger.[3]

This week I took action on a new case from North Carolina involving the Machinists Union. Although the basic issue of exclusion practiced by the Machinists Union is as yet unresolved, it occurred to me that this would be an important opportunity to bring one of the pending cases up-to-date. It also affords an opportunity to test out certain statements made by Mr. Harvey Brown, President of the Machinists, in a conference with Messrs. Hook and Evans of Region IV.[4]

I have treated at some length the conference with Mr. Robert Goodwin, Executive Director of the War Manpower Commission, in a separate memorandum.[5]

Region VII informed me this week that the Aluminum Company of America was expected to employ one thousand soldiers released from the Air Corps for production. I have taken this matter up with the War Department since we have a pending case against this company. The region also reports that ALCOA does not properly utilize Negro labor.[6]

A new report from the Post Office Department came in this week on the Houston Post Office in Houston, Texas. Although the report indicates that Negro women are now being employed and apparently resolved one of the issues in the case, the other items were treated in a very negative fashion and it will be necessary to make a careful analysis of the file before taking further action.[7]

ASSIGNMENTS

The following cases were received from the regions:

1. Watson Bros. Transfer Company, 9-BR-414.
2. International Association of Machinists, 4-UR-502 (2/14/45).
3. Wright Automatic Machinery Company, 4-BR-510 (2/14/45).

The following FDR's were received and acted upon by me during the past week:

Region VI-	4	Region VIII-	1
Region VII-	1	Region XII-	11

cc: Mr. Davidson
     Mr. Davis
     Mr. Johnson
     Mr. Jones

MS: copy, FEPC RG228, Office Files of Clarence Mitchell, DNA.

1. See report of 2/26/45. For other efforts to provide training opportunities in Macon, Georgia, see 12/4, 12/11, 12/18, 12/26, 12/29/44.

2. No such information has been found.

3. See the headnote on the Aircraft Industry. For the Legal Division's position on the Vultee plan, see Mitchell to W. Don Ellinger, teletype, 2/28/45, which states the position as follows:

Quote. Understand company's plan is to be as follows: Negroes are to be transferred on segregated basis to certain occupations in drop hammer and foundry departments, whites now in those occupations to be transferred to other departments and whites in other occupations in drop hammer and founry departments to remain there; Negroes so transferred are to be trained for upgrading in drop hammer and foundry departments to occupations temporarily retained by whites; additional Negroes are to be recruited to replace those transferred; and plan is to be extended to other departments if successful.

Quote. Assume that upgrading of Negroes within drop hammer and foundry departments is contemplated only on a segregated basis, i.e., when enough Negroes qualify to take over other occupations, with ultimate result of departmental rather than occupational segregation. Assume that recruitment to replaced Negroes transferred is to be on segregated basis also, thereby maintaining segregation at the lower job levels. Effort therefore is simply an extension of the system of department segregation. Extension of such a system is not in any sense a step toward compliance because it cannot possibly lead to equal job opportunity.

Quote. Only possible basis on which such a plan could be considered would be if upgrading within drop hammer and foundry departments were to be accomplished as Negroes qualified individually and if recruitment for replacement purposes were non-discriminatory, even though few if any whites would be available for such recruitment. With these modifications plan might be acceptable as a step toward compliance, provided that we reserved the right to process individual cases of discrimination and that the plan covered most of our outstanding complaints. Unquote.

Mitchell's 8/28/45 telegram confirmed the information Ellinger had provided the associate director in a memorandum on 2/9/45. HqR3, Office Files of George M. Johnson. Clarence Mitchell.

4. See the section on the International Association of Machinists in the headnote on the FEPC and Unions.

5. See Mitchell, memorandum, 2/28/45.

6. Mitchell informed Truman K. Gibson, civilian aide to the secretary of war, that the FEPC's regional office had forwarded a front-page story in the *Knoxville News-Sentinel*, 2/11/45, that reported the army's intention to send one thousand men to ALCOA. Given ALCOA's practice of racial discrimination, Mitchell wanted to know whether the War Department had examined the firm's hiring policies before agreeing to use military personnel to ease its labor shortages. Mitchell told Gibson that the Committee's regional staff would be available to work with the War Department to obtain a "greater utilization of Negro labor." The War Department subsequently responded that black laborers had not in fact been available in the area when the army personnel were sent in. Mitchell to Gibson, 2/27/45, HqR67, Central Files. Reports, U.S. Government, War Department. For FEPC complaints regarding ALCOA, see also 5/1, 7/31, 9/14/43, 5/24/44.

7. See the section on the Post Office Department in the headnote on Relationships with Federal Agencies.

Memorandum on Telephone Company Cases

March 8, 1945

TO: Mr. George M. Johnson
            Deputy Chairman and Acting Chief of Legal Division

FROM: Clarence M. Mitchell
            Associate Director of Field Operations

SUBJECT   Telephone Company Cases

I have read with interest Mrs. Cooper's memorandum of March 7, concerning the telephone company cases. Pursuant to my expressions in the staff meeting on March 7, I am preparing this memorandum so that you may know my position. I have devoted a great deal of time to the telephone cases in general and specifically the cases against the Chesapeake and Potomac Company of Baltimore and the New Jersey Bell Company in Atlantic City.[1]

As I understand Mrs. Cooper's memorandum, three things are up for consideration: First, the argument of the telephone company that applicants with more than two to two and one half years of high school education are not acceptable as operators. By this standard Mrs. Cooper indicates that most of our complainants would be over qualified. Secondly, it is expected that the assistance of community groups will be helpful in getting the local telephone companies to follow the New York pattern and employ Negroes as operators. Thirdly, she suggests that because there may be some changes in the telephone companies' policies, the cases should be returned to the regions for further processing.

I disagree with all three of these points. It may be that the telephone company has a policy of employing as operators persons with a maximum of two to two and one half years of high school education. However, this has never been advanced by any of the local companies as a reason for refusing to employ colored applicants. In every instance refusal has been based on the alleged possibility of a strike among white operators if Negroes are brought in to work with them. I wish to direct attention to a letter dated December 26, addressed to me by Mr. Andrew P. Monroe, Vice President of the New Jersey Bell Telephone Company. In this letter Mr. Monroe states the following on page 2:

"We are not at the present time employing Negroes as telephone operators because we have found that if the same objections to their inclusion in the force had occurred in a group directly engaged in giving telephone service, such as we initially experienced in Camden, (when Negroes were employed as clerical workers.) a serious impairment or interruption of the service would result. . . . However, as indicated in my last letter to Mr. Fleming, dated October 18, 1944, it should be emphasized that 'this company's position with respect to employing negroes in the capacity of telephone operator refers entirely to the present situation without implication that our attitude on this subject may not change at some future time.'"

In almost every conference with telephone officials this thought has been expressed on the subject of employing colored women as operators. It was my opinion that some useful purpose would be served if I could have a conference with Mr. Monroe, after the New York experiment was a success. I did not hold this conference with him because his letter clearly indicated that in spite of the success of the New York undertaking, the New Jersey company was not yet ready to move.

So far as assistance from community groups is concerned, the Chesapeake and Potomac file from Region IV is replete with efforts on the part of the Committee to obtain this type of assistance in adjusting complaints. You will recall that at my request Mr. Joseph P. Healey of the Governor's Commission in Maryland was called to a Committee meeting on August 28, 1944. At that time Mr. Healey offered assistance in the settling of the complaints and expressed the hope that within sixty days he would have something definite to report. It is with considerable regret that I must point to his failure. Mr. Healy has shown no disposition to date which would lead me to believe that he can give any real assistance in settling these cases. I feel that any plan for pulling in other community groups to do FEPC's job would be destined to a similar failure.

In my opinion the only way to settle these cases is to have a hearing and make a determination of the facts involved. It would be extremely discouraging and I feel a great waste of time, if we sent them back to the regions for processing by the regional director. I recommend that the Committee hold hearings on the New Jersey Bell and Chesapeake and Potomac Telephone Company cases at its first opportunity.

I believe that I should point out that the Baltimore community has been extremely patient in the telephone cases as well as the Baltimore Transit cases which remain unsettled. This community has great enthusiasm for the work of FEPC and it is regrettable that in spite of numerous complaints we have had no hearings there at all.

MS: LH, DI, HqR8, Office Files of Evelyn N. Cooper.

1. Cooper's memorandum is in appendix 1. See immediately related texts at 1/2, 3/13, 5/21/45. For background on the New York cases, see Lawson to Maslow, memorandum, 10/17/44, HqR3, Office Files of George M. Johnson. Will Maslow; headnote on the Telephone Industry.

Memorandum on Southern Pacific Railroad and Brotherhood of Railroad Trainmen Cases

DATE March 10, 1945

TO: Mr. George M. Johnson
             Deputy Chairman and Acting Chief of Legal Division

FROM: Clarence M. Mitchell
             Acting Director of Field Operations

SUBJECT   Southern Pacific Railroad, 13-BR-281
             Brotherhood of Railroad Trainmen, 13-UR-435

Mr. Ellinger, in the attached memorandum dated March 6, asks us whether we will have a hearing on the Southern Pacific case. I have discussed this matter with Mr. Hubbard and he informed me that the committee does intend to hold a hearing on this company.[1]

Please let me know whether I may send this information to Mr. Ellinger.

Attachment

MS: LH, DI, HqR5, Office Files of George M. Johnson. Maceo Hubbard.

1. Johnson said that the Legal Division discussed the Southern Pacific case at its meeting on 3/20/45 and agreed that an examiner-type hearing should be held as soon as possible. He said plans called for assigning A. Bruce Hunt as hearing examiner and Simon Stickgold as trial attorney. A final decision, however, would be made after a review of possible hearings for the remainder of the year against budgetary limitations. In the end, no hearing was held. Johnson to Mitchell, memorandum, 3/23/45.

In this case, the newly hired complainant charged that upon seeing him in the train's cab, the superintendent telephoned the hiring office and demanded an explanation for how someone whose skin color was so dark was able to "get by." Upon ascertaining that the man was an African American, the division examiner said a mistake had been made and fired him. Related materials are in HqR38, Memoranda, Maslow, Will, 1944, and Metzger, Stanley. For earlier preparation for previous hearings, see Hubbard to Johnson and Cramer, 12/22/42, HqR38, Central Files. Memoranda, Houston, Charles.

Weekly Report

March 13, 1945

Mr. Will Maslow
    Director of Field Operations
Clarence M. Mitchell
    Associate Director of Field Operations
Weekly Report for the Week Ending Saturday, March 10, 1945

IMPORTANT EVENTS AND PROBLEMS

This week the War Department called to offer assistance in the settlement of the General Cable case. It appears that Mr. A. L. Fergensen, Counsel for the company, visited the War Department apparently in an effort to have the hearing, which is set for March 9, postponed. After conferring with Mr. Johnson, Deputy Chairman, and a long distance call to Mr. Simon Stickgold, trial attorney, we arranged a conference with War Department, plant, and FEPC representatives in St. Louis. I wish to compliment Mr. Stickgold and Mr. [Theodore E.] Brown who succeeded in getting favorable results from this conference. The company has agreed to employ and upgrade Negroes. A special representative was sent from its Long Island plant by plane to aid in the successful operation of the program.[1]

The Post Office Department has sent letters giving the results of its investigation of complaints against the Post Offices in Houston, Texas and Los Angeles, California. These reports are highly unsatisfactory and we are continuing action on them. I have sent the Post Office Department a request for additional information (previously requested but not given) and I am also asking Mr. Ellinger to make certain follow-up checks in the field. The Los Angeles report indicates that the complainants have been ousted by the National Postal Alliance. I have requested the Los Angeles office to check on the validity of this statement. On the whole, the Post Office Department has shown great zeal in "proving" that there was no discrimination, but little interest in getting at the facts.[2]

This week I joined the Chairman and Mr. John Davis of the Division of Review and Analysis in a conference at the Veterans Administration on retraining and employment problems.

The Murray Gin Company case, 10-BR-327 has been returned to the region because the CIO states that Mr. Boyd Wilson of the United Steel Workers will make a special trip at our request to Dallas to investigate this case.

On Friday I met with Major Cross, Major Keck, Lieutenant Visceral and Mr. Foster of the War Department in the office of the Chairman to discuss St. Louis. Mr. Ross gave his appraisal of the St. Louis situation and Mr. Johnson also was present. It was agreed in this meeting that Major Cross, representing Ordnance, would have a conference with Mr. Hoglund in St. Louis. This conference is set for Wednesday, March 14. This meeting will involve problems at the McQuay-Norris Company.[3]

I have prepared a memorandum recording my position on the telephone cases. As you will note, I believe that a hearing should be held on the Chesapeake and Potomac Telephone cases in Baltimore and the New Jersey Bell case in Atlantic City.[4]

No change has occurred in the attitude of the Machinists Lodge 751 in Durham, North Carolina, although Mr. Harvey Brown, President of the Machinists, some time ago assured Region IV that he had asked the Lodge to destroy a discriminatory letter sent to the Wright's Automatic Machinery Company.

We are making an effort to work out problems in the Norris Stamping Company with the Navy Department and the War Department.

I note that the Consolidated Vultee case is in a somewhat uncertain status. I believe that we should continue with our plans for a hearing.

ASSIGNMENTS

The following cases were received from the regions during the week:

1. Naval Air Station, Jacksonville, Florida, 7-GR-559.
2. Big Four Lines: New York Central System, Brotherhood of Railway, Steamship Clerks, Freight Handlers, Express and Station Employees, 6-BR-671 and 6-UR-676.

The following cases were returned to the regions during the week:

1. Bechtel McCone and Parsons, 12-BR-468.
2. Arabian American Oil Company, 12-BC-454.[5]
3. Murray Gin Company, 10-BR-327.

The following FDR's were reviewed and acted upon by me during the week:

Region VIII-	1	Region XII-	12
Region IX-	14	Region XIII-	8
Region X-	1		

cc: Mr. Davidson
     Mr. Davis
     Mr. Johnson
     Mr. Jones

MS: copy, FEPC RG 228, Office Files of Clarence Mitchell, DNA.

1. See 3/13/45 memorandum to Johnson on General Cable; headnote on Major Cases in St. Louis. Also possibly related to work on this case is Stickgold's memorandum to Johnson on nondiscrimination clauses in contracts, 2/19/45, in appendix 1.

2. See the section on the Post Office Department in the headnote on Relationships with Federal Agencies.

3. See the headnote on Major Cases in St. Louis.

4. Mitchell's suggestion is in keeping with his 3/8/45 response to Evelyn Cooper's 3/7/45 recommendations, in appendix 1. He expressed the above position to Joseph Evans. Mitchell to Evans, memorandum, 5/15/45, HqR5, Office Files of George M. Johnson. His response was prompted by the history of the Chesapeake and Potomac's refusal to change its policies, as Muriel Ferris showed in a memorandum of 5/28/45 to Evans. She said from 7/42 to 8/43, organizations such as the Union for Democratic Action (Sidney Hollander, president) and the *Afro-American* newspaper, and the twenty-four women who had unsuccessfully applied for operator's jobs in response to newspaper ads, had been unable to change its policy. Conferences, she said, had been held with, in addition to Haneke, Lawrence Fenneman, the WMC's state director, and Joseph P. Healey, chairman of the Governor's Commission on Interracial Cooperation. As of August 1943, about 200 blacks out of a total of 5,500 were employed by the company. That represented an increase of 125 black workers over a twelve-month period. As a result of this continued opposition by the company to hire black women as operators, the Division of Field Operation recommended to Johnson that a hearing be held on this matter.

Ferris's memorandum is in HqR76, Office Files of Will Maslow. Relations with other Agencies. An excerpt of the Ferris memorandum is also used at 7/5/43.

On 5/28/45, Joseph Evans would report that on 2/24/45, when he had his most recent conference with August B. Haneke, vice president of Chesapeake and Potomac, he noted that the company had hired blacks in clerical and supervisory capacities. Those jobs were in the separate commercial office and the segregated accounting unit. Evans explained to him that to be in full compliance with EO 9346, the company would have to hire blacks also as switchboard operators. Haneke explained that he was considering the step but an educational program would have to be instituted to avoid friction and a walkout. He also expressed fear of the related unions' angry response. HqR76, Office Files of Will Maslow. Relations with Other Agencies. For an overview, see earlier contacts with Haneke at 7/5/43; headnote on the Telephone Industry.

5. See 1/9/45, note 4, for information on the Saudis' attitude toward blacks.

Memorandum on General Cable Case

DATE March 13, 1945

TO: Mr. George M. Johnson
Deputy Chairman and Acting Chief of Legal Division

FROM: Clarence M. Mitchell
Associate Director of Field Operations

SUBJECT: General Cable Case– 9-BR-267, 9-BR-1155

This will confirm our conversation on March 6, concerning the General Cable case. At that time I informed you that the War Department called and suggested that a meeting be arranged between Mr. Stickgold of the Legal Division and representatives of the War Department to discuss the General Cable Company. The company also was to have representatives at this meeting and it was suggested that it be held in the office of the General Cable Company in St. Louis. The War Department stated that it would be represented in the meeting by Colonel Niehaus of the Signal Corps and Captain Morgan also of the Signal Corps. Mr. A. L. Fergensen, attorney for the company, had come to Washington and indicated a willingness to try and settle this case without a hearing. You agreed that an effort would be made to settle it without having a hearing and called Mr. Stickgold to make this suggestion.

Mr. Stickgold and Mr. Brown met with the company and War Department officials on March 8 and Mr. Stickgold drew up an excellent stipulation which appears to have resolved the problem. Mr. Stickgold has informed me that the commissioner type hearing was adjourned for thirty days in order to give the company time to work out its adjustment of complaints. A Miss Evelyn Johnson of the General Cable's Long Island Plant flew to St. Louis for the purpose of assisting in the correction of the company's discriminatory practices.

MS: LH, DI, HqR5, Records of the Legal Division (entry 14), Office Files of George M. Johnson,. Simon Stickgold.

A copy of the stipulation, case no. 8, as well as Stickgold's "Statement of Principles," 2/20/45, is filed with this text. See also related materials in HqR5, A. Bruce Hunt. Stickgold had recently joined the Committee's legal staff. On the settlement of this case, see the headnote on Major Cases in St. Louis.

Memorandum on Conference with Navy Department Regarding Norris Stamping and Manufacturing Company, Los Angeles, California

DATE March 13, 1945

TO: Mr. Will Maslow
         Director of Field Operations

FROM: Clarence M. Mitchell
         Associate Director of Field Operations

SUBJECT   Conference with Navy Department re Norris Stamping and
         Manufacturing Company, Los Angeles, California, 12-BR-1350

On the above date I met with Captain George Keller, Head of Personnel Relations Branch, Shore Establishments and Civilian Personnel Division, and Lieutenant Paul Herzog of the Labor Relations office in the Navy Department, to discuss the Norris Stamping Company.[1]

Captain Keller expressed some concern about the fact that a Naval Inspector had gone into the Norris Stamping Company in connection with a complaint of discrimination. He agreed that FEPC was not to blame for this in that we had properly talked with the Commandant of the Naval District, Lt. Commander Fox. Captain Keller expressed the fear that Naval Inspectors would not be as sympathetic on matters of this kind as they might be. He also stated that the Navy Department has, in his opinion, one sanction only that it can apply in cases where contractors refuse to comply with Executive Order 9346. This sanction is cancellation of contract, he stated. Naturally the Navy Department would not consider the application of this sanction, Captain Keller said, unless the Committee had made a formal finding of discrimination. I pointed out that in the Norris Stamping case we were seeking an adjustment without the necessity of a hearing and we feel that the Navy Department could persuade the employer to comply with the clause in the contract prohibiting discrimination.

Lieutenant Herzog also pointed out that the Army has a major interest in the Norris Stamping Company according to information he received in a long distance call to Lt. Commander Fox. However, Captain Keller said that this would not prohibit the Navy Department from reminding the contractor that he should comply with the non-discrimination clause.

The Navy officials expressed an interest in seeing copies of actual 510 reports submitted by the WMC and also asked certain additional information on the case which we did not have in the file. I agreed to request the region to submit this information and I sent a teletype for it on March 13.

At my request Lieutenant Herzog checked with the Bureau of Ships on the status of our request for action on the Mingledorff Shipbuilding case, 7-BR-493, Savannah, Georgia. The Bureau of Ships informed him that a letter had been sent to a Navy representative at the company concerning the non-discrimination clause in the contract. No reply has come in as yet however.

During the course of our conversation Lieutenant Herzog asked whether FEPC wanted the Navy Department to make determinations of whether discrimination had occurred in a given company. I informed him that we did not wish the Navy Department to make such determination[s] but we did desire action in assisting with compliance after FEPC had determined that there is discrimination. I reminded him, however, that the Executive Order applies to all government agencies and that the Navy Department as a contracting agency does have an obligation to see that the requirements of the Executive Order are followed by its contractors.

He (Lieutenant Herzog) asked whether FEPC finds that the new operating agreement affecting shore establishments is worthwhile. I told him that in general it appeared to be an improvement over some of our previous relationships but some regional offices still feel critical of certain aspects of the agreement. I mentioned Mr. Rutledge's complaint about the Navy's policy of denying FEPC representatives access to certain witnesses for and against the complainant. I suggested that possibly Lieutenant Herzog and Captain Keller would like to come to FEPC for a talk on our general working relationships at some time in the future. Lieutenant Herzog seemed eager to do this and I shall try to arrange a small meeting during the regional directors' conference with Lieutenant Herzog and Messrs. Kingman, Lawson, Fleming, and Dodge, who have the most frequent contacts with Naval Shore Establishments.

On the whole I thought that the conference was friendly and, although I do not necessarily believe that it will result in a settlement of the Norris Stamping case, it does give us a fifty-fifty chance on this particular complaint.

MS: LH, DI, HqR84, Correspondence Relating to Cases. (L–S) Norris Stamping Co.

1. In 3/45 (exact date on microfilm copy of teletype is smudged), Mitchell told Johnson:

Re Norris Stamping 12-BR-1350, employing 1874 no non whites. ES-510 August 15, 1944 charges company refused to employ Negroes on production work. Plant has contracts with army and navy for shell cases and ammunition. Regional Office of FEPC, local army and navy officials unable to get relaxation of discriminatory hiring practice. Company states it will not hire Negroes but may reconsider its position if given "directive from higher authority." Case sent to DFO March 9, 1945 with recommendation that hearing be held. (HqR3, Office Files of George M. Johnson. M.)

Mitchell said the conclusion of a War Department official with whom he had spoken was that Norris would not "willingly hire Negroes." Mitchell to Hubbard, memorandum, 4/23/45, HqR84, Correspondence Relating to Cases. (L–S) Norris Stamping Co. See Hunt's correspondence to Johnson in HqR5, Office Files of A. Bruce Hunt.

For further action regarding this company—which began major hiring cutbacks before significant progress could be made, thus rendering a hearing useless—see 3/20, 3/22, 4/12, 4/23, 8/17/45.

Weekly Report

March 20, 1945

Mr. Will Maslow
    Director of Field Operations
Clarence M. Mitchell
    Associate Director of Field Operations
Weekly Report for the Week Ending Saturday, March 17, 1945

IMPORTANT EVENTS AND PROBLEMS

This week Region IX requested that we give some additional help in processing its case against the National Carbon Company in St. Louis. I have talked with the War Department on this matter and have asked Mr. Lawson to get in touch with the company's national office in New York City. This is a vital St. Louis plant under the jurisdiction of the Signal Corps and one of the companies listed in our letter to General Greenbaum on February 19, 1945.[1]

We have had considerable action on the Norris Stamping Company case in Los Angeles. This case was sent to the DFO on March 9, 1945 by the regional office and I have been discussing it with the Navy Department and the Ordnance Branch of the War Department. I am proposing that these agencies join us in a conference on the case. In this connection I had a conference with Captain Keller of the Navy Department and communications addressed to him and to Major Richard M. Keck of Ordnance are attached to this report.[2]

The Post Office Department reported on our Dallas, Texas cases. The report confirms an understanding reached with the Postmaster General by Mr. Ross and myself on November 25, 1944. This understanding is that postal employees who accept war service appointments are entitled to their old jobs at the cessation of hostilities if they cannot be retained in the positions to which they were promoted. The Post Office Department also confirms employment of Negro carriers which was one of the issues of the case. However, there are certain other aspects of the case which are unresolved and I have written to the region for comments. I informed the First Assistant Postmaster General that he would hear from us.[3]

I have been giving considerable thought this week to the weighty problem of segregation which lies heavily on the shoulders of Dr. Dodge and Mr. Ellinger especially. Dr. Dodge has submitted to us a program of upgrading and new employment opportunities proposed by the Bell Aircraft Corporation of Atlanta. I have attempted to surround these matters with the sufficient brakes and safeguards and have sent the position of the Central Office to Dr. Dodge in a separate memorandum.[4] I believe that we will be able to settle our current cases against Bell Aircraft by following the company's proposal. However, inevitably we will have further trouble "up the road" resulting from the segregated arrangement. The plan proposed by Bell Aircraft is in some respect similar to that of the Consolidated Vultee submitted by Mr. Ellinger.[5] We, of course, are not telling the companies that we approve [of] these programs of segregation. We are merely insisting that they comply with the Executive Order.

ASSIGNMENTS

The following cases were received from the regions:

1. Brown Shipbuilding Company, 13-BR-323 and 436.
2. Norris Stamping and Manufacturing Company, 12-BR-1350.

The following cases were returned to the region:

1. Dallas Post Office, 13-GR-210 and 250.

The following FDR's were reviewed and acted upon by me:

Region VI-	8	Region XII-	3
Region VII-	1		

cc: Mr. Davidson
     Mr. Davis
     Mr. Johnson
     Mr. Jones

MS: copy, FEPC RG 228, *Office Files of Clarence Mitchell*, DNA.

1. See also 2/6, 2/19 (both texts), 2/20, 2/26, 3/29, 4/12, 5/18, 5/21/45.

2. See Mitchell, memorandum, 3/13/45, and notes.

3. See Mitchell, report, 11/27/44.

4. See Mitchell to Dodge, 3/17/45; Dodge to Mitchell, 3/12/45; Bell Aircraft to Emanuel Bloch, n.d., all in HqR83, Correspondence Relating to Cases. (A–K) Bell Aircraft Company, Marietta, Ga.

5. For the Consolidated Vultee proposal, see the undated Outline of Plan Relative to Increasing Employment of Negro Men and Women, Consolidated Vultee Aircraft Corporation, Fort Worth Division, Fort Worth, Texas, and accompanying texts in HqR83, Correspondence Relating to Cases.

(A–K) Consolidated Vultee Aircraft Co. See also Mitchell, report, 3/5/45, and notes; headnote on the Aircraft Industry.

Memorandum on Norris Stamping and Manufacturing Company

DATE March 22, 1945

TO   Mr. George M. Johnson
            Deputy Chairman and Acting Chief of Legal Division

FROM: Clarence M. Mitchell
            Associate Director of Field Operations

SUBJECT   Norris Stamping and Manufacturing Company, 12-BR-1350

As you have noted from my letter of March 16, 1945 to Major Richard M. Keck of the Ordnance Branch of the War Department, we asked for additional assistance in the Norris Stamping case. Major Keck was called out of town but he turned the matter over to Major Everett N. Goulard, who informed me on March 21 that the War Department will take additional action as FEPC has requested.

Major Goulard stated that the War Department is very anxious to correct this problem without the necessity of a hearing and is considering the advisability of sending a special Washington representative to the West Coast on the matter. In any event, either this special representative or Captain Doub, who is now on the West Coast, will again visit Mr. Brown of the Los Angeles office to work out a correction of this problem.

After my conversation with you concerning the Committee's action of authorizing a hearing at its last meeting on March 17, I called Major Goulard and told him that his representative should also deal with Mr. A. Bruce Hunt of the Legal Division and I suggested that a program similar to that used in the General Cable case might be worked out between FEPC, [the] company, and the War Department's representative on the West Coast.

I am also working with the Navy Department on this matter but it is not yet possible to say what will be done by that agency. However, Major Goulard informed me that he had discussed the case with the Navy Department and, off the record, it appears that the Navy will again ask some action from Lt. Commander S. E. Fox. I have had some off the record discussions with the Navy Department concerning this plant which make me feel that some favorable action will be taken.

Since writing this memo the Navy has sent a pledge of cooperation which is attached in letter dated March 21 from Captain G. M. Keller.

MS: LH, DI, HqR3, Office Files of George M. Johnson. M.

See Mitchell's memoranda of 3/13 and notes, 4/23/45. For the related texts, see HqR84, Correspondence Relating to Cases. (L–S) Norris Stamping Co. On General Cable, see the headnote on Major Cases in St. Louis.

Memorandum on Shell Oil Company, Houston, Texas

DATE: March 26, 1945

TO   Mr. George M. Johnson
       Deputy Chairman and Acting Chief, Legal Division

FROM: Clarence M. Mitchell
       Associate Director of Field Operations

SUBJECT   Shell Oil Company, Houston, Texas

On March 23, Mr. Ellinger called us from Houston, Texas to say that there was an impending walk-out at the Shell Oil Company in Houston.[1] According to Mr. Ellinger, approximately three weeks ago the company upgraded some Mexican workers in accordance with an agreement formulated on December 30, 1944 with FEPC. This was accomplished apparently without incident. On March 22, the company upgraded six Negroes to helper's jobs and there were two work stoppages by white employees. The company removed the Negroes from the job and the whites resumed work. However, the workers then made a request that the Mexicans also be removed. The company would not do this and Mr. Ellinger stated that officials of the plant were given a dead line of midnight, March 23 for getting the Mexicans off the job to which they had been upgraded. (One Mexican was promoted to a truck driver and the other as a car-man's helper.) Mr. Ellinger asked for assistance from the Army and Navy in persuading the workers to remain on the job. He stated that the officials of Local 367 of the Oil Workers International were very cooperative and he was calling from their office. He indicated that the meeting would be held at 9 p.m. and approximately one thousand persons were expected to attend. He stated it would be at the Union Hall in Pasadena, Texas just outside of Houston. The plant employs 1800 workers of whom 140 are Negroes and 30 are Mexicans.

I agreed to make an effort to get Navy and Army representatives at the meeting. It appears from what Mr. Ellinger said that the workers did not have official sanction of the local of the Oil Workers International. I called Colonel Gow and Mr. Jack Ohley of the Army Service Forces, Industrial Personnel Division. Mr. Ohley agreed to try to get an Army representative at the meeting but said that the nearest person was in Fort Worth or Dallas. I also called Captain George Keller, Head of Personnel Relations

Branch, Shore Establishments and Civilian Personnel Division of the Navy Department. Captain Keller said he would try to get a representative, but later called and said that the nearest person was in New Orleans and it was impossible for this man to be at the meeting. Colonel Nelson of the War Department attended the meeting as a representative of the War Department.

I also called Mr. George Dewey, Manpower Counselor of the Petroleum Administration for War in the Department of Interior. Mr. Dewey has a labor representative in Houston and I asked that this individual be sent in to assist in adjusting the problem. Mr. Dewey stated that his representative was Mr. Robert V. Shirk, telephone—Charter 4–4731 in Houston, Texas. This office is in the Melli-Esperson Building. Mr. Shirk was in Lake Charles, Louisiana, but Mr. Dewey promised that he would get him into Houston as rapidly as possible.

I also called Mr. George Weaver of the CIO who in turn called Mr. Knight of the Oil Workers Union in Texas. Mr. Knight informed Mr. Weaver that two vice presidents were suspended for the part they played in causing the strike. He also said that the union would request the dismissal of any worker who caused a walkout.

On Saturday I called Mr. Ellinger concerning the outcome of the meeting. He said that the company, through Mr. Foster, had an agreement with the union that the two Mexican workers would not be taken off the job until the meeting was held. Mr. Foster violated his agreement and the men were taken off the job at 4 p.m. on Friday.

Mr. Ellinger said that 700 persons attended the Friday night meeting and vigorously opposed the upgrading of Negroes and Mexicans. The union appointed a committee to negotiate with management for the re-upgrading of the Negroes and Mexicans. Mr. Ellinger states that management will not upgrade the workers again unless it has assurance that there will be no strike. The union committee is to give a report of progress in settling the matter at a meeting on Tuesday. Mr. Ellinger will remain in Houston until Tuesday.

MS: LH, DI, HqR85, Correspondence Relating to Cases. (Sh–Z) Shell Oil Company.

1. See Mitchell's report to Maslow on the Shell Oil Company at 3/27/44. For background, see the headnotes on the FEPC and Unions, on the Oil Industry, and on Mexican Americans.

Memorandum on Conference
with WMC Executive Director

March 28, 1945

Mr. Will Maslow, Director of Field Operations
Mr. John Davis, Director of Review and Analysis

Clarence M. Mitchell
   Associate Director of Field Operations
Conference with WMC Executive Director

On the above date three of us had a luncheon conference in the office of Mr. Robert Goodwin, Executive Director of the War Manpower Commission, also present was Mr. Don Kingsley, Deputy Executive Director. The following is what took place:

1. Mr. Goodwin stated that Mr. Kingsley now has the function of coordinating the activities of the placement, utilization, training, and planning bureaus of the War Manpower Commission. Mr. Kingsley will serve as FEPC's liaison and will also keep us informed of important War Manpower planning which may affect our agency. He, in turn, will be expected to make specific recommendations on matters which we believe require changes in War Manpower's operations as they affect the requirements of Executive Order 9346. Mr. Kingsley also agreed that it would be proper to talk with Mr. Collis Stocking on matters affecting planning if we so desire. However, it appears that the more desirable approach should be through Mr. Kingsley. It was agreed that we would furnish specific recommendations on the administration of the pending manpower legislation if this is given to the War Manpower Commission as one of its functions.

2. Mr. Kingsley is to send us a written proposal on how FEPC's representatives in the field will have proper liaison with the War Manpower Commission's labor priority committees. The question was discussed at some length and it appears that the WMC will expect us to maintain this liaison through its Area Directors. These Directors will be expected to determine from FEPC whether the hiring policies of plants seeking priority comply with Executive Order 9346. It was agreed that FEPC's regional directors would submit lists of companies not complying with Executive Order 9346 to WMC. Also it was agreed that WMC representatives would receive recommendations from FEPC regional men (to effect compliance with E. O. 9346) concerning firms seeking priority. This proposal will be discussed further at our regional directors' meeting.[1]

3. We discussed the specific problems of Region IV concerning ES 270 reports and ES 510's. Mr. Goodwin stated that he had talked with Mr. Triede (WMC Regional Director) on the matter and Mr. Triede said that FEPC does have access to the ES 270 reports but he imposes the restriction that such reports could not be used for publicity purposes. We pointed out that it is our understanding that such reports are confidential and we do not use them for publicity purpose. We stated that FEPC's Region IV contends that it does not have access to those reports but that since Mr. Triede says we do, we would again ask Mr. Evans to get in touch with WMC's Region IV Director on this question. Mr.

Triede was also quoted as saying that he did not submit any ES 510 reports because he was trying to resolve the problems before referring them to FEPC. We stated that even though WMC might wish to resolve the problems, there was no reason why the copy of the report should not be sent to us. We pointed out that the sending out of such reports would give FEPC some proof that Mr. Triede is attempting to correct discriminatory problems and would also enable us to know whether WMC is working on a given company when a complaint is sent to us. It was agreed that we would again talk with Mr. Goodwin on this matter if Mr. Evans has no success with Mr. Triede.

It was also agreed that the conference would be summarized and the important points verified by letter from Governor Paul V. McNutt, Chairman of the War Manpower Commission, to Mr. Ross.

cc: Mr. Johnson
      Mr. Jones
      Mr. Evans

MS: copy, HqR3, Office Files of George M. Johnson. M.

1. The regional directors' meeting was held in 4/45. For the background to these FEPC-WMC negotiations, see the section on the WMC and USES in the headnote on Relationships with Federal Agencies.

To enhance the current FEPC negotiations with the WMC over ways to improve their working relationships, particularly with regard to discriminatory actions of USES offices or their failure to report discrimination by employers, Maslow had on 3/23/45 requested each regional director to send a summary of the worst example of a USES violation of the nondiscrimination program. Their responses, dated from 3/27 to 4/26/45, can be found in FEPC RG 228 (entry 40, PI 147), Office Files of Clarence M. Mitchell, box 14, WMC-FEPC Relations, and in HqR76, Office Files of Clarence Mitchell. WMC-FEPC Relations. Despite improvements, complaints of USES accommodation of discriminatory work orders continued after the war. See, for example, George Crockett, report, 3/20/46, HqR2, Reports.

Weekly Report

March 29, 1945

Mr. Will Maslow
    Director of Field Operations
Clarence M. Mitchell
    Associate Director of Field Operations
Weekly Report for the Week Ending Saturday, March 24, 1945

IMPORTANT EVENTS AND PROBLEMS

This week the New York office was very helpful in handling problems affecting plants in the St. Louis Kansas City area. Region IX requested that we ask the national office of the Remington-Arms Company to instruct its Kansas City plant that complaints of discrimination involving Negro women should be adjusted. Through Mr. Madison Jones of the New York office, the company took this action and it appears that we may expect adjustment of the cases. Mr. Robert Jones handled the National Carbon problem and also obtained a favorable commitment from the company's New York office. In the latter case, we are also dealing with the Labor Branch of the Signal Corps in Washington. This case is adversely affected by the General Cable Corporation where we have not yet obtained the transfer of Negro women from the paid training program to the actual production. We are optimistic, however, with regard to the outcome.[1]

There was considerable activity in the Central Office concerning the Shell Oil case over the weekend. Action taken on this matter is set forth on a separate memorandum.[2]

The Navy Department and the War Department are continuing action on the Norris Stamping case as requested by FEPC. I believe it is desirable that we continue preparation for a hearing so that no time will be lost in the event that negotiations end in failure.[3]

The War Department reports that the Consolidated Vultee Corporation has inducted fifty Negroes into a paid training program in the Drop Hammer Department. Additional Negroes are being recruited. I am expecting a written report from the War Department on this matter.[4]

ASSIGNMENTS

The following cases were received from the regions:

1. Brown Shipbuilding Company, 13-BR-435
2. Letterman General Hospital, 12-GR-606
3. Union Pacific Railroad, 9-BR-336.
4. Office of Inspector of Naval Engineers Material, 3-GR-189. (Referred from Mr. Davidson)
5. Gulf-Colorado and Santa Fe, 13-BR-368, 458.
6. Brotherhood of Railroad Trainmen, 13-UR-369, 459.

The following case was referred to the Legal Division:

1. Big Four Lines, 6-BR-671, 6-UR-676.

The following cases were returned from the Legal Division:

1. Los Angeles Railway Company cases, 12-BR-1150.
2. General Cable Company, 9-BR-1155, 1252, 1286, 1311.

The following case was returned to the region:

1. Los Angeles Railway Company cases, 12-BR-1150.

The following FDR's were received by me during the week:

Region VI-	2	Region IX-	7
Region VII-	10	Region XII-	8

cc: Mr. Davidson
      Mr. Davis
      Mr. Jones
      Mr. Johnson

MS: copy, FEPC RG 228, Office Files of Clarence Mitchell, DNA.

1. See also 2/6, 2/19 (both texts), 2/20, 2/26, 3/20, 3/29, 4/12, 5/18, 5/21/45; headnote on Major Cases in St. Louis.

2. See memorandum of 3/26/45.

3. See memorandum of 3/13/45 and notes.

4. See report of 3/5/45 and notes.

Otome Saito, Memorandum of Clarence Mitchell's Telephone Conversation with Mr. Ellinger, New Orleans, Louisiana

3/31/45

Mr. Clarence M. Mitchell

Otome Saito

Your Telephone Conversation with Mr. Ellinger, New Orleans

You called Mr. Ellinger in New Orleans on the above date for information on the Shell Oil problem.[1] Mr. Ellinger stated that during the meeting with Mr. Quilty and Mr. Knight there was some discussion as to who was responsible for the situation, but all were in agreement that something had to be done. Mr. Ellinger stated that he had requested that the company restore the two Mexicans to their upgraded positions and that Mr. Quilty pointed out that there was still some time before the lapse of their ninety day period. Mr. Ellinger stated that Mr. Knight, Mr. Quilty and the union committee had meetings on Thursday afternoon and Friday morning in which it has found that there are forty Mexican[s] and Negroes immediately eligible for promotion on the basis of seniority. Arrangements are to be made for the upgrading of these people immediately and the company proposes to give the white workers assurance that in the next six months there would be no other upgradings because there would be no one eligible. Mr. Ellinger stated that he informed the men that FEPC could have no part in this settlement, but that if this plan could get by the workers without trouble and did not interfere with the rights of the workers to be upgraded, it might be done.

Mr. Ellinger informed you that when help is hired from the outside everyone is first employed as a laborer. Mr. Ellinger informed you of the plan agreed upon to inform the workers of the integration of Negroes and Mexicans. He stated that a local meeting is to be held Tuesday night (April 3). Then on April 15, a meeting is to be held either in the local high school or the union hall with Mr. Knight, Mr. Quilty, Mr. Ellinger and other interested representatives. This is to be held for the purpose of informing the workers of the general policies and not the present difficulty at the plant. At the local meeting scheduled for the following night, the specific question of upgrading Negroes and Mexicans into skilled categories will be presented to the workers. It is hoped that through these meetings there will be compliance before the end of the ninety day period (April 27).

It was Mr. Ellinger's opinion that if management cooperated something could be worked out more peacefully. PAW's position on this matter was that it did not usually get into this type of situation, but it was hoped that a representation of PAW will be present at the meeting of April 15.

MS: copy, HqR85, Correspondence Relating to Cases. (Sh–Z) Shell Oil Company.
   1. For sources and cross references, see the headnote on the Oil Industry.

Weekly Report

April 3, 1945

Mr. Will Maslow
    Director of Field Operations
Clarence M. Mitchell
    Associate Director of Operations
Weekly Report for the Week Ending Saturday, March 31, 1945

IMPORTANT EVENTS AND PROBLEMS

The Navy Department this week informed me that the Mingledorff Shipbuilding Company, a Navy contractor in Savannah, Georgia, has been reminded of the necessity of complying with Executive Order 9346 as provided in its contract. I have relayed this information to Dr. Dodge with the request that he renew his negotiations with this company.

Our conference this week with the War Manpower Commission (Mr. Goodwin and Mr. Kingsley) seems to augur well for a more cooperative relationship between the Committee and the Commission.[1]

The Maritime Commission reported its activities in connection with complaints against the Todd Houston Shipbuilding Company of Houston, Texas. The Commission states that its regional representatives are cooperating with Mr. Ellinger on this matter. I talked with the Commission and later wrote a letter on this matter at Mr. Ellinger's request in order to insure full cooperation at the local level.

A representative of the Ordnance Branch of the War Department called this week to state that he would go to Los Angeles as we requested to aid in the settlement of the Norris Stamping case. Since he is not leaving until April 9, I asked him to meet with Messrs. Kingman and Brown while they are here for the regional directors' meeting. He agreed to do this and I will arrange a meeting some time during this week.[2]

Miss Saito has prepared a digest of a telephone conversation with Mr. Ellinger on the Shell Oil case. Briefly the present plan is that all Mexicans and Negroes eligible for promotion are to be upgraded. This amounts to forty persons. The company proposes that no other upgrading take place from these groups for six months thereafter. Mr. Ellinger was not entirely satisfied with this plan and it remains to be seen whether it will be acceptable to the union membership when it is presented. Mr. Ellinger informed me that the Petroleum Administration for War had communicated with the Shell Oil Company concerning our case. I gave the latest information on the status of this case to PAW [Petroleum Administration for War] and it was agreed that that agency will send a representative to a planned meeting in April at Houston.[3]

We are taking up with the Surgeon General a very interesting case involving a Negro nurse in San Francisco. This individual sought employment at the Letterman General Hospital and was refused because of her race. The Civil Service Commission is taking the matter up with the Secretary of War and Mr. Ross is seeking appointment with the Surgeon General on this matter.[4]

ASSIGNMENTS:

The following cases were received from the regions:

1. San Antonio Post Office, 10-GR-531.
2. Portsmouth Navy Yard, 1-GN-157 (Referral from Mr. Davidson)
3. National Lead Company, 9-BR-1159, 1394
4. Curtiss Wright Corporation, 9-BR-1086, 1153

The following cases were referred to the Legal Division:

Norris Stamping & Manufacturing Co., 12-BR-1350.
Union Pacific R. R., 9-BR-336.

The following cases were returned from the Legal Division: (Returned to regions)

1. U.S. Cartridge, 9-BR-69
2. Bussman Manufacturing Co., 9-BR-172
3. Carter Carburetor, 9-BR-141
4. Amertorp Corporation, 9-BR-164
5. Wagner Electric, 9-BR-157
6. St. Louis Shipbuilding and Steel Co., 9-BR-85
7. McQuay Norris, 9-BR-79, 80, 81, 82, 83.

The following cases were returned to the regions:

1. (8) U.S. Naval Drydock, 12-GC-1101
2. (9) General Cable, 9-BR-1252, 1286, 1311, 1155

The following FDR's were received and acted upon by me:

Region VI-	4	Region VIII-	2
Region VII-	13	Region IX-	2
		Region XII-	5

Messrs.   Davidson
          Davis
          Johnson
          Jones

MS: copy, FEPC RG 228, Office Files of Clarence Mitchell, DNA.

1. See Mitchell's memorandum, 3/28/45. John A. Davis added that the agreements reached with Goodwin and Collis Stocking brought to a conclusion all the FEPC's proposals regarding programming. One point on which they agreed was that Donald Kingsley, deputy executive director of the WMC, keep in touch with Davis regarding their programming techniques and especially with regard to the results of proposed legislation for a permanent committee. Davis to Ross, memorandum, 3/30/45, HqR5, Office Files of George M. Johnson. Misc.

2. See memorandum of 4/23/45.

3. See digest of 3/31/45.

4. On this case, see also 4/12, 4/24/45.

Memorandum on Kurz-Kasch Company

April 3, 1945

Miss Carol Coan

Clarence M. Mitchell
    Associate Director of Field Operations

Kurz-Kasch Company, 5-BR-271

The above case illustrates a situation in which the War Manpower Commission applied sanction to an employer who failed to comply with Executive Order 9346.[1] The company is located in Dayton, Ohio and manufactures vital equipment for aircraft such as radio, radar, ignition, and electrical installations.

On December 21, 1943, we received an ES 510 report charging that the concern failed to employ three non-white women applicants. The individuals were told there were no openings for the position, although the USES had open orders at the time and white applicants were still being considered for the job. The plant employs seven hundred persons many of whom are female. Six non-white males are at the service level and one non-white woman also at the service level. Unions having bargaining relationships with the company are: International Moulders of North America, Local 193; IAM, Lodge 13; and the International Brotherhood of F. E. and B., Local 196.

FEPC was unable to adjust the case at the regional level and referred the case for a hearing on July 27, 1944. Mr. Duncan of the War Manpower Commission requested the Regional Director, Mr. McKnight, to explore the possibility of obtaining a WMC sanction on the company.

On February 23, 1945, WMC asked the company to comply with Executive Order 9346. This resulted in the hiring of two Negro women who were employed on production on Thursday, March 22 and there was a walkout of the white employees. This walkout lasted until Thursday, March 29, when Colonel Strong of Army Air Forces went into Dayton and settled the problem. The workers are now back on the job and the Negro women are still employed.[2]

MS: copy, HqR2, *Office Files of Malcolm Ross. Material for Final Report.*

1. On the use of sanctions to enforce nondiscrimination, see the headnote on Relationships with Federal Agencies.

2. For additional background, see the headnote on Strikes and Work Stoppages.

Weekly Report

April 12, 1945

Mr. Will Maslow
    Director of Field Operations
Clarence M. Mitchell
    Associate Director of Field Operations
Weekly Report for the Week Ending Saturday, April 7, 1945

IMPORTANT EVENTS AND PROBLEMS

During the past week at the urgent request of Region XII Mr. Ross had a conference with General Kirk, Surgeon General of the U. S. Army, concerning a complaint filed by a Negro nurse against the Letterman General Hospital. Mr. Ross has informed me that General Kirk has agreed that the complainant should be hired, although it appears that a revision of the Army's plan will result in the dismissal of all civilian nurses at this establishment within approximately thirty days. It is interesting to note that the Surgeon General's office was critical of the attitude (described as "pressing") of Mr. Rutledge. Mr. Kingman in a conference with Mr. Ross stated that he was present at the meeting with the War Department representatives at the Letterman Hospital and the relationships were most cordial. This incident should remind us that whenever our examiners are conscientious in the field it is likely that we will receive a criticism concerning their "aggressiveness."

The settlement of the General Cable case emphasized the soundness of the position taken by most of us in the meeting with Major General Harrison and General Greenbaum on Monday, April 2. This position, as you will recall, was that the company should go forward with its compliance as quickly as possible.[1]

During this week I had a number of conferences with the War Department, P.A.W. and union officials on Shell Oil. At present the War Department and the Petroleum Administration for War report that they have been in touch with the company's top management and stressed the necessity of compliance with Executive Order 9346.

After discussions with Mr. Ellinger and Mr. Ross we have agreed that the original mass meeting planned to "educate white employees" would be inadvisable and therefore neither the War Department or PAW will be expected to send representatives to this meeting. However, both of these agencies will be expected to maintain a continuing interest in the problem. So far, they have agreed to do this.

The Post Office Department reported on its investigation on complaints against the Philadelphia Post Office. So far, this has been the most searching of the Post Office Department's inquiries on questions of discrimination. It appears that there have been some adjustments of complaints but, as like the other cases, it is not yet finally settled.

During the past week I arranged a conference with Messrs. Kingman and Brown on the Norris Stamping case. Major Everett M. Goulard of the Ordnance Department joined us in this conference and he promised assistance from the War Department in settling this case. He left for San Francisco and Los Angeles. While on the coast he will handle this case and also join Messrs. Brown and Hunt in conferences on it. The Legal Division has requested Mr. Hunt to return from Arizona and be available in Los Angeles.[2]

I also planned a conference between Messrs. Theodore Brown and Hoglund and Lieutenant Colonel Cross of the War Department on St. Louis. The War Department, however, misunderstood our request and sent instead Colonel Sidney Sufrin of its

Labor Branch. Nevertheless we discussed the St. Louis area and I will have a follow-up meeting with Major Cross myself.

Mr. Brown and Mr. Hoglund reported on the Remington-Arms Company in Kansas City and the National Carbon Company in St. Louis. They stated that both of these companies, following action by the central office and the New York office of FEPC (at our request), are now hiring Negro women and it appears that the complaints against them are being adjusted.[3]

ASSIGNMENTS

The following cases were received from the regions:

1. U. S. Employment Service:

Columbia, S. C.	7-GR-478
Greenville, S.C.	7-GR-479
Anderson, S.C.	7-GR-480
Spartansburg, S.C.	7-GR-481

2. Amarillo Army Air Base   10-GR-445

The following FDR's have been reviewed and acted upon:

Region VI-	4	Region IX-	20
Region VII-	2	Region XII-	17
Region VIII-	1	Region XIII-	11

cc: Mr. Davidson
       Mr. Davis
       Mr. Johnson
       Mr. Jones

MS: copy, FEPC RG 228, Office Files of Clarence Mitchell, DNA.

1. See also 2/6, 2/19 (both texts), 2/20, 2/26, 3/20, 3/29, 4/12, 5/18, 5/21/45; headnote on Major Cases in St. Louis. The General Cable Company of St. Louis, on which the Committee had held an examiner-type hearing, was working to comply with the directives that were then issued. At its 3/31/45 meeting the Committee agreed that the chairman should use his discretion to give the company time after 4/9 fully to comply. HqR1, Summary Minutes of Meetings. For more information, see HqR2, Office Files of Malcolm Ross. Difficult Cases; HqR4, Office Files of George M. Johnson. Bloch; and HqR6, Office Files of George M. Johnson. Misc.

2. See 3/13, 3/22/45.

3. The various Washington meetings mentioned in this report were supplementary activities of the regional directors' meeting held in April.

Memorandum on Appointment of Rutledge as Examiner-in-Charge of the San Francisco Office

April 12, 1945

Mr. Will Maslow
  Director of Field Operations
Clarence M. Mitchell
  Associate Director of Field Operations
Appointment of Rutledge as Examiner-in-Charge of the San Francisco Office

As you know, Mr. Kingman has a special arrangement on the West Coast under which he designates Mr. Edward Rutledge as Examiner-in-Charge of the San Francisco Office.[1] In view of the excellent work performed by Mr. Rutledge and the considerable territory under Mr. Kingman's supervision, it is my belief that we should take official notice of this designation and so inform Mr. Rutledge.

I believe that all of our regions should have examiners-in-charge of offices in the regional cities. This should enhance the statu[r]e of our regional directors and make for better operating relationships between our agency and other branches of the Government. In Philadelphia, for example, it would enable Mr. Fleming to maintain a liaison with the regional office of the War Manpower Commission and the examiner-in-charge could handle any necessary relationships with the Area Directors of WMC which fall within the Philadelphia territory.

After listening to Mr. McKnight's conversation concerning his region, I am convinced that regional directors would have more time for supervision and handling of extremely difficult cases if we could make such an arrangement.

I suggest that we take the action immediately in San Francisco and as soon as it is practical in other regions.

MS: copy, HqR3, *Office Files of George M. Johnson. M.*

1. Rutledge was appointed examiner in charge of the San Francisco office and served for a short time (see biographical directory). Rutledge was the only example of an examiner in charge acting in the same area as the Regional Director. Other examiners in charge ran offices in different major regional cities from that of the regional director. Examples include Robert E. Brown in Los Angeles, Milo Manly in Pittsburgh, Edward Swan in Detroit, and Harold James in Cincinnati. FEPC budget cutbacks precluded implementation of Mitchell's suggestion.

Memorandum on Communication from War Department Regarding Consolidated Vultee Aircraft Corporation at Fort Worth, Texas

April 12, 1945

Mr. Maceo Hubbard
    Chief, Legal Division
Clarence M. Mitchell
    Associate Director of Field Operations
Communication From War Department Re Consolidated Vultee
    Aircraft Corporation at Fort Worth, Texas

At my request the War Department addressed the attached letter to Mr. Ross concerning the status of a program for upgrading Negroes at the Consolidated Vultee Aircraft Corporation in Fort Worth, Texas.[1]

I presume you will wish to have the appropriate member of the Legal Division consider this communication in connection with the handling of the case. I believe it would also be appropriate to have a brief conference on this matter at your convenience. Attachment

MS: copy, HqR83, Correspondence Relating to Cases. (A–K) Consolidated Vultee Aircraft Co.
    For other immediately related texts, see 1/3, 1/4, 1/9, 2/12, and 4/23/45. See also the headnote on the Aircraft Industry.
    1. The attached letter, Ralph F. Gow to Ross, n.d., is filed with this text.

Memorandum on Conference with Oil Workers Regarding Shell Oil

April 12, 1945

Mr. Emanuel Bloch
    Hearings Commissioner
Clarence M. Mitchell
    Associate Director of Field Operations
Conference With Oil Workers Re: Shell Oil

The following is my understanding of what we agreed to in our conference with Messrs. Knight and Stewart of the Oil Workers Union on Saturday, April 7:

1. As a first step on the part of the company to demonstrate good faith, the two Mexican employees will be reinstated to their jobs of truck driver and carmen's helper.
2. The Union will undertake an educational program within the next three or four weeks with its various locals and representatives in Texas. This program will be designed to create a favorable climate for the upgrading of other employees at the Shell Company.
3. The one Mexican and seven Negroes who were offered jobs as helpers but turned down because of the threatened strike will be again upgraded.

MS: copy, HqR85, Correspondence Relating to Cases. (Sh–Z) Shell Oil Company.

See also Mitchell to Ellinger, 4/11/45, and other related texts in the file; headnote on the Oil Industry.

Memorandum on Continental Can Company, Norwood, Ohio

DATE: April 14, 1945

TO: Mr. Eugene Davidson
Assistant Director of Field Operations

FROM: Clarence M. Mitchell
Associate Director of Field Operations

SUBJECT: Continental Can Company, Norwood, Ohio

On Wednesday, April 11, Harold James, Examiner-in-Charge of the Cincinnati office called after closing time to report on the status of the strike at the Continental Can Company at Norwood, Ohio.[1]

Mr. James stated that he was faced with the following choices and wanted to know what position he should take:

1. The company could dismiss its two Negro employees and then such persons would file complaints with FEPC. Mr. James stated that, in his opinion, the company intended to dismiss the Negroes and thereby get the white individuals back on the job.
2. Management would agree to keep the colored employees on the job even though the white workers did not immediately return to their employment.
3. The company would remove the Negro workers, but would enter into a signed agreement with FEPC that it (the company) would embark on an educational program designed to have Negroes employed by summer.

I informed Mr. James that "1" and "3" would be undesirable. I suggested that our experience has shown that once workers are placed on the job new difficulties arise if they are removed.

MS: LH, DI, HqR77, Office Files of Eugene Davidson. Strikes.

1. On 4/14/45, Harold James informed Maslow by telegram (attached to text) that management subsequently agreed to hire two African American workers. The men were told to report to work inside the plant but they refused, fearing they would be subjected to violence. The company then had them sign statements that they had resigned voluntarily. James said that was "a flagrant case of collusion between management and striking workers. Management paid salary of all striking workers for the full time the plant was shut down and made absolutely no effort to settle the stoppage on the basis of the issues." On such incidents, see the headnote on Strikes and Work Stoppages.

Memorandum on Consolidated Vultee Aircraft Corporation, Fort Worth, Texas

April 23, 1945

Mr. Emanuel Bloch
    Hearing[s] Commissioner
Clarence M. Mitchell
    Associate Director of Field Operations
Consolidated Vultee Aircraft Corporation, Ft. Worth, Texas

For your information I am attaching copies of material sent to me by Colonel Ralph F. Gow, Director of Industrial Personnel Division, Army Service Forces. It appears that some progress is being made by the company.

Please include this in the file.

Attachment

MS: copy, HqR83, Correspondence Relating to Cases. (A–K) Consolidated Vultee Aircraft Co.

For immediately related texts, see 1/3, 1/4, 2/12, 4/12/45. For the probable enclosures, see the documents filed with this text.

Memorandum on Norris Stamping Case

April 23, 1945

Mr. Maceo Hubbard
    Acting Director, Legal Division
Clarence M. Mitchell
    Associate Director of Field Operations
Norris Stamping Case, 12-BR-1350

As you know, Major Everett Goulard of the Ordnance Branch of the War Department made a special investigation of the Norris Stamping case at the request of FEPC. Major Goulard talked with me on Monday, April 23, concerning his visit to Los Angeles and his conference with Messrs. Norris, Hunt, and Brown.

Major Goulard stated that Mr. Norris' position, briefly summarized, indicates that the company will not willingly hire Negroes. Mr. Norris is quoted as saying that if the Government insists, the company would have to hire Negroes, but he would not then be responsible for keeping production up to its present level. Major Goulard stated that although many persons have talked in terms of the possibility of a strike if Negroes are employed, Mr. Norris himself apparently does not expect anything so dramatic as a strike. His views is that there will be a gradual dropping off of certain employees who are important and a general fall in the efficiency of production.

Paradoxically, there is a considerable turnover at the plant, but Major Goulard said that it appears that the bulk of the employees are long term workers. By his estimates one thousand people form the nucleus of the company's working force and are very stable employees. The remaining seven hundred are those who are responsible for the turnover. Seventy-five per cent of those who are responsible for the turnover have been with the company less than ninety days according to Major Goulard.

It now appears that we have exhausted all possible action short of a hearing. I told Major Goulard that we would inform him when the date was set.[1] I will appreciate it if you will let me know this so that I may give him that information.

cc: Mr. Johnson

MS: copy, HqR84, Correspondence Relating to Cases. (L–S) Norris Stamping Co.
   See Mitchell's memoranda of 3/13, 3/22/45, as well as the several documents filed with this text.
   1. No hearing was held because the company began major cutbacks in employment. See 8/17/45.

Bi-Weekly Report

April 24, 1945

Mr. Will Maslow
    Director of Field Operations
Clarence M. Mitchell
    Associate Director of Field Operations
Bi-Weekly Report—April 9–21, 1945

In line with the procedure being following by regional directors, I am submitting a bi-weekly report instead of the former weekly arrangement.

During the past two weeks I have met with officials of the National Lead Company concerning complaints in St. Louis. One of the cases will be satisfactorily adjusted by the company and it appears that two others will be dismissed on merits unless St. Louis can furnish us with a refutation of the arguments that the company says it will present in writing. However, the basic issue of upgrading is still unresolved because of a case pending before the War Labor Board. I have arranged to have a conference with WLB on this matter.

Mr. Bloch and I have been following closely developments in the Shell Oil case. The War Department is very active on this matter as well as PAW.[1]

The Navy Department is at work on complaints against the Brown Shipbuilding Company in Houston, Texas as requested by me.

A strike occurred at the Combustion Engineering Company in St. Louis when a Negro was placed on the job as a welder. Unfortunately the issue was not resolved because the employee quit before the Boilermakers Union took action to order the strikers back on the job. I discussed this matter with Mr. Boris Shiskin of the Committee, who promised to call Mr. McGowan in Kansas City. I have had no report from Mr. Shiskin, but I have asked Mr. Hoglund to determine what action was taken by the Boilermakers at Mr. Shiskin's request.[2]

In a separate memorandum I have discussed my conference with Mr. Ivan Willis, National Manager of Industrial Relations for the Wright and Curtis Wright Companies.[3] We talked about complaints filed against the St. Louis plant.

ASSIGNMENTS

The following cases were returned to the regions during the period of April 9–21:

> Amarillo Army Air Base, 10-GR-445
> Letterman General Hospital, 12-GR-606

The following FDR's have been reviewed and acted upon by me:

Region VI	17
Region VIII	1
Region XII	7

cc: Mr. Davidson
Mr. Davis
Mr. Jones
Mr. Johnson

MS: FEPC RG 228, Office Files of Clarence Mitchell, DNA.

1. See Mitchell's memorandum of 4/12/45; texts in HqR84, Records Relating to Hearings. Shell Oil Company, Inc., & Oil Workers International Union, Local 367, CIO; headnotes on the Oil Industry and on Mexican Americans.

2. See the section on the Boilermakers in the headnote on the FEPC and Unions.

3. Memorandum not found, but see Mitchell at 5/18/45, where he discusses a later meeting with Willis.

Memorandum on Action on Machinists Cases

May 2, 1945

Mr. George M. Johnson
    Deputy Chairman
Clarence M. Mitchell
    Acting Director of Field Operations
Action on Machinists Cases

Region XII has again directed to our attention complaints against the Aeronautical Lodge 751 of the IAM. As I stated in my memorandum of March 7, 1945,[1] the regional offices are faced with unresolved cases involving this union and I will appreciate it if I could have an opportunity to confer with the sub-Committee handling this matter.[2] My objective, of course, would be an early conference with Mr. Harvey Brown.

The new complaints against Lodge 751 allege that Negro workers are charged permit fees but at the same time are denied membership solely because of their race.

MS: copy, HqR38, Central Files. (entry 25) Memoranda, Johnson, George M., 1/44–.

For other sources and cross-references, see the section on the International Association of Machinists in the headnote on the FEPC and Unions.

1. Memorandum not found, but see Mitchell's weekly reports of 3/5, 3/13/45.

2. The subcommittee consisted of Boris Shishkin and Charles Hamilton Houston.

Bi-Weekly Report

May 7, 1945

Mr. Will Maslow
    Director of Field Operations
Clarence M. Mitchell
    Associate Director of Field Operations
Bi-Weekly Report for the Period—April 23 to May 5, 1945

IMPORTANT EVENTS AND PROBLEMS

On May 4, 1945, I joined the Chairman [Ross], Deputy Chairman [Johnson], and Mrs. Evelyn Cooper in conference with other Government agencies on plans for handling problems which may arise in the Capital Transit case. A memorandum on our discussion has been prepared and will be submitted to you shortly.[1]

At the request of Mr. Henderson I have taken up with the War Department the question of having the Wilson Packing Company delete a question asking for religion of applicants from its pre-employment forms. Mr. Henderson considers this case important in his region. Although we do not have sufficient evidence of discrimination to warrant a hearing, it does appear that the company is not justified in keeping this type of question on its application form.[2]

New cases involving the International Association of Machinists have been sent in from Region XII. These complainants allege that they are charged permit fees but are not admitted to full union membership. I hope that I will have an opportunity to discuss this at the Committee meeting in Chicago on May 11, where I am to review events in the Shell Oil case and the present status of the St. Louis hearing cases.[3]

The National Lead Company has written as I expected paving the way for a satisfactory adjustment of one complaint. It appears that two others may be dismissed on merits and the basic complaints of upgrading are as yet unresolved. Additional meetings with the company are scheduled.

At the request of the Chicago office I obtained from the General Accounting Office statistical information on the number and grade of Negro employees in the Chicago GAO.

Also, we have received a considerable volume of correspondence from Chicago residents concerning the post office in that city. Although I am following this matter closely and will discuss it with Mr. Henderson on May 11, I have taken no action in Washington as yet.

The CIO has sent in a favorable report making possible the adjustment of a complaint involving the Paper Workers Organizing Committee which had a discriminatory clause in a contract with the Hinde-Dauch Paper Company of Kansas City. The clause has been eliminated.

Apparently the War Department is following through on the St. Louis cases in that I received notification of the employment of Negroes by the Carter Carburetor Company and, also, information on plans of the McQuay-Norris Company for the use of Negro women. I forwarded this information to Mr. Brown in St. Louis and he has verified that portion of his dealings with the Carter Carburetor Company.

Also, I should note that the National Carbon Company, which required the attention of the DFO and our office in New York, is now employing Negro women in production capacities. The company was instructed to take favorable action by its New York office after matters in St. Louis had reached a stalemate.[4]

Colonel Ralph Gow of Army Service Forces has submitted an additional report on the Consolidated Vultee Aircraft Corporation indicating that the company is making progress in the upgrading of Negroes. It should be noted that in this case we have enjoyed some rather unusual help from the War Department, although the problems are not yet settled.

On May 2, I spoke at a meeting of young women at the Washington YWCA. Most of these are Government employees. I do not know that my remarks were very informative, but I learned something from the group. One young lady stated that her supervisor had informed her that she need not worry about efficiency ratings because they were of no importance. Several others seemed to have had a similar experience. It would appear that this tended to verify a rumor that Negro Government employees are receiving low efficiency grades and told not to worry about them. This may be worth checking on.

ASSIGNMENTS

The following case was received from the region:

Indianapolis Railways Inc., 6-BR-717.

The following cases were referred to the Legal Division:

1. Indianapolis Railways Inc., 6-BR-717.
2. Curtis Wright Corporation, 9-BR-153; 1086.

The following case was returned to the region:

1. Maritime Service, 7-GR-580.

The following FDR's have been reviewed and acted upon by me:

Region VI-	13	Region X-	18
Region VII-	5	Region XII-	29
Region VIII-	1	Region XIII	6
Region IX-	20		

cc: Mr. Davidson
    Mr. Davis
    Mr. Johnson
    Mr. Jones

MS: copy, FEPC RG 228, Office Files of Clarence Mitchell, DNA.

1. See Mitchell to Maslow, "Summary of Meeting on Capital Transit—May 3, 1945," memorandum, 5/9/45.

2. See the headnote on Race, Creed, Color, or National Origin on Employment Application Forms.

3. At its meeting on 5/11/45 the Committee voted to hold a committee-type hearing on the IAM cases of Locals 79 and 751 of Seattle and on the Richmond Shipyard in California. See Mitchell's report of 5/21/45; Minutes of 5/11/45, HqR1, Summary Minutes of Meetings. For the context, see the section on the International Association of Machinists in the headnote on the FEPC and Unions.

4. According to the Final Disposition Report of 5/30/45, this case, which involved the company's refusal to hire Negro women for production jobs, was closed as satisfactorily adjusted because "this Company changed its policy so that its records reflected within one month 105 Negro women out of a total of approximately 900; further because this Company has not only agreed to favorably consider all duly qualified women without regard to their race, creed, color or national origin, and has agreed to integrate them in all occupations; and finally because further checks have indicated that this Company is hiring numerous Negro women applicants, and there have been, since the adjustment, no complaints against the Company." HqR60, Central Files. FDRs, Region IX.

Summary of Meeting on Capital Transit Company

May 9, 1945

Mr. Malcolm Ross
    Chairman
Clarence M. Mitchell
    Associate Director of Field Operation
Summary of Meeting on Capital Transit—May 3, 1945

Those present at the meeting in the Chairman's office on May 3 were: Messrs. Riley and Flannagan of the Public Utilities Commission, Captain S. M. Peyser and Mr. Lemuel Foster of Army Service Forces, Mr. Roberts of ODT [Office of Defense Transportation], and Mr. Donald Kingsley of the War Manpower Commission. Those present for FEPC were: Mrs. Cooper, Mr. Ross, Mr. Johnson, and myself.

Mr. Ross outlined the status of the Capital Transit case and pointed out that union officials have offered the company their cooperation in getting Negroes on platform jobs. Mrs. Cooper said that the union estimates that approximately four hundred persons will quit if Negroes are placed on the job; that the company's estimate based on the Lunt report is somewhat less: and that both the union and the company contemplate a breakdown in service. Mr. Ross added that FEPC has not asked the War Manpower Commission to stop servicing the company and we would also make a request that the company be given a higher priority than it now has in order to fill the vacancies which might be created by quits. It was emphasized that our purpose was not that of coercing the company but of seeking for it full Government aid and support to the end of averting a disruption of transportation service. Also, it was explained that we considered the estimates of resignations to be grossly exaggerated but nevertheless thought it wise to program on the basis of the gravest prediction.

Mrs. Cooper pointed out that at present there is very little talk of a strike or violence, but there is considerable talk of how individuals will simply walk off the job if Negroes are placed in platform jobs. She reported that although Colonel Kelly of the Police Department was not present, we do have assurance that there will be full cooperation from the Police Department.

The following precautionary measures were suggested by Mrs. Cooper:

1. Temporary schedules would be worked out for the utilization on key lines of those operators willing to stay on their jobs. This would involve the suspension of certain less important operating lines with the understanding that OPA would give supplementary gas rations to individuals living in outlying areas.

2. The War Manpower Commission would not give certificates of availability to individuals quitting jobs on Capital Transit. If they return to the USES in search of jobs, they would be referred back to the Capital Transit Company in all cases. Also, it was proposed that the company be given a larger recruiting area than it now has.

3. The War Department would supplement the available manpower with military personnel having civilian experience in the operation of busses or street cars.

Mr. Roberts of the ODT said that if the company's service is to be cut, plans have already been made for ten, twenty, or thirty per cent curtailment at the request of the Office of Defense Transportation. These plans were made necessary by the gas and tire shortage in 1943. Although they were not related to a manpower situation, it was felt that it would be useful to determine whether they would be adaptable to an emergency shortage of four hundred operators, in lieu of the abandonment of certain presently scheduled lines.

The Public Utilities representatives agreed to explore this further.

Mr. Roberts also made the assertion that under the present circumstances it appears that OPA would be in a position to give supplemental gas rations to individuals who might need it.

Captain Peyser agreed to request information on the available number of former bus driver and trolley operators in the vicinity of the Washington military district. Mr. Ross is to request Secretary Patterson for planning for the assignment of such military personnel as may be needed. Captain Peyser stated that if plans are properly developed such persons could be available for use by the company within an hour's time.

Mr. Kingsley agreed that the War Manpower Commission would give FEPC full cooperation on this matter. Among other things, he is to determine the extent to which the company's recruitment area can be enlarged, and whether it can be given a higher recruitment priority.

MS: copy, HqR1, *Office Files of Malcolm Ross. Documents [for 6/3/45 meeting].*

See background materials cited in 1/22/44, note 4. Additional significance for the Lunt study is provided by Davis's analysis submitted to Johnson 2/8/45. Davis's principal point was that the Committee did not recommend to the company the preparation of an "attitude study." It was clear from the summer of 1943, he said, that Lunt's company did not have the experience to conduct a study of the company's hiring African Americans as platform men. Consequently, the FEPC recommended three persons with general training in industrial sociology, specific managerial experience, and experience in "the business of integrating Negroes in industries." Davis's evaluation can be found in HqR4, Office Files of George M. Johnson. John A. Davis. For other sources on the Capital Transit struggle, see HqR1, Office Files of Malcolm Ross. T and Difficult Cases; HqR2, Office Files of Malcolm Ross. Materials for the July 26 Meeting; HqR5, Office Files of George M. Johnson. Legal Division; Watson, *Lion in the Lobby,* 149, note 33.

Memorandum on Report of WMC
on Capital Transit Company

May 17, 1945

Mr. Malcolm Ross
    Chairman
Clarence M. Mitchell
    Associate Director of Field Operations
Report of WMC on Capital Transit Company

On May 16 I talked with Mr. Donald Kingsley, Deputy Executive Director of WMC, concerning the Capital Transit case. He stated that he had taken follow up action on FEPC's suggestions.[1]

Mr. Kinsley informed me that the Capital Transit Company now has a "5" priority rating but WMC will be willing to move it up to the higher bracket if there is a shortage of workers resulting from quits on the part of white workers who object to the employment of Negroes as platform operators. Mr. Kingsley stated to me also that he met with Mr. Triede, Regional Director of WMC in Washington, and it was agreed that in the event there are a number of quits on the Capital Transit, all persons regardless of race will be referred to the company. Also, any Capital Transit employee who seek USES assistance in obtaining a new job will be referred only to the Capital Transit Company. Concerning the enlargement of the company's recruiting area,

Mr. Kingsley stated that this could be done but he did not believe it would be very effective.

He asked me to keep him informed of developments in the Capital Transit case and to give him ample notice of the issuance of Committee directives. He believes that this is very important and trust that I will have an opportunity to inform him of these directives before they are published in the newspapers.[2]

MS: copy, HqR39, Central Files. (entry 25) Memoranda, Ross, Malcolm, 1/45–.

1. See memorandum, 5/9/45.

2. The reference probably is to the War Department's earlier complaints about learning of the FEPC's rapid issuance of its directive on the Los Angeles Railway case through the newspapers, despite Mitchell's assurance that such directives were not issued immediately after hearings. See Mitchell to Ross, telegram, 8/10/44.

Memorandum on Meeting with Mr. Ivan Willis of Curtiss-Wright Corporation

CONFIDENTIAL

May 18, 1945

Mr. Will Maslow
    Director of Field Operations
Clarence M. Mitchell
    Associate Director of Field Operations
Meeting with Mr. Ivan Willis of Curtis-Wright Corporation

Mr. Ivan Willis, Manager of Industrial Relations for the Curtis-Wright Corporation, came to the office on Thursday, May 17, to discuss the St. Louis complaints against his company's installation in that city. As he promised in a previous meeting, Mr. Willis had been to St. Louis and discussed the whole situation with his local management.[1] He stated that while management had gone ahead with his plans for using Negroes for certain jobs in the Salvage Department of the main plant, there was no indication that there would be general integration. Thus, the company will retain its segregated plan for Negro employees engaged in general production work.

Mr. Willis also said that war contracts held by the St. Louis plant will be concluded in October. The company does not expect any new orders and its Kentucky plant

511

which received certain material from St. Louis will be closed July first. Mr. Willis stated that the St. Louis plant will have some civilian production and as a matter of over-all policy, Curtis-Wright has not decided whether St. Louis or Buffalo will be the home of its major post-war operations. If St. Louis is selected the company will eventually do away with its segregated plant and integrate Negroes in the main building.

Mr. Willis assured me that as a matter of national policy, Curtis-Wright and the Wright Aeronautical Corporation will continue the employment of Negroes in the post-war period. However, the company's total operations will dwindle from 170,000 employees to 10,000 when it reaches normal production. At present the company has 17,000 Negroes employed in all of its installations. Naturally there will be a drastic cut-back among Negro employees.

Mr. Willis stated that as the St. Louis plant lays-off individuals it may eventually become necessary to move certain Negro employees into the main plaint. When this is done management expects some trouble he stated. However, he indicated that he had informed the local management to stand firm on this policy. He also said that under the stress of labor difficulties, resulting from integration of Negroes, the local management may seek to abandon a program of integration because it would not wish to have any interference with its program of non-war production.

In view of certain statements which have been made recently about the possibilities of converting certain aircraft plants into other production, I asked Mr. Willis for his opinion on this. He is in a position to know a great deal about the employment prospects of the industry, because he is also Chairman of the Industrial Relations Committee of the National Aeronautical Chamber of Commerce. He said that he did not feel that it would be proper to comment on specific installations of other companies, but he could say that it was very unlikely that any of them could be used for production of anything other than aircraft. He estimated that the aircraft industry will drop from a million and a half employees to approximately fifty or sixty thousand. The maintenance of aircraft plants as presently constructed is so expensive that most companies will have to abandon large wartime structures Mr. Willis stated. I mentioned Bell Aircraft specifically and he said that while he could not comment on this officially, it was perfectly obvious that the Marietta, Georgia plant could not be used for any post-war work except aircraft and this is unlikely.[2]

All in all he presented a rather gloomy picture of the aircraft industry in general but he did say before leaving that it is his opinion that the aircraft industry in general will continue the employment of some Negroes in the post-war period and it is unlikely that Negroes will suffer extensive losses in the occupations they now hold. There will, of course, be tremendous numerical losses as with all other persons employed in this industry.

This memorandum may be useful for several purposes, but since Mr. Willis and I were talking somewhat informally, I believe that it should be kept confidential.

cc: Mr. Davis
       Mr. Johnson

MS: copy, HqR3, Office Files of George M. Johnson. M.

1. On Mitchell's earlier meeting with Willis, see 4/24/45. For the broader employment picture for blacks in St. Louis, see also 2/6, 2/19 (both texts), 2/20, 2/26, 3/20, 3/29, 5/21/45; headnote on Major Cases in St. Louis.

2. Looking at the overall prospects for black workers in the aircraft industry, Robert Weaver concluded, "it is reasonable to assume that the Negro will emerge as a small part of the industry's labor force, provided we do not have general, mass unemployment. Tens of thousands of colored workers in aircraft during the war, however, will be forced to seek new jobs." Weaver, *Negro Labor,* 268. According to Birch Matthews, work at the government-owned Bell-operated bomber plant in Marietta ended immediately after the war. The government closed the plant shortly thereafter. See Matthews, *Cobra!* 378; Pelletier, *Bell Aircraft,* 13; headnote on the Aircraft Industry.

Bi-Weekly Report

May 21, 1945

Mr. Will Maslow
>   Director of Field Operations

Clarence M. Mitchell
>   Associate Director of Field Operations

Bi-Weekly Report for the Period—May 7 to 19, 1945

IMPORTANT EVENTS AND PROBLEMS:

As you know from a memorandum already sent to you, the Curtis-Wright Corporation in St. Louis is due to complete its war contracts in October and this may have an important bearing on the current cases. I am requesting Mr. Brown of our St. Louis office to give me his reaction to this new development.[1]

At its meeting on May 11, I talked with the Committee on the Shell Oil and Machinists cases. I also presented the summary of the current status of the St. Louis cases. The Committee voted approval on the action taken by the Chairman, Mr. Bloch, myself, and other members of the staff in the Shell Oil case. It was also agreed that there would be a hearing on the Machinists cases and I suggested that the Richmond, California and the Seattle, Washington cases were best. The Committee took the digests of the St. Louis cases for study, but did not act on them.[2]

While in Chicago I discussed with Mr. Henderson complaints he is processing against the Chicago post office. He states that the Postmaster in that city is anxious to maintain a good reputation in the Negro community and will probably adjust most of the complaints. I trust that this is true because it will have a very helpful effect on any future negotiations with the Post Office Department.[3]

I discussed the status of the Illinois and Wisconsin Bell Telephone cases with Mr. Henderson and Mr. Gibson. It appears that Illinois Bell has indicated that it will employ Negroes as operators, but cases submitted to FEPC are not valid and we have no real test of whether the company is sincere in its intentions.[4] The Wisconsin Bell has agreed to a conference with Mr. Gibson and I have told him about the developments in the New Jersey case.

The War Manpower Commission has reported its action on the Capital Transit case as we requested and it appears that the Deputy Executive Director did the things requested by FEPC.[5]

The War Labor Board has informed me that a decision was reached in the National Lead case in favor of Mr. Junious Cole. However, some additional information is being obtained before this decision is sent to the company.

I have had a conference with the War Department on the Clinton Engineering Company in Tennessee and expect to take some action on this as previously discussed.[6]

A conference is being planned on policy affecting Americans of Japanese ancestry on the West Coast. The Civil Service Commission has verified Mr. Kingman's statement about exclusion of such persons from Naval establishments in Washington, Oregon, California, and Hawaii.[7]

ASSIGNMENTS

The following cases were received from the regions:

1. International Association of Machinists, 4-UR-502
2. Wright Automatic Machine Company, 4-BR-501
3. Southeastern Shipbuilding Company, 7-BR-58
4. BISBHA, 7-UR-484
5. Mingledorff Shipyards, 7-BR-493

The following cases were referred to the Legal Division:

1. Gulf Colorado & Santa Fe, 13-BR-368, 458
2. Brotherhood of Railroad Trainmen, 13UR-369, 459

The following cases were received from the Legal Division:

1. International Brotherhood of Teamsters, Chauffeurs, Warehousemen of America, 12-UR-327
2. New Jersey Bell Telephone Company, 3-BR-646.

The following cases were returned to the regions:

1. New Jersey Bell Telephone Company, 3-BR-646
2. International Brotherhood of Teamsters, Chauffeurs and Warehousemen of America, 12-UR-327

The following Final Disposition Reports were reviewed and acted upon by me:

Region VI-	6	Region IX-	1
Region VII-	20	Region X-	1
Region VIII-	1	Region XII-	7

cc: Mr. Davidson
      Mr. Davis
      Mr. Johnson
      Mr. Jones

MS: copy, FEPC RG 228 (entry 40 PI-147), Office Files of Clarence Mitchell, Malcolm Ross, DNA.

1. For other developments involving St. Louis war production plants, see 2/20, 2/26, 5/18/45.

2. See report, 5/7/45, and notes; headnotes on the Oil Industry and on the FEPC and Unions. On 3/17/45, the Committee ratified the stipulation entered into between its representatives and Shell Oil. Shell and the union agreed to eliminate discrimination in their contract and subsequently attempted to comply with the agreement. But while initially accepting the upgrading of Mexican workers, white workers blocked the upgrading of African Americans. At its 5/11 meeting, the Committee agreed to adhere to its position that even though white workers requested a strike vote on whether to accept the upgrading of Mexicans and African Americans, EO 9346 should be enforced. The IAM cases mentioned at the meeting were those of Locals 79 and 751 of Seattle and the Richmond Shipyard case in California. See Minutes of 3/17/45, HqR1, Summary Minutes of Meetings.

3. See the section on the Post Office Department in the headnote on Relationships with Federal Agencies.

4. On the Illinois Bell case, see Gibson to Henderson, report, 12/18/44, HqR76, Office Files of Will Maslow. Relations with Other Agencies. For background on the telephone company cases generally, see Evelyn Cooper's 3/7/45 memorandum in appendix 1 and Mitchell's 3/13/45 report for his response to three of her suggestions; headnote on the Telephone Industry.

On 5/10/45, Andrew P. Monroe, vice president of New Jersey Bell, whom Mitchell had been pressing to change the company's racial policies, informed the Committee that, in the wake of the conference he held on 5/4/45 with Ross and members of his staff, the company had

> reconsidered its position with respect to the employment of Negroes as switchboard operators. As a result of such reconsideration, I wish to formally advise you that our position has been changed and that we will employ qualified negroes as operators. In order to settle the complaint of discrimination which is before your Committee, we will immediately offer employment in Atlantic City as switchboard operators to qualified Negro applicants and, as requested in your letter of December 4, 1944, will give first consideration to Miss Miriam R. Yearwood, Miss Susie Harris and Mrs. Lillian Monk.

On 5/14/45, Cooper wrote Lee Craig, vice president of American Telephone and Telegraph, thanking him for his efforts in obtaining those results. She told him the Committee would similarly confer with A. B. Haneke of the Chesapeake and Potomac Telephone Company and inform Craig of the results. Both letters are in HqR5, Office Files of George M. Johnson. Telephone Companies. On 7/21/45, Mitchell told Cooper that Fleming had informed him that, regarding the New Jersey Bell case, two women had been placed in training in Atlantic City. "Their pictures have appeared in the weekly press," he added. A complainant in Newark was also offered an operator's job, but she turned it down because of the shift she had to work. Instead, she accepted a job as a messenger. Mitchell concluded: "Under the circumstances it appears that there is no need for further action in Washington on the New Jersey Bell cases." For Mitchell's anticipation of these results, see HqR8, Office Files of Evelyn N. Cooper; 2/14/45, note 1.

5. See memorandum, 5/9/45.

6. See introduction for discussion on the Atomic power industry.

7. In a letter of 5/15/45 to Captain E. E. Sprung, acting director of the Division of Shore Establishments and Civilian Personnel, Navy Department, Mitchell stated that Kingman's office had reported

what appeared to be official Navy Department policy, which was that American citizens of Japanese ancestry would not be certified by the Civil Service Commission to Naval establishments in California, Oregon, Washington, and Hawaii. Kingman said the policy was "especially flagrant in that it applied to veterans as well as non-veterans." Furthermore, Kingman said, in other states, appointments of Japanese Americans were subject to an investigation that was not made of German Americans. Kingman suggested that discussions in Washington with Civil Service representatives might also include questions of why, before appointing a Japanese American to a government agency, the commission required that agency to stipulate that the job was not closely related to the war nor was it confidential. If that was not stipulated, an investigation was required that took considerable time and materially increased the difficulty of the applicant's getting the job. See Kingman's memorandum, Mitchell's letter to Sprung, and other related materials at HqR66, Central Files. U.S. Government, Aliens in Defense (Japanese); related texts at 5/26 (Conference with Navy Department Re the Employment of Nisei in West Coast Navy Yards, May 23, 1945), 8/9/45; headnote on Japanese Americans.

Memorandum on Portsmouth Navy Yard

May 26, 1945

Mr. Eugene Davidson
    Assistant Director of Field Operations
Clarence M. Mitchell
    Associate Director of Field Operations
Portsmouth Navy Yard, I-GN-157

On May 23 I met with Commander W. E. Thomas of the Employee Investigation Department of the Navy Department and two of his assistants, Lieutenant Heinback and a Mr. Walker. We discussed the complaint of Mr. Fred G. Korn, who alleged that he had been dismissed from the Navy Yard at Portsmouth, New Hampshire because of his national origin.

I mentioned Admiral Crisp's letter dated May 7, 1945. This letter states that: "After careful reconsideration of the entire matter, on December 8, 1941, Mr. Korn's request was granted and he was discharged without prejudice, under which circumstances he was eligible for employment elsewhere in government upon determination or certification by the U. S. Civil Service Commission."

Lieutenant Heinback contended that the whole case had been reviewed and a definite indication of disloyalty had been established. He said however that the complainant might not necessarily be ineligible for other type[s] of work. I pointed out that Mr. Korn was working in a plant supplying materials for the Navy Department. Lieutenant Heinback contended that this was not necessarily improper because the complainant would not be in a position to observe movements of ships and personnel as he would in the Navy Yard or find out important information from Naval personnel.[1]

The Navy representatives stated that so far as their investigations were concerned, they were not made for Civil Service or any other Government agencies. Another part of the Navy explanation dealt with the complainant[']s alleged request for a dismissal without prejudice. Mr. Korn, as you know, contends that a Navy representative urged him to make this request. Lieutenant Heinback stated that the complainant offered to resign and signed a statement absolving the Navy Department from all blame in connection with his termination of service. I then offered to attempt a solution of the matter by having the complainant request that his case be reopened.

Commander Thomas made this observation: "We presume that FEPC would not wish to mislead its complainants." When I stated that we had no desire to mislead anyone, the Commander stated that if we had advised the complainant to seek the re-opening of his case it would be useless. The Commander did not explain whether he meant that the Navy had so much evidence against the complainant that a finding showing his disloyalty would be inevitable or whether he meant that with or without evidence the Navy officials would find the complainant guilty. Lieutenant Heinback argued that he himself was of German origin and was convinced that there had been no discrimination against the complainant because of his ancestry.

MS: copy, FEPC FR2, Region I. Closed Cases G–Z, Portsmouth Navy Yard, 1-GN-157.

1. On this case, see Eugene Davidson to Edward Lawson, memoranda, 5/17, 5/28/45, both filed with this text. Davidson informed Lawson on 5/28 that whether or not Korn's dismissal was justified in the interest of national security, the FEPC did not have evidence to the contrary, nor did it have sufficient evidence of discrimination because of national origin. Consequently, he recommended that the case should be "*Dismissed on Merits*" (emphasis Davidson's) unless the complainant could "furnish suffi-cient additional evidence of discrimination because of national origin to justify further contact with the party charged."

Memorandum on Conference with Navy Department Regarding Employment of Niseis in West Coast Navy Yards, May 23, 1945

May 26, 1945

Mr. Will Maslow
>Director of Field Operations

Clarence M. Mitchell
>Associate Director of Field Operations

Conference with Navy Department Re Employment of Niseis
>In West Coast Navy Yards, May 23, 1945

In keeping with a request from Mr. Harry Kingman, Director of Region XII, I dis-cussed with Captain S. H. Ordway, Jr., Head of the Employment Branch, Division of

Shore Establishments and Civilian Personnel, Navy Department, a Navy regulation which forbids the employment of American citizens of Japanese ancestry in Naval establishments of California, Oregon, Washington, and Hawaii.[1]

Captain Ordway stated that the policy had been established by Admiral Nimitz for "military reasons." The Navy's present policy permits the employment of Niseis in other sections of the country on all types of vital war work but bars them for the West Coast where at present there is a critical need for workers. Captain Ordway stated that the basic reason for refusing to employ Niseis was the recognition that the men in the Armed Services will fight people better when they hate them. He stated that the training program of the Navy has tended to promote hatred of the Japanese by Americans and naturally a number of men who will return from the Pacific war zone would not distinguish between the enemy and American citizens of Japanese ancestry. He said that if Naval personnel observed Niseis at work in the various yards there would undoubtedly be considerable violence.

I called to his attention the statement of Admiral H. R. Heinz, Chief of Staff of the Twelfth Naval District, pointing out the loyalty of the returning Niseis and urging Naval personnel to refrain from molesting them. Captain Ordway observed that he (the Admiral) had better not make that statement public because if he did it would be rather bad for him. I did not mention the name of the Admiral although I had previously intended to do so.

According to Captain Ordway the Navy Department has absolutely no objection to Niseis in its other establishments and had circulated a statement to its various local representatives indicating that it was Navy policy to employ them without discrimination because of their ancestry. I asked for a copy of this statement but while Captain Ordway let me read it, he declined to give it to me to keep. He stated that he did not wish to see any publicity on the Navy Department's policy and felt that it would be inadvisable to release the statement to me. I explained that I was not interested in getting this for any publicity purposes, but as part of Government record. He still declined to give it. Essentially, the statement is summarized in the second paragraph of his letter of May 19.

In my opinion we should determine whether the Civil Service Commission is referring qualified Niseis to other Naval establishments when they apply. Since this regulation affects veterans as well as non-veterans and is directly opposite to the purposes of Executive Order 9346, I believe that this matter should be submitted to the Committee for a determination of what further steps can be taken to correct it.

cc: Mr. Harry Kingman

MS: copy, FEPC FR103, Region XI, Administrative Files A–Z, Policy, American-Japanese.

This text is enclosed in Mitchell to Harry L. Kingman, 5/26/45.

1. See Ordway to Mitchell, 5/19/45, HqR66, Central Files. U.S. Government, Aliens in Defense (Japanese); Mitchell, weekly report, 5/21/45; headnote on Japanese Americans.

Memorandum on Processing of Cases in Which Complainants Are No Longer Available for Employment

May 31, 1945

Mr. Will Maslow
    Director of Field Operations
Clarence M. Mitchell
    Associate Director of Field Operations
Processing of Cases in Which Complainants Are No Longer
    Available for Employment

I have noted in recent weeks several important cases which consumed a great deal of time in our regional offices and resulted in satisfactory adjustments, but the complainants were not available for employment. In view of our limited staff it would seem that in all cases we should determine whether complainants will be available for employment before undertaking lengthy negotiations in their behalf.

If the question raised in the complaint concerns broad policies of the party charged, of necessity we would continue the processing of it regardless of whether the individual bringing the charge would be available for the individual redress. However, if the complaint concerns one person only and that person states he is no longer interested in receiving a job at the particular establishment it would seem proper to forego action in favor of more pressing matters.

I believe we should consider this as a basis for a possible field instruction.[1] I should like to get your reaction.

cc: Mr. Davidson
       Mr. Davis

MS: copy, HqR76, Office Files of Clarence Mitchell. Maslow.
    1. No such instruction is among those filed in HqR78, Field Instructions, 8/43–6/45.

Bi-Weekly Report

June 5, 1945

Mr. Will Maslow
    Director of Field Operations

Clarence M. Mitchell
    Associate Director of Field Operations
Bi-Weekly Report for May 21–June 2, 1945

IMPORTANT EVENTS AND PROBLEMS:

At our request Mr. George Weaver, of the CIO's Committee to Abolish Discrimination, communicated with Mr. Knight, of the Oil Workers Union, concerning the Shell Oil case. As a result of his conversation it was agreed that Mr. Weaver would go to Houston in an effort to work out a proper settlement before June 7, the date scheduled for the strike vote. We arranged plane priority for Mr. Weaver. I also advised Mr. Ellinger that the CIO official would be in Houston.[1]

A current review of the post office cases indicates that an important element of their solution may be found if we can arrange a meeting between representatives of the Postal Alliance and Post Office Department heads. I have spoken to a representative of the Chicago Postal Alliance who feels that it would be a good idea. Currently, I am planning to schedule this meeting for some time in July or August.

I have set forth in detail the happenings at a conference with Navy officials concerning that agency's policy with regard to the employment of Americans of Japanese ancestry in its West Coast establishments. I believe this matter should have prompt Committee attention.[2]

The War Department, through Colonel Barker, has promised a full investigation of complaints against the Tennessee Eastman Corporation sent to us as unadjustable in Region VII.

ASSIGNMENTS

The following cases have been referred to the Legal Division:

1. International Association of Machinists, 12-UR-265, 263, 174.
2. St. Louis Public Service, 9-BR-1204.

The following cases have been received from the regions:

1. St. Louis Public Service, 9-BR-1204
2. Aeronautical Chart Plant, 9-BR-1445
3. Murray Gin Company, 13-BR-327
4. Vendo Company, 9-BR-45, 234, 346, 351
5. John Hopkins University, 4-GR-539 (From Mr. Davidson)
6. Percy Kent Bag Company, 9-BR-273
7. Textile Workers Union of America, 9-UR-431
8. Goodenow Textile Company, 9-BR-371
9. Loose Wiles Biscuit Company, 9-BR-275
10. United Retail Wholesale & Department Store Employees of America, 9-UR-417

The following FDR's have been received:

Region VII—	42
Region XII—	4

cc: Mr. Davidson
    Mr. Davis
    Mr. Johnson
    Mr. Jones

MS: *copy, FEPC RG 228, Office Files of Clarence Mitchell, DNA.*

1. Owing to its structure, its mass-organization program, and the large number of African Americans within its ranks, the CIO did a better job than the AFL had in barring discrimination against black workers. The CIO established its National Committee to Abolish Racial Discrimination to implement its nondiscrimination policies and to facilitate their enforcement. The committee, run by a full-time director (George Weaver), had similar antidiscrimination committees in local, county, and state industrial union councils. By the end of 1944 the CIO had eighty-five such local committees. Weaver, *Negro Labor*, 219–20. See also the headnote on the FEPC and Unions.

2. For Mitchell's other activities on this issue, see 5/21, 5/26 (Conference with Navy Department Re the Employment of Nisei in West Coast Navy Yards, May 23, 1945), 8/9/45; headnote on Japanese Americans.

Memorandum on U.S. Cartridge Corporation, St. Louis, Missouri

June 6, 1945

Mr. John Davis
    Director, Review and Analysis Division
Clarence M. Mitchell
    Associate Director of Field Operations
U. S. Cartridge Corporation, St. Louis, Missouri

On June 5, I had a conversation with Mr. William Sentner of the UERMWA in St. Louis. He stated that the U. S. Cartridge plant's program for integrating Negroes in units with whites is progressing satisfactorily. Where there was formerly one unit in which this was done, there are now two. Knowing that you are working on a pamphlet I thought that this information would be useful to you.

The company plans to keep one of the integrated units through the post-war period, according to Mr. Sentner. I have asked Mr. Theodore Brown to give you a detailed, but brief, statement on this.

MS: *copy, HqR85, Correspondence Relating to Cases. U.S. Cartridge Co.*
    See the headnote on Major Cases in St. Louis.

Bi-Weekly Report

June 19, 1945

Mr. Will Maslow
    Director of Field Operations
Clarence M. Mitchell
    Associate Director of Field Operations
Bi-Weekly Report for June 4–16, 1945

IMPORTANT EVENTS AND PROBLEMS

In spite of the critical problems facing FEPC, the field staff has carried on in a courageous and constructive fashion. I am pleased to report that as the result of work by Mr. Edward Rutledge three Negroes were placed as electricians on two ships, the S. S. Wild Wave and the S. S. St. Lawrence Victory. These individuals would not have their employment today if Rutledge had permitted himself to stop his activities because of the discouraging Washington picture.[1]

Similarly, the reports of other regional directors, especially Messrs. Castaneda, Ellinger, Fleming, and Henderson show that they are still at work on important cases. In my opinion we have every reason to be proud of the tenacity shown by these members of the staff.

I have had a conference with George Weaver of the CIO on the Shell Oil Company and a report on this conference is documented in a separate memorandum.[2] Mr. Weaver went to Houston at the request of FEPC and Mr. Knight of the Oil Workers Union. It appears that he did a constructive job while in the area.

At the request of the Division of Review and Analysis I attended two War Production Board meetings on cutbacks in the aluminum industry and reconversion in refrigeration. From these meetings I obtained one or two interesting items which were relayed in the field.[3]

ASSIGNMENTS

The following cases were received from the regions:

1. Todd Houston Shipbuilding Corporation 13-UR-528, 13-BR-316, 317, 434
2. Todd Galveston Shipbuilding Company 13-BR-352, 405, 468, 480
3. BISBHA, IA, 13-UR-479
4. Post Office, New Castle, Pa., 3-GR-1867 (From Mr. Davidson)
5. Post Office, Pittsburgh, Pa., 3-GR-1855 (From Mr. Davidson)
6. Post Office, Jacksonville, Fla., 7-GR-101

The following case was returned to the region:

1. Midland Radio & Television School, 9-BR-454

The following cases were referred to the Legal Division:

1. Vendo Company, 9-BR-45, 234, 346, 351.

The following FDR's have been received by me:

Region VI—	10
Region VII—	6
Region VIII—	1
Region IX—	38
Region X—	7
Region XI—	8
Region XII—	38
Region XIII—	17

cc: Mr. Davidson
   Mr. Davis
   Mr. Johnson
   Mr. Jones

MS: copy, FEPC RG 228, Office Files of Clarence Mitchell, DNA.

1. The "discouraging Washington picture" involved Congress's cutting the FEPC's budget, which led to staff resignations, layoffs, and office closings. During the phaseout period Maslow resigned, effective 7/45, and Mitchell became acting director, then director of field operations, and was given responsibility for reducing and ultimately for closing down the FEPC's field offices. Eugene Davidson assumed the associate director's post in 7/45 and also was assigned at various times the roles of regional director for Regions III and IV. However, many texts for the period continue to use Mitchell's and Davidson's old titles.

2. Memorandum not found, but on George Weaver's role, see 3/26, 6/5/45 texts.

3. On the FEPC's interaction with the WPB, see the headnote on Relationships with Federal Agencies.

Memorandum on Todd-Johnson Shipbuilding Company

July 24, 1945

MEMORANDUM

TO: Mr. George Johnson
      Deputy Chairman

FROM: Clarence M. Mitchell
        Acting Director of Field Operations
SUBJECT: Todd-Johnson Shipbuilding Company
           New Orleans, Louisiana

On Tuesday, July 17, workers at the Todd-Johnson Shipyard located in Algiers, Louisiana, a small community outside of New Orleans, went on strike because a Negro was employed as a boilermaker's helper. The company is repairing LST's for the Navy Department and converting merchant vessels to troop transports for the Army. It also has some contracts with the War Shipping Administration. The yard employs three or four hundred Negroes in laboring jobs out of approximately three thousand workers. It was desperately in need of skilled employees and had obtained clearance for inter-regional recruitment for several thousand workers.

Under the compromise, apparently engineered by the Army and Navy, the Negro employee either quit under pressure or was terminated. In any event, he is no longer employed at the yard. In addition, the company has stated that it will not use Negroes in any jobs other than those which are unskilled. The union, which is a local of IUM-SWA [International Union of Marine and Shipbuilding Workers of America, CIO], is undertaking what is described as an educational program upon the workers.

MS: LH, DI, HqR3, Office Files of George M. Johnson. (A–M) M.
    Maslow had departed and Mitchell had assumed his job.
    See Mitchell's detailed 7/28/45 report on the strike and the headnotes on Strikes and Work Stoppages and on the Shipbuilding Industry.

Memorandum on War Department Inquiry
Concerning Designations of Race
and Religion on Application Forms

July 25, 1945

MEMORANDUM

TO: Mr. George M. Johnson
      Deputy Chairman
FROM: Clarence M. Mitchell
        Acting Director of Field Operations

SUBJECT: War Department Inquiry Concerning Designations of Race
and Religion on Application Forms

On the above date Mr. Lemuel Foster, ASF, called to say that the War Department was holding a conference with the Wilson Packing Company at 2 p.m. concerning FEPC's request that the provisions of Mr. James P. Mitchell's memorandum of August 3, 1942 be followed. The Mitchell memorandum provides that War Department contractors will be <u>required</u> to delete references to race and religion from their application forms. On May 2, 1945, we requested the War Department to ask the contractor to delete from the application for employment form a question asking for the religion of persons seeking jobs. Mr. Foster stated that the Quartermaster Corps had cited the Committee policy appearing on page 56 of the First FEPC Report in which it is stated, "the requiring of applicants for employment to state their race or religion, or both, on application forms, or otherwise, does not violate the provisions of the Executive Order . . ."

At Mr. Foster's suggestion I talked with Major Domenico Gagliardo, Chief Labor Officer, Quartermaster Corps and Mr. Samuel Silver, Assistant to the Major, and explained to them that while the Committee does not state that the inclusion of race or religion on application form[s] is in itself discriminatory, nevertheless, such requests in many instances lead to discrimination and therefore it is desirable to have them eliminated. I read to them the excerpt from the Committee meeting of August 9, 1943 (2A). Major Gagliardo stated that he would have to act within the framework of the War Department policy and therefore advise the contractor that the request for race or religion should be left off the application form but he indicated that in his opinion it is unfair for the Committee to push the War Department "ahead of its own (FEPC) policy."

I believe that this matter will not end here and we may shortly be required to review this whole situation with the War Department.

MS: copy, HqR3, Office Files of George M. Johnson. (A–M) M.
See the headnote on Race, Creed, Color, or National Origin on Employment Application Forms.

Memorandum on Meeting on Todd-Johnson Dry Docks

ROUGH DRAFT

Date: July 28, 1945

To: Mr. Malcolm Ross
           Chairman

From: Clarence M. Mitchell
           Acting Director of Field Operations

Subject: Meeting on Todd Johnson Drydocks

On the above date the following persons met in your office to discuss with you problems at the Todd Johnson Drydocks in New Orleans, Louisiana: Lt. Colonel Sidney Sufrin; Mr. Edward J. Tracy, Director of Shipyard Labor Relations, Maritime Commission; Lieutenant Fenton Gentry, Navy Department,: and Lieutenant, (j.g.) D. L. Robertson, also of the Navy. The Navy representatives were from the Bureau of Ships.

Colonel Sufrin stated that the company is greatly in need of workers but is unable to recruit through the United States Employment Service because of its refusal to make proper utilization of Negro workers. He requested that FEPC approve the company's effort to have this restriction relaxed. We did not agree to this, but did agree that we would have a meeting with the company (Mr. Obst from Todd's New York office) and Mr. John Green, President, IUMSWA. This meeting is to be held on Monday or Tuesday in Washington.

[The following two documents are integral extensions of the 7/28/45 memorandum.]

SUMMARY OF STRIKE AT TODD JOHNSON DRYDOCK
NEW ORLEANS, LOUISIANA

On July 17, 1945, the Todd Johnson Drydock Company employed a colored man as a boilermaker's helper. According to information received by FEPC, white workers immediately went on strike. This resulted in the stopping of production and approximately three thousand persons were idle. It is difficult to know at this point how many of those idle were on strike or off because the individuals who did strike had made it impossible for others to work. This situation lasted for 8 days and the colored employee was eventually removed or voluntarily left the job. In any event he is not now employed by the company.

FEPC requested the company and the union to join us in a conference on this matter shortly after the strike occurred. It was our hope that some program could be worked out under which Negro employees in the yard would obtain proper upgrading.

Mr. John Green, president of the IUMSWA, agreed to this kind of meeting, but we were told by the company that their representative could not participate until September. Meanwhile, it appears that Negro employees in the yard are concerned about their upgrading and a report summarizing the present situation was sent to me by Mr. J. H. Morton of our New Orleans. A copy of this report is attached.

PRESIDENT'S COMMITTEE ON FAIR EMPLOYMENT PRACTICE

8-10-45

To: Clarence C. Mitchell
         Assoc. Dir. of Field Operations, FEPC
From: J. H. Morton
         Examiner, Region XIII
Subject: Todd-Johnson labor situation

Since the conclusion of the unauthorized strike by white workers and members of the Industrial Union of Marine & Shipbuilding Workers of Am. (CIO) local 29, at Todd-Johnson, there has been a growing unrest among Negro workers at the yard. There are rumors of a pending strike.

On Thursday evening, Aug. 9, 1945 three unions affiliated with CIO met with representatives of local 29 to discuss the strike possibilities. The unions represented were: Transport Workers Union of America, Local 206; International Longshoremen's & Warehousemen's Union, Local 7; and the National Maritime Union.

These unions took a definite stand against supporting an unofficial strike by Negro workers and urged Negro representatives, Local 29, to comply with this stand.

In the absence of a strike or walkout, they pledged support in the establishment and maintenance of CIO National policy within the local.

The representatives, local 29, did not commit themselves on a no-strike pledge awaiting the outcome of a mass meeting of Negro workers on Sunday Aug. 12, 1945.

Local branches of the N.A.A.C.P. and the Urban League are active in the discussions. The Negro Press, local, is keeping in close contact with the situation.

From the best evidence now available it is quite unlikely that there will be a walkout of Negro workers on Monday, Aug. 13, 1945 which is the date toward which present planning points. Future action will depend largely upon the guidance and leadership provided by the CIO Council.
(Handwritten report)

MS: LH, HqR2, Office Files of Malcolm Ross, 6/40–6/46—M, Interdepartmental Memos.
    See 7/24/45 for earlier report; headnotes on the Shipbuilding Industry and on Strikes and Work Stoppages.

Proposed Program for Division of Field Operations

(ROUGH DRAFT)

PROPOSED PROGRAM FOR THE DIVISION OF FIELD OPERATIONS*

[ca. July 31, 1945]

It is proposed that the Division of Field Operations adopt the following program for the fiscal year beginning July 1, 1945. Major points of the new program are listed in order and each item is thereafter discussed more extensively.

---

*This program was proposed in part some time ago by Harry Kingman. [A copy of Kingman's suggestions, as given in his report of 1/22/45, is in RG 228, Office Files of Clarence Mitchell, box 458, DNA.]

1. Cultivation of friendly relations with large employers, government agencies, and important labor union[s].
2. Processing the most significant cases in the more important industries and government agencies which will be operating in peace time.[1]
3. Investigating policies of important industries such as public utilities, food processing, and heavy merchandise manufacturing which do not now employ minority workers but against whom we have received no specific complaints.
4. Making compliance checks with greater frequency to expand gains already made and offer services to employers who face specific difficulties which may have arisen as a result of changes in employment policies with regard to minority groups.
5. Making a greater utilization of our agreements with industries, labor, and government agencies in the handling of routine problems.

CULTIVATION OF FRIENDLY RELATIONS

Although the Committee has operated effectively in the past, too frequently our contact with parties charged is when we must make a visit on the basis of specific complaints. It is proposed that this approach be expanded to permit the regional director to discuss the FEPC program on an informal basis at luncheons, in offices, and wherever possible, with government officials, heads of industries, and labor leaders. Such discussions would be designated to bring out operating suggestions from these persons which may be later used by FEPC.

PROCESSING MOST SIGNIFICANT CASES

A careful inspection should be made of all new and pending cases for the following criteria:

1. Is it likely that industry will continue its war production until V-J Day? (e.g., certain types of production such as small arms and ammunition are being cutback at present. A case in this group would be low on the list. On the other hand, the manufacture of radios would be given a high position.)
2. Will the company return to peace time production in the near future?
3. Will the company's operations have peace time significance? (e.g., the National Cash Register Company in Dayton may now be making war materials but at the end of hostilities will revert to its peace time program.)
4. Do the issues involve broad policies which if changed would result in substantial progress in correcting discrimination against minority groups. (e.g., elimination of discriminatory auxiliary set-ups in a labor union or correction of policies which prevent the employment of Negroes in skilled jobs in the textile industry.)

INVESTIGATING POLICIES OF IMPORTANT AGENCIES, COMPANIES, AND UNIONS

The regional director by studying labor market data, ES 270 reports and other official records on labor problems should determine occupations and industries from which minorities are barred by policy or custom although shortages exist in these fields. Using these data the regional director will hold conferences with industry, labor, and government groups for the purpose of correcting the problem even though no complaints have been filed with FEPC. In government this would involve a greater utilization of FEPC's power to recommend. (e.g., the study of employment of minorities in government agencies made by the Division of Review and Analysis shows that although there is a reasonable number of Negroes employed in Washington, the field offices of various government agencies have very few. The contents of this Review and Analysis report should be used as a basic program in the regions to expand employment opportunities on the basis of merits.)

INCREASING THE COMPLIANCE CHECKS

The substantial gains made as a result of examiner contacts in the field and Committee hearings should be reviewed and, wherever it is practicable to do so, follow up visits should be made for the following reasons:

1. Obtaining a source of experience from employers which will be useful in passing on techniques of utilization and integration to other individuals who may need such material.
2. Determining the degree of success in existing programs and the possibilities for expanding in other occupations where FEPC has not yet received complaints but in which the company's positive program of utilizing a new source of labor has not yet resulted in inclusion of minorities.
3. Offering to employers advice on meeting new problems such as absenteeism, cleanliness taboos, and other matters.

MAKING A GREATER UTILIZATION OF AGREEMENTS WITH INDUSTRY, LABOR AND GOVERNMENT AGENCIES

The FEPC agreements with the UAW, U. S. Steel, the Civil Service Commission, and the War Department provides machinery for handling certain routine cases which we cannot hope to deal with on the basis of a contact with the party charged.[2] A percentage of these cases may be settled to the satisfaction of complaints through these channels. Therefore, some time should be devoted to pointing out the weaknesses in the processing of cases by these agencies in the past and urging them to strive for better results in view of FEPC's staff limitations. It might be well for the Division of Review and Analysis to make a short appraisal of FEPC's past experience with these agreements. It will be an important talking point, for example, if we are able to say to the War Manpower Commission that in a specific number of cases, the Commission was unable to affect adjustments but subsequently FEPC succeeded in correcting the policy. Thus demonstrating that a little more time and effort on the part of the agency or union with which we have the agreement might have similar results in the future.

MS: copy, FEPC FR89, Region IX. Memoranda, 1945–46, St. Louis, DNA.

This copy of the draft proposal was enclosed in Mitchell to Regional Director Roy A. Hoglund, memorandum, 7/31/45, but other copies were sent to regional directors and FEPC staff members with requests for comment. Hoglund replied on 8/7/45. See FR89, Region IX, Memoranda, 1945–46, St. Louis. The proposal was required owing to Congress's cutting the agency's appropriation in half (to $250,000) for fiscal year 1946. At its 7/21/45 meeting, the Committee voted to cut its staff from 117 to 51 and to close five of its fifteen field offices. Other actions taken accordingly are in the minutes of the meeting, HqR1, Summary Minutes of Meetings.

1. For examples of FEPC's increasing focus on industries with postwar significance, see Mitchell's memoranda of 10/7, 10/10/44, 5/18, 8/8, 10/9/45.

2. For the FEPC's working agreements with these federal agencies, see HqR66, Central Files. U.S. Government, Civil Service Commission; undated digest of agreements with other agencies in Files of John A. Davis, Agreements with Other Agencies, in HqR68. For the background, see the headnotes on Relationships with Federal Agencies and on the FEPC and Unions. On the UAW agreement, see Hill, Black Labor, 260–62.

Memorandum on Discrimination in Organized Baseball

August 3, 1945

MEMORANDUM

TO: Mr. George M. Johnson
             Deputy Chairman

FROM: Clarence M. Mitchell
             Director of Field Operations

SUBJECT: Discrimination in Organized Baseball

As you will note in the attached memorandum dated July 17, Mr. Lawson raises the question of whether it is possible to obtain an informal opinion on whether FEPC has jurisdiction over the employment practices of major league baseball teams.

I do not know whether we would have jurisdiction over this problem, but, as a matter of policy, I would recommend that we take no action on it if we do. The baseball problem is unfortunate, but I can think of many other things which are much more important. If you agree, I will convey my sentiments to Mr. Lawson. Attachment

MS: LH, DI, HqR38, Central Files. Memoranda, Mitchell, Clarence.

In his response of 8/6/45, Johnson agreed with Mitchell. The exchanges of correspondence are all filed with Mitchell's text. Lawson's memorandum of 7/17 indicated his query was in response to appeals from a number of organizations in New York who wrote the regional office asking the FEPC to "do something" about discrimination against African Americans in organized baseball.

Memorandum on Conference with Mr. Robert Goodwin of the War Manpower Commission

August 8, 1945

MEMORANDUM

TO: Mr. Malcolm Ross
           Chairman

FROM: Clarence M. Mitchell
           Director of Field Operations

SUBJECT: Conference with Mr. Goodwin of the War Manpower Commission

During our conference with Mr. Robert Goodwin, Executive Director of the War Manpower Commission, on the above date, we agreed upon the following things:

1. WMC will make an effort to obtain and make available information on how the employment of minority groups is affected by reconversion and cutbacks. It was agreed that Mr. Louis Levine of WMC would come to your office on Friday at 2 p.m. to talk further on the mechanics of doing this.
2. It was agreed that Mr. Goodwin will discuss the employment policies of the textile industries with Mr. Dillard Lassiter, Atlanta Regional Director of WMC. We mentioned specifically the conflict between a program of full labor utilization and South Carolina laws requiring segregation in the textile industry. Mr. Lassiter will be in Washington in the near future and Mr. Goodwin will talk with him on the possibility of affecting changes in the hiring policies of the industry.[1]

3. It was agreed that there would be a meeting between Mr. Triede, Mr. Evans, Mr. Goodwin, and myself to discuss cooperation between WMC and FEPC in Region IV. At this meeting it is expected that we will also review the current status of the Capital Transit case.[2]

MS: copy, HqR39, Central Files. (entry 25) Memoranda, Ross, Malcolm, 1/45–.

1. Regional Director Witherspoon Dodge informed Lasseter of this agreement on 9/7/45 and expressed interest in learning the results of his talk with Goodwin. Subsequent appeals indicate he received no response, and the unclosed textile cases were referred back to Washington when the regional office shut down in 12/45. See FR81, Region VII. Active Cases (A–Z) U.S. Employment Office, Columbia, S.C.; related texts in FR80, Region VII, Administrative Files, Textile Cases.

2. No record of such a meeting has been found.

Memorandum on Civil Service Regulation on Employment of Americans of Japanese Ancestry on West Coast Naval Establishments

August 9, 1945

MEMORANDUM

TO: Mr. Malcolm Ross
Chairman

FROM: Clarence M. Mitchell
Director of Field Operations

SUBJECT: Civil Service Regulation on Employment of Americans of Japanese Ancestry on West Coast Naval Establishments

In letters dated May 25 and June 29, Mr. Arthur S. Fleming, of the Civil Service Commission, answers inquiries made by me on a policy in the Navy Department which prevents the employment of qualified Americans of Japanese ancestry in naval establishments on the West Coast and in Hawaii. This policy of exclusion affects not only persons who have been in civilian status throughout the war, but also those persons who are honorably discharged veterans. I have explored this policy with the Navy Department at the request of Mr. Kingman and did not obtain a satisfactory answer on why the policy was established.

The Civil Service Commission clearly states on pages E16.01.03–.031 that this is policy which will be followed in recruitment and placement of American citizens of

Japanese ancestry.[1] This is a clear violation of the Executive Order and, in my opinion, we are entitled to a more detailed explanation than a simple indication of "security reasons." On page E16.01.04, provision is made for the employment of persons of Japanese origin in local positions in Hawaii. Thus it appears that persons in Hawaii have a better opportunity for employment in the Navy Department even though they may not have veteran status, while persons released from the Army have no chance at all in California, Oregon, and Washington.

I believe that when we have our conference with Mr. Fleming, we should discuss this matter thoroughly.

Attachments

MS: LH, DI, HqR66, Central Files. U.S. Government, Aliens in Defense, Specific Groups, Japanese.

1. Regarding Section E16.01 of the Civil Service regulations covering the hiring of Japanese, Arthur S. Fleming, Commissioner of the Civil Service Commission, told Malcolm Ross that the section was adopted "for reasons of national security." Following up in a letter of 11/5/45, Mitchell asked Fleming whether given the defeat of the Japanese "it would appear that the security reasons advanced by the Navy Department for the refusal to employ qualified citizens of Japanese ancestry no longer applies." No response was found to Mitchell's inquiry. Fleming's and Mitchell's letters are in HqR66, Central Files. U.S. Government, Civil Service Commission. See earlier texts on this issue at 5/21, 5/26 (Conference with Navy Department Re Employment of Nisei in West Coast Navy Yards, May 23, 1945), 6/5/45; headnote on Japanese Americans.

Memorandum on Upgrading of Mr. Bernard Ross on West Coast

August 10, 1945

MEMORANDUM

TO: Mr. Malcolm Ross
Chairman

FROM: Clarence M. Mitchell
Director of Field Operations

SUBJECT   Upgrading of Bernard Ross on West Coast

Mr. Theodore Jones has given me a copy of his memo to you dated August 10, discussing his opinion regarding the upgrading of Mr. Bernard Ross as Regional Director during the period of Mr. Rutledge's absence. I regret that it has been necessary to change our plans on several occasions concerning Region XII, but the tragedy which hit the Rutledge family seems ample justification for the revision.[1]

In my opinion all of our actions should be geared to relieve Mr. Rutledge of any undue pressure in reaching his decision. At the same time we must do justice to FEPC's program and the individual who is willing to serve on a temporary basis. I note that Mr. Jones has asked for a review of your decision. I most earnestly urge that he be requested to seek some legal way in which we can take this action. It would be extremely regrettable if it would be necessary to rescind the action simply because of administrative complications, which may not apply in this case.

I shall be happy to join with Mr. Jones in this exploration.

cc: Mr. Johnson
        Mr. Jones
        Mr. Davidson
        Mr. Kingman

MS: copy, HqR3, Office Files of George M. Johnson. (A–M) M.

1. Rutledge, who became regional director after Harry Kingman resigned, had taken leave of absence and returned with his children to New York after his wife died in childbirth. Bernard Ross served as acting director until the regional office shut down in 12/45. See Kingman to Witherspoon Dodge, 8/20/45, FR80, Region VII. Administrative Files (A–Z), Regional Offices; Kingman, "Citizenship in a Democracy," 116–17.

Memorandum on Adapting Local Employment Office Operations to Meet Reconversion Requirements

August 17, 1945

MEMORANDUM

TO: Mr. Malcolm Ross
           Chairman

FROM: Clarence M. Mitchell
           Director of Field Operations

SUBJECT Adapting Local Employment Office Operations
           to Meet Reconversion Requirements

After reading the above mentioned War Manpower Commission Instruction No. 831, I talked with Mr. Donald Kingsley, Deputy Executive Director of the War Manpower Commission, for the purpose of pointing out that treatment of minority problems is not mentioned in this instruction.

He stated that this was gotten together in a rapid fashion to meet the V-J Day requirements, and is a preliminary document only. Mr. Kingsley said that there is a longer WMC program in the making which will amount to about fifty pages, and in this document, there is considerable treatment of the minority problem. This will be sent to us for suggestions before it goes out. He hoped to have it ready for our perusal within the next week or two. I will keep you informed of developments.

MS: LH, DI, Papers of Clarence Mitchell, Baltimore.

This effort to obtain cooperation from the WMC, in keeping with Mitchell's request to the regional directors in a memorandum on 7/27 for "Suggestions on New Ways for Operation for Maximum Results," conforms with Carlos Castañeda's response on 8/2/45. See Castañeda to Mitchell, memorandum, 8/2/45, FEPC RG 228, box 469, Trimble Files, DNA. For context, see the section on the WMC and USES in the headnote on Relationships with Federal Agencies.

Memorandum on George M. Johnson's August 1 Memorandum on Cases Recommended for Hearing

August 17, 1945

MEMORANDUM

TO: Mr. George M. Johnson
          Deputy Chairman

FROM: Clarence M. Mitchell
          Director of Field Operations

SUBJECT: Your Memorandum of August 1 on Cases Recommended For Hearing

A review of the present situation shows that no useful purpose will be served if hearings were held against Consolidated Vultee Aircraft Corporation in Fort Worth, Texas; George Detterback Company, Chicago, Illinois; Norris Stamping Company, Los Angeles, California; and St. Johns River Shipbuilding Company, Jacksonville, Florida. In each of these cases there are substantial cutbacks or revisions in production which mean that there are now or will be substantial lay-offs. In one case the plant will close entirely.

You also discussed the Southwest mining cases and it is my understanding that Mr. Hunt has recommended that no action be taken on these.

It appears that the machinists cases are still among those in which we could expect some long range results if we obtain satisfactory adjustment, but because of the end of the war, I presume that we will have to restudy our jurisdiction before taking any action.

I have written this memo merely to complete your record.

MS: copy, HqR38, Central Files. Memoranda, Johnson, George M.–3, 1944.

This memorandum was Mitchell's response to an 8/1/45 memorandum from Johnson, who, based on the Committee's recommendations at its 7/21 meeting, suggested that the cases be reexamined to determine whether hearings were then advisable. Even as the Committee clearly was on its deathbed, Johnson explained that it was developing an overall program for the current fiscal year. Further emphasizing the FEPC's imminent demise, Johnson suggested that the Southwest Mining Cases and the IAM cases also be added to determine whether they too merited hearings. HqR38, Central Files. (entry 25) Memoranda, Johnson, George M., 1/44–. For background on these cases, see the headnotes on the Shipbuilding Industry, on the Aircraft Industry, and on the Mining Industry.

Memorandum on FEPC Case Activity—July

August 18, 1945

MEMORANDUM

TO: Mr. Malcolm Ross
           Chairman

FROM: Clarence M. Mitchell
           Director of Field Operations

SUBJECT: FEPC Case Activity—July

In spite of the difficulties we faced during the month of July, our field offices closed a total of 160 cases. Of these, 44 were satisfactorily adjusted. The San Francisco office was the highest with ten satisfactory adjustments out of thirty-two cases closed. The New York office was second with six satisfactory adjustments out of twenty-two cases closed. The number of active cases dropped from 1822 to 1693.

I believe that our regional representatives deserve commendation for their ability to carry on under very trying circumstances.[1]

MS: LH, DI, FEPC RG 228, Office Files of Clarence Mitchell, DNA.

1. Mitchell also praised the ongoing efforts of the regional offices in his report of 6/19/45.

Memorandum on Important Active FEPC Cases

August 20, 1945

MEMORANDUM

TO: Mr. Malcolm Ross
            Chairman

FROM: Clarence M. Mitchell
            Director of Field Operations

SUBJECT: Important Active FEPC Cases

Regional offices (except V and X) have reported on the cases which they are handling pending establishment of a definite operating policy. As you will recall, these cases were to be grouped into four categories. The first is that in which there is a possibility for immediate settlement. Secondly, there are those cases against government or private parties charged in which there are public relations values and/or long range possibilities for policy changes which will be helpful to minority groups. Thirdly, there are those cases which the director intends to refer for hearing because they are unadjustable at the regional level, but which also require further additional action on his part. Fourthly, there are those cases that are already referred to the central office for hearing but which require additional checking to be brought up to date.[1]

The regions' reports show a total of 257 cases in these groupings. Region[s] V and X have not reported because the closing of the offices in New Orleans, Cincinnati, and Cleveland has resulted in certain mechanical difficulties of analyzing the case loads. The regional offices state there are approximately 105 cases (Group I) which they believe can be settled immediately.

I presume that we are most interested in group II where there are ninety-two cases listed by the regions reporting. These cases include government complaints against the Veterans Administration, Navy Department, War Department, and the Post Office Department. In the field of private industry there are cases involving rubber, oil, transportation, food processing, tobacco, steel, and commercial air lines.

The unadjustable cases (Groups III and IV) which will require hearing are fifty-five in number. These include such industries as communication, transportation, local utilities, and textiles. As you know, there are before us unresolved matters affecting the International Association of Machinists, shipbuilding, oil, the maritime industry, street railways, and inter-state carriers. If in addition to the cases already heard by the Committee, we concentrate on those cases in Groups II, III and IV with certain additions from regions which have not reported, we will be able to make a sizeable contribution to the orderly utilization of minorities during the reconversion period.

cc: Mr. Johnson
      Mr. Jones
      Mr. Davis
      Mr. Davidson

MS: LH, DI, HqR3, *Office File of Malcolm Ross. Misc.*

Owing to Congress's cutting the FEPC budget in the National War Agencies Appropriation Act of 1946 to $250,000 with the stipulation that "in no case shall this fund be available for expenditure beyond June 30, 1946," the Committee began this assessment of its workload. See FEPC Chronology; Maslow to Ross, memorandum on "Congressional Debate on FEPC Appropriation," 5/27/44, in appendix 1.

1. For an example of this breakdown, see "The Nature of Satisfactory Adjustments (Sent 1944)" in the file with the text.

Memorandum on Jurisdiction over Federal Bureau of Prisons

August 24, 1945

Mr. Maceo Hubbard
     Acting Director, Legal Division
Clarence M. Mitchell
     Director of Field Operations
Jurisdiction Over Federal Bureau of Prisons

Attached is a communication we have received from Miss Frieda L. Lazarus, Chairman of the Conscientious Objectors Problems Committee.[1] You will note she states that there is discrimination against Negro prisoners in the Federal Prison Industries, Inc. I do not know whether we have jurisdiction over this matter and I am submitting it to you for a determination of whether it is within the scope of Executive Order 9346.

In addition, I will appreciate it if you will join me in discussing with the Deputy Chairman whether we wish to take action on such matters, even though we may have jurisdiction. My personal opinion is that it will not be good policy for us to handle this type of case.

Attachment

MS: *copy, HqR38, Central Files. (entry 25) Memoranda, Hubbard, Maceo.*

1. The attachment has not been found. The response was probably similar to that depicted in 8/3/45 and notes.

Memorandum on Important Activities and Trends Reported by Field Offices

August 25, 1945

MEMORANDUM

To: Mr. Malcolm Ross
            Chairman

FROM: Clarence M. Mitchell
            Director of Field Operations

SUBJECT: Important Activities and Trends Reported by Field Offices

GOVERNMENT EMPLOYMENT

San Antonio: Sharp reduction expected at Kelly Field. Out of eighteen thousand employees thirty per cent are Latin-Americans and ten per cent are Negroes.

Detroit: Many Negroes who received low efficiency ratings failed to appeal them and consequently now face extensive lay-offs. Several cases have been handled by FEPC.

PRIVATE INDUSTRY

San Francisco and Los Angeles: Ship repair is still holding up on the West Coast in the Bethlehem plants at Alameda and San Pedro, as well as in the Cal-Ship Company. All of these are large employers of Negroes. Aircraft has, as was expected, dramatically reduced force. Hardest hit at present is Douglas at Santa Monica which employs a considerable number of Negroes. Lockheed is holding up at present.

Kansas City, Mo.: Four plants: Hercules Powder, Pratt-Whitney, Remington Arms, and North American will release approximately five thousand Negro workers. Already three thousand are off. So employment possibilities are not bright.

Chicago: Wisconsin Bell Telephone Company still refuses to employ Negro operators after FEPC conferences. It is significant also to note that extensive lay-offs at the Missouri Valley Bridge and Iron Works in Evansville failed to develop anticipated community problems in that displaced workers left the area immediately.

All regional offices have been asked to investigate persistent reports that employment compensation is being denied Negroes who refuse to accept low paying jobs.

Philadelphia, on the other hand, reports that one USES office refers male whites to jobs but does not refer Negroes to any jobs. It does expedite payment of unemployment compensation for non-whites.

PUBLIC RELATIONS

With help of former Regional Director Ellinger, Texas citizens have formed an advisory group to counsel with FEPC's regional office.

Region XII reports definite efforts on the part of California AF of L to assist in promoting FEPC's good relations with labor groups.

Atlanta indicates new Ku Klux and related activities in the South will require attention.

cc: Mr. Johnson
       Mr. Jones
       Mr. Davis
       Mr. Davidson
       Mrs. Lawson

MS: copy, HqR3, Office Files of George M. Johnson. (A–M), M.

In July 1945, upon becoming director of the Division of Field Operations, Mitchell instructed the field directors to submit to him monthly rather than biweekly reports; in August he told them to send in the reports on the fifteenth of each month. The remaining regional directors submitted reports until at least 2/46, and Mitchell digested them into his reports to Ross. In 3/46 the directors submitted voluminous reports for the FEPC's *Final Report*. See, for example, Correspondence (Unarranged), Telegrams Received, Field Reports, Region II, FEPC Field Records, and related folders, HqR3.

Memorandum on WMC's Program on Minority Groups

August 28, 1945

MEMORANDUM

TO: Mr. Malcolm Ross
           Chairman

FROM: Clarence M. Mitchell
           Director of Field Operations

SUBJECT: WMC's Program on Minority Groups

On Saturday, I talked with J. Lawrence Duncan by telephone concerning WMC's plans for handling minority problems.[1] Among other things, he stated that it is contemplated that there will be a Form 209. This form will show the number of discriminatory orders received by a USES office; the number of firms involved; the number of referrals against such orders; and the amount of discrimination against those persons referred. This will be taken on non-war as well as war employers. In many respects this will be a valuable index to the broad policies of industries in a given area. I do not know whether this will be put into practice by WMC, but it is under consideration.

We also discussed the rumor that USES offices are forcing non-white workers to take low paying jobs in spite of skills used in previous employment. Mr. Duncan stated that this is particularly true in Michigan and does not affect non-whites only. He stated that the Michigan law is so worded that it says in effect that persons must be willing to accept jobs on which they have had the greatest work experience. Thus, an individual who has been a cook for most of his life may now have acquired a skill in war time, but under the Michigan law, as interpreted by the Unemployment Compensation Commission, he would have to accept a job as a cook or forfeit the compensation. Apparently, this matter is the subject of some concern to the UAW in the area.

MS: LH, DI, HqR4, Office Files of George M. Johnson. Wage Increases.

1. For ongoing developments related to reconversion, see also Minutes of 8/27/45, HqR1, Summary Minutes of Meetings.

Memorandum on Apprentice Training Program for Building Trades

August 28, 1945

MEMORANDUM

To: Mr. John A. Davis
           Director of Review and Analysis

From: Clarence M. Mitchell
           Director of Field Operations

Subject: Apprenticeship Training Program for Building Trades

Thank you for the release dated August 20 concerning the WMC's Apprenticeship Training Program for the building trades. I have discussed this matter with Dr. Philip S.

Van Wyck, Chief of Training for the War Manpower Commission, and Mr. Cleary of the Apprenticeship Training Program. It appears that not much consideration was given to the problems of minority groups. I am asking for material on how the program will operate and, after studying it, I hope to be in a position to determine where we will tie in.

Mr. Cleary stated among other things that it seems to be generally recognized by the unions that if a veteran was of an apprentice age at the time he went into the armed service, even though he is past that age now, he will still be considered for such training upon release.

MS: copy, HqR39, Central Files. (entry 25) Memoranda, Review and Analysis Division.

These concerns reflected the Committee's deep anxiety over the impact of reconversion on minorities. See, for example, Minutes of 7/21, 9/4, 9/15/45, HqR1, Summary Minutes of Meetings.

Memorandum to Regional Directors

President's Committee on
Fair Employment Practice
September 6, 1945

TO: ALL REGIONAL DIRECTORS

THE PRESIDENT TODAY INFORMED CONGRESS THAT FEPC WILL CONTINUE DURING THE RECONVERSION PERIOD AND URGED THE ESTABLISHMENT OF A PERMANENT AGENCY. PENDING FURTHER ADVICE FROM THE CENTRAL OFFICE, DOCKET AND PROCESS CASES ACCORDING TO THE PRIORITY SCHEDULE IN MY MEMORANDUM OF JULY 27. FOR THE PRESENT, ASSUME JURISDICTION OVER COMPLAINTS AGAINST GOVERNMENT AGENCIES, EMPLOYERS EXECUTING GOVERNMENT CONTRACTS, EMPLOYERS ENGAGED IN ACTIVITIES FORMERLY REGARDED AS ESSENTIAL TO THE WAR EFFORT, EMPLOYERS OPERATING PARTIALLY OR TOTALLY RECONVERTED INDUSTRIES, AND LABOR ORGANIZATIONS OF EMPLOYEES OF SUCH EMPLOYERS.

CLARENCE M. MITCHELL
DIRECTOR OF FIELD OPERATIONS

MS: copy, MP.

At its 9/4/45 meeting the Committee heard that the chairman and deputy chairman had been "advised informally" that the president would not issue a new executive order; neither would he send a letter to Congress clarifying the agency's status. Instead, in his message he would say that the FEPC would continue during the reconversion period and that he would request that Congress pass legislation creating a permanent FEPC. It was acknowledged that the FEPC might not continue for another six months after the war had ended because there was nothing in EO 9346 that suggested that it might. An important concern underlying this and subsequent discussions was the extent of the FEPC's jurisdiction. Without a new executive order, some argued, the FEPC's jurisdiction over war industries and reconversion industries had ended. The Committee then agreed to contact the president and get a clarification as to what he thought the FEPC's jurisdiction would cover.

At its 9/15 meeting, after the issuance of the president's statement on 9/6, the Committee agreed to send a memorandum to the president, noting his comment that it "would continue during the reconversion period" and stating that they interpreted it to mean that "the Committee is expected to assume jurisdiction over Government agencies, Government contractors and war industries, whether still engaged in war activities or reconverted to peacetime production and unions of their employees." The memorandum indicated that was the Committee's preferred course of action, but if the FEPC had misunderstood the intent of the president's statement, the alterative was that the Committee "should confine its jurisdiction to Government agencies, Government contractors and remaining war industries and union of their employees."

In the absence of contrary instructions, the Committee continued for the remainder of the year to handle cases involving some private industries. Mitchell reported on 9/27/45 that regional offices were taking action on various cases and that, "so far, the question of FEPC jurisdiction over these companies has not arisen." In the absence of such challenges, he suggested the FEPC could carry on "an aggressive program with the hope that we can make the most of what voluntary cooperation we can obtain." In December, President Truman issued EO 9664, authorizing the FEPC to investigate, make findings and recommendations, but not to issue directives. It was to report discrimination in industries contributing to military production or to the effective transition to a peacetime economy. The fruits of such investigations, which the FEPC originally intended to present at hearings in Chicago, were instead incorporated into its *Final Report*. See memoranda of 9/14, 9/27/45; headnote on Jurisdictional Issues; Minutes of 9/4, 9/15/45, HqR1, Summary Minutes of Proceedings; "Salaries and Expenses, Committee on Fair Employment Practice, Fiscal Year, 1946, Justification for Continuation of Functions and the Appropriation during Period of Reconversion," HqR3, Office Files of Malcolm Ross; John A. Davis's undated memorandum to Ross on "Jurisdiction of FEPC during Transition Period," HqR6, Office Files of George M. Johnson. Miscellaneous; Reed, *Seedtime*, 329–32, 337.

Memorandum on Meeting with First Assistant Postmaster General

September 12, 1945

MEMORANDUM

TO: Files

FROM: Clarence M. Mitchell
         Director of Field Operations

SUBJECT: **Meeting with First Assistant Postmaster General**

On September 5, 1945, I met with Mr. J. M. Donaldson, First Assistant Postmaster General, on complaints submitted to us by the Pittsburgh Branch of the United States

Post Office. A written summary of these complaints was left with him for further in-quiry and investigation.

Mr. Donaldson expressed the fear that he would not be able to accomplish a great deal on these specific cases because the problems of returning war veterans would be given priority by the Post Office Department. He stated that many persons who would receive promotions may find themselves displaced by returning veterans. I stated that since most of the complaints in the Pittsburgh case seem to have a number of years of experience, it is unlikely that they will be displaced by veterans. I also stated that the matters concern broad policies which should be corrected if minority group vet-erans are to receive proper consideration in the Post Office Department.

We had a general discussion on the attitudes of various postmasters in the country. He stated that the postmasters in Houston, Texas, and New Orleans, Louisiana, were reluctant to appoint Negro clerks. Previously, the Post Office Department has insisted that there was no discrimination in the Houston Post Office. Currently, we have com-plaints against the New Orleans Post Office, but the individuals who have told us about the cases have asked that action be withheld until further notice from them.

Mr. Donaldson has agreed to let me know the results of his inquiry, and we expect to have additional conferences on other problems.

MS: copy, FEPC RG 228, Office Files of Clarence Mitchell, box 461, Unarranged, DNA.

See the section on the Post Office Department in the headnote on Relationships with Federal Agencies.

Memorandum on Proposed Budget for Division of Field Operations for the Fiscal Year 1946

September 14, 1945

MEMORANDUM

TO: Mr. George M. Johnson
Deputy Chairman

FROM: Clarence M. Mitchell
Director of Field Operations

SUBJECT: Proposed Budget for Division of Field Operations for the Fiscal Year 1946

I have read the proposed budget for FEPC during the present fiscal year and find that it contemplates the elimination of all field offices of the Committee on January first. This is a complete and unpleasant surprise in that I cannot see how the proposed program, beginning on page 12, can be accomplished without any field staff. As I understand the fiscal situation, closing of the field offices in the third quarter would cost us approximately $14,000 in terminal leave, to be paid 23 field employees. The operation of the offices would cost approximately $22,000 in salaries.

In view of the President's statement that he desires that the Committee continue during the reconversion period, I think it is altogether proper that we request the necessary supplementary funds to make possible the effective operation of our offices.[1]

A number of our field representatives have had other opportunities for employment which they have declined to accept because they preferred to remain with FEPC, even thought our future was uncertain. It would be a serious blow to their morale if they discovered we contemplated terminating them but did not so inform them at an early date.

I respectfully request that the budget be revised to include operation of field offices and that Congress be asked to give us the necessary funds.

MS: copy, HqR38, Central Files. (entry 25) Memoranda, Johnson, George M., 1/44–.

1. On the president's statement of 9/6/45 and its impact on FEPC, see Mitchell's telegram of that date, and notes. No supplementary funds were obtained; all but three regional offices closed by the end of the year.

Memorandum on Conversation with Mr. Robert Goodwin, Executive Director, War Manpower Commission

September 26, 1945

MEMORANDUM

TO: Mr. Malcolm Ross
Chairman

FROM: Clarence M. Mitchell
Director of Field Operations

SUBJECT: Conversation with Robert Goodwin,
Executive Director, War Manpower Commission

On the above date I called Mr. Goodwin for the purpose of arranging an informal meeting with him to discuss our new relationships. He stated that he would not be in a position to talk as well this week on plans as he would be in the coming week.

The War Manpower Commission is operating as formerly although it is within the Department of Labor. Mr. Goodwin assured me that the operating agreement between FEPC and WMC remains in effect.[1]

I shall have further conversations with Mr. Goodwin at a later date.

MS: copy, FEPC RG 228, Office Files of Clarence Mitchell, box 458, Malcolm Ross, DNA.

1. See the section on the WMC and USES in the headnote on Relationships with Federal Agencies.

Memorandum on Important Activities and Trends Reported by Field Offices

September 27, 1945

MEMORANDUM

TO: Mr. Malcolm Ross
         Chairman

FROM: Clarence M. Mitchell
         Director of Field Operations

SUBJECT: Important Activities and Trends Reported by Field Offices

JURISDICTION OF FEPC

Regional offices continue to report various visits made to plants, or to our offices by parties charged, in connection with the processing of cases. So far, the question of FEPC jurisdiction over these companies has not arisen.[1] It was particularly impressive to read the following sentence in a report from the West Coast: "Mr. B. L. Winslow, general employment manager of the Pacific Telephone and Telegraph Company, in a visit to the office, said that Mr. Hambrook, vice president and general manager, 'was so impressed with the friendly and positive approach made by Kingman that he sent me here to lay our cards on the table and try to work things out.'"

Miss Joy Schultz of the Chicago office visited the Indianapolis area recently and conferred with management representatives of eight firms. In all of these cases she was able to obtain information on some of the future plans of these companies.[2]

In Washington, through the War Production Board, we have been in touch with the Continental Can Company in East St. Louis, and directly with the Washington representative of the National Lead Company. Neither of these firms questioned our jurisdiction. All of this tends to support the belief during this interim period that we should carry on an aggressive program with the hope that we can make the most of what voluntary cooperation we can obtain.

GOVERNMENT EMPLOYMENT

My report of August 25th stated that the Detroit office reported that many Negroes had received low efficiency ratings and now face layoffs. A similar problem is before us in Los Angeles where colored employees of the Naval Dry Docks at San Pedro have visited our office or called to allege that their efficiency ratings have suddenly dropped from the high 80's and low 90's to the low 60's.

PRIVATE INDUSTRY

Region I reports that sharp reductions have taken place in the employment of Negroes in small arms and ammunition plants. At Winchester Arms, which formerly had about 2,300 Negro workers, there are now only 500; Remington, which had about 800, now has 100. Three hundred Negroes were laid off in Hartford at the Pratt and Whitney Aircraft Company. The regional director feels that many of the Negroes who migrated to New England from the South are returning to their homes.

On the constructive side of the register, Region I reports that the New England Telephone Company is interviewing colored girls for jobs as operators. The agreement to employ these girls came largely as a result of the work of Examiner Madison Jones. Although none of the girls were employed as of September 18th, Mr. Lawson feels that they will soon be on the job.

Region III reports that the Telephone Company in Philadelphia called in several persons who had previously filed applications for jobs as operators and gave them jobs as clerks. The region is continuing in its effort to obtain employment of Negroes as operators.

Region III also reports that W.A. Briggs Bitumin Company promises that in its new peacetime operations its policy of non-discrimination will be made known to all of its employees.

Region VII reports growing tensions in Southern communities.

The St. Louis office states that 35,000 persons have been laid off in the St. Louis area since August 14, 1945. Seventy thousand persons have been laid off in the last six months, and to date there have been only 10,102 job openings, most of which pay comparatively low wages. Unemployment among Negroes is described as critical. The Scullin Steel Company, with approximately 20 per cent Negroes, has shut down its South Plant, resulting in the layoff of 2,200 colored persons.

MS: LH, DI, HqR3, Office Files of Malcolm Ross. Unarranged.

1. See Mitchell, telegram, 9/6/45, and notes.

2. Schulz's report to Elmer Henderson, 9/6/45, on the Indianapolis field trip is filed with this memorandum.

Memorandum on Future Operations of Western Cartridge Company and McDonnell Aircraft Corporation

October 9, 1945

MEMORANDUM

TO: Mr. George M. Johnson
         Deputy Chairman

FROM: Clarence M. Mitchell
         Director of Field Operations

Subject: Future Operations of Western Cartridge Company
         and McDonnell Aircraft Corporation

On October 1, 1945, you sent me a memorandum asking for information on the status of the Western Cartridge Company in East Alton, Illinois, and the McDonnell Aircraft Corporation in St. Louis, Missouri. The following communications have been sent to us by Mr. Elmer W. Henderson, director of Region VI, and Mr. Theodore Brown, examiner in Region IX:

(1) From Mr. Henderson:

"Reurtel. Western Cartridge already reconverted to civilian production, although reductions still in effect. Expect employment of 4500 workers by end of year. This plant in small arms ammunition production 50 years and will continue indefinitely. Urge findings be issued immediately."[1]

(2) From Mr. Brown:

"Regarding your teletype McDonnell Aircraft Corporation still in operation and plans to continue indefinitely."

MS: copy, HqR76, Office Files of Clarence Mitchell, box 458, E–R, Johnson.
1. See the headnote on Major Cases in St. Louis.

Memorandum on Closing of Philadelphia Office

October 22, 1945

MEMORANDUM

TO: Mr. Malcolm Ross
          Chairman

FROM: Clarence M. Mitchell
          Director of Field Operations

SUBJECT: Closing of Philadelphia Office

I have been giving some thought to the relative value of keeping open our offices in Philadelphia and Los Angeles. This is, of course, a difficult decision to make because both are important industrial centers.

We have received disturbing reports from San Francisco and Los Angeles, indicating serious racial tensions and possibility of further trouble in the offing. We have on the Coast, as you know, the diversified minority problem involving Latin-Americans, Negroes, and Nisei. The distance between San Francisco and Los Angeles is so great that adequate coverage from either city alone is not possible.

At one time I had hoped that our curtailed budget would enable us to do a limited amount of traveling between Los Angeles and San Francisco as well as between San Francisco and the Northwest. Hence, I was of the opinion that the San Francisco office would be able to handle a sizeable part of the problems before us in all three of the areas. I felt, therefore, that the Los Angeles office might be closed. We now know that money for any reasonable amount of travel is not available. It is, therefore, imperative that the Los Angeles office be kept open.

Although the problems in Philadelphia are very serious and could best be handled by having an office in that city, geography at least is on our side. I propose that the states of Pennsylvania and New Jersey be handled by New York, and Delaware be handled by Region IV. With the saving from the closing of Region III's office, we should be able to keep Los Angeles open for the remainder of the fiscal year.[1]

MS: copy, FEPC RG 228, Office Files of Clarence Mitchell, DNA.
1. All the regional offices closed in December 1945, except those in Detroit, Chicago, and St. Louis, which survived a few months longer.

Memorandum on Proposed Amendment to Executive Order 9346

October 29, 1945

MEMORANDUM

TO: Division of Field Operations

FROM: Clarence M. Mitchell
         Director of Field Operations

SUBJECT: Proposed Amendment to Executive Order 9346

As a result of an FEPC conference with the Department of Justice, a proposed amendment to our Executive Order is being studied. If issued, this amendment would clarify FEPC's jurisdiction over reconverted industries.

This information is submitted to you in order that you may know we are actively pressing for some solution of our problems.[1] It must be regarded as strictly confidential.

Meanwhile, I trust you are keeping in mind that the provisions of my telegram on the processing of cases are still in effect.[2]

MS: copy, FEPC FR89, Region IX. Memoranda 1945–46, St. Louis.
   1. The "problems" to which Mitchell referred was the closing down of the FEPC.
   2. See Mitchell's telegram of 9/6/45 and notes; headnote on Jurisdictional Issues.

Memorandum of Clarence M. Mitchell and John A. Davis on Decisions of Conference between Clarence M. Mitchell, Marjorie M. Lawson, and John A. Davis with Regard to the Proposed Chicago Hearing

DATE: Nov. 2, 1945

TO   Mr. Malcolm Ross, Chairman

FROM: Mr. Clarence M. Mitchell, Director of Field Operations
        John A. Davis, Director, Division of Review and Analysis

SUBJECT: Decisions of conference between Clarence Mitchell, Marjorie M. Lawson and John A. Davis with regard to the proposed Chicago hearing.

Half way through our discussion of planning data for the proposed Chicago fact finding hearing we ran head on into the problem of what staff would be available for this hearing.[1] A careful perusal of the budget with Mr. Jeter indicated that several field offices would have to be closed up in January if a skeleton staff is to be kept to the end of the fiscal year. With the consideration of a hearing of this size the question arose whether money would be available to keep a single regional office open after January. It seems first of all necessary to decide what staff would be available to collect data, how much money would be available for travel and the payment of witnesses, how much would be available for central office travel and participation.

It was furthermore decided that it is doubtful that more material on individual cities will be available by Nov. 8 when the Committee meets. It cannot be obtained from the field in this time. It was our feeling that the following cities should be included in the hearing: St. Louis and East St. Louis, Chicago, Evansville, Kansas City, Detroit, Cleveland, Minneapolis and St. Paul.

A check with USES indicated that the Oct. 15 ES 270 reports are just as bad as the Sept. 15 reports with regard to data on non-white reporting. It is apparent then that we will have to rely on our regional men and the USES in the selected areas. We decided that the regional men should immediately begin to prepare the way in the following fashion:

(1) Check each firm in the selected cities which hired Negroes during the war in any considerable number. This material would be gathered by getting copies of the ES 270 reports from the USES. Where this is not possible an employer should be approached directly or the union where it is cooperative. If a firm is going out of business the number of nonwhite persons who have been laid off should be obtained and the type of skills of the Negroes fired should be noted. Where the firm is reconverting not only should the layoffs be noted by the type of skill lost to Negroes but by the present composition of labor force broken down by skills and by Negroes should be indicated as well as the future plans of the firm with regard to total and Negro employment.

(2) The USES should be requested to keep statistics on discriminatory requests, their number, their percentage of the total, the type of occupation. They should also be classified in terms of our jurisdiction but this will have to wait on the issuance of a new executive order if there is to be one. However, decision in this regard seems imminent.

(3) USES should also be requested to collate placements by race, occupation and salary. Placement data is kept by race, occupation and salary but USES reports are only by race without any further breakdown.

(4) Most important of all once our jurisdiction has been made clear, field men should spend their time working up complaints of discrimination against those

industries which still have war contracts or which are converting to regular peacetime activities.

(5) Agencies within the selected cities should be contacted for social and economic data which describes conditions affecting the Negro's ability to obtain and hold employment. This includes material on immigration, housing, transportation, recreation, and health services.

(6) Expert agencies within the cities selected should be advised of plans of the FEPC and should be asked at an early date to get together material on the reconverted prospects of the city and on Negro industrial assimilation. These agencies should include the local Committee for Economic Development, the Urban League, the local race relations committee, local union, the central union or industrial councils, and the local Chamber of Commerce.

MS: LH, DI, HqR68, *Office Files of John A. Davis. Mr. Ross.*

1. Due to the crippling budget cuts, the Chicago hearing was not held. Instead, the remaining skeleton staff began collecting material for the FEPC's *Final Report.* On the data collection process, see also Davis to Robert C. Goodwin, 12/14/45; Goodwin to WMC Regional Directors for Regions V, VI, VIII, IX, in HqR2.

Memorandum on Cases against the Post Office Department

November 8, 1945

MEMORANDUM

TO: Mr. Eugene Davidson
Assistant Director of Field Operations

FROM: Clarence M. Mitchell
Director of Field Operations

SUBJECT: Cases Against the Post Office Department

Attached is a copy of a letter sent to Mr. Joseph F. Gartland, Chairman of the Board of Operations in the Post Office Department, by Mr. Ashby B. Carter, President of the National Alliance of Postal Employees. Also attached is a copy of my letter to Mr. Carter. These letters are sent to you in order that you may be informed of current developments.[1]

When the Alliance representatives were in Washington recently they visited the Post Office Department and obtained what they describe as "new understandings" with Mr. Gartland and the Operations Board. It is our belief that these new relationships will lead to a settlement of many of our problems.

Until we have confirmation of Mr. Ashby's position from the local branches of the Alliance, we shall consider cases already submitted to us as still active. Also, if the grievance machinery in the Post Office Department does not operate to the satisfaction of those filing complaints, we shall process the cases as before.

Sent also to:

Dr. Witherspoon Dodge
Regional Director, VII

Dr. Carlos E. Castaneda
Regional Director, X

MS: copy, HqR8, Office Files of Evelyn N. Cooper, Trial Attorney, 9/44–12/45. Misc.

1. See Carter to Gartland, 10/15/45, in which he said that Gartland's "suggestion that we try to settle all grievances within the framework of the Department before appealing to outside agencies" was being "followed to the letter"; Mitchell to Carter, 11/8/45, both in HqR8, Office Files of Evelyn N. Cooper. Misc. For context, see the section on the Post Office Department in the headnote on Relationships with Federal Agencies.

Memorandum on United Steelworkers of America, CIO

DATE: April 8, 1946

TO: Mr. Malcolm Ross, Chairman

FROM: Clarence M. Mitchell, Director of Field Operations

SUBJECT: United Steelworkers of America, CIO

Mr. Wilson mentioned the Hughes Tool Company and the Murray Gin Company in his communication of March 29th.[1] The International Union gave very excellent cooperation in handling the problems in these cases. However, the collapse of the War Labor Board prevented us from achieving any positive results.[2] In these cases the issue was discriminatory wage rates.

Our experience in Region III, where numerous strikes took place, would seem to indicate that the Negro workers either did not fully utilize the union machinery or did not have confidence in what could be achieved by their representatives, in many instances. At this distance, it seemed very surprising that a union with the Steelworkers' record did not have greater control over its Negro members in some of the larger plants. On the other hand, Mr. Wilson has always been available to assist us in handling complaints and usually made a favorable impression on our local representatives in St. Louis and New Orleans.

MS: LH, DI, HqR2, Office Files of Malcolm Ross. Materials for Final Report.

1. Boyd Wilson, international representative, United Steelworkers of America, to James B. Carey, chairman, National CIO Committee to Abolish Racial Discrimination, 3/29/46. Wilson told Carey that upon assuming jurisdiction "in an industry in which large numbers of minority group employees worked," the Steelworkers "realized in the beginning of our organizing efforts, that any plan carrying hope of success, must of necessity include these groups on equal basis." The Steelworkers' study of the history of past efforts to organize the industry, however, "revealed a lack of knowledge of the fundamental principles of the labor movement, particularly in the application of the principles of solidarity among all workers regardless of race, or nationality." He said the "industry was quick to recognize the weakness of such a policy." They readily saw "the possibility of successful resistance through the medium of fear and division among their employees." See HqR2, Office Files of Malcolm Ross. Materials for Final Report; *Final Report,* 59.

Wilson's letter was in response to requests for information on union experiences with racial and religious discrimination that Malcolm Ross had sent to the National CIO Committee to Abolish Discrimination on 3/5/46. Responding, James Carey, chairman of the committee, wrote several unions on 3/7 requesting information from them. See Ross to George L. P. Weaver, 3/5, Weaver to Ross, 3/8, and Carey to E. J. Thomas, 3/7/46, all also in the Materials for Final Report. Mitchell used some information from the reports on unions in his article "Labor Problems Affecting Negroes," epilogue.

2. For background on the NWLB, see 4/13/44, note 1, and the headnote on Relationships with Federal Agencies.

Memorandum on United Automobile Workers of America, CIO

April 8, 1946

Mr. Malcolm Ross, Chairman

Clarence M. Mitchell, Director of Field Operations

United Automobile Workers of America, CIO

The UAW statement is a reflection of the experience we have had with this union and the industry it covers during the war.[1]

I am glad to say that the principle plant in Baltimore with an integrated employment program was the Eastern Aircraft Corporation, whose work is represented by the UAW. On the other hand, in Dallas, the Local which represented workers at the North American plant did give some trouble in that certain employees charged that they were not properly represented. Most of this difficulty was corrected, however.

MS: copy, HqR2, Office Files of Malcolm Ross. Materials for Final Report.

1. For the union's statement, see "Sixteen Months of UAW-FEPC (Highlights of Report—October 15, 1944 to February 15, 1946)," in *The Fight against Discrimination,* a newsletter by Geo. W. Crockett Jr. The UAW was one of several unions that signed operating agreements with the FEPC. See Maslow's Field Instruction no. 38 to all regional directors, 8/8/44, noting the UAW-CIO's agreement outlining procedures for its War Policy Division to follow in resolving complaints to the FEPC. These materials are filed with the above text. See also *Final Report,* 61, and the headnote on the FEPC and Unions.

Memorandum on United Packinghouse Workers of America, CIO

April 8, 1946

Mr. Malcolm Ross, Chairman

Clarence M. Mitchell, Director of Field Operations

United Packinghouse Workers of America, CIO

In general, the statement of the Packinghouse Workers is a factual presentation of their problems and their progress. Although FEPC has not had extensive experience in the meat-packing industry, it has been my good fortune to be reasonably well informed on conditions in this industry because of knowledge gained in St. Paul.[1]

Although a considerable number of Negroes are employed in many plants, they are excluded from the cleaner jobs—especially those dealing with the packaging and grading of meat which is ready for the consumer, such as ham, bacon, etc. This has a particularly adverse effect on Negro women in that these are the jobs that are suitable for female employment.

Before I came to FEPC, we (with Dr. Weaver in WMC, WPB and OPM) had numerous complaints against the meat-packing plants in Omaha. Most of these involved the employment of women. We made some small progress in settling them. Usually we could depend on the representatives of the Packinghouse Workers' Organizing Committee to be of assistance. From time to time, the complaints which FEPC received were sent by this group.

MS: copy, HqR2, Office Files of Malcolm Ross. Materials for Final Report.

1. As with other industries, a major concern was retaining or finding new jobs for African Americans. *Final Report,* 50–56. On Mitchell's experiences with the Urban League in St. Paul, see Watson, *Lion in the Lobby,* 120–22; on discrimination in the meat-packing industry, see Weaver, *Negro Labor,* 78, 194, 232–33, 294.

Memorandum on National Maritime Union, CIO

DATE: April 8, 1946

TO: Mr. Malcolm Ross, Chairman

FROM: Clarence M. Mitchell, Director of Field Operations

SUBJECT: National Maritime Union, CIO

The National Maritime Union representatives were very vigorous throughout the war in promoting a policy of no-discrimination in the maritime industry. We have a number of cases in which the representatives called on FEPC to adjust cases in which Negroes, Chinese, and other minority seamen were refused employment solely because of their race.

Some of the complaints presented by NMU gave an interesting insight into the pattern of discrimination. In one case, against the Standard Brands, Inc., Mr. Ferdinand C. Smith stated that two Negroes were refused employment by the Chief Officer who said "the ship was not built for colored seamen and only white seamen will be permitted aboard." In another case against the Isbrandtsen Steamship Company which was sailing a vessel under the Panamanian flag, the NMU charged that the company maintained either all white, all Negro, or all Chinese in the Stewards' Department.

I believe you will recall the case submitted to us by the Marine Cooks and Stewards in New Orleans. As you know; in this case the NMU replaced the SUP crew and retained the Negro steward who was alleging discrimination.[1]

MS: LH, DI, HqR2, Office Files of Malcolm Ross. Materials for Final Report.

1. See the material on the National Maritime Union in the headnote on the FEPC and Unions; Weaver, *Negro Labor,* 233–34. Jamaican-born black union leader Ferdinand C. Smith was the NMU's secretary.

Memorandum on Oil Workers International Union, CIO

DATE: April 8, 1946

TO: Mr. Malcolm Ross, Chairman

FROM: Clarence M. Mitchell, Director of Field Operations

SUBJECT: Oil Workers International Union, CIO

As you know, FEPC made extensive investigations in the oil industry in Texas. These investigations involved such major companies as Shell, Humble, and Sinclair. It is difficult to know whether we made substantial progress because certain individual complaints were adjusted but there is little to indicate that the over-all pattern of these companies changed. One of those in which we noted satisfactory adjustment was the Humble Company. I am attaching a Final Disposition Report on that case for your information.[1]

In my opinion, the Oil Workers have given a very realistic statement, especially concerning the International workers of their union as we saw it. You will recall that during the Shell Oil controversy the International officers were considerably ahead of the Local Union representatives.

I believe that the Oil Workers made a very unfortunate mistake when they accepted the Shell upgrading chart which was the basis of the discriminatory practices in the plant. Some of the union men indicated that this chart was accepted in order to give the union a foothold in the plant. These individuals believed that if a non-discriminatory chart had been proposed by the CIO, the company would have been able to keep the workers in a company-dominated union.

MS: LH, DI, HqR2, *Office Files of Malcolm Ross. Materials for Final Report 2.*

1. This case was based on a wage discrimination complaint that was satisfactorily adjusted on 1/23/44, when the complainant's classification was raised to "A" (previously reserved for whites only), along with the corresponding salary. FDR, 2/10/44, HqR2, Office Files of Malcolm Ross. Interdepartmental. See also A. Bruce Hunt to Ross, "Failure to Obtain Compliance, Etc.—Shell Oil Company," memorandum, 4/10/46, HqR2, Office Files of Malcolm Ross. Difficult Cases, which gives background on the struggle with Shell dating back to 1943; headnotes on the Oil Industry and on the FEPC and Unions.

EPILOGUE

Labor Problems Affecting Negroes

By Clarence M. Mitchell, Jr., NAACP Labor Secretary

June 28, 1946

On May 3, 1946, the Fair Employment Practices Committee, without funds to pay debts properly and lawfully incurred, hastily closed its doors. The Congress had just refused to appropriate the small sum of $30,000 with which the agency intended to pay the annual leave due its employees and wind up its work by June 30. In this fashion, there ended the five troubled years of FEPC's fighting existence.

This agency of Government had been the victim of the most cynical political short-changing ever since it was established by President Roosevelt on June 25, 1941. Always its operations were curtailed by a lack of funds. At a time when the Nation was spending millions of dollars to win the war and save democracy, there was ever present in the Bureau of the Budget and Congress the threat to cut its slim monies. More frequently than not, its accomplishments were made in spite of its supposed supporters rather than because of them. The end of the Committee really began in July, 1945, when, by parliamentary brigandage in the United States Senate, its modest request for $500,000 was cut to $250,000. This was a so-called compromise engineered by Senator McKellar of Tennessee after Eastland of Mississippi and some of his colleagues had spent several days transforming the upper branch of the national legislature into something between a burlesque show and a Georgia police court.

WHAT FEPC ACCOMPLISHED

The FEPC's program was responsible for the rise in non-white employment in war industries from 3 per cent to 8 per cent. Through the work of its field representatives thousands of colored war workers were admitted to training courses which qualified them for better paying jobs. Because of the FEPC, colored men are today operating street cars in Los Angeles and Philadelphia. It was also this agency, in cooperation with other groups, which brought about the hiring of colored operators in the telephone companies of New York and New Jersey. A graphic sample of its success was shown in a checkup after its hearings in Birmingham, Chicago, Los Angeles and New York. Thirty-one companies were cited at these hearings employed 4,000 non-white workers. A little over a year later these same companies employed a total of 23,000 non-whites.

Many of its successes were accomplished without hearings. Sometimes by the simple action of writing a letter or making a visit the representatives of the agency could correct a discriminatory practice. At other times, the negotiations required months before a settlement could be reached. At the peak of its activity FEPC had handled 12,000 cases and settled satisfactorily more than a third of them. It was receiving approximately 300 new cases each month.

Although the high priest of falsehood, Senator Bilbo, has accused FEPC of stirring up trouble, most of its settlements were accomplished peacefully. During the period between July, 1943 and December, 1944, less than 2 per cent of all strikes in the country were due to racial issues. More than half of these were started by colored workers themselves as protests against discriminatory employment policies.

The successes would have been more numerous, if the agency had enjoyed the support of the important war agencies such as the War Department, the War Production Board, and the War Manpower Commission. All too frequently these agencies crippled the action of FEPC.

WAR DEPT. OBSTRUCTION

For example, when FEPC sought the assistance of the War Department in an effort to gain employment for colored women at the General Cable Company in St. Louis, Mo., it was rebuffed by Truman K. Gibson, Jr., then civilian aide to the Secretary of War. However, when the president of the company informed the War Department that he intended to follow the requirements of the executive order under which the FEPC operated, high ranking officials of the department came to FEPC's offices in an effort to stop the action. While the conference was under way in Washington, a telephone call to St. Louis revealed that the company had already begun the successful integration of colored women a few hours before.

Again the War Department blocked a joint FEPC-WMC effort to end discrimination in the hiring practices of the Western Cartridge Company in East Alton, Ill. The management of this plant contended that it had to recruit workers on a national scale because of severe manpower shortages but could not use Negroes since they were barred from the town by custom. Dr. William H. Spencer, former dean of the Business School of the University of Chicago, who was regional director of the W.M.C. and Elmer W. Henderson, the FEPC director in Chicago, agreed that the company should be denied workers unless it accepted them in a non-discriminatory basis. This plan was vigorously opposed by the War Department and finally vetoed in Washington.

In the South, the War Department [Manpower] Commission constantly undermined the Committee's work by continuing services to employers who submitted discriminatory orders. This was true especially in the case of large employers like the Bell Aircraft Company of Marietta, Georgia and the Consolidated Vultee Company of Fort Worth, Texas. The New Orleans office of W.M.C. refused to accept a non-discriminatory order from the Sefton Fibre Can Company after the plant submitted one in keeping with an FEPC request.

There were in Government a handful of right thinking people like Mrs. Anna Rosenberg, the New York WMC director, James P. Mitchell, director of the industrial personnel division of the Army Service Forces, and others. It was Mrs. Rosenberg who first dramatized the discriminatory practices of the Boilermakers Union of the West Coast when she refused to permit the recruiting of New Yorkers for work in Oregon shipyards on a discriminatory basis. Mr. Mitchell was the author of a War Department memorandum requiring contractors to delete racial specifications from application forms. Some officials of the War Shipping administration were attacked by the Smith Committee in Congress for following a policy of no discrimination in the referral of seamen to merchant vessels.

But mainly it was the courage of the Committee and its staff which gained such successes as were achieved. I wish to pay a tribute to these Jews, Negroes, Latin Americans, Southern whites, Americans of Japanese ancestry and persons of various faiths who worked together for the common goal of ending industrial discrimination. The majority of them were people from fields in which they had already attained national recognition and to which they have since returned.

Now the minorities of the country face a crisis. Many firms are returning to their old discriminatory practices. Discriminatory orders submitted to the employment offices are on the increase. The newspapers are again running ads for "White Christians Only."

In the construction industry it is estimated that two million workers will be employed by September. Yet there is no provision in the NHA program to insure the full use of colored carpenters, painters, plasterers, electricians and plumbers. We are now back where we were at the beginning of the defense program when it was the custom in Durham, North Carolina; Ravenna, Ohio; and Pine Bluff, Arkansas to employ colored laborers and refuse work to skilled craftsmen solely because of race. We are again seeing a crazy-quilt pattern of employment which will send recruiting agents scurrying around the country looking for skilled workers but ignoring the Mexicans, the Negroes and the Jews at home. Unless we exert great pressure on the National Housing Agency, the Federal Housing Authority and the United States Employment Service, minority workers will get no consideration.

Because of the strong non-discrimination policies of the United Automobile Workers and the United Packing House Workers, it can be expected that in these two industries there is a fighting chance to hold the war time gains. This is also true of the steel industry, although there are many jobs from which Negroes are still barred because of race.

There remains unsolved the problems of discrimination against minority workers in the transit industry, the telephone companies, the railways and the textile industry.

PRESIDENT BLOCKED FEPC

Non-whites constitute approximately 6 percent of the workers in the transit industry. It is true that they operate buses and street cars in Los Angeles, Philadelphia, Pittsburgh, Cleveland, Chicago and Detroit. In other big cities like Baltimore, St. Louis, Indianapolis, and Washington, Jim Crow employment practices are still rampant. The stubborn opposition of the Capital Transit Company's officials in Washington has spread like a cancer to other cities. When President Truman forbade FEPC to issue directives against this company, he strengthened the opposition in the industry and scared off forward-looking officials who possibly would have changed their hiring practices, if the Government had employed colored platform men when it operated the Capital Transit Company.

Here, as a digression, I wish to say that the Capital Transit case illustrates how a few misguided planners and high strategists muffed the ball. These people thought that we could have a permanent FEPC only if we did not create any trouble by insisting that Negroes be hired as platform men. I do not know who presented this rubber check in the first instance, but it is now clear that neither in the White House nor in Congress was there a real intention to establish a strong, permanent FEPC, if it could possibly be avoided. Everyone was waiting to see whether the minorities would get down to serious, unified agitation for the legislation. Had it not been for the dramatic resignation of the Honorable Charles Houston from FEPC and the militant fighting of the National Council for a Permanent FEPC, there never would have been a showdown as happened in the Senate. The agency would have been put to sleep with the issuance of some dehydrated reports. The lesson to be learned from this is that in the fight for economic justice minorities should never exchange immediate possibilities for real progress for mere promises of future action. Anyone who means to be fair will give both. The people must scrutinize closely those who profess to have liberal convictions to be sure that the spoken word will be followed by the concrete act.

RAILROADS DISCRIMINATE

To return to the industrial predicament in which we find ourselves, let us look at the railway industry. It employs over a million workers in normal times. The Supreme Court, in the Steele and Tunstall cases, has outlawed the practice of unions and employers putting into effect agreements which discriminate against Negro firemen. The FEPC has accomplished the upgrading of a few waiters to jobs as stewards and in some shops, such as those of the Missouri Pacific, we have obtained promotion of workers. There remains, however, the uncomfortable truth that colored men are still denied firemen's jobs on northern roads, they are still given mainly laboring jobs in the shops and in most places they are excluded from jobs as flagmen, switchmen and baggagemen.

The textile industry, with nearly half a million workers engaged in the spinning and weaving of cotton, is the seat of some of the worst discrimination in the country. Recently a southern firm published on slick paper what was called the "Story of Cotton." One photograph showed a colored man driving a mule hitched to a wagon load of cotton. Said the caption, "Neither is aware of the part he plays in this great industry." I cannot vouch for the truth of the statement because I have not talked with either subject of the picture. I do know, however, that in the textile industry, as presently operated, a mule has a better chance for full utilization of his skills than does a colored man or woman.

This is not because the jobs in the industry are so complicated. Studies have shown that 65 per cent of the workers in this industry can be trained to reach average productivity in less than six months. Rather the problem lies in the discriminatory practices which are so serious that even at the peak of manpower shortages during the war the companies obtained the release of soldiers from the army before they would make use of available colored workers. Three-fourths of the spinning and weaving of cotton in the United States is done in the coastal states of the southeast. The largest concentration of wage earners and spindle capacity for the country as a whole is in North Carolina and the states next in importance are South Carolina and Georgia. There is a law in South Carolina which forbids the employment of Negroes and whites on the same jobs in the same rooms. The law specifically states that they may not use the same windows or stairways—except when the colored persons are scrubbing floors or serving in some other menial capacity.

The country is honey-combed with firms like the Crosley Corporation of this city (Cincinnati) which during the war employed nearly 5,000 workers but used less than a dozen Negroes and these only as janitors.

FEDERAL GOVT., TOO

The Federal Government takes its place among the discriminators. Among the worst offenders are the General Accounting Office, the State Department and, of course, the Department of Justice. This last named agency still requires racial designation on application for employment forms. These departments are headed respectively by Lindsay Warren of North Carolina, James Byrnes of South Carolina and Tom Clark of Texas. But even if they were under the direction of a Henry Wallace or a Wendell Willkie they would continue to be as they are unless we strike at the roots of the evils which create these conditions. This injustisce springs from (1) the weakness of the Federal Civil Service Commission which can never find discrimination even though the party charged is ready to admit that he refused to appoint an individual because of race, creed or color, (2) the personal bias of small fry appointing officials who decide to keep their departments lily white, (3) the failure of heads of departments to back up the national policy against discrimination because all too frequently they do not believe in it themselves, and (4) the cowardly practice of some congressmen and senators serving on appropriation committees who cut the funds of agencies with liberal policies on the race question.

There remain in the Federal Government today only a few Negroes who have any chance of influencing policy. Mr. Hannegan and a few "fixers" try to play up insignificant appointments. However, a glance at the Congressional Directory and the Government Manual will show that the various bureaus are like Mr. Hannegan's Post Office Department. That is, they have numerous assistants, dozens of deputies, scores of administrative assistants and other functionaries but all of these are white. The so-called black cabinet has long since become an almost invisible gray.

BIG ELECTION JOB

We also have a job to do in the November elections. It is simply this: Washington has numerous scrub water politicians. These are men without honorable motives, men who will plot and traffic with the enemies of human progress whenever it serves their personal advantage or their party's gain. In the voting booth, you can pull the stopper and send them whirling down the drain.

Today thousands of workers have laid aside their tools in the ordnance plants. The song of the riveting gun is silent in many aircraft factories and the cranes in dozens of shipyards are motionless against the sky. From Kearny, N. J. to Mobile, Ala., there are thousands of colored men and women who for the first time in their lives drew a living wage when they worked in war plants. These people are jobless and without a real hope for work at their newly learned skills. But in the barber shops, in the churches, in the union meetings and on a hundred street corners there is expressed the resolve that never again will they work for starvation wages in the hotels, the kitchens and the cotton fields. In California, Oregon and Washington the immigrant workers who built the Boeing planes, launched the Kaiser Ships and performed a hundred new tasks under the generous California sun are there to stay. They will not return to the Jim-Crow, low wage, narrow-minded environment of Arkansas, Texas and Louisiana.

These people are awake to the employment possibilities in the nation's industry. They feel as never before that they are part of this democracy. They are determined to fight with every weapon at their command for full employment on jobs for which they are qualified.

There is now a great opportunity to move forward. This powerful network of branches that makes up the NAACP must help see that we have permanent state and national FEPC legislation and that it is effectively administered. The people of New York, New Jersey and Massachusetts have FEPC laws which make possible a frontal attack on discrimination in industry. But these laws will not be worth anything unless the people demand that they be administered fairly and forcefully. The Indiana and Wisconsin FEPC laws mean little and must be strengthened.

EXPOSE JIM CROW FIRMS

Now is the time to give plenty of publicity to the industries in our local communities which discriminate in their hiring and upgrading policies. Persistently we must demand a square deal in employment.

Again we must join hands with organized labor and get non-discrimination clauses in contracts. And we must see that these clauses are enforced. Let us encourage and support those locals of discriminating unions, such as are within the machinists, which are at present trying to change the Jim Crow policies of their internationals.

The accomplishment of full and fair employment in this country will not be easy. But difficult tasks have never stopped the NAACP. The same fighting heart and tenacity of purpose which have brought victory on so many other fronts will insure the attainment of industrial democracy for all.

After Mitchell left the FEPC in 1946, Walter White hired him as labor secretary working out of the NAACP's Washington bureau. This is the speech he gave at the NAACP National Convention in Cincinnati. It was published in *NAACP Bulletin,* July 1946, 10–11. NAACP IIA30. DLC.

Plate 21. Integrated war workers at Sun Shipbuilding in Philadelphia, exemplifying patriotism where once there was racial strife. *Temple University Libraries, Urban Archives, Philadelphia, Pennsylvania*

Plate 22. Riot damage in downtown Philadelphia following Philadelphia Transportation Company strike, August 2, 1944. *Temple University Libraries, Urban Archives, Philadelphia, Pennsylvania*

Plate 23. An injured man arrested as a "hoodlum" in the Philadelphia riot.
Temple University Libraries, Urban Archives, Philadelphia, Pennsylvania

Plate 24. The War Department announces its takeover of the PTC system.
Temple University Libraries, Urban Archives, Philadelphia, Pennsylvania

Plate 25. The army restores order in downtown Philadelphia. *Temple University Libraries, Urban Archives, Philadelphia, Pennsylvania*

Plate 26. In a victory at home, a black motorman is trained on a PTC streetcar. *Temple University Libraries, Urban Archives, Philadelphia, Pennsylvania*

Plate 27. Alabama Dry Dock and Shipbuilding Company. *Addsco Collection, University of South Alabama Archives*

Plate 28. Bethlehem Steel Shipyard, Fairfield division. *News American Photo, University of Maryland Photo Services*

Plate 29. Black and white workers at Bethlehem Steel Shipyard, Fairfield division. *News American Photo, University of Maryland Photo Services*

Plate 30. Bethlehem Steel Company, Sparrows Point. *Enoch Pratt Free Library, Baltimore, Maryland*

Plate 31. Earl Browder, general secretary of the Communist Party, at a rally at Union Square, New York, September 24, 1942, calling for the opening of a second front. *Wide World Photos*

Plate 32. Rally at Union Square, New York, September 24, 1942, organized by the New York State Communist Party. *Wide World Photos*

Plate 33. Brown-shirted Nazi sympathizers of the Verein der Saarlanders meet in midtown New York's German section, March 12, 1937. *Wide World Photos*

Plate 34. Nearly one thousand Nazis passed the reviewing stand at the German-American Bund's camp at Sussex Hills, New Jersey, on July 18, 1937. Attending was Dr. Salvatore Caridi of Union City, spokesman for the Italian-American Fascists. *Wide World Photos*

Plate 35. Salinas Assembly Center, California. *Clem Albers photo, March 1942. National Archives, Courtesy of the National Japanese American Historical Society*

Plate 36. Japanese Americans bidding farewell at Tule Lake, California. *Jack Iwata photo. National Archives. Courtesy of the National Japanese American Historical Society*

Plate 37. Evacuee farm hands irrigating crops at Tule Lake, California, September 10, 1942. *National Archives. Courtesy of the National Japanese American Historical Society*

Plate 38. Japanese Peruvians in a Federal High School classroom in Crystal City, Texas, in 1944. *Violet (Nozaki) Tsujimoto. Kanji Nishijima collection. Courtesy of the National Japanese American Historical Society*

Plate 39. The Sashihara family, formerly of Los Angeles, leaving the camp at Heart Mountain, Wyoming. *Hikaru Iwasaki photo, March 1944, National Archives. Courtesy of the National Japanese American Historical Society*

Plate 40. Military recruitment of Japanese American internees in camp at Topaz, Utah.
Courtesy of the National Japanese American Historical Society

Plate 41. Malcolm Ross, the new chairman of the FEPC, is being sworn into office on October 19, 1943, by Justice Henry Edgerton of the U.S. Court of Appeals. Attending the ceremony are Monsignor Francis J. Haas, retiring chairman, and Dr. Frank Graham, public member of the National War Labor Board. *Photo by Roger Smith, OWI. Schomburg Center for Research and Black Culture*

Plate 42. Members of the reorganized policymaking committee of the FEPC at their first meeting in 1943. *Left to right:* Sara Southall, supervisor of employment and service, International Harvester Company, Chicago; P. B. Young Sr., publisher, *Norfolk Journal and Guide;* Samuel Zemurray, president, United Fruit Company; Malcolm Ross, assistant to the chairman; Monsignor Francis J. Haas, chairman; George Johnson, chief investigator; John Brophy, CIO; Milton P. Webster, international vice president, Brotherhood of Sleeping Car Porters; and Boris Shishkin, AFL. *Photo by Roger Smith, OWI. Schomburg Center for Research and Black Culture*

Plate 43. The staff and regional directors gathered for the second annual conference of regional representatives of the FEPC in April 1945. *Standing, left to right:* Elmer Henderson, St. Clair Bourne, unknown, Harry Kingman, Joseph Evans, William McKnight, Theodore Brown, Carlos Castañeda, Edward Lawson, unknown, Milo Manley, Roy Hoglund, unknown, G. James Fleming, Don Ellinger, and unknown. *Seated, left to right:* Clarence Mitchell Jr., Marjorie Lawson, Theodore Jones, Will Maslow, Malcolm Ross, George M. Johnson, John A. Davis, Eugene Davidson, and Maceo Hubbard. *Surlock Studio. Courtesy of Elmer Henderson Papers*

APPENDIX 1

Related Documents

[October 20–21, 1941]

In April of this year, Mr. Knudsen, Director General, and Mr. Hillman, Associate Director General of the O. P. M. sent a letter to all defense contractors making clear the position of the O. P. M. that "Every available source of labor capable of producing defense materials must be tapped in the present emergency."[1]

That letter drew from the President a memorandum to them on June 12 of this year which is really the keystone of our national policy on the subject. I quote that memorandum:

"Memorandum for:

    Hon. William S. Knudsen.

    Hon. Sidney Hillman.

"Complaints have repeatedly been brought to my attention that available and much-needed workers are being barred from defense production solely because of race, religion, or national origin. It is said that at a time when labor stringencies are appearing in many areas qualified workers are being turned from the gates of industry on specifications entirely unrelated to efficiency and productivity; also, that discrimination against Negro workers has been Nation-wide, and other minority racial, national, and religious groups have felt its effects in many localities. This situation is a matter of grave national importance, and immediate steps must be taken to deal with it effectively.

"I note with satisfaction that the Office of Production Management has recognized the seriousness of this situation, and that on April 11, 1941, it addressed a letter on the subject to all holders of defense contracts. As Chief Executive of the Nation, I place the full support of my office behind your statement to the effect that "all holders of defense contracts are urged to examine their employment and training policies at once to determine whether or not these policies make ample provision for the full utilization of available and competent Negro workers. Every available source of labor capable of producing defense materials must be tapped in the present emergency."

"No nation combatting the increasing threat of totalitarianism can afford arbitrarily to exclude large segments of its population from its defense industries. Even more important is it for us to strengthen our unity and morale by refuting at home the very theories which we are fighting abroad."

"Our Government cannot countenance continued discrimination against American citizens in defense production. Industry must take the initiative in opening the doors of employment to all loyal and qualified workers, regardless of race, national origin, religion, or color. American workers, both organized and unorganized, must be prepared to welcome the general and much-needed employment of fellow workers of all racial and nationality origins in defense industries."

"In the present emergency it is imperative that we deal effectively and speedily with this problem. I shall expect the Office of Production Management to take immediate steps to facilitate the full utilization of our productive manpower.

FRANKLIN D. ROOSEVELT"

On June 25, the President issued Executive Order No. 8802 to which I have referred. So that there may be no misunderstanding about its terms, I quote the Order:

"EXECUTIVE ORDER NO. 8802"

REAFFIRMING POLICY OF FULL PARTICIPATION IN THE DEFENSE PROGRAM BY ALL PERSONS, REGARDLESS OF RACE, CREED, COLOR, OR NATIONAL ORIGIN, AND DIRECTING CERTAIN ACTION IN FURTHERANCE OF SAID POLICY.

"WHEREAS it is the policy of the United States to encourage full participation in the national defense program by all citizens of the United States, regardless, of race, creed, color, or national origin, in the firm belief that the democratic way of life within the Nation can be defended successfully only with the help and support of all groups within its borders; and

"WHEREAS there is evidence that available and needed workers have been barred from employment in industries engaged in defense production solely because of consideration of race, creed, color, or national origin, to the detriment of workers' morale and of national unity:

"NOW, THEREFORE, by virtue of the authority vested in my [me] by the Constitution and the statutes, and as a prerequisite to the successful conduct of our national defense production effort, I do hereby reaffirm the policy of the United States that there shall be no discrimination in the employment of workers in defense industries or government because of race, creed, color, or national origin, and I do hereby declare that it is the duty of employers and of labor organizations, in furtherance of said policy and of this order, to provide for the full and equitable participation of all workers in defense industries, without discrimination because of race, creed, color, or national origin;

"And it is hereby ordered as follows:

1. All departments and agencies of the Government of the United States concerned with vocational and training programs for defense production shall take special measures appropriate to assure that such programs are administered without discrimination because of race, creed, color, or national origin;

2. All contracting agencies of the Government of the United States shall include in all defense contracts hereafter negotiated by them a provision obligating the contractor not to discriminate against any worker because of race, creed, color, or national origin;

3. There is established in the Office of Production Management a Committee on Fair Employment Practice, which shall consist of a Chairman and four other members to be appointed by the President. The Chairman and members of the Committee shall serve as such without compensation but shall be entitled to actual and necessary transportation, subsistence and other expenses incidental to performance of their duties. The Committee shall receive and investigate complaints of discrimination in violation of the provisions of this order and shall take appropriate steps to redress grievances which it finds to be valid. The Committee shall also recommend to the several departments and agencies of the Government of the United States and to the President all measures which may be deemed by it necessary or proper to effectuate the provisions of this order.

FRANKLIN D. ROOSEVELT

THE WHITE HOUSE

June 25, 1941.

(F.R. Doc. 41-4544; Filed, June 25, 1941; 12:17 p.m.)"[2]

MS: copy, HqR77, Office Files of Eugene Davidson. Unarranged, Statements.

1. A copy of Hillman's public letter to contractors of April 11, 1941, appears in "A Word from OPM," *Crisis,* 5/41, 151, reprinted in Foner and Lewis, *Black Worker,* 211–12; see also *NAACP Papers* microfilm, 13-B-11. Knudsen had opposed sending out the nondiscrimination letter. He relented when Robert Weaver threatened to resign, but his signature did not appear on the document. The letter also was not entered in the *Federal Register* and had no legal weight. See Kryder, *Divided Arsenal,* 246, note 6; and Kersten, *Race, Jobs, and the War,* 15–16.

2. See *Federal Register* 6, no. 125 (June 27, 1941): 4544. For the instructions developed to implement this order, see Operations Bulletin No. I, President's Committee on Fair Employment Practice, War Manpower Commission, a copy of which is in the F.E.P.C. files, Papers of the NAACP Washington, D.C., Branch, DHU-MS.

Report on Discrimination in the Southwest
by Ernest G. Trimble

[ca. 12/42]

MEMORANDUM TO: MR. LAWRENCE W. CRAMER

FROM: ERNEST G. TRIMBLE

SUBJECT: DISCRIMINATION IN THE SOUTHWEST

This report is a summary of the facts, conclusions and impressions gathered as a result of a stay of ten weeks in the Southwest studying charges of discrimination against workers of Spanish, Mexican and Latin-American extraction in the industries of that region.[1] This study was begun as a result of numerous reports that reached the Committee on Fair Employment Practice alleging that those workers were discriminated against in favor of workers of Anglo-Saxon origin. For convenience sake the latter group will be referred to hereafter in this report as Anglos—the term commonly used in the Southwest—and the former groups will be referred to as Mexicans. Further, the term "industries" is used in a general sense without intending to convey the impression that all employers in the Southwest discriminate against certain employees. The conditions described in this report are believed, however, to obtain pretty generally in the Copper industry and also in many other establishments against whom no individual complaints were received.

The temporary field office of the Committee was opened in El Paso, Texas on July 21 and was closed September 26 [1942]. The office had a staff of two secretaries and four field investigators. Visits were made by our investigators into those industrial areas from which we had received complaints of discrimination. Contacts were made with labor leaders, the individual workers who made complaints, regional offices of the United States Employment Service, interested citizens and the Management of the Companies against whom we had received complaints. Contacts were made with the Management in order to get the employer's side of the cases involving alleged discrimination. Efforts were also made to negotiate with the Management a settlement of the complaints without a public hearing and without any publicity. Our efforts in this respect, however, have so far availed nothing. Negotiations with two companies are still pending.

As a basis for settling the complaints without a public hearing, the companies were asked to implement their obligation to observe Executive Order 8802 by (1) giving instructions to their personnel officers to hire, promote and pay their employees in accordance with the Order, (2) to notify United States Employment Service that they will accept referrals without regard to race, creed, color or national origin, and (3) to notify their employees through the Unions with which they have contracts, or by posting notices on bulletin boards, of the company's intention to observe the terms of the Executive Order.

The companies, however, generally took the position that they could not comply with No. 1 except with the qualification that they would comply with the Executive Order insofar as it could be done "consistent with an efficient and harmonious operation of the plant". The origin of this phrase was attributed by an executive of the Phelps-Dodge Company to Dr. Taylor of the War Labor Board and eventually found its way into the contract which the Phelps-Dodge Company [signed] with the Union. This qualification we have refused to accept.

In addition to complaints of a general nature made by interested citizens and labor leaders, we received approximately one hundred and fifty individual affidavits from employees who felt that they had themselves been discriminated against because of their race, color or national origin in their employment or attempts to get employment. There was also much evidence that discrimination existed or was thought to exist in a number of industrial areas where the workers expressed fear to make a formal complaint lest they be penalized by their employer. This situation prevailed in areas where Unions did not exist, or existed but were too weak to protect, or for other reasons could not protect their members.

We received formal complaints against the following Companies:

Phelps-Dodge—operations scattered throughout Arizona,

(Complaints against following operations:)

Smelter at Douglas, Arizona
Mine at Bisbee
Mine and Smelter at Clifton, Arizona
Refinery at El Paso, Texas
Miami Copper Co., Miami, Arizona
Inspiration Consolidated Copper Co., Inspiration, Arizona
International Smelter & Refining Co., Inspiration, Arizona
Nevada Consolidated Copper Co. at Hurley, New Mexico
    "   "   "   " " Ray, Arizona
United States Potash Co., Carlsbad, New Mexico
McKee Construction Co., El Paso, Texas
United States Post Office, El Paso, Texas

It will be noted that most of the companies against whom we received complaints, are engaged in some phase of the Copper business. All of the big Copper companies are involved. Nevada Consolidated is owned by the Kennecott Company, the biggest producer of copper in the country; Inspiration Copper Company is owned, I believe, by Anaconda, the second largest producer; and Phelps-Dodge, the third largest producer, in most of its operations is involved. The Copper companies against whom we received individual complaints, employ approximately 15,000 men, of whom approximately 5,000, or one-third, are Mexican, Indian and Negro. Because the Mexican workers constitute the bulk of cheap labor for the Copper industry, most of the complaints are from workers of Mexican extraction. With few exceptions, these complainants are citizens, most of them native born.

The complainants allege four kinds of discrimination:

(1) It was alleged that Mexicans were paid lower wages for the same kind and amount of work than Anglo workers were paid.

(2) It was alleged that in order to avoid criticism for the first type of discrimination, employers would sometimes hire new Anglo workers but start breaking them in on jobs paying relatively high wages, instead of starting them on the labor gang and letting them work their way up. When this was done, experienced Mexican workmen would teach the new Anglo how to do his job, after which the Mexican would return to his own position. While the Anglo was being taught his job, he would be receiving a higher rate of pay than his Mexican teacher, and would often after a short time with the company, be advanced to a still better job. The Mexican would remain on the labor gang at his low wage. This scheme, it was alleged, continued the discrimination in a different way.

(3) It was alleged that Mexican employees were not upgraded beyond certain un-attractive jobs paying low wages. These come, therefore, to be known as Mexican jobs, while the better paying jobs became known as Anglo jobs.

(4) There were a few complaints by Negroes that they were denied jobs or promotions because of their race. The number of Negroes, however, in the Copper industry is not large and so the number of Negro complaints was comparatively small.

The companies employing large numbers of Mexican workers were usually accused of the first three types of discrimination. The complainants alleged that often when they applied for a new job or for promotions to higher positions, they were told by the Superintendent that the coveted positions was for Anglos. When they offered any protest about being denied promotions, they were reportedly told, "You do as you are told or get the hell out of here", or "We don't want to hear the Mexican side". When one boy was told that he could not be placed on a certain job because it was for Americans, he replied that he was born in the United States. The foreman is reported to have said, "I don't give a damn if you were born in China, you are still a Mexican". In many cases Mexicans have worked as common laborers for ten, twelve, twenty, or even thirty years without having been promoted. In many cases they have not asked for a promotion because, they said, they "knew there was no use for a Mexican asking for a promotion".

As was explained above, in every case the Management of the Company complained against, was communicated with and given a chance to explain the policy of the Company. The wage differential for the same work was generally denied and failure to upgrade Mexican employees was in some cases denied. When it was denied, examples of a few Mexican employees who were holding well-paying jobs were cited to show they were not discriminated against. Failure to upgrade was, however, admitted in some cases, the Management saying, "Many jobs in the Copper mines are traditionally white and I wouldn't think of putting a Mexican on them". Where the failure to upgrade was admitted, the Management would usually allege that the Unions or the Anglo workers would not work with the Mexicans or accept them into the crafts. The Anglo workers and Union officials, however, would usually put the blame on the Management. It was often difficult, therefore, to place the responsibility for discrimination. In some cases, competition between the A.F. of L. and C.I.O. facilitated discrimination against the Mexican worker and also added to the difficulty of placing the responsibility for such discrimination. This was particularly true, as in the operations of Nevada Consolidated at Hurley, New Mexico, where the upgrading of Mexicans from the labor gang to a skilled or semi-skilled position meant taking them out of the C.I.O. and placing them in A.F. of L. Unions.

It is no doubt true that the competition between these two labor groups, together with the current campaign to unionize the industry, has complicated the situation throughout the Copper industry. In the operations of the Nevada Consolidated at Hurley, New Mexico, referred to above, the Company has a contract with Locals 63 and 69 of the Mine, Mill and Smelter Workers Union which contains a provision that workers shall not be discriminated against "because of race, creed, color or national origin"; it also has a contract with the Chino Metal Trades Council (A.F. of L.) which contains the same non-discriminatory clause except for the term, "national origin", and a contract with two of the Railway Brotherhoods which contains no provision applying the principle of Executive Order 8802. The Phelps-Dodge Corporation at its smelter in Douglas, Arizona, has a contract with the Mine, Mill and Smelter Workers Union (C.I.O.) which does not contain this prohibition, but has a seniority clause providing for the promotion of employees on a basis of merit and seniority, which, if applied strictly, would have the effect of applying the Executive Order. The rest of the Phelps-Dodge operations, except the refinery at El Paso, have contracts with A.F. of L. Unions, all of which I am told contains a non-discrimination clause, except for the term "national origin". The Phelps-Dodge refinery at El Paso, Texas is in the process of negotiating a contract with the Mine, Mill and Smelter Workers Union (C.I.O.). The Miami Copper Company and the Inspiration Copper Company have both recently had labor board elections conducted but as yet do not have contracts with unions. The operations of the Nevada Consolidated at Ray, Arizona, have no contract with a labor union, although I believe an organizing campaign is on. Most of the individual complaints which we have received, however, were made since these union contracts have been in operation.

CONCLUSIONS

To pass judgment on the individual complaints which we have received would require that one formulate an opinion without having heard all the evidence. However, the writer feels that certain tentative conclusions can safely be drawn as to the situation in the Southwest generally relative to discrimination. Such conclusions are, he believes, justified by uncontroverted evidence and by admissions on the part of some employers. These conclusions are:

1. There is a general pattern of social and economic discrimination against people of Mexican extraction throughout the Southwest. In the field of industry the discrimination takes the following forms:

   (a) General failure to upgrade Mexican workers beyond certain low-paying jobs. This is true in spite of some "token" employment of Mexicans on comparatively well-payed jobs.

   (b) There has been and still is, to some extent, a practice of paying Mexican workers a lower rate of pay for the same work or work that is so slightly different as not to furnish any reasonable basis for a wage differential; in other words, artificial classification of jobs is used to justify paying the Mexican employees a lower rate of pay for the same work.

   (c) Companies employing both Mexicans and Anglos segregate them. Applicants for jobs are placed in two groups, one for Anglos, the other for Mexicans and Negroes. They are separated similarly when they receive their pay. Separate toilet facilities are provided for the two groups of employees, and where recreational facilities are provided at all by the employer, separate facilities are maintained.

   (d) New Anglo employees are often brought in from the outside and are started on high-paying jobs and are broken in by experienced Mexican employees instead of the Mexican employees themselves being promoted to fill the positions.

2. There is present among employers, too, a belief that Mexicans are an inferior people; that they cannot assume responsibility, that they are not sufficiently advanced to use additional income wisely, and that they do not have the mentality to advance very high in the educational process. It is difficult to determine whether this is an honest belief or merely a defense mechanism to justify treating them as an inferior people.

3. There is a universal feeling among the Mexican employees (and among Anglos who are sympathetic with the demand of Mexicans for equal treatment), that they are discriminated against and do not have an equal chance of advancement with the Anglos.

4. This feeling among the Mexican employees has without a doubt resulted in a lowering of morale, and provides fertile ground for enemy and subversive propaganda. Loyal Mexican workers reported that they were laughed at by Communists and Fascists alike for wanting to be good Americans. They are told that this is a land of equal opportunity and are being asked to sacrifice their lives if need be for their country and yet in their daily efforts to earn a living are having it impressed upon them that there is not equality in opportunity. As was indicated above, many of them have been discriminated against for so long that they have lost hope of being able to get out of the common laborers class regardless of their efforts. In short, the worker tends to become

   > "A thing that grieves not and that never hopes,
   > Stolid and stunned, a brother to the ox".[2]

RECOMMENDATION

The writer is convinced that the employment practices of the industries of the Southwest have become so traditional and the Companies complained against have for so long dominated the political as well as the economic life of their communities, that it will be difficult to get them to change their ways. The one thing that they seem to fear and the one thing that inspires hope on the part of the employees, is the prospect of a public hearing at which the practices of the industries would be exposed. The writer believes that the mere opening of the office in El Paso had a beneficial effect. Quite a few Mexican workers were promoted during the period that the office was maintained. Many of these men had filed complaints with us. Several local employees were promoted the day following their having filed complaints with us. One company against which we had complaints, and which had previously maintained three wage scales for its common laborers—two of which were below the average for the industry—abolished the lower two scales, thus raising all of its laborers, most of whom are Mexicans, up to the standard wage for laborers. These changes the local labor leaders attributed to our presence in the field. The writer further believes that the chief obstacle to getting a satisfactory settlement of these complaints without a hearing was the belief held by some of the Executives of the Copper companies—a belief that apparently had been formed on information secured in Washington—that a public hearing would not be held. It is therefore firmly recommended that such a public hearing be held in El Paso, Texas or in Phoenix, Arizona.

MS: copy, HqR19, Records Related to Hearings. Mining.

1. Dating of this text is based on the receipt date stamped on the text and on the time of Trimble's investigations in 1942.

For reports on subsequent FEPC investigations of the mining industry, see Mitchell's memorandum of 7/17/44 and the enclosed report by Stanley D. Metzger. For additional background on discrimination in the Southwest, see the headnotes on Mexican Americans, on the Mining Industry, and on the Oil Industry.

2. This quotation is from Edwin Markham's poem "The Man with the Hoe" (1899).

Executive Order No. 9346, Further Amending Executive Order No. 8802 by Establishing a New Committee on Fair Employment Practice and Defining Its Powers and Duties

EXECUTIVE ORDER
#9346

[May 27, 1943]¹

FURTHER AMENDING EXECUTIVE ORDER NO. 8802 BY ESTABLISHING A NEW COMMITTEE ON FAIR EMPLOYMENT PRACTICE AND DEFINING ITS POWERS AND DUTIES

In order to establish a new Committee on Fair Employment Practice, to promote the fullest utilization of all available manpower, and to eliminate discriminatory employment practices, Executive Order No. 8802 of June 25, 1941, as amended by Executive Order No. 8823 of July 18, 1941, is hereby further amended to read as follows:

"WHEREAS the successful prosecution of the war demands the war demands the maximum employment of all available workers regardless of race, creed, color, or national origin; and

"WHEREAS it is the policy of the United States to encourage full participation in the war effort by all persons in the United States regardless of race, creed, color, or national origin, in the firm belief that the democratic way of life within the nation can be defended successfully only with the help and support of all groups within its borders; and

"WHEREAS there is evidence that available and needed workers have been barred from employment in industries engaged in war production solely by reason of their race, creed, color, or national origin, to the detriment of the prosecution of the war, the workers' morale, and national unity:

"NOW, THEREFORE, by virtue of the authority vested in me by the Constitution and statutes, and as President of the United States and Commander in Chief of the Army and Navy, I do hereby reaffirm the policy of the United States that there shall be no discrimination in the employment of any person in war industries or in Government by reason of race, creed, color, or national origin, and I do hereby declare that it is the duty of all employers, including the several Federal departments and agencies, and all labor organizations, in furtherance of this policy and of this Order, to eliminate discrimination in regard to hire, tenure, terms or conditions of employment, or union membership because of race, creed, color, or national origin.

"It is hereby ordered as follows:

"1. All contracting agencies of the Government of the United States shall include in all contracts hereafter negotiated or renegotiated by them a provision obligating the contractor not to discriminate against any employee or applicant for employment because of race, creed, color, or national origin and requiring him to include a similar provision in all subcontracts.

"2. All departments and agencies of the Government of the United States concerned with vocational and training programs for war production shall take all measures appropriate to assure that such programs are administered without discrimination because of race, creed, color, or national origin.

"3. There is hereby established in the Office for Emergency Management of the Executive Office of the President a Committee on Fair Employment Practice, hereinafter referred to as the Committee, which shall consist of a Chairman and not more than six other members to be appointed by the President. The Chairman shall receive such salary as shall be fixed by the President not exceeding $10,000 per year. The other members of the Committee shall receive necessary traveling expenses and, unless their compensation is otherwise prescribed by the President, a per diem allowance not exceeding twenty-five dollars per day and subsistence expenses on such days as they are actually engaged in the performance of duties pursuant to this Order.

"4. The Committee shall formulate policies to achieve the purpose of this Order and shall make recommendations to the various Federal departments and agencies and to the President which it deems necessary and proper to make effective the provisions of this Order. The Committee shall also recommend to the Chairman of the War Manpower Commission appropriate measures for bringing about the full utilization and training of manpower in and for war production without discrimination because of race, creed, color, or national origin.

"5. The Committee shall receive and investigate complaints of discrimination forbidden by this Order. It may conduct hearings make findings of fact, and take appropriate steps to obtain elimination of such discrimination.

"6. Upon the appointment of the Committee and the designation of its Chairman, the Fair Employment Practice Committee established by Executive Order No. 8802 of June 25, 1941, hereinafter referred to as the old Committee, shall cease to exist. All records and property of the old Committee and such unexpended balances of allocations or other funds available for its use as the Director of the Bureau of the Budget shall determine shall be transferred to the Committee. The Committee shall assume jurisdiction over all complaints and matters pending before the old Committee and shall conduct such investigations and hearings as may be necessary in the performance of its duties under this Order.

"7. Within the limits of the funds which may be made available for that purpose, the Chairman shall appoint and fix the compensation of such personnel and make provision for such supplies, facilities and services as may be necessary to carry out this Order. The Committee may utilize the services and facilities of other Federal departments and agencies and such voluntary and uncompensated services as may from time to time be needed. The Committee may accept the services of State and local authorities and officials, and may perform the functions and duties and exercise the powers conferred upon it by this Order through such officials and agencies and in such manner as it may determine.

"8. The Committee shall have the power to promulgate such rules and regulations as may be appropriate or necessary to carry out the provisions of this Order.

"9. The provisions of any other pertinent Executive order inconsistent with this Order are hereby superseded."

FRANKLIN D. ROOSEVELT

THE WHITE HOUSE,
May 27, 1943

MS: copy, NAACP, II A 269, DLC.

1. This executive order appeared in *Federal Register* 8, no. 106 (May 29, 1943): 7183–84.

Field Investigation Report on Alabama Dry Dock and Shipbuilding Company by Ernest G. Trimble and Clarence Mitchell Jr.

PRESIDENT'S COMMITTEE ON FAIR EMPLOYMENT PRACTICE
WASHINGTON, D. C.

FIELD INVESTIGATION REPORT

Date of Report -June 8, 1943

Names of Fair Practice Examiners -Ernest G. Trimble

Clarence M. Mitchell

Name of Company - - - - - - - - - - - - - -Alabama Dry Dock and Shipbuilding Company

Dates of Contract -May 27 to May 31 inclusive

Names and Titles of Persons Conferred with—

Captain Walter K. Graham
U. S. Maritime Commission

Burton R. Morley
Area Director
War Manpower Commission

David R. Dunlap
President
J. W. Griser
Vice President
W. T. Daly
Personnel Manager
Alabama Dry Dock and
Shipbuilding Company

Charles Hansen
J. L. Bouche
Elijah Jackson
Industrial Union of Marine and
Shipbuilding Workers of America, C.I.O

Total Number of Persons Employed -29,315

Total Number of Negroes Employed -6,750

Semi-skilled -1,930

Unskilled -4,820

Name of Union -Industrial Union of Marine
and Shipbuilding Workers
Method of Training -VTWW and In-plant Training

SUMMARY OF BACKGROUND MATERIAL

The Alabama Dry Dock and Shipbuilding Company is located at Mobile, Alabama. On November 19, 1942, the President's Committee on Fair Employment Practice sent a directive to the company instructing it to cease and desist from discriminatory hiring practices against Negroes.[1] The Company states that its first effort was made to upgrade Negroes from laboring jobs to chipping and caulking. At this time there was some friction, but the Management and the Union overcame it.

The second step in the plan to comply came on May 24, 1943, when the company placed twelve Negro welders on the night shift as part of a plan to expand its Negro labor force and to make use of Negroes in this trade for the first time. This move on the part of the company was accompanied by mob action on the part of white employees to drive Negroes from the yard.

At the time of the violence on the part of the white workers none of the Negro welders were on the job. On May 27, Messrs. Ernest G. Trimble and Clarence Mitchell, Principal Fair Practice Examiners, left Washington to represent the President's Committee in conferences with the company in Mobile. This move to send the Committee representatives to Alabama was taken following a telephone conversation between Mr. Lawrence W. Cramer, Executive Secretary for the Committee, and Mr. Daniel S. Ring, Director of Shipyard Labor Relations, Maritime Commission.

The bargaining agent for employees at the plant is the Industrial Union of Marine and Shipbuilding Workers of America, C. I. O. The IUMSWA was chosen to represent employees in an NLRB election held on April 23, 1942. At that time 8,968 persons were eligible to vote. The following returns were tabulated:

C.I.O. -3,080
Metal Trades Council, A.F. of L. - - - - - - - - - -1,254
No Union -117
Void Ballots -37

On February 28, 1943, a second NLRB election was held for the company guards and firemen. In this voting the results were as follows: 402 voting for the C. I. O.; 10 voting against the C.I.O.; and 1 ballot was challenged. There were 547 persons eligible to vote.

The following information concerning the company's hiring needs was obtained from the United States Employment Service 270 reports.

January, 1943

Total employment - - - - - - - - - - - - - - - -25,792
Non-white -5,237

Skilled Non-white -0

Semi-skilled Non-white - - - - - - - - - - - - -1,056

Unskilled non-white - - - - - - - - - - - - - - - -4,181

May, 1943

Total employment - - - - - - - - - - - - - - -29,315

Non-white -6,750

Skilled Non-white -0

Semi-skilled Non-white - - - - - - - - - - - - -1,930

Unskilled Non-white - - - - - - - - - - - - - - -4,820

ANTICIPATED HIRES BY OCCUPATION FOR

SIX MONTHS PERIOD BEGINNING JANUARY, 1943

OCCUPATION	OCC. CODE NO.	JANUARY	MARCH
TOTAL		11,476	11,075
Clerical, sales & service	1-00.000	695	100
Unskilled	8-00.000	3,095	2,000
Anglesmith	4-86.010	8	
Welder, Electric (arc)	4-16.212	3,525	2,000
Boilermaker	4-83.100	300	
Welder, arc.	4-85.020	500	1,000
Boilermaker helper	6-93.411	125	
Acetylene burner opr.	6-85.215	200	400
Welding & flame cutter	4-x6.214	200	600
Carpenter, ship	5-25.640	8	
Steelplate caulker	6-84.910	25	
Chipper	6-78.925	200	585
Electrician, reapiring motors, etc.	4-x6.167	600	150
Electrician, ship	4-97.210	300	300
Pipefitter II	5-30.010	125	
Metal plumbing, installing	4-x6.311	200	
Shipfitter	4-84.012	200	1,100
Heavy metal structural assembly	4-x6.301	675	1,000
Machinist, outside	4-75.150	50	250
Sheetmetal worker	4-88.622	100	100
Light metal structural assembly, etc.	4-x6.303	145	
Rigger, ship	5-05.570	125	450
Loftsman	5-17.210	25	25
Coppersmith	4-80.080	50	15

Machinist II	4-75.010	150
Tank tester	4-84.110	50
Pipefitter	5-30.015	800

MEETING OF MAY 27 WITH COLORED LEADERS, MOBILE, ALABAMA

On the above date a meeting was held with the following colored leaders concerning the Alabama Dry Dock and Shipbuilding Company labor troubles: Mr. Conrad Dean, who is a member of the CIO and employee of the Alabama Dry Dock and Shipbuilding Company; Mr. Sherman Guy, 456 Cedar Street, who heads the Boilermakers Colored Auxiliary of the A.F. of L.; Dr. E. T. Belsaw, 502½ Dauphin Street, and Mr. Clarence Mitchell, representing the President's Committee on Fair Employment Practice.

The meeting was held at Dr. Belsaw's home at Mr. Mitchell's request. He informed the labor representatives that in view of the trouble that had occurred at the yard their cooperation was needed in working out a settlement. Dr. Belsaw also took this position, and, because of his prominence in the community, was able to sell the two men on the idea of close cooperation with comparative ease.

Mr. Dean said that the men at the yard who were upgraded to jobs as chippers and caulkers a month prior to May 25, worked without any trouble at all. I asked these men what they thought could be done to adjust the situation satisfactorily and provide for the return of the workers to the yard. From my discussion with these gentlemen I reached the conclusion that so far as the citizens of Mobile were concerned the plan which was finally worked out would be satisfactory to most of them. It is to be expected that there will be some who may raise an objection, but it is expected that the majority of the workers will agree with the solution.

We then discussed the protection of those who were working in the yard. It was the concensus of opinion at the meeting that the Commanding Officer in charge of the troops in the yard should make a public statement showing that the soldiers were there to protect lives as well as property, Dr. Belsaw stated that he had been asked to assist in doing something about the disturbance by a number of persons interested in interracial goodwill. One of these he said was a Reverend Satterlee, Rector of an Episcopal Church in the community. Dr. Belsaw said that he declined to join with those working on the interracial end of the program because he felt that the Ministers and others did not know too much about what they were doing. Dr. Belsaw is perhaps the best known colored man in the community of Mobile. (In a later discussion with Mr. R. B. Chandler, publisher of the Mobile Press-Register newspapers, I received some indication of the high regard which white persons in the community have for Dr. Belsaw.) All of the men agreed that it would be a great mistake to remove Federal troops until the situation has been thoroughly settled.

There were many rumors in Mobile that colored persons had been killed during the disturbance at the yard. However, Mr. Clifton McKinnis, 362 Cubis Street, has the embalming business for the colored employees at the Alabama Dry Dock and Ship-building Company. Mr. McKinnis has his establishment at 600 St. Francis Street, the Johnson & Allen Funeral Home. He stated that he had received no bodies from the yard, and as far as he had been able to determine from officials of the City Morgue, no deaths had occurred. I was in his funeral parlor daily and at no time did I see any bodies from the yard.

MEETING ON ALABAMA DRY DOCK AND SHIPBUILDING COMPANY AT AREA MANPOWER OFFICE — 9:00 A. M.

At 9:00 A. M. on May 28, the following persons met at the Area Office of the War Manpower Commission in the annex of the First National Bank Building: Com-mander Hal T. Wright, representing the Navy Department; Captain W. K. Graham of the U. S. Army, but representing the Maritime Commission; Mr. Burton Moreley, Area Director of the War Manpower Commission; Mr. Ernest G. Trimble and Mr. Clarence Mitchell, representing the President's Committee on Fair Employment Practice.

As near as it could be determined, the racial conflict at the company began on May 25, at 9:30 A. M. Twelve welders had been assigned to work on the night shift on May 24. This was in keeping with the plans of the company as announced to the War Manpower Commission in a letter dated May 22. The sequence of this correspon-dence resulting in the letter of May 22, will be mentioned later in this statement.

According to Captain Graham, between 8 and 10 persons were injured. (Later FEPC investigations place the injured at approximately 50.) There were many reports of the killing of some colored persons. None of those present had any information to verify such reports of fatalities. (FEPC investigations revealed no deaths.) According to Commander Wright and Captain Graham, approximately twelve Negro welders worked on the night shift on May 24. After these men went home, the rioting broke out at 9:30 A. M. on Tuesday, May 25, but no Negro welders were involved. At the time the trouble began, Commander Wright stated, the working situation was no different from what it has been for the last forty years. (Later this was verified by the com-pany.) Negroes were working in unskilled and helper's capacities only, with the ex-ception of a few chippers and caulkers. Captain Graham said that the company had planned to have a separate way for Negroes and the employment of the welders on the night shift was the first step in meeting the requirement of the plan. (FEPC in-vestigations found this to be slightly inaccurate.) The Captain also stated that two thousand five hundred additional welders are needed at the yard. If these require-ment are to be met, he said, it is urgent that Negroes be used as welders.

Mr. Morley stated that he had been instructed by Dr. B. F. Ashe, Regional Director of the War Manpower Commission in Atlanta, to take the position that the company was not necessarily complying with the requirements of Executive Order 8802 when it employed welders. He stated that Dr. Ashe had talked with company officials con-cerning the use of Negroes on a separate way. Mr. Morley gave the following sequence of correspondence between his office and the Alabama Dry Dock and Ship-building Company:

May 3, 1943 - - - - -A letter from Mr. Morley to Mr. John Griser, Vice President and General Manager, ADDSCO. This letter expressed approval on part of the War Manpower Commission of the plan for employing Negroes on a separate way.

May 20, 1943 - - - - -Mr. Morley again communicated with the company requesting an answer to his letter of May 3.

May 22, 1943 - - - - -Mr. D. C. Knerr, Manager, ADDSCO, wrote to Mr. Morley saying that on Monday, May 24, the company intended to place crews of Negro welders on the third shift on ways 1, 2, 3, and 4. Mr. Morley responded on the plan and stated he would not take the responsi-bility of any of the developments, resulting from the action.

May 28, 1943 - - - - -Mr. Morley wired to Mr. W. T. Daly, Employment Manager of the yard, stating that workers requesting releases were entitled to get them under the area stabilization plan. He cited paragraph IV-A, of the plan, which requires the employer to grant a certificate of sepa-ration to the workers who terminate their employment.

Under the agreement, this certificate of separation is supposed to be granted within 24 hours, after the person requests it. However, the section also provides that no employee shall leave his employment pending action on his request for separation.

Commander Wright stated that in his opinion the trouble at the yard could be summarized by the statement that most of the new white workers were opposed to having Negroes in any skilled capacity in the yard. He said that in his opinion it was not a question of whether the Negroes were put on separate ways or whether they were to be integrated with the whites. So far as some of the whites were concerned, as he put it, "They are not satisfied to work with Negro mechanics in the yard regardless of where the Negroes are — even if they are 10 miles away". Both Captain Graham and Commander Wright expressed an opinion that there was some subversive activ-ity going on in the yard which was causing the trouble. In response to a direct ques-tion, however, Commander Wright took the position that it was absolutely necessary that Negro skilled workers be used in the yard. Captain Graham took a similar posi-tion. He also stated that since approximately 2,500 additional welders would be needed for work in the yard, it was inescapable that a great many Negroes would be taken on the force. Mr. Morley countered by saying that he had never had a clear statement from the yard about its hiring needs and in his opinion it might be diffi-cult for the Alabama Dry Dock and Shipbuilding Company to prove that it was in need of 2,500 welders. This precipitated a brief discussion between Captain Graham and Mr. Morley. Captain Graham and Commander Wright took the position that the company was accurate in its estimates of its needs.

From the discussion that ensued we got the impression that there were some dif-ferences between the opinion of the Maritime Commission and Navy Department representatives, and the War Manpower Commission representative, Mr. Morley.

We then came to a discussion of the meeting which was shceduled [scheduled] in the morning between company officials, union representatives and Maritime Commission representatives. This meeting was set for 10:00 A. M. The representatives of the President's Committee on Fair Employment Practice stated that they would like to be present at this meeting in order to work on the agreement which presembly would be reached concerning the employment and upgrading of Negroes. Captain Graham expressed the opinion that this would not be necessary because the intention was to hold the number of persons participating in the meeting to an absolute minimum. Commander Wright also took this position and Dr. Morley mentioned that the War Manpower Commission would be represented when he was present. Mr. Mitchell took the position that the War Manpower Commission area representative could not express the views of the President's Committee on Fair Employment Practice. He also stated that if an attempt was made to hold a meeting without representatives of the President's Committee on Fair Employment Practice present, the agreement would not be considered one which was binding and we would have a meeting of our own with the company officials. Mr. Trimble called the company's attorney and reminded him that the company had an obligation to the Committee; called his attention to the meeting being held without the representatives being present; and told him that we desired a meeting with the company officials. During the lunch hour Mr. Trimble discussed the matter with Captain Graham. He informed Captain Graham that the representatives of the President's Committee on Fair Employment Practice would not recommend the approval of any settlement if the Committee's representatives had not had access to the facts and opinions on which the settlement was based. (As a result of these positions which were taken by the Committee's representatives, we were notified to attend the meeting which is discussed at length in a later section of this report.)

Further discussion of releases arose. Mr. Mitchell took the position that the War Manpower Commission could not grant Negro and white workers releases simply because there had been a disturbance. Mr. Morley said that the Commission was powerless to insist that any persons work at the yard under the terms of the area stabilization agreement. Mr. Mitchell asked Mr. Morley to name one section of the agreement which would permit workers to leave the yard because of the current conditions. Mr. Morley said that any worker who is off the job for a seven-day period through no fault of his own was entitled to a release. Mr. Mitchell pointed out that the trouble occurred on Tuesday; that the meeting was being held on Friday; and that only 4 days had elapsed, so that even under the seven-day provision, none of the workers were yet entitled to releases. The area stabilization agreement carries provisions that workers who seek separations must continue on the job until their cases have been reviewed by the War Manpower Commission. Since the white workers were not on the job and had not observed the requirement that they remain on duty, they too were not entitled to the right of obtaining a release. Mr. Mitchell advised Mr. Morley against encouraging Negroes to obtain releases from their employment at the yard. Here it should be said that Mr. Morley frequently allured to the fact that "other" work was available for Negroes but colored persons were not taking it.

It should be kept in mind that according to the reports which we received from Mr. Cy W. Record when he was reviewing the Mobile situation, Mr. Morley had repeatedly taken the position that Negroes should be satisfied with the kind of work that could be given them and not attempt to be upgraded until the whites were ready for them to be used in higher types of jobs.

The meeting ended when Mr. Morley and Captain Graham left for the morning session with the company and union officials at the shipyard.

LIST OF COLORED WELDERS AT
ALABAMA DRY DOCK AND SHIPBUILDING COMPANY

NAME	BADGE NUMBER
T. E. Latham	24941*
W. Edwards	26723
J. George	22100
A. T. Williams	21811*
L. Tucker	22990
E. R. Shephard	22768
J. J. Smith	21317
J. C. Snow	22436
H. Haynes	22052
P. Hampton	20156
J. Callen	24798

* Welded as late as 5–29–43

STATEMENTS BY WITNESSES

(Made to FEPC Representatives)

1. Mrs. Alice Gamble
555 Short Cedar Street

Mrs. Gamble stated that on the morning of May 25, at about 9:00 A.M., she was working on what she described as "No. 6 and 7" in the ship construction section of the Alabama Dry Dock and Shipbuilding Company. Her duties were to sweep off iron. According to Mrs. Gamble, she did not know anything about a disturbance of any kind until two colored men passed her running. These men told her that she should leave because some trouble had started. Before she could get away, Mrs. Gamble stated, she was struck in the back by some white person. She started to run and continued to do so under a hil [hail?] of missiles of various kinds. Mrs. Gamble was asked what the white persons had said to her and she stated that one said, "Get going, Nigger. This is our shipyard". Mrs.

Gamble stated that she had a minor injury of the back and was willing to return to work if she could be certain of Federal protection. She did not know of any person who was killed during the upheaval.

2. **Mr. Jesse Aubrey**
457 Ingay Street
Mr. Aubrey stated that he was working as a carpenter's helper for A.B.C. Steel. He said he was present on what he called "248". Other persons around him were laborers and sweepers, Mr. Aubrey said. The first thing he saw, according to his statement, was a group of whites going off their jobs and congregating at the end of a slip. He stated that they "closed up the end of the dock". According to Mr. Aubrey, approximately 4,000 persons with pipes, clubs and everything, as he put it, that was "killable" were in the group. Mr. Aubrey stated that he though[t] the whites were striking for more money. According to his statement, a white man knocked a colored man and woman into the river. Mr. Aubrey said that he did not see either of these persons come up again. (A close investigation of his statement failed to reveal any indication that two persons were drowned as his statement implied).

Mr. Aubrey said that his white foreman shut him in a locker for safety around 9:30 or 9:45 A. M. The disturbance became greater and the foreman evidently left because Mr. Aubrey stated he remained in this locker until 1:30 P. M. when an electrician who was tracing a wire looked into the locker and saw him there. The white electrician turned him over to the Guards, and he was escorted from the yard without injury. Mr. Aubrey said he did not know the persons who appeared to have been knocked into the river, but the women looked to be about 30 and the man seemed to be about 35. In response to further questioning, Mr. Aubrey stated that he has a son and two brothers in the Army. One of his brothers is in Australia and the other is in North Africa. Mr. Aubrey said that one of the statements he heard a white person make was "put those God dam buckets and brooms down, Niggers". Although the colored persons did not fight, the white persons beat them anyway, Mr. Aubrey told the Committee's investigators.

3. **Mrs. Eliza Vincent**
460 Bizelle Street
Mrs. Vincent said that on the morning of May 25, she was picking up paper on one of the ships. She stated that her job is that of a laborer. Someone told her that the white persons employed by the company were striking. Then a man ran by who appeared to have been injured and told her that a fight was going on. She stated that the foreman said that all of the colored workers were to leave for safety. She did not imply that the foreman was doing this for any reason other than to protect the people in her immediate vicinity. Mrs. Vincent stated that she ran through a crowd of whites and they showered her with sticks and bricks. She stated that she saw one colored man struck and knocked down with a piece of iron. She did not know who he was. Mrs. Vincent stated that she would be willing to return to work at the yard if her safety could be

guaranteed. She also stated that she was struck in the back and had been hurt but did not receive any medical attention.

4. Mrs. Evelyn Walker
460 Bizelle Street

Mrs. Walker gave a brief statement indicating that at the time of the disturbance she was picking up paper. The first she heard of any difficulty was from other colored persons who said that trouble was developing. She said she would not be willing to go back to the yard unless adequate protection could be given to her. She also stated that she did not expect to return any way because she hoped to come to Washington to join her husband.

5. Mr. L. T. Welch
463 Bizelle Street

Mr. Welch stated that on the morning of May 25, he was working in the engine room of a ship. He is classified as a laborer. Mr. Welch stated that did not see any disturbance but a colored man came to him and told him that there was a fight in progress. Shortly after that a white man walked up to him and said, "Nigger, jar the ground". Mr. Welch added that the white man then said, "Every Nigger on this boat get off". Mr. Welch said that he was cut off from escape but went down any way. Just as he got to the ground level from the job, 10 white men were beating another colored man, he said. One of them threw a board at him (Mr. Welch) which struck him in the eye causing an injury. Mr. Welch is married and has one child. One of his brothers is in the Army at Camp Wheeler. He states that he did not see any colored persons killed.

6. Mr. William Welch
962 Davis Avenue

Mr. Welch stated that he is a pusher in the labor gang. According to his statement he came out of the hull of the ship to get some rags with which to soak up some water. A white man interfered with him as he was about to get the rags. Mr. Welch stated the white man told him to "Get the Hell away". Mr. Welch said he asked his foreman whether he might leave the yard because there seemed to be some disturbance. The foreman refused to let him go, but when the situation became worse he (Mr. Welch) decided he had better get the other colored employees out. As he attempted to leave the scene of the disturbance, Mr. Welch stated, he was attacked by three white men one of whom hit him in the chest with a piece of iron. Mr. Welch stated further, "Then a white lady hit me over the head with a broom handle". Mr. Welch stated that he did not see any colored persons killed. He is married and has two nephews in the Army. Both of them are still in this country. He has worked at the company since April 6, 1942.

7. Mr. Warren Robinson
412 N. Franklin Street

Mr. Robinson stated that he works with the riggers. On the morning of May 25, according to his story, he was down in the engine room of a ship when a white man said, "Boy, you had better get out of here. They are raising Hell out there". As he attempted to run from the scene, Mr. Robinson said, a white man tried to hit him with a piece of iron. Mr. Robinson succeeded in blocking the blow with his arm, but this caused an injury which necessitated treatment. He is married, but does not live with his wife. Mr. Robinson also said that he did not see any colored persons killed.

8. Mr. Thomas Johnson
402 Clairborne Street

Mr. Johnson stated that on the morning of May 25, he was picking up trash for a clean up gang. He states that he saw 8 or 10 white men chasing a colored man. He said that he thought it simply one of the usual disturbances that occur between white and colored persons in some parts of the South and did not investigate it. Later, he said, four of five whites began beating up a colored woman. At that point, Mr. Johnson stated, he decided it would be better to run away. He was struck but apparently was not seriously hurt. Mr. Johnson has a son in the Army who is at present somewhere in a theatre of action.

9. Mr. Adam Thomas
361½ N. Broad Street

Mr. Thomas stated that he was working with a rod gang pulling up cables on what he said was A-7 Deck. He said the first indication he had of any trouble was when he saw three colored women running. There were four or five white women throwing various missiles at them. Mr. Thomas stated he also heard a white man yell, "No Nigger can put iron together here". He stated that he stayed on the boat until the soldiers came, but was not injured. He did not know any whites who participated and did not see any colored persons killed.

10. Mr. Willie Wiggam
402 N. Franklin Street

Mr. Wiggam stated that on the morning of the riot he was working on what he described as the last pier, when the disturbance reached its height. He stated that a brick thrown by some unknown person struck him in the head. He said that he has not been back to work since the disturbance. He began his employment in the yard in September 1942.

11. Mr. Moses Summer
402 Cleveland Street

Mr. Summers stated that he was working with a contractor as a painter when the disturbance occurred. He stated that a guard told him that he had better run. He was able to find protection and was not injured. He returned to work on Thursday, May 27, however.

12. Mr. Zenith Dock
90 Chicapin Street

Mr. Dock stated that he works in the yard as a chipper. His employment in the yard itself began 10 months ago but he was upgraded two months ago. According to his statement he was busily engaged in his duties when whites attacked him and beat him about the head and shoulders. Mr. Dock's head was bandaged and he stated that he had two large scalp wounds. He also had two three inch lacerations on his check and contusions on his upper lip.

According to his statement, a number of white men were beating him while he was lying on the ground and he feels his life was saved by a Mr. Bailey, white, who intervened in his behalf. When the white man tried to protect him, Mr. Dock stated, the rioters attacked the white man and Mr. Dock was able to escape. Mr. Dock was not certain that the white individual who came to his rescue was named "Bailey", and it may be that this person was another white individual by the name of Davis who also was injured.

13. **Mr. A. Greene**
652 Peach Street
Mr. Green stated that he began work at the Alabama Dry Dock and Shipbuilding Company on January 9, 1943. At the time of the disturbance, he stated, he was on a tanker pulling rods. This is a laboring classification. He stated that he had "pulled 5 or 6 rods" for white men with whom he was working when , as he put it, the whites began "raising cain". He did not state exactly what happened from then on, but he did say that one white man ran by him and struck him and then another. Altogether six white men struck him, Mr. Green stated. A white man named Albert Odd got him out of his difficulties, Mr. Green stated. He had head injuries, and according to his story, the doctor who treated him advised him not to return to work until he makes a second visit.

14. **Mr. Frank Thomas**
756 Elmira Street
Mr. Thomas stated that he had been at the yard since April 13, 1943. His job is that of a laborer and cleaner. When the disturbance began he stated that he was on top of a ship. He said he saw a number of people looking over the rails and then saw a number of colored people running. Mr. Thomas thought that it was just a usual disturbance so he went back to work. He had not been working long when a colored man walked up to him and told him he had better get off because there was a fight going on. He stated that as he was attempting to follow the colored man's suggestion, a white man struck him in the face and knocked out his glasseye. He stated another white man was getting ready to hit him when someone attracted the would be assailant's attention. Mr. Thomas was able to escape.

15. **Mr. Charles Williams**
506 Liveoak Street
Mr. Williams stated that during the disturbance he was kicked severely in the groin and beaten about the face and head. He did not have a clear picture of how the trouble started.

16. **Mr. R. Roland Hobdy**
1355 Hercules Street
Mr. Hobdy stated that he is working in the personnel department under Mr. R. H. Bailey. Mr. Hobdy was one of the persons who was supposed to have

disappeared, and there was a rumor that he had been killed. According to his story, when he reported for work he noticed that there was a general "tenseness" on Tuesday morning. He said that he felt things were not safe and had told other colored workers of his views. White persons chased him when the disturbance started and threw a number of bricks in a building where he was hiding but did not catch him. He explained his alleged disappearance by saying that he had spoken at a meeting urging the colored workers to return to their jobs. After that he left for Selma, Alabama, and did not return immediately.

17. Mrs. Virginia Richardson
1214 Davis Avenue

Mr. J. L. LeFlore of the National Association for the Advancement of Colored People said he interviewed Mrs. Richardson and found that she was working on a deck of a ship when the disturbance occurred. As she was trying to escape, Mr. LeFlore said, a white man threw a piece of iron at her and struck her in the pelvic region. She is now in the hospital and Mr. LeFlore states that it is believed her pelvis is broken.

18. Mr. Harold Joseph Love
1112 Rotterdam Street

Mr. Victor Bernstein representing PM newspaper, called me concerning Mr. Love's case. He stated that the complainant said that he was climbing a ladder on one of the ships on Thursday, May 27, when a white man struck him over the head with a hammer. Mr. Bernstein stated that the complainant said he was unconscious for 1½ hours. I gave the company the name of this man and an investigation is promised.

19. Mr. J. Calhoun
306 Armstead Street

Mr. Calhoun stated that he was working in the scaffold gang when the trouble occurred on May 25. He said that he did not see the disturbance developing and did not know much about it until someone hit him across the eye with a piece of steel. He stated that he was being treated by a private physician and was unable to return to work.

SUMMARY

Although the company reports only eight or ten persons injured, these individuals were those actually contacted and talked with in all cases except the two given by the National Association for the Advancement of Colored People and PM representatives. There were at least twenty others who stated that they had minor injuries and a large number of persons who had been hurt were present on the ferry when the men returned to work.

It is our opinion that fifty would be a conservative estimate of the number of persons injured. Mr. J. M. Griser, Vice President of the Company, informed us that a Mr.

R. D. Bell was making a check of the injured for the company and would attempt to handle the cases of those who were hurt. Mr. Bell's extension is 96 at the company. The telephone is #28841 in Mobile. We suggested that any persons who felt that they had been injured should report to Mr. Bell. Mr. Griser agreed to this. We are also suggesting that the names of these persons who made statements be submitted to the company and the Department of Justice for any possible follow-up action on prosecuting those individuals who caused the trouble.

MEETING WITH SHIPBUILDING OFFICIALS

The session with the company and union officials opened at 3:00 P.M. on Friday, May 28, in the office of the Vice President, Mr. J. M. Griser. In addition to Mr. Griser, the following persons were present: Captain W. K. Graham, representing the U. S. Maritime Commission; Mr. Burton Morley, representing the War Manpower Commission; Mr. David R. Dunlap, President of the Alabama Dry Dock and Shipbuilding Company; Mr. W. T. Daly, Personnel Manager, Alabama Dry Dock and Shipbuilding Company; Mr. Charles Hansen, Regional Representative of the Industrial Union of Marine and Shipbuilding Workers of America, CIO; Mr. J. L. Bouche, representing the Union at the local level; Mr. Elijah Jackson, colored organizer for the Union; Mr. Sam Bordelon, Director of the Southern Area, National CIO Committee for American and Allied War Relief; and the representatives of the President's Committee on Fair Employment Practice, Messrs. Ernest G. Trimble and Clarence Mitchell.

Captain Graham presided at the meeting. He opened the discussion by saying that a number of suggestions had been made for settling the problem at the Alabama Dry Dock and Shipbuilding Company. One of these suggestions he said was made by Mr. Hansen and provided that the Negro welders be taken off the job and that an educational program would be undertaken before any effort was made to place Negroes on such jobs. Captain Graham agreed with this plan.

The representatives of the President's Committee on Fair Employment Practice pointed out that so far as the educational program was concerned, there was no time for that. Messrs. Trimble and Mitchell stated that the company had had since November 1942, to work out some kind of scheme for making full use of the Negro labor supply in accordance with the provisions of Executive Order 8802. Messrs. Trimble and Mitchell said that any plan for handling the situation should go into effect immediately and there should be no retreat from the program of upgrading the Negroes. The representatives of the Committee said that if the Government should retreat from its position which was dictated by the Executive Order and the necessities of war production, it would be very possible that at a later date opposition from workers would be even more vigorous than it was at present. It is interesting to note that Mr. Griser concurred with this point of view. Mr. Griser said that the company needed approximately 2,500 men to man a way, therefore it would be impractical to think of manning an entire shipway at this time with Negroes as had been proposed by the area office of the War Manpower Commission.

Mr. Trimble asked how long it would take to get enough men for a way. Mr. Griser said that if the company set aside a way at the time construction began it could organize enough men to get started in three or four days, but could not get them as fast as they would be needed. A second suggestion, Captain Graham said, had come from the company. Mr. Hansen then said, "If the company has a plan, let us hear it".

Mr. Griser stated that the company had been giving this matter of upgrading Negroes considerable thought since the Birmingham hearings before the President's Committee on Fair Employment Practice in June 1942. He said that after a thorough exploration of the idea that a separate way could be set up for Negroes, the company had decided it was not practical. He said that at certain points in the construction the need for skilled workers would make it necessary to bring in white persons. This would mean that it would be necessary to keep certain colored employees idle if there were no other places to which colored workers of certain skills could be sent. Mr. Griser said that the company had decided that after it had upgraded Negroes to chippers and caulkers at a reasonably later date, Negroes would be used as welders. This was to be the second step in compliance with the requirements of Executive Order 8802. He said that it was decided that these colored welders would be placed on the third shift. When this action was taken, Mr. Griser said, trouble developed. He added further that on Wednesday night following the trouble which occurred Tuesday morning, 4 colored welders reported for duty. He said that this resulted in a walk out of the whites on Thursday morning. Mr. Mitchell interposed to say that this seemed to indicate that those who were fomenting the trouble were confined to the day shift since Negroes had worked at night on two occasions without trouble. Mr. Griser stated that he was inclined to agree with this. He said further that he was afraid that since the company had started the upgrading of Negroes, if he stropped or withdrew and tried an education program, the minute the proposition was brought up again the element which felt that it had won a victory when it created a disturbance on Tuesday, would feel that it could try similar tactics again.

Mr. Griser proposed that a mass meeting be held on the island. This mass meeting was to start at 3:30 P. M. at a time when the morning shift would be going off and the afternoon shift would be coming in. A flag-draped platform would be constructed, Mr. Griser said, and some outstanding military official should be the principal speaker. He suggested Admiral Vickery, Admiral Fisher or some outstanding General.

Mr. Griser suggested that the officers of the company and the union along with a few other outstanding persons should be on the platform. He said that his proposal would not at the beginning cover entirely the provisions of Executive Order 8802. Mr. Griser felt that at the start there would be a probability of the company's being accused of segregation or discrimination. He proposed, however, that the Committee, as he put it, "close its eyes" to segregation for a time. His plan called for the use of colored craftsmen on the construction of hulls on 4 ways in the North end of the yard. He said that the working conditions in the repair yard would remain unchanged, but that any workers who felt they should be upgraded could be moved out into the 4 ways set up for Negro craftsmen. He said that this would cause some slight delay but in the end would probably facilitate production generally. Mr. Griser proposed that the plan be announced to workers and that those in favor would raise their hands. He said all of those who opposed would be asked to step forward to the front of the assembly of workers and it was his plan that those who opposed would be asked to leave.

Mr. Bordelon asked how soon this plan could be put into effect. Mr. Griser stated that it could be very promptly entered into. Mr. Bouche said that everyone should keep in mind that the point we were faced with was the fact that the whites as well as Negroes were off the job and some educational program was needed to convince the white workers that this proposition was necessary. Mr. Griser responded by saying that as far as the company had been able to determine none of the skilled craftsmen who were essential to production in the yard had participated in the demonstration. He stated that it had been caused by the "young bucks" and girls among the whites who thought that they had highly developed skills. Mr. Bouche proposed that the yard be divided into 4 sections and that each foreman would be asked to get a man from each craft to attend a meeting at which the proposal for upgrading Negroes could be discussed. Mr. Bouche stated that this should be done before calling a mass meeting. Mr. Griser said that the company had thought about that also, but felt that those persons not friendly to the plant would start a lot of agitation before the meeting and thereby make it unsuccessful. He contended that there were some saboteurs in the yard and that the Federal Bureau of Investigation was working to apprehend them. These saboteurs, he felt, would disrupt and defeat the plan before it could get into operation if it was discussed with the workers before the meeting.

Mr. Hansen said that the thing to do would be to take a firm policy and the program would go over. Mr. Jackson said that it was his impression that the Negroes would be gotten back to work with some effort on the part of the union. Mr. Morley stated that the War Manpower Commission had called him to say that he could officially endorse any proposal which seemed reasonable and likely to bring the situation back to normal. This was interesting to note because at the morning meeting in the area War Manpower Commission office, he was opposed to going ahead with any plan for the use of Negro welders at this time.

Captain Graham stated that he had talked with Washington during a brief absence from the meeting and had been informed that the Maritime Commission had been in touch with the White House and that the White House wanted to see the thing through and did not want any back-tracking on using Negro welders. As a result of the conference which lasted from its time of beginning at 3:00 P. M. until approximately 9:00 P. M. that night, the attached agreement was reached and signed by those present.

Mr. Trimble and Mr. Mitchell raised the question of whether it was understood that under the agreement the same conditions which had obtained in the repair departments would continue. It was agreed that they would be continued but that Negroes working in these departments could be upgraded to other jobs in the four Ways covered by the plan. It was suggested that this understanding be placed in the written agreement but Mr. Griser said that this was unnecessary since the principle of upgrading was covered by the union contract. It was the understanding of those present, therefore, that every capable Negro worker would have an opportunity to be upgraded under the plan agreed upon.

Mr. Trimble and Mr. Mitchell emphasized that, while the agreement did not mention the inclusion of Negroes in machinists jobs, pipefitting, marine electrical trades and certain other skills, nothing was agreed upon which would exclude Negroes from such trades. It was agreed that when the plan was announced there would be no statement by the person or persons making the announcement which would indicate or hint that Negroes would be barred from such trades. Mr. Griser agreed with this. Later, in talking with Mr. Trimble and Mr. Mitchell, Mr. Griser stated that the company definitely expects to use Negroes in the types of work mentioned.

During the discussion of the plan the representatives of the President's Committee on Fair Employment Practice took the position that the question of whether Executive Order 8802 should be obeyed could not be submitted to the workers to vote on. But they agreed that the proposed plan for carrying out the Executive Order could be submitted to the workers.

Mr. Morley promised that the War Manpower Commission would take immediate steps to arrange for training as soon as the program had final approval from the agencies in Washington concerned with it. Before the meeting adjourned, Mr. Jackson of the Union raised the question of what could be done to give compensation to workers injured during the fight. Mr. Dunlap said that this matter was being taken up with the insurance company handling the Alabama Dry Dock and Shipbuilding Company's business. It was also stated that two persons were actually under arrest for the disturbance and that a third was being sought for causing the trouble. The two under arrest are, Mr. C. T. Willingham, who is charged with inciting a riot, and Mr. James Melvin Jackson, who is charged with assault. Both of these men are white. The third person the company expected to have arrested was Paul Babcock. Mr. Babcock is a welder in the yard and a former officer of the CIO union. It was alleged that he went to various sections of the yard telling white workers that they should object to the upgrading of Negroes.

Mr. Babcock appeared before the President's Committee on Fair Employment Practice during the Birmingham hearings on June 19. At that time he was Vice President of Local 18, IUMSWA, in the Alabama Dry Dock and Shipbuilding Company: He stated that his union stood by the principle expressed in its constitution that there shall be no distinction made with regard to race, creed, color or sex, and that consequently his union will cooperate with the company in its policy of elevating Negroes to skilled positions where they are qualified. (Later it developed that Babcock was not under arrest by May 31, 1943. On June 4, the Office of War Information informed us that Mr. Clifford L. Williams, white, had also been arrested on the charge of assaulting one of the colored workers.)

After an agreement was reached, a statement was drawn up for release to the press, a copy of which is attached.

MEETING WITH PUBLISHER OF
MOBILE PRESS-REGISTER, MAY 29, 1943

At the invitation of Mr. R. B. Chandler, publisher of the Mobile Press-Register, the two representatives of the President's Committee on Fair Employment Practice held a conference with him on Saturday, May 29. Others present at the conference were Mr. Russel Cox of the news staff and Mr. McDonald, also of the news staff.

Mr. Chandler expressed a keen interest in the happening out at the shipyard and said that he was anxious to see the situation corrected. He blamed the company for not having a proper guard force and also said that there was a great of trouble stemming from the fact that many of the new employees of the company had some from the poor rural sections of Georgia and Mississippi and were what he called "poor white trash". The publisher declared that the chief concern he had in mind was preventing a recurrence of rioting. He expressed a feeling that the white persons at the yard who had attacked the colored persons were the kind of people who would soon attack the better thinking and local resident whites if allowed to go "uncurbed". He said also that recently there was a demonstration on the part of these same whites because of the ferry rates. (Here he had reference to the fact that the workers at the shipyard who use the ferry to get to their jobs must pay five cents to go over and five cents to return each day.) According to Mr. Chandler, the workers visited the City Hall in a mass protest and threatened to march on the homes of the City commissioners.

Speaking of the Negroes in Mobile, Mr. Chandler said that there has been a great deal of race mixing in the community. The publisher described the Negro population as French, Spanish, West Indian and other elements. These persons were not like other Negroes, according to Mr. Chandler, and he expressed the fear that they might retaliate for the trouble that they had with the whites.

On the whole, Mr. Chandler had a very cooperative attitude and we discussed with him the advisability of being present in the yard when the workers returned to their jobs. He felt that this would have an important bearing on demonstrating that it was safe to return to work. Mr. Chandler expressed the opinion that this was a situation in which everyone agreed that the Negroes were entirely free from blame. Throughout the interview Mr. Chandler emphasized that the proper solution for the problems arising out of race conflict was that of segregation.

MEETING WITH MR. R. ROLAND HOBDY,
1355 Hercules Street, Mobile, Alabama*

Mr. Hobdy stated that he is employed as a personnel representative in the Alabama Dry Dock and Shipbuilding Corporation under Mr. R. H. Bailey. Mr. Hobdy said that he received 75 cents an hour for his job and I assumed that it was something

---

* Interview by Clarence Mitchell.

comparable to a pusher. It was not possible to determine the exact duties Mr. Hobdy performed. He stated that he began working in the yard as a laborer and later was up-graded to the job he holds at present. According to this informant only 480 Negroes had reported for work on the morning of the disturbance. It was not possible to check this statement but it is very unlikely that it is correct. Mr. Hobdy listed a num-ber of complaints which he said the workers had against the company. Among those complaints are the following:

1. Negroes are dissatisfied with the way their white foremen handle them.
2. Frequently workers, Negro and white, supposed to receive their checks on a certain date and do not get them.
3. There is a feeling that adequate attention is not given to grievances which are brought to the personnel department by workers.

These elements in Mr. Hobdy's conversation seemed to have little significance so far as the general situation is concerned. All of them are matters which can be handled by the company's personnel department. I include his statement merely because Mr. R. B. Chandler, publisher of the Mobile Press Register had mentioned Mr. Hobdy as a former janitor at the newspaper who is alleged to have disappeared following a speech he made urging workers to return to their jobs.

MEETING WITH CAPTAIN RICE, OFFICE[R],

in charge of federal troops at the Alabama Dry Dock and Shipbuilding Company, MAY 31, 1943 AT 9:30 A. M.

Captain Rice stated that there were 150 troops per shift scattered throughout the yard. The yard is divided into four strategic posts and officers in jeeps are patrolling other sections of the yard. According to Captain Rice, 1,000 additional troops could be brought into the yard on short notice.

It is interesting to note that he felt that the presence of troops would serve to keep alive the recollection of the trouble. It was his view that such troops should be with-drawn gradually until only a small number would remain. I mentioned that when I arrived at the yard at 6:00 A. M., the ferries crossing the river did not have any troops on them. He stated that this situation had been corrected and when I returned to the mainland, Federal troops were aboard the ferries.

MEETING WITH WORKERS, MAY 30, 1943

A "back to work" meeting was held on Sunday, May 30th. Approximately 300 to 400 workers of the Alabama Dry Dock and Shipbuilding Company were present. It was held on lots owned by the Davis Avenue Community Center in Mobile. It was called by the Industrial Union of Marine and Shipbuilding Workers. There were a number of speakers including Colonel Robert Joerg, Commander of the Alabama State Militia, Mr. Franklin O. Nichols, of the National Urban League, Mr. J. L. Bouche of the Union, Mr. J. L. LeFlore of the Mobile Branch of the National Association for the Advancement of Colored People, Mr. Charles Hansen of the Union, Mr. Conrad Dean of the Union and Mr. Elijah Jackson of the Union, and Clarence M. Mitchell, of the President's Committee on Fair Employment Practice.

The meeting was a success in that the general note struck was return to work and at the close of it workers were asked to raise their hands if they were willing to return to the job. The majority of them agreed to do this on the following day. There were no incidents.

JUNE 2, 1943

MR. J. M. GRISER

ALABAMA DRY DOCK AND SHIPBUILDING COMPANY

MOBILE, ALABAMA

THE PRESIDENT'S COMMITTEE ON FAIR EMPLOYMENT PRACTICE AP-PROVES AS A PRACTICAL SETTLEMENT OF THE EXISTING SITUATION THE QUOTE PROPOSED SOLUTION FOR SETTLEMENT OF DIFFICULTIES AT SHIP-YARD OF ALABAMA DRYDOCK AND SHIPBUILDING COMPANY UNQUOTE DRAWN UP BY THE CONFERENCE COMMITTEE ON MAY 28 ON WHICH THIS COMMITTEE WAS REPRESENTED BY ERNEST G. TRIMBLE AND CLARENCE MITCHELL, UNDER WHICH SETTLEMENT ALL EMPLOYEES USED ON BARE HULL ERECTION ON WAYS ONE THROUGH FOUR WILL BE NEGROES. YOU WILL READILY UNDERSTAND THAT THE COMMITTEE ON FAIR EMPLOY-MENT PRACTICE CANNOT APPROVE RESTRICTIONS FOR THE FUTURE WITH RESPECT TO THE UPGRADING OF NEGROES INTO THE OUTFITTING CRAFTS SUCH AS ELECTRICIANS, PIPEFITTERS, ETC., WHICH RESTRICTIONS WOULD CONFLICT WITH THE PROVISIONS OF THE EXECUTIVE ORDER, AND WE FEEL SURE YOU WOULD NOT EXPECT THE COMMITTEE TO DO SO.[2]

FRANCIS J. HAAS

CHAIRMAN

STATEMENT OF PROPOSED SOLUTION FOR SETTLEMENT OF DIFFICULTIES AT SHIPYARD OF THE ALABAMA DRY DOCK AND SHIPBUILDING COMPANY BY THE CONFERENCE COMMITTEE REPRESENTING THE FOLLOWING AGENCIES - U. S. MARITIME COMMISSION, WAR MANPOWER COMMISSION, THE PRESIDENT'S COMMITTEE ON FAIR EMPLOYMENT PRACTICE, INDUS-TRIAL UNION OF MARINE AND SHIPBUILDING WORKERS OF AMERICA (C. I. O.) AND ALABAMA DRY DOCK AND SHIPBUILDING COMPANY:

All working conditions in the two repair plants, shipbuilding department Ways Nos. 5 -12, inclusive, Outfitting Department and its Piers, all shops, Warehouses,

Platens, and Yards, except building ways Nos. 1 to 4, inclusive, are to remain the same as they were prior to the time Chippers were upgraded.

Conditions on Ways Nos. 1 to 4 inclusive, or the North Building Yard, will be as follows:

Negro labor will be used in all crafts pertaining to bare hull erection beginning on No. 1 way then extending through the other three (3) ways of the aforesaid area as rapidly as the Craftsmen can be obtained.

Regular Outfitting Craftsmen shall start the work of outfitting hulls on these ways when hulls have progressed to the point where these installations are necessary.

When Hull Erection has reached the launching stage it will be turned over entirely to the Outfitting Department for completion and delivery. The Hull Erection Crews will proceed to other hulls on these four ways.

This will cause some daily in delivery of vessels to be constructed on these four ways, but at the same time the transferring of white hull erection craftsmen to ways Nos. 5 to 12 inclusive, should increase production on these ways.

NEWS RELEASE   MOBILE, ALABAMA
                                                    May 28, 1943

After an all-day conference, a Committee comprised of representatives of the U. S. Maritime Commission, the President's Committee on Fair Employment Practice, the War Manpower Commission, the Alabama Dry Dock and Shipbuilding Company, and the Industrial Union of Marine and Shipbuilding Workers of America, C. I. O., has unanimously agreed on a plan for solving the difficulties which have arisen in the yard of the Alabama Dry Dock and Shipbuilding Company.

This plan is now being submitted to Washington for the approval of the Governmental agencies concerned. Upon approval of this plan by these agencies in Washington, it will be submitted completely and in detail to the employees for their approval at a mass meeting to be held on Pinto Island.

This is democracy at work. Let us help to keep that democracy. We call upon every loyal American worker to return to work immediately, in order that the ships which are so vitally needed to carry the tools to our boys at the fighting fronts may continue to slide down the ways.

Captain Walter K. Graham
U. S. Maritime Commission

E. G. Trimble   Clarence M. Mitchell
President's Committee on Fair Employment Practice

Burton R. Morley
War Manpower Commission

David R. Dunlap   J. M. Griser
Alabama Dry Dock & Shipbuilding Co.

W. T. Daly
Alabama Dry Dock & Shipbuilding Co.

Charles Hansen   J. L. Bouche   Elijah Jackson
Industrial Union of Marine and Shipbuilding Workers of America, C. I. O.

This plan is to be submitted to the workmen at a Mass Meeting for their acceptance.[3]

s/ WALTER K. GRAHAM
Captain Walter K. Graham
U. S. Manpower Commission

s/ E. G. TRIMBLE   s/ CLARENCE M. MITCHELL
E.G. Trimble   Clarence M. Mitchell
President's Committee on Fair Employment Practice

s/ BURTON R. MORLEY
Burton R. Morley
War Manpower Commission

s/ DAVID R. DUNLAP   s/ J. M. GRISER
David R. Dunlap   J. M. Griser
Alabama Dry Dock and Shipbuilding Company

s/ W. T. DALY
W. T. Daly
Alabama Dry Dock and Shipbuilding Company

s/ CHARLES HANSEN   s/ J. L. BOUCHE   s/ ELIJAH JACKSON
Charles Hansen   J. L. Bouche   Elijah Jackson
Industrial Union of Marine and Shipbuilding Workers of America, C. I. O.

Part of the crafts used in bare hull construction are as follows:

Crane gangs, erectors, regulators, fitters, welders, burners, chippers, caulkers, testers, buffers, painters, blocking, shoring and scaffolding crews.[4]

MS: copy, HqR6, Office Files of George M. Johnson.

1. For a copy of this directive and records of the investigation of Alabama Dry Dock resulting from hearings held in Birmingham in 1942, see "Summary of the Hearings of the President's Committee on Fair Employment Practice" held in Birmingham, Alabama, June 19, 1942, with "Findings and Directives"

in the case of Alabama Shipbuilding and Dry Dock Corporation, Mobile, Alabama, HqR3, Office Files of Malcolm Ross. Misc. The full Birmingham hearings records are in HqR17.

2. According to Haas, composition of this telegram "cost us about half a day to prepare." On the FEPC's appearing to create a precedent for government approval of segregated work places, see the transcript of the FEPC meeting of 7/6/43, 19–59, HqR64, Central Files. Both of the African Americans on the committee strongly opposed the acceptance of segregated shipways and all of the members objected to the FEPC's approval of segregation. The NAACP attacked it. Monsignor Haas was criticized for approving the settlement by himself before the new Committee was appointed. After extended discussion, when Mitchell explained and defended the settlement under the prevailing circumstances, the committee issued the following resolution: "The Committee accepts the accomplished fact of the settlement made in Mobile to end a crisis in war production, except that the Committee cannot give its approval to the complete segregation of Negroes on the four ways and does not consider this a precedent." Milton Webster, though, voted against it. See the Summary of Actions Taken by the Committee at its meeting in Washington, D.C., on July 6 and 7, 1943, which is dated 7/13/43, in HqR1, Summary Minutes of Meetings; the full transcript of the meeting of July 6 and 7, 1943, in HqR64, Central Files; and the NAACP *Annual Report*, 1943, 27–28. For additional background and discussion of the case, see Mitchell's memorandum of 6/1/43, and the headnotes on Strikes and Work Stoppages and on the Shipbuilding Industry.

3. In his testimony (p. 23) before the FEPC on 7/6/43, Mitchell said this meeting was cancelled at the urging of the Maritime Commission and Navy Department. Their representatives said it "wouldn't be desirable to present this plan to any kind of mass meeting to the employees." A suggestion by vice president Griser that prominent military officials make a dramatic announcement of the settlement when the morning shift was leaving the yards and the afternoon shift was coming on was also vetoed by the Maritime Commission and other officials who feared that action "might be just inviting more trouble." See the transcript of the FEPC meeting of July 6 and 7, 1943, in HqR64, Central Files.

4. Copies of the report were submitted to members of the FEPC for discussion at the first meeting of the new committee on July 6 and 7, 1943. Additional copies are in many FEPC files, indicating it was widely distributed among the staff, both in the national and the regional offices.

Office of Labor Production Report on Committee on Fair Employment Practice

Office of Labor Production
Chief Economic Adviser
JLM—July 13, 1943[1]

COMMITTEE ON FAIR EMPLOYMENT PRACTICE

Executive Order No. 8802, dated June 25, 1941, first established the Committee on Fair Employment Practices in the Office of Production Management. The Order provided that the Committee should consist of a Chairman and four other member (amended to be five, on June 26, 1941), to be appointed by the President.[2]

The Executive Order set forth the policy that "there shall be no discrimination in the employment of workers in defense industries or government because of race, creed, color, or national origin; it is the duty of employers and labor organizations . . . to provide for the full and equitable participation of all workers in defense industries, without discrimination because of race, creed, color, or national origin." The Order provided also that " . . . vocational and training programs for defense production (shall be) administered without discrimination; . . . all contracting agencies of the Government shall include in all defense contracts hereafter negotiated by then a provision obligating the contractor not to discriminate against any worker because of race, creed, color or national origin."

The Executive Order directed that "the Committee shall receive and investigate complaints of discrimination in violation of the provisions of this order and shall take appropriate steps to redress grievances which it finds to be valid. The Committee shall also recommend to the several departments and agencies of the Government of the United States and to the President all measures which may be deemed by it necessary or proper to effectuate the provisions of this order."

The Committee, appointed on July 23, 1941, consisted of Mark Ethridge, Chairman (from the Louisville Courier Journal). William Green, President of the AFL, Philip Murray, President of the CIO, David Sarnoff, Radio Corporation of America, Earl Dickerson, Chicago Attorney and Negro leader, and Milton Webster, vice president, Sleeping Car Porters Union, all to serve without compensation, and to meet periodically. Lawrence Cramer, former governor of the Virgin Islands, was appointed full-time executive secretary on August 12, 1941.

In January 1942 Mr. Malcolm Maclean, President of Hampton Institute, Hampton, Virginia, succeeded Mr. Ethridge as Chairman, Mr. Ethridge remaining as seventh member of the Committee.

Under Executive Order 9024, of January 16, 1942, and Executive Order 9040, January 24, 1942, the Committee of Fair Employment Practice was transferred from the Office of Production Management to the War Production Board. It was transferred from the WPB to the War Manpower Commission by Presidential letter on July 30, 1942.

New Committee. Executive Order 9346, dated May 27, 1943, established the Committee as an independent agency in the Office of Emergency Management. The Right Reverend Monseigneur Francis J. Haas, Dean of the School of Social Science of Catholic University, was appointed as new Chairman of the Committee on May 27, 1943. The new Executive Order provided that upon designation of a new Chairman and appointment of a new committee, the old committee was automatically abolished. This occurred on July 6, 1943, when Monseigneur Haas was designated as full-time Chairman for the new Committee, the six other members then appointed being: Sara Southall, Supervisor of Employment and Service at the International Harvester Company, Chicago; P. B. Young Sr., Publisher of the Norfolk Journal and Guide, Norfolk, Virginia; Samuel Zemurray, President, United Fruit Company, New Orleans, Louisiana; Boris Shishkin; Economist, AFL; John Brophy, Director of Industrial Councils, CIO; and Milton Webster, Vice-President, Sleeping Car Porters Union.

The new Committee contemplates establishing a field staff with 12 regional offices, one in each War Manpower Region. There is now a field office in New York City.

Procedure: In the two years of its existence the Committee has gradually built up the procedure enumerated below. Resort is had to each succeeding step only when the preceding step has not resulted in complete adjustment of the case being handled, unless otherwise specified.

1. Complaints of discrimination are received by the Committee from individuals and organizations. Evidence of discrimination is also received by the Committee, either in the course of its activities, or by reports from other agencies.

2. The complainant or other source is checked by the Committee to make sure that bona fide discrimination exists, and that such discrimination lies within the jurisdiction of the Committee. If a prima facie case exists, that is, discrimination has caused employment to be barred, or prevented employees from being utilized at their highest skill, or employees have been denied opportunity for training and upgrading on that account, the Committee takes step 3.

3. The Committee attempts to adjust the matter with the "party charged." The party charged may be an employer, a union, a government agency, or a training agency. The party charged may make satisfactory explanation showing that discrimination did not in fact exist. If a valid grievance does exist, the Committee endeavors, through consultation with management, labor, Federal agencies involved, such as the WPB, the WMC, the WLB to effectuate removal of the discrimination by the party charged.

4. (Procedure under old Committee; may be procedure under new). Where circumstances warrant, the Committee presents the case to the contracting agency which, under letter of July 2, 1942, signed by the Secretaries of War, Navy, and the Chairman of the Maritime Commission, have agreed to take steps to adjust discrimination cases.

5. The Committee holds a public hearing at which the party charged is requested to appear. At the hearing, the Committee presents a statement of its case, and the party charged is requested to make a statement on its employment, training, or other policies and practices as they bear on the complaint. Where, as a result of both the statement by the Committee and that by the party charged, it appears that the policies or practices of the party charged are not in accordance with the national policy as expressed under the Executive Order, the party charged is asked to make a statement as to whether he will adjust his policies or practices to conform with the national policy. Usually the party charged makes a formal statement at the hearing that he will so comply. If he does agree to comply, the Committee proceeds with steps 6 and 9. If not, the Committee proceeds with steps 6 and 7, etc.

6. The Committee prepares a summary, findings, and recommendations or directions to the party charged.

7. Again makes an effort to get the party charged to comply, through consultation.

8. Publishes statement issued to party charged (see 6).

9. Follows up on whether party charged is complying with the Committee's recommendations.

10. Again enlists aid of contracting government agencies (4 above).

11. Certifies case to the President of the United States, for his intervention.[3]

The Committee has found it necessary to hold six public hearings, as follows:

1. Los Angeles, October 20 and 21, 1941
2. Chicago, Illinois, January 19 and 20, 1942
3. New York City, February, 1942
4. Birmingham, Alabama, May 25, 26, 27, 1942
5. Pittsburgh Plate Glass Co., Clarksburg, West Va.
   (directive issued to company 11. 29. 42)[4]

The Committee has found it necessary to refer only one case to the President, that involving the International Association of Machinists locals in San Francisco and Seattle. The International Association of Machinists, by means of a secret ritual, bar Negroes form membership, and hence from employment in shape where the Machinists had closed shop agreements. This case was taken up first with the local unions, second with the International Officers of the Union, and lastly with the President of the United States, use successfully intervened.

The International officers directed the local unions to take whatever steps were necessary to remove the bar to the employment of Negroes. Work permits were issued for this purpose, although in some areas, locals now have Negro members (by emitting or liberal interpretation of the secret ritual.)

Prior to its dissolution, the old Committee had projected hearings for Detroit, St. Louis, Cleveland, Baltimore, and Philadelphia. Of these, the new Committee has tentatively scheduled hearings for Detroit on July 28 and 29. The other cities have not been considered as yet. The Committee will also proceed with the cases involving discrimination on railroads, and the Capitol Transit Company of Washington, D.C.

Since its inception to date, the Committee has received some 12,000 complaints of which approximately 75 percent were bona fide. Data is not available as to the number of cases which have been adjusted and the number remaining unadjusted. During the period October 1941 through May 1942, however, the Committee held six hearings: in Los Angeles, New York City, Birmingham, Alabama, twice in Chicago, and a hearing at the Pittsburgh Plate Glass Co. in Clarksburg, West Virginia. These hearings covered 90 complains and 47 "parties charged." Findings of discrimination were made with respect to 27 companies. Most of those for which findings of discrimination were not made occurred in the first hearings at Los Angeles, when the procedure of making specific findings had not been developed.

Detroit Race Riots. The Committee established a temporary field office in Detroit on January 1943, in anticipation of holding hearings on the numerous complaints of discriminatory employment practices it had received from that city. When the Detroit race riots occurred, a group drawn from local government and civic circles was formed to deal with the situation. The Committee's Detroit representative was requested to meet with this group, on the basis of his knowledge of employment discrimination conditions in Detroit, and of the history of other race riots occurring in the past, although, actually, the riots lay outside the jurisdiction of the Committee on Fair Employment Practice. The Committee's representative pointed out to the local group the necessity for calling in Federal troops immediately.

The Committee on Fair Employment Practice has stated that the riots were in no way connected with employment in war plants. Father Haas, in a press conference announcing the formation of the new Committee, cited "wartime crowding in houses, busses, and recreation grounds" as breeding "irritation among decent people" and affording "irresponsible persons the opportunity for shameful mob violence . . . <Last week in Detroit> . . . the workers in was plants did not lose their heads at the time when hoodlums were rioting in the street of Detroit."

<u>Congested Labor Area</u>. The Committee finds that the problem of discrimination in employment and training practices is most acute in such congested labor areas as Detroit, Baltimore, St. Louis, etc. In these cities there are reserves of minority groups which are not being properly used.[5]

MS: copy, HqR3, Office Files of George M. Johnson. Memoranda.

1. The editors have rendered these initials as "JLM" based on an unclear carbon copy. An alternative reading may be "JLW."

2. On the manuscript, June 26 is crossed out and replaced with July 18, which is also crossed out. A few additional changes are marked on the text but have not been noted.

3. For complaints regarding proposed changes in some of these procedures, see Proposed Program for the Division of Field Operations [ca. July 31, 1945] and notes.

4. On this manuscript, the phrase "directive issued to company 11.29.42" is circled and the date Dec. 21, 1942 is written in the right margin.

5. This text is stamped as received on July 27, 1943.

Memorandum on Mitchell's Telephonic Report on Bethlehem Shipyard at Sparrows Point

July 31, 1943

To: Francis J. Haas

From: George M. Johnson

Subject: **Telephonic report on Bethlehem Shipyard at Sparrows Point on July 31 from 9:35 to 9:43.**[1]

Mitchell: Yesterday when I called you our colored men had gone back to work and I met with them last night and I determined that for the most part they stayed on the job as long as possible. When they first went back to work everything was quiet at first, but some agitators began going from group to group and ship to ship and pulling white people off (not physically) apparently telling them they should come off, so they began coming off and holding little meetings in the yard in groups. I had an understanding with the Company that they were going to have enough policemen down there that if anything like that happened they would break it up. Apparently they didn't break it up. The thing grew and crowds began to assemble. Management and Rye from the Conciliation Service all went down and tried to talk to them. Van Gelder from the union tried to talk, but they could not do anything with them. After all these meetings the Company decided they would call the Maritime Commission and get permission to close the yards, they did call and were given permission to close at noon. They sent them home at 12:00 noon and those men who I talked with last night, they said they stayed on the job until that time. All of the difficulty seems to have come from the white people. They also told me last night they are perfectly willing to come back on Monday. They said they have one or two alternatives. Either they go back with Federal protection or they will provide their own.

We had a meeting down at the yard yesterday with a joint committee. Six men from the white riveters group and six colored men. The colored men were trainees in the school. I was opposed to the meeting, however they were already in process of having it so there was nothing else for me to do but to join them since I had been invited. At the meeting the Negroes were very reasonable. The only thing they were asking was that the school should be reopened with fifteen whites and three Negroes. The whites said they wanted no school, the training on the jobs and strict seniority. When they held out for seniority the question was raised as to how many white people would be ahead of the Negroes. They said sixty-two. They didn't know how many of the sixty-two could be interested in taking the training. One man who was there who was in the riveting department said he would not be interested, and another man said he would not be interested. The way it looks the majority of the people there might want to take training. That of course was an impossible situation. In addition they have a number of training programs at the yard and the only one in which seniority is recognized as a reason for admission is in the Welding Department. In all the others, it is not on the basis of seniority, the company picks their own people.

We are having another meeting at 11:00. Colored and white will be there. After that meeting, I have suggested to some of the citizens here that they might come over to Washington and I think it will give their morale a shot in the arm. Unfortunately I don't know how soon the meeting will be over.

Johnson: I believe you stated to me yesterday morning that the Army was prepared to go in from the standpoint of plant protection.

Mitchell: There was a Major Roach and another Colonel. I do not remember his name but it is in my notes, who came into the yard on Thursday evening after I left and had a talk with management. They offered to provide troops if they needed them on Friday morning. Yesterday I raised the question with management and J. B. Knotts, representative of management, said he thought his policemen were able to handle the situation. Cooley from Ring's office and I suggested that they ought to have troops ready to come in case they are needed and to come fast.

Johnson: Could you get any inkling as to what the discussion was about that provoked this milling around yesterday morning. Was it still over the training?

Mitchell: Some of it was over that and a part of it was because the Negro crane operators were back on the job.

Johnson: Had they been off?

Mitchell: Yes. When the trouble started, they walked off in sympathy on Wednesday. On Thursday when they arrested some colored people for inciting a riot the colored crane operators went off the job and that meant they couldn't do hardly anything on the job because these men had to move things around. On Friday morning when the colored crane operators got back on the job, some of the whites told them to come down off their job. They were up in the air about some hundred feet or so, and felt safe so did not come down.

Johnson: Was there any violence in the yard?

Mitchell: No, there was no indication that there was any violence at all. I was down there the whole time. The police had an arrangement where most of the whites came out by themselves and the Negroes came out by themselves, but in most instances there were some whites among the Negroes and some Negroes among the whites.

Johnson: Those arrests that took place was that on plant property?

Mitchell: On plant property and management had called a sort of meeting of the colored people who were milling around because they were protesting about the riveting school. Knotz got them together and took them into a little room and began talking to them. They appointed some representatives to go in and work on the problem. When they got the agreement settled Knotz wanted a colored man to announce it and they wanted Knotz to announce it. It was the statement I read to you yesterday. Finally it was agreed that they both should announce it. When they got outside and Knotz went to make his announcement and introduced the Negro, he said, "Boys they wanted me to sell you down the river but I wouldn't do it."

Johnson: You said you read me a statement yesterday. I don't remember you reading me a statement, what was the substance of it:

Mitchell: The Company agreed that the school would reopen with the same conditions that prevailed on Monday with fifteen white and three Negroes, and that the men who were off the job would receive time and a half for some of the time they had lost.

Johnson: What was the Negroes objection to joining in that statement?

Mitchell: There was no objection to that, but this fellow, his name is Jacobs, they didn't have the statement in writing and he thought they were backtracking and he was going to beat them at it, but when they got the statement down in writing that was one of the things that helped to get the people back to work and I read the statement to them and they all agreed that everything was o.k.

Johnson: We got the statement yesterday that five thousand whites walked out. Was that a walkout or was there a cessation of work?

Mitchell: A cessation of work. I was right at the place where everybody had to go out, the bulk of the workers did not leave the yard until around noon when the company officials let them go.

Johnson: Now many Negroes normally working in the entire yard?

Mitchell: About twelve hundred out of approximately eight thousand workers.

Johnson: Some working in the steel mill?

Mitchell: No, the steel mill is entirely separated and that has not been affected. I am bringing one of the representatives of the steel mill over today and the management people down at Bethlehem-Fairfield said it has not been affected at all.

MS: DI, HqR1, Office Files of Malcolm Ross. J.

1. Mitchell was the FEPC's field representative during the walkouts at the Bethlehem Steel Shipyard at Sparrows Point, Baltimore. See Mitchell to George Johnson and to Maslow, 11/1/43 (and notes), Mitchell's field investigation report, 8/6/43, in appendix 1, and the headnotes on Strikes and Work Stoppages and on the Shipbuilding Industry.

Analysis of Executive Order No. 9346

ANALYSIS OF EXECUTIVE ORDER #9346

[ca. July 1943]

I.   Authority for Issuance

The Order was issued by virtue of the authority vested in the President by "the Constitution and the statutes, and as President of the United States and Commander in Chief of the Army and Navy . . ."

II.   Purpose of the Order

A. "To promote the fullest utilization of all available manpower" regardless of race, creed, color or national origin.

B. To further "the prosecution of the war, the workers' morale, and national unity."

III. National Policy Reaffirmed

"that there shall be no discrimination in the employment of any person in war industries or in Government by reason of race, creed, color or national origin

IV. Duty Imposed Upon Employers Including Federal Government and Labor Organizations

"To eliminate discrimination in regard to hire, tenure, terms or conditions of employment, or union membership because of race, creed, color or national origin."

V. Duty Expressly Imposed Upon Other Government Agencies

A. All governmental contracting agencies "shall include in all contracts hereinafter negotiated or renegotiated by them a provision obligating the contractor not to discriminate . . . and requiring him to include a similar provision in all subcontracts."
B. All governmental vocational and training agencies "shall take all measures appropriate to assure that such programs are administered without discrimination."

VI. Committee Organization

A. Committee entitled "Committee on Fair Employment Practice" and established in the Office for Emergency Management of the Executive Office of the President.
 1. Consists of Chairman and not more than six other members, all appointed by the President.
 2. Chairman is a full-time, salaried officer; Committee members receive travel expenses, a per diem allowance of not more than $25 and subsistence expenses (of $6.00 a day) on such days as they are actually engaged in the performance of their duties.
 3. New Committee comes into existence "upon the appointment of the committee and the designation of its Chairman."

VII. Powers of the Committee

The Committee is given express power to perform the following functions:

A. To formulate policies to achieve the purposes of the new Order.
B. To make recommendations to various Federal departments and agencies and to the President, which the Committee deems necessary and proper to make effective the provisions of the new Order.
C. To recommend to the Chairman of the War Manpower Commission "appropriate measures for bringing about the utilization and training of manpower in and for war production without discrimination because of race, creed, color, or national origin."
D. To receive and investigate complaints of discrimination forbidden by the new Order.
E. To conduct investigations and hearings necessary in the performance of its duties.
F. To make findings of fact.
G. To take appropriate steps to obtain elimination of discrimination forbidden by the new Order.
H. To assume jurisdiction over all complaints and matters pending before the old Committee.
I. To utilize the services and facilities of other Federal departments and agencies.
J. To utilize such voluntary and uncompensated services as may from time to time be needed.
K. To accept the services of State and local authorities and officials and act through these officials and agencies in such manner as it may determine.
L. To promulgate appropriate or necessary rules and regulations.

VIII. Powers of the Chairman

In addition to the powers vested in any chairman by virtue of his position as chairman, the new chairman is given express power to:

A. appoint and fix the compensation of such personnel for the Committee as may be necessary to carry out the new Order; and
B. make provision for supplies, facilities and services.

IX. Sanctions

No specific sanctions are fixed in the Order. The Order does not say that Committee "policies," "recommendations," "findings" or "appropriate steps" are binding upon any governmental or private agency, nor does it fix penalties for breaches of the non-discriminatory provisions required in all government contracts.

The President, however, as Commander in Chief of the Army and Navy may take action to enforce the Committee's powers. (Such action has been taken on behalf of the War Labor Board)

X.   Budget

The Order authorizes expenditures "within the limits of the funds which may be made available." No reference is made to the source of the funds and presumably money will be made available from the President's special fund or by Congressional appropriation.

XI.   Distinctions Between Executive Orders 9346 and 8802

A. 9346 was issued under the President's additional powers as Commander in Chief of the Army and Navy.

B. Under 9346, an additional duty is required of labor organizations to eliminate discrimination in regard to union membership.

C. Under 9346, discrimination is expressly forbidden "in hire, tenure, terms or conditions of employment" instead of merely generally.

D. Under 9346, discrimination is expressly forbidden against "applicants for employment" as well as existing employees.

E. Under 9346, contractual provisions proscribing discrimination are required in all sub-contracts as well as principal contracts.

F. Under 9346, the Committee is established in the Executive Office of the President, not in the Office for Production Management or the War Manpower Commission.

G. Under 9346, the Chairman is a full-time, salaried officer.

H. Under 9346, the Committee is given specific power to conduct hearings and make findings of fact.

I. Under 9346, the Committee is expressly allowed to utilize volunteer and uncompensated services, the services of State or local authorities, and the service and facilities of other Federal agencies.

J. Under 9346, the Committee is expressly authorized to promulgate rules and regulations.

K. Under 9346, all inconsistent Executive Orders are hereby superseded.

INTERPRETATION OF PARAGRAPH
NUMBERED 1 OF EXECUTIVE ORDER 9346

In a letter dated July 2, the Secretary of the Interior advised the Chairman of the Committee that it had been necessary for him to determine whether Executive Order 9346 applies to contracts let by formal advertising and bidding. The letter stated that the Secretary of the Interior had concluded that the Order did apply to such contracts and had approved a memorandum from his solicitor, a copy of which was enclosed.

Paragraph numbered 1 of Executive Order 9346 contains the phrase "all contracts hereafter negotiated or renegotiated" and the point discussed in the Solicitor's memorandum submitted by the Secretary of the Interior is as to whether contracts let by formal advertising and bidding are contracts "negotiated." As pointed out in the memorandum of the Solicitor in the Department of the Interior, it would seem that the words "all contracts hereafter negotiated or renegotiated" mean all contracts made or amended or modified. If the Committee concurs in this position, it is suggested that they do so by appropriate resolution in order that this resolution may be used to indicate the Committee's position to interested parties. The following is a proposed resolution:

> The President's Committee on Fair Employment Practice, established under Executive Order 9346, interprets the words "all contracts hereafter negotiated or renegotiated" appearing in paragraph numbered 1 to mean all contracts made, amended or modified by contracting agencies of the Government of the United States.[1]

MS: copy, HqR2, Office Files of Malcolm Ross. Meetings, Materials from July 26 Meeting.

1. For FEPC adoption of this resolution, see verbatim transcript for 7/26/43, 110–12, HqR64, Transcripts. This analysis was probably composed by George Johnson, who introduced discussion of the resolution at the FEPC meeting.

Memorandum on Telephone Calls on Bethlehem Shipbuilding Company at Sparrows Point

August 1, 1943

MEMORANDUM

SUBJECT: Telephone Calls on Bethlehem Shipbuilding Company and Sparrows Point, Maryland[1]

11:00 A. M.

Governor Herbert O' Connor 'phoned from Annapolis saying that he was going into a conference with General Reckord with respect to troop protection at Sparrows Point Monday, August 2. In response to my question, Governor O'Connor declined to say that he would not interpose any objections to the moving in of Federal troops. He stated that he would let me know what resulted from the conference he was about to hold with army officials and asked me to 'phone him in Baltimore—Plaza 4300—if any additional information on the situation came to me.

1: 30 P. M.

Jonathan Daniels, Administrative Assistant to the President, telephoned me and agreed that Federal troops must be on hand at Sparrows Point tomorrow, regardless of the Negro-white conference which is to be held today at Sparrows Point from one to four o'clock.

4:30 P. M.

Clarence Mitchell, FEPC representative, and Mr. Knotts, Personnel Manager of the Bethlehem Shipbuilding Company, phoned me from Sparrows Point saying that the Negro-white conference held this afternoon agreed upon nothing. Knotts read me the proposal which the management made to the conferees. It is:

> "The Company considers the establishment and maintenance of courses a management function but is willing to agree to conduct riveting crew training on the following basis:
>
>> Applicants will be placed in a school for tryout and preliminary training. The applicants who successfully complete this preliminary training and prove their likelihood of becoming proficient in riveting will be placed on a list from which positions in the riveting gang will be filled. When it is necessary to increase the number of riveting gangs, all men in the present gang will be entitled to promotion in line with their ability and length of service. On the job, training will be provided so that in a practical way men presently in the crews, as well as men who are added from the school, may have an opportunity to become qualified for the job ahead. The service date of all men presently in the riveting department as well as all men assigned from the ground school is the date on which their continuous service record in the riveting department started."

Knotts and Mitchell reported that the Negroes rejected this proposal. They said that the Negroes held that Negroes who came out of this school should be eligible for top jobs and this proposal excludes them from eligibility.

The whites thought the proposal could be made workable but did not endorse or accept it.

Knotts said the riveting school will open tomorrow and will have four Negroes and eight whites, and that there must be troop protection at the plant.

Mitchell said: "The colored will be back to work tomorrow."

5:30 P. M.

I telephoned Governor O'Connor at Baltimore and informed him of the outcome of the conference this afternoon. He evaded my question "will you request Federal troops at Sparrows Point tomorrow or will you at least raise no objection to their coming in." His answer was that he has been thinking of the whole matter for 48 hours. He further said that the plan he is working out with the army, State police and local police is to have the Federal troops available in the event they are needed.

5:45 P. M.

Jonathan Daniels telephoned to say that Admiral Emory S. Land has been working all afternoon on the War Department to assure adequate troop protection tomorrow at Sparrows Point.

8:30 P. M.

Clarence Mitchell telephoned from Baltimore to say that the Executive Board of Local 33, Marine and Shipbuilding Workers Union, had accepted the proposal made to the Negro-white conference this afternoon with management and the Executive Board added an amendment making the whole offer of management a bit more palatable to Negroes. Mitchell asked me whether I, as Chairman of FEPC, would approved of this agreement and I instructed him to tell the Negro workman that our approval or disapproval rests with them entirely.

MS: LH, HqR3, *Office Files of Malcolm Ross. Father Haas Memoranda.*
    This memorandum was prepared by Father Haas. On the Bethlehem Steel case, see the digest of 7/31/43 and Mitchell's field report of 8/6/43, both in appendix 1, and for background, the headnotes on Strikes and Work Stoppages and on the Shipbuilding Industry.

Field Investigation Report on Bethlehem Steel and Shipbuilding Company, Baltimore, Md.

PRESIDENT'S COMMITTEE ON FAIR EMPLOYMENT PRACTICE

WASHINGTON, D. C.

FIELD INVESTIGATION REPORT

Date of Report -August 6, 1943
Name of Examiner -Clarence M. Mitchell
Name of Company - - - - - - - - - - - - - - - -Bethlehem Steel and Shipbuilding Company,
Baltimore, Maryland

Dates of Contact -July 29 to August 2 inclusive

Names and Titles of Persons Conferred with -J.B. Knotts
Management Representative
Francis G. Wrightson
Assistant General Manager
Bethlehem Steel and Shipbuilding Company

Philip Van Gelder
Secretary–Treasurer
Industrial Union of Marine
and Shipbuilding Workers
Eugene Crocetti
President, Local 33
Edward Denhardt
Business Agent, Local 33

L. F. Rye
Commissioner of Conciliation
U. S. Department of Labor

Richard Cooley
Maritime Commission

Julius H. Gardner
War Manpower Commission

Charles W. Mitzel
War Production Board

Major Roach
Internal Security Division
Third Service Command

Total Number of Persons Employed -8,468

Total Number of Negroes Employed -1,452

Name of Union -Industrial Union of Marine
and Shipbuilding Workers

Method of Training -VTFW and In-plant Training

Progress Report

August 6, 1943

TO: Mr. George M. Johnson
   Assistant to the Chairman

FROM: Clarence M. Mitchell
   Associate Director of Field Operations

RE: Bethlehem Steel Shipbuilding Company,
           Sparrows Point, Maryland[1]

Investigation by: Clarence M. Mitchell

I. Brief Summary of Complaint

On Thursday morning, July 29, Mr. Randall Tyus, Executive Secretary of the Baltimore NAACP, informed the President's Committee on Fair Employment Practice that the Bethlehem Steel Shipbuilding Company had excluded Negroes from a training course set up for the riveting department. He also stated that because of this exclusion, Negro employees walked out of the plant, and some of them had been arrested. I was sent to Baltimore at noon. Negro passers in the riveting department and Negro crane operators had walked out of the yard after the company had closed its school. The training had been stopped originally because of objections by whites employed in the riveting department.

II. Description of Party Charged

The July 270 report of the USES shows that the Bethlehem Steel Shipbuilding Company employs 3,468 persons. Of these, 1,452 are Negroes. The company has increased its Negro employment steadily during the past year. It is building vessels for the Maritime Commission. This company is part of the Bethlehem Steel interest. Adjacent to the shipyard at Sparrows Point is the Bethlehem Steel Mill which employs approximately 20,000 persons. Of these, 5,000 are Negroes. The steel mill was not involved in the controversy.

The company states that it is employing Negroes as shipfitters, tack welders, crane operators, riggers, and in other jobs. However, management admits that for a long time the yard has had a practice of setting aside certain jobs for Negroes and certain jobs for whites. This has resulted in a heavy concentration of Negroes in unskilled jobs. White women are being employed for production work, but Negro women are used in service jobs only.

The company has a contract with Local 33 of the Industrial Union of Marine and Shipbuilding Workers of America. A majority of employees and almost all of the persons in the riveting department are member of the union. From meeting with the Negro employees it appeared that many of them are in the union but only a few attend the meetings.

III. Prior or related cases involving the party charged.

The Committee has not received any previous complaints against this company.

IV. Efforts of the War Manpower Commission to obtain compliance.

The War Manpower Commission has made several contacts with the company for the purpose of obtaining greater use of Negro labor supply in the Baltimore area. As a result of such contacts management inaugurated a program of using Negroes as welders and in the ship-fitting department. The company apparently decided to train Negroes and whites in riveting because of a need to increase the number of rivets driven such week from 60,000 to 90,000.

V. Efforts to obtain compliance.

Meetings were held with the following company officials; Mr. J. B. Knotts, Management representative in charge of industrial relations for the shipyard, and Mr. Francis G. Wrightson, Assistant to the General Manager of the Bethlehem Steel Plant. Conferences were also held with Mr. Philip Van Gelder, Secretary-Treasurer of the International Union of the Industrial Union of Marine and Shipbuilding Workers, Mr. Eugene Crocetti, President of Local 33, and Mr. Edward Denhardt, Business Agent for the local, Mr. L. F. Rye, Commissioner of Conciliation for the U. S. Department of Labor, Mr. Richard Cooley of the Maritime Commission, Mr. Julius M. Gardner of the War Manpower Commission, Mr. Charles W. Mitzel of the War Production Board, and Major Roach of the office of Colonel Johnson C. Brady of the Internal Security Division of the Third Service Command.

The dispute had its beginning on Monday, July 26, when four Negroes were assigned to the riveting school. In protest, between 125 and 150 white employees in the riveting department stopped work. The white employees contend they stopped working because the school would interfere with promotions as originally planned. The Negroes charge that the sole issue was the presence of colored trainees. Mr. Knotts informed the white workers that the school was necessary to increase the driving of rivets from 60,000 per week to 90,000. The whites answered this by saying they could drive that many. The school was closed to give the whites the opportunity to prove they could drive an additional 30,000 rivets per week.

On Wednesday, July 28, approximately 30 Negroes employed as passers in the riveting department walked off the job as protest against the closing of school. Later they were joined by Negro crane-men and finally by most of the colored employees on the day shift (approximately 800). On Thursday, July 29, the company agreed to reopen the school but when the Negroes began to return to the job a misunderstanding arose and they thought the school was not open. Hence, some of them did not go to work. As the men began to mill around some disorders occurred. Six Negroes were arrested during the disturbance. Three charged with inciting to riot were released. Two charged with assault with deadly weapons were fined. One charged with having a deadly weapon was released for lack of proof that he had it in his possession.

In the beginning I explained to management and the union representatives that (1) the school would have to remain open with Negroes in it, (2) I would try to get the colored men to return to the job, (3) the union should take the responsibility of keeping its own members in line, and, (4) every effort should be made to preserve order in the yard by using all available resources plus any other type of assistance needed.

I met with approximately 500 Negro employees in a somewhat stormy meeting on Thursday night at the Elks' Hall in Baltimore. The men voted to return to work with the understanding that the school would stay open. They kept their pledge. The yard reopened on Friday, July 30, but it appears that certain white individuals persuaded fellow workers to leave their jobs when they found the school was open. It also appears that although the company had ample warning that trouble might occur, very little was done by the police to prevent the activities of those stirring up arguments. Many whites and almost all of the Negroes remained on their jobs, but the company feared that fights would ensue. The yard was closed at noon on Friday, with the Maritime Commission's permission.

A Committee of six Negroes and six white persons met to discuss the problems raised by the opening of the riveting school. I attended all of these meetings although I did not agree that it was wise to have them. The conferees met almost all day Friday, part of Saturday, and from 12:30 p.m. to 4:00 p.m. on Sunday. Counter proposals were made by each group and when no agreement was reached, the Executive Board of Local 33, voted that the school would be reopened with colored and white trainees. They also voted that when these trainees finished their period of instruction they would be returned to the jobs previously held and all upgrading would be on the basis of strict departmental seniority. This means that in the future there must be fully mixed crews of Negroes and whites. In the past, Negroes have worked with white crews, but only as passers which is the lowest grade in the department.

The yard was reopened on Monday, August 2. Almost all of the Negroes and most of the whites reported for work. Some of the whites walked off the job, but the yard continued operations. Present to maintain order were, State, County and company police. At Logan Field, two miles away, United States Troops were encamped after what the local internal security representatives of the Army described as a "practice march". Actually, these troops were to move in to maintain order if serious trouble occurred, according to Major Roach.

Most of the employees who left the jobs were working in the riveting department. Some shipfitters and erectors also left. These workers held a meeting after they walked out and voted to return to work the next day. On Tuesday morning, they did return to work and the union threatened to discipline any members who walked off the job. The workers went on the job at 7:00 A. M. There was a rumor that a walkout would occur at 9:00 A. M. when workers normally go to the lunch room to buy milk. The union sent shop stewards throughout the yard to squelch this rumor. The stewards were successful and no walk-out occurred. The yard operations are now normal. The Negroes are in the training school. No white trainees were in the school on Tuesday, August 3, but since there were only two gangs this does not seem to present a serious problem.

VI. Attached are copies of statement made by: the company, the union, the two committees, and individual employees.

VII. <u>Recommendations for further action.</u>

Because of the recent trouble at the yard, in my opinion it would not be wise to attempt an adjustment of further problems immediately. However, I have discussed with management some of the complaints which must be handled in the future. I recommend that when a director is appointed in Region IV, this company receive his immediate attention. As will be noted in my report, some of the matters which will require steps are as follows:

1. Checking to make certain that the seniority scheme in the riveting department works equitably.
2. Correction of hiring practices which cause concentration of Negroes in laboring jobs.
3. Setting up plans to make use of Negro women for Production work.

(ATTACHMENTS)

[Attachment 1: Statements by the Company]

SUBSIDIARY COMPANIES OF BETHLEHEM STEEL CORPORATION
SPARROWS POINT, MD.

July 29, 1943

This is to certify that the Riveting School has been reopened, and will continue in operation on the same basis as Monday, July 26, 1943.

The men who did not work Wednesday, July 23, 1943, will be paid time and one-half for Saturday, July 31, and double time if they work Sunday, August 1, 1943, provided they do not lose any other days.

J. B. Knotts
Management's Representative

DISPOSITION OF CASES OF PERSONS ARRESTED AT THE BETHLEHEM STEEL SHIPYARD, July 29, 1943

The following men were arrested on a charge of inciting to riot: John A. Jacobs, George E. Boulding, and Willie Saunderlin. All three of them were dismissed.

Charles Shelton was arrested on a charge of assault with a deadly weapon. He was alleged to have pointed a knife at a white guard. Shelton testified that he had a knife in his hand while showing his badge to the guard. The guard said that the knife was open and the blade was pointed at his stomach. He also testified that Shelton seemed to be "poking" at him with the knife. Shelton argued that the blade was open but pointed away from the guard. The accused also said he had been working on his fingernails, hence he had the knife open. A fine of $26.45 was placed on Shelton. He paid this and was released.

McKinley Parker was also arrested on a charge of assault with a deadly weapon. He testified that he was "playing" when he cut a fellow colored employee with a knife. He was fined $11.45 which he paid. The accused was then released.

Frederick Johnson was charged with having a deadly weapon in his possession. The weapon exhibited was a home-made club or black-jack which seemed to weigh several pounds. The two white witnesses testified that Johnson made the weapon by wrapping friction tape around pieces of metal. Johnson testified that he made the weapon but did not know what he was going to do with it. He was released without a fine when it was found he did not have it in his possession at the time of his arrest.

[Attachment 2: Statements by the Union]

<u>NEWS RELEASE</u>

July 30, 1943

The disturbance at the Sparrows Point Shipyard which resulted in the management's shutting down the plant at noon today to prevent a riot, were caused by irresponsible individuals and agitators, who were not officers or members of the Union.

Stoppages of negroes and white workers developed on a large scale Wednesday, Thursday and Friday. They were occasioned by differences of opinion as to opportunities for training, for Negroes and whites. These differences could have been settled without any great trouble in peaceful discussions within the Union if the aforementioned agitators had not magnified the issue, and incited the stoppages.

The Union's position is firmly against any form of racial discrimination and this policy has been reaffirmed by the Local #33 Executive Board within the last two (2) days. The Union will not permit under any circumstances the removing of negroes from a job or barring him from an opportunity, because of his color.

We will not compromise an inch of this issue, which we consider fundamental to true Americanism, and in accordance with President Roosevelt's Executive Order 9346. At the same time we will not permit the worsening of wages or working conditions for any Shipyard workers.

This was no good reason for the stoppages in the yard and the Union Officers, Shop Stewards, and Committeemen did everything in their power to prevent the stoppages and keep the men from ganging up in the yard where they were inflamed by hysterical soap box orators. Anti-union elements which provoked the disorder should be disciplined by management.

The Union urges that all men return to work Monday morning in a calm and peaceful manner and redouble their efforts to get out the ships needed to win the War. If all the Sparrows Point Workers will cooperate earnestly in this effort, we can perhaps atone for the disgraceful events of the past few days.

Any legitimate dispute or grievance that any men have can and must be settled by and through the Industrial Union of Marine and Shipbuilding Workers, Local #33 which is the only legal representative of the men at the Sparrows Point Yard.

Industrial Union of Marine and
Shipbuilding Workers of America
Philip M. Van Gelder
Nat. Sec't—Treas.

NEWS RELEASE OF I.U.M.S.W.A.*

August 1, 1943

The question of the riveters school at Sparrows Point was settled by the Union Executive Board and agreed to by the Company this afternoon preparatory to reopening of the Shipyard tomorrow morning.

The discussions of the last few days resulted this afternoon in a written proposal by the Bethlehem Company which was accepted by the Union with a single amendment. This proposal embodied the principle of seniority which had been insisted upon by the Union and also the principle of no racial discrimination.

The school is to continue in operation as originally started with both white and colored trainees. In addition there will be training on the job in the riveting department. Graduates of the school and training program will be put on the higher skilled jobs in the department on a strict seniority basis, regardless of color. As openings occur for riveters they will be filled by the holder-ons on the basis of their length of service in the department. When holder-ons are needed they will be taken from the heaters, and heaters jobs will be filled by the passers. The amendment proposed by the Union and accepted by the Company was that no skilled men from the outside will be hired as long as qualified men are available in the department.

Further details of the agreement will be worked out by the Union's Grievance Committee, the Negro Committee and riveters committee with the Management tomorrow morning.

On the basis of this settlement all men are expected to return to work without disorder.

* The Union executive committee also voted unanimously that troops should be in the yard to maintain order.

[Attachment 3: Statements by the Committees]

The Riveting Department made the following proposal:

The Riveting Department is willing to train men any time the conditions warrant. They desire that this be done on the basis of Departmental Seniority, and that it be done by sending the trainee with a regular gang, under actual conditions on the boat.

They are opposed to the ground school on the basis that past experience has shown that that system does not afford a fair opportunity to the men already working in the Department.

(SIGNED) Andred Fits
Michael Fets
Willie Zieler
W. Burtholdt
George Lubin
William Malloy

CM: mem

7–30–43

PROPOSAL MADE BY THE NEGROES REPRESENTING THE TRAINING SCHOOL:

The proposal of the Committee for the Riveting School is to open the school as originally planned, to be open to both white and colored trainees.

(SIGNED) Abner Lee
Louis Brown
Clarence Gilliam
Charles Alford
Walter White
Stokes

CM: mem

7–30–43

[Attachment 4: Statements of Individual Employees]

Statements by Persons Employed at the Bethlehem Steel Shipbuilding Company, Sparrows Point, Maryland

The following statements were made by workers at the Bethlehem Steel Shipbuilding Company on Friday, July 30 and Saturday, July 31. All of these statements were obtained to determine what was the cause of the walk-out of some white workers on Friday following the return of the Negroes who had been off the job on Thursday. Those white workers who did leave the yard on Friday hampered operations to some extent. The company feared that there would be racial trouble and requested permission from the Maritime Commission to close the yard. The statements of the workers given seem to indicate that if proper steps had been taken to prevent the stirring up of trouble by certain individuals it might not have been necessary to close the yard. Unless otherwise indicated, the persons making the statement are Negroes.

1. Statement of Mr. Joseph Gilden

Mr. Gilden is white and works in the S. C. Department. On Saturday, July 31, he stated that on Friday morning almost all of the persons in his department were at work. This amounts to approximately 1800 persons. The men in his department continued to work until the yard was officially closed at noon, Mr. Gilden stated.

2. Statement of Mr. Harold Williams

Mr. Williams is white and a shop steward in the sheetmetal department. He stated that in his opinion 85% of the men in his shop remained on their jobs on Friday, July 30, until the yard was closed at noon by the company. He also stated that he walked through the yard when the first white workers left on Friday morning and many persons who were standing around did not know what was causing the disturbance.

3. Statement of Mr. Walter White

Mr. White is a shop steward and works in the crane department. He described what he saw on Friday morning, July 30. He stated that from his crane he noticed whites at #6 slip seemed to be congregating and he learned that they were threatening not to work if the Negro crane operators remained on the job. Mr. White stated that as near as he could determine about 90 Negroes working in the crane operation department were on the job on Friday morning. He stated that the company has about 30 Negro crane operators. Other Negroes work in various capacities in this department.

4. Statement of Mr. Douglas I. Parker, 602 Pitcher St., Baltimore, Md.

Mr. Parker is employed in the welding department as a tacker. He stated that he saw riveters meet on #6 way. They formed a group and started to one of the company's offices. According to his statement, they were led by Mr. George Lubin, who is shop steward in the riveting department. The man stopped in front of # 4 way, he said.

Some other men went to other boats to get white workers to come off. A white person who was working as a leadermen on # 4 Boat where Mr. Parker is employed suggested that the colored men go into the hold of the ship. There were 14 Negroes working at the time in this section, Mr. Parker stated, but none of them accepted the advice of the white leadermen. No one threatened them, Mr. Parker said, and they finally left the job at approximately 10:30 a. m.

5. Statement of Mr. Edward Harris, 1315 E. Riddle Street, Baltimore, Md.

Mr. Harris, a crane operator, stated that he was at his job when he saw white men coming up from #6 way. At #2 way, he said, the whites stopped and yelled at a crane operator named James Jones to come out of the crane. Mr. Harris stated that one of the whites named Arthur Streets appeared to make a speech. Mr. Streets went on the # 2 slip, Mr. Harris stated, and began urging whites to come off the boat. Mr. Harris did not leave his crane and stated that he made three lifts during the day. He left his post at noon. These lifts, Mr. Harris stated, were as follows: The first two were made by taking boxes from # 2 slip to # 3 for the "Y" department. The third was when he took empty gas tanks to the head of the slip for refilling. Mr. Harris said that a Lieutenant of the police in the yard suggested that some of the Negroes allow the whites to leave first when the yard was closed at noon. On his way to get his card to punch out, Mr. Harris said, two white men mentioned that it was a shame that the colored people were not getting the proper treatment.

6. Statement of Mr. Bernard Hills, 1116 Central Avenue, Baltimore, Md.

Mr. Hills is a brakeman in the crane department on the wet dock. He stated that on Friday, July 30, all of the Negroes in his department reported for work. This amounted to approximately 17. His department had 100% cooperation from the white employees. There was no violence and work stopped only when the company closed the yard at noon, Mr. Hills said.

7. Statement of Mr. Collis Williams, 1922 Madison Avenue, Baltimore, Md.

Mr. Williams is a crane conductor working between ways 5 and 6. He stated that he was told to take his proper place in the crane and did so. He would have operated the crane, he said, but white men began to gather on the track. However, he remained at his post until noon when the company closed the yard.

8. Statement of Mr. Edward Palmer, 518 Baker Street, Baltimore, Md.

Mr. Palmer is a tacker in the welding department on the wet dock. He stated that he is working on Boat 94. Around 10:15 A. M. on Friday, July 30, a white man suggested that the tackers get off the boat, Mr. Palmer said. Mr. Palmer did not know this man's name but said he was "some kind of a boss". About 6 or 8 colored men came off the boat in response to this order, Mr. Palmer said. Before 10:15 there did not seem to be any trouble, Mr. Palmer said, but when he left his job at 8:50 A. M. to get some milk for the white workers all of the whites walked off during his absence. This took him by complete surprise, Mr. Palmer said, because he was buying milk for a number of whites and still had their money.

9. Statement of Mr. Roy Elam, 526 Druid Hill Avenue, Baltimore, Maryland

Mr. Elam is a crane conductor. He stated that he reported for work at 7:00 A. M. on July 30 and remained until noon when the company closed the yard. He stated that he did not see any of the whites he ordinarily contacted begin work.

10. Statement of Mr. W. S. Foster, 821 Eye Street, Sparrows Point, Md.

Mr. Foster works in the labor department and on July 30 was employed in the sorting yard. He stated that 15 or 20 colored persons are ordinarily in this group and all of them were on the job. He remained in the yard until noon when the company closed it. On the way to the men's room, Mr. Foster stated, he heard a white man say, "Grab him". However, no one touched him.

11. Statement of Mr. Douglas Mise, 1212 W. Lanvale Street, Baltimore, Md.

Mr. Mise is a tack welder in the South yard. He stated that on July 30 he arrived on the job at approximately 7:40 A. M. When he entered he saw white persons going to #6 slip. However, he did not find out why they were going. Mr. Mise said that he would have worked on what was called the bulkhead skids but the crane (which is operated by a white person) was not in service and work materials, therefore, were not available. He stayed in the yard until noon and went home on a street car. A number of whites were in the car but none of them seemed in a mood to cause trouble.

12. Statement of Mr. R. W. Lester, 1207 Druid Hill Avenue, Baltimore, Md.

Mr. Lester is a tack welder in the South yard. He stated that he works in the fluter plate department. He got on the job about 6:40 A. M. on Friday, July 30, and three other colored workers who normally are with him were also there, he said. When he got his tools to work with none of the whites said anything to him, Mr. Lester said.

However, the white crane operators would not service the departments so it was impossible to work. Mr. Lester said he left at noon when the yard was closed and did not have any trouble.

MS: copy, HqR85, Office Files of St. Clair T. Bourne, Information Officer, July 1943–Nov. 1945. (A–Z), Sparrows Point.
    1. Mitchell was serving as FEPC's field investigator during walkouts at the Bethlehem Steel Shipyard at Sparrows Point in Baltimore. See also his memorandum of 11/1/43 and the digests of his telephone conversations of 7/31 and 8/1/43, in this appendix. For background, see the headnotes on Strikes and Work Stoppages and on the Shipbuilding Industry.

Cases Currently Being Handled by Clarence M. Mitchell

CASES CURRENTLY BEING HANDLED

By

Clarence M. Mitchell – 9/14/43

*1. International Union of Mine Mill and Smelter Workers—v. Basic Magnesium Inc., Las Vegas, Nevada. - 12-BR-125.

*2. Region IX W.M.C. Report on Failure of Emerson Electric Co., St. Louis, Mo., to Supply E. S. 270 Information - 9-BR-40.

3. International Union of Hod Carriers and Building Laborers, Local 826 v. Daniel Construction Company, Charleston, S. C. - 7-BR-108.

*4. Wiley A. Hall, Richmond, Va., v. Russell and Wise Construction Co. building McGuire Hospital, Richmond, Va.

5. Region IX W.M.C. Report on Aluminum Co. of America, Vernon, California, failure to hire Negroes because of housing shortage.

6. U.S.E.S., Stockton, California, 510 Report on Army Ordnance Deport, Stockton, California - 12-GR-115.

*7. W.P. B. Report on Jones and Laughlin Steel Co., Aliquippa, Pennsylvania (Threatened Strike of Negro Employees). - 3-BR-209.

8. James J. Nicholas v. War Shipping Administration - 10-GR-11.

9. Mrs. Sarah Davenport v. Patterson Field, Fairfield, Ohio - 5-GR-327.

*10. Miss Ruby Bell v. U. S. Weather Bureau - 2-GR-147.

11. Citizens' Committee of Columbia, S. C. v. Columbia, S. C. USES - 7-GR-113.

12. Miss Louise Sellers v. Cincinnati USES.

*13. Point Breeze Employees Association v. Western Electric Company, Baltimore, Maryland.

14. Misses Artie L. Cox, Evelyne A. Benson and Willie G. Pope v. War Department, Dayton, Ohio - 5-GR-83.

15. Miss Josephine B. Jones v. Civil Service Commission, St. Louis, Mo. - 9-GR-35.

16. Miss Catherine Valentine v. Army Ordnance Depot (Referred for final disposition by New York office)

17. Abram Rose v. Oklahoma City Air Depot.

18. Miss Daisy Lemon v. American Bridge Company, Leetsdale, Pa. - 3-BR-101.

19. Miss Cora Page v. Natta Motors Co., Braddock, Pa. - 3-BR-102.

*20. Denver Colored Civic Association, Denver, Colorado v. West Construction Company of Seattle, Washington - 12-BR-85.

21. Mrs. Vernie Wilson v. Amertorp Corporation, St. Louis, Mo.

*22. Karl Kemp and Savannah Trades and Labor Assembly v. Southeastern Shipbuilding Corporation, Savannah, Georgia - 7-BR-80.

*23. Citizens Committee of Los Angeles, et al, v. Los Angeles Street Railway Co.

24. Citizens Committee of San Diego v. San Diego Electric Railway Co., San Diego, Cal.

25. Miss Fern Webb v. Cable Spinning Company, Topeka, Kansas - 9-BR-36.

26. R. H. Anderson v. Holmes Construction Co., Wooster, Ohio,-5-BR-276.

27. Miss Carolyn A. Palmer v. Owens Illinois Bottle Co., Glassboro, N. J.

28. William Opher, 916 W. Franklin Street, Baltimore, v. American Smelting and Refining Company, Baltimore, Maryland - 4-BR-54.

29. Nathaniel Oban, Inlay City, Mich. v. War Food Administration

30. Miss Mary Nathan v. North American Aviation Co., Dallas, Texas.

31. Anon. v. 11th Naval District, North Island, San Diego, California,-12-GC-118.

32. Mrs. Catherine Martinez v. Bethlehem Steel Co., Bethlehem, Pa. - 3-BR-135.

33. Miss Mary Jane Lewis v. Erdette Hosiery Mills, Cuowensville, Pa.

34. Sidney D. Kirby v. J. A. Jones Construction Co., Brunswick, Ga. - 7-BR-89.

35. Mrs. Edith C. King v. Todd Shipbuilding Corporation, New Orleans, La.

*36. Mrs. G. T. Hamilton et al. v. J. A. Jones Construction Co. recruiting in Atlanta, Georgia - 7-BR-119.

37. Catherine Curry v. Strickland Aircraft Co., Topeka, Kansas - 9-BR-51.

38. Nathaniel Churchwell v. Civil Service Commission, Philadelphia, Pa.

*39. St. Louis NAACP v. McQuay Norris Company, St. Louis, Mo. - 9-BR-24.

40. Clairton NAACP v. Carnegie Illinois Steel Company, Clairton, Pa.

41. Rev. O. G. Butler v. North American Aviation Co., Kansas City, Kan. - 9-BR-1.

42. Mrs. Ida F. Binion v. Lockheed-Vega Aircraft Corp. - 12-BR-92.

*43. American Steel Foundries Co., Indiana Harbor, Indiana (Referred by Justice Department. Possible Race Trouble).

44. David Beans and Sanders Washington v. Buick Aviation Co., Melrose Park, Ill.

45. Frank Abercrumbie v. Bricklayers Union No. 2 - 3-UR-130.

46. Andrew J. Adams v. Westinghouse Electric Company, Farrell, Pa.

47. National Maritime Union v. War Shipping Administration in behalf of Crew Members of the S.S. Lawrence D. Thyssen.

*48. W.P.B. Report on Possible Labor Trouble among Negroes of Andrews Steel Co., Covington, Ky.

49. Joseph E. Baker v. American South African Lines, San Francisco, California. 12-BR-23.

50. Mrs. Mary Jackson v. USES of St. Louis, Missouri - 9-GR-10.

51. Mrs. Sarah Dinkins v. Remington Arms Inc., Independence, Mo.

*52. James E. Carter v. Kansas City Power and Light Co., Kansas City, Mo.

53. Heber Votaw in behalf of Sabbatarians (Action Awaiting Committee Policy).

54. Mrs. Beatrice Johnson v. Warner Robins Air Depot, Macon, Ga. - 7-GR-105.

55. Mrs. Elizabeth Roach v. State of Montana - 11-GA-3.

*56. Leonard D. Smith v. Oklahoma City Air Depot, Oklahoma City, Okla.

57. John W. Nicholas v. Civil Service Commission, Spartanburg, S. C. and Washington, D. C. - 7-GR-115.

58. J. F. Gilcrease v. Algernon Blair Co., Prichard, Alabama - 7-BR-64.

59. Gladys I. Norwood v. Aeronautical Map Plant, Army Air Forces, St. Louis, Mo.

60. Hod Carriers and Building Laborers Union v. Knutson Construction Company, Houston, Texas - 10-BR-10.

61. Robert Haskins v. Bechtel Price and Callahan Company - 12-BR-138.

*62. USES (Youngstown, Ohio) v. Railway Retirement Board, 510 Reports.

**63. Investigation of Employers in Cincinnati, Ohio Area by E.G. Trimble.

*64. Dallas Negro Chamber of Commerce v. U. S. Office of Education and Director of Training, W. M. C.

65. Mrs. Edith Myers v. North American Aviation Company, Dallas, Texas.

66. Citizens Committee on Jobs and Training, Birmingham, Alabama v. U. S. Office of Education and Director of Training, W. M. C.

67. Citizens Committee on Jobs and Training, Birmingham, Alabama v. Bechtel McCone Parsons Aircraft Conversion Plant, Birmingham, Ala.

68. Total War Employment Committee v. Chesapeake and Potomac Telephone Co., Baltimore, Maryland - 4-BR-3.

69. Benjamin Davis et al v. Swift Manufacturing Co, Columbus, Ga. - 7-BR-65 to 7-BR-75.

*70. Davison Chemical Corporation, Baltimore, Md. (discriminatory advertising) - 4-BR-104.

71. Miss Estelle Lingham v. U. S. Civil Service Commission, Washington, D. C.

72. Anon. v. Office of Defense Transportation, Mobile, Alabama (Adjustment Made).

73. USES 510 Report on U. S. Department of Agriculture, Stockton, California - 12-GR-127.

74. Mrs. Esta W. Stringer v. Lockheed-Vega Aircraft Co., Los Angeles, California - 12-BR-21.

---

*Important cases on which further correspondence may be necessary before I return.

**I have discussed these cases with Mr. Johnson. The file is still in our Central Office, but I am taking a copy of Mr. Trimble's report with me to Cleveland.[1]

MS: copy, HqR3, Office Files of George M. Johnson. M.

1. Mitchell was about to depart on extended field trips to the Midwest and Far West. Based on his memoranda for the period, he visited Cleveland and Detroit (Region V) on 9/22 and 23, then possibly returned to Washington and left again, visiting Chicago from 9/29 to 10/2, Minneapolis on 10/4, Dallas by 10/12, Portland, Oregon, from 10/18 to 10/22, and Los Angeles from 10/22 to 10/28. See Mitchell's memoranda of 9/22 and 9/25, 10/8, 10/12, 10/18–23, 10/26–/27, 11/1, and 11/6; and the references to his mission in the transcript of the FEPC meeting of 10/18/43, in HqR64. See also the headnote on the Shipbuilding Industry. The Trimble report referred to was probably his report to George Johnson of 9/10/43 on Investigation of Discrimination against Negroes in War Industries in Cincinnati, a copy of which is in HqR48, Central Files. Company Reports to and from the Field (A–J). There is also an earlier Trimble report to Haas of 6/8/43 in which, based in his visit to Cincinnati, he had found that the most difficult problem was the failure to upgrade blacks because employers had found it easier to recruit "new white workers and start training them immediately for skilled and semi-skilled positions than to find new employees for the labor crew to take the place of any of the old employees who were upgraded from the labor crew." Trimble said he learned that "this failure to upgrade applied also somewhat to white men in the labor crew so it was not only a matter of race." Another problem, he said, arose from the belief among employers that blacks were unreliable workers. The Reynolds Metal Corporation and the Voigt Machine Company, he reported, were particularly difficult in that they had never cooperated with either the FEPC or the WMC. HqR38, Central Files. Memoranda, Haas, Francis J.

Bibliography on the Negro Worker and the War

BIBLIOGRAPHY ON THE NEGRO WORKER AND THE WAR[1]

[ca. September 1943]

This is not an attempt to list all of the important books and articles about Negroes. It is a selected list of publications which deal either directly with the Negro's participation in war industries or the environmental patterns which influence the attitudes of colored workers. Since the periodical material is more current it is listed first.

Periodical and Pamphlets

American Management Association, The Negro Worker. Special Research Report No. 1. New York: American Management Association, 1942. 32 pp.

Branson, Herman, "The Training of Negroes for War Industries in World War II," Journal of Negro Education, Summer Number, 1943. pp. 376–85.

Brown, Earl and Leighton, George R., The Negro and the War. New York, Public Affairs Committee, Inc., August 1942. 32 pp.

Clark, Kenneth B. "The Morale of the Negro on the Home Front," Journal of Negro Education, Summer Number 1943. pp. 417–28.

Davis, John A., How Management Can Integrate Negroes in War Industries. New York: New York State War Council, Committee on Discrimination in Employment, 1942. 43 pp.

_____, "The Negro Outlook Today," Survey Graphic, November, 1942. pp. 500–03; 562–63.

Feldman, Herman, "The Technique of Introducing Negroes into the Plant," Personnel. New York: American Management Association, September 1942. pp. 461–66.

Fortune, "The Negro's War," June 1942. pp. 79 et seq.

Fortune, "Whose Manpower?" January 1943. pp. 79 et seq.

Granger, Lester B., et al. Toward Job Adjustment. New York: Welfare Council of New York City, 1941. 78 pp.

_____, "Barriers to Negro War Employment," The Annals of the American Academy of Political Science, September 1942. pp. 72–80.

_____, "Negroes and War Production," Survey Graphic November 1942. pp. 469–71; 543–44.

Gosnell, Harold F., "Symbols of National Solidarity": The Annals of the American Academy of Political and Social Science, 1942, pp. 157–61.

Johnson, Charles S., "The Negro Minority," The Annals of the American Academy of Political and Social Science, September 1942.

——————— "Striking the Economic Balance," Survey Graphic, November 1942. pp. 496–98; 555–56.

Kirkpatrick, Forrest H., "Color in the Production Line," International Quarterly, Summer 1942. pp. 25 et seq.

Locke, Alain, "The Unfinished Business of Democracy," "Survey Graphic, November 1942, pp. 455–59.

Modern Industry, "Found: A Million Manpower," May 1942. pp. 28–31.

National Urban League, Putting Victory First, New York, 1942. 5 pp.

Nichols, Franklin O., "Employment of the Colored Worker," Personnel, July 1942. p. 409 et seq.

Northrup, George, "Organized Labor and the Negro, "Journal of Political Economy, June 1943, pp. 206–21.

Ransom, Leon A., "Combatting Discrimination in the Employment of Negroes in War Industries and Government Agencies," Journal of Negro Education, Summer Number 1943. pp. 405–16.

Roberts, Thomas N., "The Negro in Government War Agencies," Journal of Negro Education, Summer Number 1943. pp. 367–75.

Sancton, Thomas, "Trouble in Dixie," New Republic, January 4, 1943 pp. 11–14; January 18, 1943, pp. 81–83; February 8, 1943, pp. 175–79

——————— , "The Race Riots," New Republic, July 5, 1943 pp. 9–12.

Social Security Board, Employment Security Review, July 1942.

Thompson, Charles H., ed., "The Position of the Negro in the American Social Order," Journal of Negro Education, Yearbook, July 1939.

——————— , "The American Negro in World War I and World War II," Journal of Negro Education, Summer Number 1943. pp. 263–67.

War Manpower Commission, Manpower: One-Tenth of a Nation, 1942. 15 pp.

Weaver, Robert C., "Racial Employment Trends in National Defense,' Phylon, Atlanta: The Atlanta University Review of Race and Culture, Part I, Fourth Quarter, 1941, pp. 337–58; Part II, First Quarter, 1942, pp. 22–30.

——————— , "With the Negro's Help," The Atlantic Monthly, June 1942. pp. 696–707.

——————— , "Defense Industries and the Negro," The Annals of the American Academy of Political and Social Science, September 1942. pp. 60–66.

——————— , "Detroit and Negro Skill," Phylon, Second Quarter, 1943. 131–143.

——————— , "The Employment of the Negro in War Industries," Journal of Negro Education, Summer Number 1943. pp. 386–96.

Books

Bond, Horace M., The Education of the Negro in the American Social Order New
York: Prentice-Hall, Inc. 1934. 501 pp.

Brown, Ina Corinne, Socio-Economic Approach to Educational Problems, Volume I of the National Survey of the Higher Education of Negroes, Washington: Government Printing Office, 1942. 166 pp.

Cayton, Horace C. and Mitchell, George S., The Black Worker and the New Unions. Chapel Hill, N.C.: University of North Carolina Press, 1939. 473 pp.

Davis, Allison and Dollars, John, Children of Bondage. Washington: American Council on Education, 1940. 299 pp.

Embree, Edwin R., American Negroes: A Handbook. New York: The John Day Company, 1942, 78 pp.

Frazier, E. Franklin, The Negro Family. Chicago: University of Chicago Press, 1939. 686 pp.

_____, Negro Youth at the Crossways. Washington: American Council on Education, 1941. 310 pp.

Johnson, Charles S., Pattern of Negro Segregation. New York: Harper and Brothers, 1942. 332 pp.

_____, Growing Up in the Black Belt. Washington: American Council on Education, 1941. 360 pp.

McWilliams, Carey, Brothers Under the Skin. Boston: Little, Brown and Company, 1943. 325 pp.

Reid, Ira DeA., The Urban Negro Worker in the United States, 1925–1926; Volume I of the Survey of the Training and Employment of White-Collar and Skilled Negro Workers. Washington: Government Printing Office, 1938. 127 pp.

Spero, Sterling D. and Harris, Abram L., The Black Worker. New York: Harper and Brothers, 1931. 509 pp.

Sterner, Richard, The Negro's Share. New York: Harper and Brothers, 1943 432 pp.

Sutherland, Robert L., Color Class and Personality. Washington: American Council on Education, 1942. 135 pp.

Weaver, Robert C., Male Negro Skilled Workers in the United States, 1930–1936: Volume II of the Survey of the Training and Employment of White-Collar and Skilled Negro Workers. Washington: Government Printing Office, 1939. 87 pp.

MS: copy, NAACP, II A 661, DLC.

1. This list, which Robert C. Weaver, then chief, Minority Group Service, WMC, sent to George Johnson on September 8, 1943, guided an annotated version prepared by the Division of Review and Analysis entitled "Suggested Readings for Staff of FEPC," December 1943, a copy of which is in HqR1, Office Files of Malcolm Ross. Weaver's letter and another copy of this bibliography are in HqR3, Office Files of George M. Johnson. Miscellaneous.

Field Instruction No. 19 on War Department

FIELD INSTRUCTION NO. 19

October 4, 1943

TO: All Regional Directors

FROM: Will Maslow
        Director of Field Operations

RE: War Department

Attached are copies of the following documents setting forth the policies and procedures adopted by the War Department to implement its obligations under Executive Orders 8802 and 9346:

1. Memorandum of the Under Secretary of War, dated June 4, 1942 (Proof of Citizenship).
2. Letter of the Under Secretary of War, dated June 5, 1942 (Employment Statistics).
3. Joint letter of the Secretary of War, etc., to the Committee dated July 2, 1942. (See Operations Bulletin, Appendix, Note 8).
4. Administrative Memorandum #55 (Religious Holidays, see Field Instruction No. 14).
5. Memorandum of Understanding of March 10, 1943 (Provost Marshal General).[1]

The following procedures shall be followed in processing complaints against:

A. <u>Government owned and government operated War Department plants</u>.

1. Determine whether a prima facie case exists by questioning the complainant and analyzing pertinent documentary and statistical data, but do not communicate with the party charged.
2. If, in your opinion, there is an apparent violation of the Executive Order which is not adjusted, submit a Request for Further Action to the Director of Field Operations.
3. The Deputy Chairman or the Director of Field Operations will then bring the matter to the attention of Mr. Truman K. Gibson, Jr., Acting Civilian Aide to the Secretary of War.

B. <u>Government owned but privately operated plants.</u> (List attached)[2]

1. Determine whether a prima facie case exists by questioning the complainant and analyzing pertinent documentary and statistical data, but do not communicate with the party charged.

2. If, in your opinion, a prima facie case exists, advise the Commanding Officer at the plant or in the area of the nature of the complaint and the results of the investigation to date, and arrange a joint conference with the party charged and the Commanding Officer. While an effort should be made to obtain the participation of the Commanding Officer or his representative, do not delay unduly the conference with the party charged.

3. Confer with the party charged and such Army representative in order to continue the investigation and/or to obtain compliance with the Executive Order.

4. If the Commanding Officer did not participate in the conference, advise him of the results thereof, and if the complaint is still unadjusted, solicit his co-operation in attempting to get compliance.

5. If there is no satisfactory adjustment within a reasonable time after the referral to the Commanding Officer, or after the joint conference with the party charged, submit a Request for Further Action to the Director of Field Operations.

6. The Deputy Chairman or the Director of Field Operations will then bring the matter to the attention of Mr. Truman K. Gibson, Jr., Acting Civilian Aide to the Secretary of War.

C. <u>Privately owned and privately operated plants</u>.

1. Determine whether a prima facie case exists by questioning the complainant and analyzing pertinent documentary and statistical data, but do not communicate with the party charged.

2. If, in your opinion, a prima facie case exists, advise the Commanding Officer at the plant or in the area of the nature of the complaint and the results of the investigation to date, and arrange for a joint conference with the party charged and the Commanding Officer. While an effort should be made to obtain the participation of the Commanding Officer or his representative, do not delay unduly the conference with the party charged.

3. Confer with the party charged and such Army representative in order to continue the investigation and/or to obtain compliance with the Executive Order.

4. If there is no satisfactory adjustment within a reasonable time after the conference, submit a Request for Further Action to the Director of Field Operations.

5. The Deputy Chairman or the Director of Field Operations will then bring the matter to the attention of Mr. Truman K. Gibson, Jr., Acting Civilian Aide to the Secretary of War.

[Attachment 1: War Department Memorandum for All Present and Prospective Army and Navy Contractors and Subcontractors signed by James Forrestal and Robert P. Patterson]

WAR DEPARTMENT
WASHINGTON

June 4, 1942

MEMORANDUM FOR ALL PRESENT AND
PROSPECTIVE ARMY AND NAVY
CONTRACTORS AND SUBCONTRACTORS

Subject: Requirement for Proof of Employees of Their American Citizenship[3]

In a memorandum dated July 16, 1941 addressed to all Army and Navy contractors and subcontractors, subject: "Requirements for Proof by Employees of their American Birth", reference was made to the provisions of certain statutes restricting the employment of aliens in connection with the performance of specific contracts (sec. 10, act of July 2, 1926, 44 Stat. 784: 10 U.S.C. 310; sec.11, act of June 28, 1940, 4 stat. 676; 50 U.S.C., App. 1), and a procedure was recommended for facilitating such employment of persons who are unable to produce birth certificates. That memorandum was concerned primarily with establishing proof of birth in the United States in cases of prospective employees who are unable, for one reason or another, to produce birth certificates. It has been the experience of recent months that the securing of the delayed certificate of birth mentioned in that memorandum has, in some instances been attended by considerable delay during which the services of the individual were not available in connection with the contracts in question. For this reason it is deemed advisable to recommend a revised procedure designed to fulfill the indicated requirements of the statutes in question.

Accordingly, the previous memorandum is suspended and in lieu of the procedure set forth therein it is recommended that contractors and subcontractors require applicants for employment in the performance of any secret, confidential, or restricted contract, or any contract for furnishing aircraft, aircraft parts, or aeronautical accessories, to sign a statement in the presence of an Army or Navy District Procurement, Factory or Plant Protection representative, to the effect that he is a citizen of the United States and that he has read and understands the pertinent provision of the act of June 28, 1940 (Public Law 671, 76th Cong.), as indicated by the enclosed form entitled "Declaration of Citizenship".

The foregoing recommended procedure does not relieve the employer from the duty of making further investigation when there is any reason to doubt the truth of applicant's declaration that he is a citizen.

Quotations from the pertinent statutes and a suggested form of declaration of citizenship are attached hereto.

Incls.

(Signed) Forrestal	(Signed) Robert B. Patterson
Under Secretary of the Navy	Under Secretary of War

[Attachment 2: Robert P. Patterson to Lawrence W. Cramer, June 5, 1942]

WAR DEPARTMENT
OFFICE OF THE UNDERSECRETARY
WASHINGTON, D.C.

June 5, 1942

Mr. Lawrence W. Cramer
Executive Secretary
President's Committee on
Fair Employment Practice
Social Security Building
Washington, D.C.

Dear Mr. Cramer:

By Executive Order 8802 of June 25, 1941, "Reaffirming Policy of Full Participation in the Defense Program of all Persons, Regardless of Race, Creed, Color, or National Origin, and Directing Certain Action in Furtherance of Said Policy", the President created a Committee on Fair Employment Practice and authorized that Committee to "investigate complaints of discrimination" in the employment of workers in defense industries because of race, creed, color or national origin.

It has come to the attention of the War Department that some contractors engaged in national defense activities under contract with the War Department have been uncertain whether this Department would approve the release of information concerning the employment of members of particular racial or religious groups in the course of their execution of such contracts.

The Committee on Fair Employment Practice is hereby advised, and is authorized to advise such contractors that the War Department approves the release of employment information and statistics to persons properly identified as employees of the United States representing the Committee for confidential use of the Committee.

As a matter of record, it would be appreciated if the Committee will transmit to the War Department, through the office of the Civilian Aide to the Secretary of War, copies of such statistics as may be furnished to the Committee by War Department contractors.

Sincerely yours,
/s/ Robert P. Patterson
Robert P. Patterson
Under Secretary of War.

[Attachment 3: Memorandum of Understanding between the President's Committee on Fair Employment Practice, the War Manpower Commission, and the Provost Marshal General, War Department]

March 10, 1943.

MEMORANDUM OF UNDERSTANDING BETWEEN

THE PRESIDENT'S COMMITTEE ON FAIR EMPLOYMENT PRACTICE
THE WAR MANPOWER COMMISSION, AND
THE PROVOST MARSHAL GENERAL, WAR DEPARTMENT

1. The policy of the United States concerning the employment of workers, whether citizens or aliens, as expressed by the President in Executive Order 8802, is that the United States encourages full participation in the national defense program by all workers, and that there is to be no discrimination in employment in defense industries because of race, creed, color, national origin, or citizenship. This policy contains no exceptions, and was reiterated and further clarified by the President in his statement of July 11, 1942.

2. On December 12, 1941, the President issued Executive Order 8972, in which, as Commander-in-Chief in time of war, he authorized and directed the Secretary of War and the Secretary of the Navy to take such action as they deem necessary to protect from injury or destruction national-defense material, national-defense premises, and national-defense utilities, as broadly defined in the

Sabotage Act. Pursuant to this order, various instructions have been issued and action has been taken in an effort to determine that all persons who have access to important national-defense material, premises, and utilities are loyal to the United States.

3. It is agreed between The Provost Marshal General and the President's Committee on Fair Employment that there shall be no objection to inquiry into race, creed, color or national origin after employment; nor with reference to the commissioning or enlistment of members of members of the Women's Army Auxiliary Corps; nor with reference to members of the armed services; nor with reference to investigations being conducted at the request of the War Relocation Authority. The Provost Marshal General agrees to write into each contract with each commercial agency making loyalty investigations pursuant to contract with the War Department an agreement on the part of such agency that without the written permission of the President's Committee on Fair Employment Practice such agency shall not divulge to anyone save the Provost Marshal General, or his duly authorized representative, any information regarding race, creed, color or national origin developed pursuant to investigations made under the contract.

4. Other instances have arisen, and will continue to arise, where by reason of the critical nature of a facility or of a plant or the products thereof with reference to the war effort, the loyalty of a worker, employed or seeking employment, is in question because of his foreign birth or citizenship, or for other reasons. In such instances the employer or any representative of the Government having knowledge of such facts may refer the case to the Provost Marshal General, or his duly authorized representative, for a loyalty investigation of such person. The final determination of whether such person shall not be employed for any such reason because of the critical nature of the facility or of the plant or the products thereof shall rest with the Provost Marshal General, acting for the War Department. In such cases it is agreed between The Provost Marshall General and the President's Committee on Fair Employment Practice that race, creed, color and national origin may be considered by The Provost Marshal General in making the necessary loyalty investigation.

Lawrence W. Cramer, Executive Secretary, for
President's Committee on Fair Employment Practice
Allen W. Gullion, Maj. Gen.
The Provost Marshal General

[Field Instruction Revision 1:
Field Instruction No. 19-A]

FIELD INSTRUCTION NO. 19-A
(Amending Field Instruction No. 19)
April 21, 1944

To: All Regional Directors

From: Will Maslow
          Director of Field Operations

RE: War Department.   Government Owned, Privately Operated Plants

In addition to procedures set forth in Field Instruction No. 19 entitled "War Department" your attention is directed to the following excerpt from a letter dated July 2, 1942 from Under Secretary of War, Robert P. Patterson to Malcolm S. McLean, then Chairman, FEPC discussing our procedures in cases involving government owned and privately operated plants:

"Under no circumstances will your Committee take formal or public action in any case until the War Department has had the opportunity to use its good offices to bring compliance with the President's Executive Order on this subject."

Because cases may arise in which commanding officers of government owned, privately operated plants are unaware of their power to discipline employees, your attention is called to the following paragraphs in the same letter:

"The Government has complete power to require the dismissal of any person employed in any of these plants, (government owned, privately operated plants) if the continued employment of such individual is, for the reason deemed to be not in the public interest. This power is specifically reserved by contract and can be exercised to remove persons who are subversive or unqualified.

"Each plant is operated subject to the supervision of a Commanding Officer."

[Field Instruction Revision 2:
Field Instruction No. 19-B]

Field Instruction No. 19 B
November 24, 1944

To: All Regional Directors
From: Will Maslow
           Director of Field Operations
RE: War Department

The letter set forth on the reverse hereof sent to the Chairman by the Under-Secretary of War supersedes that portion of Field Instruction No. 19 which forbids our field staff to communicate directly with the party charged (Paragraph A-1) in cases involving government-owned and government-operated plants. Henceforth, you are encouraged to deal directly with the commanding officer in such plants in an effort to adjust cases involving such plants at the regional level.

If you encounter any difficulties in such dealings, please report them, preferably through the weekly report.

[Field Instruction Revision 3: Robert B. Patterson to Malcolm Ross, November 23, 1944]

WAR DEPARTMENT
OFFICE OF THE UNDER SECRETARY
WASHINGTON, D. C.

Nov. 23, 1944

Mr. Malcolm Ross, Chairman
Fair Employment Practice Committee,
Standard Oil Building,
Washington, D.C.

Dear Mr. Ross:

Reference is made to your request that Regional Representatives of the Fair Employment Practice Committee be authorized to discuss directly with appropriate War Department field representatives complaints of alleged racial discrimination before the filing of formal complaints with the War Department. Under the present arrangement, your field representatives are expected to submit formal complaints to the War Department for investigation. They have not been expressly authorized in the past to discuss charges directly with Army representatives, although I understand in many installations there has been considerable contact between them and Army representatives.

Within the necessary limits imposed by Army methods and regulations, I agree that a useful purpose may be served in having full discussions of charges on a local level before the preparation and submission of formal complaints. Undoubtedly, by doing this many charges can be amicably disposed of, thereby obviating the subsequent necessity of formal investigations. Such a reduction in the volume of cases will enable a more expeditious handling of those cases submitted for formal action.

Accordingly, Army field representatives are being advised that they may in the future confer with Fair Employment Practice Committee Regional Representatives with a view toward adjusting as many charges of discrimination as possible on the local level. This, however, does not impose any obligations on Army officers to report to the representatives, nor does it in any way affect or change the handling of complaints by the War Department. I am certain that all Army representatives will continue to carry out in every way possible the War Department policy which requires that Executive Order 9346 be fully complied with.

Sincerely yours,
(Signed) Robert P. Patterson
ROBERT P. PATTERSON
Under Secretary of War

MS: copy, HqR78, Field Instructions, Aug. 1943–May 1945. (entry 46) Field Instructions 1–19.

   1. For the significance of these texts, see the headnotes on Relationships with Federal Agencies.

   2. The attached lists are filed with this field instruction in HqR78.

   3. On problems involved in implementing these procedures, see Mitchell's memorandum to Cramer, 3/4/43.

National Policy against Racial or Religious Discrimination

THE NATIONAL POLICY AGAINST

RACIAL OR RELIGIOUS DISCRIMINATION[1]

[February 8, 1944]

The national policy of equality without regard to race, color, or creed, is rooted in the Constitution of the United States and a score of federal statutes.

The First Amendment provides that "Congress shall make no law respecting an establishment of religion, or prohibiting the free exercise thereof . . ." The Fourteenth Amendment gives all inhabitants "the equal protection of the laws." The Fifteenth Amendment gives all citizens the right to vote without regard to "race, color, or previous condition of servitude.["]

The Civil Rights Law (8 U. S. C. Sec. 41, 42, 43, 44) confers upon all persons equal rights under the law, including the right to make and enforce contracts, to sue and be sued, to testify, to enjoy property, and to serve on juries.

In 1890 the Agricultural College Act (U. S. Stat. Vol. 26, p. 418) applied public lands to the endowment of agricultural and other colleges. The Act forbids "distinction of race or color" in the "admission of students."

Since 1933, no less than 23 statutes have been enacted forbidding discrimination because of race, color, or creed. The 1933 Act for relief of employment (U.S. Stat. Vol. 48, p. 23) provided that "in employing citizens for the purposes of this Act, no discrimination shall be made on account of race, color, or creed."

The Civilian Conservation Corps Act of 1937 (U.S. Stat. Vol 50, p. 320) provides that "no person shall be excluded on account of race, color, or creed. . . ."

The Emergency Relief Appropriation Act of 1937 (U.S. Stat. Vol. 50, p. 357) forbade exclusion of persons because of race or religion.

Similar prohibitions were contained in the Emergency Relief Appropriations Acts of 1938, 1939, 1940, 1941, 1942, and 1943.

The Civilian Pilot Training Act of 1939 (U.S. Stat. Vol. 53, p. 856) provided that "none of the benefits of training or programs shall be denied on account of race, creed, or color."

The Act of November 20, 1940 extending the Civil Service Classification Act (U.S. Stat. Vol. 54, p. 1214) forbade discrimination "against any person or with respect to the position held by any person, on account of race, creed, or color."

The Appropriation Acts of 1940, 1941, and 1942 for the National Youth Administration forbade discrimination by reason of race, color, or creed (U.S. Stat. Vol. 54, p. 593, etc.)

The Selective Service Training Act of 1940 (U.S. Stat. Vol. 54, p. 885) gave all persons "regardless of race or color" an opportunity to volunteer and provided further that in the selection and training of men there shall be no discrimination against any person on account of race or color.

The Appropriation Acts for the Federal Security Agency for the years 1940, 1942, 1943, and 1944 (U.S. Stat. Vol. 54, p. 1035, etc.) appropriated monies for the training of defense workers but forbade discrimination because of sex, race, or color.

The Lanham or Defense Housing Appropriations Act of 1941 (U.S. Stat. Vol. 55, p. 363) provides that in determining the need for public works "no discrimination shall be made on account of race, creed, or color."

The Nurses Training Act of 1943 (U.S. Stat. Vol. 57, p. 153) forbade discrimination in its administration on account of race, creed, or color.[2]

MS: copy, HqR6, Office Files of Emanuel H. Bloch, Hearing Examiner. July 1944–Jan. 1946, National Policy against Racial or Religious Discrimination.

1. This document was prepared by Emanuel H. Bloch and printed by the Division of Field Operations. For Bloch's assignment to draft this report, see Mitchell's weekly report of 2/5/44. For other digests of antidiscrimination policy, see Power of the President to Issue Executive Order No. 9346, n.d. [after May 1944], in appendix 1; State Legislation Forbidding Discriminatory Employment Practices, 2/8/44, in Files of Max Berking, HqR3; and 1/18/45 (RG 228, Entry 15), in HqR78, Field Letter 22, A folder; and Declarations of the United States in the Realm of Foreign Policy Against Discrimination Because of Race, Creed or Color, 3/15/46, also prepared by Bloch, in RG 228, Entry 5, Records of the Office of the Chairman, Outgoing Correspondence, Aug. 1941–May 1946, DNA.

2. Congressional defenders of the FEPC employed data from this report. For example, in *All Manner of Men* (114), Malcolm Ross quotes similar information used in Congress by John Vorys (R-Ohio), whom he identifies as a former Yale classmate.

Important Cases Being Handled at the Regional Level

April 22, 1944
(Supplement 4/18)

IMPORTANT CASES BEING HANDLED AT REGIONAL LEVEL[1]

Region	Name, Location and Docket No.	Brief Description of Problem & Present Status
II	1. Yamashita, et al V. War Shipping Administration 2-GR-262, New York, N. Y.	The complainants charge they have been denied employment on Merchant vessels solely because they are American citizens of Japanese origin. This was taken up with the State Department, Navy Department and War Shipping Administration by DFO (Mitchell). Loyal U.S. Citizens of Japanese ancestry are to be given sailing permits. The case was returned to Region II for follow-up with complainants. See Mitchell memo to Lawson, April 21.
V	1. Goodyear Aircraft Corp* Akron, Ohio.	A strike occurred at this plant on April 17 when Negro workers were transferred out of the gas mask department because of a production cutback and wage problems are also involved. See McKnight report of April 19.
	2. Chevrolet Transmission Plant* Toledo, Ohio	White worker[s] at the plant struck because of upgrading of Negro women. Regional report awaited.
VI	1. Gary Street Railways, Gary, Indiana	Examiner Gibson of Chicago office has been assigned to check on complaints of refusal to hire Negroes as street car operators.
VII	1. Bell Aircraft Company Marietta, Georgia 7-BR-215	Corporation refuses to supply pertinent employment data. Examiner Tipton still investigating individual cases. (Weekly Report 4/18/44)

	2. Firestone Tire and Rubber Co. 7-BR-204	Corporation and USES still discriminating against Negro trainees seeking employment. (Weekly Report 4/15/44)
	3. Consolidated Vultee Aircraft Nashville, Tenn.	Regional Office (at request of Review and Analysis) checking on compliance with Committee Directives (Weekly report 4/15/44)
X	1. Texas and Pacific Railroad 10-BR-27-40, 126, 275, 276, 277. Dallas, Texas	Complaints on failure to upgrade Negroes appears to be settled. (weekly report April 15)
	2. North American Aviation 10-BR-288, Dallas, Texas	Foremen, accused of hostile acts toward Negro employe[e]s in metal segregation, were dismissed. (Weekly report April 15)
XII	1. Los Angeles Street Railway Co. 12-BR-1150 Los Angeles, California	Citizen's Committee and Mayor of Los Angeles assisting in attempts to settle case. (Weekly report April 15)

*Denotes a strike

May 8, 1944
(Supplement 5/2)

IMPORTANT CASES BEING HANDLED AT REGIONAL LEVEL

Region	Name, Location and Docket No.	Brief Description of Problem & Present Status
I.	Missouri Valley Bridge and Iron Works, Evansville Shipyard, Evansville, Indiana	Threatened violence if company employs additional Negro welders to meet shortage of workers in this occupation. WPB reports possible hiring of Negroes with assistance of Blacksmiths and Laborers Unions (AF of L). See memorandum May 4 to Henderson.
	Monsanto Chemical Company, 6-BR-306	Conference with WPB representatives in Chicago FEPC office. See Henderson report May 1.
	Gary Street Railway, Gary, Indiana	Company states it has no policy of discriminating against Negro applicants. None have been hired as platform operators, however. See special report of Examiner Gibson April 28.

VII.	Bell Aircraft Company, Marietta, Georgia, 7-BR-215	Regional office held conference with company vice president on May 3. Further developments awaited. See Hunt report May 4.
	Firestone Company, Atlanta, Georgia, 7-BR-204	Region report on May 1 states that USES problems continue. However, other communications from region show that, in this case, Negro trainees have been referred to the company by USES offices.
IX.	Missouri-Pacific Railroad, 9-BR-187 and 9-BN-188	Since complaint in this case was filed, the carrier and the union are negotiating on the problem of upgrading Negroes and Mexicans to stewards' classifications. See Weekly Report of May 1.
	North American Aviation Company, 10-BR-268	New contacts with company being made by regional office. See Weekly Report of April 29.

May 15, 1944
(Supplement 5/2/44)

IMPORTANT CASES BEING HANDLED AT REGIONAL LEVEL

Region	Name, Location and Docket No. Brief	Brief Description of Problem & Present Status
IV	Baltimore Transit Company, 4-BR-6	The company continues refusal to employ Negroes on platform operations. Regional Director conferred with company during week ending April 22. Forthcoming union election caused Regional Director to suggest delaying further FEPC action pending this election. Weekly Report of Acting Regional Director mentions a conference with NLRB on aspects of this case. See Weekly Report May 8.
VI.	Missouri Valley Bridge and Iron Works, Evansville Shipyard, Evansville, Indiana	Threatened violence if company employs additional Negro welders to meet shortage of workers in this occupation. Examiner from regional office again visited Evansville to confer with WPB representatives and officials of the Boiler Makers Union. See Henderson report dated May 9.

VII. Firestone Company, Atlanta, Georgia, 7-BR-204

In this case, USES offices refused to refer qualified Negro trainees for employment at the company. Regional Director states local USES office referred Negro trainees to Firestone but, so far, there is no indication that any of these people have been hired. See Weekly Report May 8.

 Bell Aircraft Company, Marietta, Georgia, 7-BR-215

This case involves discriminatory practices of the company in collaboration with the USES offices. Regional Director reports one trainee referred to Bell Aircraft by USES. See Weekly Report May 8.

X. Delta Shipbuilding Company, New Orleans, Louisiana, 10-BR-128 and 187

This case has been returned to the region following a conference with the Maritime Commission on problems affecting the employment of Negroes and outbreaks of violence between Negroes and guards. See Mitchell memorandum May 5.

May 22, 1944
(Supplement 5/2)

IMPORTANT CASES BEING HANDLED AT REGIONAL LEVEL

Region	Name, Location and Docket No.	Brief Description of Problem & Present Status
VI.	Western Cartridge Company, East Alton, Illinois, 6-BR-347	Region expects to abrogate agreement of December 2, 1943, and prepare case for submission to central office. See Weekly Report of Region VI dated May 13.[2]
	Missouri Valley Bridge and Iron Works, (Evansville Shipyard, Evansville, Indiana), 6-BR-670	Unproductive conference held in Evansville May 11 with WPB, management, and union officials. Conference between Regional Director and Navy representative scheduled. See Weekly Report of Region VI for May 13.
VII.	Bell Aircraft Company, Marietta, Georgia, 7-BR-215	Regional Director has informed Air Corps of new complaints against the company. See Weekly Report of Region dated May 15.
	Consolidated Vultee Corporation, Nashville, Tennessee	Regional office has discussed this case with Air Corps representatives. See Weekly Report of Region dated May 13.

III.	Los Angeles Street Railway, 12-BR-1150	Los Angeles office continues effort to assist Mayor Bowron's Committee of Six. However, complainants with specific cases are being interviewed. See Sub-Regional Weekly Report of May 13.
	E. I. du Pont de Nemours Company, Inc., Pasco, Washington, 12-BR-103	In this case, various charges of discrimination were filed against the company. However, the Region has dismissed the case for insufficient evidence. A review of the FDR (dated May 19) shows that the dismissal is proper. Nevertheless, the Region indicates that it will take follow-up action with the War Department on August 1, 1944.
	Marinship Corporation, San Francisco, California	Conference between Chairman, staff, Mr. Shishkin of the Committee, and Head of Boiler Makers' Union scheduled for May 23, 1944.

MS: copy, HqR39, Central Files. (entry 25) Memoranda, 1944.

1. Mitchell told Ross and Johnson of his preparation of these reports in his memorandum of 4/21/44, "Important Cases Being Handled at Regional Level." This compilation was prepared from the regional directors' weekly reports, which can be found in HqR50–55.

2. Copies of the memorandum of agreement of 12/2/43 can be found in HqR85, Correspondence Relating to Cases. Western Cartridge Co., 6-BR-273; and in HqR20, Records Related to Hearings. Western Cartridge Co. The agreement was officially terminated by a letter sent to Western Cartridge, signed by William H. Spencer, A. Harry Brawner, and Elmer W. Henderson on 5/20/44 (HqR20, Records Related to Hearings. Western Cartridge Co.). For background, see headnote on Major Cases in St. Louis.

Report on FEPC Action in Race Strikes

5/25/44

Mr. Malcolm Ross

John A. Davis

FEPC Action in Race Strikes

As a result of a staff discussion,[1] and as a result of a request from Field Operations that the Division of Review and Analysis attempt to formulate some standards with regard to our behavior in race strike situations, I discussed the matter with those members of the staff who have settled race strikes,[2] Messrs. Mitchell,[3] Manly,[4] Metzger,[5] and McKnight.[6]

It seems to me that the Committee should make a general statement of policy to the effect that it is against strikes in industry on a racial basis as a violation of public policy and of labor's pledge to the Government and as dangerous to the war effort. It should instruct the staff in all situations to attempt to get workers back to work as quickly as possible. This is as far as Committee action need go. It is a statement of policy.

FEPC's value in racial strike situations lies in the fact that it has the confidence of the Negro workers. It has no authority to settle strikes and was not established for that purpose. It operates on a basis of appeal and persuasion and its powers to enforce a decision vary with the nature of a situation and the degree to which other powers of the Federal Government can be brought into play. It is clear now that hearings are not always effective in forcing violators of Executive Order 9346 to comply.

When Negro workers have struck because of unbearable discrimination and FEPC instructs them to return to work and assures them that it can handle their grievances in a satisfactory manner, it should be sure that it has gathered up enough support in the given situation in order to actually settle the grievances involved. It should go about gathering this support in the same way it does in all its other cases, by enlisting the aid of the contracting agency, the company, the union, and other Government agencies. FEPC needs to fail in only one or two of these situations and it will lose its ability to handle these strike situations, since its ability results only from its good name. Getting men back to work does not arise from our telling them to go but from their belief that we can handle the situation.

It is high time that a field instruction be developed on strike situations because we are coasting along dangerously without policy. Our behavior in two strikes is already questionable. At the Dravo plant in Neville Island, Pittsburgh, 50 striking Negroes were fired for protesting their discrimination in this fashion. FEPC handled the case and remedied the discrimination, but did nothing about the 50 Negroes. In October, 1943 there was a race strike at the Dodge plant in Detroit which FEPC settled without taking up the problem of the 15 Negroes who were fired for protesting their discrimination in terms of a strike.[7]

The following principles can be developed from the experiences of examiners Mitchell, Metzger, McKnight, and Manly:

1. The examiner should attempt to achieve commitments from the company, the Government contracting agencies, the union, and other Government agencies involved, to the effect that they wish FEPC intervention, and that they will support its decisions, before he contacts the workers. He will then be able to tell the workers to go back to work and that he will handle the situation when he first sees them.

2. Where FEPC has the backing of all parties concerned, it is often possible for him to wire or call by long distance leading workers instructing them to return to work before he arrives on the scene and promising them a settlement of the case.

3. Where the local union is recalcitrant, the examiner can usually achieve support by going up the line to a higher official of the union.

4. Where the local company is recalcitrant, the examiner can usually achieve support by going up the line to higher officials of the company, either in that vicinity or elsewhere.

5. Where either the company or the union is recalcitrant or weak in their positions, but where the examiner is strongly backed up by the contracting agencies, he should feel safe in accepting responsibility.

6. Where the examiner feels shaky about FEPC support from the other parties involved in the controversy, he can notify the workers to appoint a delegate to go along with him to report constantly to the main body of the workers.

7. An FEPC examiner should always attempt to establish a union and managerial policy which can be policed by him from time to time and which will prevent all future work stoppages.

8. Where FEPC has complaints and where a racial strike has occurred, it should continue to process these complaints. When strikes originally break out, they are properly within the jurisdiction of the company, the union, the contracting agency, or the conciliation service. It is erroneous to fail to continue processing the complaints, especially when the settlement of such complaints might result in the workers returning to work.

9. When the company or the union or both are recalcitrant and the contracting agencies are unwilling to back FEPC's handling of the case, and where we have complaints, the examiner should continue to process the complaints, at the same time telling the workers to return to work. In this situation, however, he should ask for worker assistance and cooperation in negotiating the settlement of the complaints. He should insist upon a worker representative going with him at all times, in order that the working group can be fully informed of the degree of progress which he has achieved.

10. FEPC examiners should always insist that striking workers be allowed to return to work if they had valid complaints of discrimination and if they had in no way been guilty of violence of destruction of company property, etc. It is hard to see why workers who strike because of racial discrimination should be penalized to any greater extent than workers who strike because of what they feel is union or working-man discrimination.

cc: Davidson
       Bloch
       Metzger

MS: LH, DI, HqR1, Office Files of Malcolm Ross. D.

1. After a year of ad hoc action by FEPC staff members in racially related strikes, the FEPC sought to formulate an official policy and to establish guidelines for its field representatives. Chairman Malcolm Ross appointed a subcommittee of three, consisting of Stanley Metzger, Emanuel Bloch, and Eugene Davidson, to review the handling of racial strikes and make recommendations. After the three failed to reach agreement, each issued his own policy statement in May 1944.

Despite staff disagreements, John A. Davis of the Division of Research and Analysis pressed for formulation of an official racial strike policy based on the cumulative experiences of key FEPC staff members who had faced such situations. After consulting Mitchell, Metzger, McKnight, and Manly, among others, Davis drafted this compromise policy statement.

The headnote on Strikes and Work Stoppages provides the earlier background. Mitchell's report of 5/10/43 provides earlier policy suggestions. For the recommendations of the three committee members, see Metzger to Ross, 5/17/44 [HqR1, Office Files of Malcolm Ross. M], Bloch to Ross, 5/25 [HqR1, Office Files of Malcolm Ross. B], Davidson to Ross, 5/22/44 [HqR4, Office Files of George M. Johnson. Strikes].

2. On the participation of the FEPC in strike settlements generally, see Eugene Davidson, Participation of FEPC Examiners in Settlement of Work Stoppages, [ca. April–May 1944], the undated summary entitled Participation of Strikes, and the Statement on Work Stoppages, all in HqR4, Office Files of George M. Johnson. Strikes; Davidson's texts and related documents found in HqR77, Office Files of Eugene Davidson, Assistant Director, Oct. 1941–Apr. 1946, Unarranged; Statements, Miscellaneous, Strikes folder; Weaver, *Negro Labor,* 223; Mitchell's *NAACP Bulletin* article of July 1946; Kryder, *Divided Arsenal,* 100; and the tables of strikes printed from FEPC records in FEPC *First Report,* 79–80; in King, *Separate but Unequal,* 243; and in Kersten, *Race, Jobs, and the War,* 143–44. See also the texts cited in the notes to the headnote on Strikes and Work Stoppages. The undated statement on work stoppages probably is the one FEPC publicist Max Berking said he composed in the summer of 1944 but which the FEPC did not then circulate because of the "delicacy" of the subject. See Berking to Joy P. Davis, 12/8/44, HqR1, Office Files of Malcolm Ross. B.

3. On the strikes in which Mitchell was personally involved, see Mitchell's field investigation reports of 6/8/43 (Alabama Dry Dock) and 8/6/43 (Bethlehem Steel, Sparrows Point), and Johnson's report of 7/31/43 on a telephone call from Mitchell, all in appendix; Mitchell's memorandum of 11/1/43, and, on the Western Electric case at the Point Breeze plant in Maryland, Mitchell's memoranda of 8/26, 11/11, 11/13, and 12/14/43.

4. For Manly's much admired role in the settlement of walkouts at the Jones and Laughlin-Hazelwood Byproducts plant in Aliquippa and the Carnegie-Illinois Steel plant at Clairton, see Mitchell's weekly reports of 3/27 and 5/1/44, memoranda of 9/29/43 and 5/4/44, and notes; the extracts from weekly reports on both cases found in HqR77, Office Files of Eugene Davidson. Unarranged; Statements, Miscellaneous, and Strikes; and the Statement on Work Stoppages, on HqR4, Office Files of George M. Johnson. Strikes. Coverage of Manly's role, based in part on the text of Statement on Work Stoppages, was also included in *First Report,* 81–83. See also Reed, "Black Workers, Defense Industries, and Federal Agencies in Pennsylvania," 374–82.

5. For Metzger's negotiations during the Monsanto Chemical Company work stoppage of March 1944 in Monsanto, Illinois, see his memorandum to Maslow of 3/17/44, in HqR77, Office Files of Eugene Davidson. (Unarranged; Statements, Miscellaneous), Strikes; and his testimony at the 4/20/44 FEPC meeting (33–54), HqR65, Central Files.

6. For McKnight's role in strike settlements in Ohio, particularly with the Wright Aeronautical plant, see the memoranda on Mitchell's telephone conversations with him of 6/6 and 6/9/44. Eugene Davidson's memorandum on participation of FEPC Examiners in Settlement of Work Stoppages and the summary cited above refer to the following cases involving McKnight as regional director for region V: Harsch Bronze and Foundry Company-Cleveland, Ohio (September 1943), and Eberhard Manufacturing Division, Eastern Malleable Iron Company, Cleveland (December 1943); on these cases, see also McKnight's memorandum to Maslow of 3/20/44, in HqR77, Office Files of Eugene Davidson. (Unarranged, Statements, Miscellaneous) Strikes. For additional cases in Ohio, see Kersten, *Race, Jobs, and the War,* 86, and 161note60.

Several other staff members also played prominent roles in strike settlements, particularly those in the Chicago, Detroit, Kansas City, and Dallas regional offices. See, for example, Mitchell's weekly report of 5/17/44 and his memorandum of 12/8/44; Edward Swan's memorandum to Maslow of 3/17/44, Edward Lawson's memorandum to Davidson to 3/20/44, and the extracts from reports by Region VI (Chicago), and other regions, all in HqR77, Office Files of Eugene Davidson (Unarranged, Statements, Miscellaneous) Strikes; and Kersten, *Race, Jobs, and the War,* 104–5.

7. On the Dravo case, handled by Manly, and the Dodge case, handled by G. James Fleming, see Mitchell's weekly report of 4/13/44; Richard Hastings, President, Local 61, IUMSWA-CIO, to Fleming, 1/1/44, and Manly to Fleming, 2/9 and 3/17/44, all in HqR77, Office Files of Eugene Davidson. (Unarranged, Statements, Miscellaneous) Strikes; and Kersten, *Race, Jobs, and the War,* 105.

Memorandum on Congressional Debate on FEPC Appropriation

May 27, 1944

MEMORANDUM

TO: Malcolm Ross
     Chairman

FROM: Will Maslow
      Director of Field Operations

RE: Congressional Debate on FEPC Appropriation[1]

The following points were made against the FEPC in the debate in the House of Representatives on the FEPC appropriation on Friday, May 26, 1944:

1. Mr. Tarver, (Georgia)

   Page 5110— Until the FEPC undertook its efforts to stir up racial trouble among its employees (Southern Railway) there had been no complaint from the great body of these Negro employees as to any unfair discrimination in employment as between Negroes and whites.

2. Page 5119— The FEPC has soft-pedaled the actions taken against those railroads in the Northeast and have made a deliberate effort to sectionalize the matter.

3. Page 5119— In the Philadelphia Transportation Company case the FEPC attempted to violate a contract of long standing.

4. Page 5119— The FEPC has "inspired" Vincent and Pollatsek in activities in the RMO.[2]

5. Page 5120— The FEPC is engaged in an effort to foist certain ideas of social not economic equality.

6. Page 5120— A. Bruce Hunt insisted upon his Negro stenographer being allowed to use the rest room provided for white women employees in Atlanta.

7. Mr. Tarver, (Georgia)

   Page 5120— The FEPC insists that employers who desire to hire white stenographers through USES must accept Negro stenographers if available.

8. Page 5120— It is even reported that in one case in California an employer was required to reduce the number of his white Caucasian employees already employed and provide for the employment of a certain proportion of clerical employees who should be Negroes or people of another race.

Mr. Whitten, (Mississippi)

9. Page 5122—   The FEPC is Negro dominated with a sprinkling of white employees to attempt to claim fairness.[3]

10. Page 5122—   What the FEPC wants, what they have done, and what they are
doing, is to discriminate in favor of the Negroes.

11. Page 5122—   If the FEPC receives its appropriation, Congress would do more
to create strife, riots, to destroy America, than anything it could possibly do.

12. Mr. Hobbs, (Alabama)

Page 5130—   What the FEPC seeks is to make their pets (Negroes) work
whether or not they are qualified.

13. Page 5131—   The FEPC seeks to oust those with white skins from employment they already have.

14. Page 5131—   It is an FEPC practice to prevent white people from obtaining
jobs, and to get white people ousted from jobs they have, so as to make a place
for Negroes.

15. Mr. Peterson, (Georgia)

Page 5134—   It is discriminatory for the FEPC to have a staff composed of
⅔ Negroes.

16. Mr. Hare, (South Carolina)

Page 5142—   It is common knowledge that FEPC has demanded and succeeded in having many positions in many or practically all of the Government
agencies in Washington filled with persons not qualified to do the work to
which they have been assigned, wholly because they happen to be colored or
happen to have a particular creed.

17. Page 5142—   When FEPC seeks to have Latin-Americans who are kept at
work below their capacity upgraded it is discriminating in their favor.

18. Page 5142—   The FEPC seeks to direct that Negro workers be given employment regardless of their fitness or qualifications.

19. Mr. Brooks, (Louisiana)

Page 5143—   The FEPC decision in the railroad case will eliminate the
seniority rights of railroad workmen.

20. Mr. Fisher, (Texas)

Page 5144—   The FEPC duplicates the functions of the War Manpower
Commission as is proven by page 539 of the hearings. (the reference is to the
operating agreement between the two agencies.)

MS: copy, FEPC RG 228, Office Files of Will Maslow, Director (Entry 39, PI-147), box 456, Congressional Record References.

1. This series of highlights was apparently prepared from the unedited transcripts of the House debate. The published pages from the debate on National War Agencies Appropriations, 1945, bill, H.R. 4879, *Congressional Record*–House, 78th Congress, 2d sess., v. 90, Part 9, UMR 250, 5026–5068, correlated with the Maslow text are accordingly: (1) 5110=5027; (2) 5119=5027; (3) 5119=5027; (4) 5119=5027; (5) 5120=5028; (6) 5120=5028; (7) 5120=5028; (8) 5120=5028; (9) 5122=5030; (10) 5122=5030; (11) 5122=5030; (12) 5130=5040; (13) 5131=5041; (14) 5131=5041; (15) 5134=5043; (16) 5142=5052; (17) 5120=5052; (18) 5142=5052; (19) 5143=5052; (20) 5144=5053. For in-depth looks at the debate, see Berman, *Politics of Civil Rights*, 181–91; and Ruchames, *Race, Jobs, and Politics*, 92–96. For Ross's responses to the congressional arguments, see Ross, *All Manner of Men*, 34–38.

2. See the headnote on Relationships with Federal Agencies.

3. When the FEPC was organized in 1943, the staff included forty African Americans and four whites. "This argued for an almost exclusive concern with discrimination against Negroes," Ross noted. However, it "was a National enterprise." Upon becoming chairman, he added, Father Haas "began to alter the racial and religious makeup of the staff. Eventually it was to include Protestants and Jews, a young Catholic priest, several Mexican-Americans and a few stenographers of Japanese ancestry." Ross, *All Manner of Men*, 32–34. According to Kersten, in mid-1944 the FEPC had 105 officials and staff members of whom 45 were white and 60 were black (*Race, Jobs, and the War*, 173, note 16).

Memorandum on Power of the President to Issue Executive Order No. 9346

POWER OF THE PRESIDENT
TO ISSUE EXECUTIVE ORDER NO. 9346[1]

[ca. May 1944]

Executive Order No. 9346 was executed by the President on May 27, 1943, to establish a new Committee on Fair Employment Practice, to promote the fullest utilization of all available manpower and to eliminate discriminatory employment practices. It recites that the successful prosecution of the war demands the maximum employment of all available workers; that it is the policy of the United States to encourage full participation in the war effort by all persons in the United States, in the firm belief that the democratic way of life within the Nation can be defended successfully only with the help and support of all groups within its borders; that there is evidence that available and needed workers have been barred from employment in industries engaged in war production solely by reason of their race, creed, color, or national origin, to the detriment of the prosecution of the war, the workers' morale, and national unity. By virtue of authority vested in him by the Constitution and statutes, as President of the United States and Commander in Chief of the Army and Navy, the President then reaffirms the policy of the United States that there shall be no discrimination in the employment of any person in war industries or in Government by reason of race, creed, color, or national origin, and declares it to be the duty of all employers, including the several Federal departments and agencies, and all labor organizations, in furtherance of this duty and of this order, to eliminate discrimination in regard to hire, tenure, terms or conditions of employment, or union membership because of race, creed, color, or national origin.

It then orders as follows:

First, that all contracting agencies of the Government shall include in all contracts thereafter negotiated or renegotiated by them a provision obligating the contractor not to discriminate against any employee or applicant for employment because of race, creed, color or national origin, and requiring him to include a similar provision in all subcontracts.

Second, that all departments and agencies of the Government which are concerned with vocational and training programs for war production shall assure that such programs shall be administered without discrimination [remainder cut off—recheck microfilm-because of race, creed, color or national origin?]

The order then establishes the Committee on Fair Employment Practice. This Committee shall formulate policies to achieve that purposes of the order, and make recommendations to the various Federal departments and agencies and to the President, which it deems necessary and proper to render effective the provisions of the order. In addition, the Committee shall recommend to the Chairman of the War Manpower Commission appropriate measures for bringing about the full utilization and training of manpower in and for war production without discrimination because of race, creed, color, or national origin. It shall receive and investigate complaints of discrimination forbidden by the order, and may conduct hearings and make findings of fact and take appropriate steps to eliminate such discrimination. It may utilize the services and facilities of other Federal departments and agencies and such voluntary and uncompensated services as may from time to time be needed. It may accept the services of State and local authorities and officials, and may perform the functions and duties and exercise the powers conferred upon it by this order through such officials and agencies and in such manner as it may determine. It is empowered to promulgate such rules and regulations as may be appropriate or necessary to carry out the provisions of the order.

The decreeing of these orders and the establishment of the Committee raise a number of legal problems, the first of which involves the pronouncement by the President of the Policy against discrimination.

As Chief Executive of the United States, the President is vested with the Executive power (Constitution, Art. II, sec. 1, cl. 1). He takes an oath that he will faithfully execute the office of President of the United States and will, to the best of his ability, preserve, protect, and defend the Constitution of the United States (Constitution, Art. II, sec. 1, cl. 7). "He shall take Care that the Laws be faithfully executed."

It would seem to follow from these constitutional mandates that the President, as Chief Executive, is authorized to proclaim as a policy of the United States, arising from the innate character of the American people, implicit, if not express, in the Declaration of Independence, in the Constitution of the United States and amendments thereto, and in bills of rights in various state constitutions, a doctrine of immunity of the workers of the land from discrimination because of race, creed, color, or national origin, and to direct that all contracting agencies of the Government shall insert a provision in all Government contracts, to be included in subcontracts, which shall maintain the policy which he has proclaimed.

Indeed, the President's pronouncement in 1941 of the policy against discrimination in Executive Order No. 8802, predecessor of Executive Order No. 9346, was not the first attempt by government in this country to resist the rise of racial and religious persecution which followed its European examples. In 1934, Illinois (Ill. Gen. Stat. (Jones) secs. 22.05-22.10) required that provisions be inserted in contracts for public works to prohibit discrimination in the selection and treatment of employees by reason of race, color, or creed. New Jersey followed in 1937 (N. J. Rev. Stat. (1937) secs. 10:2-1-4). New York in 1935 (N. Y. Labor Law, secs. 220-3) and Pa. in 1936 (Pa. Stat. (Purdon 1936) Title 43, sec. 153. Since 1933 New York has declared it to be unlawful for a public utility corporation to refuse to employ any person in any capacity in the operation or maintenance of a public service because of his race, color, or creed (N. Y. Civil Rights Law, sec. 42). Of well-known and earlier origin is state legislation to prevent racial and religious discrimination in places of public accommodation, most of which was enacted after the Federal Civil Rights Act of 1875 (18 Stat. 335) was held to be unconstitutional (Civil Rights cases, 109 U. S. 3 (1883).[2]

In 1938 New York wrote into its Constitution (Const. Art. 1, Sec. 11) that:

> No person shall be denied the equal protection of the laws of this State or any subdivision thereof. No person shall, because of race, color, creed or religion, be subjected to any discrimination in his civil rights by any other person or by any firm, corporation, or institution, or by the state or any agency or subdivision of the State.

Since the President's original order of June 25, 1941 (Executive Order No. 8802) five states have adopted statutes which make unlawful discrimination in employment under defense contracts. (Ill. Rev. Stat. 1941 (Smith-Hurd Ill. Ann. Stat.) ch. 29, secs. 24a-g):

> Discrimination in employment under defense contracts. 24a, sec. 1. "In construction of this act the public policy of the state of Illinois is hereby declared as follows: To facilitate the rearmament and defense program of the Federal government by the integration into the war defense industries of the state of Illinois all available types of labor, skilled, semi-skilled and common shall participate without discrimination as to race, color or creed whatsoever."

> 24e, sec. 5. "Any war defense contractor, its officers, agents or employees who shall violate any provisions of this act shall, upon conviction thereof, be fined in a sum of not less than five hundred dollars in any court of competent jurisdiction in the county in which the defendant shall reside."

In 1943 the Illinois legislature approved the following (63rd General Assembly, 1943, Vol. 1, p. 210. House bill No. 208, approved July 1, 1943):

Sec. 1. "There is created in the office of the Attorney General a Division to be known as the Division for the Enforcement of Civil and Equal Rights. The Division, under the supervision and direction of the Attorney General, shall investigate all violations of the laws relating to civil rights and the prevention of discriminations against persons by reason of race, color or creed, and shall, whenever such violations are established, undertake necessary enforcement measures."

New Jersey legislature in 1942 prefaced its somewhat similar legislation with the following statement of policy. (Laws N.J. 1942, ch. 114, p. 386):

"Whereas, a state of war exists between the United States, Japan, Germany and Italy, and

"Whereas, During the present state of war it is essential to the interest and welfare of the people of the State of New Jersey that the utmost effort be expended in order to create the necessary war materials to carry said war to a successful conclusion; therefore

"BE IT ENACTED, by the Senate and General Assembly of the State of New Jersey:

"It is declared to be the public policy of the State of New Jersey that it opposes discrimination in the engagement of persons employed on defense contracts or public works, by reason of race, color or creed."

A statement in the New York Civil Rights Law (sec. 44, 1942) reads:

"It shall be unlawful for any person, firm or corporation engaged to any extent whatsoever in the production, manufacture or distribution of military or naval material, equipment or supplies for the state of New York or for the federal government to refuse to employ any person in any capacity on account of the race, color, creed or national origin of such person."

Section 1 in a Nebraska statute (Laws of Nebraska, 1943, p. 400) provides:

"It shall be unlawful for any person, firm or corporation, engaged to any extent whatsoever in the State of Nebraska in the production, manufacture or distribution of military or naval material, equipment or supplies for the State of Nebraska or the government of the United States, to refuse to employ any person in any capacity, if said person is a citizen and is qualified, on account of the race, color, creed, religion or national origin of said person."

Pronouncement of policies by Presidents is a long-established practice. While differing in kind, yet based on a similar authority, are such Presidential proclamations as that of Flag Day, the pronouncement of the Four Freedoms in the Atlantic Charter and, more remotely, the declaration of the Monroe Doctrine. There is sufficient moral and patriotic justification to sanction the declaration of each of these, including the declaration of a policy of nondiscrimination against workers because of their race, creed, color, or national origin.

The power of the President to prescribe terms and conditions in a Government contract has been clearly recognized by the Supreme Court in Perkins v. Lukens Steel Co., 310 U.S. 113, 127.

> "Like private individuals and businesses, the Government enjoys the unrestricted power to produce its own supplies, to determine those with whom it will deal, and to fix the terms and conditions upon which it will make needed purchases."

Although the Perkins case dealt with wage provisions to be inserted in Government supply contracts pursuant to the Public Contracts Act (49 Stat. 2036, U.S.C. Title 41, section 35), there is nothing in the opinion which would limit the application of the quotation to provisions or conditions provided by statute, or which would prevent the President, in absence of Congressional restriction, from prescribing terms and conditions of a contract, at least when such terms and conditions are reasonable.

In time of war and of labor shortage, the powers of the President, not only as Chief Executive but as Commander in Chief of the Army and the Navy of the United States (Constitution, Article II, Section 2, Clause 1), would seem to emphasize the President's power and to reaffirm the reasonableness of his direction in the present instance.

Nor is it any less certain that the President, as Chief Executive, may instruct the proper departments and agencies of the Government to assure that training and vocational programs shall be administered without discrimination because of race, creed, color, or national origin. In time of war his power to do this becomes even more obvious and his direction to prevent such discrimination, more reasonable.

As to the formation of the Committee on Fair Employment Practice and the enumeration of its functions, it would seem manifest that in time of peace the President, as Chief Executive, would be empowered to establish such a committee. The Committee is not a contracting agency of the Government. It duties are investigatory and advisory. In pursuance of the policy declared by the President, it makes recommendations to achieve the purpose of the order. It is difficult to perceive wherein the President can be said to have transcended his power as Chief Executive by providing that such investigations, declarations of policy, and recommendations shall be carried on for him by the Committee on Fair Employment Practice.

The case of Myers v. United States clearly recognizes that the President may delegate his administrative powers (272 U. S. 52, 117):

> "The vesting of the executive power in the President was essentially a grant of the power to execute the laws. But the President alone and unaided could not execute the laws. He must execute them by the assistance of subordinates. This view has since been repeatedly affirmed by this Court. Wilcox v. Jackson, 13 Peters 498, 513; United States v. Eliason, 16 Peters 291, 302; Williams v. United States, 1 How, 290, 297; Cunningham v. Neagle, 135 U. S. 1, 63; Russell Co. v. United States, 261 U.S. 514, 523. As he

is charged specifically to take care that they be faithfully executed, the reasonable implication, even in the absence of express words, was that as part of his executive power he should select those who were to act for him under his direction in the execution of the laws."

When the powers of the President as Commander in Chief are added to those of Chief Executive, and when the function of investigation by the Committee on Fair Employment Practice is that of encouraging the fullest utilization of the Nation's manpower for the successful prosecution of the war, it is further difficult to perceive wherein this activity constitutes an unconstitutional exercise or delegation of powers by the President.

Ex-President Taft once contended "that the President can exercise no power which cannot be fairly and reasonably traced to some specific grant of power or justly implied and included within such express grant as proper and necessary to its exercise. Such specific grant must be either in the Federal Constitution or in an act of Congress passed in pursuance thereof." Accordingly "there is no undefined residuum of power which he (the president) can exercise because it seems to him to be in the public interest, and there is nothing in the Neagle case and its definition of a law of the United States, or in other precedents, warranting such as inference." Taft, Chief Executive and His Powers, pages 139–140.

Later as Chief Justice, Mr. Taft wrote the opinion of the Court in Myers v. United States, 272 U. S. 52, 128, upholding the President's power to remove from office a postmaster of the first class. In supporting this ruling, the Chief Justice said:

"The difference between the grant of legislative power under Article I to Congress, which is limited to powers therein enumerated, and the more general grant of the executive power to the President under Article II, is significant. The fact that the executive power is given in general terms strengthened by specific terms where emphasis is appropriate, and limited by direct expressions where limitation is needed and that no express limit is placed on the power of removal by the executive, is a convincing indication that none was intended."

Mr. Taft quoted freely from the works of Alexander Hamilton (pages 137–139):

"'The second article of the Constitution of the United States, section first, establishes this general proposition, that "the Executive Power shall be vested in a President of the United States of America."

"'The same article, in a succeeding section, proceeds to delineate particular cases of executive power. It declares, among other things, that the President shall be commander in chief of the army and navy of the United States and of the militia of the several states, when called into the actual service of the United States, that he shall have power, by and with the advice and consent of the Senate, to make treaties; that it shall be his duty to receive ambassadors and other public ministers, and to take care that the laws be faithfully executed.

"'It would not consist with the rules of sound construction, to consider this enumeration of particular authorities as derogating from the more comprehensive grant in the general clause, further than as it may be coupled with express restrictions or limitations; as in regard to the co-operation of the Senate in the appointment of officers and the making of treaties; which are plainly qualifications of the general executive authority, would naturally dictate the use of general terms, and would render it improbable that a specification of certain particulars was designed as a substitute for those terms, when antecedently used. The different mode of expression employed in the Constitution, in regard to the two powers, the legislative, and the executive, serves to confirm this inference. In the article which gives the legislative powers of the government, the expressions are "All legislative powers herein granted shall be vested in a congress of the United States." In that which grants the executive power, the expressions are "The executive power shall be vested in a President of the United States."

"'The enumeration ought therefore to be considered, as intended merely to specify the principal articles implied in the definition of executive power; leaving the rest to flow from the general grant of that power, interpreted in conformity with other parts of the Constitution, and with the principles of free government.

"'The general doctrine of our Constitution then is, that the executive power of the nation is vested in the President; subject only to the exceptions and qualifications, which are expressed in the instrument.'"

Concerning the Myers case, Mr. Willoughby says in his work on Constitutional Law (1929, vol. 3, p. 1474):

"However, as will appear in the chapter dealing with the constitutional power of the President to remove Federal officers from office, the court, in Myers v. United States deduced this power not only from the President's power to appoint but also from the fact that, the power to remove being essentially executive in character, is to be regarded as included with the general and unqualified grant to him by the Constitution of the executive power. There can be no question but this holding marks a new departure in the construction of this provision of the Constitution, and that it opens up at least the possibility of declaring that other and still more important specific executive powers are vested in the President."

Charles Warren wrote in his "The Making of the Constitution" (1928, 1 p. 526n.)

"That there were powers of the President which were to be implied from the specific grants was recognized by Edmund Randolph in the Virginia Convention, June 10, 1788 (Elliot's Debates, III, 463), when he said: 'Let us take an example of a single department; for instance, that of the President, who has certain things annexed to his office. Does it not reasonably follow that he must have some incidental powers? The principle of incidental powers extends to all parts of the system. So, too, in The Federalist, No. 79, Hamilton stated as to the specific power granted to the President to require opinions from heads of departments: 'This I consider as a mere redundancy; as the right for which it provides would result of itself from the office.'"

The Neagle case, mentioned by Mr. Taft, involved the shooting of Judge Terry by Deputy United States Marshall Neagle, in protecting the life of Justice Field. A statement in Justice Miller's opinion in that case is clearly in point both as to the President's Constitutional powers and as to his authority to delegate administration of them to subordinate officials (135 U. S. 1, 63):

> "The Constitution, section 3, Article 2, declares that the President shall take care that the laws be faithfully executed, and he is provided with the means of fulfilling this obligation by his authority to commission all the officers of the United States, and by and with the advice and consent of the Senate, to appoint the most important of them and to fill vacancies. He is declared to be commander-in-chief of the army and navy of the United States. The duties which are thus imposed upon him he is further enabled to perform by the recognition in the Constitution, and the creation by acts of Congress, of executive departments, which have varied in number from four or five to seven or eight, the heads of which are familiarly called cabinet ministers. These aid him in the performance of the great duties of his office, and represent him in a thousand acts wo [to] which it can hardly be supposed his personal attention is called, and thus he is enabled to fulfill the duty of his great department, expressed in the phase that "he shall take care that the laws be faithfully executed.'
>
> "Is this duty limited to the enforcement of acts of Congress or of treaties of the United States according to their <u>express terms</u>, or does it include the rights, duties and obligations growing out of the Constitution itself, our international relations, and all the protection implied by the nature of the government under the Constitution?"

That the President's duty is not limited to the express terms of statutes and treaties, the <u>Neagle</u> case stands as historic authority.

Edwards Corwin in his book entitled "The President, Office and Powers" page 133, summarizes the argument thus:

> "Historically, executive power <u>is</u> residual power, Mr. Taft to the contrary notwithstanding; and the idea that the opening clause of Article II is to be a grant of power affords this conception an open route into constitutional law and theory."

And when we again turn to the President's power as Commander in Chief of the Army and Navy in time of war, authority is no less reassuring both as to the existence of the President's power and as to the reasonableness of its exercise when he executed Executive Order No. 9346. The limits to this power would seem to be measured by the conditions which confront the President in time of war. Former Chief Justice Hughes once said that "the power to wage war is the power to wage war successfully." (Senate Document No. 105, p. 7, 65th Congress, 1st Sess., No. 7265). This is a day of total war. Chief Justice Stone recently emphasized this well-known fact when, in upholding the President's Japanese curfew orders in <u>Hirabayaski</u> v. <u>United States</u>, 320 U. S. 81, 93, he said that the war power "extends to every matter and activity so related to war as substantially to affect its conduct and progress. The power is not restricted to the winning of victories in the field and the repulse of enemy forces. It embraces every phase of the national defense. . ."

Only two years ago in a resolution which declared the existence of a state of war with the German Government, the Congress resolved that "to bring the conflict to a successful termination, all the resources of the country are hereby pledged by the Congress of the United States." (U.S.C. Title 50, app. supp. 3, note preceding sec. 3).

On May 9, 1944, Judge MacSwinford [Mac Swinford] discussed the President's powers, aside from statute, to seize the plant of the Ken-Rad Tube and Lamp Corporation, in these words (No. 132 D.C. Western Dist. KY):

"I further conclude that without an act of the Congress there was sufficient authority by the terms of the Constitution itself to justify the action of the President in this case. The President has no power to declare war, that belongs exclusively to Congress. But when war has been declared and is actually existing, his functions as Commander-In-Chief become of the higher importance and his operations in that connection are entirely beyond the control of the legislature. There develops upon him by virtue of his office a solemn responsibility to preserve the nation and it is my judgment that there is specifically granted to him authority to utilize all resources of the country to that end. * * * *

"Charged with the grave responsibility of preserving a government which guarantees the property rights of individuals the chief executive as commander-in-chief must not be hampered in the prosecution of the war effort. His exercise of authority to this end is subject only to the review by the court that his actions are not arbitrary or without reasonable justification. With this limitation there need be no fear that constitutional government as we know it in these United States will be abolished, destroyed or impaired."

Theodore Roosevelt thus stated his views of the high duty and responsibility which are imposed on the President (Works, Vol. XX, page 347):

"My view was that every executive officer, and above all every executive officer in high position, was a steward of the people bound actively and affirmatively to do all he could for the people, and not to content himself with the negative merit of keeping his talents undamaged in a napkin. I declined to adopt the view that what was imperatively necessary for the Nation could not be done by the President unless he could find some specific authorization to do it. My belief was that it was not only his right but his duty to do anything that the needs of the Nation demanded unless such action was forbidden by the Constitutions or by the laws."

President Wilson was hardly less emphatic (Constitutional Government in the United States, page 69):

"His (The President's) office is anything he has the sagacity and force to make it.
"That is the reason why it has been one thing at one time, and another at another. The Presidents who have not made themselves leaders have lived no more truly on that account in the spirit of the Constitution than those whose force has told in the determination of law and policy."

MS: copy, HqR6, Office Files of Emanuel H. Bloch, Hearing Examiner. July 1944–Jan. 1946 (A–Z) (entry 15), Constitutionality of E.O. 9346.

1. This report probably was based on work Bloch began when assigned to prepare materials for submission to the Smith Committee early in 1944 but used for the congressional hearings and debates on FEPC appropriations later in the year. See Mitchell's report of 1/14/44, Bloch's memorandum of 2/8/44, and Maslow's memorandum on Congressional Debates on FEPC Appropriations, 5/27/44, in appendix 1. For a greatly condensed version that includes many excerpts from this text, see Constitutionality of Executive Order No. 9346, Further Amending Executive Order No. 8802 by Establishing a New Committee on Fair Employment Practice and Defining its Powers and Duties, n. d., also in HqR6, Office Files of Emanuel H. Bloch, Constitutionality of E. O. 9346. The last date referred to in both texts is May 9, 1944, the date of Judge Swinford's decision, which the condensed text states was a recent one. The editors have therefore dated this text as ca. May 1944.

2. For other digests of state antidiscrimination policy, see State Legislation Forbidding Discriminatory Employment Practices, 2/8/44, in Files of Max Berking, HqR3, and 1/18/45 (RG 228, Entry 15), on HqR78, Field Letters. Aug. 1943–June 1945, Field Letter 22, A.

Memorandum on General Motors, Delco-Remy Division

Nov. 30, 1944

Mr. George M. Johnson
Deputy Chairman and Acting Director, Legal Division

Emanuel H. Bloch
Hearing Examiner

General Motors, Delco-Remy Division[1]
6-BC-6, 275, 276, 277, 278, 280, 281, and 282

These cases involve the discharge of Seventh Day Adventists because of their refusal to work on their Sabbath.

The Delco-Remy Division of the General Motors Company, Anderson, Indiana is implicated in these complaints of creedal discrimination. This Division manufactures aircraft engine parts and electrical equipment. This activity indisputably subjects this establishment to our jurisdiction.[1]/

The complaints in issue were filed with the Washington office of the FEPC during the period January 25, 1943 to March 11, 1943.

In response to our inquiry regarding the first filed complaint, the general manger of the Delco-Remy plant replied by letter of 2/16/43 that the employee was not discharged because of her religion but "for the reason that she was habitually absent from work on our Saturday."

This communication declares further, "This company does not have any objections to any religion that any employee may have, however, it is a condition of employment that an employee must work whenever there is work available."

Reference is made to the serious problem of absenteeism on Saturdays and Sundays and the necessity of disciplining employees who do not work on these days. This disciplinary policy was effectuated by the practice of warning for the first offence, of imposition of a disciplinary lay-off for the second offence, and of dismissal for the third violation. Attention is directed to the inability "to excuse certain employees for various reasons as this would give other employees good cause for claiming discrimination." Finally, it is asserted, "Under the present war conditions it is necessary to produce our products on schedule. Therefore, it is necessary to have all employees at work when they are needed."

The record discloses no further connection with the party charged in the instant cases until 9/29/44. This delay appears to have been occasioned by a train of unfortunate circumstances, including the inadequacy of our Washington staff in early 1943 to cope with the case load, the lapse of time in the opening of our field offices, the assignment of the file to our Detroit office in an attempt to adjust the grievances with the Detroit home office of the subject,2/ the return of part of the file to the Director of Field Operations, the remittance of the whole file to Region V and the apparent loss of the of the file in this region for a considerable period of time, the transfer of the file to Region VI, the preparation of final disposition reports by Region VI recommending dismissal for "other reasons,"3/ followed by the refusal of the central office of Field Operations to confirm this disposition and its direction to the region to determine whether the complainants are still interested in the case and, if so, to "make an effort to obtain a satisfactory adjustment,"4/ the discharge of this instruction resulting in affirmative expressions of abiding attentiveness from five of the complaints and culminating in the renewed request to the company to reinstate the complainants on an adjusted schedule so as to permit their observance of the Saturday religious holiday.

The answer of the general manager of Delco-Remy, under date of 10/31/44 denied the request asserting that present circumstances prevent resolving the matter in favor of our proposals. He stated also that the dismissal of the complainants "definitely precludes the reestablishment of their seniority," and refers to the "seniority employees" who were "laid off" in addition to a great many others who were acquiring seniority. The people of this status have priority over the nine former employees who have appealed to your office. He concludes "in view of the above, it is impossible for me to state what the future relationship of these people will be with this company. It is a matter which can be determined only by giving consideration to all of the circumstances which may prevail at some time in the future when the factors which currently prevent their being reemployed do not exist."

On November 1, 1944 the region reopened the cases and referred them to the Director of Field Operations on the ground that attempts at adjustment of these complaints at the regional level "would be futile." The matter comes before us pursuant to referral from the Director of Field Operations.5/

The file reveals that all of the complainants but one have worked for the company up to their discharge for periods ranging from nine and one half to sixteen and one half years. During all of this time, including fourteen months of the war period, they encountered no difficulty with the company in accommodating their Saturday worship to their employment. We can reasonably infer from this history the absence of any rigid prejudice of management against creedal observance of Sabbatarians and a fortification of the company's contention that the war necessity to maintain production schedules without interruption of work dictated the discharge.

The Committee has formulated and adopted its policy on Sabbatarian cases. Its statement of policy reads:

> "In cases in which it is alleged that a person has been discriminated against in connection with employment in war industries or government service, because of creed, and it appears upon investigation, that such person has been denied employment or dismissed from employment because he or she on account of his or her creed conscientiously cannot perform secular work on certain days the Committee takes the position that if it is possible even at considerable inconvenience, for the party charged to arrange work schedules so as to permit such persons to absent himself or herself from work on days on which he or she because of creed conscientiously cannot perform secular work, failure to arrange such work schedules will be regarded as a violation of the provisions of Executive Order 9346."6/

There is no serious dispute that the complainants cannot perform secular work on Saturdays because of their religious scruples. We turn then to an examination of the evidences to determine whether the party charged failed to arrange its work schedules, even at considerable inconvenience, to allow these Sabbatarian disciples to absent themselves from work on Saturdays.

The burden rests on the Committee to show the failure of an employer to discharge this duty. Proof of such nonfeasance is an indispensable prerequisite to a determination that the Executive Order has been violated.

We find the record in an ambiguous state on this vital element of the case. There are persuasive statements that the plant was operating on a 6-day 48-hour work schedule at the time of the dismissal,7/ which, if true, furnish some corroboration of the company's position. We have already made some concessions to this position when Henderson stated to the company in his letter of 9/29/44, "our Committee recognized the handicap that your company was under in adjusting the work schedules of these employees under the new 7-day program then in operation.

On the other hand, there are allegations that the company was operating some departments on a 5-day week basis and refused to cooperate in the transfer of one complainant to this department,8/ "some are working on Sunday; but the most of the employees are only working 48 hours,"9/ specifying that two "Preacher" toolmakers never worked on Sunday, "although toolmakers were for a long time working 9 hours a day, 5 days a week and on Saturday and Sunday 8 hours," and the department of one complainant was on a 6-day week, but other departments worked Sundays and he could have been transferred.11/ These assertions, however, lack any substantiation.

This whole picture is beclouded and inconclusive. For want of more concrete and convincing evidence, we entertain doubts whether a prima facie case of contravention of the provisions or the interpretations of Executive Order 9346 has been established. Under such circumstances, it is plain that the cases are not ripe for hearing.

Nevertheless, in recognition of the fact that dismissal at this stage may be construed as a cavalier disposition of the matter, and in order to procure adequate information upon which to base a factual decision on the merits, it is recommended that the field investigate and report on the specific issue whether the company could have rearranged its work schedules, even at considerable inconvenience, at the time of the discharges, to continue the complainants in employment at their skills while permitting them to be absent on Saturdays.

Relevant investigatory data should include (1) normal and special weekly work schedules of the company, particularizing the days, hours per day and various shifts (2) the volume and type of operations performed on Sunday, if any, with a breakdown of the categories of jobs engaged in the performance of work on this day.

This interlocutory disposition does not mean that the Regional Director's reasons for a final closing of the cases have been overlooked or overruled. On the contrary, they are undoubtedly impressive but their practical consideration must be held in abeyance until the report suggested herein has been received and evaluated.

It is recognized that the fulfillment of the assignment of this special investigation and report will entail further direct communication with the company. Consequently it is competent to notify the field that the company's contention that the discharges "definitely preclude the reestablishment of (the complainants') seniority" is untenable and arbitrary. For, if it is found that the dismissals were discriminatory and violative of the Executive Order, the complainants should be made "whole" and be restored to the status quo ante.

It is customary for the National Labor Relations Board, in unlawful discharge cases, to provide for reinstatement with substantially equivalent employment without loss of seniority or other rights. The courts have sustained the propriety of such relief 12/. The Fair Employment Practice Committee, under its powers "to take appropriate steps to obtain elimination of such discrimination," may direct reinstatement and restoration of seniority rights for the purpose of redressing a grievance based on discrimination forbidden by the Order.13/

It is, therefore, recommended that the Division of Field Operations be directed to conduct the investigation and prepare the report thereon pursuant to the instructions herein. Final decision will be postponed in the interim.

FOOTNOTES

1/ Statement of the President's Committee on Fair Employment Practice, adopted September 9, 1944, relating to its jurisdiction over "war industries," etc. IA, — Appendix AI.

2/ There is no demonstration that such assignment was performed.

3/ July 31, 1944 — The reasons for the action were stated: "In view of the fact that the case involves a discharge that occurred a year and a half ago, it is felt that further processing would serve no useful purpose whatsoever. In addition it is believed that the revival of this specific issue at this time would jeopardize the success of other dealings which this office expects to have with Delco-Remy in the near future. Finally, it appears highly improbable that further contact with the complainants after a year of silence would result in any service to them or would be valuable from the public relations angle."

4/ Memo, Mitchell to Henderson, August 19, 1944.

5/ Memo, Maslow to Johnson dated November 10, 1944 — Maslow acquiesces in the correctness of Henderson's original disposition because the cases are "old" but, nevertheless, turns them over to the Legal Division on the theory that only two sources are open, either a hearing or disposition under "other".

6/ Summary of Essential Actions taken by the President's Committee on Fair Employment Practice September 14, 1943 meeting — paragraph 3.

7/ Letter of complainant, Ethel Mae Smith, to Committee — 3/24/43.

8/ Complaint of Nellie Hackleman, dated 3/11/43.

9/ Letter, Letha Stimson Lawson (complainant) to Committee 3/28/43.

10/ Supra, 9 — We are unimpressed with this information in view of its apparent references to an indefinite past.

11/ Letter, Otto Dubaique (complainant) to Committee, 3/14/43.

12/ In the Matter of Botany Worsted Company, 106 Fed. (2nd) 263, 269.
In the Matter of Carlisle Lumber Company, 99 Fed. (2nd) 533, 539.
In the Matter of Quality Art Novelty Company, 127 Fed. (2nd) 903,906.
In the Matter of Valley Mould Co. 116 Fed. (2nd) 760, 762.
Skinner vs. Kennedy, 113 Fed. (2nd) 667, 671.

13/ Executive Order 9346, paragraph 5 — of. Summary of Essential Actions taken by the President's Committee on Fair Employment Practice at its September 30, 1944 meeting — 2(h), in which it stated, "The problem of minority rights as affected by discrimination was discussed. The Committee agreed that in connection with any case where an applicant for employment receives employment after a discriminatory bar has been removed, his seniority so far as the Committee is concerned dates from his actual employment and not from the date when he would have been employed but for the discriminatory bar. On the general question of seniority, it was agreed that the Committee should act as a mediating agency and develop on a case by case basis policies and procedures for effective mediation.

MS: copy, HqR83, Correspondence Relating to Cases. A–K.

1. For directly related texts, see Mitchell to Maslow, 11/18/44, and in appendix 1, Bloch to Johnson, 11/30/44, and Johnson to Maslow, 12/6/44. For immediately related texts in the file, see Maslow to Johnson, 11/20/44, and Johnson to Bloch, 11/22/44.

Memorandum on General Motors, Delco-Remy Division

December 6, 1944

Mr. Will Maslow, Director of Field Operations

George M. Johnson, Deputy Chairman & Acting Director, Legal Division

General Motors, Delco-Remy Division
6-BC-6, 275, 276, 277, 278, 280, 281 and 282

Attached hereto is the file relating to the above subject together with two copies of Mr. Bloch's memorandum with respect to the same. It seems unfortunate that this whole case should be reopened at this time, and yet I am persuaded by Mr. Bloch's argument that a dismissal at this stage may be open to criticism.[1]

I concur therefore in his recommendation.

MS: copy, HqR83, Correspondence Relating to Cases. A–K.
   1. See Mitchell to Maslow, 11/18/44, and in appendix 1, Bloch to Johnson, 11/30/44.

Memorandum on Nondiscrimination Clause

February 19, 1945

Mr. George M. Johnson, Deputy Chairman & Acting Director, Legal Division
Simon Stickgold, Trial Attorney
Non-discrimination clause (Federal Register, February 15, 1945)

On February 15, 1945 the Federal Register published a series of amendments to the various procurement regulations of the United States Army. Section 803-325 of Procurement Regulation No. 3, entitled "anti-discrimination clause", makes mandatory the inclusion in every contract "regardless of subject matter or amount", the following clause "without deviation":

"Anti-discrimination. (a) The Contractor, in performing the work required by this contract, shall not discriminate against any employee or applicant for employment because of race, creed, color, or national origin.
"(b) The Contractor agrees that the provision of paragraph (a) above will also be inserted in all of its subcontracts. For the purpose of this article, a subcontract is defined as any contract entered into by the contractor with any individual, partnership, association, corporation, estate, or trust, or other business enterprise or other legal entity, for a specific part of the work to be performed in connection with the supplies or services furnished under this contract: Provided, however, That a contract for the furnishing of standard or commercial articles or raw material shall not be considered as a subcontract."

Sections 809.984 and 809.985 deal with "Executive Order No. 9346" and "Interpretations of Executive Order No. 9346 by the Committee on Fair Employment Practice," respectively. Under Section 809.984 paragraphs 1 and 2 of the Executive Order are quoted and briefly discussed. Under Section 809.985 the 12 point interpretation of these paragraphs, issued by the Committee on September 30, 1944, is duplicated, in toto.

Section 809.986 discusses the amendment of existing contracts and subcontracts not containing anti-discrimination clauses and directs the incorporation of such clauses in proper cases.

These amendments appear to contain a concise formulation of the Committee's position with respect to the inclusion of non-discrimination clauses in government contracts.

MS: copy, HqR38, Central Files. Memoranda, Johnson, George M.—3, Jan. 44.

Memorandum on Telephone Company Cases

CONFIDENTIAL

MEMORANDUM

March 7, 1945

TO: Committee Members

FROM: Evelyn N. Cooper

SUBJECT: Telephone Company Cases[1]

On March 1, 1945 I conferred in New York City with Mr. Cleo F. Craig, Vice President-in-Charge of Personnel, American Telephone and Telegraph Company, about our telephone cases. The purpose of this conference was to "sound out" A.T. & T.'s policy regarding the employment of Negroes as telephone operators and to solicit A.T. & T.'s aid in the adjustment of pending cases. The conference was partially successful. Likelihood of adjustments was indicated and the way left open for further discussion, if needed.

A.T. & T. is the holding company of the various telephone companies charged with discrimination. It does not formulate nor dictate the employment policies of the subsidiary companies but it clearly influences such policies; especially as regards operators since it maintains "long line" operators in each telephone exchange, all long distance calls being handled over A.T. & T. wires. This was evidenced not only by Mr. Craig's remarks but by our own files which show a uniform policy and, furthermore, an almost uniform defense among the companies charged.

During the past two years there has been in effect within the Bell System a <u>pressure for the integration of Negroes. In the last year it has been intensified.</u> (*) The following cases have been referred for hearing to the Legal Division: Ohio Bell Telephone Company (Columbus, Ohio), Southern Bell Telephone Company (Louisville, Kentucky), Chesapeake and Potomac Telephone Company (Baltimore, Maryland), and New Jersey Bell Telephone Company (Atlantic City, New Jersey). Informally, Region XII's files on the Pacific Telephone & Telegraph Company (San Francisco and Palo Alto, California and Spokane, Washington) have been referred, although the regional office still has hope of adjustment.

The program calls for the employment of colored girls as messengers, elevator operators, receptionists, clerks, etc., and ultimately as operators. (Job opportunities for men in the Bell System are limited at the lower wage levels but the program apparently includes Negro men as well as women, as is indicated by the recent employment of Negroes as coin collectors in Baltimore.) Negroes were previously employed only in menial, unskilled jobs. Nowhere are they yet otherwise employed in large numbers and progress under the program has been variant. In terms of the categories of positions held by Negroes, substantial progress has been made by Chesapeake and Potomac Telephone Company (Baltimore) and Ohio Bell Telephone Company (Columbus), and in a somewhat lesser degree by New Jersey Bell Telephony Company (Camden). In the Ohio Bell Telephone Company some of the colored girls have already been upgraded from service to clerical jobs.

Oddly enough, though the operator job category has been set aside as the last in which integration is to be tried, operators are among the lowest paid of the Bell System's "white collar jobs". In New York City, for example, messengers and clerks have the same starting wage, better hours and with more opportunity for advancement. Again, in New York City, the maximum salary for operators is $34.00 per week and than maximum can be achieved only after eleven years service. The result is that Negro girls are now employed by some of the companies charged in clerical jobs paying more than operators jobs. Two of the companies charged (New Jersey Bell and Ohio Bell) have offered to consider the complainants for clerical jobs at wages comparable to operators jobs, while refusing to employ them as operators. The reason given for this apparent incongruity is that the operators work in such close proximity to each other, having to lean across one another's boards. By employing Negro girls as messengers and elevator operators and as clerks in the personnel and various other offices, it is thought that the operators will thereby become conditioned to ultimate integration in their job category. Otherwise, work stoppages are feared.

Offsetting this reasoning is the fact that the National Federation of Telephone Workers, of which the operators like the other categories of employees are a part, is virtually company-dominated so that the chance of work stoppages among white operators because of the employment of Negro operators seems minimum. New operators, moreover, are trained by supervisors rather than by other operators. In New York City the telephone company accomplished integration through the supervisors, that is, by "selling" them on the idea. But, on the other hand, a strike is reported to have been threatened by some of the national officers of the union at the time Negro operators were first employed in New York, and in Baltimore it is claimed that there is now more tension among the white operators than before. Earlier there was a one-day stoppage in Camden, New Jersey when Negroes were first employed there in clerical jobs.

In any event, the real reason for the separate treatment of the operator job category under the integration program seems to lie in a long standing Bell System policy. As indicated, the wage level of the operators is very low–so low in fact that WMC has exempted operators from all recruitment controls. As part of the same policy, the companies have provided the operators with exceptionally nice rest areas, recreational and eating facilities, thereby giving them a sort of compensatory "social status" among telephone company workers. Also, the job qualifications established for operators are calculated in normal times to permit only those girls to qualify who would not be apt to protest low wages nor be able to qualify for higher paid work elsewhere because of limited education. Thus it is required that an operator have not more than $2–2^1/_2$ years of high school. This is important to our cases because practically all of the complainants are "over-qualified." In a few instances this has been given as the reason for refusal of employment.

In defense of the integration program and the present failure to employ Negroes as operators, it is contended that the companies are undertaking a thorough-going job intended to carry over into peace time, that they are in a somewhat different position than war-time industries, and that they are using the best-known integration techniques. All of this, I think, must be conceded. The principle criticism is with the timing. I mean by that that if a similar program were to be presented to the committee as a step toward compliance it would probably be acceptable as such, provided that employment in all job categories as assured within a reasonably short period of time. However, in Baltimore, for example, the program seems to be stalemated. Integration has been accomplished in all but the operator job category and the company is doing nothing to prepare for it there, feeling that the time is not yet opportune. Similarly in the case of the New Jersey Bell Telephone Company. All of the complaints against that company originated in Atlantic City where the only telephone jobs are operators jobs and where, again, it is felt that Negro girls cannot yet be employed without a work stoppage.

Mr. Craig said he thought the problem of integration in those two cities was peculiarly difficult but, speaking generally, intimated that it might be worthwhile for us to try again for adjustment since conditions within the companies had changed substantially since most of our cases first arose. (With the exception of the West Coast cases, they all date back to at leas[t] 1943.) Conditions have changed as indicated, but it is known that in Baltimore the company's position as to operators is unchanged. The same can be assumed in Louisville, Kentucky (Southern Bell). What it might now be in Columbus (Ohio Bell) cannot be opined. Nevertheless, all of the companies in the Bell System have been informed of the New York City experiences and Mr. O.H. Taylor, operating Vice President of the New York Bell Telephone Company, freely expresses his pleasure about it. More recently his company has put a Negro girl in training in Buffalo. All of this is bound to have an effect upon the other telephone companies, not only because of the very acute shortage of operators, but because of the tradition of uniformity of policy among the companies–some of the companies charged have said so in the past that they would hire Negroes as operators when they were employed in that capacity by other companies in the System. Presumably it has already had some effect on the West Coast where Region XII is optimistic about adjustment.

Edward Lawson, whose opinion I value in this matter because of his success in New York, feels that telephone companies elsewhere (except in the deep South) will follow the New York lead rather quickly, particularly under pressure of favorable public opinion. Specifically, in Atlantic City, he suggests that the weatherman who has recently

hired a Negro girl to prepare weather reports, and one of the City Commissioners who has a Negro secretary, could be of help. The Mayor, I understand, might also be helpful. In Baltimore too there seems to be room for resort to public opinion. (The Regional Director for Region IV concedes as much and is willing to explore the possibilities.)

For these several reasons, it is my recommendation that the cases be sent back to the regions for further attempts at adjustment, except that the Southern Bell case be held in abeyance in the national office until adjustment is assured elsewhere. There are legal reasons too for this recommendation. In all but the Baltimore and New Jersey cases where the companies admit refusal to hire Negroes as operators, the position of the companies charged is that they do not discriminate but, on the contrary, employ Negroes for jobs for which they are best suited on the basis of their qualifications. Where the complainants are over-qualified, our cases against these companies are therefore difficult of proof, if not exceedingly weak. In the Ohio Bell case the one and only complainant is over-qualified. The complainants are over-qualified also in the Southern Bell case. In the West Coast cases the educational background of only one of the three complainants is shown and she too is over-qualified. Admission of discrimination by the Baltimore and New Jersey companies makes those cases much stronger but nevertheless all but one of the 22 Baltimore complainants is over-qualified. Policy-wise this fact is weighty. From the file in the New Jersey case, it is impossible to tell whether or not the complainants satisfy the educational requirement.

Another requirement of operator applicants, which is as strictly adhered to as the educational requirement, is that they have no small children or if so that they have some means of having them cared for. This is because operators are subject to call at all hours of the day and night and their assigned hours are frequently irregular. To the extent that any of the complainants might qualify educationally, it is not known whether they would qualify in this respect. A complete list of the requirements used by the New York Bell Telephone Company is appended. It is understood that they are the same throughout the System.

In addition to the use of favorable public opinion, it is suggested that a few outstanding girls who appear to meet all of the requirements be presented at the proper time to the management of each of the various companies charged, as evidence of the sort of colored girls who are available for operators jobs. This suggestion is predicated upon Mr. Lawson's experience. A caution is necessary, however,—that is, that the girls should really want operators jobs. In New York City many of the girls who were obtained as applicants for operators jobs after these jobs were opened to Negroes actually took clerical jobs instead because of better wages, hours, and opportunities for advancement.

I make this recommendation of referral back to the field after some hesitation, realizing the difficulty of starting anew on a case which has long been under negotiation—to the point even of becoming a cause celebre. I feel however that there is more to be gained at this time by trying again for adjustment than there would be in going to hearing. I say this in the belief that if adjustment efforts fail again in the field, adjustment can probably be secured through the American Telephone and Telegraph Company.

Attachment

Qualifications

1) 2 years high school (1/2 year more or less allowed)
2) Record of citizenship.
3) Age 17 to 40

After referral to company, applicants are given

1) Preliminary interview of 5 minutes
2) More intensive interview of 30 minutes (*)
3) Physical examination

(*) For this purpose, following criteria are used

1) Reading test for voices, enunciation and diction
2) Reach of arm length (3 boards)
3) Eyesight (color blindness disqualifies)
4) Adaptability (compatibility)
5) Memory
6) Appearance
7) Dependability

MS: copy, HqR4, Office Files of George M. Johnson. Mrs. Evelyn Cooper.

1. Responding in his memorandum of 3/8/45, Mitchell disagreed strongly with three of Cooper's assertions, especially that regarding the 2½-year education requirement throughout the industry. In a memorandum of 3/8/45 to Maslow, Johnson noted:

As you know, for some time now the Committee has been considering holding hearings in connection with one or more of the several telephone cases which have been referred by Regional Directors. At its meeting in Chicago on February 12, the Committee considered a general report on these cases and agreed that hearings should be held case by case, rather than attempt a single industry wide hearings.

Mrs. Evelyn N. Cooper of the Legal Division has had several conferences with Mr. Mitchell, Associate Director of Field Operations with respect to these cases. On March 1, 1945 she conferred with officials of the A.T. & T. and as a result of this conference she has come to certain conclusions with respect to the manner in which the cases should be approached at this time. A copy of her proposed memorandum to the Committee in which she makes certain recommendations is attached hereto.

At the staff meeting on March 7, 1945 she discussed briefly some of her recommendations and the reasons therefore. It appeared that there were some rather basic differences of opinion among members of the staff, and for this reason I am requesting that you submit a memorandum commenting upon Mrs. Cooper's proposed recommendations.

Johnson then expressed his desire to join Mitchell, Maslow, and Davis in another meeting with Cooper. The text is in HqR3, Office Files of George M. Johnson. Will Maslow.

APPENDIX 2

Documents Not Published

September 22, 1943, Memorandum to William McKnight on Important Problems of Region V (HqR3, Office Files of George M. Johnson. A–M, M)

November 26, 1943, Memorandum to Will Maslow on Final Disposition Report on Western Union Telegraph Company, 4-BA-184 (FR45, Region IV. Closed Cases, Western Union Telegraph Company, Washington, D.C., 4-BA-184)

December 23, 1943, Memorandum to Robert C. Weaver on Report from William McKnight (HqR39, Central Files. Memoranda, Weaver, Robert C.)

December 31, 1943, Memorandum to Emanuel Bloch on Biltmore Hotel, Los Angeles, California (HqR83, Correspondence Relating to Cases. A–K, Biltmore Hotel, Los Angeles, Calif.)

[1943], Memorandum to Mr. Barron, Dr. Landes and Dr. Trimble on Findings and Recommendations on Seth Major of Library of Congress (HqR3, Office Files of George M. Johnson. A–M, M)

January 12, 1944, Memorandum to George M. Johnson on St. Louis and San Francisco Railroad Company, Fort Scott, Kansas (HqR38, Central Files. Memoranda, Johnson, George M., Jan. 1944–)

February 19, 1944, Memorandum to Stanley D. Metzger on USES Investigation (HqR38, Central Files. Memoranda, Metzger, Stanley D.)

February 24, 1944, Eleanor F. Rogers Memorandum to Mitchell on Telephone Conversation with A. Bruce Hunt, Director of Region VII, Re. Bell Aircraft Visit (HqR83, Correspondence Relating to Cases. A–K, Bell Aircraft Co., Marietta, Ga.)

March 11, 1944, Memorandum to Will Maslow on Active DFO Cases (HqR38, Central Files. Memoranda, Maslow, Will, 1944)

March 17, 1944, Memorandum to St. Clair Bourne on Spot Radio Announcements in Region II (HqR39, Central Files. Memoranda, Region II)

March 27, 1944, Memorandum to Eugene Davidson on his Comment on National Biscuit Company Case. (HqR38, Central Files. Memoranda, Davidson, Eugene)

April 11, 1944, Memorandum to Will Maslow on General Box Company, Kansas City, Missouri (HqR83, Correspondence Relating to Cases. A–K, General Box Company)

April 22, 1944, Memorandum to Mrs. Alexander, Miss Baker, Miss Blanche, Miss Clifton, Miss Hoffman, and Mrs. Whiting on Communications addressed to Region XII (HqR38, Central Files. Memoranda, A–C)

April 23, 1944, Memorandum on Norris Stamping [not found]

April 29, 1944, Memorandum to Emanuel Bloch and Stanley D. Metzger on Handling of Regional Reports (HqR38, Central Files. Memoranda, Bloch, Emanuel)

May 12, 1944, Memorandum to Emanuel Bloch and Stanley Metzger on Division of Agencies (HqR38, Central Files. Memoranda, Bloch, Emanuel)

July 11, 1944, Memorandum to George M. Johnson on Line Material Company (HqR84, Correspondence Relating to Cases. L–S, Line Material Co., Zanesville, Ohio)

July 17, 1944, Memorandum to George M. Johnson on International Harvester Company (HqR38, Central Files. Memoranda, Johnson, George M., Jan. 1944–)

July 22, 1944, Memorandum to George M. Johnson on Kraus Super Service (HqR83, Correspondence Relating to Cases. A–K, Kraus Super Service)

July 27, 1944, Memorandum to George M. Johnson on Complaint of the National Maritime Union Against Hotel Senator (HqR85, Correspondence Relating to Cases. United Seamen's Service, Region X)

August 7, 1944, Memorandum to George M. Johnson, Memorandum on Security-First National Bank and Bank of America (HqR84, Correspondence Relating to Cases. Security First National Bank of America, 12-BR-1325-26)

September 23, 1944, Memorandum to Mitchell prepared by Eleanor F. Rogers of Telephone Call from G. James Fleming re Stoppage at Carnegie-Illinois Steel Company, Clairton, Pennsylvania (HqR38, Central Files. Memoranda, Mitchell, Clarence)

September 30, 1944, Eleanor F. Rogers, Memorandum to Mitchell on His Telephone Call to W. Don Ellinger on Post Office Cases (HqR38, Central Files. Memoranda, Mitchell, Clarence)

October 5, 1944, Memorandum to L. E. Beane, Industrial Secretary, Washington Urban League, on [Mitchell's membership on the Industrial Committee of the Washington Urban League] (HqR38, Central Files. Memoranda, Mitchell, Clarence)

November 27, 1944, Memorandum to Frank D. Reeves, Trial Attorney, on International Brotherhood of Electric Workers, Local 302 Case (HqR39, Central Files. Memoranda, Reeves, Frank)

December 2, 1944, Memorandum to George M. Johnson on Wilson and Company Case (HqR38, Central Files. Memoranda, Johnson, George M., Jan. 1944–)

December 16, 1944, Memorandum to Hayes Beall on Status of Transit Cases Handled by Regional Offices (HqR38, Central Files. Memoranda, Beall, Hayes) [not found]

January 9, 1945, Memorandum to Files on Telephone Call from Mr. William McKnight (HqR84, Correspondence Relating to Cases. L–S, Line Material Co., Zanesville, Ohio)

February 8, 1945, Memorandum to Hayes Beall on Most Important FEPC Cases (HqR38, Central Files. Memoranda, Beall, Hayes)

February 19, 1945, Memorandum to Mrs. Evelyn Cooper on Bechtel McCone & Parsons, 12-BR-468 DFO [on Arabian cases] (HqR8, Office Files of Evelyn N. Cooper. Correspondence)

March 3, 1945, Otome Saito Memorandum to Mitchell on His Telephone Conversation with Dr. Dodge and Mr. McKay (HqR68, Central Files. Reports, Files of John A. Davis, Mr. Mitchell)

March 20, 1945, Memorandum to Will Maslow on Resignation of George D. McKay (FEPC RG 228, Division of Field Operations, Office Files of Clarence Mitchell, box 458, E–R, Maslow, Will, DNA)

March 24, 1945, Memorandum to George M. Johnson on Wilson & Company (HqR85, Correspondence Relating to Cases. Wilson & Co., Region VI)

April 12, 1945, Memorandum to Emanuel Bloch, Hearings Commissioner, on Shell Oil Company, Houston, Texas (HqR21, Records Relating to Hearings. Shell Oil Company, Inc., & Oil Workers International Union, Local 367, CIO)

April 12, 1945, Memorandum to Emanuel Bloch, Hearings Commissioner, on Conference with Oil Workers Re: Shell Oil (HqR21, Records Relating to Hearings. Shell Oil Company, Inc., & Oil Workers International Union, Local 367, CIO) [not found]

May 25, 1945, Otome Saito Memorandum to Mitchell on Telephone Conversations with Mr. G. James Fleming on May 22 and 24, 1945, on New Jersey Telephone Case (HqR68, Office Files of John A. Davis. Mr. Mitchell) [not found]

July 21, 1945, Memorandum to Mrs. Evelyn Cooper on New Jersey Bell Telephone Case (HqR8, Office Files of Evelyn N. Cooper, Telephone Company Cases) [not found]

July 30, 1945, Memorandum to Theodore A. Jones on Allotment of Travel Funds for the Quarter Ending September 30, 1945 (HqR3, Office Files of George M. Johnson. A–M, M).

August 3, 1945, Memorandum to John A. Davis on Information in FEPC's First Report (HqR39, Central Files. Memoranda, Review and Analysis Division)

August 11, 1945, Memorandum to Hayes Beall on FEPC-WMC Cases (HqR38, Central Files. Memoranda, Beall, Hayes)

August 27, 1945, Memorandum to Malcolm Ross on Proposed WAE Employees (HqR39, Central Files. Memoranda, Ross, Malcolm, Jan. 45–)

November 1, 1945, Memorandum to Sara E. Southall on Employment of Negroes in New Orleans (HqR39, Central Files. Memoranda, Southall, Sara E.)

December 4, 1945, Memorandum to Eugene Davidson on Resignation of Charles Houston (RG 228, Division of Field Operations, Office Files of Clarence Mitchell, box 457, A–D, Davidson, Eugene)

APPENDIX 3

FEPC Organizational Chart

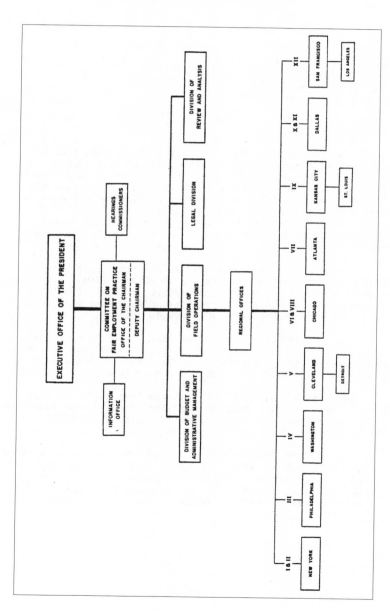

APPENDIX 4

Processing a Complaint

Precision Plastics
1742 West Indiana Avenue
Philadelphia, Pennsylvania

<u>Attention: President</u>

Gentlemen:

The President's Committee on Fair Employment Practice
has received a report from the United States Employment
Service that you have submitted to it a discriminatory request
for workers. This report indicates that on October 6, 1942,
you specified that only white persons be referred for consideration as Assembly Laborers(Plastic) 8-52.61 (female). The
report further indicates that efforts of the United States
Employment Service officials to obtain a change in this specification in your requisition were unsuccessful.

Executive Order 8802 prohibits discrimination in war
industries and activities essential to the war effort because
of race, creed, color or national origin, and this Committee
is required to investigate complaints of such discrimination
and to redress grievances which it finds valid.

You are requested to furnish this Committee with any
facts you may have regarding this report on your requisition
to the United States Employment Service, and to indicate
whether or not this report represents your employment policy.

In view of the question which has been raised by this
report concerning your employment policy, you are also requested
to implement your obligations under Executive Order 8802 in
the following manner:

1. Issue written instructions to all of your personnel officers
   and employees to carry on their activities in the recruitment, training, or upgrading of workers or prospective
   workers solely on the basis of the qualifications of applicants or workers without regard to their race, creed, color

App. 4.1. Notice of violation

Precision Plastics
January 13, 1943   Page 2

or national origin, and in the case of qualified aliens, to submit to the Secretary of War or Secretary of the Navy applications for consent to employ such aliens in accordance with War-Navy regulations;

2. Issue written instructions to the appropriate officer of your Company to delete from Application for Employment forms any reference to race or religion which may be included on them;

3. Give written notice to any employment agency, whether public or private, through which your Company recruits workers, that it will accept needed workers for any and all classifications of work solely on the basis of their qualifications without regard to their race, creed, color or national origin;

4. Give written notice to any training institution or agency through which your Company recruits or trains workers for upgrading that your Company will accept workers for any and all classifications of work solely on the basis of their qualifications and without regard to their race, creed, color or national origin;

5. Give written notice to all labor unions with which your Company has labor contracts that it will comply fully with its contract obligation not to discriminate against workers because of their race, creed, color or national origin in recruitment, upgrading, or in any other terms or conditions of employment;

6. Furnish the President's Committee on Fair-Employment Practice with a copy of each of these instructions and notices.

7. Submit a monthly report beginning January 31, 1943, indicating the number of Negroes employed, the number in employment at the skill levels (skilled, semi-skilled and unskilled), the number in employment as Assembly Laborer (Plastic) 8-52.61 (female), and similar statistics covering white workers.

Your immediate response and compliance are requested.

Sincerely yours,

George M. Johnson
Assistant Executive Secretary

Davidson:vl:lf

App. 4.1. Notice of violation (cont.)

RADCLIFF 4233

PARK 2467

PRECISION PLASTICS COMPANY

1724 W. INDIANA AVENUE   PHILADELPHIA, PA.

011188

July 19, 1943.

President's Committee on
Fair Employment Practice
War Manpower Commission
Washington, D. C.

Attention: Mr. George M. Johnson

Gentlemen:

In accordance with your letter of April 9th, we
submit herewith, a monthly report as requested by
your office.

Yours very truly,

PRECISION PLASTICS COMPANY

E. W. DANIEN
PRESIDENT

EWD:lp
enc.

App. 4.2. Reply of company

CASE SHEET

Assigned to: _George Fleming_   Docket #3- _75_

Date Assigned: March 29, 1944

21 W on market

I.   Party Charged: Precision Plastics Company, 1724 W. Indiana Ave., Phila., Pa.

(a) War contracts

II.   Party Aggrieved: USES-510 report (12-4-42)   M ☐ F ☐

III. Labor union, if any:

IV.   Summary of complaint:

Order placed with Phila. USES 10-6-42 for white, female, assembly laborer, (plastic). Insisted that they would not hire non-white female referrals. Employer advised that they do hire non-white men but not non-white women.

Jan. 12, 1943, Geo. M. Johnson, Washington FEPC, advised company to discontinue discriminatory hiring and to submit monthly reports to the Committee showing breakdown of their employees, white and nonewhite. Company has complied with this latter request; last report dated Feb. 22, 1944.

V.   Investigation conducted by means of:

A. Correspondence   B. Field visits

C. Office interview   D. Other

Comments:

4655 Stenton ave

near Wayne.

VI.   Date and type of final disposition:

CLOSED
DATE 8-25- _____ 4
REASON _Satis. adj._
BY _AJ_ _BJ_ _Hf_

FEPC-III-4-44

App. 4.3. Case sheet

Region III
503-4 Stephen Girard Building
Philadelphia 7, Pa.

September 1, 1944

Precision Plastics Company
1724 West Indiana Avenue
Philadelphia, Pennsylvania

        Attention: Miss W. G. Harvey, Assistant Secretary

        In reply refer to <u>Case Number 3-BR-757</u>

Dear Miss Harvey:

        This regional office of the President's Committee
on Fair Employment Practice was forwarded a report that your company
placed with the U. S. Employment Service a discriminatory order on
October 6, 1942, for assembly laborers, female.

        We have noted the monthly employment reports sub-
mitted by you from April 9, 1943 to July 24, 1944, and find that
approximately 10% of your total employees are non-white males and
females.

        In the light of the foregoing, this office holds
that you have shown compliance with the requests outlined to you on
January 12, 1943, by Mr. George M. Johnson, the then Assistant
Secretary of the President's Committee. We are pleased to advise,
therefore, that it will no longer be necessary for you to submit
monthly reports to this agency, and have reported this case to our
National office as satisfactorily adjusted.

        Very truly yours,

        G. James Fleming
        Regional Director

GJF:gvb

App. 4.4. Compliance letter

FINAL DISPOSITION REPORT

TO: Mr. Will Maslow, Director of Field Operations

FROM: G. James Fleming, Regional Director

RE: Precision Plastics Company

Investigation by: G.M. Johnson, Correspondence

Date: August 30, 1944

Region: III

Case Number: 3-BR-757

Report by: Gergas

A. Chronology:

    1. Date of discrimination:
    2. Date of filing complaint:
    3. Dates of personal contact with complainant:
    4. Date of docketing:
    5. Date of first contact with party charged:
    6. Dates of personal visits to party charged:
    7. Date of closing:
    8. Date of submission of FDR:
    9. Type of final disposition:

October 6, 1942
August 21, 1944
None
August 21, 1944
January 12, 1943
None
August 25, 1944
August 30, 1944
Satisfactory Adjustment

B. Description of party charged:

    Primarily engaged in manufacturing plastic materials which include cellulose
    plastics (nitro-cellulose, synthetic resins, casein, soybean and lignin
    plastics) etc. No ES-270 reports available.

C. Date and summary of complaint:

    An ES-510 report submitted to FEPC, dated December 4, 1942, stated that on
    October 6, 1942 an order for assembly laborers (plastic) female, "white only,"
    was placed with USES. USES suggested use of non-white females. Employer
    stated non-white males were employed but could not yet employ non-white fe-
    males. USES efforts to persuade company to relax discriminatory specifications
    were futile.

D. Background:

    None.

E. Date and type of final disposition:

    August 25, 1944 - Satisfactory Adjustment

G. Details of satisfactory adjustment:

    On January 12, 1943, George M. Johnson wrote a 1 - 7 letter to company and,
    among other things, requested the submission to FEPC of monthly employment
    reports to begin January 30, 1943. On March 16, 1943, the company replied,
    stating that it did not discriminate in hiring workers; that it had always
    employed both white and non-white help and workers of all religions. On

App. 4.5. Final disposition report

695

August 30, 1944
Case Number: 3-BR-757

April 1, 1943, Mr. Johnson (FEPC) insisted that since there was a variance in statements made by the company and the report (510) by USES, the company submit monthly employment reports as he previously requested, commencing April 1, 1943 instead of January 30, 1943. The company forwarded to FEPC on April 9, 1943, copies of the notice to their personnel staff and USES regarding the company's non-discriminatory policies. It was also stated that the company did not use application for employment forms, no training institutions or agencies and that it did not have any affiliation with labor unions.

Monthly employment reports, indicating skilled, unskilled, white, Negro, male and female employees have been submitted from April 1, 1943 to July 1, 1944. These reports show that the company has, over the aforementioned period, employed a total of 539 employees, 34 of whom are Negro females and 29 Negro males, who are working in skilled and unskilled capacities.

In the light of the above, it has been considered that the company has complied fully with the requests made of it under Executive Orders 8802 and 9346. The case has, therefore, been closed as satisfactorily adjusted and the company advised to discontinue the submission of monthly employment reports.

Gorgas/ep

App. 4.5. Final disposition report *(cont.)*

COMPLIANCE REPORT

TO: Mr. Will Maslow, Director of Field Operations   Date: April 10, 1945

FROM: G. James Fleming, Regional Director (III)

RE: Precision Plastics Company   Case Number: 3-BR-757
     (Moved to 4655 Stenton Avenue, Phila.)   Case Closed: August 25, 1944

Investigation by: W. Johnson (Correspondence)   Compliance check by: Risk

I. Date of compliance check

March 27, 1945

II. Employment figures

A. As of date of adjustment — 30 workers, all skilled, including 3 Negroes, of whom 2 were males, and one female. The 27 white workers consisted of 16 females and 11 males.

B. As of date of compliance check — 50 workers of whom 24 are skilled (10 female and 14 male; one male Negro, skilled; no Negro women are currently employed.

III. Findings

In compliance.

V. Findings of compliance

Mr. Klein, treasurer and factory manager, explained that USES still furnishes most of his workers. There has been a rapid turnover in workers, evidently due to low wage rate (50 cents an hour and up). A worker becomes skilled in less than a month. Mr. Klein stated that the rapid turnover of Negro workers has been no greater than that of others; all turnover is considerable.

While at the moment Mr. Klein has no Negro woman employed, he feels this is not unusual. It changes from day to day.

The firm, according to Mr. Klein, experienced no particular difficulties when Negro women were employed for the first time in May of 1943; nor, for that matter, since then.

When the company moved to its present location two months ago, it lost almost all of its workers. With the exception of about seven or eight old timers, the labor force is new.

App. 4.6. Compliance report

, Will Maslow
Compliance Report
April 10, 1945

- 2 -

V. <u>Findings of compliance (Cont'd)</u>.

Mr. Klein voiced his objection to a USES practice. Each time he phones in an order for workers he is asked, "Will you take Negroes?" Mr. Klein stated that on each occasion he goes through the formality of saying, "It makes no difference to us."

Note: William Smith of WMC advised this examiner, when informed of this, that a few interviewers persist in asking this question, contrary to instructions.

RIBK:mm

App. 4.6. Compliance report *(cont.)*

APPENDIX 5

FEPC Progress Charts

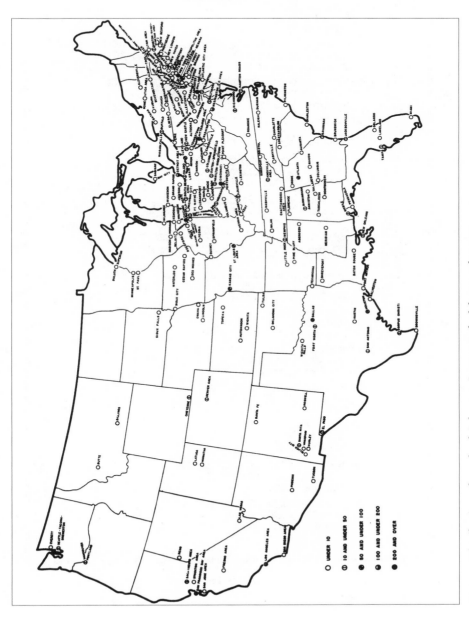

App. 5.1. Distribution of case load, July 1943–June 1944, by labor market area

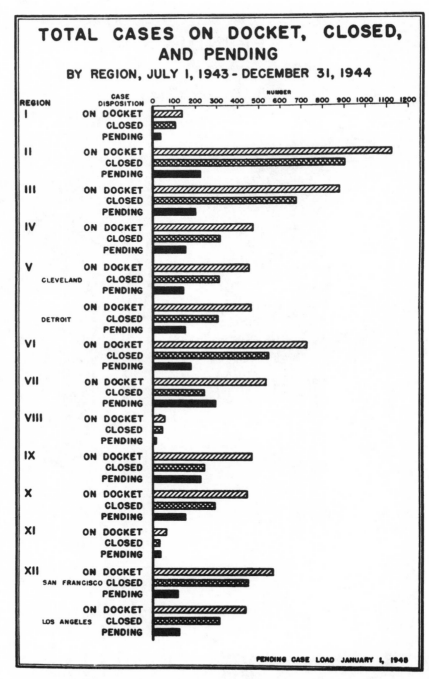

App. 5.2. Total cases on docket, closed, and pending, by region, July 1, 1943–December 31, 1944

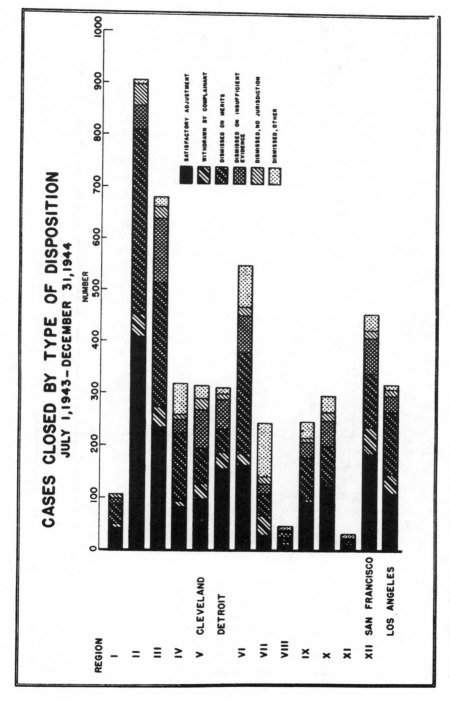

App. 5.3. Cases closed by type of disposition, July 1, 1943–December 31, 1944

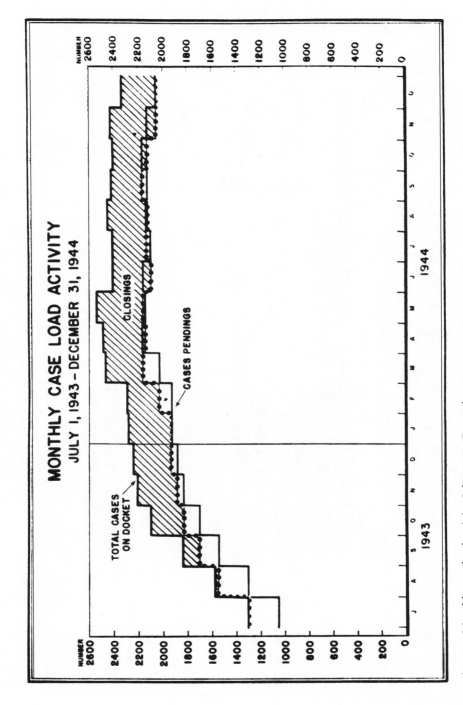

App. 5.4. Monthly case load activity, July 1, 1943–December 31, 1944

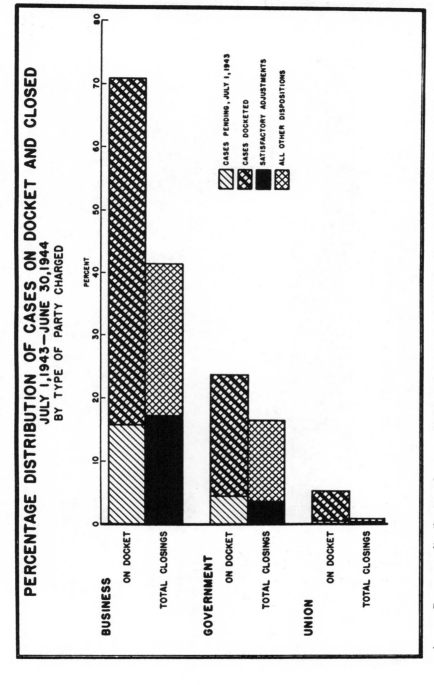

App. 5.5. Percentage distribution of cases on docket and closed, July 1, 1943–June 30, 1944, by type of party charged

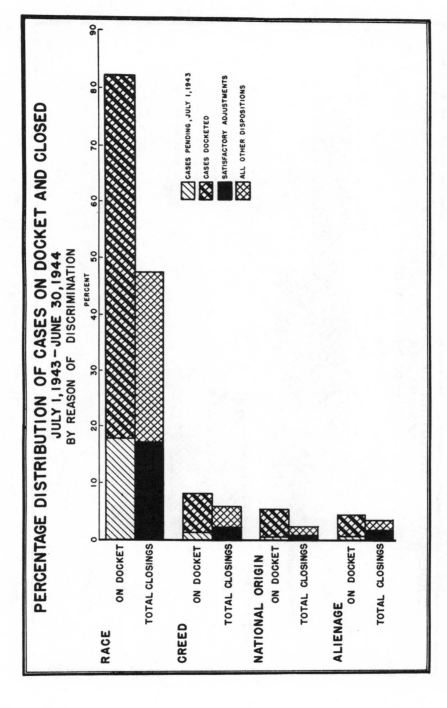

App. 5.6. Percentage distribution of cases on docket and closed, July 1, 1943–June 30, 1944, by reason of discrimination

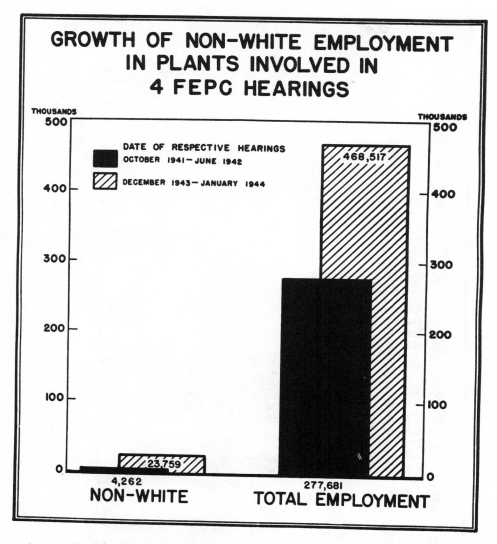

GROWTH OF NON-WHITE EMPLOYMENT
IN PLANTS INVOLVED IN
4 FEPC HEARINGS

THOUSANDS

DATE OF RESPECTIVE HEARINGS
OCTOBER 1941 – JUNE 1942
DECEMBER 1943 – JANUARY 1944

468,517

23,759

4,262
NON-WHITE

277,681
TOTAL EMPLOYMENT

App. 5.7. Growth of nonwhite employment in plants involved in four FEPC hearings

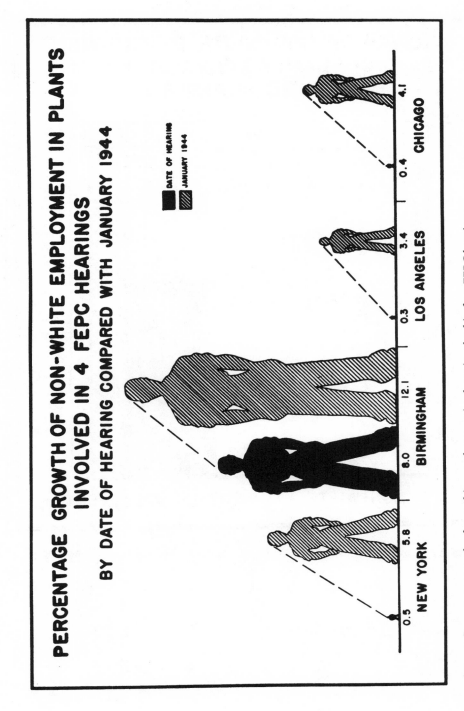

App. 5.8. Percentage growth of nonwhite employment in plants involved in four FEPC hearings

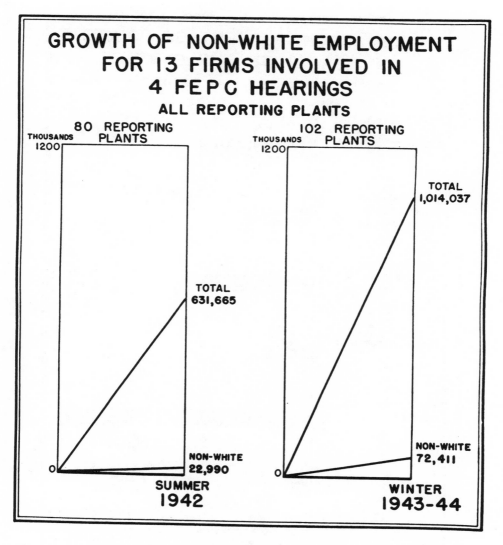

App. 5.9. Growth of nonwhite employment for thirteen firms involved in four FEPC hearings

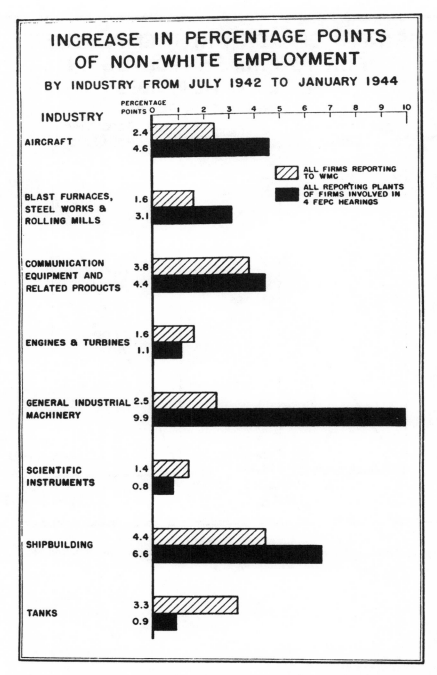

App. 5.10. Increase in percentage points of nonwhite employment by industry, July 1942–January 1944

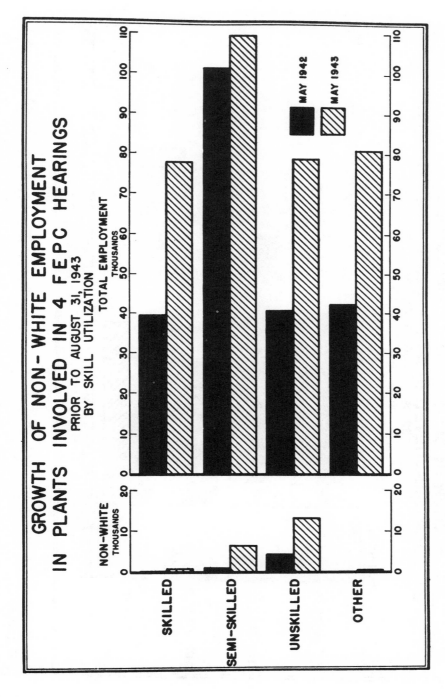

App. 5.11. Growth of nonwhite employment in plants involved in four FEPC hearings, prior to August 31, 1943, by skill utilization

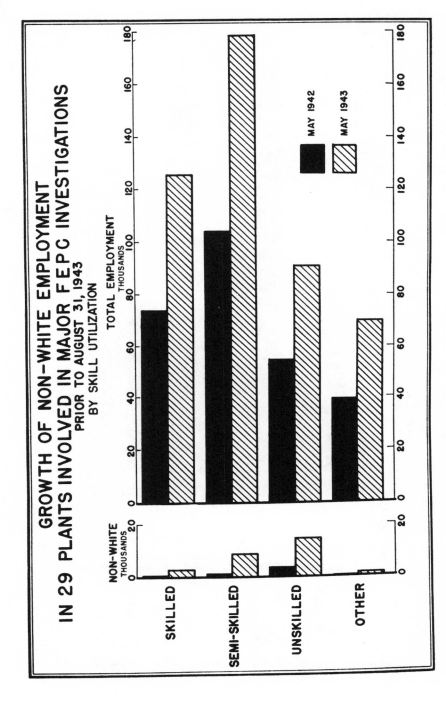

App. 5.12. Growth of nonwhite employment in twenty-nine plants involved in major FEPC investigations, prior to August 31, 1943, by skill utilization

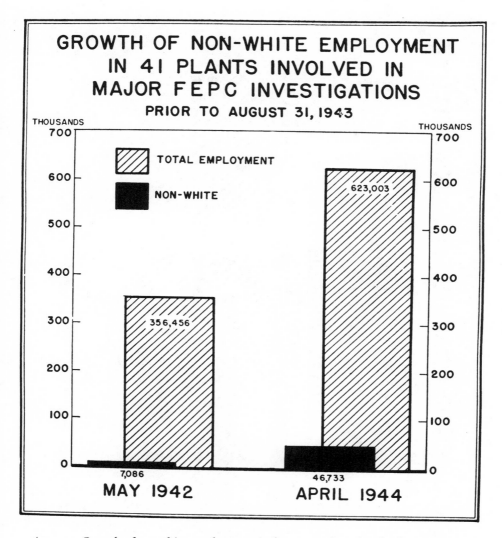

GROWTH OF NON-WHITE EMPLOYMENT
IN 41 PLANTS INVOLVED IN
MAJOR FEPC INVESTIGATIONS
PRIOR TO AUGUST 31, 1943

THOUSANDS

TOTAL EMPLOYMENT

NON-WHITE

623,003

356,456

7,086

46,733

MAY 1942

APRIL 1944

App. 5.13. Growth of nonwhite employment in forty-one plants involved in major FEPC investigations, prior to August 31, 1943

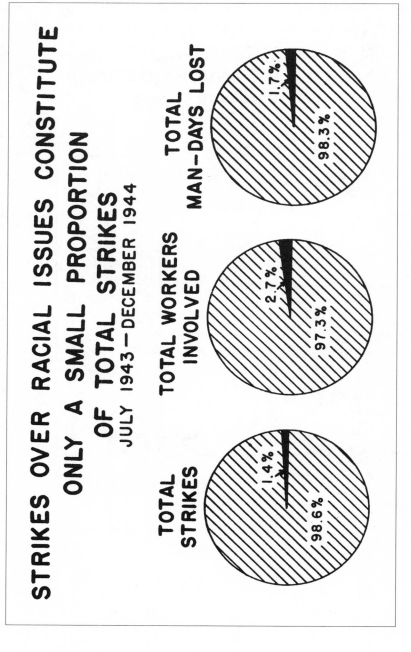

App. 5.14. Strikes over racial issues as proportion of total strikes, July 1943–December 1944

APPENDIX 6

Corporate Directory

Profiles of Corporations and Companies Significant to the FEPC's Work

Alabama Dry Dock and Shipbuilding Company

Shipbuilding and repair facility in Mobile, Ala., opened in 1917. Emergency yards built on its site in 1941 with funding from U.S. Maritime Commission; large new yard built on Pinto Island; built Liberty ships (the emergency WWII cargo ship), other cargo vessels, and tankers. Peak employment of 18,500, of which about 6,000 were African Americans. Investigated by FEPC in 1942 and directed to end discriminatory hiring and promotion policies. After serious racial violence over upgrading of black workers led to temporary shutdown, operated segregated facilities with one separate shipway reserved for blacks. Shipbuilding and repair functions separated, and shipbuilding placed under new management in August 1943. Remained open after WWII. Company and its union investigated in 1970 by Office of Federal Contract Compliance and Maritime Commission for continued employment discrimination, especially in skilled and white-collar positions; agreements reached in 1971 and 1972.

Alan Wood Iron and Steel Corporation

Alan Wood Steel Company, founded in 1857 and incorporated into Alan Wood Iron and Steel Corporation in 1901, was huge steel plant in Conshohocken, Pa.; threatened with strike by white workers in 1944 over upgrading of black workers.

Aluminum Company of America (ALCOA)

Aluminum firm in many locations with defense contracts for producing high-strength aluminum sheeting, tubing, and other metal products. FEPC successfully negotiated with firm in Bridgeport, Conn., in 1943 over in-plant segregation, opportunities for African Americans for upgrading and admission to training programs, and employment of black women on same terms as white women. There were also FEPC complaints against plant in Vernon, Calif., regarding failure to hire African Americans there because of housing shortage and other complaints regarding failure to utilize available black workers in its Southern plants.

713

American Bemberg Corporation

German-owned (later Dutch-owned) rayon manufacturer founded by German rayon company in 1925 in Elizabethtown, Tenn. Manufactured parachute cloth during WWII; became Bemberg Industries but closed in 1970s. FEPC received complaint from German-born complainant over dismissal because of alienage; FEPC action suspended because it was alienage case over which jurisdiction was not determined.

American Smelting and Refining Company (ASARCO)

Corporation formed in 1899 through consolidation of several earlier plants; smelted lead, zinc, and copper ores; at one time had largest lead refinery in world; continued in operation after war. FEPC investigated complaints against operations in El Paso, Tex., Ariz., and Baltimore.

American Steel Foundries

Incorporated in New Jersey in 1902, was largest maker of steel castings in U.S.; had plants in East St. Louis, Ill., Granite City, Ill., Alliance, Ohio, Chicago, Pittsburgh, Sharon, Pa., and Chester, Pa. Produced shells as well as castings used for manufacturing atomic bombs. In July 1944, black workers at Granite City site launched wildcat walkouts over wage dispute and alleged abuse by white foreman. Its Indiana Harbor Works was referred to FEPC by Justice Department in 1943 as place of possible race trouble.

American Telephone and Telegraph Company

Incorporated in N.Y. in 1885 as subsidiary of American Bell Telephone Company to handle long-distance telephone operations; in 1899, acquired assets of its parent, American Bell, and became parent company of Bell Telephone System network that, until its settlement with Justice Department in 1974, had near monopoly on long-distance service and included Bell Labs and 22 local Bell telephone companies around nation. FEPC negotiated with AT&T to facilitate efforts to increase black employment at various Bell companies, particularly hiring of black women as operators and in clerical positions.

American Trading and Production Corporation (ATAPCO)

Founded in 1931; privately-held corporation in Baltimore consisting of businesses connected to Blaustein family, founders of AMOCO; involved in oil and gas, real estate, security systems, and office products; recently restructured into 3 firms, including ATAPCO Inc. Complaint against firm investigated in 1944.

Amertorp Corporation

St. Louis firm producing submarine torpedoes on which FEPC held hearings in August 1944 over its refusal to hire black women; directed to cease discriminatory practices, develop and publicize nondiscriminatory policy for employment and promotions, and educate white workers on nondiscrimination policy; little compliance.

Anaconda Copper Mining Company

Vast copper mining and manufacturing firm founded in 1875 in Mont., but with mining operations in Ariz., Nev., and many other areas worldwide; second-largest U.S. copper producer during WWII; held contracts for many types of wire needed by military. Investigated by FEPC for discrimination against Mexicans, Indians, and African Americans; complaints involved wage discrimination, segregation, and restriction to laborer positions.

Anniston Warehouse Corporation

Operators of army's Anniston Ordnance Depot; FEPC negotiated regarding complaints of discriminatory work orders and discriminatory layoffs and reinstatements aggravated by segregated work arrangements. War Department officials failed to cooperate with FEPC, leading to breakdown of negotiations in 1943.

Arabian American Oil Company (ARAMCO)

Oil company founded in 1933 when Saudi Arabia granted oil concession to California Arabian Standard Oil Company (Casoc), affiliate of Standard Oil of California (later Chevron). Texas Company (later Texaco) acquired 50 percent ownership in 1936, and other oil firms also later became owners. Name changed to Arabian American Oil Company in 1944. FEPC received complaints regarding refusal to hire African Americans or Jews for overseas positions in Arabia; but it was determined that FEPC had no jurisdiction over these jobs. Case led to FEPC queries regarding Arabian employment policies. Ownership later acquired by Saudi Arabian government and name changed to Saudi Arabian Oil Company (Saudi Aramco).

Athenia Steel Company

Steel manufacturing plant in Clifton, N.J., owned by National Standard Company; continued in operation until 1988. Investigated by FEPC in 1944 for discriminatory questions on employment application.

Atkinson, Guy F., Company

San Francisco–based multinational construction firm; did major construction on West Coast during 1930s and 1940s; served as subcontractor for construction on Hanford Engineering Works in Wash. Discrimination complaints referred to War Department in 1944 and successfully resolved by FEPC. Filed for bankruptcy in 1997 and was acquired by Clark Construction Company.

Atlanta Joint Terminals

Southern railroad company signatory to Southeastern Conference Agreement blocking promotions of blacks to railroad firemen positions, against which FEPC held hearings in 1943. FEPC issued directive setting aside agreement as discriminatory, supported by Supreme Court decisions in *Steele* and *Tunstall* cases.

Atlantic Coast Line Railroad Company

Southern railroad signatory to Southeastern Conference Agreement blocking promotions of blacks to railroad firemen positions, against which FEPC held hearings in 1943. FEPC issued directive setting aside agreement as discriminatory, supported by Supreme Court decisions in *Steele* and *Tunstall* cases. Challenged FEPC directive. NAACP fought segregated seating on line in 1950s.

Baldwin (W. F.) Company

Real estate and property management firm founded in N.C. in 1928. Complaint against firm investigated in 1944. Now W. F. Baldwin & Son., Inc.

Baldwin Piano Company

Major U.S. piano manufacturer founded in Cincinnati as music store in 1862 and as piano manufacturer in 1890s. During WWII, ceased piano production and manufactured airplane parts. Returned to piano manufacturing in 1945. Investigated in 1942 for submitting discriminatory hiring request to USES and for refusal to comply with executive order against discrimination.

Baltimore and Ohio Chicago Terminal Railroad Company

Railroad company not signatory to Southeastern Conference Agreement but investigated in FEPC hearings in 1943 for failure to hire or upgrade black workers in skilled and better-paying positions.

Baltimore and Ohio Rail Road Company

Railroad not signatory to Southeastern Conference Agreement but investigated in FEPC hearings in 1943 for failure to hire or upgrade black workers in skilled and better-paying positions. After war, NAACP fought requirement that employees join segregated union local.

Baltimore Transit Company

FEPC unsuccessfully sought to induce it to hire African Americans for "platform" positions as drivers or conductors.

Basic Magnesium, Inc. (BMI)

Wartime plant opened in 1941 near Las Vegas to produce magnesium for use in bullets, bombs, planes, and tire rims. Government-owned but privately operated, first by BMI, then by Anaconda Copper. Workforce of over 13,000 at peak, including black workers imported into area. FEPC investigated complaints and reported on racial tensions. WPB closed plant in November 1944.

Bechtel, McCone, and Parsons

Civil engineering firm formed in 1930s from partnership of W. A. Bechtel and John McCone's engineering firms. Bechtel bought out McCone's share at end of WWII; McCone became head of Atomic Energy Commission and later of CIA. Company became Bechtel Corporation. Involved in many wartime contracts, including aircraft and shipyards, such as Evansville Shipyard in Ind. FEPC received complaints regarding denial of training for black workers from Citizens Committee on Jobs and Training of Birmingham, Ala., against firm's aircraft conversion plant in Birmingham, which worked on B-24 and B-29 bombers.

Bechtel, W. A., Company

Firm founded in 1898 in Calif.; involved in railroad, highway, and dam construction, notably Hoover Dam. Constructed Bechtel's Marinship shipyards in Sausalito, Calif., during war; partner in construction and operation of Evansville Shipyard in Ind. Evolved into Bechtel Group, privately held San Francisco–based corporation, one of world's largest engineering, project management, and construction firms; still major government contractor. Also built many projects in Saudi Arabia, Kuwait, Iraq, and many other nations.

Bechtel-Price-Callahan

Temporary partnership of W. A. Bechtel Company, H. C. Price Company, and W. E. Callahan Company, which contracted with War Department to build giant wartime construction project known as CANOL Sub-Arctic Pipeline and Refinery Project in Alaska. FEPC's Region XII referred complaints against firm to national FEPC; case was referred to Legal Division for possible hearing but then returned to region. Company investigated by Truman Committee, 1941–43, which strongly criticized firm for cost overruns and mismanagement.

Bell Aircraft Corporation

Aircraft manufacturing firm based in Buffalo, N.Y., that operated unit in Marietta, Ga., under government contract. Produced B-29s and other military planes. Investigated for failure to employ blacks in skilled positions. FEPC initially was denied access to plant, and company refused to supply employment data. Firm continued in operation after war, concentrating operations in South and leaving Buffalo in late 1940s; later became Bell Helicopter and Bell Aerospace; acquired by Textron.

Bell Telephone Company

A group of 22 Bell telephone companies under parent company AT&T. FEPC negotiated with various firms to increase black employment, especially hiring of black women as telephone operators and clerical workers. FEPC succeeded in reaching agreements with New York Bell, New Jersey Bell, and other branches; failed to secure black employment at Chesapeake and Potomac Bell and Wisconsin Bell.

Bendix Aviation Corporation

Airplane parts producer with plants in several locations; held many defense contacts. In Philadelphia, FEPC successfully negotiated its employment of black women trained in government program for light manufacturing; FEPC also listed it as Baltimore-area firm with segregated toilet facilities.

Bethlehem Alameda Shipbuilding Corporation

Operated shipyard at Alameda, Calif.; acquired during WWI by Bethlehem Steel Corporation, San Francisco, and was only major shipbuilder on West Coast prior to WWII. Converted to ship repair after WWI, but modernized and returned to ship production in WWII, building troop ships for U.S. Maritime Commission. Continued shipbuilding until mid-1950s and ship repair until 1970s. Was one of firms Mitchell listed as having prospects for continued employment.

Bethlehem Fairfield Shipbuilding Corporation

Operated emergency, or wartime, shipyard, which opened as subsidiary of Bethlehem Steel in Baltimore in 1940 to build Liberty ships (385) and Victory ships for Maritime Commission; also built amphibious-warfare ships for U.S. Navy. Employed 27,000 workers at wartime peak. Closed at end of war. Discontinued hiring women after complaints regarding refusal to hire African American women.

Bethlehem Steel Corporation

Founded in 1904 in Pa.; major war contractor during WWI. Largest shipbuilding company in world at time of WWII; owned or operated 15 shipyards during war, with contracts with navy and Maritime Commission; also second-largest steel corporation after U.S. Steel. Produced steel plate for ships and tanks, structural steel for defense plants, and forgings for guns, shells, and aircraft engines. Employed nearly 300,000 workers at peak of war, 180,000 of whom were in shipbuilding; produced over 1,121 ships, more than any other shipbuilder. FEPC had to deal with discrimination complaints and strikes over hiring or upgrading of black workers at several of its yards and plants. Continued in operation after war; exited shipbuilding in 1990s; bankrupt in 2001; plants acquired by International Steel Group.

Bethlehem Steel and Shipbuilding Corporation–Sparrows Point

Operated shipyard at Sparrows Point, Md., just outside of Baltimore; major pre-war merchant shipbuilder; opened in 1914 and was fully operational at start of war; builder of oceangoing tankers, as well as cargo and passenger ships. Produced for private industry and under military contracts with Maritime Commission throughout war. Continued in operation as shipbuilder and repairer until 1990s, when it was acquired by Baltimore Marine Industries. Had racial strike over training and upgrading of black workers to skilled positions; listed as one of area firms with segregated toilet facilities.

Bethlehem Steel Corporation–Sparrows Point

Iron and steel plant opened in 1889, adjacent to Bethlehem Steel Shipyard at Sparrows Point. Racial strike at shipyard did not affect steel plant.

Boeing Aircraft Corporation

Based in Renton and Seattle, Wash.; produced B-29s and other military planes. Black workers suffered from housing discrimination in Renton. In 1941, had no black workers in workforce of 41,000. Machinists Union had contract with company and barred black union membership; union initially blocked employment of blacks, then agreed to issue temporary work permits for them but charged fees similar to union dues without conveying union benefits.

Brand and Puritz Manufacturing Company

Kansas City clothing manufacturing firm whose white workers went on strike in 1943 because company upgraded black workers to sewing machine operator positions.

Brecon Bag Loading Company

Subsidiary of Coca-Cola Company associated with ordnance plant built in Flora, Miss., and operated by General Tire and Engineering Company of Akron, Ohio; investigated by local FEPC officials and during FEPC's Birmingham hearings in 1942. Despite 55 percent black population in area, it refused to employ African Americans, particularly black women, in production jobs, restricting them to unskilled labor positions; it insisted black women were unqualified and that black and white women could not work together on production jobs in that area. FEPC directed firm to end such discriminatory practices; firm ultimately complied to some degree.

Breeze Aircraft Company

Newark, N.J., aircraft manufacturer investigated for discrimination in 1942.

Brewster Aeronautical Company

Long Island City, N.Y., airplane manufacturer with wartime contracts for bombers and fighter planes. Opened large, government-built plant in Pa. in 1941; advertised for over 5,000 workers. FEPC negotiated with firm in 1942 for inclusion of black workers in employment and training. Production delays investigated in congressional hearings in 1943, and some contracts cancelled; plant closed in 1944; site taken over by navy.

Briggs Company

Briggs and Stratton, Milwaukee-based engine manufacturing company producing many forms of equipment during WWII. White workers at one of its plants went on strike in 1943 over employment of black workers, but union action quickly ended walkout. Continues in operation.

Brown Shipbuilding Company

WWII emergency shipyard opened in Houston in 1941 for construction of destroyer escorts for navy. FEPC received complaints regarding refusal to hire African Americans for skilled positions. Sold to Todd shipbuilding after war, becoming Todd Houston; closed in 1985.

Brunswick Marine Shipbuilding Company

See Jones, J. A. Construction Company.

Brunswick Pulp and Paper Company

Brunswick, Ga., firm about which FEPC had complaints in 1944; became subsidiary of Georgia-Pacific Corp; sold to Koch Cellulose, LLC, in 2004.

Buckeye Cotton Oil Company

Memphis, Tenn., cotton oil company with numerous mills in South; founded by Procter and Gamble in 1901. Produced cellulose used for many wartime synthetic products. Under investigation in 1945 for wage discrimination and failure to upgrade black workers.

Bussman Manufacturing Company

Large St. Louis–based electronics manufacturer on which FEPC held hearings in August 1944 over failure to hire black women; firm directed to cease discriminatory practices, develop and publicize nondiscriminatory policy for employment and promotions, and educate white workers on nondiscrimination policy; little compliance. Continued in operation; now part of international corporation of Cooper Bussman.

California Shipbuilding Company (CALSHIP)

"Emergency" shipyard built at start of WWII at Terminal Island, Los Angeles, by Todd and Kaiser companies, with funding from U.S. Maritime Commission; Kaiser bought out Todd's interest in 1942. Built Liberty ships (336), Victory ships, and tankers; at its peak, employed 40,000 people. Closed at end of war.

Capital Transit Company

Public transportation company for Washington, D.C., operating bus lines needed for government and defense workers. Refused to employ African Americans in platform positions (drivers and conductors), restricting them to low-level maintenance jobs. Object of FEPC investigation, hearings, and directive to cease discrimination, which it disregarded; enforcement of directive blocked by President Truman in 1945 for fear of strikes.

Carbide and Carbon Chemicals Corporation

West Virginia petrochemical firm established in 1920; unit of Union Carbide and Carbon Company. Built and operated government plant in Institute, W.Va., for production of butadiene and styrene in WWII (used for synthetic rubber and cable insulation). WPB conferred with it over hiring of African American workers in 1943. Ran atomic laboratories at Oak Ridge, Tenn., and Paducah, Ky., from 1940s until 1984. After war, NAACP continued to negotiate with firm to hire and train skilled black workers.

Cardinal Engineer Company

Construction firm in region II; complaints against firm in 1944 sent to FEPC central office and successfully adjusted through intervention of Maritime Commission with which company had contract.

Carnegie Steel Company

Steel company founded by Andrew Carnegie; became part of U.S. Steel. FEPC assisted in settlement of strike by black workers at Carnegie-Illinois Clairton Works steel plant in Pittsburgh over discrimination in upgrading to better positions.

Carter Carburetor Company

St. Louis firm producing carburetors and fuel pumps. MOWM marched on its plant in 1942, protesting its refusal to hire black workers; FEPC held hearings on firm in August 1944 over continued refusal to hire black women; FEPC directed it to cease discriminatory practices, develop and publicize nondiscriminatory policy for employment and promotions, and educate white workers on nondiscrimination policy; little was done to comply.

Central of Georgia Railway Company

Southern railroad signatory to Southeastern Conference Agreement blocking promotions of blacks to railroad firemen positions, against which FEPC held hearings in 1943. FEPC issued directive setting aside agreement as discriminatory, supported by Supreme Court decisions in *Steele* and *Tunstall* cases. Firm challenged FEPC directive.

Chesapeake and Ohio Railway Company

Railroad not signatory to Southeastern Conference Agreement but investigated in FEPC hearings in 1943 for failure to hire or upgrade black workers in skilled and better-paying positions.

Chesapeake and Potomac Telephone Company

Bell Telephone Company serving Baltimore and Washington, D.C. FEPC sought unsuccessfully to require employment of qualified African American women as operators. NAACP subsequently continued to press for enforcement of nondiscrimination clause in its government contracts.

Chevrolet Motor Company

General Motors subdivision that declined to provide racial statistics to FEPC in 1943. White workers at transmission plant in Toledo, Ohio, went on strike over upgrading of black women to production jobs in 1944.

Chicago and North Western Railway Company

Railroad not signatory to Southeastern Conference Agreement but investigated in FEPC hearings in 1943 for failure to hire or upgrade black workers in skilled and better-paying positions.

Chicago Transportation Company

Chicago transit system that successfully upgraded African Americans to platform positions as drivers and conductors in 1943. Management, labor, FEPC staff, and local civil rights leaders all cooperated in process.

Clinton Engineering Works

Name of Manhattan Project atomic facility built in Tenn. in 1942–43; produced plutonium for atomic bomb. Became Oak Ridge National Laboratory in 1948. FEPC negotiated with plant for inclusion of black workers, especially in skilled positions. FEPC also received complaint of dismissal because of national origin.

Collins and Aikman Company

Michigan-based auto parts and accessories company. USES complained in 1943 firm did not accept African American workers referred to it. Case investigated by FEPC. Firm continued in operation after war.

Colt's Patent Firearms Company

Manufacturer of revolvers, pistols, rifles, and machine guns in Hartford, Conn. Founded in 1836 in Paterson, N.J., and incorporated in Conn. in 1855. Held contracts for machine guns and automatic cannons. Complaints against company were referred to FEPC's hearings division in 1944.

Combustion Engineering Company

St. Louis firm whose white workers went on strike in 1945 when company employed black worker as welder.

Consolidated Steel Corporation

Consolidated's Shipbuilding Division operated shipyard which was investigated in FEPC hearings in 1943. Built in Wilmington, Calif., in 1941 with funding from U.S. Maritime Commission, yard built cargo ships, troop ships, and landing vessels. Peak employment of 12,000. Black workers protested being forced to join and pay dues to segregated union auxiliary as condition for employment. Closed at end of war.

Consolidated Vultee Aircraft Corporation (Convair)

San Diego, Calif.–based aircraft and airplane parts manufacturer. Had plants in Tex., Tenn., Ariz., and Fla. that also held defense contracts; had contracts with Machinists Union, which barred black membership; southern plants generally refused to hire blacks, except in laboring positions. Investigated during Birmingham hearings in 1942 and directed to cease discrimination. FEPC negotiated with firm on issues of employment, upgrading, and access to training for African American workers.

Continental Can Company

Container manufacturer in Ill., Ohio, and elsewhere. Had contracts for shells, recoil and percussive mechanisms, detonators, and other materials. Directed in 1942 by first FEPC to cease discriminatory practices. White workers in Norwood, Ohio, plant went on strike in April 1945, protesting employment of black workers who then resigned for fear of violence. FEPC considered this a case of collusion between management and strikers.

Cramp Shipbuilding Company

Philadelphia shipbuilder dating back to 1830 but idled since 1927. Reactivated by navy in 1940; closed at end of war. FEPC listed it in 1943 as shipyard employing black workers.

Crosley Radio Corporation

Cincinnati firm developing and assembling fuzes (detonators for antiaircraft projectiles) for Bureau of Ordnance. Investigated for employment discrimination against blacks in 1943; hearings held in 1945. Company had closed-shop agreement with IBEW, which barred black membership and refused to permit hiring of black workers. Union refused to comply with any nondiscrimination order, predicting strike if company tried to hire blacks. Company employed over 7,000 workers during war but only 6 African Americans, used exclusively as janitors.

Curtiss-Wright Corporation

Airplane and airplane engine manufacturer derived from merger in 1929 of firms related to Curtiss Aeroplane and Motor Company (major WWI aircraft manufacturer) and Wright Aeronautical (designer and manufacturer of airplane engines); major WWII contractor producing fighter planes, bombers and transports, aircraft engines and propellers; quotas and segregation at firm's plant in St. Louis limited black access to employment. Complaints against firm were settled by negotiation without hearing. It had workforce of about 170,000 during war, of which 17,000 were African Americans. Despite considerable reductions in workforce, it continued in operation after war and diversified into multifaceted firm active in both private and military-related industries.

Davison Chemical Corporation

Baltimore, Md., firm investigated by FEPC in 1943 for discriminatory employment advertising. Manufacturer of catalysts and silica; later based in Columbia, Md., and acquired by Grace, Inc., in 1954.

Delco-Remy Division of GM

General Motors subsidiary in Ind.; had contract with UAW local dominated by southern whites that restricted black employment to 5 low-level positions. Union also barred black members from using its union hall or recreational activities or attending union activities apart from official union meetings. FEPC negotiations failed to change discriminatory patterns. FEPC also received creedal discrimination complaints of dismissals of Seventh-day Adventists and Jehovah's Witnesses.

Delta Shipbuilding Company

Located in New Orleans, La; built 188 Liberty ships, as well as tankers and colliers, under contract with U.S. Maritime Commission. Investigated by FEPC in 1942 and directed to open skilled labor positions to African Americans. Had closed-shop agreement with Boilermakers Union, which banned black members; because of labor shortage, union eventually established auxiliaries to permit black employment. Violence against black workers led to black walkout in 1944; refusal to change upgrading policies led to negotiations with U.S. Maritime Commission, and agreement to place some black welders on job in 1945.

Denver and Rio Grande Railroad Company

Railroad investigated for discriminatory employment advertising in 1944.

Detterback, George L., Company

Complaints against this Chicago company were referred to Legal Division of FEPC for possible hearings in 1944; no hearings were held because cutbacks in 1945 made hearings unlikely to produce any long-term results.

Dick, A. B., Company

Printing and graphic arts supplier in Niles, Ill., founded in 1887; bankrupt in 2004. Discrimination complaint against company filed with FEPC in 1944.

Douglas Aircraft Company

Airplane and aircraft parts manufacturer founded in 1921; based in Santa Monica, Calif., with plants in El Segundo, Dogget, and elsewhere in Calif. and parts of Midwest. Largest aircraft manufacturer in U.S. by end of war. Employed large numbers of blacks but suffered substantial cutbacks at end of war. Major producer of commercial planes and military planes during Korean War and Cold War. Merged with McDonnell Aircraft to become McDonnell Douglas in 1967.

Dow Chemical Company

Chemical company founded in 1897 in Midland, Mich. Plants held many important contracts for magnesium- and aluminum-related products, industrial chemicals, electrical equipment, and many other items. FEPC held hearings on Midland in September 1943. Continued in operation; second-largest chemical company in world, after Dupont; world's largest plastics producer and major player in petrochemical industry.

Dravo Corporation

Small, pre-WWII shipbuilder in Pittsburgh, Pa.; in continuous operation since 1919. Also operated wartime shipyard in Wilmington, Del. Built LSTs (landing ships), submarine chasers, barges, and other vessels for navy, as well as floating crane barges for army. Returned to barge-building and ship-scrapping after war; ceased shipbuilding in 1980s.

Dupont de Nemours Company, E. I.

Chemical manufacturer based in Wilmington, Del., with plants throughout nation holding defense contracts to produce chemicals, explosives, detonators, rayon, and other goods. Oversaw construction and operation of Hanford Engineering Works and other atomic facilities until end of war.

Emerson Electric Company

St. Louis firm producing electrical equipment and gun turrets, on which FEPC held hearings in August 1944; directed to cease discriminatory practices, develop and publicize nondiscriminatory policy for employment and promotions, and educate white workers on nondiscrimination policy; little compliance.

Farquhar, A. B., Company

Agricultural machinery and steam engine manufacturer in York, Pa., founded in 1889. Black employees complained that they were denied membership by Machinists Union and denied upgrading by company because of pressure by union. Acquired in 1952 by Oliver Farm Equipment Company and subsequently ceased to exist.

Federal Cartridge Company

Minnesota ammunition manufacturing company that operated Twin City Ordnance Plant. Its president, Charles Horn, became member of FEPC.

Federal Shipbuilding Company

Subsidiary of U.S. Steel; shipyard based in Kearny, N.J., was one of 5 major pre-WWII shipbuilders; fully operational at start of war and expanded with naval funding; its discriminatory policies, investigated by first FEPC in 1942, were changed in response to Executive Order 8806; however, some complaints continued regarding discriminatory refusal to hire at highest skill level. Built passenger and cargo ships for U.S. Maritime Commission. Developed second wartime yard at Port Newark with naval funding. Both yards closed at end of war.

Federal Telegraph Company

San Francisco–based telegraph company; produced transmitters; became part of IT&T. First FEPC investigated it in N.J. in 1942 for failure to accept black applicants.

Ferguson, H. K., Company

A leading industrial construction and engineering firm with offices in New York, Washington, and Cleveland that contracted with Manhattan Project in 1944 to design and build thermal diffusion plant that was part of atomic facility in Oak Ridge, Tenn. Also built army's chemical warfare facilities and other major projects. Complaints were filed with FEPC in 1944 regarding failure to hire black carpenters for Oak Ridge site. By 1945, regional FEPC officials induced company to hire them.

Firestone Rubber Company; Firestone Rubber and Latex Company; Firestone Tire and Rubber Company

Related firms originally founded as Firestone Tire & Rubber in Akron, Ohio, in 1900. Produced tires for carriages, then automobiles; principal tire supplier for Ford Motor Company; expanded into tire and automobile services and retail of varied consumer products. Praised for its nondiscriminatory policies in 1943, including use of African American women in production jobs. Acquired by Bridgestone Corporation of Japan in 1988, making Bridgestone/Firestone largest manufacturer of tires and other rubber products.

Ford Motor Company

Automobile and parts manufacturing firm with contracts for producing tanks, armored cars, and other military vehicles. Also involved in aircraft production, particularly at Willow Run plant near Detroit, about which black workers complained of poor transportation and lack of housing. Ford reduced hiring of African Americans after 1942, especially at its huge River Rouge plant; policy triggered protests by black workers. FEPC negotiated employment of black women, but they were confined to small, segregated plant rather than River Rouge. Like GM, it declined to provide racial employment statistics to FEPC.

Gary Street Railway Company

Gary, Ind., transit company which, despite FEPC efforts, did not integrate African American workers into platform positions as drivers or conductors.

General Box Company

Kansas City firm at which black workers requested strike vote after dismissals they alleged were due to workers' union activities. FEPC lacked jurisdiction on issue of company discrimination or retaliation against unionism.

General Cable Company

Communications cable producing firm founded in N.J. in 1927 and headquartered in N.Y. By 1945 it produced 80 percent of battlefield communications wire used by Allies and 50 percent of navy's power and communications cable. At one major plant in St. Louis area, white workers opposed hiring of skilled black workers. Strike was threatened over attempt to mix white and black women workers. Firm's president, Dwight Palmer, succeeded in persuading workers to accept African American employees, and strike was averted. Continued in operation after war.

General Chemical Company

Company against which German employee complained that he had been dismissed because of alienage. After FEPC intervention, complainant was offered job back, but he declined.

General Electric Company

Giant electronics, lighting, appliance, and aircraft engine firm formed in 1892, based on companies started by Thomas Edison. FEPC negotiated discrimination complaints against firm at its headquarters in Schenectady, N.Y., in 1944.

General Motors Corporation

Automobile and parts manufacturer in Mich. whose units held multiple contracts for tanks, armored cars, trucks, parts, and other equipment. Refused to submit statistics on race or religion of its employees. FEPC investigated various subdivisions, including Chevrolet, Oldsmobile, and Delco-Remy, for discrimination.

General Steel Castings Company

Granite City, Ill., firm whose workers were on strike in 1944. FEPC reported that, although most strikers were black, issues were not racial but involved complaints of abuse of workers by white foreman.

General Tire and Engineering Company

Akron, Ohio, firm operating ordnance plant in Flora, Miss., that hired African American women only as maids and custodians.

Georgia Railroad

Southern railroad signatory to Southeastern Conference Agreement blocking promotions of blacks to railroad firemen positions, against which FEPC held hearings in 1943. FEPC issued directive setting aside agreement as discriminatory, supported by Supreme Court decisions in *Steele* and *Tunstall* cases.

Goodrich, B. F., Rubber Company

Rubber products firm in Akron, Ohio, founded in 1871; developed vinyl and synthetic rubber; had contracts for tires, rafts, landing gear, and various rubber products; praised by FEPC in 1943 for nondiscriminatory employment policies, including employment of African American women in production jobs. Continued in operation after war, turning increasingly to aircraft and aerospace industry, including space suits; ended tire manufacturing in 1988. Name changed from B. F. Goodrich Company to Goodrich Corporation in 2001.

Goodyear Aircraft Company

Goodyear subdivision in Akron grew out of zeppelin division founded in 1920s. Had contracts for blimps, Corsair airplanes, and aircraft parts. Black workers walked out in April 1944 over transfers during work cutbacks. FEPC hearings held in Akron, Ohio, in May 1945 regarding failure to upgrade black workers. Continued in operation after war, especially in missile development and computers; now part of Lockheed Martin.

Goodyear Tire and Rubber Company

Rubber products firm founded in Akron, Ohio, in 1898; became world's largest tire company; praised by FEPC in 1943 for nondiscriminatory employment policies, including employment of African American women in production jobs.

Gulf Oil Company

Oil and refining company founded in 1901 and incorporated in 1907 in Tex.; FEPC investigated complaints against it for wage discrimination and refusal to upgrade Mexican and African American workers beyond position of laborer in 1943; now part of Chevron.

Gulf Shipbuilding Company

Shipyard at Chickasaw, Ala., built various types of naval vessels for navy; investigated in 1942 and directed to upgrade African Americans into more skilled positions; had closed-shop agreement with Boilermakers Union, which banned black members and resisted establishment of black auxiliaries. Company had hiring agreement with Mobile Metal Trades Council of AFL, which, despite labor shortages, refused to refer black workers.

Gulf, Mobile, and Ohio Railway Company

Railroad not signatory to Southeastern Conference Agreement but investigated in FEPC hearings in 1943 for failure to hire or upgrade black workers in skilled and better-paying positions.

Hanford Engineering Company

Plutonium production complex provided fuel for nuclear reactors for Manhattan Project, developers of atomic bomb. Five-hundred-thousand-acre site developed in Columbia River basin in sparsely populated area around Hanford, Richland, and Pasco, Wash., in 1943. Required construction not only of plant but of highways, rail lines, housing, and other facilities for over 45,000 workers building site. Workers recruited nationwide, but particularly in Midwest and Southwest by Dupont (managers of project) and by army. Hanford had population of over 50,000 by mid-1944. FEPC investigated discriminatory recruitment for site. Continued in operation after war under management of Atomic Energy Commission.

Hegemen Harris Company

New York–based contracting company handling large construction projects in U.S. and Panama; submitted discriminatory work order for typists to USES in 1942, stating that "Christian" applicants were preferred. Company denied complaint, and subsequent FEPC checks indicated workers were being employed without discrimination.

Higgins Industries

Small New Orleans shipyard that expanded to 8 factories with 30,000 workers at peak of war. Built over 20,000 landing craft used for D Day and in Pacific, as well as other specialized craft. Its workforce was first racially integrated one in New Orleans and used blacks in skilled positions. FEPC sought to have black welders released by company during cutbacks in 1944 employed by Delta Shipbuilding.

Hinde and Dauch Paper Company

Paper and packaging company founded in Sandusky, Ohio, but with units elsewhere in U.S. and Canada. Kansas City branch had contract with paper workers union that included discriminatory clause that was eliminated in 1945 with assistance of CIO. Merged with West Virginia Paper Company (Westvaco) in 1953.

Houston Shipbuilding Company

Employed many African Americans in low-level positions but refused to admit them to training courses in 1943. In 1944, FEPC reported that company had ceased to discriminate against Latin Americans but still discriminated against African Americans.

Hughes Tool Company

Manufacturing firm producing oil drill bits founded in Tex. by Howard Hughes Sr. in early 1900s; became known as Toolco; parent company of Hughes Aviation, founded by Howard Hughes Jr. in 1932, Hughes Electronics, and other firms. Subsidiary firms had many contracts; produced armaments and radio equipment during war. FEPC received complaints against firm for wage discrimination that were still unresolved in 1946 despite support from steel workers union. Divisions continued and expanded after war in aircraft, helicopters, satellite communications, and other industries. Descendant firms include Hughes Electronic Corporation, subsidiary of

General Motors; Hughes Space Company, now Boeing Satellite Systems; and helicopter division, acquired by McDonnell Douglas.

Humble Oil Company

Houston, Tex., affiliate of Standard Oil of N.J.; FEPC investigated complaints of wage discrimination and refusal to upgrade Mexican and African American workers beyond position of laborer.

Illinois Central Railroad Company

Railroad not signatory to Southeastern Carriers Conference Agreement but investigated in FEPC hearings in 1943 for failure to hire or upgrade black workers in skilled and better-paying positions. After war, NAACP investigated complaints regarding segregation and mistreatment of porters by railroad.

Ingalls Iron Works

Had small yards in Decatur, Ala., then in Birmingham and Chickasaw, before developing Ingalls Shipbuilding yard at Pascagoula; built tugs for navy; continued in operation after war. Reported to FEPC in 1942 as employing black workers, including in some skilled positions.

Ingalls Shipbuilding Corporation

Developed in Pascagoula, Miss., in 1938 in anticipation of U.S. Maritime Commission's long-term shipbuilding program; had funding from USMC and navy; built oceangoing cargo and passenger ships for U.S. Maritime Commission. Employed substantial numbers of blacks, but was accused of failure to upgrade. Continued in operation after war; subject of complaints with Office of Federal Contract Compliance because of continued discrimination by company and its unions. Affirmative action agreement signed in 1970. Company sold to Litton Industries, then to Northrop-Grumman; now one of 6 major U.S. shipbuilders.

Inspiration-Consolidated Copper Company

Copper mining company in Miami, Ariz.; founded in early twentieth century. Investigated by FEPC for discrimination against Mexicans; complaints involved wage discrimination, segregation, and restriction of workers to laborer positions.

International Harvester Corporation

Tractor and agricultural machines manufacturer and steel works based in Chicago. Held contracts for aircraft parts, torpedoes, and other munitions. Sara E. Southall, its supervisor of employment and personnel, was member of FEPC, 1943–46.

International Telephone and Telegraph Company

Conglomerate originally formed from smaller companies, including Federal Telegraph and international telephone monopolies sold by Western Union to avoid antitrust action. Subdivisions held contracts. Investigated in N.J. by first FEPC in 1942 for failure to hire black applicants.

Isbrandtsen Steamship Company

New York City–based shipping company founded in 1939; sailed primarily to Far East; had cargo contracts with War Shipping Administration during WWII. NMU complained to FEPC in 1946 about company's employment discrimination based on segregation; it maintained either all-white, all-black, or all-Chinese staff in Stewards' Department. Later merged into American Export Isbrandtsen Lines, Inc.

Jacksonville Terminal Company

Southern railroad signatory to Southeastern Carriers Conference Agreement blocking promotions of blacks to railroad firemen positions, against which FEPC held hearings in 1943. FEPC issued directive setting aside agreement as discriminatory, supported by Supreme Court decisions in *Steele* and *Tunstall* cases.

Jones, J. A., Construction Company

Major engineering, facilities management, and construction firm based in Charlotte, N.C.; had large shipyard in Panama City, Fla.; built Liberty ships, transports, and aircraft carriers at its Wainwright shipyard; also managed shipyard in Brunswick, Ga., built by Brunswick Marine Construction Corporation. Funded by U.S. Maritime Commission; Ga. yard built 85 Liberty ships; peak employment 17,000; closed after war.

Company also contracted with Manhattan Project to build much of atomic facility at Oak Ridge, Tenn. FEPC received complaints regarding failure to hire black carpenters; by early 1945, local FEPC staff had negotiated agreement with company to hire them. Company continued in operation after war as unit of J. A. Jones, Inc.; parent company bankrupted in 2003, and various divisions were sold.

Jones and Laughlin Steel Company

Large, Pittsburgh-based steel company founded in nineteenth century; had army and navy contracts. Black workers at its Aliquippa, Pa., plant went on strike over discrimination in upgrading in 1943. FEPC successfully negotiated end of strike. Black workers also walked out in May 1944 at company's Hazelwood By-Products Plant in Pittsburgh over access to employment in pusher positions at plant. Again, FEPC negotiated end to strike and clarification of procedures for promotion. Continued in operation after war; merged with Republic Steel to became part of LTV Steel Corporation.

Kaiser Companies

Large group of related firms holding many WWII contracts; headed by Henry J. Kaiser, New Yorker who migrated to Wash.; corporations founded in British Columbia in 1914 and in Calif. in 1920s, with headquarters in Oakland; built roads, bridges, and dams in 1920s and 1930s; first company to manufacture steel on West Coast (1942); formed partnerships with Todd Shipyards and Bath Iron Works, of Maine; owned or operated 7 shipyards and factories producing Liberty ships, aircraft carriers, landing vessels, cargo ships, escorts, aircraft, steel, cement, and magnesium for bombs and artillery shells; shipyards based primarily in Richmond, Calif., Vancouver, Wash., and Portland, Ore. Launched more ships (1,490) than any other shipbuilder. Required massive immigration of workers, especially from Southwest. Labor shortages required extensive use of women and minority workers but led to disputes over union denial of admission of black workers and over upgrading and promotion. At Kaiser's Richmond yard, 6,000 African Americans were employed, 1,000 of them women. Individual shipyards and other facilities were closed at war's end, but Kaiser Industries remained major manufacturing, housing, and health care conglomerate.

Kaiser Shipbuilding Company, Inc.

Kaiser shipyard in Vancouver, Wash. Built by Kaiser with funding from U.S. Maritime Commission; had closed-shop agreement with Boilermakers Union. Black workers recruited by Kaiser were concentrated in Vancouver yard because Boilermakers banned black membership and initially set up segregated auxiliary for that area that permitted employment of black workers. Black workers objected to auxiliary and to concentration in Vancouver, alleging it was temporary and marginal yard not likely to provide continued employment. Yard closed at end of war.

Ken Rad Tube and Lamp Corporation

Manufacturer of lighting and radio tubes in Owensboro, Ky., under contracts with navy. Dating back to 1902, it assumed that name in 1929 when it started producing vacuum tubes. Company seized by federal government under presidential executive order in 1944. Acquired by General Electric in 1945; later part of GE's Microwave Products Division; became part of MPD, Inc., in 1987.

Kennecott Copper Corporation

Largest U.S. copper producer during WWII; started with copper mining in Alaska in 1906. Owned Nevada Consolidated Copper Company units in N.Mex. and Ariz. Investigated by FEPC for discrimination against Mexicans, Indians, and African Americans; complaints involved wage discrimination, segregation, and restriction of minority workers to laborer positions.

Key System

Transit company operating bus and streetcar lines in Berkeley and Oakland, and into San Francisco. Its AFL-affiliated closed-shop union, Amalgamated Association of Street, Electric Railway, and Motor Coach Employees of America, did not accept black members and thereby prevented their being hired. Despite labor shortages, union remained adamant against hiring of blacks and company acquiesced. FEPC hearings held in Oakland and San Francisco in 1945. Local black protests and FEPC negotiations failed to secure employment of any African American as operator or mechanic during WWII.

Liggett & Myers Tobacco Company

Giant tobacco company whose plant in St. Louis had strike by its black workers in 1944.

Lockheed-Vega Aircraft Corporation

Calif.-based multinational aircraft manufacturer that grew to peak employment of more than 90,000 workers during war, with $2 billion in military contracts. Produced bombers, fighters, and transports. Vega Airplane Company was subsidiary of Lockheed Aircraft Corporation that was absorbed in 1943. FEPC listed Lockheed plant in Dallas in 1943 as apparently not employing any black workers. Company experienced fewer cutbacks than other aircraft manufacturers in 1945. Continued in operation producing military, stealth, and reconnaissance planes, missiles, rockets and satellites; now part of Lockheed Martin.

Lone Star Defense Corporation

A subsidiary of B. F. Goodrich Rubber Corporation, it managed Lone Star Army Ammunition Plant constructed for army at beginning of WWII in Texarkana, Tex. Adjacent to plant was Red River Ordnance Depot; both units were combined into Texarkana Ordnance Center. Plant was ammunition loading plant for shells, bombs, fuzes, and other items; continued in operation after war. FEPC Region X investigated complaints against both units in 1944.

Los Angeles Railway Company

Los Angeles bus and trolley system on which hearings were held and directives issued on integrating African Americans into platform positions as drivers and conductors. Despite strike threats by white workers, directive was peacefully and successfully enforced in 1944.

Louisiana & Arkansas Railway Company

Railroad not signatory to Southeastern Carriers Conference Agreement but investigated in FEPC hearings in 1943 for failure to hire or upgrade black workers in skilled and better-paying positions. FEPC also received complaints that railroad practiced wage discrimination based on race.

Louisville and Nashville Railroad Company

Southern railroad signatory to Southeastern Carriers Conference Agreement blocking promotions of blacks to railroad firemen positions, against which FEPC held hearings in 1943. FEPC issued directive setting aside agreement as discriminatory, supported by Supreme Court decisions in *Steele* and *Tunstall* cases.

Marinship Corporation

Opened in 1942 in Sausalito, Marin County, Calif., by W. A. Bechtel Company and other investors to produce Liberty ships, oilers, and tankers for U.S. Maritime Commission and navy, as well as landing barges for army. Employed 20,000 workers at peak. Because of labor shortages, it recruited and trained minority workers; workforce was eventually 25 percent women and 10 percent black. Investigated by FEPC and taken to court because its union refused to admit African Americans to membership and required them to join auxiliary unions or be dismissed. Case led to *James v. Marinship* decision by Calif. Supreme Court asserting that unions with closed-shops could not bar blacks as members. Shipyard closed at end of war and land was turned over to Army Corps of Engineers.

Maryland Dry Dock Company

Baltimore shipbuilding and repair company that employed black workers.

Matson Navigation Company

Oakland-based shipping line against which alienage complaint was filed in 1944; case successfully resolved by FEPC.

McDonnell Aircraft Corporation

St. Louis firm founded in 1938. Produced aircraft and airplane parts; had contract with Machinists Union which barred black membership and blocked employment of blacks in many positions. Investigated for refusal to hire blacks for production and clerical jobs or to upgrade them from janitor positions. FEPC held hearings in August 1944; directed company to cease discriminatory practices, develop and publicize nondiscriminatory policy for employment and promotions, and educate white workers on nondiscrimination policy; little compliance gained. It experienced cutbacks at war's end, but later grew into leading aircraft and spacecraft company; merged with Douglas Aircraft to become McDonnell Douglas in 1967.

McIntosh Hemphill Foundry Company

Foundry in Midland, Pa., threatened with strike over discriminatory dismissal of black worker in 1944.

McQuay-Norris Manufacturing Company

St. Louis firm producing various types of fuzes, bullet cores, piston and sealing rings, and bearings. FEPC held hearings in August 1944 over its continued refusal to hire black women; directed to cease discriminatory practices, develop and publicize nondiscriminatory policy for employment and promotions, and educate white workers on nondiscrimination policy; little compliance gained. Continued in operation after war as auto parts manufacturer.

Merrill-Stevens Drydock Company

Shipyard founded in 1866 and incorporated in 1885 in Jacksonville, Fla.; grew to one of largest shipyards on Atlantic Coast by WWII. Had government contracts for ship conversion. FEPC investigated union complaints of wage discrimination by company in 1944. Still in operation as yacht brokerage, service, and maintenance firm.

Metcalfe-Hamilton Construction Company

Major construction company holding contract for building Alaska-Canada Highway (Alcan). There were several complaints against firm in 1944, including one by black worker alleging he was discriminated against in Canada.

Miami Copper Company

Founded in early twentieth century in Miami, Ariz.; investigated by FEPC for discrimination against Latinos; complaints involved wage discrimination, segregation, and restriction to laborer positions.

Miller Printing Machine Company

Privately owned and operated plant in Pittsburgh for which FEPC requested War Department assistance in negotiating settlement of discrimination complaint.

Mingledorff Shipbuilding Company

Savannah shipyard with naval contract; directed to comply with nondiscrimination clause in contracts.

Missouri, Kansas, & Texas Railway Company

Railroad not signatory to Southeastern Carriers Conference Agreement but investigated in FEPC hearings in 1943 for failure to hire or upgrade black workers in skilled and better-paying positions.

Missouri Pacific Railroad Company

Railroad investigated for employment discrimination against blacks and Mexicans in upgrading to positions above laborer classification; FEPC negotiated promotions for African Americans in 1944.

Missouri Valley Bridge and Iron Works

Leavenworth, Kans.–based company; chief contractor for Evansville Shipyard facility in Ind. during war; had contracts with navy; largest producer of landing vessels in country; peak work force of 19,200. FEPC negotiated with WLB and navy to resolve complaints against yard regarding failure to hire blacks for skilled positions. Company began to comply, but white workers threatened violence if more black welders were employed to meet labor shortages. Yard had extensive layoffs, then closed, in 1945, before any significant advancement for African Americans. Most shipyard workers left Evansville area after war.

Monsanto Chemical Company

Monsanto, Ill., chemical company with numerous contracts for coal tar–based products and chemicals. Had strike by black workers in 1944 over transportation issues. FEPC and WPB sought to negotiate settlement.

Montgomery Ward Company

Chicago-based department store and mail-order catalog company founded in 1872; had few federal contracts during WWII. FEPC declared it did not have jurisdiction over firm, except for units directly tied to contracts. Filed for bankruptcy in 2000 and closed.

Moore Dry Dock Company

A ship repairer and shipbuilder in Oakland, Calif., in continuous operation since 1909; had military contracts for shipbuilding in WWI; built oceangoing passenger and cargo ships under contract with U.S. Maritime Commission and navy during WWII; closed after war. FEPC negotiated upgrading of black workers to higher-paying and more skilled positions.

Morgan and Rice Manufacturing Company

Kansas City firm manufacturing WAAC uniforms that FEPC induced to employ black workers as power sewing machine operators, but on segregated basis.

Murray Gin Company

Atlanta-based cotton oil and gin machinery company with contracts for production of shells. Its plant in Dallas, Tex., investigated by FEPC because its contract with United Steel Workers barred promotion of blacks beyond laborer. FEPC negotiated case with CIO; was still unsuccessfully trying to resolve wage discrimination complaints against firm when it closed in 1946.

National Carbon Company

A unit of Union Carbide and Carbon Company; owners of Eveready Battery (later Energizer); produced batteries and lighting products; had major plant in St. Louis. Produced batteries for fuzes under contract with Bureau of Ordnance during WWII. FEPC negotiated with firm both in St. Louis and then successfully at New York company headquarters to employ black women in production jobs in 1945. Energizer, with headquarters in St. Louis, became world's largest manufacturer of batteries and flashlights.

National Lead Company

St. Louis, Mo., firm producing steel cartridge cases under military contracts. Had 31 percent black workforce but declined to admit African Americans to certain departments traditionally reserved for whites, fearing that whites would walk out. Black employees then went on strike because of company's failure to upgrade or hire them in certain classifications. FEPC and CIO negotiated to end strike.

Nevada Consolidated Copper Company

Mining company incorporated in 1904; subsequently acquired by Kennecott Copper in 1932. Investigated by FEPC for discrimination against Mexicans; complaints involved wage discrimination, segregation, and restriction to laborer positions.

New Britain Machine Company

Part of New England Gas and Electric System; produced screw machine systems; held military contracts. FEPC visited firm in 1943 and reported use of black workers, including black women, in production work. FEPC intervened successfully in complaint regarding failure to upgrade black worker.

New York Central Railroad Company

Railroad not signatory to Southeastern Carriers Conference Agreement but investigated in FEPC hearings in 1943 for failure to hire or upgrade black workers in skilled and better-paying positions. Its union opposed employment of blacks in certain positions and barred black membership, requiring black workers to join separate union auxiliaries as condition for employment.

New York Shipbuilding Company

Shipyard in Camden, N.J., producing battleships during WWII; closed in 1967. Investigated by Mitchell in 1942; was reported to be hiring African Americans in 1943.

Newport News Shipbuilding and Drydock Company

Located in Newport News, Va.; one of 5 major prewar shipbuilders; in continuous operation since 1891 and fully operational at start of WWII; expanded with funding from navy; built aircraft carriers and cruisers; peak employment, 35,000; built oceangoing passenger and cargo ships under contract with U.S. Maritime Commission; employed large numbers of black workers; continued in operation after war as shipbuilder and repairer; currently largest U.S. shipbuilder; merged with Northrop-Grumman in 2001. Investigated for employment discrimination by EEOC and subjected to lawsuit in federal court in 1960s; settlement reached in 1971.

Nicol, R. A., and Company, Inc.

New York City–based firm that chartered liberty ships to War Shipping Administration. Discrimination complaint on West Coast referred to NYC office of FEPC to handle in 1944.

Norfolk Southern Railroad Company

Southern railroad signatory to Southeastern Carriers Conference Agreement blocking promotions of blacks to railroad firemen positions, against which FEPC held hearings in 1943. FEPC issued directive setting aside agreement as discriminatory, supported by Supreme Court decisions in *Steele* and *Tunstall* cases.

Norris Stamping and Manufacturing Company

Cartridge firm in Los Angeles and San Francisco; had contracts with both army and navy for shell cases and ammunition; refused to employ African American workers, despite nondiscrimination clauses in its contracts. FEPC sought assistance of naval officials and War Department in resolving complaints. Considered holding hearing on firm in 1945, but severe cutbacks made such effort futile. Continued in operation after war as Norris Industries.

North American Aviation Company

Calif.-based aviation corporation founded in 1928, with wartime plants in Dallas and Kansas City; producer of largest number of aircraft during WWII, especially fighter planes, trainers, and bombers. Peak employment of 91,000; dropped to 5,000 in 1946. In 1943, FEPC was negotiating for fuller employment and upgrading of African American workers; complainant believed black workers referred by USES were not being hired. Seventh-day Adventists also complained of religious discrimination. Employment policies produced racial tensions at Dallas plant in 1944. Foreman accused of hostile treatment of black workers was dismissed. FEPC negotiated cases through Calif. headquarters. Dallas and Kansas City plants closed, but company continued in operation after war in aircraft, missiles, and aerospace in Calif. and Ohio. Merged with Rockwell in 1967 and with Boeing in 1996.

North Carolina Shipbuilding Company

Wilmington, N.C., wartime shipyard developed by Newport News Shipbuilding Company in 1941 with funding from U.S. Maritime Commission. Peak employment of 15,000; built 243 Liberty ships and other cargo vessels; employed substantial number of black workers, including in riveting positions. Preserved as standby yard until 1950s, then liquidated.

Northern Pump Company

Minnesota firm with wartime contracts against which discrimination complaint was filed in 1944. Continued in operation after war; now division of McNally Industries, Inc.

Northwest Mining and Exchange Company

Coal mining company in Pa. on which FEPC held hearing in October 1943.

Oregon Shipbuilding Company

Emergency shipyard built in Portland, Ore., at start of WWII by Todd and Kaiser Companies with funding from U.S. Maritime Commission; Kaiser bought out Todd's interest in 1941. At its peak, it employed over 35,000 people, 30 percent of them women; built Liberty ships (322); closed after war. Had closed-shop contract with Boilermakers Union; involved in West Coast hearings over requirements for black workers to join segregated union auxiliary as condition of employment.

Palmer-Bee Company

Detroit manufacturer of conveyors and radar equipment that had brief strike because it hired citizen of Japanese ancestry; company indicated that, nevertheless, additional loyal citizens of Japanese ancestry would be hired.

Pennsylvania Railroad Company

Railroad not signatory to Southeastern Carriers Conference Agreement but investigated in FEPC hearings in 1943 for failure to hire or upgrade black workers in skilled and better-paying positions. One of its unions barred employment of blacks as machinists, machinist helpers, machine operators, and painters. Another barred blacks as members and blocked their access to positions as trainmen, brakemen, and supervisors of dining car service. FEPC also received complaints that company refused to hire black cleaning women because it lacked separate toilet facilities for them.

Percy Kent Bag Company

Kansas City, Mo., bag manufacturer founded in 1875 on which FEPC received complaint in 1945.

Phelps-Dodge Copper Corporation

The largest U.S. copper mining and copper products manufacturing company. Held many federal defense contracts for copper wire, rods, tubes, and other products. Operated mines and smelters in Ariz. and refinery in El Paso, Tex. Investigated by FEPC for employment discrimination against Mexican Americans and Native Americans, particularly refusal to upgrade them beyond level of laborer, janitor, or gardener; considered particularly uncooperative with FEPC, which believed reform of this company especially likely to change behavior of entire industry.

Philadelphia Transportation Company

Operators of Philadelphia transit system of buses, trolleys, and subway. Refused to hire African Americans for platform positions of drivers or conductors, allegedly because of union opposition. Wildcat strike by white workers in 1944 after blacks were accepted as trainees for platform position was ended by military intervention. Black workers then successfully trained and upgraded into platform positions and into leadership positions of CIO local.

Pitney Bowes

Postage stamp meter company founded in 1920; now major business mailing and communications company headquartered in Stamford, Conn. FEPC negotiated with firm after Mitchell made inspection visit there in 1943.

Pittsburgh Plate Glass Company

Company in Clarksburg, W.Va., whose employees insisted on dismissal of Jehovah's Witnesses who refused for religious reasons to stand during national anthem or to participate in flag-raising ceremonies in 1942. After hearing on this case in December 1942, FEPC ruled that, in violation of Executive Order 8802, company had unjustly dismissed them because of their creed.

Pratt and Whitney Aircraft

Pratt and Whitney Aircraft founded in 1925 with support from Pratt and Whitney Tool Company of Hartford to produce aircraft engines. Its engine was the most produced during WWII. Black workers at Kansas City plant were denied membership by Machinists Union but charged similar fees for permission to work. Continued in operation as major manufacturer of aircraft engines and aerospace equipment.

Procter and Gamble

Cincinnati-based soap and candle manufacturer founded in 1837. One of Cincinnati firms investigated by FEPC in 1943.

Pullman Company of Chicago

Railroad car manufacturer. Produced aircraft wing assemblies, submarine chasers, landing tanks, escorts, other vessels, gun carriers, and shells under military contracts.

White workers walked out in 1944 at its shipbuilding division in Chicago over up-grading of black employee to skilled position.

Quaker Oats Company

Midwestern oat-processing and cereal company founded in 1901 from merger of previous mills; now division of Pepsico. Complaints investigated in 1944.

Radio Corporation of America (RCA)

New York City–based radio and parts manufacturer founded as radio monopoly in 1919 by General Electric; formed National Broadcasting System; had WWII contracts for radio equipment and fuzes. Also owned RCA-Victor phonograph company. RCA's president, David Sarnoff, was member of FEPC; RCA was investigated regarding racial questions on its application forms. Continued in operation after war in radio, phonographs, television, and satellite communications. Sold to GE in 1986, which, in turn, sold some divisions to other companies.

Remington Arms Company

Small-arms manufacturer based in Bridgeport, Conn.; owned by Dupont Corporation; FEPC negotiated with firm's headquarters to employ black women in production jobs at firm's Kansas City, Mo., plant; investigated complaint against plant in Independence, Mo., in 1943; investigated discriminatory layoffs in 1945.

Republic Oil Company

Texas City, Tex., oil and refinery company; FEPC investigated complaints against it for wage discrimination and refusal to upgrade Mexican and African American workers beyond position of laborer.

Retail Credit Company

Atlanta-based company conducting investigations of employees for various companies, including many with military contracts. FEPC received complaints about its use of questions regarding race and religion on employment applications and during its background checks on employees in 1944. Cases investigated locally, but FEPC ruled that it lacked jurisdiction over private employment and credit agencies.

Reynolds Metal Corporation

Richmond, Va.–based aluminum products company founded in Ky. in 1928 through merger of various firms; during WWII, had plants around country producing military-related lightweight aluminum materials under government contract, especially for aircraft. Plant in Macon, Ga., investigated for discrimination in hiring and training. Cincinnati plant also investigated in 1943; management described as uncooperative with WMC and FEPC. FEPC secured admission for blacks in its Ga. training program in 1945 with help of Navy Department. Company continued in operation after war, producing siding, foil, and other forms of packaging; acquired by Alcoa in 2000 to form largest aluminum products producer in world.

Rheem Manufacturing Company

Nationwide manufacturing and shipbuilding firm with many defense contracts. Opened in Calif. in 1920s, manufacturing water heaters; became major producer of heating and cooling products. Produced bombs, powder containers, and other munitions. Operated shipyards producing Liberty ships for U.S. Maritime Commission; Machinists Union restrictions on black membership blocked black employment at its yard in Richmond, Calif.

San Diego Electric Railway Company

Investigated by FEPC because of refusal to hire blacks for platform positions. Strike threatened by white workers in 1944 over hiring of black trainee for platform job.

Seaboard Airline Railway Company

Southern railroad signatory to Southeastern Carriers Conference Agreement blocking promotions of blacks to railroad firemen positions, against which FEPC held hearings in 1943. FEPC issued directive setting aside agreement as discriminatory, supported by Supreme Court decisions in *Steele* and *Tunstall* cases. Firm challenged FEPC directive.

Seattle-Tacoma Shipbuilding Company

Shipyard with contract with Machinists Union, which barred black workers from membership but charged permission fee similar to dues to permit them to work there.

Sefton Fibre Can Company

New Orleans firm from which FEPC obtained commitment of nondiscrimination; its attempt to place nondiscriminatory order with local USES was blocked by USES officials.

Shell Oil Company (Royal Dutch Co., Shell Oil Co., Inc.)

Shell Oil Company was U.S. unit of global Anglo-Dutch conglomerate; founded in Calif. in 1915; headquartered in Houston, Te. Had contracts for production of gasoline and other fuels during WWII. Investigated for discrimination in wages and in hiring and promotions against both blacks and Mexicans; had contract with Oil Workers Union limiting both groups to laborer, janitor, and gardener positions. FEPC held hearing on company in December 1944; negotiated agreement on upgrading of eligible black and Mexican workers; white workers threatened walkout if upgrading occurred, and subsequent negotiations failed to reach agreement.

Sinclair Oil and Refining Company

Oil company now operating primarily in Midwest and West; founded in 1916; provided fuel and petrochemicals for military use during WWII; FEPC investigated complaints against its Houston refinery for wage discrimination and refusal to upgrade Mexican and African American workers beyond laborer positions. Made successful transition to peacetime economy at end of war.

Southeastern Shipbuilding Company

Located in Savannah, Ga.; built 88 Liberty ships for U.S. Maritime Commission. CIO, then organizing at company, supported efforts to end discrimination in 1943. In 1945, FEPC sought USMC assistance to end discrimination in upgrading, but cutbacks at that point prevented any significant upgrading of black workers.

Southern Pacific Railroad Company

FEPC planned to hold examiner-type hearing on discrimination complaints regarding this railroad in 1945, but none was ever held.

Southern Railway Company

Signatory to Southeastern Carriers Conference Agreement blocking promotions of blacks to railroad firemen positions. Included in hearings FEPC held on railroads in 1943. FEPC issued directive setting aside agreement as discriminatory, supported by Supreme Court decisions in *Steele* and *Tunstall* cases. Firm challenged FEPC directive.

St. John's River Shipbuilding Company

A small shipyard built with U.S. Maritime Commission funding in Jacksonville, Fla., by Merrill-Stevens, shipbuilding and repair company in operation since 1866. Built 82 Liberty ships during World War II. FEPC received complaints over refusal to train or hire African Americans for skilled positions. White workers threatened violence if black welders and burners were hired. Significant layoffs in 1945 prevented further progress in upgrading black workers. Continued in operation after WWII as repair yard until 1980s, then closed.

St. Louis Shipbuilding and Steel Company

St. Louis firm on which FEPC held hearings in August 1944; directed to cease discriminatory practices, develop and publicize nondiscriminatory policy for employment and promotions, and educate white workers on nondiscrimination policy; little compliance gained.

St. Louis-San Francisco Railway Company

Signatory to Southeastern Carriers Conference Agreement blocking promotions of blacks to railroad firemen positions. Included in hearings FEPC held on railroads in 1943. FEPC issued directive setting aside agreement as discriminatory, supported by Supreme Court decisions in *Steele* and *Tunstall* cases. Firm challenged FEPC directive.

Standard Brands, Inc.

Shipping company against which NMU complained to FEPC in 1946 about employment discrimination based on segregation; company refused to employ African Americans because of unwillingness to mix black and white crews.

Standard Oil Company

Nationwide oil trust first founded in 1868 in Pa.; broken up into smaller regional units in antitrust action in 1911; some units continued to bear Standard Oil name. FEPC induced Kansas City–based unit to submit nonwhite employment statistics in 1943; FEPC was located in Standard Oil Building in Washington along with other federal agencies and protested discrimination in segregated lunchroom facility there in 1944. FEPC also investigated complaints against company in N.Y. in 1944.

Strickland Aircraft Company

Aircraft manufacturer headquartered in High Point, N.C.; St. Louis plant investigated by FEPC in 1944.

Sun Shipbuilding and Drydock Company

Of Chester, Pa.; developed by Sun Oil in 1917, and one of 5 major pre-WWII shipbuilders, especially of tankers; fully operational at start of war; expanded into largest single shipyard during WWII; peak employment 40,000; built tankers, hospital ships, and oceangoing passenger and cargo ships under contract with U.S. Maritime Commission; continued in operation as shipbuilder after war until 1989. Employed large numbers of African Americans on segregated basis; suffered brief strike by black workers over upgrading and hiring policies; workers experienced severe housing shortages.

Swift Manufacturing Company

Textile firm in Columbus, Ga., founded in 1882, against which FEPC investigated numerous complaints of wage discrimination and failure to upgrade black workers from 1943–45, with little result.

Tampa Shipbuilding Company

Small prewar shipbuilder in Tampa, Fla.; in operation since 1915; involved in U.S. Maritime Commission's prewar long-range shipbuilding program; also received additional navy funding; employed 16,000 at peak; built naval vessels, tugs for Army, and oceangoing passenger and cargo ships for USMC; closed at end of war.

Tennessee Eastman Corporation

Chemical division of Eastman Kodak Company founded in Tenn. in 1920; major contractor operating Manhattan Project uranium facility at Oak Ridge, Tenn.; now Eastman Chemical Company. FEPC engaged in extensive negotiations with firm to get black workers and trainees, especially women, hired for higher skilled positions.

Texas and Pacific Railway Company

FEPC investigated complaints over failure to upgrade black workers; succeeded in negotiating training and promotions in 1944.

Texas Oil Company (Texaco)

Oil company first founded in Beaumont, Tex., in 1902; partner with Standard Oil of Cal. in Arabian-American Oil Company (Aramco); FEPC investigated complaints against it for wage discrimination and refusal to upgrade Mexican and African American workers beyond position of laborer. Company's proposal to institute segregated deck crews on its tankers was opposed by FEPC. Continued in operation after war; now merged with Chevron and with Shell Oil.

Timken Roller Bearing Company

Founded in 1901; based in Canton, Ohio; produced steel, alloys, and industrial bearings. FEPC cases regarding firm involved segregation and failure to hire African American women because of opposition of white women workers.

Todd-Houston Shipbuilding Corporation

Originally called Houston Shipbuilding Company, it was wartime shipyard built in Houston, Tex., by Todd and Kaiser companies with funding from U.S. Maritime Commission; managed by Todd Shipbuilding; built 208 Liberty ships under contract with USMC. At its peak, it employed 23,000 people; ownership of yard reverted to government at end of war, and it was closed. FEPC investigated its refusal to hire trained black welders for any position higher than laborer.

Todd-Johnson Dry Docks, Incorporated

One of Todd Shipbuilding's ship repair yards; located in Houston, Tex. White workers went on strike over promotion of African Americans as boilermakers helpers; black workers threatened strike over working conditions in yard. Its dry docks in Algiers, La., and Galveston, Tex., also listed as refusing to upgrade black workers.

Todd Shipyards Corporation

Founded in 1916, it operated shipyards and dry docks in various parts of country. Received large number of WWII contracts from navy and Maritime Commission; operated 5 shipyards and 5 repair yards during war, handling over 23,000 ships. FEPC received various complaints, particularly about southern yards, regarding refusal to hire or train blacks for skilled positions.

Union Carbide and Carbon Corporation

Manufacturer of carbon products, chemicals, gases, and alloys; originally formed in 1917 through merger of 4 prior firms. Parent company of National Carbon Company, Carbide and Carbon Chemicals Company, and others. Headquartered in New York during WWII. Primarily produced petrochemicals and batteries. Ran atomic laboratories at Oak Ridge, Tenn., and Paducah, Ky., from 1940s until 1984. After war, it became giant multinational corporation that produced chemicals, electronic components, plastics, and other products; name changed to Union Carbide Corporation in 1957; financially damaged by liability for explosion of its plant in Bhopal, India, in 1984; acquired by Dow Chemical in 2001.

Union Pacific Railroad Company

Not signatory to Southeastern Carriers Conference Agreement but was investigated in FEPC hearings in 1943 for failure to hire or upgrade black or Mexican workers to skilled and better-paying positions.

United Fruit Company

Huge banana-importing corporation with extensive operations in Latin America; founded in 1898 through merger of several companies. Marketer of Chiquita banana. Reduced its shipping operations during war because of submarine danger; many of its ships contracted to government as cargo vessels. Its president, Samuel Zemurray, became member of FEPC. Expanded and diversified after war; after merger, became part of United Brands.

United States (U.S.) Cartridge Company

Component of Olin Industries, biggest small-arms manufacturer in world; operated huge new plants in St. Louis area; hired large numbers of African American workers but under quotas and on segregated basis. It was one of several firms on which FEPC held hearings in St. Louis in 1944. Directive issued against it to cease discrimination. Firm, with union support, eventually was able to introduce black workers into new nonsegregated work settings.

United States (U.S.) Potash Company

Carlsbad, N.Mex., potash mining and refining company formed in early 1930s against which first FEPC received complaints of discrimination against Mexicans in 1942. Potash was used not only for fertilizer but also in manufacturing for military uses, particularly of high-octane gasoline and black powder.

United States (U.S.) Rubber Company

Rubber manufacturing conglomerate formed in 1892 from Samuel Colt's merger of earlier companies; later became Uniroyal, and then acquired by Michelin. When workers objected to upgrading of black workers at Detroit plant in 1943, Rubber Workers Union president came and informed union local it had to observe rights of upgraded black workers. WPB also agreed to check on company's employment situation in W.Va. during inspection tour there in 1943.

United States (U.S.) Steel Corporation

Pittsburgh-based conglomerate founded in 1901 was one of largest steel producers and largest corporation in world. Still largest integrated steel producer in U.S. Peak employment during WWII was 340,000 workers. FEPC investigated its subsidiary, Federal Shipbuilding, in 1942 and succeeded in lessening discriminatory employment policies. FEPC field representative Milo Manly negotiated settlement of strike by black workers at company's Carnegie-Illinois steel plant at Clairton over issues of seniority and upgrading in 1944. FEPC also negotiated operating agreement with U.S. Steel creating mechanism to resolve routine discrimination complaints. During

1950s, NAACP conducted negotiations with firm regarding employment and housing discrimination at its large new plant in Bucks County, Pa.

United States (U.S.) Sugar Corporation

Large, diversified, privately held agribusiness firm with headquarters in Clewiston, Fla. Founded in 1931, it is best known for its role in sugar and citrus production. Mitchell questioned accuracy of Department of Agriculture information about wages and working conditions among firm's sugarcane workers in Fla. in light of Justice Department's later investigation of peonage charges against firm in 1942.

Vendo Company

Vending machine company founded in 1937 in Kansas City, Mo. Provided vending machines for soft drinks for soldiers and also produced radar detection equipment during war. Complaint against company in 1945 referred to FEPC's Legal Division, but no action was taken. Greatly expanded after war and moved to Fresno, Calif.

Victor Electric Company

Hearings were held on company in Cincinnati in March 1945.

Virginian Railway Company

Not signatory to Southeastern Carriers Conference Agreement but was investigated in FEPC hearings in 1943 for failure to hire or upgrade black workers to skilled and better-paying positions.

Wagner Electric Company

St. Louis firm on which FEPC held hearings in August 1944; directed to cease discriminatory practices, develop and publicize nondiscriminatory policy for employment and promotions, and educate white workers on nondiscrimination policy; little compliance gained.

FEPC held hearings in March 1945 on company's Cincinnati plant because of its refusal to hire blacks other than as laborers. Company had closed-shop agreement with IBEW, which banned black membership and refused to permit hiring of black workers other than as janitors, predicting strike if company did so. Union continued to refuse to comply with any nondiscrimination order.

Ward Baking Company

Large-scale manufacturer of bread and other baked goods; founded in Pittsburgh in 1878 and expanded into other urban areas, including New York; makers of Wonder Bread. FEPC handled complaints regarding company in 1944.

Western Cartridge Company

Component of Olin Industries, biggest small-arms manufacturer in world; formed in 1898 as subdivision of Equitable Powder Company founded by Franklin W. Olin in 1892; both based in East Alton, Ill., a town barring black residence or employment. Sanctioned by WMC for refusing to hire black workers referred to it. Negotiated settlement broke down once firm no longer needed large numbers of workers; FEPC held hearings in February 1945. Citing local community opposition, firm made no concessions, and FEPC considered case complete failure; subdivision, Winchester Repeating Arms Company in Conn., was, however, noted for its nondiscriminatory employment policies.

Western Electric Company

Founded by Western Union in 1869 and later acquired by American Bell Telephone Company (later AT&T) in 1882 to become its manufacturing arm of telecommunications equipment and other electrical devices. During WWII, produced radio and wire communications equipment including radar systems for army and navy; provided federal government with more than 30 percent of all electronic gear for war. Operated through Hawthorne and Kearny, N.J., and Point Breeze, Md., plants and used numerous satellite plants and subcontractors. Company remained heavily involved in defense work after war in communications, guided missiles, radar—including erection of radar posts in Artic (Distant Early Warning Line, or DEW Line)—and atomic energy. Following antitrust action against Bell System by Justice Department, telephone service and research and manufacturing divisions were split. Old Western Electric Company and Bell Labs became AT&T Technologies and subsequently evolved into Lucent Technologies.

During WWII, company's employment policies were generally nondiscriminatory, and some of its executives were considered for appointment to FEPC. However, because of local segregation policies, Point Breeze Works in Baltimore was involved in racial disputes and white worker walkout demanding continuance of segregated toilet facilities. During negotiations after War Department seized plant, FEPC had to grudgingly accept adoption of informal segregation system for toilet and lockers facilities.

Western Pipe and Steel Company

Small prewar shipyard in San Francisco, Calif., in operation since 1917; built cargo ships in WWI; reactivated by U.S. Maritime Commission at start of WWII; built oceangoing passenger and cargo ships under contracts with commission; built second yard in San Pedro for naval shipbuilding; closed at end of war.

Western Union Company

Telegraph company and money transfer firm first formed in N.Y. during 1850s. Now primarily financial services firm. Compliant against it investigated in 1944.

Westinghouse Electric and Manufacturing Company

Electrical equipment manufacturer with army and naval contracts; Mitchell negotiated with company and its union in 1942 over dismissal of African American trainee because of white worker opposition to admission of blacks to training program; FEPC investigated complaint in Pa. in 1943; also listed as one of Baltimore area companies that had segregated toilet facilities.

Will and Baumer Candle Company

Prominent Syracuse, N.Y.–based candle manufacturer. Complaints against it investigated in 1944.

Willamette Iron and Steel Corporation

Portland, Ore., small shipbuilder founded in 1904. During war, contracted to build Liberty ships and other types of vessels; continued as repair yard and occasional shipbuilder after war; closed in 1990s. Listed in 1943 as employing some black workers.

Winchester Repeating Arms Company

Founded in 1866 and acquired in 1931 by what became Olin Industries; based in New Haven, Conn.; division of Western Cartridge Corporation, which employed

62,000 people and manufactured 15 billion rounds of ammunition during WWII and developed U.S. carbine and M-1 rifle; Winchester was considered model of nondiscrimination in employment during war.

Wright Automatic Tobacco Packing Machinery Company

Durham, N.C., firm with closed-shop contract with Machinists Union. During FEPC negotiations with company in 1942 over its failure to employ African Americans, union stated that its ban on black membership meant that company could not employ blacks as mechanics.

Young, L. A., Spring and File Company

Detroit manufacturer that laid off but then recalled number of black workers in 1944.

Youngstown Sheet and Tube Company

Firm's Indiana Harbor Works in East Chicago produced steel ingots, bars, tin plates, and other metal goods; suffered racial strike in 1944 over employment of blacks in positions not previously open to them.

LIST OF OTHER CORPORATIONS
SIGNIFICANT TO THE FEPC'S WORK

ABC Railroad

Algernon Blair Company, Montgomery, Ala.

American Bridge Company, Coraopolis, Pa.

American Bridgeworks, Gary, Ind.

American Can Company, Cincinnati, Ohio

American Radiator and Standard Sanitary Company
(American Standard), Richmond, Calif.

American South African Lines, San Francisco, Calif.

American Tool Company, Cincinnati, Ohio

Andrews Steel Company, Newport, Ky.

Angelica Jacket Company, St. Louis, Mo.

Associated Shipyards, Seattle, Wash.

Atlanta Gas Light Company, Atlanta, Ga.

Atlantic Basin Iron Works, Brooklyn, N.Y.

Atlantic City Transportation Company, Atlantic City, N.J.

Atlas Powder Company, Wilmington, Del.

Baldwin Locomotive Company, Philadelphia, Pa.

Bendix Corporation, Elyria, Ohio (headquarters); Baltimore, Md.

Bryant Electric Company, Bridgeport, Conn.

Bryant Roofing and Home Improvement, Baltimore, Md.

Buick Aviation Corporation, Melrose Park, Ill.

Cable Spinning Company, Topeka, Kans.

California Street Railway Company, San Francisco, Calif.

Canfield Rubber Company, Bridgeport, Conn.

Caterpillar Tractor Company, Peoria, Ill.

Central Soya Company, Fort Wayne, Ind.

Champ Manufacturing Company, St. Louis, Mo.

Chicago Motor Coach Company, Chicago, Ill.

Chicago Railroad, Chicago, Ill.

Chicago Surface Lines, Chicago, Ill.

Chrysler Corporation, Detroit, Mich.

Cice Steel Company, Houston, Tex.

Cincinnati Bickford Tool Company, Cincinnati, Ohio

Cincinnati Milling Machine Company, Cincinnati, Ohio

Columbus and Greenville Railway Company, Columbus, Miss.

Commercial Iron Works, Portland, Ore.

Conrady Construction Company

Consolidated Engineering Company, Baltimore, Md.

Crane and Breed Casket Company, Cincinnati, Ohio

Crown Cork and Seal, Baltimore, Md.

Cuneo Press, Chicago, Ill.

Curtis Company

Daneiger Oil Company

Daniel Construction Company, Charleston, S.C.

Del Mar News Agency, Wilmington, Del.

Donnelly, R. R., and Sons, Chicago, Ill.

Dorn, R. J., Company

Eastern Aircraft Company, Baltimore, Md.

Eastern Machinery Company, Cincinnati, Ohio

Electric Alloid Metallurgical Company

Electronics Mechanics, Incorporated

Elliott, H.W., Company

Fairchild Aviation, Hagerstown, Md.

Federal Prison Industries, Incorporated, Washington, D.C.

Fifth Avenue Coach Company, New York, N.Y.

Formica Company, Cincinnati, Ohio

Freeman Shoe Company, Beloit, Wis.

Fulton Sylphon Company, Knoxville, Tenn.

General Baking Company, New York, N.Y.

General Electronics, Incorporated

Goodenow Textile Company, Kansas City, Mo.

Graham Construction Company

Gulf-Colorado and Santa Fe Railroad

Hammond Instrument Company, Evanston, Ill.

Hannon Machine Works

Hercules Powder Company, Hercules, Calif.

Higgins Aircraft Corporation, New Orleans, La.

Holmes Construction Company, Wooster, Ohio

Hoover Ball Bearing Company, Ann Arbor, Mich.

Hydraulic Machinery, Incorporated

Illinois Bell Telephone Company, Chicago, Ill.

Indianapolis Railways, Incorporated, Indianapolis, Ind.

Inland Steel Company, East Chicago, Ind.

International Paper Company, Moss Point, Miss.

International Smelter and Refining Company, Inspiration, Ariz.

Johnson and Johnson Company, New Brunswick, N.J.

Jones Machine Tool Company, Cincinnati, Ohio

Kahn, E., and Sons, Cincinnati, Ohio

Kansas City Power and Light Company, Kansas City, Mo.

Kansas City Stock Yards Company, Kansas City, Kans.

Kentucky Chemical Industries, Incorporated, Cincinnati, Ohio

Key Company

Kinsey, E.A., Company, Cincinnati, Ohio

Knickerbocker Canvas Company

Knutson Construction Company, Houston, Tex.

LeBlond, R. K., Machine Company, Cincinnati, Ohio

Line Material Company, Zanesville, Ohio

Lodge and Shipley Machine Tool Company, Cincinnati, Ohio

Loose Wiles Biscuit Company (Sunshine Biscuits,
Incorporated), Kansas City, Mo.

Luckenbach Steamship Company, New York City, N.Y.

Mahon, R. C., Company, Detroit, Mich.

Market Street Railway Company, San Francisco, Calif.

Maryland Bolt and Nut Company, Anne Arundel County, Md.

McEvoy Company

McKee Construction Company, El Paso, Tex.

Metro Envelope Company

Michigan Bell Telephone Company, Detroit, Mich.

Millhiser Bag Company, Richmond, Va.

Mountain City Copper Company, Mountain City, Nev.

Nashville, Chattanooga, and St. Louis Railroad, Nashville, Tenn.

National Cash Register Company (NCR), Dayton, Ohio

National Foods Corporation, Chicago, Ill. (headquarters); Washington, D.C.

National Smelting Company, Cleveland, Ohio

National Tube Company, Lorain, Ohio

Natta Motors Company, Braddock, Pa.

New England Telephone Company, Boston, Mass.

New Jersey Bell Telephone Company, Newark, N.J. (headquarters);
Atlantic City, N.J.; Camden, N.J.

New York Bell Telephone Company, New York City, N.Y.

Ohio Bell Telephone Company, Cleveland, Ohio (headquarters); Columbus, Ohio

Old Dominion Box Company, Madison Heights, Va. (headquarters); Charlotte, N.C.

Owens Illinois Bottle Company, Glassboro, N.J.

Owl Drug Company, Los Angeles, Calif.

Pacific Electric Company, Los Angeles, Calif.

Pacific Enamel Works, Richmond, Calif.

Pacific Telephone and Telegraph Company, Palo Alto, Calif.; San Francisco, Calif.; Spokane, Wash.

Pennsylvania Bell Telephone Company, Philadelphia, Pa.

Pennsylvania Central Airlines, Pittsburgh, Pa.

Philco Radio Corporation, Philadelphia, Pa. (headquarters); Watsontown, Pa.

Press Wireless Incorporated, Chicago, Ill.

Pyramid Company, St. Louis, Mo.

Quality Family Laundry

Russell and Wise Construction Company, Richmond, Va.

Rustless Iron and Steel, Baltimore, Md.

Sacramento Transit Company, Sacramento, Calif.

Sangamo Electric Company, Springfield, Ill.

Schick Razor Blade Company, Stamford, Conn.

Scullin Steel Company, St. Louis, Mo.

Sebastian Lathe Company, Cincinnati, Ohio

Shelter Island Oyster Company, Greenport, N.Y.

Sherwin-Williams Company, Cleveland, Ohio

Sinclair Contractors

Southern Alkali Corporation, Corpus Christi, Tex.

Southern Bell Telephone and Telegraph Company, Atlanta, Ga. (headquarters); Louisville, Ky.; New Orleans, La.

Southern California Telephone Company, Los Angeles, Calif.

Southwestern Bell Telephone Company, St. Louis, Mo.

St. Louis Aircraft Company, St. Louis, Mo.

Standard Wholesale, Phosphate, and Acid Works, Baltimore, Md.

Texas and New Orleans Railroad, Houston, Tex.; New Orleans, La.

Tichnor Brothers, Incorporated, Boston, Mass.

Todd-Galveston Shipbuilding, Incorporated, Galveston, Tex.

Tubular Alloy Steel Company, Gary, Ind.

Twin City Rapid Transit Company, Minneapolis-St. Paul, Minn.

United Cigar-Whelan Stores Corporation, Washington, D.C.

W.A. Briggs Bitumen Company, Philadelphia, Pa.

Walker-Turner Company, Plainfield, N.J.

Washington Telephone Company, Washington, D.C.

Watson Brothers Transfer Company, Lincoln, Neb.

West Construction Company, Seattle, Wash.

Whalen Drug Company, Washington, D.C.

Wilson and Company

Wilson Packing Company, Chicago, Ill.

Wisconsin Bell Telephone Company, Milwaukee, Wis.

Wright Aeronautical Company, Paterson, N.J.

Zip Baggage and Express Company

APPENDIX 7

Biographical Directory

Abbott, Olcott R. (1912–2000), of Ohio, white FEPC examiner, Region V (Aug. 1945).

Acker, Charles E. (1895–1990), secy.-treas., Baldwin Locomotive Co., Phila.; contact person for FEPC complaints against his company.

Addes, George F. (1910–90), intl. secy.-treas., UAW-CIO; leader, more left-wing faction of union; assisted in settlement of strike at Wright Aeronautical Co. (1944); backer of permanent FEPC.

Aldrich, Kildroy P. (1877–1964?), longtime postal employee, rose through ranks (1897–); first asst. postmaster gen. (1943–45); attended conferences with FEPC officials on discrimination complaints (1944); criticized by Mitchell in congress. testimony for failure to acknowledge or act on discrimination complaints against post office (Dec. 1947).

Alexander, Will W. (1884–1956), Methodist minister, Southern spokesman for more liberal racial policy; dir., Commission on Interracial Cooperation (1917–44); asst. administrator, Resettlement Admin.; dir., FSA; founder, pres. (1931–35), Dillard U.; vice pres., Rosenwald Fund (1940–48); dir., Minority Groups Branch (1941–42); special asst. for Minority Affairs, WMC (1942–43); consultant on race relations for several other agencies.

Allen, Alexander J. (1916–?), applicant for position with FEPC but not hired; industrial secy. for Baltimore Urban League (1943); active in antidiscrimination campaigns related to Western Electric, Chesapeake and Potomac Telephone, and Baltimore Transit cases; exec. dir., Baltimore Urban League (1944–50), Pittsburgh Urban League (1950–60), New York Urban League (1964–66); then vice pres. for programming, Natl. Urban League. Born in Boston; BS, Wilberforce U. (1937); BD, Yale (1940); MSSW, Columbia (1942).

Altmeyer, Arthur J. (1891–1972), exec. dir., WMC (May–Dec. 1942); chair, Social Security Board (1937–52); later denied charges of discrimination in his dept.

Anderson, Mary (1872–1964), dir., Women's Bureau, U.S. Dept. of Labor; investigated statements of Elsie Wolfe (of her dept.) on employability of black women in Miss.; told officials of General Tire and Engineering Co. that Wolfe's statements were contrary to bureau's policy.

Appley, Lawrence A. (1904–97), dep. chair, exec. dir., WMC (June 1943–June 1944); pres., American Mgmt. Assoc. (1948–68).

Arnold, Mr., of Postal Alliance; assisted FEPC complainant on discrimination at LA post office.

Aronson, Arnold (1911–98), Harvard educated supporter (in assoc. with A. Philip Randolph) of proposed March on Washington that led to FDR's order establishing FEPC; secy., Chicago Fair Employment Practice Council; member, Industrial Council of Chicago Urban League; secy., Natl. Council for a Permanent FEPC (1943); exec. dir., Bureau of Jewish Employment Problems, Chicago; consultant to Region VI, FEPC; candidate for regional dir., Region VI, FEPC; dir., Natl. Jewish Community Relations Advisory Council; secy., Emergency Civil Rights Mobilization (1950); a founder, secy., Leadership Conference on Civil Rights

(1950–80); a planner of 1963 March on Washington; founder, pres., Leadership Conference on Civil Rights Education Fund (1980–98).

Ashe, B[owman]. F., Dr. (1885–1952), pres., U. of Miami (1926–52); regional dir., WMC, Region VII (Atlanta office); assigned to ensure blacks received aircraft training in Ala. (1942); issued statement that Ala. Dry Dock and Shipbuilding Co. was not necessarily in full compliance with EO 8802 when it employed black welders but in segregated units.

Atkinson, Hamilton R. (ca. 1890-?), commissioner, Baltimore Police Dept. (1943). Mitchell called him about strike at Western Electric's Point Breeze plant (1943).

Ballinger, E[dwin]. Ray (1891–1967), of D.C., dir. of personnel, GAO (1944); consulted on employment rights of Japanese Americans (WWII).

Barber, William J. (b. ca. 1919), PTC track worker whose upgrading as one of eight blacks training as street car operators precipitated Phila. transit strike (Aug. 1944); one of three trainees interviewed by FEPC on background to strike.

Bard, Ralph A. (1884–1975), Chicago business exec.; asst. secy. of navy (1941); undersecy. of navy (1944–45); dep. U.S. rep. to UN (1947). Various FEPC, NAACP complaints on naval discrimination referred to him.

Bardsley, William W., chair, Regional Labor Supply Committee, Phila. area (1942); assisted in settlement of labor dispute over hiring of blacks at Westinghouse; acting asst. in charge of operations, WMC; regional rep. to USES (1943).

Barnes, Eugene, black member, Point Breeze Employees' Assoc.; chair, committee of Western Electric employees; at WLB hearing, disputed many of the PBEA's claims about demands for separate facilities for white and black workers at Western Electric plant (1943); in related company meetings (1944).

Barron, Harry I., administrative asst., then chief, Compliance Div., FEPC (1943); exec. secy., Bureau on Jewish Employment Problems; testified on problems of minority workers in training and job placement at Chicago FEPC hearings (Jan. 1942); exec. secy., Jewish Community Council, Cleveland (after WWII).

Beall, W[illiam]. Hayes (1910–89); FEPC examiner (1944–45); previously asst. chief of the migratory labor camp program of Dept. of Agriculture (1943–44); chief of youth activities, official military govt., U.S. War Dept., Berlin (1945–47); a dir. for coop programs, Superior, Wis., Chicago (1948–56); a dir., Kidney Foundation, Chicago (1967–70); lobbyist, Ore. Consumer League (1970s). Active in Democratic Party, Ill., Ore.; Ore. delegate to natl. convention (1972). Born in Colorado Springs; BA, Willamette U. (Salem, Ore.) (1932); MDiv, Yale (1935).

Beatty, W. Barton, black candidate for FEPC examiner, Region X (Dallas), not appointed because had only recently arrived.

Beecher, John (1904–80), writer, reporter, poet, English prof., administrator in various New Deal agencies, esp. Farm Security Admin. Sr. field rep. for FEPC in South (1941–42); handled most organizing, investigation for Birmingham hearings (June 1942). Placed in charge of FEPC's New York office (July 1942); resigned (Mar. 1943), wrote articles in *New York Post* exposing inadequacies of FEPC. Officer on liberty ship *Booker T. Washington*, first integrated ship in American war effort (May 1943–45). Raised in Birmingham.

Bell, [Isaac] Vaughn (1888–1957), industrial relations mgr., Bell Aircraft (1940–48); personnel dir., Bell plant in Buffalo; in FEPC efforts to overcome employment discrimination at Bell plants (1944). Previously associated with Hirsch Mercantile Co., La. (1916–40).

Belsaw, Edward T., Dr. (d. 1952), black dentist, influential leader in Mobile; attended meeting with Mitchell to discuss settlement of racial conflict at Ala. Dry Dock and Shipbuilding.

Belschner, Carl E., treas., Point Breeze Employees' Assoc.; wrote WPB on creation of separate restrooms at Western Electric's Point Breeze plant (1942); queried whether unions were considered discriminatory if they refused to admit blacks.

Bennett, L. Howard (1913–?), of Charleston, S.C.; educated at, became principal of Avery Normal Inst., Charleston. FEPC complainant on behalf of black women denied employment at Charleston Navy Yard (1943); reported women were being hired. J.D., U. of Chicago (1950), municipal judge, Minneapolis; joined Dept. of Defense (1963); civil rights dir., DOD (1965); acting dep. asst. secy. of defense for civil rights (1968–70).

Benowitz, C., of Long Beach, Calif., one of eight white members of Boilermakers Union, Local 92, who met with Mitchell, regional FEPC officials to oppose union's policy of requiring blacks to join auxiliary unions. Possibly Charlotte Benowitz, born in New York (1915), died in L.A. (1997).

Bergemann, Russell A[rthur]. (1909–1991), of L.A., mgr. of industrial relations, Calif. Shipbuilding Co.; Gave information on firm to FEPC during its investigations of shipbuilding industry (1943).

Bernstein, Victor H[eine]. (1904–1992), of PM, New York daily newspaper (1940s); reported complaints of black man injured in racial violence at Ala. Dry Dock (1943). Berlin correspondent, Jewish Telegraph Agency (1937–39); returned to Berlin to cover issues like liberation of concentration camps, war crimes trials (1945). Wrote *Final Judgment* (1947); managing editor of *The Nation* (1952–63).

Berryman, Milton (prob. 1912–94), welder forced into auxiliary of Boilermakers Union after union learned he was black; denied promotion to welding instructor because of race. Complainant to FEPC. Born in La.

Biddle, Francis B. (1886–1968), U.S. solicitor gen. (1940); U.S. atty. gen. (1941–45); chief U.S. rep. at Nuremberg trials (1945–46); FDR's letter to him (Nov. 5, 1943) affirmed mandatory nature of nondiscrimination clauses in EOs.

Bilbo, Theodore G. (D-Miss.) (1877–1947); U.S. sen. (1935–47); governor (1916–20, 1928–32); racist opponent of FEPC; in filibuster against appropriations for FEPC (June 1945); investigated for taking gifts, services, political contributions from military contractors, others seeking favors (1946); CIO convention called for his ouster from Senate (1946); NAACP supported his removal.

Blackburn, W. W., Rev., of Jackson Coll.; consulted by Cy W. Record on discrimination against blacks at Brecon Bag Loading plant, Flora, Miss. (1942).

Blackwell, E. V., secy., business agent, Local 92 (Cal., Nev.), IBBISHA; said blacks could not be admitted into union except as auxiliary members (1941); warned that after WWII, if admitted, blacks would have to be retained by union, but auxiliaries would be disbanded.

Blakeney, Andrew (1898–1992), black jazz trumpeter, band leader, welder, L.A.; FEPC complainant after he was dismissed from Calif. Shipbuilding Co. for failure to pay dues to black auxiliary. Mitchell recommended him as witness for Boilermakers hearing in L.A. (Nov. 1943). Had his own band (1940s–60s); toured with "Legends of Jazz" (1970s). Born in Miss.

Bloch, Emanuel H[irsch]. (1901–54), hearings examiner, Legal Div., FEPC; also served on staff of Div. of Field Operations, FEPC (1943–45); recruited to FEPC by Maslow; noted defense lawyer for leftist sympathizers and Trenton Six; defense lawyer along with his father, Alexander, in espionage trial of Ethel and Julius Rosenberg (1950–53); guardian of Rosenbergs' children until his sudden death by heart attack.

Block, Harry (1908–1988), of Phila.; vice pres., United Electrical Workers (1936–46), Intl. Union of Electrical Workers (1949–72); secy.-treas., Pa. Council, CIO (1946–60); member, WSB, WLB, WPB during WWII. As asst. to James P. Casey, labor rep. on Regional Labor Supply Committee, Phila. area, assisted in settlement of labor disputes over hiring of blacks at Westinghouse (1942).

Blunt, Royden A. (1892–1985), area manpower dir., WMC, Baltimore; investigated complaints on Chesapeake and Potomac Telephone Co. (1942).

Boardman, J[oseph]. Griffith (1904–60), insurance exec., founder, Boardman, Haas, and Geraghty of Phila. (1938–45); dir., Region III, WPB (1944); board member, Brewster Co., Hatboro, Pa.; conferred with on FEPC complaints against company.

Bond, J[ames]. H., acting dep. exec. dir., WMC (Jan. 1943–Mar. 1944); dir., Region X (Dallas), WMC (1944); conferred with on labor stabilization agreements, FEPC-WMC relationship; ensured that WMC staff provided data that FEPC needed.

Boullon, Armando (prob. 1918–85), FEPC complainant, witness at FEPC hearings on Boilermakers' union, Portland, Ore. (Nov. 1943). Employee, Swan Island shipyard, Kaiser Co.; denied promotion because of race.

Bourne, St. Claire T. (1910–?), black reporter, columnist, editor, *New York Age* (1931–36), *Amsterdam News* (1937–42), *The People's Voice* (1942–43); field examiner, New York office, FEPC (1942–43); information officer, FEPC (July 1943–Nov. 1945); then, publicity dir., New York Dept. of Labor; present in Phila. during transit strike, Aug. 1944.

Bowers, A[ndrew]. C. (1895–1957), works mgr., Miss. Ordnance Plant–Brecon Bag Loading Plant; contacted on discrimination in hiring of black women. Said black women did not have needed skills and that blacks would be confined to low-level positions.

Bowles, Chester (1901–86), administrator, OPA (throughout WWII); FEPC asked him to reaffirm policies of his predecessor on racial discrimination (1943). Held several UN posts (1946–51); governor of Conn. (1948–50); ambassador to India (1951–53, 1963–69), U.S. rep. (1959–60); foreign policy adviser; writer, lecturer on natl., foreign affairs.

Bowron, Fletcher (1887–1968) (D-Calif.), lawyer, judge; mayor of L.A. (1938–53) who requested postponements of FEPC hearings on Street Railway discrimination, saying he feared racial conflict.

Brawner, A[lexander]. H[arrison]., Lt. Col. (1899–1995), chief, Labor Branch, Sixth Service Command (1943); involved in settling strike at American Steel Foundry, East Chicago, Ind.; later, a dir., Fireman's Fund Insurance Co., Del Monte Corp. Born, died in San Francisco. Princeton graduate (1921).

Brin, Leonard M[ilton]., of San Antonio; recruited to FEPC by Maslow; dir., Region X (Dallas), FEPC (Jan.–June 1944); consultant, Region VII (1944–45); active on FEPC cases involving Republic Oil, Delta Shipbuilding, North American Aviation; formerly field examiner, NLRB; employee, OSS; previously special agent for div. of investigation of WPA, working with Bureau of Foreign and Domestic Commerce, Commerce Dept.; asst. U.S. trade commissioner to Mexico, Argentina. Coauthored *Parana Pine Lumber Industry of Brazil* (1927).

Brooks, Overton (1897–1961) (D-La.), U.S. rep. (1937–61); opponent of FEPC appropriations (1944).

Brophy, John (1883–1963), of D.C.; English-born labor leader, UMWA; dir., Industrial Union Councils, CIO (1951–61); member, FEPC (1941–45); wrote letter of support for state FEPC legislation in W.Va. (1947).

Brotman, Herman B. (1909–1986), moved to D.C. (1935), helped draft Social Security Act, worked with Social Security Admin.; then, worked for WMC; served in army in Europe, later, became chief of labor and social admin. during military occupation in Austria, then labor attaché, U.S. embassy there until 1952; worked with HEW; asst. commissioner in admin. of aging, helped draft Older Americans Act of 1965. Sent Mitchell information on employment in street railways (1943). Born in Phila. BA, MA, CCNY.

Brown, Harvey Winfield (1883–1956), vice pres., IAM (1921–38), acting pres. (1938–39), pres. (1940–48); a vice pres., AFL (1941–56); assisted with settlement of FEPC cases involving discrimination by machinist union locals.

Brown, Prentiss M. (1889–1973), administrator, OPA (1943); issued statement on OPA policy on implementing EO 8802.

Brown, Robert Elmer, Jr. (ca. 1905–?), regional Negro affairs rep., NYA, San Francisco; examiner, Region XII, FEPC (1943); later, examiner in charge, LA suboffice, Region XII, FEPC (end of 1945); later, worked for Los Angeles Juvenile Guidance Dept. BA, Morehouse Coll.; MA, Fisk.

Brown, Theodore E. (1915–1983), black labor economist; a leader of Midwest March on Washington Movement; examiner in charge, St. Louis suboffice, FEPC (1943–45); economist, editor, researcher, field agent, Brotherhood of Sleeping Car Porters, AFL; exec. dir., American Negro Leadership Conference on Africa; testified on revision of Taft-Hartley Act (Mar. 1949). BA, Northwestern; MA, U. of Chicago.

Bruton, Philip G. (1891–1960), col., Army Corps of Engineers; dep. administrator, War Food Admin.; told FEPC (1943) that imported Bahamian, Jamaican, Mexican agricultural workers would be covered by nondiscrimination provisions of EO 8802.

Bullitt, Orville Horwitz (1894–1979), of Pa., banker; partner in W. H. Newbold's Son and Co., Phila. Dir. of Region III (Phila. office), WPB, in efforts to get Phila. transit strikers back to work (Aug. 1944).

Burke, Jack B., FEPC examiner, Detroit (1943), Region XII (1944–45); previously junior administrative asst., Labor Div., OPM. During anti-FEPC debates in Congress, Rep. Malcolm Tarver alleged that his real name was Jack Burton Burkowitz and that he had had "his nose operated on and his name changed in Pennsylvania."

Burns, William R., asst. to dir., Regional Construction Office, East Coast (Phila. office), U.S. Maritime Commission; represented commission in meeting with FEPC on Southeastern Shipbuilding Co., Savannah.

Byrnes, James F. (1879–1972) (D-S.C.), U.S. rep. (1910–25), sen. (1930–40); Supreme Court justice (1941–42); liaison officer for OEM (WWII); did not support FEPC; secy. of state (1945–47); as governor of S.C. (1951–55), moderate on social programs but opposed desegregation.

Cansler, G[eorge]. H. (1908–91), pres., Local 367, OWIU, Shell Oil, Houston; said no changes would be made in company's discriminatory upgrading policy (1944).

Carey, James B[arron]. (1911–73), chair, Natl. CIO Committee to Abolish Racial Discrimination during WWII; member, President's Commission on Civil Rights (1946); pres., IUERMW-CIO (1949–65); secy.-treas., CIO; vice pres. (1955–65); in meeting with Labor Secy. Lewis B. Schwellenbach on nondiscrimination by USES offices.

Carmichael, Leonard J., Dr. (1898–1973), psychology prof., experimental psychologist; pres., Tufts U. (1938–52); secy., Smithsonian Inst. (1953–64); vice pres. for research, exploration, Natl. Geographic Society (1964–73); dir., Natl. Roster of Scientific and Specialized Personnel, WMC (1940–44); FEPC conferred with him on questions of race on application blanks for inclusion on roster; such questions subseq. removed.

Carney, Frank P., Phila. Transportation Co. motorman, pres., PTC employees union that was replaced as rep. of transit workers by CIO's Transport Workers Union (early 1944). Leader of Phila. transit strike (Aug. 1944) protesting hiring of black trainees as streetcar operators; arrested and fired.

Carrington, Walter R., a leader of SNOV, the local organization of black shipbuilders in Portland, Ore., that sought to overcome discrimination by shipbuilding companies, relevant unions there. Denied promotion to leaderman because of race. Testified at Portland FEPC hearing on Boilermakers cases (Nov. 1943).

Carter, Ashby B. (1898–1953), black postal clerk in Chicago (1913–at least 1950); Chicago branch pres., NAPE (WWII); involved with protests against post office discrimination and against placing FEPC under WMC's control; later, board member, Natl. Council for a Permanent FEPC; as natl. pres., NAPE (1945–53), pledged donation for NAACP's 40th anniversary (1949). Born, educated in W.Va.

Case, George Wilkinson (1880–ca. 1974–76), civil engineer; prof., dean of engineering, U. of N.H. (1925–45); on leave to work on wartime programs (1940–45); dir., Engineering Science Management War Training program (1942–45); FEPC held discussions with him on limits to number of Jews, other minorities in program. Born in Ind.

Casey, James P., former pres., IUERMW; labor rep. to Regional Labor Supply Committee, Phila.; regional rep., Office of Labor Production, WPB; scheduled for radio talk urging strikers to return to work during Phila. transit strike (1944), but broadcast cancelled at request of mayor.

Castañeda, Carlos E[duardo]., Dr. (1896–1958), Mexican American scholar of Southwest history; librarian, U. of Tex.; special asst. to FEPC chair on Latin American Affairs; acting dir. (1943), later, dir., Region X (Dallas), FEPC; acting dir., Region XI (San Antonio); esp. active on FEPC cases involving discrimination against Latin Americans, particularly by oil companies, mining industry.

Chandler, Ralph B. (1891–1970), publisher of *Mobile Press, Register* newspapers, who provided information on racial conflict at Ala. Dry Dock; charged with contempt for criticizing judge's sentencing to only $2,000 peace bond of white man charged with inciting the violence.

Charters, W[errett] W[allace]., Dr. (1875–1952), teacher, prof., educational administrator; acting dir., Bureau of Training, WMC (1943–43). Born in Ontario.

Chew, Claude C., supt. of industrial relations, Western Electric; conferred with Mitchell on difficulties at integrated Point Breeze plant, Md.; defended company's stand against providing separate facilities for black and white workers in statement at WLB hearing, Baltimore (1943); replaced by Jack Gainey (1944).

Chubb, Sally, clerk-stenographer, Atlanta office, FEPC (1944–45).

Clifton, N. Jeanne, clerk-stenographer, central office, FEPC (1943–45).

Clore, Lethia Warren, black former teacher, social worker, race relations specialist; employment counselor, USES; personnel supervisor, NYA; field examiner, New York office, then Detroit, Cleveland, Cincinnati offices, FEPC (1943–45); briefly examiner in charge of Cincinnati suboffice (1945); field rep., Natl. Committee for a Permanent FEPC (1945).

Clymer, Lewis Walter (1910–2001), black lawyer, Kansas City, Mo.; minorities group specialist, Region IX (Kansas City), WMC (1941–45); then, asst. prosecuting atty., municipal and circuit court judge, Mo. LLD, Howard.

Coan, Carol, of New York, compliance analyst, FEPC (Sept. 1943–Aug. 1945). Bryn Mawr.

Coburn, Frank, a leader of Phila. transit strike (Aug. 1944); as a union spokesman, cited "customs" clause in union's contract as restricting employment or upgrading of blacks to certain jobs.

Cochran, Clay Lee (1914–82?), of Amarillo; examiner, Region X (Dallas), FEPC (1943); left office when drafted to serve in WWII.

Cooley, Richard, active in negotiations over unrest at Bethlehem Steel and Shipbuilding Corporation–Sparrows Point, Md. (1943). Possibly mistaken reference to Russell Cooley.

Cooley, Russell, special asst. to dir. of shipyard relations, U.S. Maritime Commission; attended FEPC meeting on Gulf Coast shipbuilding companies (1944).

Cooper, Evelyn Neilson (1913–?), atty., hearings examiner, Legal Div., FEPC (1944–45); transferred from Portland, Ore., branch of OPA (Apr. 1944); active in Capital Transit case, telephone company cases, among others.

Corwin, Edward (1878–1963), noted constitutional scholar at Princeton U.; consultant on constitutional issues like FDR's court reorganization plan (which he supported), Bricker

Amendment to restrict presidential treaty-making powers (which he opposed). Quoted in FEPC text on presidential power to issue, enforce exec. orders.

Covington, Floyd Cornelius James (1901–89), exec. secy. of Los Angeles Urban League 1928–53); accompanied Mitchell on interviews with leaders of Boilermakers union A-35. Later, group relations adviser for Federal Housing Authority (1953–75). Born in Denver.

Craig, Cleo F. (1893–1978), vice pres. in charge of personnel, AT&T; FEPC conferred with him on employment of blacks as operators in telephone companies (1945).

Cramer, Lawrence W[illiam]. (1897–1978), of New Orleans; instructor in govt., Columbia U. (1926–31); lt. governor, St. Croix, Virgin Islands (1931–35); governor, Virgin Islands (1935–41); first exec. secy., FEPC (Aug. 1941–June 1943); resigned after FEPC placed under WMC and its chair, Paul McNutt, canceled hearings on discrimination in railroad industry; later, exec. secy., Caribbean Commission.

Crisp, Frederick Grafton, Adm. (1892–1970), dir. of shore establishments, civilian personnel, U.S. Navy; asst. secy. of navy; conferred with FEPC on discrimination in training programs (1944); wrote letter on FEPC case involving shipyard worker of German origin dismissed after loyalty investigation.

Crockett, George William, Jr. (1909–97), black lawyer from Fla.; sr. atty. in Solicitor's Office, Dept. of Labor (1939–43); appointed hearings examiner, FEPC (1943); member of Detroit law firm (1946–66); lawyer for UAW; vice pres., Lawyers Guild; controversial Detroit Records Court judge (1967–1979); Democratic congressman from inner city Detroit (1980–1991). Morehouse Coll.; U. of Mich. Law School.

Cross, Ira B., Jr. (1912–96), of Calif.; Maj., Lt. Col., War Dept.; intervened in settlement of FEPC cases in St. Louis; area coordinator of labor branch, Industrial Personnel Div., War Dept. (1943). Son of prominent Calif. economist, Ira B. Cross Sr. (b. 1880).

Crum, Bartley C[avanaugh]. (1900–59), liberal San Francisco lawyer; a founder of Natl. Lawyers Guild and of PM; special counsel for FEPC working on railroad cases (1943); member, Natl. Legal Committee, NAACP; later, lawyer for Hollywood 10 who refused to answer questions from HUAC; labeled as fellow traveler by HUAC, kept under surveillance during investigations into Communist Party, associated organizations. Committed suicide.

Cushman, Edward L. (1914–92), Mich. dir., WMC (1943–46). FEPC sought his intercession on General Motors' policy of refusing to supply information on nonwhite employees (1944). Prof., public admin. (1946–54), exec. vice pres. (1966–84), Wayne State U.; vice pres., American Motors (1954–66).

Cutietta, Vincent A. (1918–81), FEPC complainant; suspended from job as machinist's helper at Murray-Ohio Mfg. Co. (1943) by order of General Eagan of Fifth Service Command, Army Service Forces; War Dept. reported the action taken for internal security. Born in Italy; arrived in U.S. 1921; resided in Cleveland.

Dalrymple, Sherman Harris (1889–1962), founding pres. (1935–45), United Rubber Workers, based in Akron; defended rights of black workers upgraded at U.S. Rubber Co.

Daniels, Jonathan W[orth]. (1902–81) (D-N.C.), newspaper reporter, editor, author; presidential aide to FDR in charge of racial and labor problems, Southern politics (1943–45); press secy. to Pres. Truman (1945); U.S. member, UN Subcommittee on Prevention of Discrimination and Protection of Minorities (1947–53); represented FDR in discussions with FEPC on Bethlehem Steel Shipbuilding case (1943), Phila. transit strike, Los Angeles Railway case (1944).

Davidson, Eugene (1896–1976), of D.C.; dir., New Negro Alliance (1930s–1940s); March on Washington Movement official; sr. field rep., FEPC (Oct. 1941–July 1943); asst. dir. of field operations, FEPC (1943–45), associate dir. of field operations, acting dir., Regions III, IV

(1945–46); board member, D.C. branch, NAACP (1927–57); pres. (1954); a leader of drive to desegregate D.C.

Davis, Henry, FEPC complainant from Iowa; witness at Boilermakers hearings in Portland, Ore. (Nov. 1943).

Davis, John Aubrey (1912–2003), prof., poli. sci., Lincoln U., Ohio State U., CCNY; member, New York State Commission against Discrimination; served with Mitchell on FEPC, heading Div. of Review and Analysis (Aug. 30, 1943–May 1946); consultant to NAACP Legal Defense and Education Fund; personnel consultant to State Dept.; prepared memorandum opposing Lodge-Gossett Bill to eliminate role of electoral college. Davis's paper argued that under circumstances then prevailing the measure would give undue political influence to the South, reduce importance of blacks, other minorities as swing voters in states with large numbers of electoral votes, lead to creation of a multiparty system, and destroy president's effectiveness in foreign affairs.

Davis, Joy A., compliance analyst, FEPC (Sept. 1943–May 1945). Wrote report on FEPC relationship with War Dept.

Dedmon, Jesse O., Jr. (1908–86), black lawyer; capt., 366th Infantry (1941–45); secy. of veterans affairs, NAACP (1945–48); later, trial judge advocate, Veterans' Affairs. Born in Ark. Degree from Howard.

Denham, Robert N. (1885–1954), trial examiner (1938–47), NLRB; in case against Ore. Shipbuilding Corp., Kaiser Co. (WWII); later, counsel gen., NLRB (1947–50); Mitchell said he reportedly had strong antiblack bias.

Dickerson, Earl B. (1891–1986), of Ill.; "dean of Chicago's black lawyers"; member, exec. committee, Chicago NAACP, NAACP national board of directors (1941–73); legal counsel, Supreme Life Insurance; first black Democratic alderman, Chicago (1938–43); appointed to FEPC in 1941; later, acting chair; not reappointed to new FEPC in 1943, considered too militant; pres. Natl. Bar Assoc. (1945–47); first black pres., Natl. Lawyers Guild (1951–59); pres., Chicago Urban League (1939–47; 1950–55).

Dietz (Deits, Detiz), Walter P., associate dir., Training within Industry (TWI) (1940–45), program transferred among various federal agencies, but primarily within WMC (1942–45); Western Electric exec. who cooperated in negotiations with FEPC over minority hiring; consulted on availability of Western Electric execs. for membership on FEPC.

Dixey, William C., Jr. (1909–88?), Phila. transit conductor; vice chair of "strike committee" of Phila. transit strike (1944); arrested for violation of Smith-Connally Act.

Dock, Zenith (1921–98), black employee of Ala. Dry Dock who testified to FEPC on racial conflict at yard.

Dodge, [David] Witherspoon, Dr. (1887–1959), white Presbyterian and Congregationalist minister; college prof.; radio minister (1930–35); labor organizer (1938–43) for the Textile Workers of America, CIO; labor rep. for WPB, Jacksonville, Birmingham (1943–44); dir., Region VII (Atlanta), FEPC (1944–45); exec. dir., Natl. Religion and Labor Council of America (1947–53). Wrote *Southern Rebel in Reverse, The Autobiography of an Idolshaker* (1961). Born in S.C.

Domínguez, Adolfo G., Mexican consul at Houston; met, corresponded with FEPC officials on discrimination complaints by Mexican workers at Shell Oil (1944); pressed for overall action on discrimination against Chicanos in Southwest.

Donaldson, Jesse M. (1885–1970), career civil service employee, first asst. postmaster gen. of Post Office Dept. (1945), postmaster gen. (1947–53). Mitchell testified against his appointment as postmaster gen. because of failure as first dep. postmaster gen. to take action against discrimination in postal system.

Donovan, Daniel R., white CIO union organizer; previously, worked for Unemployment Compensation Bureau, Social Security Board; labor relations adviser, WPA; labor member,

NRA; examiner, field rep., FEPC (1941–45); active on cases in Ariz., Detroit, St. Louis; examiner, Cleveland office (1943); transferred to New York office as sr. fair-practice examiner (1943–45).

Doram, Thomas Madison, admitted to Boilermakers union; refused to transfer to auxiliary when union learned he was black. Arrested after conflict with white worker in Calif. Shipbuilding plant (1943). Gave Mitchell a statement for use in Boilermakers hearings.

Douty, Kenneth (1910–91), of WMC; in conference on black employment at Chesapeake and Potomac Telephone Co. (1943).

Dreyfus, Benjamin (1910–83), Calif. lawyer; member, Natl. Lawyers Guild; FEPC special counsel for hearings on railroads, Boilermakers union, L.A. (Nov. 1943). Degrees from Stanford U., Stanford Law.

Duncan, J. Lawrence (1907–?), black Detroit resident; supt., Dept. of Public Welfare, Detroit (1931–36); state supervisor, Mich. Unemployment Compensation Commission (1938–41); asst. to Robert Weaver in OPM's Negro Employment and Training Branch (1941); race relations specialist, working with OPM, WPB, WMC, FEPC (1943–45); negotiated jobs for blacks in auto industry; dir., Region V (Cleveland), WMC. Later, employment specialist, USES; racial relations officer, PHA; equal opportunity dir., Housing and Home Finance Agency, HUD (1950s–70s). Born in Ala.; educated in public admin., Wayne State, U. of Mich.

Dunlap, David R[ichardon]. (1879–1968), of Mobile; pres. (1916–44), Ala. Dry Dock during racial incident in its shipyard (1943); chair of board (1944–56, 1963–68).

Eastland, James O. (1904–86) (D-Miss.), U.S. sen. (1941, 1943–78); segregationist; leader of opposition to permanent FEPC and, later, civil rights legislation; later, pres. pro tem of Senate; chair, Judiciary Committee.

Ellinger, W. Don, of Dallas; white labor organizer; rep. of ILGWU, AFL, in Tex.; examiner in charge, then acting dir., Region X (Dallas); recruited to FEPC by Maslow; dir., Region XIII (New Orleans), FEPC (1944–45); CIO field rep. (1946–50); natl. rep., field dir., CIO PAC (1950–56); area dir., AFL-CIO Committee on Political Education (1956–61) in union areas 8, 9 (Kans., Mo., N. Mex., Okla., Tex.).

Ethridge, Mark F. (1896–1981), of Ky.; publisher of *Louisville Courier-Journal;* member, first chair, FEPC (1941); observer of elections in Bulgaria, Romania (1945), who warned of undemocratic processes, Russian interference in E. Europe; moderate on desegregation (1950s).

Evans, Joseph H. B. (ca. 1892–?), black teacher, St. Louis; insurance agent, Atlanta; returned to D.C.; social economist, race relations specialist, FSA (1935–40); consultant, chief, Negro Relations Section, NYA (1940); regional affairs officer (Denver), NYA (1942); successively, field examiner, acting dir., dir. of Region IV (D.C.), FEPC (1943–45); associate exec. secy., President's Committee on Equality of Treatment and Opportunity in the Armed Services (Fahy Committee), created in 1948. Born in D.C. BA, U. of Mich.

Ewing, Oscar R. (1889–1980), head of FSA (1947–52); consulted by NAACP on exec. order banning discrimination in public employment (1948); appointed committee to review discrimination, segregation in Bureau of Old Age and Survivors Insurance (Social Security Administration) (1948); chair, Democratic Natl. Committee, who proposed creation of liberal advisory group to counter conservative influences on pres.; ended exclusion of black doctors from white hospitals in D.C.; supported federally financed health insurance but defeated by AMA opposition. Later Truman wished to create dept. of HEW and make Ewing head, but was blocked by some congressmen because of backlash against his health plan, other liberal policies.

Fahy (Fahey), Charles (1892–1979), counsel, NLRB (1935–40); U.S. solicitor gen. (1941–45); chair, President's Committee on Equality of Treatment and Opportunity in the Armed

Services (Fahy Committee) (1948–50); judge, U.S. Court of Appeals for the District of Columbia (1949–67). Mitchell conferred with him on FEPC case on Western Electric.

Farmer, A[rchie]. A[rrington]., Brig. Gen. (1892–1963), commanding officer, Phila. Signal Depot (1941–42); commanding gen., Signal Corps Eastern Signal Service (1942–46); operated Western Electric's Point Breeze plant for War Dept. after govt. took it over for three months following strike by white workers demanding resegregation; conferred with Mitchell in Baltimore (1944). Born in N.C.

Fenneman, Lawrence (1902–86), of Baltimore; Md. State dir., WMC; in conference on black employment at Chesapeake and Potomac Telephone Co. (1943).

Fenton, Francis Patrick (Frank) (1895–1948), Boston labor leader; alternate for William Green, FEPC; resigned (Dec. 1942), replaced by Boris Shishkin; dir. of organization, CIO; member, Natl. Labor Committee, NAACP; intl. labor rep. of AFL at time of his sudden death.

Ferris, Muriel, examiner, FEPC central office (Aug. 1945); prepared report on Chesapeake and Potomac Telephone case (1945).

Field, Stephen J. (1816–99), justice, U.S. Supreme Court (1863–97); judge, U.S. Court of Appeals, 9th Circuit. Life threatened by David Terry; his bodyguard, David Neagle, shot Terry; case led to the influential opinion on presidential power found in *Cunningham v. Neagle* (1890), cited in FEPC text on presidential power to issue, enforce exec. orders.

Fisher, C[harles]. W., Rear Adm., chief of shore establishments, Navy Dept.; in conference with FEPC (1943).

Fisher, Ovie Clark (1903–94) (D-Tex.), U.S. rep. (1943–74); opponent of FEPC appropriations (1944).

Flaherty, John J., Lt., naval officer representing U.S. Army Engineers in labor matters, Region VII, WMC (1945); in negotiations to reduce discrimination at Tenn. Eastman Corp., contractor for top-secret Manhattan Project.

Fleming, G[eorge]. James (1904–90), black political scientist from Phila.; edited traditionally Republican black newspaper *Phila. Tribune;* member, Gunnar Myrdahl's research group on race in America; headed first Chicago field office of FEPC (opened 1941); FEPC field rep., El Paso (1942), of discrimination against Chicanos in copper mines of N.Mex., Ariz.; examiner in charge, Detroit office, FEPC (1943); dir., Region III (Phila.), FEPC (Sept. 1943–Nov. 1945). Important in negotiations with PTC that led to Phila. transit strike (1944). Became race relations secy., American Friends Service Committee (Nov. 1945). Editor, *Amsterdam News;* prof., Morgan State Coll. PhD (poli. sci.), U. Penn (1948); diss.: "The Administration of Fair Employment Practice Programs." Born in Virgin Islands.

Flemming, Arthur S. (1905–96), chief of labor supply, OPM; member, WMC (WWII); member, CSC (1939–48); consulted by FEPC on policies on hiring of Japanese Americans at naval establishments. Pres., Ohio Wesleyan U. (1948–51); dir., ODM (1953–58); secy., HEW (1958–60).

Ford, Aaron L. (1903–83) (D-Miss.), U.S. rep. (1935–43); gen. counsel, Smith Committee (Special Committee to Investigate Exec. Agencies) (1944); responded to FEPC query on lawyer mistakenly assumed to be part of committee's investigations.

Foster, Lemuel Lewis (1890–1981), race relations specialist, Army Service Forces; in discussion on FEPC Capital Transit case (1945); exec. secy., Atlanta Urban League; supervisor, Div. of Negro Economics, Dept. of Labor; race relations officer, Federal Works Admin.; exec., R. H. Macy and Co. (1945–49); independent consultant on race relations (1949–). Born in Miss. Graduate of Fisk U.

Furfey, Paul Hanly, Fr. (1896–1992), Irish Catholic sociologist; prominent member, sociology dept., Catholic U. of America (1925–66), chair (1934–64); prolific writer in sociology; member, board of D.C. Urban League; cofounder, Fides Neighborhood House, Il Poverello

House, experiments in interracial living, D.C.; recommended by Mitchell for position as hearing commissioner for FEPC (1944). Born in Mass.

Gagliardo, Domenico, Maj. (1895–1955); prominent labor economist, U. of Kans.; chief labor officer, Quartermaster Corps (1945); questioned FEPC policy on elimination of race, religious specifications on contractors' employment forms.

Gallup, E. H., Capt. (later, Maj.), rep. of Army Ordnance Dept. during efforts to settle strikes at Jones and Laughlin Steel (1943) and Carnegie-Illinois Steel Corp., Clairton, Pa. (1944).

Gardner, Julius M., of Region IV, WMC; in investigations of Baltimore and Potomac Telephone Co. (1942), negotiations at Bethlehem Steel and Shipbuilding Corporation–Sparrows Point, Md. (1943).

Garrett, Sylvester (1911–96), of Pa., labor arbitrator. As chair of Phila. Regional Office, of WLB (1942–45), in meetings related to 1944 and certified that case for natl. action to NWLB chair, William H. Davis.

Gartland, Joseph Francis (1880–1949), chief of Operations Board, Post Office Dept.; dir. of budget and administrative planning, Post Office Dept.; in negotiations to resolve FEPC complaints against various post offices (1944–45).

Gee, Raymond L., FEPC complainant, witness at Boilermakers hearings, Portland, Ore. (Nov. 1943).

Gibson, Harry H. C. (1913–98), black atty. from Chicago; brother of Truman K. Gibson Jr.; member, exec. committee, Chicago branch, NAACP; examiner assisting Elmer Henderson in FEPC's Chicago Office, 1944–45; active on telephone company cases, 1945.

Gibson, John Strickland (1893–1960), lawyer; U.S. rep. (D-Ga.), 1941–47; opponent of FEPC.

Gibson, Truman Kella, Jr. (1912–), black lawyer; member, exec. committee, Chicago branch, NAACP; acting civilian aide to secy. of war (1943–45); handled FEPC complaints brought to attention of War Dept.; criticized by Mitchell for obstructing some FEPC initiatives; member, Truman's Advisory Committee on Universal Military Training (1946); won Medal of Merit Award for Civilians (1947); boxing mgr., promoter, dir., secy., Joe Louis Enterprises; returned to private practice, Chicago (1960s).

Gifford, Walter Sherman (1885–1966), business exec.; asst. secy., asst. treas., Western Electric (1905–8); exec., AT&T (1911–50), exec. vice pres., then pres., chair of board (1948–50); in FEPC negotiations on Western Electric (1943). U.S. ambassador to Great Britain (1950–53). Born in Mass.; educated Harvard.

Gohr, William K. (1901–1987), German American aeronautical engineer, designer, St. Louis; removed from employment by army or navy contractors by order of the Army Air Corps (1943). Case appealed to Industrial Employment Review Board, FEPC. Came to U.S. (1925); naturalized (1931).

Golightly, Cornelius L. (1917–76); instructor, Howard U. (1942–43); compliance analyst, FEPC (Oct. 1943–Sept. 1945); sought commission in U.S. Naval Reserve (1944), but blocked by racial quotas. Prof., philosophy, U. of Wis., Wayne State; member (1970–76), pres. (1973–76), Detroit School Board. Born in Miss.; PhD, U. of Mich.

Goodwin, Robert C[lifford]. (1906–99), dir., Region V (Cleveland), WMC (1942–45); exec. dir., WMC (Feb.–Sept. 1945); dir., USES (1945–48); FEPC conferred with him on prevention of discrimination by USES after its return to state control. Administrator, BES (1949–69); exec. dir., Defense Manpower Admin. (1950–53); associate manpower administrator for unemployment insurance, DMA (1969–70s). Born in Ind.

Goott, Daniel D. (1919–), of New York; associate chief, NLRB (1942–43); as member of WPB, contacted Mitchell about negotiations on separate restrooms at Western Electric's Point Breeze plant. Later held many govt. posts, esp. for State Dept.

Goulard, Everett M[aurice]., Maj. (1913–94), staff member, Ordnance Branch, War Dept. (1941–46); in FEPC meeting with War Dept. personnel on cases in St. Louis (1945); in

FEPC's case against Norris Stamping Co.; later, vice pres. of personnel, Pan American Airlines. LLB, Harvard (1937).

Gow, Ralph F., Col., Army Service Forces; contacted on Shell Oil case; reported on FEPC case against Consolidated Vultee Aircraft.

Graham, Frank Porter, Dr. (1886–1972) (D-N.C.), Southern white liberal; first chair, Southern Conference for Human Welfare (1938–48); candidate for chair, FEPC (1943); public member, WLB; wrote WLB ruling in Southport case that as wartime labor policy no employer under board jurisdiction could pay different wage rates to black and white employees for same work; member, Truman's Committee on Civil Rights; U.S. sen. (1949–50); pres., U. of N.C., Chapel Hill (1930–49); UN mediator (1950?–67).

Graham, Walter K., Capt., Gulf region labor rep., U.S. Maritime Commission; investigated racial conflict at Ala. Dry Dock (1943); said use of black manpower was necessary for yard; attended FEPC meeting on region's shipbuilding companies (Dec. 1944).

Grant, David M. (1903–85), black lawyer, civil rights leader, local Democratic Party leader, St. Louis; organized first black picket against economic injustice, against local Woolworth store, continued to organize such pickets against other discriminating firms (1931); a leader of St. Louis March on Washington Movement (1942–45); gathered evidence on discrimination in employment, esp. against black women, and requested FEPC hearings in St. Louis; leader, Interracial Council of St. Louis; challenged Jim Crow in interstate transportation (1946); lawyer for NAACP on desegregation cases. Attended U. of Mich., Howard U. Law School.

Green, John (1896–1957), pres., IUMSWA (1935–51); board member, Natl. Council for a Permanent FEPC; founding member, Americans for ADA; FEPC conferred with him on FEPC complaints against Todd Johnson Dry Docks Co., New Orleans (1945).

Green, William (1873–1952), Ohio leader of UMW (1913–24) and AFL, pres. (1924–52); member, FEPC, many other New Deal, WWII boards.

Greenbaum, Edward Samuel, Brig. Gen. (1890–1970); exec. asst., Office of the Under Secy. of War (1940–45); in negotiation of FEPC cases in St. Louis (1945).

Greenblat, Mildred R., psychologist, N.J. Dept. of Institutions and Agencies (1934–42); field examiner, FEPC, New York, then Phila. office (1943–45). BS, Syracuse U.

Grew, Joseph (1880–1965), ambassador to Japan (1932–42); special asst. to secy. of state Cordell Hull (1942–44), heading Far Eastern Div.; undersecy. of state (1944–45); acting secy. of state (Jan.–Aug. 1945). FEPC obtained information from him on employment of Japanese Americans (1944).

Grinnage, Willard T., examiner Region III (Phila.), FEPC (1944–Aug. 1945).

Griser, J[ohn]. M[illen]. (1896–1957), of Mobile; vice pres., gen. mgr., Ala. Dry Dock Co. (1943); later, pres.

Guy, Moses, black member, grievance committee, IBEW, Local 48; initiated proposal that black welders blocked from admission to Boilermakers' union be admitted to IBEW instead. Plan opposed by SNOV, local organization of black shipbuilders, for fear it would harm efforts to force Boilermakers to change their discriminatory policies.

Haas, Francis J., Monsignor (1889–1953), labor mediator; dean, School of Social Sciences, Catholic U.; supporter of New Deal, held various New Deal posts; chair, FEPC (1943); resigned when appointed bishop of Grand Rapids (Oct. 1943); appointed to Truman's Committee on Civil Rights (1946), signed 1947 report *To Secure These Rights*. Born, educated, ordained in Wis. PhD, Catholic U. (1922).

Hambrook, Richard Edward (1899–1968), of San Francisco; as vice pres., gen. mgr., Pacific Telephone and Telegraph Co., praised Harry Kingman's approach in negotiating FEPC complaints against his firm (1943); later, the company's exec. vice pres. (1954–68).

Haneke, August B. (1894–1971), of Baltimore, vice pres., gen. mgr., Chesapeake and Potomac

Telephone Co.; reported on progress of black hiring (1943); opposed FEPC attempts to compel hiring of black telephone operators; pres., Baltimore Transit Co. (1948–52).

Hannegan, Robert E[mmet]. (1903–49) (D-Mo.), local party leader, Truman supporter; commissioner, IRS (1943); chair, Democratic Natl. Committee (1944); postmaster gen. (1945–47).

Hardin, Walter T., black organizer for UAW-CIO; former member, IWW and Communist Party; considered an esp. effective speaker; spoke at Urban League conference (1943). Born in Tenn.

Hare, Butler B. (1875–1967) (D-S.C.), U.S. rep. (1925–33, 1939–47); opposed FEPC appropriations (1944).

Harris, Ray Guy (1891–1971), of Tex.; brig. gen., Army Air Force, commander, Midwestern Dist., Army Air Force Air Training Service Command (1942–45); in settlement of Consolidated Vultee case with FEPC (1945).

Harrison, Marvin C., prominent Cleveland lawyer; former Ohio state sen.; trial atty. for many labor unions; FEPC special counsel, Boilermakers hearings, Portland, Ore. (Nov. 1943).

Harrison, William Henry, Maj. Gen. (1892–1956), communications engineer, telephone company exec.; vice pres., chief engineer, AT&T, NYC (1938–45); vice pres., dept. of operational engineering (1945–48); pres. and dir. (1948–56); dir. of subsidiary companies, OPM (1941–42); dir. of production, WPB (1942); dir. of procurement and distribution service, Office of Chief Signal Officer (1943–45); in settlement of FEPC's General Cable case (1945). Born in Brooklyn.

Hastie, William Henry (1904–76), chair, Natl. Legal Committee, NAACP; asst. solicitor, Dept. of Interior (1933–37); helped draft Organic Act for Restructuring of Governance of Virgin Islands (1936); federal judge, U.S. Dist. Court, Virgin Islands (1937–39); prof., dean, Harvard Law School (1939–45); civilian aide on Negro affairs to secy. of war (1940–43); governor, Virgin Islands (1946); appointed to U.S. Court of Appeals, 3rd Circuit (1949); chief justice (1968–76). B.A., German and mathematics, Amherst Coll. (1925); LLB, Harvard Law School (1930).

Hawkins, L[ayton]. S., Dr. (1877–1960), dir. of war training, WMC; chief of vocational training for war production workers, U.S. Office of Education; FEPC conferred with him on discrimination against blacks in such training (1944).

Hay, Charles M. (d. 1945), gen. counsel, Legal Service, WMC (July 1943–Aug. 1944); dep. chair, exec. dir., WMC (June 1944–Jan. 1945).

Hayes, Philip, Maj. Gen. (1887–1949), career military officer; commanding gen., 3rd Service Command, Army Service Forces (1943–46); rep., War Dept., during Phila. transit strike (1944); called for full resumption of work; when that failed, called for federal troops.

Healey, Joseph P., chair, governor's Commission on Interracial Cooperation, Md.; board member, Md. Trust Co., Baltimore Transit Co.; unsuccessful as mediator in attempts to integrate the Chesapeake and Potomac Telephone Co.

Hein, Herbert R., Adm., chief of staff, 12th Naval Dist. (1945); issued statement on loyalty of returning Japanese American veterans, urged naval personnel to restrain from molesting them.

Henderson, Elmer W. (1913–2001), research dir., Ill. State Commission on Urban Colored Population (1940–41); acting exec. secy., Chicago NAACP Branch (Apr.–Sept. 1941); field rep., FEPC (Nov. 1941–Aug. 1943); personally challenged railroad segregation during trip South, leading to major court case (1942); dir., Regions VI, VIII (Chicago), FEPC (Aug. 1943–May 1946); research associate, Rosenwald Foundation Study on Segregation in the Nation's Capital (Jan.–July 1947); exec. secy., Natl. Council for a Permanent FEPC (1947–48); lobbyist, exec. dir., American Council on Human Rights (1948–55); counsel,

House Committee on Operations, D.C. Regarded as particularly effective negotiator, lobbyist. Recruited Mitchell to work with FEPC. BA, Morgan State U.; MA, U. of Chicago (1939); LLD, Georgetown (1952).

Hennighausen, H[arry]. G[eibel]. (1913–1981), replaced V. L. Dorsey as leader of Point Breeze Employees' Assoc. (1943–44), which sought segregated bathroom, locker facilities at Western Electric's Point Breeze plant.

Herrell, Russell H. (ca. 1895–?), dir. of personnel, administrative asst. to public printer, GPO; handled charges of discrimination at GPO.

Herzog, Paul M. (1906–86), chair, N.Y. State Labor Relations Board (1942–44); lt., staff member, labor relations office, Navy Dept. (1945); in negotiations with FPEC on Norris Stamping and Mfg. Co. case; chair, NLRB (1945–53); referred NAACP views on provisions of Taft-Hartley Act to NLRB (1949).

Hill, T. Arnold (1888–1947), black special asst. to administrator on racial matters, OPA (1943); FEPC conferred with him on OPA policy on discrimination.

Hillman, Sidney (1887–1946), Jewish labor leader; pres., Amalgamated Clothing Workers Union; member, OPM, WPB, various other New Deal and wartime boards; labor adviser to FDR (1943–); wrote to General Tire and Engineering Co., Wright Automatic Tobacco Packing Machinery Co. on their employment policies. Born in Lithuania.

Hobbs, Samuel Francis (1887–1952) (D-Ala.), U.S. rep. (1935–51); opposed FEPC appropriations (1944).

Hobdy, R. Roland, black employee of Ala. Dry Dock; testified to FEPC on racial conflict at yard; falsely rumored to have been killed in that incident.

Hoffman, Clare E. (1875–1967), Mich. lawyer; U.S. rep. (R-Mich.), 1935–63; opponent of FEPC.

Hoglund, Roy A. (ca. 1898–1962?), of Kans., white high school principal (1926–32), supt. of schools (1932–40); dir. of student work, state dir., NYA (1940–43); dir., Regions IX (Kansas City) (1943–45), (St. Louis) (1946), FEPC.

Hollander, Sidney (1881–1972), Jewish pharmaceutical manufacturer in Baltimore; pres., Md. Pharmaceutical Co., Rem Co. (1900–56); pres., Natl. Council of Jewish Federations and Welfare Funds (1938–46); board member, Urban League (1945–72); active on boards of many community relations, social welfare organizations; candidate for member, FEPC (1943), but not appointed; board member, Natl. Council for a Permanent FEPC.

Hook, Frank E. (1893–1982), U.S. rep., (D-Mich.), 1935–43, 1945–47; dir., Region IV (D.C.), FEPC (Nov. 1943–Apr. 1944); resigned to seek reelection to Congress.

Hoover, J. Edgar (1895–1972), Justice Dept. clerk, asst. to atty. gen. (1915–21); asst. dir., Bureau of Investigation (1924); dir. (1925); established natl. fingerprint file (1925); established FBI (1935), remained its head until 1972. Periodically leveled charges against black leaders and their allies as subversives, Communists, or fellow-travelers.

Hope, John, II (1909–?), black economist from Atlanta; economics instructor, Morehouse Coll., Spelman Coll., Atlanta U.; FEPC examiner, Region VII (Atlanta) (1943–45); later, member, Race Relations Inst., Fisk U.; wrote *Equality of Opportunity: A Union Approach to Fair Employment* (1956) (on the Packinghouse Workers Union), *Minority Access to Federal Grants in Aid: The Gap between Policy and Performance* (1976). In Office of Civil Rights; member, President's Committee for Equal Employment Opportunity (1960s–70s). BA, Morehouse.; MA, Brown. Son of John Hope (1868–1936), pres., Morehouse Coll., Atlanta U.

Horn, Charles L[illey]. (1888–1978), Minneapolis lawyer; pres., Federal Cartridge Corp. (1921–75), chair of board (1975–78); operated Twin Cities Ordnance plant, for which he hired many blacks; member, second FEPC (1944–46); member, natl. committee, Urban League. His progressive employment policies set a new pattern for employment of blacks in Minneapolis area. Born in Iowa.

Hosford (Hossford), William, F[uller]. (1882–1958), vice pres., Western Electric (1928–58); in FEPC negotiations with his firm; considered candidate for FEPC, but not appointed. Born in W. Chicago, Ill.

Houston, Charles Hamilton (1895–1950), black D.C. lawyer; partner with father and William Hastie, then Joseph Waddy; dean, Howard U. Law School; created NAACP legal dept.; special counsel, NAACP (1925–40); member, NAACP Legal Committee (1940–50); member, NAACP Natl. Board, NAACP Natl. Labor Committee; gen. counsel, Assoc. of Railway Employees; resigned as FEPC special counsel for railroad cases after hearings were postponed (1943); reappointed, served when FEPC hearings rescheduled for Sept. 15–18, 1943; member, FEPC (Mar. 1944–Dec. 1945); resigned after Truman blocked FEPC action against Capital Transit Co. BA, Amherst; LLB, Harvard.

Houston, Theophilis J. (b. ca. 1890), black D.C. lawyer; FEPC examiner, central office and Region IV (D.C.) (1943–45). Born in Ind.

Hovde, Frederick Lawson (1908–83), exec. asst. to chair, Natl. Defense Research Committee (1942–43), chief of div. III (1943–45); pres., Purdue U. (1946–71). Mitchell reported (1943) that because Hovde's agency (NDRC) conducted secret, technical military-related research for army, navy, it was hard to tell whether his agency was following FEPC employment guidelines.

Howell, Clark, Dr. (1894–1966), of Atlanta; pres., publisher, *Atlanta Constitution* (1936–66); dir., Associated Press (1936–42); adjutant gen. of Ga. (1943–44); candidate for FEPC (1943).

Hubbard, Maceo W. (1898–1991), black lawyer, Phila. (1927–42); sr. field rep. (1942), hearings examiner, Legal Div. (Jan. 1943–Jan. 1946); acting dir., Legal Div., FEPC (Apr. 1945–Jan. 1946); appointed special asst., U.S. atty. gen. (1946); member, Civil Rights Div., Justice Dept. (–late 1970s). Born in Ga. Degrees from Lincoln U. (Pa.) (1922), Harvard (1926).

Huff, Theodore, placement supervisor, Portland office, USES (1943). Gave information to FEPC on employment policies of Kaiser shipyards (1943); referred blacks to Vancouver, Wash., yard only after repeated efforts to end discrimination by Boilermakers in other yards failed.

Hughes, Charles Evans (1862–1948), associate justice, U.S. Supreme Court (1910–16); secy. of state (1921–25); chief justice, Supreme Court (1930–41). Moderately conservative, he often was swing vote in court rulings on constitutionality of New Deal legislation; views quoted in FEPC text on presidential power.

Hunt, A. Bruce (ca. 1908–?), white lawyer from Va.; reviewer, then trial examiner, NLRB (1939–43); disputes dir., West Coast Region, NWLB (1943); FEPC field investigator of copper industry cases in Southwest on discrimination against Chicanos; FEPC trial atty. assigned to hearings on Southwest cases (1944); dir., Region VII (Atlanta), FEPC (1944); perceived as militant, ordered to leave by Atlanta City Council; returned to FEPC legal div. as hearings examiner, Western counsel (Nov. 1944); worked on important cases in L.A., Southwest.

Ivey, Clarence E. (1890–1964), black porter, part-time asst. personnel mgr., Kaiser Co.; gave Mitchell information on firm (Oct. 1943); told USES that black workers were no longer interested in placement as sheet-metal worker's helper; testified for company at rehearing (1944).

Jackson, Lillie Mae Carroll (1889–1975), mother of Juanita Jackson Mitchell, wife of Clarence Mitchell Jr.; pres., Baltimore NAACP Branch (1935–70); led struggles along with Juanita, a lawyer, that desegregated Md., including public parks, schools, beaches, swimming pools.

James, Harold, of San Francisco; FEPC examiner, Region XII (1944–45); examiner in charge, Cincinnati office, FEPC (1945); previously employed by USDA and War Relocation Authority; resigned May 1945 to take job with UNRRA.

Jeter, Sinclair V., administrative officer, Central Office, FEPC (1943–45). Discussed impact of budget cuts with Mitchell, other FEPC staff members planning for Chicago hearing in 1945.

Joerg, Robert E., Lt. Col., commander of Ala. State Guard during racial incident at Ala. Dry Dock shipyard in Mobile, May 1943; spoke to black workers urging them to return to their jobs under guarantees of protection from violence.

Johnson, Clarence R. (1903–83), black Californian; field rep., minorities consultant, Negro Employment and Training Branch, Labor Div., WMC, L.A. (Region XII); cooperated with, gave information to FEPC on Boilermakers cases (1942), Consolidated Steel Corp.'s Shipbuilding Div. (1943).

Johnson, George M. (1900–?), black lawyer, law prof. from Calif.; member, NAACP Natl. Legal Committee; asst. exec. secy., FEPC (Oct. 1941–July 9, 1943); dep. chair, FEPC (July 13, 1943–Feb. 1946); acting gen. counsel, dir., FEPC Legal Div. (1943–45); assoc. prof., Howard U. Law School, later dean (1946–58); later human rights commissioner; vice-chancellor, U. of Nigeria. AB, LLB, JSD, U. of Calif., Berkeley.

Johnson, Reginald A., worked with Mitchell for Negro Manpower Service of OPM; replaced him as regional rep. in Phila. office (1942); minorities rep., WMC, Phila. (1943); provided information about grievances at Jones and Laughlin Steel plant (1943). Resigned in protest over the attitudes of regional WMC toward strengthening its minority group efforts (Sept. 1943).

Jones, Madison S[umner]., Jr. (ca. 1910–?), youth dir., NAACP (1940–43); examiner, New York office, FEPC (1944–45), working primarily on Region I (New England) cases; negotiated with New York office of Remington Arms Co. to adjust FEPC complaints against Kansas City plant; negotiated agreement with New England Telephone Co. for hiring blacks (1945); administrative asst., NAACP natl. office; assisted in negotiations with AT&T on discrimination complaints against telephone companies (1948); assisted with effort to desegregate restaurants in D.C. (1950). BA, St. John's U.

Jones, Robert G. (ca. 1905–?), black staff member, USES (1937–43); field examiner, New York office, FEPC (1942–43); rehired, served until Aug. 1945; facilitated negotiations in Natl. Carbon Co. case (1945).

Jones, Theodore A. (1912–2001), black CPA in Chicago; administrative mgr. (1942–43); dir. of budget, administrative mgmt., FEPC (1943–45); partner in T. A. Jones and Co. (later Jones, Anderson); regional dir., Office of Economic Opportunity (1966–67); pres., Chicago branch, NAACP; member, NAACP natl. board. Educated U. of Ill.

Kadish, Frank (ca. 1915–?), of LA; one of eight white members of Boilermakers Local 92 who met with Mitchell, regional FEPC officials in 1943 to express opposition to union's policy of requiring blacks to join auxiliary unions. Born in Ill. of Lithuanian-Jewish descent.

Kahn, Alice R., of N.Y., Mass.; junior fair-practice examiner, FEPC Region IV (1943–44); internship with Natl. Inst, of Public Affairs, D.C. Poli. sci. degree, Smith Coll.

Kaiser, Edgar F. (1908–81), vice pres., gen. mgr., Ore. Shipbuilding Corp., Kaiser Co., Portland, Ore., Vancouver, Wash. (1941–45); during the war his firm imported many workers from New York, other eastern cities. Submission of whites-only employment orders, supposedly in deference to segregated unions, and failure to keep training and upgrading promises made to black workers brought about formation of Shipyard Negroes Organization for Victory and complaints to FEPC. Testified for his firm at FEPC hearings in Portland, Nov. 1943. Pres., dir., Kaiser Motors Corp. (1945–56); pres. Kaiser Industries Corp. (1956–67); chairman, dir. of the various affiliated Kaiser companies. Medal of Freedom (1969) as backer of low-, moderate-income housing programs, various labor-mgmt. innovations. Son of Henry J. Kaiser, founder of Kaiser companies.

Kaiser, Henry J. (1882–1967), founder of Kaiser Industries; arranged meeting to deal with concerns over his importation of black workers into Portland as part of his recruitment efforts for company shipyards in area.

Kasper, Sydney H. (ca. 1912–2000), writer; editor, public affairs officer with several govt. agencies; as editor, *Employment Security Review,* sought information for article on FEPC (1943). PhB, U. of Chicago.

Keck, Richard M., Maj., staff member, Ordnance Branch, War Dept.; in settlement of FEPC cases with military contractors in St. Louis.

Keenan, Edward Louis, Jr. (1911–?), regional rep., BES, for Ohio, Mich., Ky. (1937–42); acting chairman, Regional Labor Supply Committee, WPB, Region V (Cleveland) (1942), where he helped form Cleveland Metropolitan Council for FEPC; dep. regional dir., WMC, Region V (1942–43); Ohio state dir., WMC (1943–45); dir., WMC, Region V (1945); dep. dir., USES (1945–48); dep. dir., BES, Dept. of Labor (1949–58); asst. exec. dir., ODM (1951), involved with full use of black labor during WWII, Korean War, esp. by Capital Transit Co. Continued to hold similar manpower posts through the 1970s. Born in N.J.; graduated Temple U. (1933).

Keenan, Joseph Daniel (1896–1988), Chicago leader of IBEW-AFL; labor adviser, OPM (1940–41); associate dir., Labor Production Board (1942); vice chairman, Office of Labor Production, WPB (1943–45); aided in reorganization of German labor movement in War Manpower Div., Germany (1945–48); special asst. for labor, Office of Defense Mobilization (1953–58); intl. secy., IBEW (1954–at least 1974); vice pres., AFL-CIO. FEPC wrote him on employment discrimination in Ind., enlisted his assistance in negotiations with Boilermakers Union.

Keller, George M., Capt., head of personnel relations branch, shore establishments, civilian personnel div., Navy Dept.; involved in enforcement of nondiscrimination clauses in military contract with Mingledorff Shipbuilding Co., Savannah (1945); contacted for assistance on settlement of case at Shell Oil; sent letter pledging naval cooperation in case against Norris Stamping Co.

Kelly (Kelley), Edward J[oseph]. (1876–1950), mayor of Chicago (1933–47) who pledged cooperation with FEPC.

Kingman, Harry Lees (1892–1982), briefly played baseball for New York Yankees (1914–16), coached freshman baseball for U. of Calif., Berkeley; headed Stiles Hall, an off-campus university YMCA that worked actively for free speech, civil rights, student participation; served in China for six years (1921–27) for Intl. YMCA, sent informal newsletters on events in China to various prominent officials; headed the West Coast office (Region XII), FEPC (1943–45). Mitchell considered him most effective of FEPC regional leaders; campaigned for state FEPC legislation in Calif.; after retirement (1956), came at Mitchell's urging to D.C., where with wife, Ruth, created Citizens Committee for Freedom and Fair Play, under which they personally lobbied for civil rights, integration, cooperative housing, statehood for Alaska and Hawaii, representation of relations with China, world peace (1957–70); helped Mitchell develop solid relationship with Sen. William Knowland (R-Calif.); active with Leadership Conference on Civil Rights; campaigned for John F. Kennedy; opposed Vietnam War; lobbied for passage of Federal Fair Housing Law. Born in China to Congregational missionary family; educated in Claremont, Calif.

Kingsley, [John] Donald (1908–72), asst. regional dir., WMC (1942–44); dep. exec. dir., WMC (Apr.–Sept. 1945); WMC liaison with FEPC; in conferences with FEPC officials (1945); held many internationally oriented public jobs after WWII.

Kirk, Norman Thomas, Maj. Gen. (1888–1960), of Md.; surgeon gen., U.S. Army (1943–47); conferred on FEPC case about employment of black nurse; criticized "pressing" attitude of FEPC examiner Edward Rutledge.

Knapp, Gerald C. (1905–81), mgr., Portland USES; sought to confirm Kaiser company statements that particular black workers were not interested in the sheet metal worker's helper positions they had previously requested.

Knight, Orie Albert (1902–1981), pres., OWIU, CIO (later Oil, Chemical and Atomic Workers Intl. Union, AFL-CIO); labor member, NWLB; vice pres., CIO (1947–), merged AFL-CIO (1955–); retired (1965); assisted in settlement of Shell Oil case, FEPC (1945).

Knudsen, William Signius (1879–1948), Danish-born automobile exec.; pres., General Motors (1933–42); dir. of production, office of undersecy. of war (1942–44); dir., Army Air Force Material and Service (1944–45).

Koeval, Joseph Karl (1908–74), of McKeesport, Pa.; organizer, United Steel Workers Union; Pittsburgh rep., Labor Production Div., WPB; in efforts to settle strike at Jones and Laughlin Steel Plant, Aliquippa, Pa. (Sept. 1943).

Korn, Fred G. (ca. 1905–?), German-born FEPC complainant who contended he was dismissed from Portsmouth Navy Yard because of natl. origin. Navy Dept. contended he was dismissed because of substantial evidence of disloyalty.

La Vista, Frank W. (1893–1963), of N.Y.; aviation pioneer, aeronautical engineer, aircraft exec.; lt. col., Army Air Force, WWII; resident rep. for AAF at Lockland plant, Wright Aeronautical Corp., Cincinnati; assisted in settlement of strike at company (1944). Aeronautics instructor, Brooklyn Technical H.S. (1932–41), returned as dept. chairman (1945–47) before resuming career as an aircraft exec., Farmingdale, Long Island (1947–57).

Lancaster, Rufus Garrison (1902–75), Phila. porter for Phila. Transit Co. whose upgrading as one of eight blacks training as street car operators precipitated Phila. transit strike (Aug. 1944); one of three trainees interviewed by FEPC on background to strike.

Land, Emory Scott (1889–1971), Adm., chief of the Bureau of Construction and Repair (1932–37), asst. chief, Bureau of Aeronautics, Dept. of Navy (1937–38); commander, U.S. Maritime Commission; chairman, Maritime Commission (1938–46); active in planning govt. response in Bethlehem Steel and Shipbuilding Corporation–Sparrows Point case (1943); FEPC complaints against maritime unions referred to him (1944); as chairman of WSA, refused (1945), despite NAACP protests, to reinstate Frank Pollatsek, dismissed for promoting social equality through nonsegregation of crews.

Landes, Ruth Schlossberg, Dr. (1908–91), social worker, anthropologist with extensive field work studying Garvey movement in Harlem and its relationship to group of black Jews, Ojibwa nation in Ontario, race relations in Brazil; daughter of Joseph Schlossberg, cofounder, longtime secy.-treas. of Amalgamated Clothing Workers of America; field rep., consultant, FEPC (1941–45); conducted investigations in Southwest in preparation for 1944 FEPC hearings; wrote many works in anthropology on Native Americans, race relations, Latin Americans in Southwest, anthropology of education; prof., McMasters U., Ontario (1965–91). Born in N.Y.; PhD, Columbia.

Lane, Layle (1893–1976), teacher, union leader, activist; a leader of March on Washington Movement, NYC; supporter of complainant in an FEPC case.

Lasseter (Lassiter), Dillard B. (1894–1993?), dir., Region IV, WMC (Atlanta) (1943–46); administrator, FSA (1946–53); encouraged cooperation with FEPC; active in efforts to limit discrimination practices by USES and to obtain USES data on minority employment for FEPC.

Lauerman, F[rank]. A[lbert]. (1894–1979), dir. of industrial relations, Consolidated Vultee Aircraft, San Diego; contact person for FEPC complaints against the firm.

Lautier, Louis R. (1896–1962), asst. to the civilian aide to secy. of war; in conferences with FEPC; gave FEPC information on discrimination by USES in New Orleans (1943); War Dept. rep. during Phila. transit strike; D.C. rep. of NNPA; reporter for *Atlanta Daily World;*

sought access to Capitol Press Galleries; first black to obtain such credentials (1947); criticized Mitchell's refusal to speak no more than five minutes at a congress. committee hearing on Taft-Hartley Act repeal.

Lawson, Edward H[oward]. (1913–?), editor, *Opportunity: The Journal of Negro Life,* a publication of the Natl. Urban League (1938–41); special asst. to administrator, WPA (1936–38); field rep. for WMC, WPB, OPM (1941–43); dir., Regions I, II (New England, N.Y., operating primarily out of NYC), FEPC (1943–45); chief of the minorities section, UN, NYC (1946–64); dep. dir., Div. of Human Rights, Office for Political and General Assembly Affairs, UN (1964–at least 1975). Born in Md.; BA, Rutgers U. (1933).

Lawson, Marjorie McKenzie (1912–2002), lawyer, judge; wife, law partner of civil rights lawyer Belford V. Lawson; compliance analyst, asst. dir., Div. of Review and Analysis, FEPC (Oct. 1942–Oct. 1945), dir. (1945–46); primary editor, FEPC's *Final Report;* vice pres., gen. counsel, Natl. Council of Negro Women; first black woman appointed federal judge, for D.C. (1965); member of President's Committee for Equal Employment Opportunity. Educated U. of Mich., Terrell Law School; JD, Columbia U. Law School (1950).

LeFlore, John L., Sr. (1903–76), exec. secy., Mobile branch, NAACP (1925–56); chairman, southern conference of NAACP branches; active in investigation of Ala. Drydock incident (1943), handled by Mitchell for FEPC; longtime post office employee disciplined for involvement in civil rights activities, eventually forced into early retirement; brought post office discrimination issues in Mobile to attention of D.C. bureau, NAACP (1953).

Leiserson, William (1883–1957), economist, labor relations consultant, arbitrator who held many govt. posts; chair, Natl. Mediation Board (1934–39, 1943–44); member, NLRB (1939–43); in case against Ore. Shipbuilding Corp., Kaiser Co.

Leland, Wilfred C., Jr. (ca. 1869–1958), son of Wilfred C. Leland, founder along with father, Harry Leland, of Cadillac and Lincoln Motor Cos.; inventor of eight-cylinder engine; staff member, office of civilian personnel, War Dept. (1943); consultant on program planning, FEPC (Sept. 1943–Dec. 1945); secy. and/or exec. dir., Minneapolis FEPC; proposed candidate for Committee on Govt. Contract Compliance (1952).

Levine, Lewis (1889–1980), of WMC, NYC stock brokerage exec., member, board of arbitration.

Lingham, Estelle L. (1906–?), college graduate of African American, American Indian descent from R.I., whose complaints to Eleanor Roosevelt, Paul McNutt, and Civil Service Commission on employment discrimination following her training course in mapmaking were referred to FEPC. Sought, ultimately received employment in Alaskan branch of Dept. of Interior.

Lotwin, Bernice, asst. gen. counsel, Legal Service, WMC (1944); acting gen. counsel (Aug. 1944–Sept. 1945); attended conference with FEPC on priority referral system; wife of Bernard Bernstein, prominent lawyer for several federal agencies, including HEW.

Luikart, Fordyce W[hitney]. (1910–2001), associate dir., U.S. Civil Service Commission, Cleveland, where he cooperated with FEPC Region V; appointed chief of investigations div. of CSC, D.C.

MacGowan, Charles J. (1887–1960), pres. of IBBISBH (1944–54); although previously had defended necessity of black union auxiliaries at AFL conventions, assisted in settlement of FEPC cases against Boilermakers union locals (1944–45).

MacLean, Malcolm S., Dr. (1894–1977), of Va.; white liberal; pres., Hampton Inst.; second chairman, FEPC (1942–43).

Mahon, William D. (1861–1949), former street car driver, union organizer in Columbus, Ohio; pres. for 53 years of Amalgamated Assoc. of Street, Electric Railway, and Motor Coach Employees of America; interceded unsuccessfully in Capital Transit case to discourage discrimination in hiring blacks for platform positions (1942).

Manly, Milo A. (1903–91), of Phila.; former Phila. parole officer, investigator, supervisor with the Pa. Dept. of Public Assistance; appointed examiner, FEPC Region III (1943), later examiner in charge, Pittsburgh suboffice; played major role in negotiating settlement of work stoppage at Clairton Byproducts plant of Carnegie-Illinois Steel Corp.; field dir., Natl. Council for a Permanent FEPC (1947–48).

Marks, Wilbourne A. (ca. 1919–?), black worker in Portland, Ore.; reported to USES that when he sought position as burner at Boilermakers Union Local 72, was queried about his race, informed he could only be hired at Vancouver, Wash., shipyard. Born in La.

Maslow, Will (1907–), white lawyer; Mitchell's superior as FEPC's dir. of field operations (July 1943–June 1945); formerly principal trial examiner of NLRB; later gen. counsel, dir. of Commission on Law and Social Action; finally exec. dir. of American Jewish Congress (1960–72); in conference with Lewis B. Schwellenbach, secy. of labor, on nondiscrimination by USES offices. Born in Kiev, Ukraine.

McDonald, Ed, dir., Region IX, WMC.

McGee, Vernon A., dep. exec. dir., WMC (1944–45); conferred with FEPC officials on cooperation between the two agencies.

McGillicuddy, Neale, intl. organizer of UEW-CIO, Local 252, Remington Arms Co., Bridgeport, Conn.; complained to FEPC on discriminatory layoffs by Remington (1944).

McGranery, James Patrick (1895–1962) (D-Pa.), U.S. rep. (1937–43); asst. to U.S. atty. gen. (1943–46). Consulted on advisability of govt. participation in radio broadcast with strikers during Phila. transit strike (Aug. 1944). U.S. dist. judge, eastern dist. of Pa. (1946–52); U.S. atty. gen. (1952–53).

McKay, George Danner, of Ind.; field examiner, investigator, NLRB (1937–44); FEPC examiner, Region VII (1944–45).

McKellar, Kenneth D. (1869–1957) (D-Tenn.), U.S. sen. (1917–53); pres. pro tem (1945–47, 1949–53); chair, appropriations committee; opponent of FEPC who initiated compromise ending anti-FEPC filibuster (1945).

McKinnie, Clifton, Mobile funeral dir. who reported that contrary to rumors no blacks were known to have been killed during racial conflict at Ala. Dry Dock.

McKnight, William T. (ca. 1902–?), of Cleveland; black lawyer; asst. atty. gen., Ohio (1937–38); atty. for U.S. Dept. of Labor (1939–43); member, NAACP legal committee (1942–?), labor committee; dir., Region V (Cleveland office), FEPC (1943–45); worked closely with J. Lawrence Duncan, regional dir. of WMC; Mitchell considered him quite effective. AB, U. of Kans.; law degree, Yale.

McMenamin, James H., transit operator, strike committee member, Phila. Transit Co. (Aug. 1944); opposed training of blacks as street car conductors; arrested, fired for role in strike.

McNamee, Francis (Frank) L., dir., WMC, Region III (Phila. office); active in meetings on Phila. transit strike (Aug. 1944); later dep. chair, WMC (1945).

McNutt, Paul V. (1891–1955) (D-Ind.), governor (1933–37); high commissioner to Philippines (1937–38); administrator, FSA (1939–45); chair, WMC (1942–45). Criticized as "Adolph McNutt" by NAACP, black press for arbitrary, dictatorial procedures when FEPC placed under his control (1943).

McSherry, Frank J[ohnson]., Gen. (1892–1980), chief of operations, WMC (May–Dec. 1942).

Meecham, Stewart, of NLRB; said he believed unions could ask for strike vote on issue of separate-but-equal bathroom facilities, in response to Point Breeze Employees' Assoc. complaints, Baltimore (1943).

Metzger, Stanley D[avid]. (1916–), fair-practice examiner, Div. of Field Operations, FEPC (recruited by Maslow) (1944); resigned for job in OPA (July 1944); asst. to legal adviser, State Dept. (1948–60); on board dealing with personnel issues, State Dept.; prof., Georgetown

Law School; wrote books on intl. trade. One work, on lowering nontariff trade barriers, recalled when some material found to be plagiarized; apparently led to his dismissal (1975).

Miles, Vincent Morgan (1885–1947), special asst., U.S. atty. gen. (1937–38); solicitor, Post Office Dept. (1938–47?); in FEPC meeting with Post Office on discrimination complaints against various post offices.

Miller, Samuel Freeman (1816–90); doctor, lawyer, first in Ky., then Iowa; Republican; first U.S. Supreme Court justice from west of Miss. R. (1862–90); FEPC text on presidential power quoted his opinion in *Cunningham v. Neagle* (1890).

Millis, Harry A[lvin]., Dr. (1873–1948), economics prof., holder of many govt. posts; member, NLRB (1934–35, 1945–48), chair (1940–45); in case against Ore. Shipbuilding Corp., Kaiser Co.

Mitchell, Clarence M., Jr. (1911–84) of Baltimore; field asst. for N.J., Del., Pa., later asst. to Robert C. Weaver, chief of Negro Employment and Training Branch, OPM (and under subsequent reorganizations under WPB and WMC) (1941–42); appointed sr. field rep., FEPC (Jan. 1943), associate dir. of field operations (July 1943), dir. of field operations (June 1945–Apr. 1946); labor secy., NAACP (Aug. 1946–July 1950); dir., NAACP Washington Bureau (Aug. 1, 1950–1978).

Mitchell, Harry B. (1867?–1955), chair, Civil Service Commission; FEPC sent him a letter (1944).

Mitchell, James P. (1899–1964) (R-N.J.), expediter, Western Electric (1925–30); staff member, N.J. Relief Admin. (1931–36), WPA (1936–40); dir., industrial personnel div., Army Service Forces, War Dept. (1941–45); supporter of civil rights; praised by Mitchell for 8/3/42 memo requiring defense contractors to delete racial specification from employment application forms; later exec. with Macy's, Bloomingdale's (1945–53); asst. secy. of army (May–Oct. 1953); secy. of labor (1953–61).

Mitchell, Juanita (1913–92), daughter of Lillie Mae Carroll Jackson, Keiffer Bowen Jackson; wife of Clarence Mitchell Jr.; founder, City-Wide Young People's movement, Baltimore (1932); special asst. to Walter White, NAACP exec. secy., Natl. Youth Dir. (1935–38); legal redress chair, counsel, Baltimore NAACP branch, specializing in constitutional law who directed all desegregation cases, including, successively, lawsuits against U. of Md.'s schools of medicine, pharmacy, dentistry, nursing, graduate dept. of sociology, undergraduate school of engineering; pres., Md. State Conference of NAACP branches. LLB, U. of Md. School of Law (1950).

Mitten, Arthur Allan, Dr. (1888–1967), board member, head of industrial relations, Phila. Transportation Co.; in negotiations over FEPC, union charges of discrimination by company, represented company in meetings during Phila. transit strike; alleged by some union leaders to have precipitated strike to weaken new CIO union at company and to induce FEPC to drop demands for employment of blacks. Born in Attica, Ind.

Mitzel, C[harles]. W., regional labor rep., WPC, Baltimore; wrote letter to rep. of union at Western Electric's integrated Point Breeze plant on separate restroom facilities; in shipyard negotiations at Bethlehem Steel and Shipbuilding Corporation–Sparrows Point, Md. (1943).

Moreton, Vivian B., FEPC complainant who sought employment in Pearl Harbor Navy Yard in 1943 in order to join her husband there; ultimately, she was offered employment.

Morgan, Robert D., Capt., rep., U.S. Army Signal Corps, Labor Div., Kansas City, Mo.; in enforcement of nondiscrimination clauses in govt. contract with General Cable Co., St. Louis.

Morley, Burton B., Dr. (1898–1982), area dir. of WMC in Ala. during racial conflict at Ala. Dry Dock. Reportedly argued that blacks should accept whatever jobs offered and not seek to be upgraded until whites were willing to accept them in higher positions.

Morrell, Fred (1880–1959), forester; chief, office of Civilian Conservation Corps Activities, USDA (1934–43); asst. dir., Agricultural Labor Admin., USDA (1943). Mitchell queried him on application of EO 8802 to Bahamian agricultural workers imported during WWII.

Morton, J[ames]. H., instructor, Wiley Coll., Marshall, Tex.; examiner, Region X (Dallas), FEPC (1944), Region XIII (New Orleans office) (1945); reported on Todd Johnson Dry Docks case. Graduated Ind. U., U. of Chicago.

Motley, A. W., chief of Field Mgmt. Div. (1942–43), dir., Bureau of Placement, WMC; in conferences with FEPC officials on cooperation between the two agencies (1944).

Mulholland, Frank L., of Toledo; counsel, IAM (1921–48); as intl. union rep., agreed that bans on admitting blacks to local lodges were wrong and that local leaders would not interfere with full utilization of black workers (1944); black workers, however, charged that agreement was not adhered to in Tex. and Pacific Railroad case.

Mulliken, Otis E. (1907–72), of Mass.; chief of labor section, Sugar Div., USDA (1935–43), whose testimony, on relatively high living standards of sugarcane workers before Civil Liberties Committee of U.S. Senate, Mitchell questioned after U.S. Sugar Corp. indicted on peonage charges in 1942; held many posts in State Dept. (1943–70). PhD, Harvard.

Murray, Philip (1886–1952), Scots-born leader of United Mine Workers of America; pres., CIO (1940–52); member, FEPC; member, NAACP natl. board.

Neagle, David, dep. U.S. marshal in Calif. who shot David Terry while on duty as bodyguard for Justice Field when serving as circuit judge for 9th circuit. Involved in Supreme Court case *Cunningham v. Neagle,* referred to in FEPC text on presidential power to issue, enforce exec. orders.

Newman, Cecil Earl (1903–76), ed., black newspapers *Minneapolis Spokesman, St. Paul Recorder;* personnel rep. for Twin Cities Ordnance Plant to resolve difficulties in employment of black workers; provided information on Charles L. Horn when he was candidate for FEPC member.

Nichols, Franklin O., industrial relations field secy., Natl. Urban League; speaker at meeting of workers to end racial conflict at Ala. Dry Dock (1944).

Nimitz, Chester William, Adm. (1885–1966), established policy forbidding employment of Japanese Americans in naval establishments on West Coast (1945).

Norris, Kenneth T., Sr. (1899–1972), founder, chief exec., Norris Stamping and Mfg. Co., Calif.; said company would not willingly hire blacks (1945); if forced to do so, expected decline in productivity from resignations of white workers.

Northrup, Herbert R. (1918–), Harvard-educated economist; consultant for FEPC; prepared report used by FEPC (1944) on discrimination by Boilermakers Union. Previously, research asst. on Gunnar Myrdal's "Negro in America" project; instructor in economics, Cornell; economist, Tool and Die Commission; member, Regional War Labor Board, Detroit. Author of *Organized Labor and the Negro* (1944). Later, prof. of industry, dir., Industrial Research Unit, Wharton School, U. Penn.

Norton, Mary T. (1875–1959) (D-N.J.), U.S. rep. (1925–51); chair, House Committee on Labor; a sponsor of permanent FEPC legislation.

O'Brian, John Lord (1874–1973), prominent lawyer in Buffalo, later, D.C.; head of War Emergency Div., Justice Dept. (1917–19); head of antitrust div. of Justice Dept. (1929–35); appointed gen. counsel, TVA (1936); gen. counsel, Natl. War Production Board (1941–44) who submitted legal opinions to FEPC (1942) confirming its gen. jurisdiction over industries essential to war effort, even if they had no federal contracts, and over transportation industries in particular.

O'Connor, Herbert R. (1896–1960) (D-Md.), of Baltimore, governor (1939–47); FEPC conferred with him on Bethlehem Steel Shipbuilding strike (1943).

O'Grady, James, administrator in charge of United Seamen's Service, WSA; FEPC conferred with him on segregation of rest camps for merchant seamen. Informed FEPC blacks could apply to camps outside South and would be given free transportation to them (1945); warned against challenging segregation in Miss.

Odum, Howard W. (1884–1954), Southern sociologist, founder of Southern Regional Council, white liberal civil rights organization; prof., U. of N.C., Chapel Hill; author of *Race and Rumors of Race* (1943); candidate for FEPC, but not chosen.

Ohly, John H. (Jack) (1911–90), atty., Office of Asst. Secy. of War (1940–46); when in office of civilian personnel, War Dept., in meeting with FEPC (1943); as member Industrial Personnel Div., Army Service Forces, assisted in attempt to settle Shell Oil case (1945); later, special asst. to secy. of defense (1947–49); held many other govt. posts.

Ordway, Samuel Hanson, Jr., Capt., USNR (1900–71), Harvard-educated New York lawyer, assoc. exec., civil service reformer, conservationist; head of Employment Branch, Div. of Shore Establishments and Civilian Personnel, Navy Dept. (1945). Mitchell conferred with him on Navy regulation forbidding employment of Japanese Americans at naval establishments on West Coast (1945).

Outland, George E. (1906–81) (D-Calif.), U.S. rep. (1943–47); social worker (1928–35); college prof. (1935–42, 1947–72); supported FEPC legislation. PhD, Yale (1937).

Palmer, Dwight R.G. (1886–1980), St. Louis–born, New York City–based pres., chair, exec. committee, board member, General Cable Corp., a military contractor whose white workers in St. Louis went on strike over effort to train black women as electrical workers. Flew from New York, successfully induced employees to accept the workers and return to work (1945). Later, member of President's Committee on Equality of Treatment and Opportunity in the Armed Services (Fahy Committee) (1948–50); chair, Pres. Eisenhower's Committee on Govt. Contract Compliance.

Parran, Thomas, Jr., Dr. (1892–1968), U.S. surgeon gen. (1936–48); longtime employee, Public Health Service; active New Dealer, strong supporter of public health measures. Gave FEPC report on susceptibility of blacks to industrial diseases (1943). Born, educated in Md. MD, Georgetown.

Parsons, Paul S. (ca. 1887–1970), dep. area dir., WMC, New Britain, Conn.; gave Mitchell information on black employment at New Britain Machine Co. (1943).

Patterson, Robert P. (1891–1952) (R-N.Y.), secy. of war (1945–47); denied existence of discrimination in his dept.; FEPC asked him to make plans for use of military personnel in event of walkout at Capital Transit Co. (1945).

Pestana (Pestano), Frank S. (1913–?), labor lawyer of Portuguese descent; FEPC examiner, Region XII (1944–45), first in S.F. then L.A. office; resigned to practice law (1945). Graduated U. of Calif., Berkeley.

Peterson, Eric (1894–1961), Swedish-born labor leader; gen. vice pres., IAM (1940), secy.-treas. (1943–59); challenged FEPC's authority to require locals to accept black members (1944).

Peterson, Hugh (1898–1961) (D-Ga.), U.S. rep. (1935–47); opposed FEPC appropriations (1944).

Pollatsek, Frank, chief, NYC recruiting and manning office, WSA; attacked by members of Smith Committee, Southern congressmen during FEPC appropriation debates (1944–45) for promoting "social equality" of blacks through nondiscriminatory, nonsegregated employment of black seamen; denied "eligibility" for continued employment with federal govt. on basis of lack of "loyalty" because he "forced white and black sailors to bunk together." NAACP efforts to get him reinstated failed.

Poston, Ted [Theodore Roosevelt Augustus Major Poston] (1906–74), prominent Ky.-born black writer; employed by *Amsterdam News,* then *New York Post;* on leave from *Post*

(1940–45) to serve as a publicist for various federal agencies, including OPM, WPB, WMC; headed Negro Press Section in OWI's D.C. news bureau; Mitchell consulted him as rep. of OWI on advisability of govt. participation with strikers in radio broadcast on Phila. transit strike of Aug. 1944.

Pretschold, Carl, reporter, *St. Louis Dispatch, PM;* gave FEPC information on discrimination at Pratt and Whitney's Kansas City plant (1944).

Quill, Michael Joseph ("Mike") (1905–66), Irish-born founder, pres., Transport Workers Union of America; CIO union leader; NYC councilman from Bronx.

Randolph, A. Philip (1889–1979); black labor leader who organized Brotherhood of Sleeping Car Porters, won recognition for it after 12 years of struggle; pres., Natl. Negro Congress (1937–40), resigned because of Communist Party control; organized March on Washington Movement (1941), inducing FDR to issue EO 8802, barring discrimination in employment by defense contractors and creating FEPC; pressured Pres. Truman to pass exec. order outlawing segregation in armed services (1941); on natl. board and Natl. Labor Committee, NAACP.

Rapellin, Louis (1898–1973), French-born welder; one of eight white members of Boilermakers Union Local 92 who met with Mitchell, regional FEPC officials to express opposition to union's policy of requiring blacks to join auxiliary unions. Mitchell recommended him as witness for FEPC hearing in L.A. (Nov. 1943).

Rarig, Frank M., Jr. (1908–95), regional dir., WMC, Minneapolis; consulted by Mitchell on need for FEPC office in Minneapolis; assured Mitchell of WMC cooperation with regional office in Chicago.

Raspberry, Wallace S. (1889–1973), black helper, Boilermakers Union; local rep., IUMSWA; met with FEPC to discuss problems at Merrill-Stevens Dry Dock Co., Jacksonville, Fla.; allegedly fired by mgmt. when his position on committee was learned.

Ray, Thomas, controversial leader, business agent of Boilermakers Local 72 (Portland, Ore.), who created black auxiliaries to get around antidiscrimination measures against segregated Boilermakers union; negotiated secret union agreements with Kaiser Industries, required segregated work crews, established other policies that brought complaints from black workers.

Raycroft, L[ouis]. B. F. (1876–1972), regional dir., WMC, mgmt. rep. on Regional Labor Supply Committee, Phila.; in settlement of wartime labor disputes over hiring of blacks, esp. Phila. transit strike.

Record, Cy Wilson (1916–98), public relations chairman, Chicago Committee on Fair Employment Practices (1942); field rep. under Weaver in Negro Employment and Training Branch and Negro Manpower Service, OPM (1942); assisted in preparations for FEPC hearings in Birmingham (1942), when he testified; later transferred to WMC; investigated black employment problems in Miss., Memphis, Charleston, among others. Gave information to Mitchell on progress in employment in Region VII after hearings were held in Birmingham; drafted (1943), served in U.S. Air Force (–1946); later, prof. of sociology, author of several works on blacks, Communist Party. Born in Fort Worth. BA (1941), MA (1949), Roosevelt U.; PhD, U. of Calif., Berkeley (1953).

Record, Milton Atchison (1879–1975); Maj. Gen., Natl. Guard; commanded 29th Div. (1934–41); XIII Corps (1943–44); 69th Div., North-West Europe (1944–45); adjutant gen., Md. (1920–65), on leave during wartime service (1941–45). Conferred with on troop use during Bethlehem Steel Shipbuilding strike (1943).

Redmond, S[idney]. D[illon]., Dr. (1871–1948), black physician, lawyer, Jackson, Miss.; Republican Party leader, natl. convention delegate (1916, 1940, 1944); NAACP rep. consulted by Cy Record on discrimination against blacks at Brecon Bag Loading Plant, Flora, Miss. (1942).

Reeves, Frank D[aniel]. (1916–73), black lawyer; trial atty., associate fair practice examiner, FEPC (Aug. 1943–Sept. 1945); assignments included preparation for hearings in Southwest on Latin American discrimination cases, during which his cautiously legalistic, individual-complaint-focused approach was criticized by Castañeda, other FEPC staff members; legal research asst., natl. office, NAACP (1942); administrative asst., D.C. bureau, NAACP (May–Sept. 1942); prof., Howard U. Law School (Sept. 1, 1942–); atty., D.C.; member, Natl. Legal Committee, NAACP; consultant, D.C. bureau, NAACP; chair, D.C. branch, NAACP Legal Redress Committee; assisted in many civil rights cases; White House staff, Kennedy admin. Born in Montreal. BA, MA, Howard U.

Reilly, Gerard D. (1906–95), Harvard-educated lawyer, Labor Dept. solicitor; member, NLRB (1941–46); in case against Ore. Shipbuilding Corp., Kaiser Co.; later helped draft Taft-Hartley Act of 1947: appointed judge, U.S. Court of Appeals, D.C. (1970).

Rhone, Robert L., Jr., FEPC complainant who testified during Boilermakers hearings in Portland, Ore., Nov. 1943.

Rhudey, J. P., Maj.; labor office, Signal Corps, in Phila.; testified at WLB hearing in Baltimore on Point Breeze plant of Western Electric; appealed against strike at plant that would lessen the supply of material urgently needed by the army.

Ring, Daniel S., dir., Div. of Shipyard Labor Relations, U.S. Maritime Commission; in FEPC meeting on shipbuilding industry in Gulf Region.

Risk, Samuel Rudolph, examiner, NYC, Phila. offices, FEPC (1943–45); previously on staff of USES for six years.

Roche, Richard J., Fr. (OMI), Roman Catholic priest from Haverhill, Mass.; examiner, central office and Region IV (D.C.), FEPC (1944–45); in negotiations with Natl. Lead Co.; author of *FEPC—A Challenge to Democracy* (pamphlet, 1945); "Catholic Colleges and the Negro Student" (thesis, 1948). MA, PhD (sociology), Catholic U. of America.

Rock, Eli (1915–2000), noted labor arbitrator; head of disputes div., Phila. regional office, WLB; in hearing relating to Point Breeze Employees' Assoc. issues (1943); in meetings to settle Phila. transit strike (1944).

Rodriquez, Julius, pres. of SNOV, local organization of black shipbuilders in Portland, Ore., that sought to overcome discrimination by shipbuilding companies, relevant unions there; opposed plan to place black welders in Electrical Workers union instead of discriminatory Boilermakers Union. Testified at Boilermakers hearings, Portland (Nov. 1943).

Rogers, Eleanor F., clerk-stenographer, central office, FEPC (1943–45); typed many of Mitchell's reports, memoranda (initialed "efr" at end).

Rogers, Maybelle, secy., Non Partisan Committee, group of black workers at Western Electric's Point Breeze plant that opposed segregation proposals of Point Breeze Employees' Assoc. (1944).

Roosevelt, Eleanor (1884–1962), U.S. first lady (1932–45); directed discrimination complaints to FEPC; member, natl. board, Natl. Labor Committee, NAACP; natl. board, Legal Defense and Education Fund, NAACP.

Roosevelt, Franklin D. (1882–1945) (D-N.Y.), U.S. pres. (1933–45) who signed EOs 8802, 9346, establishing, strengthening FEPC.

Roosevelt, Theodore (1858–1919), U.S. pres. (1901–9); N.Y. politician, author; officer of Rough Riders, Spanish American War; elected governor (1898); elected vice pres. (1900), became pres. upon assassination of William McKinley. Views on strong exec. power "unless expressly forbidden by law or the Constitution," cited in FEPC text on presidential power to issue, enforce exec. orders.

Rosenberg, Anna M. (1902–83), dir. of Social Security Board (SSB) of New York State (1940); dir., Region II, WMC, praised by Mitchell as esp. effective, supportive; blocked discriminatory recruitment of workers in N.Y.; supporter of permanent FEPC legislation; asst. secy. of defense (1950–53); involved with development of universal military service legislation, desegregation of armed forces, increasing role of women in military; prominent N.Y. liberal Democrat active in civil rights, UN, municipal issues.

Ross, Bernard, former Portland Housing Authority official; appointed examiner, San Francisco office, FEPC (end of 1944); regional dir. after resignations of Harry Kingman, Edward Rutledge (Aug., 25, 1945).

Ross, Malcolm (Mike) (1895–1965); author, editor; in Army Air Force (WWI); dir. of information, NLRB (1936–42); dep. chair, then chair, FEPC (1943–46). Born in Newark, N.J. Graduated Yale (1919).

Rotnem, Victor W. (ca. 1900–?), New York lawyer; chief, Civil Rights Section, Dept. of Justice; handled case against U.S. Sugar Corp., which was indicted on peonage charges (1942). Consulted by Mitchell on wages, working conditions of sugarcane workers in Fla., La., and on advisability of govt. participation in radio broadcast with strikers during Phila. transit strike (Aug. 1944). Born in Minn.

Ruchel, Horace A. (1895–1975), trial examiner, NLRB, Chicago; reported to FEPC on Western Cartridge Co.

Russell, Richard B., Jr. (1897–1971) (D-Ga.), U.S. sen., opposed FEPC, civil rights legislation; originated Russell Amendment, requiring congress. authorizations of appropriations for presidential agencies in existence more than one year; introduced segregation amendment to draft legislation (1950).

Rutledge, Edward (1915–2002), asst. prof. of economics, Colo. State U. (1937–41); examiner in charge, Region XII (San Francisco office), FEPC in 1945; appointed regional dir upon Kingman's resignation, but unable to serve; replaced by Bernard Ross; praised by Mitchell, criticized by others for zeal in FEPC cases; later defended by Mitchell, Kingman in loyalty investigation (1955); later, dir. of race relations, Office of Housing Expediter, Seattle; Federal Housing Admin., L.A.; Public Housing Admin., NYC (1946–55); housing dir., New York State Commission for Human Rights (1955–64); exec. dir., Natl. Committee against Discrimination in Housing, NYC (1964–72); consultant on race relations; special asst. for policy development (1975–79), regional dir., mid-Atlantic region, U.S. Commission on Civil Rights (1979–80s). BA, Cornell; M.A., U. of Mo.

Ryan, John Augustine, Msgr. (1869–1945), American Catholic Church's expert on economic, social questions in first half of 20th century; taught at Catholic U., Trinity College, D.C.; in several New Deal federal posts; headed Social Action Dept., Natl. Catholic Welfare Council (1920–45). Considered for position on FEPC, but did not serve. Testified to congress. committee in favor of permanent FEPC legislation (Chavez-Norton Bill) (1944); member, exec. committee of Natl. Council for a Permanent FEPC. Born, educated in Minn. PhD (sacred theology), Catholic U. of America (1906).

Rye, Lucien F., commissioner of conciliation for Dept. of Labor; in efforts to settle walkouts, labor unrest at Bethlehem Steel and Shipbuilding Corporation–Sparrows Point, Md.; involved with complaints of Point Breeze Employees' Assoc. on Western Electric's refusal to provide separate facilities for white and black employees (1943). Held that separate-but-equal facilities would not be discriminatory.

Saito, Otome A., Japanese American clerk-stenographer, field operations office, FEPC (1943–45).

Samuel, Bernard (1880–1954), acting mayor, Phila. (1941–44), mayor (1944–45) during transit strike (Aug. 1944). Having said neither he nor police could control strike, federal troops brought in.

Sandvigen (Sanvigen), I[ngval]. A. (1895–1984), business agent, Lodge 79, IAM; consulted on rights of black workers to join or be represented by union local.

Sarnoff, David (The General) (1891–1971), of New York, Russian-born pres. of Radio Corp. of America (1930–47), chair of board (1947–69); career employee of Marconi Wireless Telegraph Co. who rose through ranks of RCA after it took over Marconi; member, FEPC; resigned after Paul McNutt canceled hearings on railroad cases (1943).

Scanlon, Thomas Edward (1896–1955) (D-Pa.), of Pittsburgh; pressman for local newspapers (1914–36); delegate to Pittsburgh Central Labor Union (1920–40); U.S. rep. (1941–45); backer of permanent FEPC bill (Dawson-Scanlon-LaFollette Bill).

Schultz, Joy, white industrial relations expert, formerly employed by Republic Drill and Tool Co., Swift and Co.; worked on large research project on black-white relations in Chicago; examiner assisting Elmer Henderson, Chicago office, FEPC (1944–45); FEPC investigator for Ill. Ordnance plant strike; FEPC praised her excellent work, esp. in public relations. BA, U. of Chicago.

Schweinhaut, Henry Albert (1902–1970), D.C. lawyer, judge; special asst. to atty. gen. (1936–45); Justice Dept. rep. in Phila. during transit strike (Aug. 1944); U.S. Dist. Court judge, D.C. (1945–56).

Scott, Hugh D. (1900–94) (R-Pa.), lawyer; U.S. rep. (1941–45, 1947–59); sen. (1959–77); minority leader (1969–77); supporter of FEPC legislation.

Sentner, William, gen. vice pres. of UERMWA, Dist. 8; member, St. Louis Race Relations Committee; FEPC conferred with him on integration of blacks at U.S. Cartridge plant in St. Louis.

Seulberger, Ferdinand George (1902–79), engineer, prof. of cooperative education; chairman, Dept. of Industrial Relations, Technical Inst., Northwestern U. (1940–44); participated in FEPC discussions on access to training programs during WWII. Later, dean of students (1944–52), asst. dean of Technical Inst. (1952–71). Born in St. Louis.

Seymour [Seymore], Virginia, clerk-stenographer, San Francisco office, FEPC (1944–45).

Sharfsin, Joseph (1898–1979), S.C.–born Phila. lawyer, business exec.; counsel to comptroller of Phila. (1933–36); city solicitor (1936–40?); public member of board, Phila. Transportation Co.; special counsel for FEPC; active in meetings on Phila. transit strike (1944); witness for FEPC at Smith Committee hearings.

Shiel, Bernard James (1888–?), auxiliary bishop of Chicago; considered for appointment to FEPC (1943); supported permanent FEPC.

Shiozaki (Shiosaki), Ronald I., Japanese American discharged from position as cost accountant with Shotwell Mfg. Co. after intervention by War Dept. Complained to FEPC that discharge was discriminatory; had previously been properly investigated, released from a war relocation center.

Shishkin, Boris (1906–84), chief economist, AFL; member, FEPC (1943–45); member, Natl. Labor Committee, NAACP.

Silverberg, Louis G. (1916–91?), of NLRB; provided information to FEPC.

Simmons, Walter L., clerk-stenographer, Div. of Review and Analysis, FEPC (Oct. 1943–Aug. 1945).

Smith, A[ntonio]. Maceo (1903–77), of Dallas; black teacher, newspaper publisher, exec. dir., Dallas Negro Chamber of Commerce; consulted on FEPC appointments in Tex.; longtime NAACP leader, member natl. board (1953–57); housing administrator, FHA, HUD (1937–72).

Smith, Ferdinand C. (1894–1961), natl. secy., Natl. Maritime Union, who presented discrimination complaints to FEPC against Standard Brands. His integrated union, considered relatively radical and having Communist members, support, strongly opposed segregation and discrimination in shipping industry. Member, Natl. CIO Committee to Abolish Racial Discrimination. Deported as subversive alien to his native Kingston, Jamaica (1948).

Smith, Howard W. (1883–1976) (D-Va.), lawyer, judge; U.S. rep. (1931–67); chair, Select Committee to Investigate Exec. Agencies (Smith Committee), which challenged jurisdiction, actions of FEPC, various other govt. agencies (1943–44).

Smith, Jack (probably Jack Clifford Smith) (1916–96), after working as reporter in Calif., Honolulu, employed by UPI (1943); later became well-known reporter, columnist for *LA Times* (1953–95).

Smith, Joseph A., dir., Region I (New England), WMC; issued appropriate operating instructions on cooperation with FEPC in his region.

Smith, Kenneth F. (ca. 1910–?), black racial relations rep. for USES in Ore. (1941–43); later, dir. of a USO in Portland; in early negotiations on black workers imported for work in area shipyards; applied for position with FEPC, but not hired. BA, U. of Kans.

Smith, Sylvia, vice pres., L.A. local of NAPE, member of its committee on discrimination; brought FEPC information on discrimination by Post Office in L.A.

Smith, William A., Jr. (ca. 1905–) black former asst. youth personnel officer, NYA, Newark, N.J.; considered for appointment as FEPC field examiner, Region III; minorities rep., Region III (Phila.), WMC; in meetings on Phila. transit strike.

Soellner, Rudolf, German American aeronautical engineer, designer; migrated from Germany (1935), naturalized (1939); resided in St. Louis; removed from employment by army or navy contractors by order of Army Air Corps (1943); case appealed to Industrial Employment Review Board and FEPC.

Southall, Sara E. (1893–1978), of Chicago, a supervisor of employment, service, Internatl. Harvester Corp.; member, second FEPC (1943–46); author of *Industry's Unfinished Business* (1950), a plea for racial tolerance in the workplace.

Spencer, William H., Dr., former dean, Business School, U. of Chicago; dir., Region VI, WMC; issued appropriate instructions to his state directors for cooperation with FEPC.

Stacy, Walter P., of Raleigh, N.C., chief justice, Supreme Court of N.C.; FDR appointed him chair, special committee on FEPC railroad cases (Jan.1944), after FEPC certified case to FDR as at an impasse in efforts to secure removal of discrimination in certain fields of railway employment. The committee failed to secure any redress.

Stickgold, Simon (1911–84), Ill. lawyer; trial atty., Legal Div., FEPC (1945); trial atty. on General Cable case; author of *Memorandum #1: Specific Methods for Promoting Good Will among Racial Groups in Illinois,* published by Ill. Interracial Commission (1943).

Stimson, Henry L. (1867–1950) (R-N.Y.), secy. of war (1911–13, 1940–45); secy. of state (1929–33); developed proposal for protecting black servicemen from civilian violence.

Stocking, Collis (1900–78), Tex.-born economist who served as asst. exec. dir., WMC, associate dir. of its Bureau of Program Planning (1941–45); also acted as chief of Reports and Analysis Service, WMC (June 1944–May 1945); asst. dir., USES (1945–48); later held other govt. posts.

Stoll, Clarence G[riffith] (1883–1967), Pa.-born pres., dir., Western Electric; considered as candidate for membership on FEPC (1943), but not appointed. His company's employment policies praised by Mitchell.

Stoll, Leo C., area dir. of War Manpower Commission; handled job requests for Kaiser Industries; conferred with Mitchell during investigation of shipyard cases.

Streator (Streater), George W. (ca. 1902–55), black asst. field employment rep. on Robert Weaver's staff in Negro Employment and Training Branch, OPM (1942); race relations specialist also with WMC and WPB (1943–45); active on FEPC case against Monsanto Chemical Co. (1944). Protégé of W. E. B. Du Bois; staff member (1933), managing editor, *The Crisis;* resigned when Du Bois did (1934); subsequently became union organizer for ACWA-CIO, ILGWU-AFL, consultant for other unions. After WWII, reporter, *New York*

Times (1945–49); editor, *The Pilot,* newspaper of Natl. Maritime Union, CIO (1949–55). Graduated Fisk U.; MA, Western Reserve U.

Strong, George E., Col., of Army Air Force; investigated, sought to resolve FEPC complaints; assisted in settlements of strike at Wright Aeronautical Co. (1944), walkout by white workers over hiring of black women at Kurz-Kasch Co., Dayton (1945).

Sufrin, Sidney C., Lt. Col. (1910–97); staff member, Labor Branch, War Dept., in discussions on FEPC cases in St. Louis, New Orleans; sought relaxation of regulations against filling of discriminatory work orders by USES at Todd Johnson Dry Docks shipyard, New Orleans; subsequently headed govt.-sponsored economic mission to Spain; held other govt. posts (through 1954); prof. of economics, Syracuse U. (1951–68), of business economics, U. of Mass., Amherst (1975–90). Graduated U. Penn (1931); PhD, Ohio State.

Swan, Edward M., of Mich., examiner in charge, Detroit suboffice, FEPC (Sept. 1943); formerly Mich. dir. of Negro affairs, NYA; later exec. secy., Detroit branch, NAACP.

Swinford, Mac (1899–1975), Ky. lawyer, legislator; judge, U.S. Dist. Court, Eastern and Western Dists. of Ky. (1937–75), chief judge (1963–69). Views cited in FEPC text on presidential power to issue, enforce exec. orders.

Tall, S. Broughton, regional chief, Station Relations Div., OWI; in Phila. during transit strike (Aug. 1944).

Tarver, Malcolm C. (1885–1960) (D-Ga.), U.S. rep. (1927–47); opposed FEPC appropriations (1944).

Taussig, Charles Williams (1896–1948), of NYC; pres., board chair, American Molasses Co.; member, Roosevelt Brain Trust; chair, Natl. Advisory Committee, NYA (1935–43); adviser on Caribbean affairs; considered for inclusion on FEPC.

Taylor, George William, Dr. (1901–72); prof., Wharton School, U. Penn; chair, NWLB (WWII).

Taylor, Jay L., Lt. Col., dep. administrator, War Food Admin.; informed FEPC that West Indian agricultural workers imported under an agreement with the British govt. would be covered under the nondiscriminatory provisions of EOs 8802, 9346; stated Mexican workers were also covered.

Terry, David S., opposed Justice Stephen Field, repeatedly threatened his life until shot by Field's bodyguard, David Neagle. Led to Supreme Court case *Cunningham v. Neagle* (1890); cited in FEPC text on presidential power to issue, enforce exec. orders.

Thomas, J. A., industrial secy., Natl. Urban League; attended NUL conference (1943), provided information on role of Natl. Assoc. of Manufacturers.

Thomas, R[olland]. J[ay]. (1900–67), Detroit union leader; pres., UAW (1939–46); a CIO vice pres.; member, WLB, other wartime boards; FEPC conferred with him on strike at Wright Aeronautical Co. (1944).

Thompson, Frank Anthony, Phila. motorman, transit strike leader (Aug. 1944) who was arrested, released on bond.

Thompson, Lewis Sylvester (ca. 1901–?), welder whose upgrading as one of eight black transit employees training as street car operators precipitated Phila. transit strike (Aug. 1944); one of three trainees interviewed by FEPC on background to strike.

Tipton, James H., Jr., of Ga., son of former rep., Ga. legislature; instructor, asst. treas., mgr. of radio program, Ga. Tech; in army (1942–43); high school principal, Clayton, Ga.; associate examiner, Region VII, FEPC (1944); temporarily blocked from investigating Bell Aircraft plant in Marietta by War Dept. regulations. BS (commerce), Ga. School of Technology.

Tobert, William E., asst. dep. administrator, Food Production and Distribution Admin., USDA; gave Mitchell information on agreement between British govt., USDA on importation of Bahamian agricultural workers (1943).

Tobin, Daniel J. (1875–1955), Irish-born pres., Teamsters Union (IBTCWA) (1907–52); vice pres., AFL (1933–52). Mitchell planned to contact him in 1944 about his union's attitudes to persons of Japanese ancestry during WWII.

Tobin, Thomas J., Fr., Roman Catholic priest active in labor mediation programs; on Portland Voluntary Appeals Board during WWII; participated in efforts to settle discrimination complaints against Boilermakers Union; gave information to FEPC.

Triede, Henry E. (1899–1962), dir., Region IV (D.C.), WMC; in disputes with FEPC, Region IV, over access to USES information on discrimination. He generally released information only when given specific orders from WMC to do so.

Trimble, Ernest Greene (1897–1972), Southern white lawyer, political scientist; prof., U. of Ky.; FEPC sr. field rep., headquarters examiner, trial atty., hearings examiner (1941–44); investigated, with Mitchell, Ala. Dry Dock case (1943).

Truman, Harry S. (1884–1972) (D-Mo.), U.S. sen. (1935–45); vice pres. (1945); pres. (1945–53); on July 26, 1948, signed EO 9980, establishing Fair Employment Board, EO 9981, creating President's Committee on Equality of Treatment and Opportunity in the Armed Forces, a desegregating order.

Tyler, Oscar P. (1903–77), FEPC complainant protesting compulsory assignment to auxiliary union at Calif. Shipbuilding Co.; recommended by Mitchell as witness for Boilermakers hearings in LA (Nov. 1943).

Unthank, Denorval, Dr. (1899–1977), of Portland, Ore.; West Coast official with WMC/USES; in meeting on importation of black workers into Portland shipyards.

Van Gelder, Philip, secy.-treas., IUMSWA-CIO; in negotiations with FEPC, other agencies over walkouts, labor unrest at Bethlehem Steel and Shipbuilding Corporation–Sparrows Point, Md.

VanWyck, Philip S., Dr., chief of training, WMC (1944–45).

Vickery, Howard L., Adm. (1892–1946), commissioner, U.S. Maritime Commission; letters written to him on FEPC cases.

Vincent, Craig S., Atlantic Coast regional rep., Recruitment and Manning Organization, WSA; attacked by Smith Committee and in Congress during debates over FEPC appropriations (1944); labeled fellow traveler for promoting "social equality" of blacks through nondiscriminatory, nonsegregated placement of black seamen on ships.

Waesche, Russell Randolph (1886–1946), Adm., U.S. Coast Guard; gave FEPC information on employment of Japanese Americans on merchant vessels.

Walker, Frank C. (1886–1959), U.S. postmaster gen.; in negotiations with FEPC on discrimination complaints against post offices; acknowledged jurisdiction of FEPC (1944).

Warren, Lindsay C. (1889–1976) (D-N.C.), U.S. rep. (1925–40); U.S. comptroller gen. (as of 1940); ruled (Oct. 7, 1943) that inclusion of nondiscrimination clauses in govt. contracts was directive, not mandatory. His statement overruled by FDR's letter (Nov. 6, 1943) to atty. gen. declaring the provisions mandatory. Warren reluctant to send FEPC a copy of GAO memorandum on employment rights of Japanese Americans.

Weaver, George L. P. (1912–?), black union leader; member, United Transport Service Employees of America; natl. dir., CIO Committee to Abolish Discrimination (1942–); asst. to secy.-treas., CIO (1942–55); exec. secy., AFL-CIO Civil Rights Committee (1955–58); member, Natl. Labor Committee, NAACP; cooperated with FEPC in settling oil company cases; conferred with FEPC on discriminatory contract by Steel Workers Union (1944); represented James B. Carey at board meetings of Natl. Council for a Permanent FEPC; asst. secy. of labor for intl. affairs (1961–69); special asst. to dir. gen., ILO (1969–at least 1975); in conference on nondiscrimination by USES offices (1946); supported NAACP-proposed antidiscrimination amendments to Taft-Hartley Law; conferred with president's Fair Employment Board (1948). Born in Pittsburgh.

Weaver, Robert Clifton, Dr. (1907–97), economist; "Black Cabinet" leader; administrator, minority affairs adviser in various New Deal agencies (1933–), including adviser to Secy. of Interior Harold L. Ickes (1933–37); special asst. to Nathan Strauss, administrator, Housing Authority (1937–40); administrative asst. to Sidney Hillman, NDAC (1940); chief of Negro Employment and Training Branch, Labor Div., OPM and WPB (1942–43); hired Mitchell as field asst. (May 1941); asst. to dir. of operations, WMC (1942); chief of Negro Manpower Service, WMC (1943–44); after WWII held many state, federal posts, posts in education and foundations; appointed administrator, HHFA (1961), highest federal administrative position then assigned to a black; appointed first secy. of HUD by Pres. Johnson (1966)—first black in cabinet post. Author of *Negro Labor: A Natl. Problem* (1946), *The Negro Ghetto* (1948), *The Urban Complex: Human Values in Urban Life* (1964), *Dilemmas of Urban America* (1965). Born in D.C. PhD (economics), Harvard (1934).

Weber, William A., Lt., asst. to Admiral Vickery, U.S. Maritime Commission; contacted FEPC about negotiations with Delta Shipbuilding Co., New Orleans (1944).

Webster, Milton P. (1887–1965), of Ill.; first intl. vice pres., Brotherhood of Sleeping Car Porters; black member, FEPC.

Werts (Wertz), Leo R, asst. exec. dir., Office of Field Service, WMC (1942–45); in discussions of labor stabilization agreements (1943); in meeting with FEPC officials on problems in Regions VII, X (1944); later, asst. secy. for admin., Dept. of Labor.

Westmoreland (Westmorland), Edgar (1890–1969), black special rep., Defense Vocational Education, Office of Education; investigated problems with wartime vocational training for blacks in Ala. (1942); conferred with on training programs in Ga. (1944); previously special rep., trade and industrial education, Interior Dept.

White, Allen Hunter ("Buck"), atty. with Phila. firm Ballard, Spahr, Andrews, and Ingersoll; gen. counsel, Phila. Transit Co., during FEPC investigation of company (1943), Phila. transit strike (1944).

White, Walter F. (1893–1955) of Atlanta; asst. secy., NAACP (1918–31), in charge of investigating lynching; exec. secy. (1931–55); friend of Eleanor Roosevelt; joined AFL (1935) in successful battle to defeat Pres. Hoover's nomination of Judge John J. Parker to U.S. Supreme Court; led successful fight (1946) to get the Senate to block seating of Theodore G. Bilbo of Miss., rabid racist who had attempted to kill FEPC by sponsoring amendment to deny it funding (1944); joined A. Philip Randolph in meeting with FDR (1941) to press demand for EO 8820; founder, dir., NAACP Washington Bureau (1942–50).

Whitmore, Julia E., FEPC complainant against War Dept., Chicago; subsequently hired for position sought.

Whitney, A. F. [Alexander Fell] (1873–1949), pres., Brotherhood of Railroad Trainmen (1928–49); appealed to regarding admission of black stewards to union.

Whitten, Jamie L. (1910–95) (D-Miss.), U.S. rep. (1941–95); opposed FEPC appropriations (1944).

Wilkins, Roy (1901–81), managing editor, *Kansas City Call* (1923–31); asst. natl. secy. (1931–49), editor (1934–49), *The Crisis;* acting natl. secy., NAACP (1949–50); administrator, internal affairs (1950–55), natl. secy., exec. dir. (1955–77), NAACP. Represented NAACP during Phila. transit strike negotiations (1943). Born in St. Louis. Educated, U. of Minn.

Williams, L[eroy]. Virgil, of Dallas; recording secy., Allied Organizations against Discrimination in Natl. Defense (1941); examiner, Region X (Dallas), FEPC (1943–44); FEPC investigator, Delta Shipbuilding case; FEPC examiner, Chicago office (1944–45); became asst. dir., Industrial Relations Dept., Chicago Urban League (Sept. 1945).

Williams, Wyatt, black lawyer in Portland, Ore., who assisted Thomas Ray in organizing Boiler-makers Union auxiliary A-42, formed to allow blacks access to shipbuilding jobs despite union's ban on black members. (Many black workers considered such unions both discriminatory and inadequate and protested payment of dues to the auxiliary.) Williams angered by NAACP's opposition to auxiliary.

Willingham, G. T., white employee charged with inciting antiblack riot at Ala. Dry Dock (1943); convicted only of threatening violence, placed under $2,000 peace bond.

Willis, Ivan, natl. mgr. of industrial relations, Wright and Curtis-Wright Companies; conferred with on FEPC cases regarding his firms. Chair, industrial relations, Industrial Relations Committee of Natl. Aeronautical Chamber of Commerce; gave FEPC information on postwar employment prospects for blacks in aircraft industry.

Willkie, Wendell (1892–1944), liberal Republican candidate for pres., 1944.

Willoughby, Westel Woodbury (1867–1945), author of Constitutional Law of the United States (3 vols.; 1910), became standard reference on subject, 1910s–20s; quoted in FEPC texts on presidential power to issue, enforce exec. orders.

Wilson, Alfretta (1903–95), FEPC complainant against Lodge 514, IAM, Kansas City (1944); denied union membership because of race.

Wilson, Boyd L. (1896–1985), black union leader from Mo., United Steel Workers; member, Natl. CIO Committee to Abolish Racial Discrimination; investigated FEPC complaint against Murray Gin Co., Dallas (1945); reported on policies of his union (1946).

Wilson, Woodrow (1856–1924); Va.-born U.S. pres. (1913–21); political science prof., pres., Princeton U. (1902–10); governor, N.J. (1911–13). Writings on presidential power cited by FEPC text on presidential power to issue, enforce exec. orders.

Wolfe, James, chief justice, Utah supreme court; traveled to L.A. (1943) to assist with FEPC complaints against Boilermakers Union, shipbuilding firms.

Woomer, George, commissioner, U.S. Conciliation Service, Dept. of Labor, 1943; tried to settle grievances at Jones and Laughlin Steel plant, Aliquippa, Pa. (1943).

Worth, Emory R. (1897–1966), of Portland; dir., Ore. State Employment Service; gave FEPC information about employment policies of Kaiser shipyards (1943).

Wright, Harold (Hal) T., Cmdr., represented the U.S. Maritime Commission at meeting on racial conflict at Ala. Dry Dock. Asserted use of black manpower was necessary.

Wright, Thomas, area dir., WMC, Chicago; in efforts to settle strike at American Steel Foundry Plant, East Chicago, Ind.

Wrightson, Francis G. (ca. 1884–?), asst. gen. mgr., Bethlehem Steel Shipbuilding; in negotiations with FEPC, other agencies over walkouts, unrest at Sparrows Point, Md., shipyard.

Yates, Frank L[loyd]. (ca. 1894–1953), longtime GAO official (1922–); asst. comptroller gen. (1943–53); issued instructions to GAO on employment rights of Japanese Americans during WWII; FEPC conferred with him on nondiscrimination clauses in govt. contracts.

Young, P[lummer]. B[ernard]. (1884–1962), of Va.; publisher, editor, Norfolk Journal and Guide; a leader of Southern Conference on Race Relations; member, second FEPC (1943–44).

Zemurray, Samuel (1877–1961), of La.; Russian-born Jewish entrepreneur; pres., United Fruit Co.; member, second FEPC (1943–44).

BIBLIOGRAPHY

PRIMARY SOURCES

Manuscript Collections

Franklin Delano Roosevelt Library, Hyde Park, New York.
  Roosevelt, Franklin Delano. Papers. Official Files 93 and 4245G.
Henderson, Elmer W. Collection. Privately held by family.
Library of Congress, Washington, D.C. Papers of the National Association for the Advance-
  ment of Colored People (NAACP).
Mitchell, Clarence, Jr. Papers. Privately held by family, Baltimore, Md.
Moorland-Spingarn Research Center, Howard University.
  Davidson, Eugene C. Papers.
  National Association for the Advancement of Colored People–Washington, D.C., Branch.
    Papers. F.E.P.C. files.
National Archives, Washington, D.C.
  Assistant Secretary of the Navy (Ralph Bard). Records. General Records of the Department
    of the Navy, 1798–1947. RG 80.
  Office of the Assistant Secretary of War. Civilian Aide to the Secretary. Records. Subject File,
    1940–1947. RG 107.
  President's Committee on Fair Employment Practice. Records. FEPC Papers. RG 228.
  War Manpower Commission. Records. RG 211.
  War Production Board. Negro Employment and Training Branch. Records. RG179.
State University of New York, College at Old Westbury.
  The Papers of Clarence Mitchell, Jr. Collection.

Microform Publications

Bracey, John H., and August Meier, eds. *Papers of the NAACP.* Part 13, NAACP and Labor,
  1940–1955. Series B, Cooperation with Organized Labor. 25 reels. Frederick, Md.: University Publications of America, 1982–.
Kirby, John B., Robert Lester, and Dale Reynolds, eds. *New Deal Agencies and Black America.* 25
  reels. Frederick, Md. : University Publications of America.
*Microfilm Record of Selected Documents of the Committee on Fair Employment Practice in the Cus-
  tody of the National Archives.* Glen Rock, N.J.: Microfilming Corporation of America, 1970.

Finding Aids and Guides to Document Collections

Brophy, John. Papers. Catholic University of America Department of Archives, Manuscripts,
  and Museum Collections. Finding aid. http://libraries.cua.edu/achrcua/brophy.html.

Eastman Chemical Company. History. East Tennessee State University, Archives of Appalachia Web site. Finding aid. http://cass.etsu.edu/archives/afinaid/a418.html [2004].

Ellinger, W. Don. Papers, 1946–61. Texas AFL-CIO records, 1918–75. University of Texas, Arlington. Finding aid.

Friend, Bruce I. *Guide to the Microfilm Record of Selected Documents of the Committee on Fair Employment Practice in the Custody of the National Archives.* Glen Rock, N.J.: Microfilming Corporation of America, 1970.

Furfey, Paul Hanley. Papers. CUA Archives. Finding aid. http://www.libraries.cua.edu.

Grant, David M. Western Historical Manuscript Collection, University of Missouri, St. Louis. Finding aid.

Haas, Francis J. Papers. CUA Archives. Finding aid. http://www.libraries.cua.edu.

Keenan, Joseph Daniel. Papers. CUA Archives. Finding aid. http://www.libraries.cua.edu.

Kennedy, Stetson. Oral history (1988), Georgia Government Documentation Project. Georgia State University Library, 1988. Finding aid.

Kingman, Harry L. Papers, 1921–75. Bancroft Library. University of California, Berkeley. Finding aid.

LeFlore, John L. Papers, 1926–76. South Alabama University Archives. Guide. www.southalabama.edu/archives/lefloreintro.htm.

Matchette, Robert B., and Jan S. Danis, comps. *Guide to Federal Records in the National Archives of the United States.* Washington, D.C.: National Archives and Records Administration, 1995.

McNeal, Theodore D.. Western Historical Manuscript Collection, University of Missouri, St. Louis. Finding aid.

O'Brian, John Lord. Papers. Law Library Archives, University of Buffalo. Finding aid.

Ramsay, John Gates. Papers. Georgia State University. Finding aid.

Ryan, John Augustine. Papers. CUA Archives. Finding aid. http://www.libraries.cua.edu.

Schomberg Center for Research, New York Public Library. Collections. Finding aid.

United States. Department of Labor. General records. National Archives, RG 174. www.nara.gov/guide/rg174.html.

———. Department of the Navy, Records. National Archives, RG 80. Guide. www.nara.gov/guide/rg80.html.

———. National War Labor Board. Records, 1942–45. Labor Archives and Research Center, San Francisco State University. Guide.

———. War Production Board. Records. National Archives, RG 179. Guide. www.nara.gov/guide/rg179.html.

U.S. Rubber Company Records/Colt Family Papers. University of Rhode Island Special Collections Web site. Finding aid. http://www.uri.edu/library/special_collections/registers/colt/seriesXIV.htm.

Zaid, Charles. *Preliminary Inventory of the Records of the Committee on Fair Employment Practice.* RG 228. Washington, D.C.: National Archives and Records Service, General Services Administration, 1962.

———. *Inventory of the Records of the War Manpower Commission.* RG 211. Washington, D.C.: National Archives and Records Service, General Services Administration, 1973.

Oral Histories

Civil Rights Documentation Project, Ralph J. Bunche Oral History Collection. Moorland-Spingarn Research Center, Howard University.

Davis, John A. Interview by Denton L. Watson. New Rochelle, N.Y., September 25, 1985. Collection of The Papers of Clarence Mitchell, Jr., SUNY College at Old Westbury.

Jones, Theodore. Interview by Denton L. Watson. New York, November 19, 1982. Collection of The Papers of Clarence Mitchell, Jr., SUNY College at Old Westbury.

Kingman, Harry L. "Citizenship in a Democracy: An Interview Conducted by Rosemary Levenson." Regional Oral History Office, Bancroft Library, University of California, Berkeley, 1973.

LeFlore, John L. Interviews. McLaurin Oral History Project, University of South Alabama Department of History. (http://www.southalabama.edu/oralhist1.htm)

Mitchell, Clarence, Jr. Interview by Merl Reed. Baltimore, Md., August 24, 1978. Private collection of Professor Reed.

———. Interview by Denton L. Watson. Baltimore, Md., January 1983. Collection of The Papers of Clarence Mitchell, Jr., SUNY College at Old Westbury.

Mitchell, Juanita Jackson. Interview by Denton L. Watson. Baltimore, Md., May 3, 1988. Collection of The Papers of Clarence Mitchell, Jr., SUNY College at Old Westbury.

Nash, Philleo. Oral history interview by Jerry N. Hess. November 29, 1966. Truman Presidential Museum and Library. http://www.trumanlibrary.org.oralhist.Nash 11.htm [2003].

Rutledge, Edward. Interview by Denton L. Watson. Washington, D.C., June 17, 1982. Collection of The Papers of Clarence Mitchell, Jr., SUNY College at Old Westbury.

Weaver, Robert. Interview by Denton L. Watson. New York, December 8, 1991. Collection of The Papers of Clarence Mitchell, Jr., SUNY College at Old Westbury.

Werts, Leo R. Oral history interview by James R. Fuchs. Washington, D.C., August 4, 1977. Truman Presidential Museum and Library.

SECONDARY SOURCES

Books and Articles

Adams, Stephen B., and Orville R. Butler. *Manufacturing the Future: A History of Western Electric.* Cambridge: Cambridge University Press, 1999.

"Alien Registration Begins." *Christian Century* 57 (August 28, 1940): 1044.

"Alien Registration Program." *Monthly Labor Review* 51 (September 1940): 569–71.

"Aliens Must Register." *Business Week* (August 3, 1940): 20.

"Aliens Register." *Survey* 76 (September 1940): 264.

Almaráz, Félix D., Jr. *Knight without Armor: Carlos Eduardo Castañeda, 1896–1958.* College Station: Texas A & M Press, 1999.

American Council on Race Relations. *Negro Platform Workers.* Chicago: American Council on Race Relations, 1945.

Amidon, B. "Aliens in America." *Survey Graphic* 30 (February 1941): 58–61.

———. "Can We Afford Martyrs?" *Survey Graphic* 29 (September 1940): 457–58.

Ashby, Warren. *Frank Porter Graham: A Southern Liberal.* Winston-Salem, N.C.: John F. Blair, Publisher, 1980.

Bailey, Robert. "Theodore G. Bilbo and the Fair Employment Practice Controversy: A Southern Senators Reaction to a Changing World." *Journal of Mississippi History* 42 (February 1980): 27–42.

Bergstrom, Herbert C., and Glenn Everett. *The FEPC Faces Crisis: The Philadelphia Strike.* Race Relations Committee of the American Friends Service Committee and Washington Newsletter of the Friends Committee on National Legislation. Philadelphia and Washington, D.C., 1944.

Berman, William C. *The Politics of Civil Rights in the Truman Administration.* Columbus: Ohio State University Press, 1970.

Bernstein, Barton J., ed. *Politics and Policies of the Truman Administration.* Chicago: Quadrangle Books, 1970.

Bernstein, Philip S. "Some Facts about Jews." *Harper's* 178 (April 1939): 501–06.

Blake, I. George. *Paul V. McNutt: Portrait of a Hoosier Statesman.* Indianapolis: Central Publishing Company, 1966.

Blantz, Thomas E. *A Priest in Public Service: Francis J. Haas and the New Deal.* Notre Dame: University of Notre Dame Press, 1982.

Bosworth, Patricia. *Anything Your Little Heart Desires: An American Family Story.* New York: Simon and Schuster, 1997.

Bracey, John H., Jr., and August Meier. "Allies or Adversaries: The NAACP, A. Philip Randolph, and the 1941 March on Washington," *Georgia Historical Quarterly* 75 (Spring 1991): 1–17.

Branson, Herman. "The Training of Negroes for War Industries in World War II." *Journal of Negro Education* 12 (Summer 1943): 376–85.

Brazeal, Brailsford R. *The Brotherhood of Sleeping Car Porters: Its Origin and Development.* New York: Harper & Brothers, 1946.

Cayton, Horace R., and George S. Mitchell. *Black Workers and the New Unions.* Chapel Hill, N.C.: University of North Carolina Press, 1939.

Chen, Anthony S. "Rethinking the Origins of Affirmative Action in Employment, 1941–1972." Unpublished paper presented at Graduate Student Research Conference, Institute for Labor and Employment, University of California, Santa Cruz, January 9, 2002.

———. "The Strange Career of Federal Fair Employment Policy, 1941–1963." Unpublished paper presented at the Miller Center for Public Affairs, University of Virginia, Charlottesville, Va., May 26, 2001.

Cole, David. *Enemy Aliens: Double Standards and Constitutional Freedoms in the War on Terrorism.* New York: The New Press, 2003.

Collins, William J. "Race, Roosevelt, and Wartime Production: Fair Employment in World War II Labor Markets." *American Economic Review* 91 (March 2001): 272–86.

Congress and the Nation: A Review of Government and Politics in the Postwar Years. Vol. 1, 1945–1964. Washington, D.C.: Congressional Quarterly, Inc., 1965.

Dalfiume, Richard M. *Desegregation of the U.S. Armed Forces: Fighting on Two Fronts, 1939–53.* Columbia: University of Missouri Press, 1969.

Daniel, Clete. *Chicano Workers and the Politics of Fairness: The FEPC in the Southwest.* Austin, Tex.: University of Texas Press, 1991.

Daniels, Roger. "Incarcerating Japanese Americans." *Organization of American Historians Magazine of History for Teachers of History* 16 (Spring 2002): 19–23.

———. *Prisoners Without Trial: Japanese Americans in World War II.* New York: Hill and Wang, 1995.

Davis, John P. "The Plight of the Negro in the Tennessee Valley." *Crisis* 42 (October 1935): 294–95, 314.

Dierenfield, Bruce J. *Keeper of the Rules: Congressman Howard W. Smith of Virginia.* Charlottesville: University Press of Virginia, 1987.

Dodge, [David] Witherspoon, and Clair M. Cooke. *Southern Rebel in Reverse: The Autobiography of an Idolshaker.* New York: The America Press, 1961.

Du Bois, W. E. B. *Black Reconstruction.* Millwood, N.Y.: Kraus-Thomson Organization Limited, 1976.

Dykeman, Wilma, and James Stokely. *Seeds of Southern Change: The Life of Will Alexander.* Chicago: University of Chicago Press, 1962.

Eagles, Charles W. *Jonathan Daniels and Race Relations: The Evolution of a Southern Liberal.* Knoxville: University of Tennessee Press, 1982.

Elphick, Peter. *Liberty: The Ships That Won the War.* Annapolis, Md.: Naval Institute Press, 2001.

"FEPC: Its Feckless Friends." Editorial. *Crisis* 53 (March 1946): 73–74.

Fite, Gilbert C. *Richard R. Russell, Jr.: Senator from Georgia.* Chapel Hill: University of North Carolina Press, 1991.

Foner, Eric. *Reconstruction: America's Unfinished Revolution, 1863–1877.* New York: Harper & Row, Publishers, 1988.

Foner, Philip S., and Ronald L. Lewis. *The Black Worker from the Founding of the CIO to the AFL-CIO Merger, 1936–1955.* Volume 7 of *The Black Worker: A Documentary History from Colonial Times to the Present.* Philadelphia: Temple University Press, 1983.

Franklin, John Hope. *The Emancipation Proclamation.* Wheeling, Ill.: Harlan Davidson, 1995.

———. "The Emancipation Proclamation, 1863–1963." *Crisis* 70 (March 1963): 133–37.

———. "History of Racial Segregation in the United States." *Annals of the American Academy of Political and Social Science* 303 (March 1956): 1–9.

Gannon, Francis X. *Joseph D. Keenan, Labor's Ambassador in War and Peace: A Portrait of a Man and his Times.* Lanham, Md.: University Press of America, 1984.

Gardner, Michael R. *Harry Truman and Civil Rights: Moral Courage and Political Risks.* Carbondale and Edwardsville: Southern Illinois University Press, 2002.

Garfinkel, Herbert. *When Negroes March: The March on Washington Movement in the Organizational Politics for FEPC.* Glencoe, Ill.: The Free Press, 1959.

Glenn, A. L., Sr. *History of the National Alliance of Postal Employees, 1913–1955.* Washington, D.C.: National Alliance of Postal Employees, 1955.

Graham, Hugh Davis. *The Civil Rights Era: Origins and Development of National Policy, 1960–1972.* New York: Oxford University Press, 1990.

Harris, William H. "Federal Intervention in Union Discrimination: FEPC and West Coast Shipyards during World War II." *Labor History* 22 (Summer 1981): 325–47.

Henderson, Alexa B. "FEPC and the Southern Railway Case: An Investigation into the Discriminatory Patterns of Railroads during World War II." *Journal of Negro History* 61 (April 1976): 172–87.

High, Stanley. "Alien Poison." *Saturday Evening Post* 213 (August 31, 1940): 9–11, 75.

———. "Jews, Anti-Semites, and Tyrants." *Harper's* 185 (June 1942): 22–29.

Hill, Herbert. *Black Labor and the American Legal System: Race, Work, and the Law.* Madison, Wis.: University of Wisconsin Press, 1985.

Hill, Robert, ed., *The FBI's RACON: Racial Conditions in the United States during World War II.* Boston: Northeastern University Press, 1995.

Houston, Charles H. "Foul Employment Practice on the Rails." *Crisis* 56 (October 1949): 269–71, 284.

Houston, Charles H., and John P. Davis, "TVA: Lily White Reconstruction." *Crisis* 41 (October 1934): 290–91, 311.

Hunt, A. Bruce, "The Proposed Fair Employment Practice Act: Facts and Fallacies." *Virginia Law Review* 32 (December 1945): 1–38.

Janken, Kenneth Robert. *White: The Biography of Walter White, Mr. NAACP.* New York: The New Press, 2003.

"John Beecher Biography." Prepared by the Manuscript Department of William R. Perkins Library, Duke University. http://www.English.uiuc.edu/maps/poets/a_f/beecher/bio.htm.

Johnson, Charles S. *To Stem This Tide: A Survey of Racial Tension Areas in the United States.* Boston: The Pilgrim Press, 1943.

Katznelson, Ira, Kim Geiger, and Daniel Kryder. "Limiting Liberalism: The Southern Vote in Congress, 1933–1950." *Political Science Quarterly* 108 (Summer 1993): 282–306.

Kersten, Andrew E. "Publicly Exposing Discrimination: The 1945 FEPC Hearings in Cincinnati." *Queen City Heritage* 52 (Fall 1994): 9–22.

———. *Race, Jobs, and the War: The FEPC in the Midwest, 1941–46.* Urbana, Ill.: University of Illinois Press, 2000.

Kesselman, Louis C. *The Social Politics of FEPC: A Study in Reform Pressure.* Chapel Hill: University of North Carolina Press, 1948.

King, Desmond S. *Separate and Unequal: Black Americans and the U.S. Federal Government.* New York: Oxford University Press, 1995.

Kryder, Daniel. *Divided Arsenal: Race and the American State During World War II.* Cambridge: Cambridge University Press, 2000.

Lane, Frederic Chapin. *Ships for Victory: A History of Shipbuilding Under the U.S. Maritime Commission in World War II.* Baltimore: Md.: Johns Hopkins University Press, 1951 and 2001.

"Legal Restrictions on Employment of Aliens." *Monthly Labor Review* 51 (December 1940): 2352–54.

"Lobbyists: Four Negroes Working behind the Scenes to Influence Congress on Civil Rights." *Ebony* (July 1950): 25–28.

Logan, Rayford W. "The United States Supreme Court and the Segregation Issue." *Annals of the American Academy of Political and Social Science* 303 (March 1956): 10–16.

Lyons, Benjamin S. B. "Liberty/Victory Ships: Several World War II Workhorses Steam on— and Welcome Passengers—Cruising through History." *Cruise Travel* (May–June 2002).

MacGregor, Morris J., Jr. *Integration of the Armed Forces, 1940–1965.* Washington, D.C.: Center of Military History, United States Army, 1981.

Maslow, Will. "FEPC—A Case History in Parliamentary Maneuver." *University of Chicago Law Review* 13 (June 1946): 407–44.

Matthews, Birch. *Cobra! Bell Aircraft Corporation, 1934–1946.* Atglen, Pa.: Schiffer, 1996.

Mayer, Kenneth R. *With the Stroke of a Pen: Executive Orders and Presidential Power.* Princeton: Princeton University Press, 2001.

McNeil, Genna Rae. *Groundwork: Charles Hamilton Houston and the Struggle for Civil Rights.* Philadelphia: University of Pennsylvania Press, 1983.

Meier, August, and Elliot Rudwick. *Black Detroit and the Rise of the UAW.* New York: Oxford University Press, 1979.

Melcher, F. G. "Civil Rights Again an Issue: Alien and Sedition Bills Now before Congress." *Public Weekly* 137 (March 9, 1940): 1069.

Milner, Lucille B., and David Dempsey. "The Alien Myth." *Harper's* 181 (September 1940): 374–79.

Mitchell, Clarence, Jr. "Labor Problems Affecting Negroes." *NAACP Bulletin* 5 (July 1946): 10–11.

———. "N.A.A.C.P.—Welcome to Baltimore!" *Crisis* 43 (July 1936): 200–201, 208.

Moreno, Paul D. *From Direct Action to Affirmative Action: Fair Employment Law and Policy in America, 1933–1972.* Baton Rouge: Louisiana State University Press, 1997.

Morgan, Chester A. *Redneck Liberal: Theodore G. Bilbo and the New Deal.* Baton Rouge: Louisiana State University Press, 1985.

Morgan, Ruth P. *The President and Civil Rights.* New York: St. Martin's Press, 1970.

Nabritt, James M., Jr. "Legal Inventions and the Desegregation Process." *Annals of the American Academy of Political and Social Science* 303 (March 1956): 35–43.

"Negroes! Jews! Catholics! (Three Days of Business in the U.S. Senate)." *Crisis* 52 (August 1945): 217–19, 237–38.

Neuchterlein, James A. "The Politics of Civil Rights: The FEPC, 1941–46." *Prologue* 10 (Fall 1978): 170–91.

Northrup, Herbert R. *Organized Labor and the Negro.* New York: Harper and Brothers, 1944; reprinted Millwood, N.Y.: Kraus, 1976.

———. "Organized Labor and Negro Workers." *Journal of Political Economy* 51 (June 1943): 206–21.

Northrup, Herbert R., and Richard L. Rowan, eds. *The Negro and Employment Opportunities: Problems and Practices.* Ann Arbor: Bureau of Industrial Relations, Graduate School of Business Administration, University of Michigan, 1965.

"On the N.A.A.C.P. Battlefront." *Crisis* 53 (March 1946): 86.

Osur, Alan M. *Blacks in the Army Air Forces during World War II.* Washington, D. C.: Office of Air Force History, 1977.

Patterson, James T. *Mr. Republican: A Biography of Robert A. Taft.* Boston: Little, Brown, 1971.

Pelletier, Alain J. *Bell Aircraft since 1935.* Annapolis: Naval Institute Press, 1992.

Perlman, Mark. *Democracy in the International Association of Machinists.* New York: John Wiley and Sons, 1962.

———. *The Machinists: A New Study in American Trade Unionism.* Cambridge, Mass.: Harvard University Press, 1961.

Pfeffer, Paula F. *A Philip Randolph: Pioneer of the Civil Rights Movement.* Baton Rouge: Louisiana State University Press, 1990.

"Philadelphia—Postwar Preview?" Editorial. *Crisis* 51 (September 1944): 280.

Pollack, J. H. "America Registers Her Aliens." *American Scholar* 10, no. 2 (Spring 1941): 194–208.

"Problems of Race before President." Editorial. *Crisis* 44 (February 1937): 46, 62.

Reed, Merl E. "Black Workers, Defense Industries, and Federal Agencies in Pennsylvania, 1941–1945." *Labor History* 27 (Summer 1986): 356–84.

———. "FEPC and the Federal Agencies in the South." *Journal of Negro History* 65 (1980): 43–56.

———. "The FEPC, the Black Worker and the Southern Shipyards." *South Atlantic Quarterly* 74 (Autumn 1975): 451–55.

———. *Seedtime for the Modern Civil Rights Movement: The President's Committee on Fair Employment Practice, 1941–1945.* Baton Rouge: Louisiana State University Press, 1991.

Reuters, E. B. "Racial Theory." *American Journal of Sociology* 50, no. 6 (May 1945): 452–61.

Roche, Richard J. "FEPC Challenge to Democracy." *America* (April 14, 1945) [also inserted into *Congressional Record* 79th Congress, May 15, 1945, by Senator David I. Walsh (D.-Mass.)].

"Roosevelt, the Humanitarian." Editorial. *Crisis* 43 (October 1936): 298–99.

Ross, Malcolm. *All Manner of Men.* New York: Reynal & Hitchcock, 1948.

Ruchames, Louis. *Race, Jobs, and Politics: The Story of FEPC.* New York: Harcourt, Brace & Co., 1946.

Schierenbeck, Jack. "Lost and Found: The Incredible Life and Times of (Miss) Layle Lane." *American Educator* 24 (Winter 2000–2001): 4–19.

Sitkoff, Harvard. "American Blacks in World War II: Rethinking the Militancy-Watershed Hypotheses." In *The Home Front and War in the Twentieth Century,* ed. James Titus, 147–53. Washington, D.C.: Government Printing Office, 1984.

———. *A New Deal for Blacks: The Emergence of Civil Rights as a National Issue.* New York: Oxford University Press, 1978.

———. "Racial Militancy and Interracial Violence in the Second World War." *Journal of American History* 58 (December 1971): 661–81.

Spaulding, Theodore. "Philadelphia's Hate Strike." *Crisis* 51 (September 1944): 281–83, 301.

Spero, Sterling D., and Abram L. Harris. *The Black Worker: The Negro and the Labor Movement.* Port Washington, N.Y.: Kennikat Press, 1966.

Taylor, R. L. "Aliens All." *New Yorker* 16 (November 9, 1940): 36.

Titus, James, ed. *The Home Front and War in the Twentieth Century.* Washington, D.C.: Government Printing Office, 1984.

Turkel, Studs. *"The Good War": An Oral History of World War II.* New York: Pantheon Books, 1984.

Watson, Denton L. *Lion in the Lobby: Clarence Mitchell, Jr.'s Struggle for the Passage of Civil Rights Laws.* New York: William Morrow, 1990.

———. *Lion in the Lobby: Clarence Mitchell, Jr.'s Struggle for the Passage of Civil Rights Laws.* Rev. ed. Lanham, Md.: University Press of America, 2002.

Weaver, Robert C. "Defense Industries and the Negro." *Annals of the American Academy of Political and Social Science* 223 (September 1942): 60–66.

———. "The Defense Program and the Negro." *Opportunity: Journal of Negro Life* 19 (1940): 324–27.

———. "Detroit and Negro Skill." *Phylon* 4 (Second Quarter 1943): 131–43.

———. "The Employment of Negroes in the United States War Industries." *International Labor Review* 50 (August 1944): 141–59.

———. "The Employment of Negroes in War Industries." *Journal of Negro Education* 12 (Summer 1943): 386–96.

———. "Housing in a Democracy." *Annals of the American Academy of Political and Social Science* 244 (March 1946): 95–106.

———. "The Negro Comes of Age in Industry." *Atlantic Monthly* 172 (September 1943): 54–59.

———. "Negro Employment in the Aircraft Industry." *Quarterly Journal of Economics* 59 (August 1945): 597–625.

———. *Negro Labor: A National Problem.* New York: Harcourt Brace and Co., 1946.

———. "Northern Ways." *Survey Graphic* 36 (January 1947): 43–47.

———. "The Problems of Race Relations in Public Administration." *Opportunity: Journal of Negro Life* 21 (1943): 108–11, 133.

———. "Racial Employment Trends in National Defense." Part I, *Phylon* 2 (Fourth Quarter 1941), 337–38; Part II, *Phylon* 3 (First Quarter 1942): 22–31.

———. "Recent Events in Negro Union Relationships." *Journal of Political Economy* 52 (September 1944): 234–49.

———. "War-Time Employment Gains." *Negro Digest* 2 (May 1944): 33–34:

———. "Whither Northern Race Relations Committees." *Phylon* 5 (Third Quarter 1944): 205–18.

———. "With the Negro's Help." *Atlantic Monthly* 169 (June 1942): 696–707.

White, Walter. *A Man Called White.* Bloomington, Ind.: Indiana University Press, 1948.

Wilkerson, Doxey A. "The Training and Employment of Negroes in National Defense Industries." *The Journal of Negro Education* 10 (January 1941): 121–32.

Wilkins, Roy. "Mississippi Slavery." *Crisis* 40 (April 1933): 81–82.

———. "Through the 1937 Floor Area." *Crisis* 44 (April 1937): 104–6, 124–26.

Winkler, Allan M. "The Philadelphia Transit Strike of 1944." *Journal of American History* 59 (June 1972): 73–89.

Wynn, Neil A. *The Afro-American and the Second World War.* New York: Holmes & Meier, 1975.

Zamora, Emilio. "The Failed Promise of Wartime Opportunity for Mexicans in the Texas Oil Industry." *Southwestern Historical Quarterly* 95 (Winter 1992): 323–350.

Dissertations and Theses

Chen, Anthony S. "From Fair Employment to Equal Employment Opportunity and Beyond: Affirmative Action and the Politics of Civil Rights during the New Deal Order, 1941–1972." Ph.D. diss., University of California at Berkeley, 2002.

Hardin, Frances Anne. "The Role of Presidential Advisers: Roosevelt Aides and the FEPC, 1941–43." Master's thesis, Cornell University, 1975.

Obadele-Starks, Ernest. "The Road to Jericho: Black Workers, The Fair Employment Practice Commission, and the Struggle for Racial Equality on the Upper Texas Gulf Coast, 1941–1947." Ph.D. diss., University of Houston, 1996.

Saucier, Bobby Wade, "The Public Career of Theodore G. Bilbo." Ph.D. diss., Tulane University, 1971.

Smith, Charles Pope. "Theodore G. Bilbo's Senatorial Career: The Final Years, 1941–1947." Ph.D. diss., University of Southern Mississippi, 1983.

Tassava, Christopher James. "Launching a Thousand Ships: Entrepreneurs, War Workers, and the State of American Shipbuilding, 1940–1945." Ph.D. diss., Northwestern University, 2003.

Government Reports

United States. Committee on Fair Employment Practice. *FEPC: How It Operates*. Washington, D.C., Government Printing Office, 1944.

———. *Final Report, June 28, 1946*. Washington, D.C.: Government Printing Office, June 28, 1946.

———. *First Report, July 1943–December 1944*. Washington, D.C.: Government Printing Office, May 1945.

———. *Minorities in Defense*. Washington, D.C.: Government Printing Office, 1941.

United States. Congress. House. *National War Agencies Appropriation Bill for 1945: Hearings before the Subcommittee of the Committee on Appropriations on HR 4879, House of Representatives*. 78th Cong., 2d sess. Washington, D.C.: Government Printing Office, 1944.

———. *To Investigate Executive Agencies: Hearings before the Special Committee to Investigate Executive Agencies [Smith Committee], House of Representatives*. 78th Cong., 1st and 2d sess. Washington, D.C.: Government Printing Office, 1944.

———. *Supplemental Federal Security Appropriations for 1949: Hearings before the Subcommittee on Appropriations, House of Representatives*. 80th Cong., 2d sess. Washington, D.C.: Government Printing Office, 1948.

———. Committee on Appropriations. *National War Agencies Appropriation Bill, 1945*. H. Rept. 1511 to accompany HR 4879, 78th Cong., 2d sess. Washington, D.C.: Government Printing Office, 1944.

———. Committee on Government Operations. *Executive Orders and Proclamations: A Study of a Use of Presidential Powers*. 85th Cong. 1st sess. Washington, D.C.: Government Printing Office, 1957.

United States. Congress. Senate. Fair Employment Practices Act, S. 2048: Hearings before a Subcommittee of Committee on Education and Labor, 30–31 August, 6–8 September, 1944. 78th Cong., 2d sess. Washington, D.C.: GPO, 1944.

———. Fair Employment Practices Act: Hearings before a Subcommittee of Committee on Education and Labor, on S. 101 and S. 459, 12–14 March 1945, 79th Cong., 1st sess. Washington, D.C.: Government Printing Office, 1945.

———. Labor-Federal Security Appropriations Bill for 1948: Hearings before the Committee on Appropriations United States Senate on HR 2700. 80th Cong., 1st sess. Washington, D.C.: Government Printing Office, 1947.

———. Committee on Appropriations. National War Agencies Appropriations Bill, 1945, S. Rept. 960 to accompany HR 4879, 78th Cong., 2d sess. Washington, D.C.: Government Printing Office, 1944.

———. Committee on Civil Service. Hearings before the Committee on Civil Service, United States Senate, on the Confirmation of Nomination of Jesse M. Donaldson to be Postmaster General and Paul Aiken to be Second Assistant Postmaster General, December 9, 1947, 80th Cong., 1st sess. Washington: Government Printing Office, 1947.

United States. Office of War Information. *United States Government Manual, 1945.* Washington, D.C.: Government Printing Office, 1945.

Data Bases and Online Sources

African-American Biographical Data Base. Alexandria, Va.: Chadwyck Healey, 2001.

Amateur Athletic Foundation of Los Angeles. "Famous Magnates of the Federal League: R. B. Ward, the Master Baker, Vice President of the Feds." http://www.aafla.org/SportsLibrary /BBM/1915/bbm3g.pdf.

Ancestry.com. Social Security Death Index. http://www.ancestry.com/search/db.aspx?dbid=3693.

———. 1930 Census Records. http://content.ancestry.com/iexec/?dbid=6224&htx=List&ti=0.

AT&T. "History of AT&T." http://www.att.com/history/history1.html.

Atkinson Construction. "Atkinson Construction Company Background." http://www.atkn.com.

Atomic Heritage Foundation. "Manhattan Project History/Oak Ridge." http://www.atomicheritage .org/oakridge.htm.

Bechtel. *Bechtel Briefs.* January 1998 http://www.bechtel.com.

Bell System. "Western Electric: A Brief History." http://www.bellsystemmemorial.com /westernelectric_history.html.

Boeing. "North American Aviation History." http://www.boeing.com/history/bna/waryr.html.

Burson, Harold. "Prepping for a Career in Public Relations: My First 25 Years." *Burson-Marsteller.* http://www.bm.com/pages/about/history/memos/2.

Center for Public Integrity. "Windfalls of War, Bechtel Group and Parsons Corp. Company Profiles." http//www.publicintegrity.org.

Colton Company. "WWII Shipbuilding Records." http://www.coltoncompany.com/shipbldg /usshipbldrs.htm.

The Columbia Electronic Encyclopedia. New York: Columbia University Press, 2000.

Curtiss-Wright. "Curtiss-Wright History." http://www.curtisswright.com/history/default.asp.

Energizer. "Energizer Company History." http://www.energizer.com/company/companyhistory .asp.

Evansville Museum. "The Evansville Shipyard on Evansville Museum Website." http://www .emuseum.org/virtual_museum/evansville.shipyard/shipyard.html.

FAS Military Analysis Network. Analyses of Hughes Electronics Corporation, New York Ship Building, Northrop Grumman, and Textron, on http://www.fas.org.

General Cable Company. "Historical Highlights." http://www.generalcable.com/Sections /About_Us/a_GCCdates.html.

General Electric. "Our Company: History." http://www.ge.com/en/company/companyinfo /at_a_glance/history_story.htm.

Global Security.Com. "Military Facilities." http://www.globalsecurity.org/military/facility.htm.

———. "Military Industry." http://www.globalsecurity.org/military/industry.htm.

Goodyear. "Goodyear Corporate History." http://www.goodyear.com/corporate/chistory.html.

Greater Astoria Historical Society. "History Topics: Industry, Loose-Wiles (Sunshine) Biscuit." http://www.astorialic.org/topics/industry/sunshine.shtm.

Hanford, Washington. "History of Hanford Site Defense Production." http://www.hanford.gov /history/misc/defn-2nd.htm.

History Makers. "Lawmakers: Biography of Truman Gibson." http://www.thehistorymakers.com.

Hoover Precision. "Company History [Hoover Ball and Bearing]." http://hooverprecision/com/history.htm.

Hyperwar. "U.S. Naval Activities World War II by State." *U.S. Navy, U.S. Navy in World War II.* http://www.ibiblio.org/hyperwar/USN/ref/USN-Act/index.html.

Information Headquarters.Com. "Bechtel Corporation Profile." http://www .informationheadquarters .com/List_of_American_Companies/Bechtel_Corporation.

Manhattan Project Heritage Preservation Association, Inc. "Manhattan Project History." http://www.childrenofthemanhattanproject.org.

Maryland Organ Service Online. "The Hammond Story." http://www.mosweb.com/knowledgebase /hammond/id44.htm.

Matson. "Matson Navigation Company Corporate Background." http://www.matson.com /about_content.html.

Morning Call Online. "Forging America: The Story of Bethlehem Steel." http://www.mcall .com/news/specials/bethsteel/archives.

MPD. "MPD History (Ken-Rad Tube and Lamp Corporation)." http://www.mpdcomponents .com/Components/mpd_history.htm.

National D-Day Museum. "D Day Historyscope." www.ddaymuseum.org.

National Park Service. "World War II Shipbuilding in the San Francisco Bay Area." *World War II in the San Francisco Bay Area.* http://www.cr.nps.gov/nr/travel/wwIIbayarea/shipbuilding.htm.

Nevada Northern & Railroads of White Pine Country. "A Corporate History of the Nevada Consolidated Copper Properties." http://nn.railfan.net/nevconhist/nevconhistory.htm.

Northern Indiana Center for History. "A B Farquhar Company Sketch." *The Oliver Farm Equipment Company History.* http://www.centerforhistory.org./oliver_corp.html.

Northrop Grumman Newport News. "About Us: History." http://nn.northropgrumman.com /about/History/wwii.stm.

Ohio History Central. "B.F. Goodrich Company History." http://www.ohiohistorycentral/org /ohc/h/05/gro/bfgc.shtml.

Olin. "Olin Company History." http://olin.www.com/about/history.asp.

Online Archives of California. "Guide to the Henry J. Kaiser Papers at the Bancroft Library, UC Berkeley." http://oac.cdlib.org/findaid/ark:/13030/tf2v19n6d)/scopecontent/288696609.

Pitney Bowes. "Pitney Bowes Company History." http://www.pb.com.

Procter and Gamble. "Procter and Gamble: Our History." http://www.pg.com/company /who_we_are/ourhistory/jhtml.

Project Liberty Ship. http://www.liberty-ship.com.

Quaker Oats. "Quaker Company History." http://www.quakeroats.com/qfb_AboutUs/history.cfm.

Saudi Arabian Information Resource. "Saudi Aramco: Summary Chronology." http://www .saudinf/com/main/d199.htm.

Sinclair Oil. "Sinclair History." http://www.sinclairoil.com/about_sinclair.htm.

Southwest Museum of Engineering, Communications, and Computation. "Radio Proximity Fuzes." http://www.smecc.org/radio_proximilty_fuzes.htm.

Tennessee Valley Authority. "History." http://www.tva.gov/heritage/hert_hist.htm.

———. "TVA Act of 1933." http://www.tva.gov/abouttva/pdf/TVA_Act.pdf.

Union Carbide Corporation. "Union Carbide History." http://www.unioncarbide.com/history /index.htm.

United Fruit Historical Society. "United Fruit Company Chronology." http://www.unitedfruit .org/chronology/chronology.html.

University of Texas. "Lone Star Army Ammunition Plant." *Handbook of Texas Online.* http://www .tsha.utexas.edu/handbook/online/articles/view/LL/dml1.html.

U.S. Centennial of Flight Commission. Douglas, Hughes Aviation, McDonnell Aircraft, Pratt & Whitney, North American Aviation and Lockheed Profiles. http://www.centennialofflight .gov/essay_cat/5.htm.

U.S. Merchant Marine. "World War II Liberty Ships Built During World War II Listed by Shipyard." http://www.usmm.net/libyards.html.

———. "Steamship Company Operators of American Flag Ships during World War II." http://www.usmm.net/operators.html.

———. "Shipyards and Suppliers for U.S. Maritime Commission During World War II." http://www.usmm.net/shipbuild.html.

U.S. Steel Corporation. "Corporate Profile." http://www.ussteel.com/corp/about.htm.

U.S. Sugar Corporation. "U.S. Sugar History." www.ussugar.com/aboutus/history.html.

Western Reserve Historical Society, Crawford Aero-Aviation Museum. "LTV Steel Sketch." http://wrhs.org/crawford/template.asp?id=410.

Western Union. "Western Union Company, About Us: Our History." http://www.westernunion .com/info/aboutUsHistory.asp.

Biographical Directories and Encyclopedias

American Men and Women of Science. New York: Bowker, 1971–.

American National Biography. Ed. John A. Garraty and Mark C. Carnes. 24 vols. New York: Oxford University Press, 1999.

Beecher, John. *Biography.* Prepared by the Manuscript Department of William R. Perkins Library, Duke University. http://www.English.uiuc.edu/maps/poets/a_f/beecher/bio.htm [2003].

Biographical Dictionary of American Labor. Ed. Gary M. Fink. Westport, Conn.: Greenwood Press, 1984.

Biographical Dictionary of American Labor Leaders. Ed. Gary M. Fink. Westport, Conn.: Greenwood Press, 1974.

Biographical Directory of the American Congress, 1774–1989. Westport, Conn.: Greenwood Press, 1989.

Biographical Directory of the Governors of the United States, 1789–1978. Westport, Conn.: Meckler Books, 1978.

Biographical Directory of the United States Executive Branch, 1774–1989. Ed. Robert Sobel. New York: Greenwood Press, 1990.

Biography Index: A Cumulative Index to Biographical Material in Books and Magazines. Ed. Bea Joseph. New York: H. W. Wilson Co., 1949–.

The Cambridge Dictionary of American Biography. Ed. John S. Bowman. Cambridge: Cambridge University Press, 1995.

Civil Rights: A Current Guide to the People, Organizations, and Events. Ed. A. John Adams and Joan Martin Burke. New York: Bowker, 1970.

Contemporary Authors: A Bio-Bibliographical Guide to Current Authors and Their Works: Permanent Series. Ed. Clare D. Kinsman. Detroit: Gale Research, 1975–.

Current Biography Yearbook. New York: H. W. Wilson Co., 1955–.

Dictionary of American Biography. New York: Charles Scribner's Sons, 1946–.

Encyclopedia of African American Civil Rights: From Emancipation to the Present. Ed. Charles D. Lowery and John F. Marszalek. New York: Greenwood Press, 1992.

Encyclopedia of African-American Culture and History. Ed. Jack Salzman, David Lionel Smith, and Cornel West. New York: Macmillan Library Reference, 1995.

Encyclopedia of the McCarthy Era. Ed. William M. Klingaman. New York: Facts on File, 1996.

Gibson, Truman. *Biography.* http://www.thehistorymakers.com/biography/biography.asp
　　?bioindex=288&category=LawMakers.

*In Black and White: A Guide to Magazine Articles, Newspaper Articles, and Books Concerning
　　More that 15,000 Individuals and Groups.* Ed. Mary Mace Spradling. 3d ed. Detroit: Gale
　　Research, 1980.

Levine, Michael, and Eleanora W. Schoenebaum, eds. *The Eisenhower Years.* Political Profiles.
　　New York: Facts on File, 1977.

————. *The Truman Years.* Political Profiles. New York: Facts on File, 1978.

National Cyclopaedia of American Biography. Clifton, N.J.: J. T. White, 1893–1984.

Notable Black American Men. Ed. Jessie Carney Smith. Detroit: Gale Research, 1999.

Notable Black American Women. Ed. Jessie Carney Smith. Detroit: Gale Research, 1991.

New York Times Biographical Service. New York: Arno Press, 1974–.

Standard and Poor's Register of Corporations, Directors, and Executives. New York: Standard and
　　Poor's, 1928–.

Who's Who among African Americans. Detroit: Gale Research, 1976–.

Who's Who in American Law. 2d ed. Chicago: Marquis Who's Who, 1977.

Who's Who in American Politics. New York: Bowker, 1968–.

Who's Who in Colored America. New York: Who's Who in Colored America, 1927–.

Who's Who in Finance and Industry. New Providence, N.J.: Marquis Who's Who, 1973–.

Who's Who in Government. Chicago: Marquis Who's Who, 1973–77.

Who's Who in Labor. New York: Arno Press, 1976.

Who's Who in the United Nations and Related Agencies. 1st ed. New York: Arno Press, 1975.

Who's Who in World Jewry. Ed. Harry Schneiderman and Itzhak J. Carmin. New York: 1955–.

Who Was Who in America. New Providence, N.J.: Marquis Who's Who, 1896–.

Women Anthropologists: A Biographical Dictionary. Ed. Ute Gacs, Aisha Khan, Jerrie McIntyre,
　　and Ruth Weinberg. Westport, Conn.: Greenwood Press, 1988.

INDEX

apparel industry: FEPC cases on, 372, 374; postwar employment significance of, 377

Appley, Lawrence A. (dep. chm. and exec. dir., WMC), **764;** correspondence with, 71–72; negotiations with, 200

application forms: elimination of discriminatory information from, 206, 216, 351, 506, 525

Appropriations Committee, House: and FEPC appropriations, clvi, ccix; hearings of, ccxxviii, 258; information to, lxxiii

Arabian American Oil Co. (Aramco), *715;* discrimination by, 436n–37n; FEPC case on, 436, 480

Arizona: discrimination against Mexican Americans in, clxx; employment stabilization plan for, 64; FEPC cases in, 325–29, 373; mining industry in, clxxi, clxxiv, clxxvii; testimony on conditions in, 325

Arkansas: discrimination against Mexican Americans in, clxx–clxxi; discrimination in training programs in, 31; segregation in, 564

Armed Forces, U.S.: desegregation of, xxx; and loyalty investigations, cxxx; and processed foods, cxxiii; segregation in, xxx; supply of, xxiv

arms and ammunition plants: layoffs at, 254–55, 547

Armwood, George: lynching of, xx–xxi, lxii, lxxvii

Army, U.S., 55, 55n; and Air Forces FEPC cases, 257; and ALCOA, 476n; and Bethlehem Steel Shipbuilding strike, 619–20, 625–27, 631, 634; and black employment, 463–65; contractors of, clii, 466, 524; contracts with, 483n; employment of Japanese Americans, lxxiii, 177, 194, 208–9; ; enforcement of exec. order against discrimination, 300, 646; FEPC relationship with, xxiii–xxiv, cxxxi, 652–53; and FEPC shipbuilding cases, 421; foreigners in, cl–cli; and General Cable case, cxxxi, ccxv; and integration of defense plants, 311; investigation by, 251; Japanese American veterans of, 533; and Jones and Laughlin Steel Co. work stoppage, 114; nondiscrimination clauses in contracts, 679; and Norris Stamping case, 482–83; and Philadelphia transit strike, xxv, lxviii, cciii–cciv, 341, 345, 346; plants occupied by, cxxviii, ccxxix; Point Breeze works, withdrawal from, 222, 247; procurement regulations of, lxxiv; and proof of citizenship, 55, 55n, 647; relationship with FEPC, 449; secret research for, 43; and Shell Oil case, clxxix; and strikes, ccxxv, ccxxvii, 166, 171, 487; and upgrading of black workers, 77; violence and protest in, 430, 921; and Western Cartridge case, ccxv; and Wright Aeronautical Co. strike, 311, 312

Army Air Forces, U.S.: and Consolidated Vultee Aircraft Corp. case, 456, 461; contractor of, 466; FEPC cases on, 207, 245, 376; regulations of, 236; and strikes, 310

Army Air Forces Depot, U.S.: FEPC case on, 201, 368; and nonwhite employment statistics, 155

Army Communications Service: FEPC case on, 265, 280

Army Engineers, Northwest Division: FEPC case on, 208, 390

Army Ordnance Depots: FEPC cases on, 638, 639

Army Signal Corps, U.S.: contractors of, 465, 466; and employment of black women, 271, 274–75, 465, 466; FEPC contact with, 21; negotiations with Labor Branch of, 491; plants under the jurisdiction of, 484

Arnold, Mr. (Postal Alliance), **764;** and FEPC cases against P.O.s, 366

Arnold Agency: FEPC case on, 347–48

Aronson, Arnold (exec. dir., Bureau of Jewish Employment Problems), **764–65;** as consultant, Region VI, FEPC, 227

Arredondo (FEPC complainant), 326

arsenals: applicability of nondiscrimination policy to, ccxxv; Japanese Americans employed at, 177

Ashe, Bowman F. (regional dir., Atlanta Office, WMC), **765;** and Alabama Dry Dock and Shipbuilding case, 595; attitude of, 41; and black access to training programs, 28

Ashley, E. W. (pers. mgr., Vancouver Yard, Kaiser Shipbuilding): and training and upgrading of black workers, 129

Associated Press (AP): dispatches of, 349–50; reporting on strikes, 405

Associated Shipyards: FEPC case on, 333, 381, 393

Athenia Steel Co. (Clifton, N.J.): *715;* FEPC case on, 206

Atkins, Capt. A. K. (Labor Rel. Sect., Navy Dept.), 108–9, 194

Atkinson, Guy F., Co., *716;* FEPC case on, 213, 237, 285, 287

Atkinson, Hamilton (commissioner, Baltimore Police Dept.), **765;** meeting with, 185

Atlanta, Ga.: black employment in, 485; FEPC cases in, 244, 246, 444, 446; FEPC regional office in, ciii, 295, 367; FEPC relationships in, 449; investigation of industries near, 42n; Mitchell's field trip to, 427, 440, 441, 448, 451; reports from USES office in, 250; segregation in, 663; training program in, 39–40

Atlanta Constitution: employment listings of, 239n–40n

Atlanta Gas Light Co.: report on, 188

Atlanta Joint Terminals, *716*

Atlanta Journal: discriminatory advertising by, 228, 239, 239n–40n; employment listings of, 239, 239n–40n; report on, 263; request regarding, 200

Atlanta School of Social Work: Mitchell's attendance at, xx

Atlantic Basin Iron Works: discrimination against blacks by, 234

Atlantic City, N.J.: black employment in, ccxi, 477, 682, 683; FEPC cases in, ccxi, 400–401, 479; telephone operators in, 515n

Atlantic Coast Line Railroad Co., *716;* FEPC case on, lxix, lxxxvi

Atlantic Joint Terminals: FEPC case on, lxix, lxxxvi

Atlantic Steel Co.: FEPC case on, 446

Atlas Powder Co.: as Army contractor, 466

atomic bomb, production of, lxxv, 92n, 447n

atomic power industry: development of, 92n; inclusion of minority workers in, lxxv, 92n, 447n

attorney general, U.S.: questions referred to, 320n; ruling of, 364

Austin, Tex.: FEPC office in, proposed, 180

automobile industry: black employment in, ccxxii, 113n, 561; citizenship requirements for work in, clxix; report on FEPC experience with, 554; unions in, xlvi

automobile plants: employment discrimination at, 113n

aviation industry: postwar significance of, clxxii; unions in, xlvi

Axis Powers: refugees from, clii–cliii

B29 bombers, clxxxii

Baba, Mr. (Japanese American FEPC complainant), 426

Babcock, Paul (VP of Local 18, IUMSA): and Alabama Dry Dock and Shipbuilding case, 608

backlash, white, xxxii

badges: racial designations on, clix, clxiii

baggagemen: blacks denied jobs as, 562

Bahamas: agricultural workers from, cxlviii, 66–67, 80–81, 89

Bailey, R. H. (Alabama Dry Dock and Shipping Co.): workers under, 609

bake shops: FEPC jurisdiction over, cxxiii

Baker, Helen F.: and affidavit, 384

Chinese: barred from naturalization, cl; discrimination against, xxiv, clxxxiii, 556; FEPC complaints from, clxviii; and union membership, clxxxix; "white," counted by union as, 432

Chino Metal Trades Council, AFL: nondiscrimination clauses in contracts of, 587

chippers: blacks employed as, 29, 98, 134, 138, 151, 337–38, 593, 595, 596, 606

Chrysler Corp.: ordance plant operated by, 255; segregation at, lix

Chrysler Tank Arsenal plant: strike at, 295, 300

Chubb, Sally (FEPC office, Region VII, Atlanta), **769**; role of, 448, 450

churches: and settlement of strikes, ccxxv

Cicero, Ill.: employment figures regarding, 97–98

Cincinnati, Ohio: employment discrimination in, 96–97; FEPC cases in, lxvii, 389; FEPC negotiations in, 257; FEPC office in, 111, 111n, 370, 537; hearings in, 391n; investigation of employers in, 96–97, 640; reports on, 641n; segregation in, clxxxi; strikes at, 295; treatment of blacks in, 36n

Cincinnati Bickford Tool Co.: discrimination by, 96

Cincinnati Milling Machine Co.: discrimination by, 96

CIO. *See* Congress of Industrial Organizations

CIO Committee to Abolish Discrimination: and Shell Oil case, clxxix, 520, 522; discussions with, 244

Citizens Committee, Columbia, S.C.: FEPC complaint of, 638

Citizens Committee of Los Angeles: as FEPC complaint, 639; and street railway cases, 656

Citizens Committee of San Diego: as FEPC complaint, 639

Citizens Committee on Jobs and Training, Birmingham, Ala.: as FEPC complaint, 641

citizenship: declarations of, clii, 647–48; employment regulations regarding, cxxv, cxlix–cl, cli–clii, cliii, clvi, clx; proof of, clii, 55, 55n, 647; questions on, on employment forms, clxi

City-Wide Young People's Forum, Baltimore: Mitchell's role in, xx, liii

civic organizations: and settlement of strikes, ccxxv

Civil Air Regulations: and aliens, 251

Civil Conservation Corps Act, 654

Civil Liberties Committee (Senate), 32

civil rights: and loyalty investigations, 73

Civil Rights Act of 1875, 667

Civil Rights Act of 1957, xxx–xxxi, xxxiii

Civil Rights Act of 1964, xxvii, xxxii, xxxiii

Civil Rights Commission, U.S., xxxi

civil rights groups: relationship to FEPC, xxv

civil rights laws: enforcement of, xxxi; passage of, during Reconstruction, lxxvi–lxxvii; southern blocking of, xxx; state, 356

civil rights legislation, xxxi, xxxii

civil rights movement: and school busing, xxxiii; fragmentation of, xxxiii; impact of, xxxiii; new generation of, xxxi

civil rights organizations: and black employment, ccxiv, cxcix; and settlement of strikes, ccxxv; and transit cases, ccv; and union discrimination, ccxvii

civil rights statutes, 653

civil service: aliens in, cxlix, clvi; prohibition on discrimination in, 245

Civil Service Classification Act, 654

Civil Service Commission, U.S.: agreements of, 275, 449; and back wages for reinstated employees, 368; clearance of FEPC staff members by, 119; cooperation of, with FEPC, 299–300; criticism of, 563; discrimination by, cxxxiv, 105, 109–10, 206; discrimination complaints referred to, 91, 95; and employment discrimination, cxxxiv, 34n;

and employment forms, clx; and employment of Japanese Americans, cxxxiv, cliii, clxviii, 515n–16n, 532–33, 533n; examinations of, and discrimination, 397; FEPC agreements with, cxxvii, cxxxiv, cxl, 529; FEPC cases on, 245, 295, 639, 640, 641; FEPC designated staff member for, 300; FEPC relationship with, xxiv, cxxxiv, 116, 210, 306; Form 57 of, clx, clxi; information from, 445; investigation by, 179; jurisdiction of, cxxxiv; loyalty investigations by, cxxxiv, clv, 516; nondiscriminatory policy of, cxxix; policies of, on citizens of Japanese ancestry, 66, 66n, 256, 514, 518, 532–33, 533n; and P.O. discrimination, 289n; and records on black employment, clxiv; on release of interned Japanese Americans, 68; and religious holidays, cxlv; regulations of, clx

Civil Service Commission (Region V): relationship with FEPC, 449

Civilian Pilot Training Act (1939), 654

Clairton, Pa.: strikes at, cxcviii, ccxxxv–ccxxxvi; walkout at, 243, 257

Clark, Howard (FEPC complainant), 135

Clark, Mr.: and Engineering Science Management War Training programs, 34–35

Clark, Tom C. (D., Texas) (atty. gen., Truman admin.): and discrimination in Justice Dept., 563

Clark, William (chm., Grievance Committee, Local 767, UER & MWA): FEPC complaint from, 384

Clearfield, Pa.: FEPC hearing in, ciii

Clemens, Hiawatha P. (FEPC complainant), 124

clerical workers: blacks employed as, cxxxvi, cci, ccxi; 2, 99, 140, 366, 400n, 403n, 447n, 477, 481n, 663, 681, 682, 684; wages of, 681, 684

Cleveland, Ohio: black employment in, ccvii, cxcix; complaints against P.O. in, 33; complaints against railroads in, 37; employment by street railways in, 76; employment stabilization plan for, 61–62, 63; FEPC cases in, 263, 367; FEPC hearings, 40, 551, 617; FEPC staff in, li; Mitchell's visits to, 641n; nonwhite employment in, 562; P.O. cases in, cxxxvi; transit system in, cxcix, ccvii, 76

Click, Commander D. G. (Indus. Rel. Section, Navy Dept.): conference with, 108–9

Clifton, Ariz.: FEPC complaints in, 585

Clifton, N. Jeanne, **769**

Cline, A. J.: FEPC meeting with, 432

Clinton County Board of Supervisors, N.Y., 263

Clinton Engineering Works (Oak Ridge, Tenn.), *724;* employment opportunities at, lxxv; FEPC case on, 206, 514

Clore, Lethia W[arren] (examiner, FEPC), li, 111, 111n, 370, **769**

closed shop contracts: court rulings on, ccxxviii–ccxix; impact of, 2, 158–59; impact of, on black workers, clxxx, clxxxi, clxxxvii, clxxxix, cxc, ccxviii–ccxix, 431, 433, 439n, 617

closed shops: court decisions on, lxx, cxcii–cxciii; and employment discrimination, ccxvii, 42n; exclusion of blacks from, 37n; gov. sanction of, ccxvii; impact of, on blacks, clxxxv, clxxxix; and union discrimination, lxx, cxcii–cxciii, 2, 321

Clow, Rev. James (pres., Portland NAACP): meeting attended by, cxcv

CLU of A (Union): complaints against job referrals by, 235

Clymer, Lewis W. (WMC rep., Region IX), **769;** and employment of black women, 90; information from, on strike, 81; and St. Louis cases, 321

coal mines: and segregation, lxi

Crocetti, Eugene (pres., Local 33, IUMSWA): and Bethlehem Steel strike, 628, 630

Crockett, George W. (legal div., FEPC), **770;** and FEPC jurisdiction, cxix; jurisdictional statements of, 288n–89n; memo of, on hospital cases, 304; newsletter of, 555n; opinions of, 303n–4n; recommendations of, 197, 218n

Crockin, Miss (union leader, Chesapeake and Potomac Telephone Co.), 100

Crosby, Amanda Lee: memo on, 195

Crosley Radio Corp. (Cincinnati), *726;* black employment at, 563; discrimination by, 96; hearings on, 391n

Cross, Maj. (Lt. Col.) Ira B., Jr., **770;** and FEPC cases in St. Louis, 479, 497–98

Crossetti, Eugene (IUMSWA): opposition to black welders of, 147n

Crown Cork and Seal: segregated facilities at, 169

Crum, Bartley C. (special counsel, FEPC), **770**

Cumberland, MD: labor stabilization plans for, 63

Cummings, A. C. (foreman, California Shipbuilding Co.): and discrimination against black workers, 152

Cuneo Press: FEPC case on, 371

Cunningham v. Neagle (1890): decision in, 669, 671–72; and presidential power, 669, 670, 671–72

Curtis Co.: FEPC cases on, 245, 249

Curtiss-Wright Aeronautical Corp., *726;* black employment at, ccxii; FEPC cases on, 247, 464, 465–66, 494, 504, 507, 511–13; FEPC negotiations with, clxxxi; impact of completion of war contracts of, 511–12, 513; quota system at, ccxii; segregation at, ccxii, 294–95, 511, 512

Cushman, Edward L. (Michigan state dir., WMC), **770;** and discrimination at Ford plants, 113; and information on nonwhite employees, 270

custodians: minority groups limited to positions as, lvii

customer service jobs: black employment in, 400n, 403n

Customs, Collector of, U.S.: FEPC case on, 264; FEPC letter regarding, 302

customs, local: concessions to, ccxiv; discrimination excused by, ccxiv; and employment discrimination, clxxviii, ccxiii

Customs Service, U.S.: FEPC case on, 440

cutbacks: impact of, clxxxii, 484n; and reconversion, clxxxi, clxxxii, ccxiii

Cutietta, Vincent A., **770;** loyalty investigation of, 225

cylinder head magnesium divisions of ALCOA: segregation ended at, 90

Czechs: access to Engineering Science Management War Training courses, 35

Dailey, Pat (Boilermakers Union): referrals by, 292

dairy industry: FEPC opinion on, 301

Dallas, Mr.: demotion of, 323

Dallas, Tex.: blacks hired as mail handlers in, 366; Bloch's field trip to, 251; dismissal of Seventh Day Adventists in, 237; FEPC cases in, 285, 364; FEPC complainants in, 175; FEPC complaints on Machinists Union in, 432–33; FEPC complaints on P.O.s in, cxxxvi; FEPC office in, 180; FEPC staff in, lii; Mitchell's visits to, 117–20, 385, 386, 387, 641n; P.O. cases in, 361, 392, 396, 397, 398, 412, 415, 462, 484–85; P.O. in, 297; segregation in, xlviii; union problems in, 246, 554

Dallas Morning News: FEPC case on, 320n

Dallas Negro Chamber of Commerce: and complaints to FEPC, 112; as FEPC complainant, 640

Dalrymple, Sherman Harrison (pres., United Rubber Workers), **770;** supports rights of black workers, 76

Daly, W. T. (pers. mgr., Alabama Dry Dock and Shipbuilding Co.): FEPC discussions with, 597, 605, 613

Daneiger Oil Co. (Texas): FEPC case on, 386

Daniel Construction Co. (Charleston, S.C.): FEPC case on, 638

Daniels, Jonathan W. (presidential aide), **770;** and Bethlehem Shipbuilding strike, 626, 627; conferences with, 189, 343–44; and discrimination against Mexicans, Mexican Americans, clxxv; and Los Angeles Street Railway case, ccxxx, 350n; and Philadelphia transit strike, 346

Daughters of the American Revolution: discrimination by, xlvii

David, Alfred E.: refusal to pay dues to union auxiliary, 135

Davidson, Carl C. (FEPC complainant), 151

Davidson, Eugene C. (asst. dir. of field operations, FEPC), **770–71;** agreement with, 399; appointed assoc. dir. of field operations, 523n; assignments of, 20, 188, 206, 212, 217, 226, 228, 258, 307, 365n, 389, 427, 468, 491, 494, 520, 522; and Bell Telephone Co. cases, 400, 413; and cases of postwar significance, 375n; cases prepared by, 238; and discrimination against aliens, cli; discusses motive as element of discrimination, 68, 74; discussions with, 367, 386, 387; and FEPC cases with postwar significance, 377–79; and hearings in New York, 22n; and information collected by USES, 74; memoranda of, 517n; memoranda to, 501–2, 516–17, 537–38, 552–53; Mitchell's relationship with, li; and Philadelphia transit strike, 345; and racial strikes, ccxxxvi, ccxxxviii, 661n; reports and memoranda sent to, 178, 179, 194–96, 199–203, 218, 317–19, 363–65, 367–69, 375–76, 382–83, 387–88, 389–91, 398–400, 404–5, 412–13, 418–19, 423–24, 426–27, 435–37, 438–41, 452–53, 456–57, 458–60, 461–63, 467–71, 473–76, 478–81, 484–86, 490–92, 493–95, 496–98, 504–5, 506–8, 513–16, 519–21, 522–23, 533–34, 539–40; reports of, 60, 447n; suggestions of, 116

Davis, Al: statement of, 135

Davis, Henry (FEPC complainant), 127, 135, **771**

Davis, James (Delta Shipbuilding Co.): conference with, 353n

Davis, Dr. John Aubrey (dir., Div. of Review and Analysis, FEPC), **771;** and Chicago hearing, 550–52; confers with Veterans Admin., 479; and employment statistics, lxxvi; FEPC, assessment of, lxxxii; and FEPC relationship with WMC, 495n; investigates complaints regarding firms in Saudi Arabia, 437n; and Los Angeles Street Railway case, ccx; and Lunt Report, 510n; memoranda of, lxxxiv, 473n; memoranda to, 209–10, 269, 488–90, 511–13, 519–21, 537–38, 539–40, 541–42; Mitchell, views on, xliv; and racial strikes, ccxxxvi, 661n–62n; report of, on racial strikes, 659–62; reports of, ccx, 36n, 229n, 343n; and reports on successful FEPC cases, 88; reports sent to, 178, 179, 367–69, 375–76, 382–83, 387–88, 389–91, 398–400, 404–5, 412–13, 418–19, 423–24, 426–27, 435–37, 438–41, 452–53, 456–57, 461–63, 467–71, 473–76, 478–81, 484–86, 490–92, 493–95, 496–98, 504–5, 506–8, 513–16, 519–21, 522–23; and telephone co. cases, 675n; and WMC, 458–60, 471, 472, 473n, 488–90

Davis, Mrs. Joy (FEPC), 209–10, **771**

Davis, R. V. (Southern Bell Co.): FEPC confers with, 402

Davison Chemical Corp. (Baltimore, Md.), *726;* discriminatory advertising by, 641

Dawson, LeRoy: as judge, 145

Dawson, William A. (D., Ill.): and permanent FEPC legislation, ccviii

Donahue, E. W. (pres., Lodge 721, IAM): letter of, on black access to union membership, 358–59

Donaldson, Jesse M. (1st asst. postmaster gen.), cxxxviii, **771;** meetings with, cxxxviii, 543–44

Donnelly, R. R., and Sons: FEPC complaint on, 211

Donovan, Daniel R. (examiner, FEPC), **771–72;** assigned to Detroit office, 111; assigned to Region V, li; and discrimination against Mexicans, Mexican Americans, clxxiii–clxxiv; discusses work stoppages, 76; field trip of, to Los Angeles, 160; investigations by; report of, clxxxvi; and shipbuilding industry, clxxxvi; transfer to New York, 272

Doolan, Jerry (pers. dept., California Shipbuilding Co.), 145

Doram, Thomas Madison (FEPC complainant), 144–46, 160, **772**

Doran, Norman: as member, Boilermakers Union, 141

Dorn, Charles H. (atty., Point Breeze Employees Assoc.): statement of, 165–67, 168–69, 170, 171

Dorn, R. J., Co.: FEPC case on, 258, 264, 272, 382, 393

Dorsey, V. L. (dir., Point Breeze Employees Assoc.): replacement of, 222–23; and segregated facilities, 100–101, 103–4

Doub, Capt. (War Dept.): and Norris Stamping case, 486

Douglas, Ariz.: FEPC complaints in, 585

Douglas Aircraft Co., *727;* black employment at, clxxxii; discrimination by, lvii; FEPC case on, lvii; and nonwhite employment statistics, 155, 156; postwar economic conditions at, 539

Douglass, Frederick, xx

Douty, Kenneth (WMC), **772;** and telephone co. case, 99

Dow Chemical Co., *727;* FEPC hearing on, ciii

draft boards: appeals to, cxxii, cxlvi

draft deferments: complaints regarding, 262n; federal policies on, 67–68; jobs qualifying for, 56n; revocation of, cxxvii–cxxviii, cxl–cxli

Dravo Corp., *728;* black employment at, 53; labor problems of, 271; strikes at, ccxxv–ccxxvi, 660; wage dispute at, 194

Dreyfus, Benjamin (special counsel, FEPC), **772;** and Boilermakers cases, 144, 150–51, 173

drinking fountains, segregation of, 167

druggists: and FEPC jurisdiction, cxxiii

Du Bois, W. E. B.: speeches of, xx

Du Pont de Nemours Co., E. I., *728;* discrimination by, 659; FEPC case involving, 659

DuBose, Elager (FEPC complainant), 135

Dudenhefer, Mr. (Delta Shipbuilding Co.): black worker rejected by, 292

Duncan, J. Lawrence (WMC rep., Region V [Cleveland Office]), **772;** and black access to training, 90; discussions with, 113, 541; and Kurz-Kasch Co. case, 496; and strike, 76–77

Duncan, James A. (IAM): as union rep., 432

Dunlap, David R. (pres., Alabama Dry Dock and Shipbuilding Co.), **772;** FEPC negotiations with, 605, 608, 613

Durham, N.C.: employment discrimination in, 431, 433; FEPC cases in, 358, 418, 419, 431, 433, 479; P.O. cases in, cxxxvi, 418, 419, 462, 469, 470

Durr, Clifford J. (Federal Communications Commission): and Philadelphia transit strike, 345

East Alton, Ill.: blacks barred from, ccxiii; defiance of FEPC in, ccxv; employment discrimination in, 298–99; hearing at, ccxiii; postwar employment in, 548; segregation in, lviii

East Chicago, Ind.: strikes in, cxcviii, ccxxvi, 86–87

East Coast, shipyards on, cxxxiii, clxxxix, clxxxix–cxc

East St. Louis: complaints against railroads in, 37; conference at, and strike, 262–63; and FEPC hearings, 551; strike at, 249–50

Eastern Aircraft Corp.: integration at, clxxxi, 170, 554

Eastern Machinery Co. (Cincinnati): discrimination by, 96

Eastland, James O. (D., Miss.), **772;** and FEPC legislation, 559; views on FEPC, clvi–clvii

Eberhard Manufacturing Division, Eastern Malleable Iron Co.: strike at, 662n

education: low levels of, in South, 451, 452; programs needed in discrimination cases, 481n

Education, Office of, U.S.: FEPC cases on, 206, 228, 640, 641; information from, 423; statistics from, 65; and training programs, 28, 30–31, 41–42, 69n, 206, 404, 419, 422, 425, 469, 474

educational institutions: FEPC jurisdiction over, cxxiii

efficiency ratings: lowering of, for blacks, 539, 547

Eisenhower, Dwight D.: and desegregation of armed forces, xxx; exec. orders of, xix–xx

El Paso, Tex.: complaints against P.O. in, 585; FEPC complaints in, 585; FEPC field office in, clxxiii–clxxiv, 584, 589; mining industry in, clxxv

Electric Alloid Metallurgical Co.: discussions with, 88

electrical industry: postwar significance of, 385

electrical work: exclusion of blacks from, clxxiv

electricians: blacks employed as, 522, 561; training as, lxxvi, 31n

Electronics Mechanics, Inc.: and Japanese Americans, 281

elevator operators: blacks employed as, 99, 681

Ellinger, W. Don (acting dir., Region X [Dallas Office]; dir., Region XIII [New Orleans Office], FEPC), **772;** advisory group formed by, 540; appointed director of Region XIII, 450n; appraisal of, lii; and cases with postwar significance, 388; conferences of, on black employment by military contractors, 462; and Consolidated Vultee Aircraft Corp. case, clxxxi, 456, 461, 474; and Delta Shipbuilding case, 352, 353n, 386, 423, 434n–35n, 439n; and ES 510 reports, 384, 471; and FEPC directives, 353n; memoranda sent to, 420–21; Mitchell's discussions with, 394; Mitchell's evaluation of, 386; and oil co. cases, clxxviii; and P.O. cases, 479; promotion of, 319, 386; and railroad cases, 478; reports of, 522; request from, 435, 436; role of, 386n; and segregation provisions in black employment proposals, 485; and Shell Oil case, clxxix, 487, 488, 492–93, 494, 497, 520; and shipbuilding cases, 386, 421; and telephone co. cases, 402; and training programs, 425

Elliot's Debates: cited, 671

Elliott, E. W., Co.: FEPC case on, 413

Elwood Ordnance Plant, 257, 279, 285

Emancipation Proclamation, lxxvi

Emergency Relief Appropriation Acts: discrimination banned by, 654

Emerson Electric Co., *728;* discrimination by, 464, 466; failure to provide employment information by, 638; and nonwhite employment statistics, 155, 156

employees: discrimination in upgrading of, 51, 52, 53, 58, 114, 129, 138, 151–52, 159, 203, 232, 233–34, 282, 326, 338, 346, 429, 466

employees, government: and efficiency ratings, 507

employees, public: investigation of loyalty of, 73

employers: compliance of, with FEPC regulations, 20; discriminatory recruitment practices of, 208, 466; FEPC contact with, 528, 529; hostility of, to FEPC, 460n; and loyalty issues, cxlix; negotiations with, xliv, xlvii; and union discrimination, cxciii

New Orleans, La.: black employment in, 51, 53; complaints against P.O. in, 33, 544; data on shipbuilding co. in, 436; discrimination at shipyard in, 204, 284; discrimination in, 204, 402, 556, 561; employment service practices in, 455; FEPC cases in, cxxxii, 287n, 291–93, 373, 402, 420, 421; FEPC representatives in, 183, 554; field trip to, 182–83; hiring of blacks at shipyard in, 423, 435; incident at shipyard in, 227, 229n; Maritime Commission office in, 449; P.O. cases in, cxxxvi; racial tensions in, 353n; shipyard cases in, cxciv; strikes in, 394

New Orleans Port of Embarkation: FEPC case on, 302

New York: antidiscrimination legislation in, 667, 668; bans on employment of aliens by, cxlix; black employment in, 400, 476, 477, 559, 681–82; constitution of, 667; and discrimination in baseball, 531n; and discriminatory work orders, cxxix; FEPC hearings in, 22n; FEPC investigations in, cxxxiii; FEPC law of, 564; and FEPC regional divisions, 216; FEPC settlement with telephone co. in, 413; labor stabilization plans for, 62, 64; recruitment of black workers in, 26–27, 129; recruitment of workers in, cxxix; workers recruited in, clxxxv

New York Bell Telephone Co.: black employment at, 682–83; job requirements, 683, 684

New York Central Railroad, 743; complaints against, lxxxvi; FEPC cases on, 372, 424, 427, 480

New York City: black employment in, cxcix, 681, 684; discrimination against aliens in, cli; discriminatory recruitment in, 27n; discussions with co. headquarters in, 484; employment by street railways in, 75; FEPC hearings in, ci, cv, 560, 617; FEPC regional office opened in, ciii; integration of workers in, 681; subway strike in, 343n; transit system in, cxcix

New York City Board of Transportation: employment statistics on, 75

New York City Omnibus Corp.: employment statistics on, 75

New York Shipbuilding Co., 743; black employment at, clxxxiv, 53; and FEPC, 22; and job discrimination, 300

New York State: admission of blacks to unions in, 356, 359; bans discrimination in union membership, 356

New York Telephone Co.: black employment at, lxxvi, ccxi, 399n–400n; FEPC case on, ccxi

New York Times: articles in, 231–35, 235n, 238

Newark, N.J.: black employment in, 515n; employment practices of firm in, 20

Newark Plan: for non-piracy of labor, 63

Newman, Cecil Earl, **785;** employment of, xlviii, 221

Newport News, Va.: complaints against P.O. in, 33; P.O. cases in, cxxxvi; P.O. discrimination in, 34n, 289n

Newport News Shipbuilding and Drydock Co., 743; black employment at, clxxxiv, 52

newspapers: conferences with owners of, 239; coverage of FEPC actions in, 420; coverage of Philadelphia transit strike in, 340, 342; coverage of strikes in, 311; discriminatory advertising in, xxv, lvii, cli, 239, 239n–40n, 561; and FEPC jurisdiction, cxxi, 320n; hostility of, to FEPC, 344; publication of FEPC directives in, 511n; wage rates listed in, 241

newspapers, black: discrimination complaints by, 38, 38n

Nichols, Franklin O. (National Urban League), **785;** and Alabama Dry Dock and Shipbuilding case, 611

Nicol, R.A., and Co., Inc., 743; FEPC case on, 381, 392, 413

Niehaus, Col. (Army Signal Corps): and General Cable Co. case, 481

night shifts: consignment of blacks to, 409

Nimitz, Adm. Chester William, **785;** exclusion of Japanese Americans from naval establishments by, 518

Nisei, on West Coast, 549

Nixon, Richard M.: and civil rights, xx, xxxiii; and Mitchell, xxxiii; and presidential election of 1968, xxxiii; and school busing, xxxiii

Non-Ferrous Metals Commission: and discrimination against Mexicans, Mexican Americans, clxxv, clxxvi; FEPC cooperation with, clxxvi; jurisdiction of, clxxvi; and mining industry complaints, cxxxv; and wage discrimination, clxxvi, clxxvii

Non-Partisan Committee (Baltimore): and Western Electric case, 266–67, 268; opposes segregated facilities, 102n; role of, 267n

Nordberg Manufacturing Co.: discrimination by, lvii; FEPC case on, lvii

Norden, Carl, Inc.: discrimination by, lvii; FEPC case on, lvii, 256

Norfolk, Va.: FEPC field trip to, 302

Norfolk Naval Hospital: FEPC case on, 264, 273, 275

Norfolk Navy Yard: black employment at, 52

Norfolk Southern Railroad Co., *743;* FEPC case on, lxix, lxxxvi

Norris, Frank: as candidate for FEPC, 50n

Norris, Kenneth T., Sr. (Norris Stamping Co.), **785;** discussions with, 503

Norris Stamping and Manufacturing Co., *744;* cutbacks at, 484n, 535; discrimination by, 482, 483n–84n; FEPC case on, 458, 482–84, 485, 486–87, 491, 494, 497, 503, 535; FEPC problems with, 479; turnover at, 503

North: black employment in, lxxxi; labor shortages in, lxxxi; segregation in, lx

North American Aviation Co., *744;* black employment at, clxxxii, 656; cutbacks at, 385; discrimination by, clxxxii, 656; FEPC cases on, 119, 183, 272, 285, 295, 639, 640, 641, 656, 657; complaints against, clxxxii; discrimination by, clxxxi; layoffs by, clxxxii, 539; Mexicans, Mexican Americans employed at, clxxxii; and processing of alien questionnaires, 232; racial tensions at, 244; Seventh Day Adventists dismissed by, clxxxii, 237; union problems at, 246

North Carolina: black employment in, 29; FEPC cases in, 279, 474; migrants from, cc; textile industry in, 563; and TVA, 36n

North Carolina Shipbuilding Co., *744;* black employment at, 29

Northern Pump Co., *744;* FEPC cases on, 373

Northrop, Dr. Herbert, **785;** and Boilermakers Union, ccxx; CIO, views on, ccxvii; and railroad hearings, ccxviii; reports of, cxciv, ccxx; research of, 202n; writings of, cxcviii

Northwest: FEPC regional office proposed for, 347n

Northwest Mining and Exchange Co., *744;* hearing on, ciii

Northwestern Railroad: FEPC cases on, 372

Northwestern Univ.: Engineering Science Management War Training courses at, 34–35

Norton, Mary T., **785**

Nurse Training Act (1943): discrimination banned by, 654

nursery and child care schools: and FEPC jurisdiction, cxxi

nurses, black: discrimination against, 494, 497

O'Brian, John Lord (gen. counsel, OEM), **785;** rulings of, cxxvi

O'Connor, Herbert R. (gov. of Maryland), **785;** and Bethlehem Steel Shipbuilding strike, 625, 626–27

O'Grady, James (War Shipping Admin.), **786;** and United Seamen's Service, 253–54

O'Neal, John (Iron Workers Union): as member of Portland Voluntary Appeals Board, 130

Panama: construction in, 233; discrimination and segregation in, 231; ships sailing under flag of, 556

Panama Canal Zone: FEPC file on, 231, 238

Panama City, Fla.: FEPC cases in, 439n, 442

paper industry: FEPC cases on, 371, 372, 374

Paper Workers Organizing Committee: complaint against, 506

Parham, Herschel (chief of recruitment and placement, GAO), 176

Parran, Dr. Thomas, Jr. (surgeon gen.), **786;** report of, 47–48

Parrish, Homer (Local 401, Boilermakers Union): discussions with, 128, 136; role of, 130, 135

Parsons, Paul S. (dep. area dir., New Britain, Conn., WMC), 54, **786**

Pascagoula, Miss.: FEPC attention to, 450

Pasco, Wash.: atomic power facilities at, lxxv; discrimination in, 270, 275, 284, 305–6; FEPC reports on, 305–6; investigation at, 251

Pasco Co.: FEPC case on, 273

Pass Christian, Miss.: segregation ordinance of, 253

Patterson, Ellis (D., Cal.): and alienage complaints, clvi

Patterson, N.J.: employment practices of firm in, 20

Patterson, Robert P. (under sec. of war; sec. of war), **786;** letters of, cxxxii, 648–49, 651; memoranda of, 645, 647–48; and Western Electric case, 268

Patterson Field (Fairfield, Ohio): FEPC case on, 638

Pauline, Kan.: and nonwhite employment statistics, 155

peacetime: continuation of nondiscrimination policies in, 547

Pearl Harbor: attack on, cl, cli; impact of, xliii; and treatment of Japanese Americans, clxvii

Pearl Harbor Navy Yard: discrimination complaint against, 206, 228; FEPC case on, 249

Pena, Luis (FEPC complainant), 241

Pendleton Shipyard: FEPC case on, 179

Pennsylvania: black employment in, 53; employment discrimination in, 84, 91, 95; FEPC complaints in, 84; handling of, by FEPC New York office, 549; hiring of black telephone operators in, 401; housing for black war workers in, 275; Mitchell as regional director over, xliv; nondiscrimination legislation of, 667; segregated work patterns in, 293; strikes in, cxcviii, ccxxxv–ccxxxvi, 106–7, 108, 262

Pennsylvania Bell Telephone Co.: complaints against, 237; FEPC case involving, 216, 250

Pennsylvania Central Airlines: FEPC cases on, 275

Pennsylvania Railroad Co., *745;* complaints against, lxxxvi; FEPC cases on, 372

Pensacola, Fla.: FEPC activities in, 450; FEPC case against USES in, 446; FEPC cases in, 439n

peonage: examples of, 37n; indictment of U.S. Sugar Corp. for, 32; investigation of, 32n–33n

Percy Kent Bag Co., *745;* FEPC case on, 520

Perdue, Saul M.: discussion with, xlv

Perkins v. Lukens Steel Company: decision in, 669; and gov. contracts, 669

permit men: blacks as, 357–58

Perry, Fred (FEPC complainant), 128–29

Perry, Leslie S. (NAACP Washington Bureau): meeting attended by, cxcv; reports of, cxcv; testimony of, cxcvii

Pestana (Pestano), Frank (FEPC examiner, Region XII), **786;** commendation of, 257; reports on union discrimination, 332, 358

Peterson, Eric (IAM), **786;** and discrimination by unions, 357

Peterson, Hugh (D, Ga.), **786;** FEPC, views on, 664

Petroleum Administration for War (PAW): and Shell Oil case, clxxix, 488, 493, 494, 497, 504

Peyser, Capt. S. M. (Army Service Forces): meeting with, 508, 509

Pfauts, Mr. (mgr., National Lead Co., St. Louis), 335

Phelps-Dodge Copper Corp., *745*

Phelps-Dodge Corp.: companies owned by, 585; complaints against, clxxiv, 325–26, 327, 585; contracts of, 587; discrimination by, clxxiv, clxxv, 369n, 585; exec. of, 585; FEPC investigation of, clxxiv; and unions, 369n; WMC relationship with, 369

Philadelphia, Pa.: black employment in, 76, 559; blacks employed as telephone operators in, 547; closing of FEPC office in, 549; discrimination at USES office in, 540; employment practices in, 21, 22; employment stabilization plan for, cciii; FEPC cases in, 195, 364; FEPC field trip to, 390; FEPC hearings in, cii, civ, cci, 40, 617; FEPC office in, cci; information from WMC in, 219; Maritime Commission office in, 449; Mitchell's interest in, xxvii; nonwhite employment in, 562; police, 341, 342; P.O. cases in, cxxxvi, cxxxviii, 33, 288–89, 295, 361, 362, 391, 396, 397, 398, 412, 418, 462, 497; postmaster of, denies FEPC jurisdiction, 398; telephone co. cases in, 186n; transit strike in, ccxxxvii 339–43, 344, 345–46

Philadelphia Navy Yard: black employment at, 53

Philadephia Quartermaster Depot: FEPC memo on, 195

Philadelphia Rapid Transit Employees Union: and blacks in platform positions, cci; challenges FEPC jurisdiction, cci; directive to, ccviii; FEPC hearings on, civ; and nondiscrimination clauses in gov. contracts, cci

Philadelphia Transit case: union-management collusion in, ccxix

Philadelphia Transportation (Transit) Co. (PTC), *746;* black employment at, cci, cciii–cciv, ccvi, 271, 318; complaints against, cci; conference on, 343, 344; contract of, 318; directives to, ccviii; discrimination by, cci, ccxix; employment statistics on, 76; FEPC case on, lxvii–lxviii, cci–cciv, 344–46, 663; FEPC hearing on, civ; Mexican, Mexican American employment at, cci; and nondiscrimination clauses in gov. contracts, cci; and Smith Committee, cciii; strike at, xxv, xxvii, xxxvi, xliv, lxvii–lxviii, cxxxv, cxl, cciii–cciv, ccxxvii, 344–46

Philco Radio Corp.: FEPC complaints regarding, 84

Philips Coach Co.: segregation at, lix

Phoenix, Ariz.: black employment in, ccvii; transit system in, ccvii

photographs on employment applications, clix, clx

photostats, use of, 187

Pickens, D. K.: as gov. relations rep., National Lead Co., 308–10

Pickens, Lonnie T. (FEPC complainant), 154

Pine Bluff Arsenal: and nonwhite employment statistics, 156

pipefitting: black employment in, 608

Pitney Bowes, *746;* FEPC case on, 70

Pittsburgh, Pa.: black employment in, cxcvii, ccvii; complaints against P.O. in, 543–44; complaints against telephone co. in, 186n; FEPC cases in, 237, 256, 522; labor problems in, 271; nonwhite employment in, 562; race strikes in, 290–91; strikes at, 284; telephone cases in, 186, 401; transit system in, ccvii

Pittsburgh Plate Glass Co., *746;* discrimination by, lvii, cxlvi; FEPC case on, lvii, cxlvi; hearings on, 617; and Jehovah's Witnesses, lvii, cxlvi, 59

Pittsfield, Mass.: labor stabilization plan for, 62

Plainfield, N.J.: employment practices of firm in, 20

plasterers: blacks employed as, 561

platform jobs: blacks barred from employment as, cxcix, 656, 657; blacks employed in, cxcix, cci, ccv, ccvi, ccvii; hiring of blacks for, 508, 509, 510, 510n

Pledge of Allegiance: refusal to say, clix

secretaries: blacks employed as, 442–43

sectionalism: FEPC accused of, 663

security: and questions on national origin, clxii

sedition: laws against, cxlix

Seff, Bernard (NLRB rep.): statement of, 166

Sefton Fibre Can Co., *749;* nondiscrimination policy of, 455, 561

segregation: of armed forces, xxx; in cafeterias, 101–2, 199n; considered nondiscriminatory, ccxiv; and Constitution, U.S., lx; cost(s) of, lix, 104n; court decisions on, xxvii, lix–lx, cxcii, 104n–5n; in defense industries, ccxv; discriminatory impact of, lxvi, lxxxiv; in employment, 244; and employment mobility, cxxiv; in employment services offices, 455; experts on, lxxxiv; in federal agencies, 33n–34n; FEPC cases involving, lix, 254n; FEPC investigation of, 89–90, 94; FEPC jurisdiction over, lviii–lxvi, cxv, cxxiii, cxxvi–cxxvii, ccxxvii; FEPC opposition to, lxvi, lxxviii, 171n, 172n, 193n–94n; FEPC policy on, lxvi, cxxxv, 293; FEPC responses to employment plans based on, 464, 468, 485; impact of, on employment opportunity, lviii; laws against, xxviii–xxix; laws mandating, 253; of lockers, ccxxvii, 266–67, 268; management opposition to, 166, 167; of Mexicans, Mexican Americans, clxxv, 588; not recommended by FEPC, 192; opposition to, lxi, cxxxv, ccxxvii, 102n, 614n; in Panama Canal Zone, 231; petitions against, 267; in public schools, lix; of recreational facilities, 588; residential, xx; and rise of black activism, xxxi; and separate but equal doctrine, xxx, lviii, lix–lx, lxiii, ccxxvii; of ship crews, lix, ccxxii; of skilled workers, 293; social pressures supporting continuation of, 223; as solution to race conflict, 609; spread of, lxii; and strikes, cxxxv; of toilet facilities, xlviii, l, lix, lxv, cxvi, cxxiv, cxxxv; in training programs, liv, 65, 422, 441; in training programs, 422; and unions, xxiv, cxcii, ccxii, ccxxiii, 42n, 147–48; and venereal disease, 168, 170, 223–24; of work arrangements, lviii, lix, lxi, lxii, lxiii, lxiv, lxxxviii, clxxviii, clxxix, clxxx, clxxxi–clxxxii, clxxxiv, cxc, cxxiii, cxxix, cxxxv, ccxv, ccxxii, ccxxvii, 26–27, 252n, 293, 294–95, 562, 588, 596–97, 606, 614n; of work crews, opposed, 147–48; of work shifts, 353n; worker demands for, 103, 104, 104n, 165–66, 167, 169, 171n

Seitzer, Lee (asst. economic analyst, Bureau of Program Planning and Review, WMC?): memo to, 51–53

Select Committee to Investigate Executive Agencies (Smith Committee): and FEPC case, ccviii, 382–83; and FEPC directives, cci–ccii; and FEPC jurisdiction, cxviii–cxix, cci–ccii; and FEPC powers, ccxxiv; and PTC, cciii; and Recruitment and Manning Org., cxxxiii; and War Shipping Admin., 561; attacks on FEPC in, clvi–clvii; complaints to, cxxxiii, clxxxviii, ccxxii; FEPC actions on, 195; FEPC, investigation of, cci–ccii, cciii, ccviii, ccix, ccxxviii; hearings of, cxviii–cxix, cxxxiii, cci–ccii, cciii, ccix, ccxxii; hearings of, on FEPC, civ; impact of, on FEPC, 354; investigation of FEPC by, cxcvi, cxcvii, 261, 262n, 379–80; materials submitted to, 674n

Selective Service, U.S.: and conscientious objectors, 59; and essentiality ratings, 230; FEPC case on, 228, 376

Selective Service Training Act: discrimination banned by, 654

semiskilled work: blacks in, lxi, cxci; training for, 641n

Senate, U.S.: budget cuts by, 559; and permanent FEPC, 562; southern control of committees of, xxx

seniority: and black workers, clxxxiii, ccxviii; charts of, 241; discrimination in, lxviii, cxcviii, ccxviii, 241, 411; FEPC accused of interfering with, 664; and layoffs, 254, 255, 293; occupations excluded from, 326; and promotions,

587; rules of, clxxix; and training programs, lxv, 619, 626, 630, 634; upgrading based on, 282, 492–93, 631; and unlawful discharges, 677; violations of, 411

seniority rights: discrimination in, 283n

seniority rules: impact of, on blacks, 254, 255; violations of, 241, 282, 411

Senter, William (UERMWA), **790;** discussion with, 521

"separate but equal" principle: and exec. orders, cxxxv, 166, 167, 168, 170, 171; and FEPC jurisdiction, lviii; and railroad facilities, lxxxiv; application of, 101, 104; compliance with, lix–lx; court cases on, lix–lx, 168; legal opinions on, 167; overturning of, xxvii, xxx, lxv–lxvi

Sepulveda (FEPC complainant), 326

Serna, Sabas (FEPC complainant), 241

servicemen, black: violence against, xxx

Seulberger, F[erdinand]. G[eorge]. (chm., Dept. of Indus. Rel., Northwestern Univ.), **790;** and access to Engineering Science Management War Training courses, 34, 35

Seventh Day Adventists: complaints by, clxxxii; complaints of, xxiv; discrimination against, cxliv, clxxxii, 59, 233, 674–79; dismissal of, clxxxii, 207, 237, 674–79; FEPC cases on, cxliv, 296, 298n, 389, 674–79; Sabbath, refusal to work during, cxliv, 674–79

sewing machine operators: black women employed as, lxii, 44, 81; FEPC complaints of, 90, 94; restriction to whites, lix, lx

sex: bans on discrimination based on, liv, 654

Sexton, Charles W. (FEPC complainant), 433

Sexton, David (FEPC complainant), 433

Seymour (Seymore), Mrs. Virginia (FEPC staff, San Francisco), 319, **790**

Shanks, Mr. (Los Angeles P.O.), 366

Sharfsin, Joseph (special counsel, FEPC), **790;** and Philadelphia transit strike, 340, 341–42, 345, 346

Sharkey, T. L. (War Dept., Army Map Service): and FEPC complainant, 109

Sharp, Robert: discrimination against, 18–19

Shea, John (works mgr., Western Electric, Point Breeze Plant): and Western Electric case, 223–24

Shell Oil Co. (Royal Dutch Co., Shell Oil Co., Inc.), *749;* discrimination by, clxxviii–clxxix; FEPC agreement with, clxxix; FEPC case on, lxvii, clxxviii–clxxix, 203, 204, 210, 215, 217, 245, 256, 305, 487–88, 491, 492–93, 497, 500–501, 504, 506, 513, 515n, 522, 557; FEPC complaints against, 119; FEPC conferences with, 203; FEPC hearings on, clxxviii–clxxix, 318; FEPC investigation of, clxxii, clxxviii; proposals of, on promotion of blacks and Mexicans, 240–43, 494, 501; strike at, 487–88, 492–93; wage discrimination by, 203

Shelter Island Oyster Co.: FEPC case on, 246, 247, 382, 392

Shepard, Mrs. Dorothy (FEPC complainant), 430

Sheridan, Thomas (utilization consultant, WMC, Region XII), 138, 139

Sherwin Williams Co.: as contractor, 191

Shiel, Bernard J., Auxiliary Bishop (Chicago Diocese), **790;** as FEPC candidate, 50, 51n

shifts: discrimination in, clxxxvii, 353n

Shiosaki (Shiozaki), Ronald I.: FEPC case on, 213, **790**

shipbuilding industry: black employment in, lxxxi, clxxxiv, clxxxviii, cxciv, ccxxv, 51–53, 78–79, 137, 322–23, 420–21, 539; and Boilermakers Union, clxxxiv; citizenship requirements for work in, cxlix; closed shop agreements in, 158–59; complaints regarding, clxxxiv; decline of, cxciv; demand for labor in, 539; discrimination in, clxxxvi–cxciv, ccxix, 322–23; employment in, ccxvii, 120–25; employment of women in, 51–52,

Van Wyck, Dr. Philip S. (chief of training, WMC), **793;** apprentice training program, 541–42; meeting with, 28; and pre-employment courses, 422

Vanadium, N.M.: FEPC investigations in, 118, 119

Vancouver, Ore.: black employment in, 52, 122, 125; FEPC cases in, cxc, 333n

Vancouver, Wash.: FEPC cases in, cxcv, clxxxv

Vancouver and Swan Island Shipyards: complaints against, during W.W.II, 124, 129, 134, 135; employment at, 122, 137, 138

Vancouver Shipyard: black workers assigned to, 122, 128, 138; complaints against, 134, 135

Vega Airplane Co.: black employment at, clxxxii; discrimination by, lvii, clxxxii; FEPC case on, clxxxii, lvii

Vendo Co., *755;* FEPC cases on, 520, 523

veterans: and apprenticeship programs, 542; blacks not employed in interviewing, 455; discrimination against Japanese-American, cxxxix, clxix, 516n; displacement of workers by, 544; and hostility to Japanese-Americans, 518; preferences for, cxxxix

Veterans Administration: FEPC cases on, 537; retraining and employment problems, 479

Vickery, Adm. Howard L. **793;** and Delta Shipbuilding Corp. case, 243, 256, 292; and discrimination in shipyards, 198; letter to, 243

Victor Electric Co., *755;* hearings on, 391n

Victory Tax: deducted from wages, 46

Vincent, Craig S. (War Shipping Admin.), **793;** congressional attacks on, 663; opposes use of all-black deck crews, 193

violence: against black employment, 421; against unions, 46–47; among workers, 309; between black and white workers, lxxix, 145, 282, 407, 599–605, 608, 609; between workers, 339n; fear of, cxcix, ccvi, ccvii, 502n; threats of, ccvi, ccxv, ccxxvii, 18–19, 19, 439n; threats of, by whites, 656, 657; and war production, 115n; by whites against blacks, lxxix, cxxxii, cxciv, 287n, 292, 407, 599–605, 608, 609

Virgin Islands: governor of, xxiii

Virginia: black employment in, 52; migrants from, cc; and TVA, 36n

Virginian Railway Co., *755;* complaints against, lxxxvi

Visceral, Lt.: and FEPC cases in St. Louis, 479

Vivian B. Moreton *vs.* Navy Department: as FEPC case, 217

V-J Day: aftermath of, 535

Vocational Education for National Defense (VEND) Program: courses under, 21

Voight Machine Co.: uncooperative with FEPC, 641n

Vorys, John (R., Ohio): and FEPC, 655n

voting rights: constitutional basis of, lxxxv, 653; court cases on, xxix, xxxvi, lxxxv

Voting Rights Act of 1965: passage of, xxix; and poll taxes, xxxvi; renewal of, xxxiii

W. A. Briggs Bitumin Co.: nondiscrimination policy of, 547

Waesche, Adm. Russell R[andolph] (Coast Guard), **793;** and employment of Japanese Americans, 265n; FEPC case submitted to, 368; information from, 263, 279

wage and hour standards: establishment of, 42n–43n

wage discrimination: xxiv, xliii, clxxi, clxxii, clxxiv, clxxv, clxxvi, clxxvii, clxxviii, clxxix, cxci, ccxviii, ccxxv, 151, 175, 203, 204, 208, 215, 236, 241, 243, 322–23, 372, 443, 444, 445, 553, 557n, 586, 588, 589; rulings against, 33n, 50n, 115n

wage scales: abolition of discriminatory, 589; for black laborers, 25

wages, regulation of, cxxxiv–cxxxv

Wagner, Martin (UGCCWA), 335, 338

Wagner Act: and affirmative action, lxxiv; bars interference with internal affairs of unions, clxxxviii

Wagner Electric Co., *755–56;* discrimination by, ccxiii–ccxiv, ccxiii; FEPC case on, 280, 302, 322n, 464, 467n, 495; FEPC letter on, 286

Wainwright Shipyard (Panama City, Fla.): black workers chased from jobs at, 428; discrimination at, 51–52

Walker, Mr. (Navy Dept.): and disloyalty charges, 516–17

Walker, Anthem (FEPC complainant), 135

Walker, Frank C. (postmaster gen.), **793;** and discrimination in P.O.s, 396; FEPC agreement with, 484; FEPC cases investigated by, 423; FEPC conference with, 362, 362n, 366, 391, 398; inability to obtain appointment with, 387; letter to, 364, 368, 391; letters of, 289n; meetings with, cxxxvii, cxxxviii, 388n; statement issued by, 409

Walker, Mrs. Lawrence (FEPC complainant), 84

Walker-Turner plant: FEPC case against, 20

Wallace, George: presidential campaign of, xxxii

Wallace, Gerald (postal worker, Los Angeles): replaces black worker, 410

Wallace, Henry: Mitchell's comments on, 563

Wallace Corporation v. National Labor Relations Board: and closed shop contracts, ccxviii–ccxix; decision on, lxix–lxx, cxciii, ccxviii; and union discrimination, ccxviii–ccxix

war, secretary of: and protection from sabotage, cxxx

war bonds: and Jehovah's Witnesses, cxlvi, 216, 262n; refusal to buy, cxvii, cxxii, cxlvi; religious opposition to purchase of, 59

War Department, U.S.: and access of blacks to training, 90, 94; and Bethlehem Shipbuilding strike, 627; black employment, report on, 90, 94; and Capital Transit case, 509; companies operated for, 227; complaints against, 90–91, 92, 436, 639; complaints investigated by, 85, 645–46; and compliance of contractors with exec. order against discrimination, 417, 456, 464, 648–49; conferences on FEPC cases, 306, 395; conferences with, on FEPC cases, 85–86, 417, 497, 514; and Consolidated Vultee Aircraft Corp. case, clxxxi, 429, 456, 462, 491; cooperation of, with FEPC, 81, 192, 250, 257, 467, 507, 560; correspondence with, 380, 381; Cramer's transfer to, xlix; and discriminatory recruitment of employees, 560; and employment of aliens, cliii–cliv, clx; employment of civilian workers by, cxxxi; and essentiality ratings, 230; FEPC agreements with, cxxxvii, cxxxi, cxl, 86n, 364, 376, 529, 649–50; and FEPC cases, 236, 256, 339, 392, 415–17, 440, 474, 479, 497; and FEPC cases in St. Louis, 463–65, 466, 470, 484, 497–98, 507; FEPC cases involving, 178, 195, 206, 207, 208, 256, 295, 537, 639; and FEPC complaints, 272, 435; FEPC complaints referred to, 90, 94, 237; FEPC designated staff member for, 300; and FEPC directives, 511n; FEPC relationship with, lvi, xxvi, cxvii, cxxx–cxxxii, clxvii, clxxxi, ccxiv, 85–86, 86n, 116, 252n, 298n, 303n, 339n, 376, 390, 391n, 396–97, 415n, 449, 453, 464–65, 560, 645–46, 648–49, 651, 652–53; and General Cable case, cxxxi, ccxv, 464, 479, 481; information from, 201, 205, 207, 375; inquiries of, on FEPC cases, 418, 520; interference of, with FEPC cases, 300–301; interference of, with FEPC officials, 275, 285; and Japanese Americans, lxxiii,cxxx, cliii, 176–77; letter to, 248; letters from, to FEPC, 399, 500; and Los Angeles Street Railway case, 350; and loyalty investigations, cxvii, cxxx, cl, clxvii, 213n, 225, 227n, 391–92, 650; memoranda of, 647–48; Mitchell as contact with, cxl; and nondiscrimination clauses in contracts, lxxii, lxxiii,